ROMAN MAR

ROMAN MARRIAGE

Iusti Coniuges from the Time of Cicero
to the Time of Ulpian

SUSAN TREGGIARI

CLARENDON PRESS · OXFORD

Oxford University Press, Walton Street, Oxford OX2 6DP
Oxford New York Toronto
Delhi Bombay Calcutta Madras Karachi
Kuala Lumpur Singapore Hong Kong Tokyo
Nairobi Dar es Salaam Cape Town
Melbourne Auckland Madrid
and associated companies in
Berlin Ibadan

Oxford is a trade mark of Oxford University Press

Published in the United States
by Oxford University Press Inc., New York

British Library Cataloguing in Publication Data
Treggiari, Susan
Roman marriage : Iusti Coniuges from the time of
Cicero to the time of Ulpian.
1. Roman empire. Marriage. Legal aspects
I. title
343.70616
ISBN 0-19-814939-5 (pbk)

Library of Congress Cataloging in Publication Data
Treggiari, Susan
Roman marriage : Iusti Coniuges from the time of
Cicero to the time of Ulpian / Susan Treggiari.
Includes bibliographical references.
Includes index.
1. Marriage (Roman law)   I. title
KJA2233.T74 1991
346.3701'6—dc20
[343.70616]
ISBN 0-19-814939-5 (pbk)

1 3 5 7 9 10 8 6 4 2

Printed in Great Britain
on acid-free paper by
Bookcraft (Bath) Ltd.
Midsomer Norton, Avon

Coniugi, Filiabus, Sororibus

Preface

THE germ of this book dates back twenty years and deliberate work on it to a sabbatical year spent in Oxford in 1976/7. It was conceived as an attempt to understand how the marital relationship worked in the late Republic and Principate. The institution of marriage and the complex webs of society, law, economics, morality, customs and feeling in which it is set offer endless scope for exploration. I aim here only to examine the themes which seem to me most important for the Roman experience of marriage. The reader will discern my preconceptions and interests. But I have tried to concentrate attention on what the Romans themselves tell us. The sources, for this as for most topics of social history in the ancient world, are scattered and diverse. I have tried to let them speak for themselves. Hence the frequent quotations, particularly from texts which readers may not have permanently at their elbow. Except where credited to others, translations are my own and as literal as possible, in the hope that the Latinless reader will gain some sense of the flavour of the original. Description and argument rest often on snippets of evidence. Critics may generously assume that I have searched in vain for counter-evidence; they are referred to the sources on which I rely so that they may choose to reject my view if they wish. It would be tedious to spell out in detail the methods I have tried to follow in assessing the usefulness of any particular ancient literary work for the present enquiry. In seeking to exploit any particular passage, one has constantly to bear in mind the genre in which it is written, the biases and purposes of the author who wrote it, the audience for which it was intended. It will appear that Tacitus often seems to me about as reliable a narrator of facts as the rhetoricians immortalized by the Elder Seneca, and that, although I think Cicero in his letters to Atticus as honest as a man can be in revealing himself to a friend, this does not mean that we have a full picture of his marriage to Terentia or of what led to their divorce. The conscientious work of Justinian's commission in digesting the opinions of earlier jurists, though a model to all later committees, leads to many uncertainties in our attempts to reconstruct the social realities which lay behind the excerpts from the works of the great lawyers. I have not troubled the reader by repeatedly inserting the caveat that conclusions drawn from such data must often be provisional. Emphasis on what the surviving texts say is dictated by an impulse to try to get as close to the minds of the Romans as possible, as well as by the conviction that we must avoid theories which conflict with sources. My last few years are dotted with the corpses of hypotheses which had to be abandoned when they clashed with evidence.

The ramifications of the subject have produced a lengthier bibliography of modern works than I could wish. I have neither attempted to give a systematic review of the scholarship on any particular topic nor to list all that I have read, but merely to acknowledge authorities whom I have followed, record alternative opinions, or suggest where the reader might look for further discussion. Where possible, I cite work in English, of recent date and of particular interest. If I have omitted items which I ought to have cited, it is by oversight, for which I apologize. Little of the work published after 1988 could be taken into account.

I was inspired by J. A. Crook's inimitable *Law and Life of Rome* (1967) to explore the interaction of law and reality (as far as we can penetrate to the real in Roman history). Since then, scholars working in many different areas of classical literature, history, and law have cast new light on Roman society. It seemed to me that there was a need for a book on the institution of marriage, which would build on but not duplicate the older work on the law of marriage and the newer scholarship on the legal position of women.

The only monograph in English on the law of marriage was published in 1930 and remains an excellent guide to the sources. Nor have changing times rendered Corbett's own views obnoxious. He remains more reliable than many of the specialized books and articles which have appeared on the Continent in the last half-century. On law in general and republican law in particular I have been much influenced by Alan Watson. Jane Gardner's survey, *Women in Roman law and society*, appeared when this book was in its late stages, but I hope I have profited from it, and our aims are similar. On particular topics of law and as examples of how to approach the material and the problems, and of how to set the law in its social context, I acknowledge a special debt to David Daube, J. A. Crook, and Suzanne Dixon.

Literary studies are at the centre of classics as the discipline is organized in most of the English-speaking world. Yet paradoxically to move between literature and history is often no easier than to move between history and law. A particular debt is owed to historians who take account of the full range of texts and to literary specialists who relate the poets to their social context. I hope the examples of J. H. D'Arms, P. A. Brunt, Peter Garnsey, Ramsay MacMullen, Fergus Millar, Sir Ronald Syme, and T. P. Wiseman among the historians and R. E. Fantham, Jasper Griffin, and Gordon Williams among the Latinists have had some effect on me. Although epigraphic sources are not prominent in this book, I am also grateful to those who have explored the ways of using tomb inscriptions to answer questions of social history, scholars such as M. K. Hopkins, Beryl Rawson, Richard P. Saller, and Brent D. Shaw.

Such categorization of scholars is unduly schematic. How can one measure or duly acknowledge the impact of what a friend, in discussion of a variety of topics, says, or does not say? They plant the seeds, by casually making a connection which turns out to be important or by suggesting an area or source to explore. The germs of ideas may come from other writers, historians in other fields, novelists, journalists, as much as from scholars deliberately studied and cited. I owe an inestimable debt to all my teachers, more especially to Margaret Pinsent, Margaret Freeman, W. F. Hicken, L. H. Jeffery, D. L. Stockton, P. A. Brunt, and David Daube. Over the years correspondence and discussion and support and friendship from many people have enriched my life as well as creating the debt which demands these acknowledgements. I retain memories of constant and generous help from members of the scholarly community and most particularly from ancient historians in Britain, Canada, and the United States, from fellow members of the Universities of Oxford and Ottawa and Stanford University, and those with whom I have worked in several learned societies. Particular thanks are owed to my Ottawa colleague Colin Wells, for sharing his store of reading, his archaeological expertise, and his insight into the nature of the Romans. His stern criticisms have improved several chapters. Suzanne Dixon of the University of Queensland, whose post-doctoral term at Stanford was an inspiration, has been generous in showing me her unpublished work and in giving illuminating comments on vast areas of scholarship. Keith Bradley, Richard Saller, and Brent Shaw have kindly brought their expertise to bear on chapters which caused me particular problems. I am grateful to William Harris, Beryl Rawson, Richard Saller, and David Kertzer for organizing workshops which exposed me to criticism and new ideas. My former students G. W. Pinard, Susan Dorken, Marianne Goodfellow, and Marie Laurence of Ottawa and Judith Evans-Grubbs of Stanford have taught me much. The sound judgement and breadth of vision of David Cherry has helped me on many problems in the law of marriage, most particularly on the Augustan legislation. He criticized successive drafts of this book. Alice Pellegrino, Livia Tenzer, Andrew Bell, and David Briney of Stanford generously helped me with the verification of references. The editors of the Press gave me firm encouragement and devoted meticulous care to the presentation of the text.

I gratefully acknowledge my indebtedness to the Social Sciences and Humanities Research Council of Canada for a Leave Fellowship and grants in aid of research, to the Pew Foundation for a research grant, and to the University of Ottawa and Stanford University. The University of Pennsylvania kindly gave me library facilities for a term. Without the Ashmolean Reading Room and the Bodleian Law Library this book would have been very different and taken much longer to complete. Above all, I am grateful to the Principal and Fellows of the King's Hall and College of Brasenose for electing me to a visiting fellowship for 1976/7 and for continuing hospitality ever since. Several chapters were drafted during summers at Brasenose and all bear the mark of hours spent in the common room or library there.

Nor would the book have been finished without the support, encouragement, and well-directed help of my family, especially my daughters Joanna and Silvia and my sisters Heather Pegg and Caroline O'Hagan. Heather Pegg supplied wise comment as well as logistical aid. My husband Arnaldo Treggiari has been an unfailing source of inspiration. He has not only tolerated but abetted my absorption in research and composition and has offered practical help beyond the imaginings of classical theorists.

Stanford   S.M.T.
1 October 1989

Contents

Abbreviations

THIS list refers chiefly to sources and standard works of reference. The unusually short forms used for abbreviations of literary texts, e.g. 'Tac. A' for the *Annals* of Tacitus, should be clear to most readers and are not listed separately here. Any doubt may be resolved by consulting the *Oxford Classical Dictionary*. Abbreviations of titles of periodicals generally follow *L'Année philologique*. Abbreviations for other books are given under their authors' names in the bibliography.

Where possible, I cite Oxford Classical Texts or Loeb texts and translations, as the most accessible to most English readers. Quotations from the *Minor Declamations* attributed to Quintilian are from Winterbottom's edition. The numbering of sections in Tacitus' *Annals* is that of Furneaux, in Dio that of the Loeb edition.

ADA	S. Riccobono (ed.), *Acta divi Augusti* i (Rome, 1945)
Alf.	Alfenus
ANRW	Hildegard Temporini (ed.), *Aufstieg und Niedergang der römischen Welt. Geschichte und Kultur Roms im Spiegel der neueren Forschung* (Berlin, 1972–)
Berger	Adolf Berger, *Encyclopedic Dictionary of Roman Law* (Transactions of the American Philosophical Society 43.2; Philadelphia, 1953)
Bruns	C. G. Bruns (ed.), *Fontes iuris romani antiqui*, 2 vols., 7th edn. by O. Gradenwitz (Tübingen, 1909)
CE	*Carmina Epigraphica*, final part of *Anthologia Latina*, ed. A. Riese, P. Buecheler, and E. Lommatsch (Leipzig, 1869–1926)
CHCL	*Cambridge history of classical literature* i. *Greek literature* (Cambridge, 1985), ii. Latin literature (1982)
Cic. *A*	Cicero *Epistulae ad Atticum*
Cic. *F*	Cicero *Epistulae ad familiares*
Cic. *QF*	Cicero *Epistulae ad Quintum fratrem*
CIL	*Corpus inscriptionum latinarum* (Berlin, 1863–)
CLE, Engström	Einar Engström (ed.), *Carmina latina epigraphica post editam collectionem Büchelerianum in lucem prolata* (Göteborg, 1911)
Coll.	*Mosaicarum et Romanarum legum collatio* = *FIRA* ii.543 ff.

D	*Digest of Justinian*
EJ	Victor Ehrenberg and A. H. M. Jones, *Documents illustrating the reigns of Augustus and Tiberius* (Oxford, 1955)
FIRA	*Fontes iuris romani antejustiniani*, 2nd edn., ed. S. Riccobono *et al.*, 3 vols. (Florence, 1968–9)
Frag. Dos.	*Fragmentum Dositheanum* = *FIRA* ii.617 ff.
Frassinetti	Paolo Frassinetti, 'Gli scritti matrimoniali di Seneca e Tertulliano', *RIL* 88 (1955) 151–88.
FV	*Fragmentum Vaticanum* = *FIRA* ii.463 ff.
G	Gaius
Gnom.	*Gnomon of the Idiologus* = *FIRA* i.99
Herm.	Hermogenianus
HS ·	Sesterces
ht	'hoc titulo' ('in this title', used in juristic references to avoid repetition of book- and title-numbers)
Iav.	Iavolenus
ILLRP	A. Degrassi (ed.), *Inscriptiones latinae liberae reipublicae*, 2 vols. (Biblioteca di Studi Superiori, 23, 40; Florence: vol. i, 1965; vol. ii, 1963)
ILS	H. Dessau (ed.), *Inscriptiones latinae selectae* (Berlin, 1892–1916)
Iul.	Iulianus
Jer. *adv. Iovin.*	Jerome, *adversus Iovinianum*, quoted from the ed. of E. Bickel, *Diatribe in Senecae philosophi fragmenta* i (Leipzig, 1915) pt. VII, *De Senecae Dialogo de matrimonio*, pp. 288–420
Lab.	Labeo
Laud. Tur.	Erik Wistrand (ed.), *The So-called* Laudatio Turiae (Göteborg, 1976)
Lenel, *Edictum Perpetuum*	Otto Lenel, *Das Edictum perpetuum*, 3rd edn. (Leipzig, 1927)
Mod.	Modestinus
MRR	T. R. S. Broughton, *The Magistrates of the Roman Republic*, 3 vols. (American Philological Association Philological Monographs 15; vols. i–ii: Cleveland, Ohio, 1951–2; vol. iii: Atlanta, Ga., 1986)
Ner.	Neratius
OLD	*Oxford Latin Dictionary* (Oxford, 1968–82)
Pap.	Papinian
Paul *S*	*Pauli Sententiae* = *FIRA* ii.319 ff.
Philadelphia Digest	Alan Watson (ed.), *The* Digest *of Justinian* (Philadelphia, 1985) [Eng. trans. with Latin text edited by Mommsen and Krüger]
*PIR*²	*Prosopographia imperii romani*, 2nd edn., 3 vols. (Berlin, 1933–)
Pomp.	Pomponius

P. Ox.	*The Oxyrhynchus Papyri*, ed. B. P. Grenfell, A. S. Hunt, *et al.* (London, 1898–)
PSI	*Papiri della società italiana per la ricerca dei papiri greci e latini in Egitto* (Florence, 1912–)
RE	*Real-Encyclopädie der classischen Altertumswissenschaft*, ed. A. Fr. von Pauly, rev. G. Wissowa *et al.* (Stuttgart, 1894–1980)
RHDFÉ	*Revue historique du droit français et étranger*
SB *A*	D. R. Shackleton Bailey (ed.), *Cicero's letters to Atticus*, 7 vols. (Cambridge, 1965–70)
SB *F*	D. R. Shackleton Bailey (ed.), *Cicero Epistulae ad familiares*, 2 vols. (Cambridge, 1977)
SB *QF*	D. R. Shackleton Bailey (ed.), *Cicero, Epistulae ad Quintum fratrem et M. Brutum* (Cambridge, 1980)
Scaev.	Scaevola
Sierl, L. E.	*Supplementum ad Othonis Lenel Palingenesiam iuris civilis ad fidem papyrorum* (Graz, 1960).
Stangl	Thomas Stangl (ed.), *Ciceronis orationum scholiastae* (Vienna, 1912: repr. Hildesheim, 1964)
SVF	J. von Arnim (ed.), *Stoicorum veterum fragmenta*, 4 vols. (Leipzig, 1903–24)
Thesleff, *Texts*	H. Thesleff, *The Pythagorean texts of the Hellenistic period* (Acta Academiae Aboensis: Humaniora ser. A xxx.1; Abo, 1965)
Tit. Ulp.	*Tituli* [or *Regulae*] *Ulpiani = FIRA* ii.261 ff.
TLL	*Thesaurus linguae latinae* (Leipzig, 1900–)
TP	R. Y. Tyrrell and L. C. Purser (eds.), *The correspondence of M. Tullius Cicero* (Dublin, 1904–33)
Tryph.	Tryphoninus
TvR	*Tijdschrift voor Rechtsgeschiedenis*
Ulp.	Ulpian
Vives	José Vives, *Inscripciones latinas de la España romana*, 2 vols. (Barcelona, 1971–2)

PART I
Matrimonium

1

Introduction

As in the days that were before the flood they were eating and drinking, marrying and giving in marriage, until the day that Noe entered into the ark.

(Matthew 24.38)

For in what stupid age or nation
Was marriage ever out of fashion?

(Samuel Butler, *Hudibras*
pt. iii, c. 1, l. 817)

MARRIAGE is such a normal part of human life that it is taken for granted. The Romans held that it had not existed at the beginning in a Latin city made up of male immigrants and fugitives, simply because there was a shortage of women and no rights of intermarriage with neighbouring peoples.[1] It was necessary to ask for alliances and intermarriage, *conubium*.[2] Rejected everywhere, Romulus arranged the kidnapping of suitable maidens by decoying whole families from nearby towns and the Sabine country to a festival. The maidens were carried off, their kinsmen fled. Romulus reassured the misdoubting women:

... patrum id superbia factum qui conubium finitimis negassent; illas tamen in matrimonio, in societate fortunarum omnium civitatisque et quo nihil carius humano generi sit liberum fore; mollirent modo iras et quibus fors corpora dedisset, darent animos; saepe ex iniuriis postmodum gratiam ortam; eoque melioribus usuras viris quod adnisurus pro se quisque sit, ut cum suam vicem functus officio sit, parentium etiamque patriae expleat

---

[1] Livy draws attention to an original mixture of Albans, Latins, and shepherds (1.6.3), bound together by Alban, Greek, and Etruscan rites and laws, *iura* (1.7.3, 8.1.3), augmented by fugitives from all the neighbouring tribes (8.6). For syntheses on the law the reader is referred to Corbett; Volterra, *Enciclopedia*; Gardner, *Women in Roman law and society*. For the Republic Watson's work is of primary importance. Brini's ambitious *Matrimonio e divorzio nel diritto romano* remains of some interest. Robleda, *El matrimonio en derecho romano*, is of limited usefulness.

[2] Livy 1.9.2. On the forms of the legend see Wiseman, 'The wife and children of Romulus'.

desiderium. Accedebant blanditiae virorum, factum purgantium cupiditate atque amore, quae maxime ad muliebre ingenium efficaces preces sunt. (Livy 1.9.14–16)

'It is the fault of the pride of your fathers, who denied *conubium* to neighbours, but you will be in marriage and will enjoy partnership of all our fortunes and of citizenship and of children, the dearest thing there is for human beings. Soften your anger and give your hearts to those to whom chance has given your bodies. Liking often arises from wrongs. You will find that your husbands will treat you better because each of them will strive not only to do his own duty towards you but to make up for your loss of your parents and country.' The men also resorted to blandishments, making passion and love the excuse for their action, the type of entreaty which is especially effective with women.

The snatching of the maidens was illicit *raptus*, aggravated by violation of religion and hospitality.[3] But in assuring them of their safety, Romulus is able to invoke criteria of honourable marriage. Livy therefore assumes that there are pre-existing Latin or Sabine customs which the Romans can adopt and which will placate their brides. Other antiquarian reconstructions of the first century BC suggested that Romulus invented a particularly fine form of indissoluble marriage in which the couple's wealth was indivisible.[4] But Livy strikes the more authentically Roman note in emphasizing the honourable status which the Sabines are to enjoy. Assimilation of customs in marriage and annexation of women are made parallel to the adoption of ritual and ceremonial and the attraction of settlers which he has already described. It is not clear whether he implies that the status of Roman wives was to be higher than that of wives among the other Latins or the Sabines. Probably not. But his narrative immediately goes on to describe the particular influence of Roman wives and the particular affection in which the Sabines were held.[5] There may perhaps be a genuine folk-memory of marriage by capture here. But historicity is unimportant. The legend has to be fitted into Livy's main theme of the small beginnings of Rome, which by bravery, conciliatory policies, and high moral standards was to grow into the leader of Italy and the mistress of an empire. Wives and mothers are to play a prominent role, particularly in the highly polished first book, with its echoes of Herodotus and of tragedy. Livy's handling of the rape of the Sabines is important for the Roman colour which he gives to these earliest marriages. The key elements are partnership in worldly

---

[3] Livy 1.9.10–14.
[4] DH *Ant.* 2.25.
[5] 1.11.2, 13.

goods, the breeding of children and the grant of citizenship to the wives.[6]

I. Concepts and Definitions

Matrimonium is an institution involving a mother, *mater*.[7] The idea implicit in the word is that a man takes a woman in marriage, *in matrimonium ducere*, so that he may have children by her. He joins her to him by marriage, or by 'his' marriage, or by marriage with himself.[8] He keeps her in marriage, *in matrimonio habere*.[9] Her family may give her into marriage, *in matrimonium dare* or *collocare*.[10] The husband receives her, *accipere*. The word *matrimonia* may also be used almost as the equivalent of 'married women'.[11] There is a tendency, then, to stress the woman's position in relation to marriage, not the man's. Only a woman can enter into *matrimonium* or a *matrimonium*, a relationship which makes her a wife and mother. A man cannot. A specific *matrimonium* may be described as her marriage with a particular man: 'A wife is she whose marriage has been made with a man.'[12] She may be in or live in a marriage 'of' a certain man.[13] She comes into a marriage.[14] So she can go away from it.[15] Her husband can dismiss or turn her out of a specific marriage, but she could not drive him out of it.[16] A *matrimonium* can be dissolved or broken by death or divorce without particular reference being made to either husband or wife.[17] It is possible to refer to a man's *matrimonium* simply from his point of view, but this is rare.[18]

---

[6] *Conubium* (right of intermarriage: see ch. 2) between Roman men and Sabine women would have been sufficient to secure legal marriage and Roman citizenship for the children. But Romulus goes further.

[7] The abstract-noun suffix *-monium* is defined by *OLD* as 'enlargement of -IVM, prob. derived from lost adjs. in *-mo*, *-monis* (*alimonium*, *matrimonium*, *testimonium*)'.

[8] *CIL* 16.18 (AD 76); Curt. 5.3.12, 6.9.30, 8.1.9; Tac. *A* 15.68.5; Suet. *Nero* 28.1; *CJ* 5.6.3.

[9] Cic. *Scaur.* 8. 'He had in marriage so-and-so' is a normal way to introduce a wife in narrative (e.g. Cic. *2Verr.* 2.89, *Caec.* 10, *Scaur.* 8; Nep. *Cim.* 1.2). Also *matrimonio tenere*: Tac. *A* 12.40.3.

[10] Plaut. *Trin.* 691; Cic. *Div.* 1.104.　　[11] *TLL* s.v. 480.

[12] *Decl. min.* 247.2 Tac. *H* 3.45 shows a British queen playing a masculine role, taking a man into her marriage and royal position. The normal Roman use is exemplified by Tac. *A* 6.51.3, 12.58.1; Suet. *DA* 62.1. The noun which looks as if it should be parallel, *patrimonium*, does not mean the position of a father, but his property. (For a play on these two words see Quint. *Inst.* 9.3.80.)

[13] Tac. *A* 1.53.2: 'fuerat in matrimonio Tiberii'; 13.45.4: 'agentem eam in matrimonio Rufri Crispini'; *CJ* 3.36.2: 'uxor tua si Metelli matrimonium tenuisse sciebas'; Suet. *DA* 62.2: 'Liviam Drusillam matrimonio Tiberii Neronis . . . abduxit.'

[14] *Ire* or *convenire*: Plaut. *Trin.* 732; *D* 23.2.15. But *coire* of both *coniuges*: *D* 35.1.31.

[15] Plaut. *Mil.* 1164–5.　　[16] Cic. *Clu.* 188; Suet. *Tib.* 49.1.

[17] *Solvere* (e.g. *D* 25.2.6.4); *dissolvere* (*D* 24.3.38); *distrahere* (*D* 24.3.33); *dirimere* (*D* 24.3.29.1).

[18] Gell. 10.15.23: 'matrimonium flaminis'.

Coniugium is a more general word for marital union, less associated with the specifically Roman institution. It can be used of foreigners, mythical persons, gods, or even animals. Because of its less legalistic tone, it is a word for poetry and high-flown prose.[19] The ancients were uncertain whether it derived from the verb *coniungere*, to join, or from *iugum*, a yoke.[20] It could be used as equivalent of either husband or wife and it does not occur in such interesting conjunctions with verbs as *matrimonium* does. On the other hand, while there is no verb related to *matrimonium*, *coniugium* is related to the convenient verb *coniungere*, 'to join together', which is, among other specific usages, used independently or with *matrimonio* to describe joining in marriage.[21] In particular, a woman is often described as *coniuncta viro* (joined to a man).[22] Again, though both husband and wife may be *coniuncti*,[23] the phrase *coniunctus uxori* (joined to a wife) seems to be absent.

The noun which describes either husband or wife, *coniunx* (or *coniux* etc.), is related to this verb. The grammarians derived it from *iugum*.[24] Although it is used in formal prose, such as oratory, and is very common in sepulchral inscriptions, it is strongly associated with poetry. It is attested as far back as the tragedians Pacuvius and Accius, in the second century BC. It is not a word we should expect to find in mundane contexts such as private letters or the writings of jurists. It is used to describe wives with much greater frequency than husbands, which might be attributed to the fact that our literary sources focus on men, so that wives appear as adjuncts to them. But it is striking that some authors completely avoid using the word to describe a husband.[25] *Coniunx* is used of the wife or husband in relation to the other partner.

There are also different words for husband and wife, *maritus* and *uxor*, etymologically quite separate from each other and from *coniunx*. *Uxor* is held to be related to a Sanskrit word meaning 'sprinkle with seed'. The function of a wife is thus made clear. It is much rarer than *coniunx* in funerary inscriptions from Rome, but preferred to it in Terence, the letters of Cicero, Pliny, and Fronto, Pliny's *Panegyric*, Juvenal, and Suetonius, evidence which demonstrates that it

---

[19] See *TLL* s.v.   [20] Isid. *Etym.* 9.7.20.

[21] *TLL* s.v. 333; e.g. G 1.59. *Coniunctio* is also used (ibid.).

[22] Verg. *E* 8.32; *D* 35.1.10 pr.   [23] e.g. *CIL* 6.1779: 'hi coniuncti'.

[24] *TLL* s.v. 341.

[25] An observation which I owe to Susan Dorken, who in 1983 under my direction undertook a survey, '*Uxores* in *Corpus inscriptionum latinarum* VI', funded by the Social Sciences and Humanities Research Council of Canada. The authors are Cicero, Horace, Curtius, and the Younger Pliny.

is the usual word in everyday speech.[26] *Uxor* is used in connection with a husband, specified or implied. *Maritus* may again be related to Sanskrit and Greek words, for an adolescent male. The word is used in prose and verse and may occur with the genitive to denote 'the husband of so-and-so'. But it is often to be translated as 'a married man'.[27] *Maritus* is also probably used, though not often, as an adjective to describe a man as married.[28] The plural noun is occasionally also used to describe married people of both sexes.[29] *Marita* of a wife or married woman is almost entirely confined to poetry and epitaphs.[30] This root also produces a verb and adjectives.[31]

The masculine noun *vir*, besides describing an adult male, in contrast to a woman, a boy, or a eunuch, is commonly used of a husband or lover. For a husband it is the normal prose word and also occurs in such verse genres as comedy, satire, and epigram.[32] *Femina*, 'female' or 'woman' (related to Sanskrit and Latin words meaning 'suck', thus a word which recalls a mammalian function), is only occasionally used to mean wife.[33] *Mulier*, the alternative word for woman, is often used of the sexually experienced woman, contrasted with the virgin.[34] It may therefore be used specifically of a man's wife or mistress, though this usage is not very common.[35] *Vir* and *femina* make the pair of 'man and woman', *vir* and *mulier* correspond more closely with 'man and wife'. *Nupta* may be used to describe a woman as married, in contrast to unmarried women, without direct reference to her husband. Finally, the resonant words *matrona* and *materfamilias* describe the legally married Roman woman. These and other semi-technical terms will be discussed later.

[26] The data are again Mrs Dorken's.
[27] e.g. Plaut. *Cas.* 291, *Merc.* 1018, contrasted with *caelebs*; Tac. *H* 3.45.2, contrasted with *adulter*.
[28] e.g. Cic. *Dom.* 37.   [29] Suet. *DA* 44.2; *D* 24.1.52.1.
[30] *TLL* s.v. 406–7. *Maritata* is a post-classical equivalent (*TLL* s.v. *marito* 402).
[31] *Marito* 'to join in marriage' is used with individuals of either sex as the object or even whole groups, as in *Lex de maritandis ordinibus*. The adjective *maritalis* may describe such things as wedding torches, union, secrets, embraces, injuries. *Maritus* is a poetic variant. Horace boldly uses *lege marita* of the Augustan Law (*Carm. saec.* 20). All the words from this root are also used of the mating of animals and the training of vines on trees.
[32] It may be used with a possessive referring to the wife, as in *vir suus* or *eius* or *mi vir*. In epitaphs *viro suo* is relatively frequent. Cf. *CIL* 6.11372: 'vir eius', 15124: 'vir et libertus', 20682: 'vir et patronus', 1815: 'prior vir Culicinae'. By itself, *vir* indicates sex, not marital status (Isid. *Orig.* 9.7.1).
[33] e.g. Prop. 2.6.24; Col. 12 pr. 8; Mart. 8.12.4. See *TLL* s.v. 458. Cf. French *femme*. Latin derivatives relate to the general sense.
[34] e.g. Cic. ap. Quint. *Inst.* 6.3.75; *D* 21.1.14.7.
[35] e.g. Suet. *DA* 69.1; *CIL* 4.8590; 6.28091: 'mulier et filii', 28687: 'mulieri meae', 33195: 'mulieri suae'; 8.9619; *D* 32.93.1. See *TLL* s.v. 1574–5. Cf. Italian *moglie*. The plural is also used to refer to the grown women in a family, 'our womenfolk' (Cic. *A* 7.13a.3, 7.14.3). A number of other Latin words derive from *mulier* in its general sense and tend to have a derogatory flavour.

Several of the words already discussed have emphasized the wife's role in procreation and child-rearing. The Romans conventionally regarded marriage as an institution designed for the production of legitimate children. A wife was given to a man for the purpose of getting children, *liberorum quaerundorum causa*. It is this purpose which defines the woman as a legal wife and the union as marriage. The parallel Greek formula had been more specific about the legitimacy of the children.[36] Although the formula and its variants occur at all periods, it is rarer than might be expected and often alluded to rather than quoted.[37] It was ingrained in Roman consciousness and could therefore be taken for granted or used for solemn or humorous effect, much as a phrase from the 'Solemnization of matrimony' in the *Prayer Book* may be. It may be noted that a man marries a wife to get children for himself, to continue his line with legitimate descendants. The technical term is not used to describe the purpose of women in marrying. As so often, literary Latin looks at the matter from the man's point of view.[38]

A wife may be defined as the woman whom a man takes for the breeding of legitimate children. No writer will stop to think of defining a husband or his function. What about defining the private relationship of marriage or the institution which was of such public importance?

It was necessary for the state that citizens should marry and

---

[36] Παίδων ἐπ' ἀρότωι γνησίων. See e.g. Apul. *Apol.* 88.

[37] Plaut. *Capt.* 889: 'liberorum quaerundorum caussa ei . . . uxor datast'; cf. Suet. *DJ* 52.3: 'uxores liberorum quaerendorum causa ducere'; Gell. 17.21.44: 'uxorem se liberum quaerundorum causa habere'; *Tit. Ulp.* 3.3. Variants and usages include 'duxit me uxorem liberorum sibi quesendum gratia' (Enn. *Trag.* 120); 'uxorem se liberum quaerundum gratia habiturum' (Gell. 4.3.2.); 'Q. Metellus censor censuit, ut cogerentur omnes ducere uxores liberorum creandorum causa' (Livy *Per.* 59); 'quia non creandorum liberorum causa coniugium intercesserat' (VM 7.7.4, of an elderly couple); 'coisse liberorum creandorum gratia' (Quint. *Decl.* 247.6); 'uxorem liberorum procreandorum causa domi habuisti' (*CJ* 5.4.9). Similarly 'liberis procreandis . . . volo te uxorem domum ducere' (Plaut. *Aul.* 148ff.); 'quaeritur . . . pueris beata creandis uxor' (Hor. *Epp.* 1.2.44–5). It appears that the *Lex Julia de maritandis ordinibus* used the phrase *liberorum procreandorum causa: FIRA* iii. 17; *PSI* vi.730; Isid. *de eccl. off.* 2.10.10; and that it was quoted in dotal contracts (ibid. and Aug. *Sermo* 51.13, PL 28.345). See further Volterra, *Enciclopedia* 739ff., Daube, *Duty of procreation* 18ff. For the obvious connection between marriage and fatherhood cf. Plaut. *Mil.* 680ff.; Cic. *Dom.* 34, *Acad.* 2.109. It is an early Christian doctrine (derived from ascetic pagan philosophy), that children should be the only purpose of marriage and that each sexual act in marriage was designed for procreation, which leads to statements such as 'matrimonium quippe ex hoc appellatum est, quod non ob aliud debeat femina nubere, quam ut mater fiat' (Aug. *c. Faustum* 19.26, PL 42.365); 'matrimonialis concubitus, qui fit causa gignendi' (Aug. *de bono coniugali* 6.6, PL 40.377); or 'concubitus coniugalis, qui . . . procreandorum fit causa liberorum' (Aug. *Civ. dei* 14.18, PL 41.426.) Cf. *TLL* s.v. *matrimonialis* 475.

[38] This is independent of the fact that the verbs *creo* and *procreo* are used of either parent.

produce new citizens.[39] But no juristic definition of marriage has been passed down to us from the heyday of Roman jurisprudence. Justinian's compilers in the sixth century chose to introduce the *Digest* title on formation of marriage (*de ritu nuptiarum*), a very short selection, with a sentence from Modestinus (early third century AD). This can scarcely be regarded as a definition:

Nuptiae sunt coniunctio maris et feminae et consortium omnis vitae, divini et humani iuris communicatio. (*Digest* 23.2.1)

Marriage is the joining together of a male and a woman, and a partnership for life in all areas of life, a sharing in divine and human law.

The virtue of the sentence was that it was flexible enough to fit both old Roman ideas and the Christian concepts of Justinian's time. It is unnecessary to regard the extract as substantially reworked by the compilers.[40] *Consortium* is used in classical Latin for the sharing of property, community of life. It was originally used in a technical sense, of the joint enjoyment of an undivided estate by coheirs, especially brothers.[41] *Consors*, a partner or sharer, was originally someone who shares an inheritance. Brothers will often therefore be *consortes*.[42] The word is then used metaphorically of partners in crime or toil. *Tout court*, it can be used of a wife, like our 'consort'.[43] *Consortium* is also used in a wider sense for sharing.[44] It is used in the context of marriage by Tacitus and Apuleius. It becomes common in this usage in Christian writings, but cannot be called non-classical.[45] It is clear that, as *consortium* was the technical description for the holding of property in common by heirs (who therefore needed to co-operate and were also likely to divide the property at some subsequent date), so it was appropriate for the fusion of property for the duration of a marriage which might be practised by husband and wife. *Communicatio* is not a very common word and not especially used in connection with marriage in classical Latin, except in the *aquae et ignis communicatio* (the sharing of water and fire), the sacrament which formed a part of at least some wedding ceremonies

[39] Gell. 1.6.6.
[40] Robleda, *El matrimonio en derecho romano* 66ff., gives a convenient list of scholars for and against interpolation. To those who believe it classical add Humbert (*Remariage à Rome* 28–9). Albertario, 'La definizione del matrimonio secondo Modestino', gives a useful list of classical parallels.
[41] *TLL* s.v. 488, citing Suet. *Cl.* 28; Gell. 1.9.12; *D* 17.2.52.8.
[42] *OLD* s.v. 1. See esp. Fest. 296M; cf. Livy 41.27.2; VM 2.7.5; *D* 27.1.31.4; *CIL* 5.2844.
[43] Partners: e.g. Cic. 2*Verr.* 3.155, *Brut.* 2; Vell. 2.74.2; Tac. *A* 1.3.3. Wives: Ov. *M* 1.319, 6.94, 10.246; *Decl. min.* 376.2. Cf. *CIL* 9.2617: 'coniugi et consorti'.
[44] e.g. Sen. *Dial.* 10.14.1, *Epp.* 48.2; Pliny *Pan.* 7.
[45] Tac. *A* 3.34.9; Apul. *Plat.* 2.260: 'dites inferiores nuptias non recusent et locupletium consortium inopes consequantur.' Cf. *TLL* s.v. 489.

and which symbolized precisely the sharing of natural resources. The idea of the sharing of worldly wealth certainly antedates Modestinus. It happened automatically in archaic marriage (when the wife's property legally belonged to the husband) or as a matter of convenience and morality in the normal classical marriage, where the wife's property remained legally separate. The idea of sharing is a prominent feature in both Greek and Roman ideology of marriage, as we shall see in Part III.[46]

The first part of the definition is very similar to one postulated in a rhetorical exercise:

Uxor est quae femina viro nuptiis collocata in societatem vitae venit. (*Declamationes minores* 247.2)

A wife is a woman who is given in marriage to a man and comes to share his life.

Such a definition seems to lie behind a number of ancient descriptions of a legal Roman marriage.[47] Nor of course is there anything unclassical or specifically Christian about Modestinus' allusion to *divinum ius*. *Omnis vitae* in vague: it could refer to the permanence of marriage, which is a pagan idea, but which pagans interpreted with much greater flexibility than Christianity was later to sanction, or to all the facets of life here and now;[48] probably both. Some support is given to the second sense by a *Digest* passage on concubines. Papinian is trying to discover when a certain relationship changed from *concubinatus* to valid marriage. The existence of the intention to be husband and wife ought to be indicated by the way the couple lived together, *vitae coniunctio*.[49] The sort of change he had in mind might include something like the modern *rite de passage* from cohabitation to a joint bank account. I take *consortium omnis vitae* as 'a partnership for life in all areas of life'.[50]

[46] See e.g. Cic. *Off.* 1.54: 'one house, everything in common'; Col. 12 pr. 8: 'There was nothing to be seen in the house which belonged to the individual'; Mart. 4.75.3–4, to Nigrina: 'It pleases you to mix your paternal wealth with your husband, rejoicing that he is your partner and shares it with you'; Quint. *Decl.* 247.11: 'he would have wished for nothing better than that his goods, even if he lived, should be shared with her.'

[47] A law attributed to Numa allegedly said, 'If a father allows his son to take a wife *to be a sharer in holy things and property* according to the laws, then the father no longer has authority to sell his son' (DH *Ant.* 2.27.4).

[48] I am not sure if this is what Humbert means (*Remariage à Rome* 28) by 'toute espèce de vie', human and divine (explained by 'humani iuris communicatio'). Albertario is clearer: not 'consortium perpetuo, finchè la vita dura' but 'consortium di ogni cosa, o lieta o triste, che ha la vita' ('Definizione del matrimonio' 184). Westrup, *Introduction to early Roman law* i.10–11, had defined it as 'complete association of life' rather than 'union for life'.   [49] *D* 39.5.31 pr.

[50] Cf. also Just. *Inst.* 1.9.1 'Nuptiae . . . sive matrimonium est viri et mulieris coniunctio individuam vitae consuetudinem continens' ('Marriage or matrimony is the union of a man and a woman implying the undivided conduct of life'). This definition has been thought to derive from Ulpian, because of similarity with *D* 1.1.1.3, but the similarity is not compelling.

Coniunctio, used in the passage of Papinian just mentioned for the common life of a couple who may or may not be married, is used of friends and also quite often of husband and wife. Ulpian in his brief remarks on the natural origin of law sets human mating in the context of the animal world just as Cicero had done:[51]

Ius naturale . . . hinc descendit maris atque feminae coniunctio, quam nos matrimonium appellamus. (*Digest* I.I.I.3, Ulpian *i institutionum*)

From natural law . . . derives the union of male and female, which we call marriage.

The jurists and philosophers do not proceed beyond such general statements.

2. Purposes

The reproductive purpose of marriage is, as we have seen, inextricably linked with the Romans' conception of the institution. This may remind us of the Anglican *Prayer Book*'s tripartite classification:

First, it was ordained for the procreation of children . . . Secondly, it was ordained for a remedy against sin, and to avoid fornication, that such persons as have not the gift of continency might marry . . . Thirdly, it was ordained for the mutual society, help, and comfort, that the one ought to have of the other, both in prosperity and adversity.

The Romans see children as the vital continuation of the blood-line and an insurance policy. A wife represents, therefore, a strengthening of the family, *firmamentum familiae*.[52] Children protect the parents' old age, are a staff for the aged, act as reinforcements, prop up the house or form its foundations, or are the pole to which the vines may cling.[53]

The Romans' idea of *stuprum* (illicit sexual intercourse), as we shall see in Chapter 9, was very different from the Church's idea of fornication (where a Latin word which describes men's commerce with prostitutes is applied to any extra-marital intercourse). The sexual instinct was recognized as the natural cause of animals' mating. But the satisfaction of the sexual instinct was not regarded as a reason for the institution of marriage.[54] Men could licitly satisfy their physical

[51] *Off.* 1.54: 'Because the urge to reproduce is an instinct common to all animals, the first sharing (*societas*) takes place in the actual mating of the pair, the next is that of the pair in their children. Then there is one house and all things in common. This is the beginning of the city and the seed-bed of the state.'   [52] Afran. *com.* 241–2.

[53] *Munire senectam*: Lucr. 4.1255–6; *bacillum*: CIL 6.18086 = *CE* 1581; *subsidia*: Cic. *Clu.* 32; Suet. *Cal.* 12.1; *fulcire domum*: Sen. *Contr.* 2.1.7; Sen. *Cons. ad Marc.* 15.2; *fundamentum*: Plaut. *Most.* 121, cf. Pliny *Epp.* 4.21.3.

[54] But note that a pair's *societas* necessarily precedes reproduction.

instincts without marriage. We might, however, expect to find it said that marriage channelled the natural desires of respectable women. As far as I know, this is not precisely stated, although to leave a girl unmarried was imprudent. Sexual activity within marriage was natural, necessary, and chaste. Women were expected to accept it. Conversely, respectable women were to abstain from extra-marital sexual relations. It had, however, occurred to pagan thinkers to wonder how young men might best be steadied. Plutarch recommends early marriage as a way of disciplining unruly desires.[55]

The third reason for the institution of marriage was officially added to the liturgy by Cranmer.[56] Unlike the second, it fits the Roman ideology of marriage. We are occasionally told that marriage ensures support. A rhetorical exercise goes so far as to say that this is the purpose for which nature itself invented the institution. 'Thus males are joined to females so that the weaker sex may obtain protection from their shared partnership.'[57] Conversely, the wife might be the prop of her husband, whether he was compared to a vine or a tottering house.[58] But the *Prayer Book* idea of sharing and partnership in good and bad fortune is particularly Roman. It may be doubted whether ordinary Romans would have defined this as a *purpose* of marriage. Rather, it was part of the ideal nature of marriage. The difference in approach between jurists and *Prayer Book* is made inevitable by the Church's insistence that marriage was instituted by God, for the good of mankind, at the time when he created Eve as a helpmate for Adam. Marriage is given a heavy mystical significance, as the preamble to the description of the three reasons shows. All three elements belong to a divine plan. The third element of Cranmer's tripartite classification has its roots in the Greek philosophical ideas to which the best Roman moralists adhered. Musonius in his lectures puts it in words close to those of Cranmer:

The husband and wife . . . should come together for the purpose of making a life in common and of procreating children, and furthermore of regarding all things in common between them, and nothing peculiar or private to one or the other, not even their own bodies. The birth of a human being which results from such a union is to be sure something marvelous, but it is not yet

---

[55] Plut. *libb. educ.* 13F. Cf. Apul. *M* 6. 23.

[56] Stone, *The Family, sex and marriage in England 1500–1800* 101. But the tripartite set of reasons goes back much further in Judaeo-Christian thought. See Isid. *Etym.* 9.7.27: 'Tribus . . . ob causis ducitur uxor: prima est causa prolis, de qua legitur in Genesi (1.28): "Et benedixit eos", dicens: "Crescite et multiplicamini"; secunda causa adiutorii, de qua ibi in Genesi dicitur (2.18): "Non est bonum esse hominem solum; faciamus ei adiutorium simile"; tertia causa incontinentiae, unde dicit Apostolus, ut (1 Cor. 7.9): "Qui se non continet, nubat."'

[57] *Decl. min.* 368.3.   [58] Tac. *A* 12.5.4; Ov. *Tr.* 1.6.5.

enough for the relation of husband and wife, inasmuch as quite apart from marriage it could result from any other sexual union, just as in the case of animals. But in marriage there must be above all perfect companionship and mutual love of husband and wife, both in health and in sickness and under all conditions, since it was with desire for this as well as for having children that both entered upon marriage. (13A trans. Cora Lutz, *YCS* 10 [1947] 89)

Musonius is right to point out that breeding can take place without marriage. But to lawyers marriage made possible the link between father and child. The father could acknowledge the child as his own and undertake to rear it. The child could succeed to his citizen status, social position, and property. The difference in viewpoint between the professional jurist and the professional philosopher was a natural one. To the former it was not of primary interest that wives be supported to enable them to bear and nurture children. To the latter the mutual duties and happiness of both husband and wife were of moral significance. Ordinary Latin discourse about the 'built-in' purpose of marriage tends to stress the legal nature of the institution. This is not to deny the parallel existence of a morality of marriage, to which we shall give more attention in Chapters 6–8.

The Romans saw marriage as a matter of human practice, varying in different cultures, but in Roman law accompanied by precise legal results. Its purpose was clear and pragmatic: the production (and consequent rearing) of legitimate children. A union could be defined as a Roman marriage if certain legal conditions were met and if both partners intended marriage. Their intention could often be proved if they produced children and the man acknowledged them.

3. Chronological Overview

The gradual and complex development of Roman customs in family life and the relationship between husband and wife cannot be reduced to a simple linear progression. Attempts to identify sudden 'reforms' which improved the position of wives in relation to husbands have, for example, been abandoned. Nor is it often possible to trace the course of important changes. Much of the evidence which would enable us to do so is simply lacking. In particular, the pivotal period of Roman law during which social priorities altered in reaction to changing circumstances and the praetors by their edicts and administration of justice modified the ancient rules in the interests of equity and of practicality is badly documented.[59] We can ascertain from

[59] For a succinct account of the development of law see Watson, *LAR*. Cf. also id., *RPL*; and 'The development of the praetor's edict'.

various scattered sources the socio-economic pressures on the upper
class which motivated the praetors, the individuals who made wills,
the senators who introduced legislation, and eventually the jurists of
the second and first centuries BC who compiled coherent accounts of
legal theory. But the social context can be reconstructed only in part,
for instance from Polybius or conjecturally from Plautus. Not only is
the archaic period from the kings through the foundation of the
Republic (c.509) down to the beginnings of transmarine imperialism
in the early third century unreliably and scantily attested, apart from
what can be deduced for the fifth century and earlier from the Twelve
Tables.[60] But so is the period of rising economic prosperity and social
unrest which followed in the wake of continued wars and annexation
of provinces in the late third and second century. Evidence concerning political developments and civil wars improves for the period after
133 BC, but in the area of private life we are poorly served until the
early speeches of Cicero, which date to the dictatorship of Sulla.
From about 80 BC until about AD 14 (the death of Augustus) contemporary sources remain relatively rich. Thereafter, informative secondary sources, particularly Tacitus and Suetonius, cover the period
of the Julio-Claudian and Flavian emperors (to AD 96). For the late
first and early second centuries AD Tacitus and Pliny become primary
sources, but for later in the second century literary sources in Latin
are again scattered. The bulk of the juristic writings which survive
are, on the other hand, concentrated in the second and third centuries. These often cast light on earlier legislation, notably the reforms of
Augustus.[61] The result of this patchiness of available sources is that in
a discussion of the development of law in its social context we cannot
focus as sharply as we should like on the transition from archaic
patriarchalism to the society we know from the letters and speeches of
Cicero in the late Republic (during the pre-classical period of law).
We are on surer ground with the radical reforms in family law
introduced by Augustus (emperor 27 BC–AD 14). For the second and
early third centuries AD, the classical period of law, we are well
informed about the interpretation of law in such sources as the
introductory textbook of Gaius and the extracts from juristic opinions
collected in the *Digest*. For light on some areas of social mores we can
turn to the funerary inscriptions, which reach their peak in that
period. But Roman literary sources give us only weak support after
Pliny and Tacitus. With the death of Ulpian (223) and of the last
Severan emperor (235) and the decline into civil war and disruption

---

[60] Watson, *XII Tables*.
[61] For fuller consideration of the nature of the sources see Wells, *Roman Empire* 33 ff.

(235–84), the juristic evidence again becomes tenuous and the literary accounts completely unsatisfactory. It is clear that after that troubled half-century, the stern reforms of Diocletian, savage persecutions, and civil wars, Constantine presided over a very different society. The reforms which he introduced in family law are symptom and cause of new or intensified social pressures, among which Christian ideals must be counted. Constantine's legislation marks the third pivotal period in the development of family law. It lies outside the focus of this book, although occasional reference will be made to it. But the sharp break in continuity which comes after 235 and the almost total disappearance of viable sources in the half-century which follows provide a practical stopping-point. It will therefore be clear that the only pivotal period which we shall examine in any detail is that of Augustus. In order to get any sense of development it will be necessary to give a conjectural account of the archaic patriarchal system, then to concentrate on the well-documented period from Cicero to Ulpian. The differences between law and society in the time of Cicero and the time of the Twelve Tables will seem obvious enough. The differences between pre- and post-Augustan society may well seem indistinct, although the legal changes are sharp.

(a) Early 'patriarchalism'

Romans long retained an institution which distinguished them from nearly all other races, *patria potestas*, paternal power. This meant that children born in legal Roman marriage were in the power of their father or his oldest male ascendant in direct male line.[62] So were those who were adopted. The male who held this power was called the father of the household, *paterfamilias*. He might have in his power his own legitimate children, his sons' children, his son's sons' children. He might free his children by a legal procedure called *emancipatio*. On his death, his children or fatherless grandchildren who had been in his power became independent, *sui iuris*. The males became *patresfamilias* in their own right. But grandchildren whose father was alive (and had not previously been emancipated) fell under their own father's power. So the death of a *paterfamilias* may create several new households, each under a new *paterfamilias*, and a number of independent women (daughters or fatherless granddaughters). In the early period, daughters on marriage often left their natal family and were automatically freed from *patria potestas*. In any case, if they

---

[62] See e.g. Watson, *Persons* 77 ff.

were legally married their children belonged to their husband's family
and their mother's father had no power over them. Those under the
power of a *paterfamilias* (*filiifamilias*, *filiaefamilias*) had no property
of their own, and anything they acquired belonged to him. On his
death they had rights of intestate succession. The *paterfamilias* had
power of life and death over his *filiifamilias* and could sell them.
Presumably he could also, at this early date, dispose of them in
marriage as he thought fit, without their consent. The institution of
patria potestas, which continued right through the classical period
of Roman law, is essential to an understanding of the early system of
marriage and continued to be intertwined with marriage throughout
the classical period.[63]

(*b*) Manus *and* matrimonium

As far as we know, marriage in early Rome was usually accompanied
by *manus*.[64] Our fullest information is gleaned, as so often, from the
textbook of law written by the famous jurist Gaius in the second
century AD. He divides persons into those who are independent, *sui
iuris* (literally, 'of their own right'), and those who are subject to
someone else's right. The latter are categorized as persons in power,
manus, or ownership.[65] Slaves and children begotten in Roman
marriage are in power.[66] *Mancipium*, a fictitious ownership when
applied to free persons, need not concern us at present. *Manus* is the
word especially though not exclusively used in relation to wives.[67]
Gaius' formal description occupies less than two pages in modern
texts, much less than his long and complex discussion of the creation
of paternal power which precedes. The beginning of the paragraph is
corrupt, but he is clearly introducing *manus*:

. . . quod et ipsum ius proprium civium Romanorum est. Sed in potestate
quidem et masculi et feminae esse solent; in manum autem feminae tantum
conveniunt. Olim itaque tribus modis in manum conveniebant: usu, farreo,
coemptione. (1.108–10)

---

[63] Gaius discusses marriage because it creates *patria potestas*: 1.55 ff.
[64] Watson, *XII Tables* 17–18. Buckland (*Textbook* 118) and Corbett (68) think it always was.
For recent views on *manus* see Gaudemet, 'Observations sur la manus'; Cantarella, 'Sui
rapporti fra matrimonio e conventio in manum'; Volterra, 'La "conventio in manum" e il
matrimonio romano' (against Cantarella); Villers, 'Manus et mariage' (supporting Volterra);
Volterra, *Enciclopedia* 755 ff.; Watson, 'Two notes on *manus*'.
[65] 1.49: 'earum personarum, quae alieno iuri subiectae sunt, aliae in potestate, aliae in manu,
aliae in mancipio sunt'.   [66] 1.52 ff. We return to this topic in ch. 2.
[67] Used of paternal power: Livy 3.45.2 and loosely 34.2.11; Sen. *Contr.* 3.3; *epit.* 1.6.3; *CJ*
7.40.1.2 Just. *Inst.* 1.12.6. Of power over slaves and freedmen: *D* 1.1.4; Livy 39.9.6; Quint.
Inst. 7.7.9. Both of these are implied by *emancipatio* and *manumissio*. Cf. Watson, *XII Tables*
19. Gaius, however, regards *in manum convenire* as restricted to women.

. . . this too is a right peculiar to Roman citizens. But both males and females may be in power; but only females come into *manus* [control, literally 'the hand']. In the old days there were three ways in which females came into it: by *usus*, *farreum*, and *coemptio*.

Convenire in manum ('to come into control') is the usual way of describing this process. *Viro* ('to a man or husband') or *mariti* ('of a husband') may be added.[68] The abstract noun *conventio* occurs in this context.[69] A wife in her husband's control is normally described in phrases such as *uxor (quae) in manu viri est*, 'a wife (who) is in her husband's hand'.[70] But the useful phrases 'marriage *cum manu*' and 'marriage *sine manu*' for marriage accompanied by or without the husband's control are modern constructs. The Romans always speak only of the wife coming into or being in *manus*, and do not even regard *her* as being 'without' it. Nor do they speak of the husband as having *manus* over the wife.[71]

It will be clearer to concentrate first on the ancients' descriptions of this custom, even though these are comparatively late. Let us begin with the three methods by which a woman might enter *manus* and then describe the results of the procedure. The three methods are always listed in the order used by Gaius: by *usus*, by emmer-wheat, and by *coemptio*.[72] Cicero also keeps the priority of *usus* when discussing the only two ways in which a certain free-born (but not upper-class) woman could have come into *manus*: 'usu an coemptione?'[73] (The third method seems to have been reserved to patricians.) Watson's argument that the traditional order was enshrined in the Twelve Tables is persuasive.

(c) Usus

Usu in manum conveniebat quae anno continuo nupta perseverabat; quia enim veluti annua possessione usu capiebatur, in familiam viri transibat filiaeque locum optinebat. Itaque lege duodecim tabularum cautum est ut, si qua nollet eo modo in manum mariti convenire, ea quotannis trinoctio abesset atque eo modo usum cuiusque anni interrumperet. Sed hoc totum

---

[68] e.g. G 1.111, 3.83, 84; Cic. *Flacc.* 84, *Top.* 14; Quint. *Inst.* 5.10.62; *Coll.* 4.2.3, 4.7.1; Boeth. ad. Cic. *Top.* 14 = Bruns ii.73 = *FIRA* ii.307; Schol. Bob. on Cic. *Flacc.* 84 (Stangl p. 106). The husband may receive a woman into *manus* as a wife (G 2.98) or she may be given *in manum* (Ter. *And.* 297).

[69] Serv. ad *A* 4.103 = Bruns ii.76. This passage also has 'in matrimonium convenire' and 'mulier in potestatem viri cedit'.

[70] e.g. G 1.115b, 136, 148; 3.3, 40, 41, 199.

[71] Gaudemet, 'Observations sur la manus' 330–1.

[72] Watson, *XII Tables* 9ff., which replaces his earlier article, 'Usu, farre(o) coemptione'. The only other texts are Boeth. ad Cic. *Top.* 14 (Bruns ii.73 = *FIRA* ii.307), which derives from *Tit. Ulp.* and so probably from Gaius (Watson, *Persons* 19), Arnobius *adv. Gent.* 4.20, and Serv. ad *G* 1.31.   [73] *Flacc.* 84.

ius partim legibus sublatum est, partim ipsa desuetudine obliteratum est. (Gaius 1.111)

A woman came into control if she remained married for a continuous year, because she was as it were acquired by usucapion because of the year's occupancy and went over into the family of the husband and obtained the position of a daughter. Therefore it was prescribed by the law of the Twelve Tables that if any woman did not wish to come into the husband's control in that manner, she should stay away for three nights each year and so break the *usus* of each year. But all this rule has partly been abolished by statutes and partly wiped out by desuetude.

Possessio (occupancy) is distinct from ownership (*dominium*, *proprietas*).[74] It was defined as physical power over a thing, accompanied by the intention to possess. Usucapion of property was dealt with in the Twelve Tables. It is defined as 'acquisition of ownership of a thing belonging to another through possession of it (*possessio*) for a period fixed by law'.[75] The possessor had to be in good faith and to have just cause. According to the Twelve Tables, uninterrupted possession of a moveable object for one year conferred legal ownership. Two years were required for immoveables, such as land.[76] This allowed, for instance, the transfer of the ownership of a slave without the need for a formal procedure. The passage shows clearly that acquisition of *manus* over a wife by *usus* antedates the fifth-century codification of the law. It also indicates that it was already accepted that not all wives entered *manus*.[77] A woman in the first year of a marriage was already recognized as a wife, though *usus* had not yet created *manus*.[78]

The *trinoctium* (interval of three nights) which interrupted possession is little attested.[79] We have, however, a learned citation of the jurist Q. Mucius Scaevola (consul 95 BC):

---

[74] Berger s.v. *possessio* 637; Buckland, *Textbook* 196 ff.

[75] Berger s.v. *usucapio*. See further Buckland, *Textbook* 241 ff.; Nicholas, *Introduction to Roman law* 122 ff.; Mayer-Maly, 'Studien zur Frühgeschichte der usucapio' 259 ff. Daube, 'Historical aspects of informal marriage' 97, makes the essential point economically: 'while, in general, a promise to be actionable had to be by way of question and answer—"Do you promise so-and-so?", "I promise"—sale and hire could be concluded in any fashion. These so-called "informal contracts" were evidently as good as the formal stipulation. The law just did not require a form for sale, hire or marriage.'

[76] Cic. *Top.* 4.23.

[77] Corbett 87 ff.; Watson, *XII Tables* 18.

[78] Cf. the slightly puzzled note by Servius (ad *G* 1.31 = Bruns ii.78–9): 'Tribus enim modis apud veteres nuptiae fiebant: usu, si verbi gratia mulier anno uno cum viro, licet sine legibus, fuisset' 'marriages [*sic*] came about in three ways among the ancients: by *usus*, if for instance a woman was with a man for a year, although without the laws [*sic*]').

[79] See Wolff, 'Trinoctium'. Arangio-Ruiz (*Istituzioni* 437) held that originally the *trinoctium* broke the marriage: I would not agree.

Q. quoque Mucium iureconsultum dicere solitum legi non esse usurpatam mulierem, quae, cum Kalendis Ianuariis apud virum matrimonii causa esse coepisset, ante diem iv Kalendas Ianuarias sequentes usurpatum isset. Non enim posse impleri trinoctium, quod abesse a viro usurpandi causa ex duodecim tabulis deberet, quoniam tertiae noctis posteriores sex horae alterius anni essent, qui inciperet ex Kalendis. (Gellius 3.2.12–13; also in Macrobius 1.3.9)

Moreover, I have read, the jurist Q. Mucius was in the habit of saying that a woman did not break usucapion if, after beginning to be with a man for the sake of marriage on 1 January, she went to break it on the following 29 December. For the *trinoctium*, for which she had to be away from her husband in accordance with the Twelve Tables in order to interrupt usucapion, could not be completed. This was because the second six hours of the third night belonged to the second year, which began on 1 January.

The jurists used *usurpatio* to mean interruption of *usucapio*.[80] The person who broke occupation by the possessor might be the legal owner. The most obvious context in which this might occur is in agriculture, where a squatter who took two annual crops of land might argue that he had become the legal owner, and the original proprietor, who had not intended to transfer the land, might reassert his rights.[81] But in our context it is the wife who intervenes in order to remain in the power of her original *paterfamilias* or to remain independent. Presumably in the first instance she acted with the approval of her male ascendant, and in the second she may still have acted on the instructions or in accordance with the wishes of her original family. It is not clear whether the husband's intentions should be taken into account. Did he agree to the *usurpatio*? Or should we assume that the initiation of *usus* implied that he expected to receive the wife into *manus*?[82] The latter seems better to fit the legal situation. But the interests of both husband and wife and their kin in whether a woman was *in manu* varied according to circumstances and over time. It is a gross over-simplification to assume that avoidance of *manus* was always in the interest of the wife. As for the practicalities of the escape-method introduced or at least ratified by the Tables, there were certain inconveniences. *Manus* through *usus* could only be brought about by lapse of a year, during which the wife presumably resided in her husband's house. (No one talks of what happened if he absented himself: presumably this was immaterial.[83] We shall discuss later the information we have about the initiation of marriage in the

---

[80] *D* 41.3.2, cf. ht 5. The use of *usurpatam*, passive in a middle sense describing the action of the wife, is interesting.   [81] Buckland, *Textbook* 242–3.   [82] Cf. Watson, *Persons* 20–1.
[83] *Pace* Arangio-Ruiz, *Istituzioni* 437–8.

husband's absence.) If the wife was called away for some valid
reason, such as a family emergency, she might involuntarily impede
manus. On the other hand, in order to prevent the automatic creation
of *manus*, *usurpatio* would need to be repeated each twelvemonth
and the dates carefully calculated. Although the custom seems to
have lasted down to the first century BC, it would certainly seem to
have been simpler for those desiring *manus* to achieve it by *coemptio*.

Watson has argued vigorously that between the discussion by
Scaevola and Cicero's speech for L. Flaccus in 59 BC a system evolved
which made the *trinoctium* unnecessary. Cicero is defending his client
against a charge that he had wrongfully taken the estate of a free-born
married woman, Valeria, who had died intestate. The prosecution
allegedly argued that she had been *in manu*. Cicero pretends that he
had not thought of that possibility, and inquires how she had entered
manus. Was it *usu*? But that would have required the consent of her
guardians, so Flaccus, who was one of them, could have refused, in
order to safeguard his rights to the property. Watson suggests that at
this time the authorization of guardians was required for *usus* to lead
to *manus* (although it was not required for marriage as such). This
rule may have been based on safeguards in the Twelve Tables which
protected the property of a woman in agnatic guardianship from
usucapion. 'The *auctoritas tutoris* was an innovation, a deliberate
misrepresentation of the XII Tables' provision, in order to allow most
marriages to be *sine manu*.' The requirement will then have been
extended to women in other kinds of guardianship and to *filiaefamilias*. 'This extension, illogical though it is, is easy to explain, since the
whole point of the exercise is to get rid of *usus*, which was no longer
wanted.'[84] The implication is that prior authorization for *manus* to
take effect twelve months after the beginning of the marriage was
now required; avoidance of *manus* by the *trinoctium* would be
unnecessary. 'Instead of contracting out of *manus* deriving from *usus*,
it would be necessary to contract in.'[85] This tendentious passage
cannot bear so much weight. We have no evidence that the consent of
patresfamilias and any kind of guardian was *not* required for the
initiation of *manus* in the period before Scaevola. Since the wife
entering *manus* took her property into the husband's family, it would
be surprising if authorization had not always been required.[86] Such
authorization would have parallels in the informal transfer of things
which led to ordinary usucapion: the possessor was expected to have

[84] Watson, *Persons* 21ff. on Cic. *Pro Flacco* 84. The rule on usucapion: G 2.47; cf. Cic. *A*
1.5.6, with SB.   [85] Gardner 13.
[86] Volterra in his review critized Watson's argument. Cf. Dixon, 'Infirmitas sexus: womanly
weakness in Roman law'.

grounds for believing he could become the legal owner. But in both cases the process could be interrupted if the previous owner or those who would otherwise have benefited from the woman's property changed their minds. Circumstances might alter. As far as we can tell, the *trinoctium* worked, in Cicero's day and in Scaevola's. But we do not know that *usus* was a frequent form of acquisition of *manus* in the first century. The passage in Cicero strongly suggests that *manus* was unusual in around 59 BC.

There seems every reason to believe that marriages in which *manus* came into being after a year's cohabitation were deeply rooted in Roman tradition. A woman was given to a man, on the clear understanding that they were beginning a marriage. By the end of twelve months it might well be clear whether the union was fertile and congenial. If it was not, or if there was room for uncertainty, the woman could avoid transferring herself and her property finally into the man's power. She would absent herself for three nights. They might then separate or try again for a further year. The method had several advantages over immediate transfer. The woman's family were not finally committed to giving her as a breeder and an accompanying dowry until the initial twelve months ended. We may compare the custom in historical times which allowed the payment of dowry in three instalments, beginning on the first anniversary of the wedding. But the origins of this would not be in economic practicality but in ancient folk custom.[87]

The history of the disappearance of *usus* is quite uncertain. It was obsolete by the time of Gaius. Since he says it was partly abolished by statute it is tempting to see the hand of Augustus. But the move away from *manus* marriage, which seems to have taken place between about 200 and 100 BC, will have been the main reason for its decay.[88]

(*d*) Confarreatio

Nothing is proved by the order of the traditional list about the relative dating of the methods for acquisition of *manus*. But the second and third methods both involved formalities. The second, generally known as *confarreatio*, was thought by Dionysius of Halicarnassus, in his idealizing account of the system set up by Romulus, to go back to the origins of Roman marriage. The crucial element, as the probable quotation from the Tables indicates, was *far*, the staple grain of the

---

[87] For a reconstruction of a gradual progression to a full marriage built into the archaic religious calendar see Torelli, *LR* chs. 2–4, esp. pp. 115 ff.

[88] Villers later abandoned an attempt to diagnose *usus* in Tac. *A* 13.46 ('A propos de la disparition de l'usus').

ancient Romans.[89] The language of the Tables describes *manus*
as created by the grain which was made up into a sacramental loaf.
It is not clear whether this was offered to Jupiter or shared by the
couple or both. The abstract noun *confarreatio*, which describes this
sacrament, did not have the same venerable antiquity.

Confarreatio was of interest to Greek and Roman antiquaries, so
that our information is richer than for the other two methods of
creation of *manus*. *Manus* and marriage were begun simultaneously.
Gaius again gives us the best account:

Farreo in manum conveniunt per quoddam genus sacrificii quod Iovi Farreo
fit; in quo farreus panis adhibetur, unde etiam confarreatio dicitur; com-
plura praeterea huius iuris ordinandi gratia, cum certis et sollemnibus
verbis, praesentibus decem testibus, aguntur et fiunt. Quod ius etiam nostris
temporibus in usu est. Nam flamines maiores, id est Diales, Martiales,
Quirinales, item reges sacrorum, nisi ex farreatis nati non leguntur; ac ne ipsi
quidem sine confarreatione sacerdotium habere possunt. (1.112)

Women come into *manus* by *farreum* through a type of sacrifice which is
made to Jupiter Farreus. A loaf of emmer is used in this, and the name
confarreatio derives from it. A number of acts and rituals take place in
performing this procedure in due order. There are prescribed and solemn
words and ten witnesses are present. This institution is still in existence
today. For the greater *flamines* (priests), that is, those of Jupiter, Mars, and
Quirinus, and also the *rex sacrorum*, are picked only from sons of parents
married by *confarreatio*, and they themselves cannot hold their priesthoods
unless married in this form.

Festus defines *farreum* as a type of sacrificial cake made of *far*. The
Elder Pliny also refers to it as carried before the bride.[90] Servius adds
that the Pontifex Maximus and Flamen Dialis officiated, joining the
pair 'through' grain of emmer and salted meal. At least at the
wedding of the *flamen Dialis* and his *flaminica*, a sheep was sacrificed
and the couple then, with their heads veiled, sat on two seats covered
by the sheepskin. The children of a confarreate marriage are said by
one authority to have been called *patrimi* and *matrimi*.[91] The religious
rituals involved stamp *confarreatio* as ancient. Modern scholars
reasonably hold that it was reserved for patricians. In any case, only
the upper classes of historical times would be able to secure the

---

[89] For the identification of *far* as emmer, *triticum dicoccum*, a husked and hardy wheat, see
Spurr, *Arable cultivation in Roman Italy* 10ff. It has often been identified as spelt.

[90] Fest. 78L (Bruns p. 8); Pliny *NH* 18.10.

[91] Ad *G* 1.31 (but according to Fest. 113L, cf. 82, 266, 267L, *patrimes/i* and *matrimes/i* are
children with both parents living), ad *A* 4.103, 374 (Bruns ii.76, 78; all quoted by Corbett 71–2),
Tit. Ulp. 9 merely repeats Gaius. Boethius on Cic. *Top.* 14, also derivative, claims (inaccurately
for the pre-Augustan period) that the ritual applied only to priests. Corbett (73–4) argues that
Servius is probably wrong to connect fire and water with this part of the wedding ceremony.

attendance of priests.[92] But there were times when the necessary priests were simply unavailable. The *flamen Dialis*, hedged about with ancient taboos, was practically restricted to the city of Rome, so confarreate marriages would have to take place there. After one *flamen* committed suicide in 87 BC, no candidates came forward and the office was left vacant until Augustus revived ancestral customs, no doubt with a certain lack of historical authenticity.[93] It is hardly surprising that in this interval, if not before, the custom of confarreate marriage lapsed. Tacitus reports the difficulty of finding three candidates, all of whom had to be born of confarreate parents, for the flaminate of Jupiter in AD 23. Few, he says, had maintained the custom, for both men and women were negligent and avoided the difficulties of the ceremony. Since the succession of *confarreati* was presumably broken before Augustus' revival, it is not surprising that there was a dearth of *confarreati* or bachelors born of *confarreati*. In the end Tiberius was able to recruit the son of the previous holder of the office, who by definition was qualified. But in order to make *confarreatio* more attractive for the future it was necessary to dilute its legal effect. In future the wife of the *flamen* was to fall under her husband's control for ritual purposes only: she was otherwise as independent as other women. Although Tacitus states specifically that a debate on this delicate point was initiated by the emperor in the Senate in 23 and a law resulted, he also thinks that Augustus furnished a precedent in modifying some harsh ancient rules to bring them into line with modern tastes. Gaius in fact attests a senatorial decree of the same effect in 11 BC. It is not clear why the problem arose again. A mistake in dating by one of our authors might be suspected. Tacitus must be right on the difficulties attending the selection of Maluginensis (to whose father he had devoted some attention). He ought to be relying on the minutes of the Senate. But it is odd that the jurist Gaius refers only to the decree of 11 BC and not to a later law which would have been authoritative in his day. So possibly it is Tacitus who is inaccurate about the law.[94]

In any case, the innovation of Augustus or Tiberius is likely to have meant that only those patricians interested in priestly office will have continued to perform *confarreatio* and that real *manus* was no longer created by the ceremony. Nevertheless, the custom survived prob-

[92] Volterra (*Enciclopedia* 764) rejects Servius' testimony that the priests officiated.
[93] Watson, *Law making* 180.
[94] *A* 4.16; 1.136 (where the beginning of the sentence is lost, but presumably referred to the *flaminica*); the decree said 'ut haec quod ad sacra tantum videatur in manu esse, quod vero ad ceteras causas proinde habaeatur atque si in manum non convenisset'. Cf. Talbert 435, 438.

ably until the end of paganism.[95] Gaius vouches for its continuance in the mid-second century AD and later the *Tituli Ulpiani* still speak of it in the present tense. An inscription put up by the people of Antium to a priest in charge of *confarreationes* and *diffarreationes* also attests some activity in the period after Commodus became sole emperor in 180.[96] *Diffarreatio* was a ritual form used to dissolve *confarreatio*. We have very little information on the topic. The text of Festus' word-list of the late second century AD as we now have it describes the institution in the past tense, as a type of sacrifice, by which a dissolution was brought about between a man and a woman. It was so called because a cake called *farreum* was used.[97] This implies that this form of dissolution was generally used for any *confarreatio*. Festus was abridging the earlier, fuller work of the Augustan grammarian Verrius Flaccus. It is not clear whether Verrius would have used the present or the past tense to describe the custom. But since Plutarch also describes a ritual dissolution for the *flamen Dialis*, it is likely that Flaccus described it as (at least theoretically) extant. According to Plutarch (late first/early second century AD), the *flamen Dialis* had to resign his post if his wife died, and he was forbidden to divorce. This in itself suggests that divorce was possible for other *confarreati*. Domitian allowed a *flamen* to divorce as an exception: 'On that occasion, the priests were present at the ceremony of divorce, and went through numerous horrible, extraordinary, and dismal rites.'[98]

What emerges clearly is that the Romans retained a sentimental respect for this form. The Elder Pliny attests it as the most solemn religious rite. The verb *confarreo*, used by Tacitus in the passive participle to describe those married in this way, is employed by Apuleius for special effect. Naturally, the gods ought to be married with sacrament. So when Cupid divorces Psyche he swears that he will unite himself with her sister by confarreate marriage. And he can also use it, with quite different nuances, of a male about to consummate a union in a public ceremony.[99] This tells us nothing of the frequency of *confarreatio*, only of the potency of the tradition.

---

[95] Corbett 78.

[96] *CIL* 10.6662. Cf. Corbett 78. Such a priestly title is odd and perhaps a late innovation.

[97] 65L (Bruns ii.7): 'Diffarreatio erat genus sacrificii, quo inter virum et mulierem fiebat dissolutio: dicta "diffarreatio", quia fiebat "farreo" libo adhibito.'

[98] *QR* 50, trans. H. J. Rose.

[99] Pliny *NH* 18.3.10; Apul. *M* 5.26, 10.29: 'talis mulieris publicitus matrimonium confarreaturus' (actually of the ass, expected to perform with a condemned woman in the amphitheatre).

(*e*) Coemptio

Unlike *confarreatio*, *coemptio*, the acquisition of *manus* by a formal purchase, could take place at any time during a marriage, not merely at the celebration of its beginning. The main text is again from Gaius:

Coemptione vero in manum conveniunt per mancipationem, id est per quandam imaginariam venditionem. Nam, adhibitis non minus quam v testibus civibus Romanis puberibus, item libripende, emit vir mulierem cuius in manum convenit. Potest autem coemptionem facere mulier non solum cum marito suo, sed etiam cum extraneo; scilicet aut matrimonii causa facta coemptio dicitur aut fiduciae. Quae enim cum marito suo facit coemptionem, ut apud eum filiae loco sit, dicitur matrimonii causa fecisse coemptionem; quae vero alterius rei causa facit coemptionem aut cum viro suo aut cum extraneo, veluti tutelae evitandae causa, dicitur fiduciae causa fecisse coemptionem. (1.113–14)

But by *coemptio* they come into *manus* by mancipation, that is, by a kind of imaginary sale. For in the presence of not fewer than five witnesses who are adult male Roman citizens, and of a scales-holder, the man into whose *manus* the woman passes buys her. But a woman can also make a *coemptio* with an outsider, not just with her husband. A *coemptio* is said to have been made either for the sake of marriage or for the sake of a trust. If a woman makes a *coemptio* with her husband, so as to have the position of a daughter in his household, she is said to have made it for the sake of marriage. But if a woman makes a *coemptio* either with her husband or with an outsider for another reason, for example in order to avoid guardianship, she is said to have made it for the sake of a trust.

The legal formality which was required for fiduciary purposes need not concern us here, except as showing how clear it was by Gaius' day that this imaginary sale was merely a convenient legal procedure.[100] Many societies have practised the purchase of brides, and it is not unlikely that the Romans once did, giving bridewealth to the woman's family in exchange for her reproductive powers.[101] But in historic times the bride-price was purely symbolic, like other formal Roman transfers of property performed with a piece of bronze and a scale. In the ordinary mancipation of a slave, for instance, the buyer pronounced a formula: 'I declare that this man is mine in accordance with the right of Roman citizens and let him be bought for me with this bronze and brazen scale.' Then he struck the piece of bronze

---

[100] Fiduciary *coemptio* was used to enable to woman to make a will and to change guardians (*FV* 325 is the latest text). Cicero complains that *coemptio* was used to allow family cults to lapse, sc. because the woman left her original family. It is not clear whether this was *coemptio* by a husband or by an outsider (Cic. *Mur.* 27). See Buckland, *Textbook* 119–20.

[101] See esp. MacCormack, 'Coemptio and marriage by purchase'.

against the scale and handed it to the seller.[102] But mancipation of a slave was a real conveyance of property and meant that the slave was *in mancipio* to his buyer. *Coemptio* did not make the woman a slave of her husband, but a free person *in manu*.[103] The sale was clearly imaginary, at least to a classical jurist. Rather than speaking of the woman as being sold, for instance by her father, the sources speak of her 'making a *coemptio*'. The husband does the same, although Gaius also speaks of him buying her.[104] Although it was the woman who was 'sold', the *coemptio* also transferred her property to the husband. 'In form a sale of the woman, in substance it is a transaction comprising, among other things, the alienation of property and the cessation of tutorship.'[105] It is for this reason that if a woman was independent the guardians' consent (which was not needed for marriage) would be needed for *coemptio*, as Cicero tells us.[106]

The precise verbal formula used for *coemptio* is unknown to us, as Cicero says it might well have been to an orator who had as his brief to defend a woman who had performed a *coemptio*.[107] We have tantalizing references to what is presumably a quite different verbal formula, an exchange between bridegroom and bride. He asked her name and she replied, 'Where you are Gaius, I am Gaia.'[108] So runs the attractive antiquarian account, transmitted by Plutarch. But unfortunately Cicero muddies the waters. In an ironical passage attacking the ingenuity of lawyers in corrupting the spirit of the law by pretended respect for the letter, he claims:

In omni denique iure civili aequitatem reliquerunt, verba ipsa tenuerunt, ut, quia in alicuius libris exempli causa id nomen invenerant, putarunt omnis mulieres quae coemptionem facerent 'Gaias' vocari. (*Pro Murena* 27)

In fact all through civil law they have abandoned equity while holding fast to the words themselves. For instance, because in someone's books they found the name 'Gaia' cited as an example, they thought that all women who made a *coemptio* were called 'Gaia'.

Cicero's complaint suggests that the lawyers had succeeded in imposing a custom he thinks inauthentic. So Plutarch may be right. His

---

[102] Buckland, *Textbook* 236. It is not clear to whom the bronze was given in *coemptio*. Cf. Corbett 80ff.; Watson, *Persons* 24. On a possible formula see Corbett 83–4.

[103] G 1.123.

[104] Cf. Cic. *de or.* 1.237; G 1.115b, 123; *Laud. Tur.* 1.14. But the view that each bought the other is a misunderstanding (Boeth. ad Cic. *Top.* 14; cf. Corbett 80). As Corbett says (82), by the time of Cicero a *sui iuris* woman is seen as the leading spirit: her *tutor*, or the father of a *filiafamilias*, merely authorizes the procedure.

[105] Corbett 82.   [106] *Flacc.* 84, with Schol. Bob. (Stangl p. 106).

[107] *De or.* 1.237: 'Neque illud est mirandum, qui quibus verbis coemptio fiat, nesciat, eundem eius mulieris quae coemptionem fecerit, causam posse defendere.'

[108] *QR* 30.

account seems to be backed by two other scholarly authorities. One, the author of a treatise on names, says that when a bride was asked for her name outside her husband's door, she gave the name 'Gaia': this may represent half of Plutarch's dialogue and it locates it. Quintilian, saying that the abbreviation 'C' is pronounced 'Gaius', adds that the inverted letter 'C' is used to indicate a woman. This is indeed true of inscriptions, where the reverse C is used generically, especially in the formula for 'freedman of a woman'. The usage occurs precisely because women did not normally have forenames. Quintilian goes on to mention that the marriage ritual clinches his point. He appears to be referring to the Plutarchan formula.[109] No one apart from Cicero links this ceremony especially with *coemptio*. Quintilian attaches it to religious ritual. If it took place in front of the bridegroom's door it is likely to have been quite separate from the procedure of imaginary sale. However, for the bride to claim that her name (even if only the forename) is now the same as the husband's would be appropriate if she was joining his family through *manus*. But an element which attracts the advocate in a bold rhetorical flight and a handful of antiquarians will not yield much certainty. Yet again we have faint traces of something hallowed by tradition, likely to be connected with a time in which brides usually entered *manus* and therefore with full religious ceremonial as well.

We also have testimony that Ulpian described a verbal formula used during the *coemptio* itself. According to Boethius, the man asked the woman if she was willing to be *materfamilias* to him. She replied that she was willing. She then asked him if he was willing to be *paterfamilias* to her and he replied that he was willing. This account is uncorroborated and is not a verbatim quotation, so little reliance can be placed upon it.[110]

It is *coemptio* which makes it very clear that *manus* and marriage were distinguished. For a woman could perform *coemptio* with a man without bringing about marriage. Or a husband and wife could perform it after they had been married some time already.[111]

---

[109] Inc. *de nominibus* 7, on forenames adopted from men's: 'Ceterum Gaia usu super omnes celebrata est: ferunt enim Gaiam Caeciliam, Tarquinii Prisci regis uxorem, optimam lanificam fuisse et ideo institutum, ut novae nuptae ante ianuam mariti interrogatae quaenam vocarentur, Gaias esse se dicerent.' The name given Priscus' wife (usually called Tanaquil) is attested also by Pliny (*NH* 8.194), who also associates her with spinning and weaving and with the spindle carried in the procession of a virgin bride. Such associations may be at the root of the otherwise surprising fact that Tanaquil is put on the list of role models for wives. (Cf. Jer. *adv. Iovin.* 320B.) Nor does Inc. explicitly say that this was the only name they might give. Quint. *Inst.* 1.7.28: 'Nam et "Gaius" C littera significatur, quae inversa mulierem declarat, quia tam Gaias esse vocitatas quam Gaios etiam ex nuptialibus sacris apparet.' Cf. Gordon, 'On reversed C (Ɔ = Gaiae)'.

[110] Boeth. ad Cic. *Top.* 14.   [111] *Laud. Tur.* 1.13, cf. 16.

Moreover, if a wife who was *in manu* because of *coemptio* divorced, the *manus* was dissolved subsequently by *emancipatio*. This also applies to *usus*. The wife could (by the second century AD) compel the husband to emancipate her, although a child in paternal power had no such right.[112] It would also be possible for a husband to emancipate his wife without divorcing her.

(*f*) *Effects of* manus

If a woman entered *manus* by any of these methods, she underwent a change known as *capitis deminutio minima*, which left her freedom and citizenship intact but altered her previous status.[113] If she had been *filiafamilias*, daughter in the paternal power of a male ascendant, she was freed from that power.[114] If the ascendant (*paterfamilias*) in whose power she had been had died or had freed her (by *emancipatio*), so that she was independent (*sui iuris*), she lost this freedom by entry into *manus*. A widow freed by his death from the control of a previous husband or a divorced woman emancipated by a previous husband would also be *sui iuris* and change this status by a subsequent entry into *manus*. If a woman married a son in his own father's power and entered the husband's *manus*, she also came under his father's power, rather as the son's property was legally owned by his father. *Manus* was removed, as we have seen, by *emancipatio* or by the death of the husband.

 The wife who entered *manus* had in fact transferred herself to her husband's family.[115] According to Cicero, it was only a wife *in manu* who had the title of *materfamilias*, mother of a household (which was independent of whether she had in fact become a mother):

A forma generis [sc. sic ducitur] quam interdum, quo planius accipiatur, partem licet nominare hoc modo: Si ita Fabiae pecunia legata est a viro, si ei viro materfamilias esset; si ea in manum non convenerat, nihil debetur. Genus est uxor; eius duae formae: una matrumfamilias, eae sunt quae in manum convenerunt; altera earum, quae tantum modo uxores habentur. (*Topica* 14)

(Arguments are drawn) from the species of a genus in the following way. (A species may sometimes, for clarity, be called a part.) 'If money was bequeathed to Fabia by her husband on condition that she was *materfamilias* to that man, and she had not come into his control, then nothing is owed to her.' Wife is a genus and there are two species, one consisting of *matresfamilias*, that is, those who have entered *manus*, and the other of those who are considered merely wives.[116]

[112] G 1.137a.   [113] G 1.162. On the effects of *manus* see Corbett 108ff.
[114] G 1.136.   [115] Gell. 18.6.9; Serv. ad *A* 11.476.
[116] Confirmed by Gell. 18.6.9; Serv. ad *A* 11.476; Boeth. ad Cic. *Top*. 14, citing Ulpian's *Institutes*; *Tit. Ulp*. 22.14.

When she entered her husband's family, the wife became part of his kindred for legal and religious purposes. Her rights were the same as those of his daughter. That is, she counted for intestate succession as if she were related to him as an agnate.[117] This artificial Roman kinship group was based on relationship through males. Two individuals were agnates if they were legitimately descended from a common male ancestor, through males. They could be described as 'those who would sacrifice to the same set of ancestors, or who would be in the same *potestas* if the common ancestor were alive'. So a brother and sister were agnates, or a woman and her brother's child, but not a man and his sister's child.[118] A wife *in manu* would share equally with his children in an intestate husband's estate. Like them, she was *sua heres*, literally 'her own heir'. She was *filiae loco*, in the position of a daughter. *Sui heredes* were those who became independent on the death of the *paterfamilias*.[119] If a wife entered *manus* after her husband had made his will, the will became invalid, because he had acquired a new intestate heir, just as it did if a posthumous child were born.[120] But, like his children who were in his power, she had no property of her own before his death. Anything she owned before entering *manus* passed to her husband:

Cum mulier viro in manum convenit, omnia quae mulieris fuerunt viri fiunt dotis nomine. (Cicero *Topica* 23)

When a woman enters the *manus* of her husband, everything which belonged to the woman becomes the husband's as dowry.

Although such property was absorbed into the husband's, by Cicero's time it was recognized as distinguishable and therefore recoverable, like the dowry which was transferred to a husband by a wife who did not enter *manus*. Any property which the wife acquired after entering *manus* also went to the husband.[121] Any liabilities which she had had before entering *manus* were extinguished by her *capitis deminutio*, but the praetor allowed creditors and others who would have suffered from this to sue.

---

[117] *Tit. Ulp.* 23.3.
[118] Buckland, *Textbook* 105.
[119] G 2.156–9; *Coll.* 16.2.1 ff. (quoted from Gaius bk. 3: the text of G 3.1 is reconstructed from this) lists *sui* according to the Twelve Tables. A son's wife who was or had been in *his* control would be in the position of a granddaughter, and a grandson's wife in the position of a great granddaughter, as long as their husbands were no longer in the power of the *paterfamilias*, i.e. had been emancipated or had died. If the husband was in his father's power, he would be *suus heres* himself. Similarly, a son's child was *suus/a* if the son was no longer in his father's power. On this see further Buckland, *Textbook* 305.
[120] G 2.139. Cf. *Laud. Tur.* 1.13–14.
[121] Corbett 110.

The consequences of *manus* are often equated with those of paternal power. Legislation lists dependants as those *in potestate manu mancipio*.[122] Like slaves and *filiifamilias*, a woman under her husband's control could not incur obligations (such as debts) to him or to anyone else.[123] A husband could sue for theft of his wife or injury to her (which counted as injury to him).[124] He could emancipate her or appoint a guardian for her in his will, just as he could for his children in power. But he could, in classical law, give his wife (though not his children) the privilege of choosing her own guardian.[125] The phrase 'in the position of a daughter' has on odd ring to modern ears. It certainly expresses a position of dependence and of membership in a family, but it does not mean that a wife *in manu* was regarded as a daughter. She was not a daughter but in the position of a daughter. Being *loco filiae* also distinguishes a wife *in manu* from a woman who has gone through fiduciary *coemptio*, who acquired no privileges in her purchaser's family.[126]

The disciplinary powers which a householder had over his slaves and *filiifamilias* are little attested in relation to wives *in manu*. From the earliest times any theoretical right of physical coercion seems to have been hedged around by social conventions. The subject will be discussed later, in the chapter on adultery.

Quite early, lawyers distinguished between wives *in manu* and adoptive children on the one hand and other children *in potestate* on the other. The former seemed less closely attached to a man. So, while the Twelve Tables allowed an ex-owner to claim his intestate freedman's estate only if he left no *suus heres*, this stipulation seemed to later praetors unjust if the *suus* was not the freedman's own child, but an adoptive child or a wife. It made a difference, no doubt, that natural children were an expense for their father, while adoptive children had normally been reared by others, and that a wife brought a dowry with her. It is interesting that this evidence shows that *manus* was not restricted to the upper classes. The law was changed to enable the ex-owner to claim half, whether or not the freedman had made a will.[127] It appears that wives were usually *in manu* during the early and middle Republic, but that by the time of Cicero this situation was relatively uncommon. Both the Augustan adultery law (*c*.18 BC) and

---

[122] *Lex Salpensana* (*FIRA* i.23), and *Lex Irnitana* (González, 'The Lex Irnitana' 22). For the abbreviation *M.M.P.* (*manu, mancipio, potestate*) see *FIRA* ii.458.
[123] G 3.104, 114. Cf. 83–4.
[124] G 3.199, 221.
[125] G 1.118, 137, 148ff.
[126] G 1.115b, 136. *Loco filiae* is used in contexts related to privilege, not disability. Other examples: G 1.111, 3.33a; *Coll.* 16.2.3; *Schol. Bob.* 106 Stangl.
[127] G 3.39ff., 46; *Tit. Ulp.* 29.1.

the Flavian municipal law mention the institution.[128] Gaius speaks of *manus* as if it were still in existence and of some importance in his day. It also occurs in some contexts in the *Tituli Ulpiani* of the second quarter of the fourth century, but this may be mere scholarly conservatism. But the emperors and Senate were still paying attention to the institution perhaps as late as the time of Severus Alexander. M. Aurelius in 178 allowed children to inherit from their intestate mother even if she had not entered *manus* and so become their agnate. The emperor's speech was followed by a detailed senatorial decree, called the *Senatusconsultum Orfitianum*.[129] This is a recognition of the blood-tie and is part of a series of social and legal shifts which improved the reciprocal rights of mothers and children, originally low in the order of succession since they counted as cognates unless the mother were *in manu*. Claudius began the reform.[130] The *Senatusconsultum Tertullianum* of Hadrianic date improved the right of a mother to succeed intestate children, as long as she had the *ius liberorum*.[131] This suggests that the law will somewhere have stated that it was not a necessary qualification that the mother had been *in manu* to the dead child's father. When M. Aurelius dealt with succession of children to mother, he was operating outside the old agnatic preconceptions, and considerations about *manus* will have been explicitly ruled out. The right of the child to succeed was founded on the blood relationship, as it was originally for illegitimate children.[132] A *Senatusconsultum Gaetulicianum*, mentioned in a fragmentary text attributed to Paul and tentatively dated to early in the reign of Alexander Severus, also mentions *manus*. It abolished the ancient rule that a wife *in manu* was *sua heres* to her husband.[133] The occasional mentions of the effects of *manus* in juristic writings which escaped revision and updating show that the rules about the rights of a wife *in manu* on a husband's intestacy and the exceptions made by

---

[128] *Coll.* 4.2.3, 4.7.1 for the adultery law. Augustus gave the father who had transferred a daughter from his own power to a husband's control the right to kill her if he took her in adultery. But the husband had no right to kill his wife, irrespective of whether she was in his control or not. Augustus seems not to have been interested in encouraging *manus* in itself. Copies of the law from Salpensa (*FIRA* i.23) and Municipium Flavium Irnitanum in Spain (González, 'The Lex Irnitana' 147ff., q.v. for bibliography) 22 show *manus* in Latin communities. On the decline and disappearance of *manus* see Watson, *Persons* 19ff.; Corbett 84–5.

[129] *Tit. Ulp.* 26.7. See Talbert 449 no. 128.

[130] *Just. Inst.* 3.3.1. For detailed discussion of changes in the law of succession between mother and child see Dixon, *RM* 44ff. Buckland, *Textbook* 372ff., remains useful.

[131] Talbert 445 no. 82.

[132] There is a whole *Digest* title (38.17) on the *SCC Tertullianum* and *Orfitianum*. In their present form none of the texts except *Tit. Ulp.* 26.7 (the chief are *D* 38.17; *Just. Inst.* 3.3, 4; *CJ* 6.56, 57; Paul *S* 4.9) have any mention of *manus*.

[133] *Frag. Berol.* 3 (*FIRA* ii.427); Talbert 453 no. 165. Cf. Volterra, 'Nuove ricerche sulla *conventio in manum*', 351–3.

the praetors about succession to freedmen were still worth repeating in textbooks.[134] But they had been steadily undermined ever since the praetorian changes, and the *Senatusconsultum Gaetulicianum* must have been the death-blow. *Manus*, if any Roman apart from a legal scholar ever thought about it in the dark days of the third century, hung on only as a pale survival affecting the *flaminica Dialis*. It has been edited out of the earlier texts collected in the sixth century for Justinian's *Digest*.

(g) *Wives not in their husband's control*

The position of wives who did not enter their husband's control is more simply defined, but it has none the less puzzled scholars who expect Roman marriage to conform more closely to modern ideas. Such members of the genus 'wife' were, according to the legalistic definition which Cicero provided for his young friend the lawyer Trebatius, 'mere wives', *uxores*.[135] They might be *filiaefamilias*, daughters in an ascendant's power (until he died or emancipated them), or *sui iuris*, independent. The latter category includes women previously released from paternal power and former slavewomen, who had no legal father. Both had guardians to supervise the administration of their property. A former owner (patron) automatically assumed this function for a freedwoman. All wives who did not enter *manus* remained members of their original families. *Filiaefamilias* retained the right to succeed to their *patresfamilias* as *suae heredes* on intestacy. They retained their places as agnates or *cognatae* (kin by blood in general) in their natal families or, if freedwomen, their obligations to their patron or patroness and his or her descendants. If, as *sui iuris* women, they acquired any property after marriage, as they might well do by will or gift, this was their own, not their husband's. If they were *filiaefamilias*, such property accrued to their fathers. As far as the law was concerned, their property was distinct and the husband had no claim on it. It was traditional to transfer some property to him as dowry on or after marriage. Children born of their marriage belonged to the husband's agnatic kin. So, if a wife were *filiafamilias*, her children were in her husband's power and had no legal connection with her own *paterfamilias*. They had no claim on her intestate father's estate as she or her brother or his children would, if *in patria potestate*.[136]

[134] e.g. *Tit. Ulp.* 22.14, 23.3, 29.1; but there is no mention at 10–11, where we would expect it. Paul *S* 4.8 ignores it in discussion of intestate succession. *Coll.* 4.2.3., 4.7.1 is citing earlier law.   [135] *Top.* 14, followed by Quint. *Inst.* 5.10.62.

[136] Pomeroy, 'The relationship of the married woman to her blood relatives in Rome', and Gratwick, 'Free or not so free? Wives and daughters in the late Roman Republic', survey parts of the topic. See also Dixon, *RM* 44 ff.

The function of such an *uxor* was to give the husband children, while herself remaining a part of her natal family. But the arrangement was not as minimalist as this might suggest. The couple did not meet to mate and then separate, the wife returning to her parents and delivering a child to the husband in due course. Roman marriage seems normally to have been patrilocal. The wife not *in manu mariti* is considered in the Twelve Tables to be living in her husband's house, which she will leave for three nights per annum in order to avoid the creation of *manus*. There are indications, as we shall see later, that dowry was expected to be used for the wife's support during the marriage.

The husband and his family received a child-breeder and the means which would at least help support her; the wife's family established a daughter. If the wife entered *manus*, her future and that of her property were, as far as human beings could control events, in the power of her husband (or his *paterfamilias*). If she did not, then the continuance of the marriage was as dependent on the will of her family as on that of the husband. Her *paterfamilias* might bring about a divorce, and so might she (in the historic period), if *sui iuris*. (This is again the legal position: the social position might be more complex, as we shall see in Chapter 13.) From the husband's point of view, marriage with a wife not under his control might seem more precarious.

Whether this kind of wife (as Cicero would put it) had existed from the beginning, alongside the wife *in manu*, is an insoluble problem. Most scholars would like to argue that 'marriage *cum manu*' has priority, the more negative 'marriage *sine manu*' being its offshoot. But these names are a mere scholarly invention, though hallowed by tradition.[137] The only real argument for this depends on the evidence of the Twelve Tables. If *usurpatio* is a means invented by the compilers for preventing *manus* being created *usu*, then it might have previously been automatic for any wife who remained in her husband's house for a year to come into *manus*. The only wives who were not *in manu* would be those who had been married less than a year or (perhaps) those who happened to have been separated from the husband for periods of time. But can we be sure that the Twelve Tables introduced *usurpatio*? The text does not allow us to decide whether the Tables merely embodied older custom here. Theoretically, the creation of *manus* by *usus* (which might logically have grown out of *coemptio*) could be much later than the type of marriage in which the wife was never intended to come into *manus*. *Usurpatio*

---

[137] Rasi, *Consensus facit nuptias*, and Volterra, *Enciclopedia*, give sufficient indication of the vast bibliography.

would then be an innovation, whether originating in the Tables
or earlier, to solve problems raised for some families by another
innovation, *usus*.

On the other hand, some see *manus* and marriage as contempor-
aneous developments but originally separate institutions, in the sense
that a man who had *manus* over a woman was not also her husband,
while other men took women as wives without controlling them,
although both situations allowed men to become fathers. Men with
manus were more powerful in relation to the woman's family and so
were able to seize her; the men who married were weaker than the
woman's kin.[138] This theory, which has a certain charm, seems
extremely far-fetched. In historic times a woman was only *in manu* to
a man if he was her husband.

The third view, that 'marriage *sine manu*' preceded 'marriage *cum
manu*', seems as unprovable as the other two reconstructions. For
what it is worth, the Augustan writer Dionysius associates *manus* with
Romulus. The only clear fact is that by the mid-fifth century some
wives were *in manu* and some not.[139]

By the end of the third century BC it was worth legislating about
wives who were not *in manu*. The Cincian Law, of around 204 BC,
which regulated gifts, allowed them between husband and wife. A
wife *in manu*, by definition, had no property to give to her husband.[140]
In 169 the reactionary Cato complained in a speech about wives who
held separate property.[141] The possibility of divorce initiated by the
father of the wife is sometimes mentioned in Roman comedy of the
late third or early second century.[142] By Cicero's time, as we have
seen, most wives seem not to have entered *manus*.

The word *materfamilias* was restricted by Cicero to wives *in manu*.
But the comic writers earlier appear to use it of any honourable wife.
In the *Stichus* two young women whose father wants them to give up
their absent husbands argue that they must honour the men to whom
their father wished them to be *matresfamilias*. *Ex hypothesi*, Plautus
cannot mean they were *in manu*.[143] The essential connotation
throughout Roman history is of dignity. The *materfamilias*, says
Cicero's contemporary Nepos, normally holds the first place in a
house and goes out on public occasions, quite unlike a Greek wife.[144]

---

[138] Rasi, *Consensus facit nuptias* 6 ff.

[139] J. Bryce, *Studies* ii.389, whose elegant exposition is still worth reading, puts this with his
usual clarity: 'This was the old Roman system, and a very singular system it was, because it
placed side by side the extreme of marital control as the normal state of things and the complete
absence of that control as a possible state of things.'

[140] Corbett 90–1.   [141] Gell. 17.6.1.

[142] Enn. *Cresph.* ap. *Rhet. ad Her.* 2.38. For Plautus see Watson, *Persons* 48 ff., and cf. 29 ff.

[143] *Stich.* 98. Cf. *Merc.* 405, Ter. *Ad.* 747.   [144] *Praef.* 6.

She is the partner of the head of the household, the *paterfamilias*.[145]
Even the jurists grew to use the word in this non-technical sense:

'Matrem familias' accipere debemus eam, quae non inhoneste vixit: matrem
enim familias a ceteris feminis mores discernunt atque separant. Proinde
nihil intererit, nupta sit an vidua, ingenua sit an libertina: nam neque nuptiae
neque natales faciunt matrem familias, sed boni mores. (*Digest* 50.16.46.1,
Ulpian *lix ad edictum*)

By *materfamilias* we ought to understand a woman who has lived not
dishonourably: for a *materfamilias* is distinguished and separated from other
women by her character. So it will not make any difference, whether she is
married or divorced or widowed, or whether she is free-born or a freedwoman: for it is not marriage or birth which makes a *materfamilias*, but good
character.[146]

Where *materfamilias* denotes a respectable married woman in relation to husband or household status, *matrona* denotes the married
woman in a less private context. She was recognizable by her dress,
the long robe worn out of doors, called the *stola*. Grammarians derive
the name from her motherhood or potential motherhood.[147] Matrons
might act as a group in public contexts, for instance in mourning
or protesting[148] and might even be called an order, *ordo*.[149] Such
concerted action was associated with the Sabine brides.

The main trend in republican development of the basic institution
of marriage was a movement away from a situation in which many, if
not most, wives had been *in manu* to a situation in which that status
was a rarity. Alongside this went a growing body of doctrine which
protected the separability and reclaimability of the property which a
wife brought into her marriage. As Rome grew from a cluster of
villages in which reciprocal intermarriage with Sabine and Latin
neighbours could arise naturally, her extended boundaries brought
her people into contact with Italians of a different culture, with
Greeks of southern Italy and Sicily and transmarine populations of

---

[145] Fest. 112L suggests that a woman would not have this title until her husband became
paterfamilias, i.e. *sui iuris*.

[146] Cf. *D* 43.30.3.6. Ulpian also uses it in contrast to *filiafamilias*, to mean a woman *sui iuris*
(*D* 1.6.4, 38.17.1.1; cf. 24.3.34, Afr.). Again, it is parallel to *paterfamilias*, which could describe
a child too young to be a father or govern a household, as long as he was free of paternal power.

[147] *TLL* s.v. See esp. Fest. 112L: 'matronas appellabant eas fere quibus stolas habendi ius
erat.' For a perverse distinction between *matrona* and *materfamilias* see Gell. 18.6.4ff. A wife's
status is emphasized by calling her *matrona stolata* (*FIRA* iii.51).

[148] Livy 2.7.4, 16.7; 22.7.7; 34.1.5; Suet. *DJ* 84.4 Cf. Purcell, 'Livia and the womanhood of
Rome' 81ff.

[149] VM 5.2.1 (grant of proper insignia, including *vittae* and purple), 8.3.3.; Sen. *Rem. fort.*
16.3. The usage is loose: see *TLL* s.v. *ordo* 961 and cf. Plaut. *Cist.* 23ff. (prostitutes compared
with the tight-knit group of married women).

many races and traditions. The question of who was eligible as a marriage partner therefore became much more difficult. Romans evolved legal answers to changing social circumstances. Their ideology of marriage, like that of citizenship, evolved in part from native roots and in part in reaction to new influences from outside.

2
Capacity and Intent

If any of you know cause, or just impediment, why these two persons should not be joined together in holy Matrimony, ye are to declare it.

(Banns of marriage)

I. CIVIL LAW

WHAT determined whether marriage was legally possible between two particular individuals? What demonstrated that a marriage existed between two people? The answer to the first question depends on the existence of certain qualifications and the absence of certain disqualifications.[1] The answer to the second depends on voluntary (at least legally voluntary) decisions by the individuals concerned. In this chapter we shall discuss the legal qualifications and the legal definition of the relationship of intent subsisting between a given couple. The question of the giving of legally valid consent at the time of an engagement and of the initiation of marriage will be treated in Chapters 4 and 5. The much broader questions of the social and moral nature of the consent of a particular couple and of the kin who did and did not have a legal role and of others who had a hand in the making of a particular match will be considered in Chapters 3 and 4. How far the *coniuges* themselves were independent agents in giving formal consent to their own marriage is a question for Chapter 5.

1. Rules of Kindred and Affinity

Roman rulings on kindred and affinity forbade marriage between ascendant and descendant even when the relationship was adoptive. If an adoptive father emancipated his daughter (freed her from *patria*

---

[1] Gaudemet, 'Justum matrimonium', provides a useful overview of the requirements for marriage.

potestas) he was still not permitted to marry her.[2] As for collaterals, marriage was forbidden between brother and sister.[3] Originally, second cousins were not permitted to marry, but gradually marriage between second and then first cousins became acceptable.[4] The emperor Claudius had a law passed in AD 49 to enable men to marry their brothers' daughters. One or two men besides the emperor took advantage of this dispensation at that time: we hear of no later examples.[5] Men were forbidden to marry the daughters, granddaughters, and great granddaughters of their sisters. Adoptive brothers and sisters could marry as long as one of them was emancipated first. So Nero, after being adopted by his uncle Claudius, was able to marry his new father's real but emancipated daughter, Octavia. If, however, a father adopted his son-in-law after the latter married his daughter, the marriage was dissolved.[6] A man might not, in classical law, marry his paternal or maternal aunt, or anyone who, by virtue of a previous marriage, stood to him in the relationship of stepmother, stepdaughter, mother-in-law, or daughter-in-law (including the former wife of an adoptive father, a former wife's stepmother, and a stepson's former wife).[7] A woman might not marry the corresponding males.

Marriages which defied these rules were incestuous and null:

> . . . si quis nefarias atque incestas nuptias contraxerit, neque uxorem habere videtur neque liberos. Itaque hi qui ex eo coitu nascuntur matrem quidem habere videntur, patrem vero non utique; nec ob id in potestate eius sunt, quales sunt ii quos mater vulgo concepit . . . (Gaius 1.64)

> . . . if anyone contracts a wicked and incestuous marriage, he is held to have neither wife nor children. So those born of such a union are held to have a mother, but no father; therefore they are not in his power, just like children whom their mother conceives in promiscuous intercourse . . .[8]

Those who made an incestuous marriage might also be punished, but it made a difference if they acted in ignorance of the law. In particular, women were not punished if they entered on a marriage which was invalid only under Roman rules about incest: they were only expected to be aware of what was accepted as incest *iure gentium*, by the common beliefs of all mankind. Papinian also cites a second-century case in which the incestuous couple had been let off

---

[2] *D* 23.2.53–5; G 1.59.   [3] G 1.60.

[4] Cf. Corbett 47 ff. for sources and discussion. In AD 384 or 385 Theodosius prohibited marriage of first cousins, but the ban was lifted in 405. See Goody, *Development of the family and marriage in Europe* 55.

[5] G 1.62; Tac. *A* 12.7.3–4; Suet. *Cl.* 26.3; *Gnom.* (*FIRA* i.99) 23; *D* 23.2.39.

[6] *D* 23.2.17 pr.–1; G 1.61; *Inst.* 1.10.2; Berger s.v. *incestus*; Paul *S* 2.19.4 = *Coll.* 6.2.

[7] *D* 23.2.12, 14 pr.–1, 15, 17.2, 39, 56; G 1.63; Paul *S* 2.19.5 = *Coll.* 6.3.3; *Tit. Ulp.* 5.2.6 = *Coll.* 6.2.3.   [8] Cf. *Tit. Ulp.* 5.7 on the status of the children.

by the emperors because of their youth and presumed ignorance: this illicit marriage had been dissolved. A stepson who had married his stepmother was also excused because he had subsequently divorced her. In general, ignorance or mistake or the fact that nobody had prosecuted the couple would help the defence. None of this applied if incest were extra-marital. The most interesting feature here is the distinction between incest *iure gentium* and incest in Roman law. The former means sexual relationships between ascendant and descendant. Some marriages between people who were related laterally were, as we have seen, forbidden in Roman law, but licit and indeed customary in other societies which were part of the empire. The most obvious example is marriages between brother and sister in Egypt. The willingness of Roman lawyers to excuse the female partner on the grounds of presumed ignorance or both on the grounds of youth or proven ignorance, and particularly, as Paul tells us, when the marriage had been perfectly open, was humane and necessary, given the complex legal and social structure of the empire.[9]

2. *Age*

Iustas autem nuptias inter se cives Romani contrahunt, qui secundum praecepta legum coeunt, masculi quidem puberes, feminae autem viripotentes, sive patresfamilias sint sive filiifamilias, dum tamen filiifamilias et consensum habeant parentum, quorum in potestate sunt . . . (Justinian *Institutes* 1.10 pr.)

Roman citizens contract valid marriages with each other, if they come together in accordance with the bidding of the laws, the males physically mature, the women capable of taking a man [i.e. of sexual intercourse], whether they are *patresfamilias* or *filiifamilias*, as long as *filiifamilias* also have the consent of the parents under whose control they are . . .

Corbett says that in very early times physical examination determined whether a girl was ready for marriage, but Watson finds no evidence of any criterion other than age, 12 being fixed, probably by the end of the Republic, as the age from which puberty might be expected to begin and therefore the minimum age for valid marriage.[10] But there seem to be traces of a dual criterion in Vergil. Describing Lavinia's situation as a desirable *parti*, he says she is 'iam matura viro, iam

---

[9] *D* 48.5.39 pr.–7; cf. 23.2.57, 68; Paul *S* 2.26.15; *Coll.* 6.3.3; *D* 23.2.68. Cf. Hopkins, 'Brother–sister marriage in Roman Egypt'. The *Gnomon Idiologi* is clear about incest rules (*FIRA* i.99.23).

[10] Corbett 51; Watson, *Persons* 39. Cf. *CJ* 5.60.3: 'quemadmodum feminae post impletos duodecim annos omnimodo pubescere iudicantur' ('as women once they have reached their twelfth birthday are always assumed to have begun puberty').

plenis nubilis annis' ('now ready for a man [husband], now marriageable of full years'). Servius comments that the expression is not
repetitious: the first half of the line refers to physical development
(*habitus*), the second to her age in years.[11] It would be logical enough
if age were the only legal qualification, but attention would surely be
given by the girl's family to her physical development, and even the
bridegroom and his family could not fail to be aware of some
symptoms of puberty or their absence. References in literature to the
readiness of girls for marriage[12] or sexual experience allude both to
physical and psychological readiness. Lyde is 'nuptiarum expers et
adhuc protervo | cruda marito' ('with no part in marriage and as yet
unripe for a demanding man'). Lalage is like a heifer not yet broken
to the yoke, not able to take her fair share of the work with a mate or
to stand the weight of a mounting bull. Chloe, however, young and
nervous, clinging to her mother, is supposed to be 'tempestiva . . .
viro' ('ripe for a man').[13]

Ancient medical theory, accommodating itself to social pressures,
held that marriage should come soon after menarche. The twelfth
birthday was postulated as the usual *terminus post quem* for adoles-
cence, but it is clear that this was only a rough guide. Menstruation
does not begin until some time after pubertal development has got
under way, nor is physical development complete for a number of
years. Individual girls differ very considerably in the timing and rate
of their sexual development. But there do not seem to be very striking
physiological differences between the Romans and twentieth-century
man. The average age at menarche in Roman times (at least for the
more prosperous and perhaps healthier classes, with whom medical
writers were most familiar) was probably 13 plus. This may be
compared with 13.2 in southern England in 1950–60.[14] According to
ancient scientific theories and male perception of the unbridled
passions of women (whether backed by observation it is difficult to
say), it was advisable to marry girls off soon after menarche, to assure
the preservation of their virginity until marriage.[15] Like menstru-

[11] Verg. *A* 7.53; Serv. ad loc. *Habitus corporis* is a technical phrase in this context. Cf. Quint. *Inst.* 4.2.5; Serv. ad Verg. *E* 8.40.   [12] e.g. Hdt. 1.107.2.

[13] Hor. *O* 3.11.11–12, 2.5.1 ff., with Nisbet and Hubbard ad loc. on the crudity and possible explicit gynaecological allusions in this metaphor; 1.23.11–12. See Fantham, 'The mating of Lalage: Horace *Odes* 2.5'.

[14] See esp. Hopkins, 'The age of Roman girls at marriage' 310 ff.; Eyben, 'Antiquity's view of puberty', gives a general account. See also Amundsen and Diers, 'The age of menarche in classical Greece and Rome'.

[15] Hopkins, 'Age' 314–15, 317–18. Cf. Macrob. ad Cic. *Somn.* 1.6.71: 'Post annos autem bis septem ipsa aetatis necessitate pubescit. Tunc enim moveri incipit vis generationis in masculis et purgatio feminarum. Ideo et tutela puerili quasi virile iam robur absolvitur: de qua tamen feminae propter votorum festinationem maturius biennio legibus liberantur'; VM 6.1.4.

ation, sexual intercourse might also be expected to be good for a girl's health.[16] But some more advanced doctors argued strongly against early intercourse and premature pregnancy.[17]

In the legal sources marriage with immature girls is referred to fairly frequently, again, as in Servius, with emphasis on either the statutory age or physical development. Labeo, in Augustus' time, insists on the physical immaturity of the prepubertal 'wife': *nondum viripotens* (not yet able to take a man) or *minor quam viripotens* (too young to take a man).[18] However, Servius Sulpicius, Cicero's contemporary, had earlier mentioned 'the right age' (*iusta aetas*) as the qualification for partners of either sex, which may suggest that the age of twelve had been fixed, by some lawyers at least, before Labeo's day.[19] The only other piece of evidence seems to be Dio's statement that Augustus, to stop men engaging themselves to very young girls in order to claim the privileges granted to husbands and fiancés in his new law on marriage, tightened up the law by disallowing engagements which did not result in marriage within two years. This meant that for the man to claim privileges under the law the fiancée had to be at least 10, since girls became marriageable at 12. If Dio's comment reflects the Augustan situation, then this passage gives us a *terminus ante quem* of AD 9 for the existence of the view that 12 should be the legal minimum age for marriage.[20] *Minor duodecim annis nupta* ('a woman married under the age of 12') is the usual formulation for the premature bride in the lawyers of the second century AD.[21] There is nowhere any trace of a higher minimum age, one, for instance, closer to the accepted *average* age of menarche.

The legal position of the girl who married before her twelfth birthday was that of a fiancée, *sponsa*, according to Julian and a rescript of Septimius Severus, but only, said Labeo, Papinian, and Ulpian, if a formal betrothal had taken place.[22] Or she was a quasi-wife, *loco nuptae*, but this was extra-legal.[23] Affection rather than

---

[16] Soranus 1.7 gives arguments on both sides.   [17] See esp. Soranus 1.8.

[18] *D* 24.1.65, Lab. *vi post. a Iav. epit.*: 'quod vir ei, quae nondum viripotens nupserit, donaverit, ratum futurum existimo'; 36.2.30, *iii post. a Iav. epit.*: 'quod pupillae legatum est "quandoque nupserit", si ea minor quam viripotens nupserit, non ante ei legatum debebitur quam viripotens esse coeperit, quia non potest videri nupta, quae virum pati non potest.'

[19] *D* 12.4.8, Ner. *ii membr.*: 'quod Servius in libro de dotibus scribit, si inter eas personas, quarum altera nondum iustam aetatem habeat, nuptiae factae sint, quod dotis nomine interim datum sit, repeti posse.' Cf. Watson, *Persons* 39.   [20] Dio 54.16.7.

[21] *D* 5.3.13.1, Ulp., 23.2.4, Pomp., 23.3.74, Herm., 24.1.32.27, 27.6.11.3, 42.5.17.1, 48.5.14.8, Ulp.; cf. 23.3.68, Pap. Cf. Plut. *Comp. Lyc. & Numa* 4; Macrob. ad Cic. *Somn.* 1.6.71, *Sat.* 5.7.7.6.   [22] *D* 24.1.32.27; cf. 27.6.11.3, 48.5.14.8.

[23] *D* 23.1.9, Ulp. Or *loco uxoris* (23.1.9), *quasi uxor* (42.5.17.1), or *ut uxor* 23.3.74), the husband *quasi maritus* (24.1.32.27).

underhand dealing might motivate a father to give his daughter early. Affection for the son-in-law or indulgence to a passionate girl? It is not clear.[24] Gifts from *sponsus* or quasi-husband to *sponsa* or quasi-wife would be valid; arrangements were made for dowry; 'divorce' might occur before the girl's twelfth birthday; she could be prosecuted for adultery *qua sponsa* by the man.[25] But if the couple were still together and still intended marriage when the girl reached her twelfth birthday, she automatically became a legal wife, her dowry became legal, legacies left to her on condition of her being a married woman became payable.[26]

Boys, as Justinian says in the *Institutes*, had to be *puberes*, able to consummate the marriage. Their physical maturity was, according to the Sabinian school of lawyers, to be established by physical examination. This is in the context of the ending of *tutela impuberum*, guardianship of minors. The Proculian school held that a boy was freed from guardianship at 14. Priscus thought that both conditions, *et habitus et numerus annorum*, should be fulfilled.[27] Quintilian refers to the two criteria as alternatives.[28] Servius regards them as going together: in law puberty is proved by both.[29] There is no reason to suppose that these criteria might not be applied to determine whether a boy was legally capable of marriage. But (although consummation was not essential for valid marriage) physical maturity was, it should be noted, the more relevant of the two criteria in the context of marriage. The entry into manhood, symbolized by the adoption of the plain white toga instead of the purple-bordered *praetexta*, and marked by the acquisition of full citizen rights, seems, for the few individuals of whom we are informed, to have taken place in the mid-teens.[30] Marriage too was a rare event for boys as young as 14. There seems to be only one allusion in the *Digest* to the possibility that a marriage might be invalid because the husband was too young:[31]

Quod Servius in libro de dotibus scribit, si inter eas personas, quarum altera nondum iustam aetatem habeat, nuptiae factae sint, quod dotis nomine interim datum sit, repeti posse, sic intellegendum est, ut si divortium intercesserit, priusquam utraque persona iustam aetatem habeat, sit eius pecuniae repetitio . . . (*Digest* 12.4.8, Neratius *ii membranarum*)

[24] *D* 27.6.11.3, Ulp., quoting Julian.
[25] *D* 24.1.32.27, Ulp., ht 65, Lab., 5.3.13.1, Ulp., 12.4.8, Ner., 42.5.17.1, Ulp.; cf. ht 18, Paul, 48.5.14.8, Ulp.   [26] *D* 23.2.4, Pomp., 36.2.30, Lab.
[27] G 1.196; cf. *Tit. Ulp.* 11.28.
[28] *Inst.* 4.2.5: 'pubertas annis an habitu corporis aestimetur?'
[29] Ad Verg. *E* 8.40.   [30] Corbett 51.
[31] In Quint. *Decl.* 279 a pre-pubertal boy is given a wife by his father. There is no allusion to any incapacity for marriage, but only for consummation; but in a sense the boy is 'not yet a husband'.

As for what Servius writes in his book on dowries, that if a marriage takes place between two persons, one of whom has not yet reached the legal age, that which has in the mean time been given as dowry can be reclaimed, we must understand this to mean that if a divorce intervenes, before both persons have reached the legal age, a claim for the money exists . . .

3. Conubium

Although after the age qualification Justinian's *Institutes* discuss the necessary consents,[32] the emphasis in classical discussions of legitimacy of children (and indirectly of valid Roman marriage) is on the legal capacity of a particular couple to marry (*conubium*) not only by reason of both parties having attained the right age and not being too closely related,[33] but also because of their citizen status.

Conubium est uxoris iure ducendae facultas. Conubium habent cives Romani cum civibus Romanis: cum Latinis autem et peregrinis ita, si concessum sit. Cum servis nullum est conubium. (*Tituli Ulpiani* 5.3–5)

Conubium is the capacity to marry a wife in Roman law. Roman citizens have *conubium* with Roman citizens, but with Latins and foreigners only if the privilege was granted. There is no *conubium* with slaves.

Uxoris ducendae facultas implies its obverse, *nubendi facultas*, the right of a woman to marry a particular man, for *conubium* is a two-way concept.[34]

Gaius fills in more detail. He is discussing *patria potestas*:

. . . in potestate nostra sunt liberi nostri quos iustis nuptiis procreavimus. Quod ius proprium civium Romanorum est . . . [Iustas autem nuptias contraxisse liberosque iis procreatos in potestate habere cives Romani ita intellegantur], si cives Romanas uxores duxerint vel etiam Latinas peregrinasve cum quibus conubium habeant. Cum enim conubium id efficiat, ut liberi patris condicionem sequantur, evenit ut non [solum] cives Romani fiant, sed etiam in potestate patris sint. (1.55–6)

. . . our children are under our control if we have procreated them in a marriage valid in Roman law. This right is peculiar to Roman citizens . . . [Roman citizens have contracted marriages valid in Roman law and have their children under their control] if they have married Roman citizens or even Latins or foreigners with whom they have *conubium*. Since indeed the effect of *conubium* is that the children follow the status of the father, it comes about that they are not only born as Roman citizens but are also in their father's power.[35]

[32] 1.10 pr. Intermarriage with non-citizens was less of an issue after the Edict of Caracalla in 212.

[33] G 1.59 says there is no *conubium* between close relatives. Cf. *Tit. Ulp.* 5.6. *Contra*, Volterra, 'La nozione giuridica del conubium' 359–60.

[34] Volterra, 'La nozione giuridica del conubium' 360, 365.

[35] Further definitions in Serv. ad *A* 1.73 (cf. Boethius *ad loc.*) and Isid. *Etym.* 9.21.

Broadly speaking, then, any adult Roman citizen had the right to marry any other Roman citizen of the opposite sex who was not within the forbidden degrees of relationship.[36] Under the Principate certain limitations were superimposed on this general rule. These may be mentioned briefly here, since they may be seen as restricting or taking away the *conubium* which an individual in a particular category, or two people in two particular categories in relation to each other, would otherwise have enjoyed. Soldiers, in the Principate and probably from Augustus on, were forbidden to be husbands during their service. Senators, their sons, and sons' sons were forbidden by Augustus to marry freedwomen, or their daughters and sons' daughters to marry freedmen. There was, by the same laws, a ban on marriage with prostitutes, probably for all free-born citizens, and further rulings to prevent senators allying themselves with women of low origins or professional connections. By imperial order, a provincial administrator was not allowed to marry a woman of the province during his tenure. Guardians and their sons were not to marry a female ward. These prohibitions will be discussed in detail later.

If a Roman citizen was taken prisoner by the enemy, his or her citizenship lapsed. Freedom and citizenship were intertwined. So, as an automatic consequence, valid Roman marriage ended with the loss of freedom and Roman rights. But a prisoner could hope to become free and recover his citizenship. Certain rights which went with citizenship might be recovered automatically by *postliminium*, if he came back to Roman territory. These had been held in suspense while he was captive, for instance his *patria potestas*. But marriage, which depended on the consent of the partner, was not automatically revived in classical law:

Non, ut pater filium, ita uxorem maritus iure postliminii recipit: sed consensu redintegratur matrimonium. (*Digest* 49.15.14.1, Pomponius *iii ad Sabinum*)

A husband does not recover his wife by right of *postliminium* as a father recovers his son, but marriage is renewed by consent.[37]

In republican times Latin cities had *ius conubii* with Rome, which meant that children of a Roman father and a Latin mother would be Roman and children of a Latin father and a Roman mother Latin

---

[36] Briefly in the 5th cent. there was no *conubium* between patricians and plebeians. (See Watson, *XII Tables* 20ff.) I agree with Watson, *Persons* 32ff., that there is no reason to believe that the intermarriage of free-born and freed persons was prohibited by law during the Republic, i.e. that they lacked *conubium* with each other. For a subtle but essentially unconvincing restatement of the opposing view see Humbert, 'Hispala Fecenia et l'endogamie des affranchis sous la république'. For *conubium* with non-citizens in the early Republic see de Visscher, 'Conubium et civitas'; Sherwin-White, *RC*, index s.v.

[37] D 24.2.1, 49.15.12.4; Buckland, *Textbook* 67ff.; Watson, '*Captivitas* and *matrimonium*'.

(since *conubium* means that children follow their father).[38] After the Social War of 91–89 BC, all citizens of Latin cities south of the Po became Roman, but Latin status for cities continued to exist in the provinces. It is uncertain if their citizens had *conubium* automatically or 'only if the privilege had been granted'. Another type of Latin, introduced by a Junian law of Augustan or early Tiberian date, was the ex-slave who had been manumitted under the age of 30, who became a Junian Latin. Such a man, if he married a Latin or Roman woman in accordance with the *Lex Aelia Sentia* of AD 4, and had a child who reached the age of 1, could apply for Roman citizenship.[39] If he was successful, he would then have *conubium* and be validly married in Roman law and the child would come under his *potestas*.[40]

Peregrini, foreigners, might have *conubium* bestowed upon them. This would mean that the children took the father's citizenship. But at some time before 90 BC a Minician law changed the rules. It had no doubt been recognized that Roman citizenship was more desirable than that of other Italian cities (from which, rather than the rest of the Mediterranean world, the peregrine partner in a mixed marriage normally came). By the Minician Law, therefore, children were to follow the status of the 'inferior' parent, so that if either parent was foreign the child was non-Roman. There are four possible types of couple involved. When the mother was a foreigner and the father Roman and there was no *conubium* between them, the child followed the mother by *ius gentium*, the law of all peoples. When the father was a foreigner and the mother Roman and they had *conubium*, the child followed the father, because the marriage was valid in his law. The position of these two sets of couples and their children was left unaltered by the new law, since the children were non-Roman. But whereas before the children of a Roman mother and a non-Roman father without *conubium* were illegitimate and therefore by *ius gentium* Roman, the Minician Law penalized them, making them follow the father.[41] The fourth type of marriage is that of a Roman man and a foreign woman with *conubium*. Gaius, before discussing

---

[38] Sherwin-White, *RC* 109, citing Livy 8.14.10: 'ceteris Latinis populis conubia commerciaque et concilia inter se ademerunt' ('they [sc. the Romans, punishing their fellow Latins in 338 BC] took away their rights of intermarriage and trade with each other and their councils').

[39] G 1.29; *Tit. Ulp.* 3.3.   [40] G 1.65–6.

[41] *Tit. Ulp.* 5.8: 'If *conubium* is present the children always follow the status of their father, if it is not they take their mother's condition, except that the child of a foreign man and Roman citizen woman is born foreign, since the Minician Law orders that if one or the other parent is a foreigner, the child follows the condition of the inferior parent.' G 1.78: 'But as for what we said, that the child of a Roman citizen man and a foreigner, unless there is *conubium*, is a foreigner, this is laid down by the Minician Law, that is, that he must follow the condition of the foreign parent. But by the same law it is laid down conversely that if a foreigner marries a Roman wife, with whom he does not have *conubium*, then their child is born with the foreign

the *Lex Minicia*, states emphatically that 'if a Roman citizen marries a foreign woman with whom he has *conubium*, a valid marriage is contracted and any child born to them is a Roman citizen and in his father's *potestas*'.[42] This is in apparent conflict with the specific statements in both Gaius and the *Tituli Ulpiani* that the *Lex Minicia* laid down that if either parent was peregrine the child was peregrine. But both these statements should be taken to be in the context only of marriage without *conubium*. The emphasis in both sources on the marriage of a Roman woman with a foreign man would then be dictated by the fact that this was the only type of marriage which was affected by the Minician Law. The law reaffirmed the foreign status of children of a Roman man and a foreign woman without *conubium* (upholding *ius gentium*) and of a foreign man and a Roman woman with *conubium*, deprived the children of a foreign man and a Roman woman without *conubium* of the benefits of natural law, and left untouched the validity in civil law of the marriage of a Roman man and a foreign woman with *conubium*.[43]

Gaius gives an elaborate set of rules about what happened in the Principate when a Roman citizen entered on a marriage with a foreigner or Latin believing him or her to be a Roman citizen.[44] After the birth and first birthday of a child, as long as the error could be proved, the spouse and child could obtain Roman citizenship under the ruling of a senatorial decree of unknown date (which must fall somewhere between the *Lex Aelia Sentia* and Hadrian) and the child would come under *patria potestas*. This generous provision did not apply to those who knowingly entered on a mixed marriage.[45]

Mixed marriages, invalid in Roman law, were nevertheless contracted by Roman citizens in the early Empire. The largest class of

citizenship. But it is in this instance that the Minician Law is particularly necessary, for in the absence of that law the child should have acquired a different status, since the child of parents without *conubium* by the law of all peoples follows his mother's status.' 'Unless there is *conubium*' is conjectural and so is the order of the pairs. The *Lex Minicia* included Latins under 'peregrini' (G 1.79).

[42] G 1.76.
[43] There is an interesting passage of Ulpian on mixed marriages involving two non-Roman partners, in which the privilege might have been conferred that the children followed the superior status of the mother, e.g. (he supposes) where the father was a Campanian but the mother belonged to the *municipium* of Puteoli. Ilium and Delphi allowed this to their women; Pompey had conferred it on Pontic women (*D* 50.1.1.2; cf. Volterra, 'Sulla D. 1.5.24', 546).
[44] 1.67ff., 87. This applied even to a Latin who married a peregrine believing him or her to be Latin or Roman (1.69–70) or a Roman who married a Latin woman because he believed himself to be a Latin, or a *peregrina* because he believed himself to be a peregrine.
[45] Cf. *Gnom.* 46: a Roman man who married an Egyptian in ignorance of her citizenship was exempt from a fine and his children took his citizenship; *contra Gnom.* 39: if a Roman of either sex married a 'townsperson' or Egyptian under a mistake about his or her status, the children followed the 'inferior' race.

such citizens must have been the soldiers, debarred (probably by Augustus) from valid Roman marriage. They naturally formed relationships, some of them stable and long-lasting, with women in the areas where they were stationed, who were largely non-citizens. Perhaps some of these unions were valid according to the custom and law of the woman's community. But lack of recognition in Roman law involved a number of very serious disadvantages, particularly the illegitimacy of children and their consequent lack of claim on the father's estate.

That mixed marriages were a possibility to be guarded against even in the higher reaches of society is suggested by a passage of Seneca, which smacks of the rhetorical school but might also reflect the social background of the provinces, such as his own Spain.

Promisi tibi in matrimonium filiam; postea peregrinus adparuisti. non est mihi cum externo conubium; eadem res me defendit, quae vetat. (*De Beneficiis* 4.35.1)

I promised you my daughter in marriage: it afterwards came to light that you were a foreigner. I have no *conubium* with an alien; this prohibition is my defence.

Senatorial governors and all other officials concerned in the administration of a province were forbidden at a date prior to the death of Septimius Severus in 211 to marry women of that province during their term of office.[46] The law seems to imply that such women would be Roman citizens with whom a valid marriage might otherwise have been contracted.

The child of a Latin man and a Roman woman, according to a senatusconsultum of Hadrian, was to have Roman citizenship in accordance with the *ius gentium*. Before there had been some doubt whether such a couple, if they married in accordance with the *Lex Aelia Sentia*, had *conubium*, so that the child would follow the Latin father.[47]

If a foreign woman obtained Roman citizenship during pregnancy, the child was Roman if it was illegitimately conceived according to the law of the non-Roman community, but non-Roman if it was conceived in a valid peregrine marriage, unless the father also acquired Roman citizenship.[48]

To sum up, in a mixed marriage with *conubium*, the child followed the father. If the father was Roman, the marriage was valid in Roman

---

[46] Dell'Oro, 'Il divieto del matrimonio fra funzionario romano e donna della provincia' 531, says that recent scholarship is unanimous in referring this law to women with Roman citizenship. He points out that governors' terms were usually short and that a relationship with a provincial citizen would not usually be construed as marriage.

[47] G 1.30, 80–1; *Tit. Ulp.* 3.3.   [48] G 1.92.

law. A mixed marriage without *conubium* was not valid in Roman law. If one partner was *peregrinus*, the children followed his or her status, after the Minician Law, unless error could be proved. The Romans probably had *conubium* with Latins under the *Lex Aelia Sentia*, as they had had in the Republic, until Hadrian allowed children of a Roman mother and a Latin father to take the superior status. Marriages between Junian Latin and Roman could be upgraded into Roman marriage, with Roman citizenship and *patria potestas* for the ex-slave, as long as a child survived to his first birthday. In mixed marriages without *conubium*, *patria potestas* did not follow; the husband, in case of a divorce, was not entitled to retain part of the dowry for the benefit of the children; husband and wife had no automatic or other rights of succession to each other; there was no valid dowry or action for recovery of dowry by the wife; the husband could not prosecute the wife for adultery *qua* husband but only as a third party (*iure extranei*), and the children were illegitimate and subject to various disabilities.[49]

Where a valid non-Roman marriage had previously existed and one of the partners received the Roman citizenship (unless there were *conubium* between the peregrine community and Rome)[50] the marriage would be invalid in Roman law and possibly in the original community too. This could be avoided either by a grant of *conubium* with the particular partner or by a direct grant of citizenship. The most generous treatment was accorded to Latin communities. When Latin magistrates left office, they were automatically granted Roman citizenship and so were their parents, wives, children born in legitimate marriage who had been in paternal power, and grandsons and granddaughters born to a son who had also been in power.[51] Volterra has collected instances where a grant of citizenship to the individual husband is accompanied by a grant to the wife (defined as the woman who is or will be his wife after the grant of citizenship to him) as well as to existing children and to his parents.[52] Grants of citizenship to the wife of a foreigner who had performed signal service to the Roman people, like Seleucus of Rhosus, or even to wives of a group of veteran auxiliaries, were, however, exceptional. The marriage could be made valid in Roman law and subsequent children made legitimate simply by granting *conubium*. As emerges very clearly in the

[49] G 1.87; *Tit. Ulp.* 5.1; Cic. *Top.* 20; *D* 38.11.1 pr., Ulp.; 48.5.14.1, Ulp.; *Coll.* 4.5.1.

[50] G 1.56, 76–7; Corbett 28; Volterra, 'L'acquisto della cittadinanza romana e il matrimonio del peregrino'.

[51] *Lex Salpensana* (*FIRA* i.23) and *Lex Irnitana* (González, 'The Lex Irnitana' 147 ff.) 21.

[52] *Enciclopedia* 778–9 and more fully in 'Sulla condizione dei figli dei peregrini cui veniva concessa la cittadinanza romana'. See e.g. *FIRA* i nos. 55, 56, 76, and cf. Sherwin-White, 'The *Tabula* of Banasa and the *Constitutio Antoniniana*'.

grants of citizenship to auxiliaries on their discharge, *conubium* was granted with the current wife, or, for bachelors, with the first woman the man chose to marry after the grant. Sometimes existing children were also given citizenship.[53]

4. Matrimonia Iusta *and* Iniusta

Marriages where the partners had *conubium* were marriages valid in Roman law (*iusta matrimonia*).[54] Marriages between two foreigners might be defined as valid foreign marriages in a particular community (*secundum leges moresque peregrinorum*).[55] But in the whole discussion of mixed marriages, Gaius speaks as if marriages where *conubium* did not exist were still marriages. Ulpian refers to such unions as *matrimonia iniusta*, the wife as *iniusta* (*uxor*). Some of the effects of marriage followed despite invalidity in Roman law. The marriage was not regarded as null.[56] This is clear as early as Cicero. He is discussing retention of part of the dowry by the husband after divorce:

Si mulier, cum fuisset nupta cum eo, quicum conubium non esset, nuntium remisit, quoniam qui nati sunt patrem non sequuntur, pro liberis manere nihil oportet. (*Topica* 20)

If a woman who had been married to a man with whom she did not have *conubium* sends him notice of divorce, since the children do not follow the father he may retain nothing on account of the children.

Here the language appropriate to marriage and divorce is retained and the husband has received a dowry. But some consequences of valid marriage have not followed.

Ut bonorum possessio peti posset unde vir et uxor, iustum esse matrimonium oportet. Ceterum si iniustum fuerit matrimonium, nequaquam bonorum possessio peti poterit, quemadmodum nec ex testamento adiri hereditas vel secundum tabulas peti bonorum possessio, nihil enim capi propter iniustum matrimonium potest. (*Digest* 38.11.1 pr., Ulpian *xlvii ad edictum*)

In order for possession of the estate to be claimed by a person *qua* wife or husband, the marriage must be valid. But if it was invalid, possession of the estate cannot be claimed at all, just as an inheritance may not be taken or

---

[53] Volterra, *Enciclopedia* 779–80; J. B. Campbell, *The Emperor and the Roman army* 439 ff. (with recent bibliography).

[54] *Tit. Ulp.* 5.2. *Iustae nuptiae*: *D* 32.38 pr., 38.4.1 pr., 38.10.4.2, 38.11.1 pr., 48.20.1.2. *Iusta uxor*: 48.5.14.1. *Iusti liberi*: *FV* 168.   [55] G 1.92.

[56] For this view see Corbett 102 ff., 139; Taubenschlag, *The law of Greco-Roman Egypt* 80–1; Gaudemet, 'Justum matrimonium' 309 ff.; Kunkel, *RE* xiv (1930) 2263; Watson, *Persons* 27. *Contra*, Volterra, 'Iniustum matrimonium', 'La nozione giuridica del conubium' 362.

possession of the estate claimed in accordance with a will. For nothing may be taken on account of an invalid marriage.

Similarly, there was no automatic succession on intestacy. However, other consequences of a valid marriage might be held to follow:

Plane sive iusta fuit sive iniusta, accusationem instituere vir poterit: nam et Sextus Caecilius ait, haec lex ad omnia matrimonia pertinet, et illud Homericum adfert: nec enim soli, inquit, Atridae uxores suas amant. (*Digest* 48.5.14.1, Ulpian *ii de adulteriis*)

Clearly whether she was a legal wife or not, her husband can charge her [with adultery], for, as Sextus Caecilius says, this law [the Julian law on adultery] applies to all marriages, and he applies the quotation from Homer, 'for not only the sons of Atreus love their wives'.

Omnia matrimonia: all sorts of marriages, fully valid in civil law or invalid for various reasons, especially different citizenships. The invalidity of the marriage, or so it could be argued by certain jurists, did not affect the right of the husband to prosecute for adultery.

What sort of marriages should be counted as *iniusta*? Certainly mixed marriages of people with different citizenships and without *conubium*.[57] When two people married and the husband was subsequently convicted of previous adultery with his new wife, Papinian tells us they would not benefit from each other's wills. Presumably this too was invalid marriage.[58] Similarly if the marriage contravened the *Lex Julia de maritandis ordinibus* or the *Lex Papia Poppaea*: again husband and wife lost the right of succession to each other. The specific examples suggested here are marriages between any citizen and a woman technically *famosa* (of ill repute) and between senator and freedwoman.[59] 'The fact that a marriage was *injustus* because one of the parties belonged to a class rendered ineligible by the *Lex Julia de maritandis ordinibus* (18 BC) did not render the woman any less liable to immediate execution or public prosecution for adultery.'[60] All these couples seem to be regarded as husbands and wives. The marriages are not null or punished. But the advantages offered by the Augustan legislation to married people do not accrue.

Nuptiae inter easdem personas nisi volentibus parentibus renovatae iustae non habentur. (*Digest* 23.2.18, Iulianus *xvi digestorum*)

If two persons marry each other for the second time, the marriage is not considered valid unless their parents consent.

---

[57] G 1.77ff.; *Coll.* 4.5.1.

[58] *D* 34.9.13, Pap., may be equating it with a marriage with a detected or convicted adulteress, which was *iniustum* under the Augustan Laws.

[59] *Tit. Ulp.* 16.2.   [60] Corbett 139, citing *D* 48.5.14.1, ht 25.3.

This passage, put in here in the title *De ritu nuptiarum* with various other points about the arrangement and non-arrangement of marriages by fathers, relations, and guardians,[61] should be linked with the normal requirements for consent of parents. Iulianus merely states that when the parties remarry after a divorce, the consent of parents (sc. *patresfamilias*) must be renewed and cannot be carried over from the initial, dissolved marriage. For our present purposes though, what is important is that such a marriage would apparently be considered *iniustum*. But it would exist.

Respondit mihi placere, etsi contra mandata contractum sit matrimonium in provincia, tamen post depositum officium, si in eadem voluntate perseverat, iustas nuptias effici: et ideo postea liberos natos ex iusto matrimonio legitimos esse. (*Digest* 23.2.65.1, Paul *vii responsorum*)

He replied, 'In my opinion, even if a marriage was contracted in a province against imperial decree, still, if after the end of a man's tenure of office he perseveres in the same intention, the marriage is made valid and therefore the children born subsequently from a valid marriage are legitimate.'

Again it seems fair to deduce that Paul would qualify this marriage as *iniustum* during the husband's tour of duty in the province to which his wife belonged. But the intention of the man was to contract a marriage. What he legally could have done was to take a provincial woman as his concubine. This—perhaps because of her social status—was precisely what he did not do. He regarded her as his wife to all intents and purposes except those of the imperial ruling (which may go back only to the late second century AD), and the moment he laid down his office the relationship was transmogrified. Clearly there was *conubium* between the specific Roman and the provincial woman about whom Paul was consulted, though it was suspended while the man was an official. Any children born after the marriage became valid were legitimate, in unfortunate contrast to any elder children born during their father's term.

5. Concubinatus

In all these discussions, the lawyers are thinking of relationships which had some of the effects of valid marriage. There are two other unions which moderns regard as quasi-marital, but which do not enter into the thinking of the Roman jurists in this area. These are *concubinatus* and *contubernium*. In *iniustum matrimonium* each member of the pair intended a marital relationship, but because of

---

[61] *D* 23.2.16, 18–22.

some incapacity the union was not fully valid in Roman law. But in *concubinatus* at least one of the couple, the man, did not intend marriage. (Some moderns confuse the issue by calling *iniustum matrimonium* concubinage. I shall use 'concubinage' and 'concubine' only where the Romans would use *concubinatus* and *concubina*.)

There is a division between literary sources, which sometimes use *concubina* of any recognizable extra-marital sexual partner, and juristic and epigraphic sources. A Roman governor or emperor might have a whole seraglio of slave or freed mistresses, according to hostile sources, and these are called *concubinae*.[62] The marital status of the man was irrelevant. But the women honoured in epitaphs and occasionally discussed by jurists appear to be living in an avowed monogamous relationship with a man who did not have a legal wife. Upper-class men are attested by literary and juristic sources as having concubines of lower social status either when they were relatively young and unready for marriage, like Augustine, or after the death of a wife who had given them enough children, like Vespasian. Concubines were chosen precisely because they were socially ineligible for marriage: the man obtained a stable sexual and presumably affective relationship with a companion and domestic partner who had no legal claim on his property and was not expected to bear him children. (If there were children, they were illegitimate, with no legal claim on his property.) The woman, presumably, obtained a higher standard of living than would have been possible with a man of her own class. Her position might be relatively secure, and substantial presents are seen as normal. The one concubine about whose feelings we know anything, Augustine's, was, on his evidence, devoted to him. But the union was asymmetrical: there is no word to describe the male partner of a *concubina*.[63]

To put the situation as briefly as possible, in Roman concubinage *affectio maritalis*, the reciprocal attitude of regarding the other as a wife or husband, was lacking. If both began to regard the other as a *coniunx*, then the relationship became *matrimonium*, as long as there was no legal disqualification.

6. Contubernium

In *contubernium*, by contrast, the will to have the sexual partner as *coniunx* might exist, but legal capacity was absent because at least one of the partners was a slave.

[62] e.g. Cael. ap. Quint. *Inst.* 4.2.124 = *ORF* no. 162.17; Tac. *H* 1.72, 3.40; Pliny *Epp.* 3.14.3; Suet. *Dom.* 22.

[63] For details see B. Rawson, 'Roman concubinage and other *de facto* marriages'; Treggiari, 'Concubinae'.

Cum servis nullum est conubium. (*Tituli Ulpiani* 5.5)

There is no *conubium* with slaves.

Inter servos et liberos matrimonium contrahi non potest, contubernium potest. (Paul *Sententiae* 2.19.6)

Between slaves and free persons marriage cannot be contracted but *contubernium* can.

Because there was no capacity for marriage, the children followed the mother's status: if she was a slave, so were they.[64] Like concubinage, *contubernium* might develop into marriage. If both partners were slaves and then both were freed and continued to live together, then they might be validly husband and wife. The change in the legal nature of their union depended on the acquisition of legal capacity —they had been freed and became Roman citizens—and also on their attitude (*affectio maritalis*). If the manumission of two slave partners was not synchronized, so that one was a freed person and the other still slave, the union remained *contubernium*. If the woman was freed and the man slave the children would be illegitimate but free-born. If the man was freed and the woman slave, the children would be born slaves. The same situation applied to a disparate couple in which one partner was free-born. These various phases in the status of the individual *contubernalis* are therefore reflected in the status of the union or of any children. Unlike marriage, which depended on the consent of the partners and of their *patresfamilias* (if any), the continuance of *contubernium* involved at least the tacit consent of the owner or owners of the slaves. But some unions did achieve relative stability and recognition, and continuance into a valid citizen marriage.[65] Much as public authorities concerned themselves with wives when granting citizenship to men, private owners might give freedom to *contubernales* when they manumitted male slaves, so that legal marriage became possible.[66]

Children born to *contubernales* were not *iusti*. They followed the status of the mother. A woman living in *contubernium* could not be accused of adultery.[67] But that someone could raise the question of adultery at all shows how *contubernium* was compared with marriage. A *contubernalis* might bring her mate a quasi-dowry and the children were recognized as offspring of the union by outsiders such as the

[64] *Tit. Ulp.* 5.9.

[65] See my '*Contubernales* in *CIL* 6'. Slaves who, because of informality in the ceremony of manumission or because they or their owners were not fully qualified under the Augustan legislation, entered the special half-free class of Junian Latins came under special rules, described in detail by Gaius at 1.65 ff.

[66] Explicit in the will of Dasumius of AD 108 (*FIRA* iii.48.40 ff.). See *D* 32.41.2 on legacy of *contubernales* to *liberti*.　　[67] *CJ* 9.9.23 pr. (AD 290).

slave-owner as well as by the father. *Contubernales* commemorate each other on tombstones far more often than a man commemorates his concubine, which suggests that the duty to do so was more strongly felt. Most significant, *contubernales* often call each other *coniunx*. So in many ways *contubernium* imitates *matrimonium iustum*.

7. Intent

If a couple had *conubium*, the other necessary condition for marriage was that each intended to be married to the other. Consent was initially signified when the marriage began.[68] The continuing will to regard the partner as *coniunx* is defined by jurists as *affectio maritalis*, literally a 'marital attitude'.[69] It may also be referred to in a number of other ways. Quintilian, for instance (though with particular reference to the initiation of marriage), says

Nihil obstat quominus iustum matrimonium sit mente coeuntium, etiamsi tabulae firmatae[70] non fuerint: nihil enim proderit signasse tabulas, si mentem matrimonii non fuisse constabit. (Quintilian *Institutio* 5.11.32)

There is no obstacle to a marriage being valid by reason merely of the will [literally mind] of those who come together, even though a contract has not been ratified. For it is useless to seal a contract if it turns out that the will to marriage did not exist.

Mens matrimonii seems to be much the same as *affectio maritalis*.

Si mulier et maritus diu seorsum quidem habitaverint, sed honorem invicem matrimonii habebant (quod scimus interdum et inter consulares personas subsecutum), puto donationes non valere, quasi duraverint nuptiae: non enim coitus matrimonium facit, sed maritalis affectio . . . (*Digest* 24.1.32.13, Ulpian *xxxiii ad Sabinum*)

Even if wife and husband have long lived apart, but have each reciprocally honoured the marriage (which we know has occurred occasionally even between people of consular rank), I think that gifts between them are not valid, on the grounds that the marriage has continued: for it is not sexual intercourse which makes a marriage, but *maritalis affectio*.

---

[68] See ch. 5. For the views expressed here cf. Volterra, *Enciclopedia* 738ff. For him what makes a marriage is 'la volontà effettiva, continua di essere uniti durevolmente in tale rapporto'. Also Corbett 92ff. *Contra*, Rasi, *Consensus facit nuptias*, with Volterra's reply, 'Precisazioni in tema di matrimonio classico'. See also the short monograph by Huber, *Der Ehekonsens im römischen Recht*.

[69] The phrase has been held to be interpolated. See for bibliography Robleda, *El matrimonio en derecho romano* ch. 3. Donatella Quartuccio argues that the expression is classical but late ('Sull'origine dell'"adfectio maritalis"'). See for convenient documentation Volterra, *Enciclopedia* 738ff.

[70] *Firmo* is used elsewhere in the context of marriage: Ter. *Hau.* 1048; Cat. 62.27.

The point that it is not sexual union, initial consummation, which makes a marriage, but consent, is made elsewhere.[71]

Since custom ruled that gifts of any importance between husband and wife were (in principle) invalid, discussions about ownership, usually after the death of at least one of the partners, often involved determining whether the couple were legally married at the time of the alleged transfer.[72] The precise moment at which consent had been given during the wedding and its preliminaries was often of vital importance, and hard to determine long after the event. A still more obscure situation might occur when a couple had been living in concubinage and then began to regard each other as husband and wife, without perhaps celebrating the change with a wedding:

Donationes in concubinam collatas non posse revocari convenit, nec, si matrimonium inter eosdem postea fuerit contractum, ad irritum reccidere quod ante iure valuit. An autem maritalis honor et affectio pridem praecesserit, personis comparatis, vitae coniunctione considerata perpendendum esse respondi. (*Digest* 39.5.31 pr., Papinian *xii responsorum*)

It is agreed that gifts bestowed on a concubine cannot be revoked, nor, if marriage is subsequently contracted between the same parties, should a gift which was previously legally valid become invalid. But, I replied, the question must be carefully weighed whether *maritalis honor et affectio* preceded the [sc. apparent] marriage, taking into account the relative standing of the parties and their union in their way of life.

Justinian in AD 530 refers to this change of mental attitude by a man and his concubine when he writes of a man living with a woman whom he could legally marry, but not at the beginning with *affectio maritalis*. His attitude towards her then changes. Alternatively, there might be instances in which lawyers decided that his attitude had been that of a husband from the beginning.[73] Ulpian, in discussing how lawyers are to determine when a gift will be invalid, says that if a marriage is in accordance with Roman customs and laws, then a gift is invalid. So if the union was between a freedwoman and a senator or a governor and a woman of the province he was ruling, both of which were prohibited by law at different periods, then the marriage was invalid and the gift

---

[71] D 35.1.15 and 50.17.30, attributed to Ulp. *xxxv* and *xxxvi ad Sab.*: 'nuptias enim non concubitus sed consensus facit.'

[72] For discussion of property transfers between husband and wife see ch. 11.

[73] CJ 5.27.11 pr.: 'non ab initio adfectione maritali', 2: 'talem adfectionem habuisse'; ht 10.2: 'talem adfectionem circa mulierem . . . habuisse' (AD 529). Instead of arguing that the phrase is Justinianic and therefore interpolated in the *Digest*, I would hold that Justinian here uses it in a classical sense, but that elsewhere in the same two excerpts in *CJ* his use of *affectio* comes near to 'affection'. Cf. e.g. *CJ* 5.27.10 pr.: 'ex eadem adfectione', ibid. 1: 'adfectio prioris subolis.'

valid. In one instance the emperor chose to regard a freedwoman as a concubine, in order apparently to let her benefit from a gift:

Divus tamen Severus in liberta Pontii Paulini senatoris contra statuit, quia non erat affectione uxoris habita, sed magis concubinae. (*Digest* 24.1.3.1, Ulpian *xxxii ad Sabinum*)

The deified Severus made the opposite decision in the case of the freed-woman of the senator Pontius Paulinus, that she was not kept with the intention of having her as a wife, but rather as a concubine.

It is clear that a concubine was distinguished from a wife by the intention of, particularly, the man.[74] The obverse is that marriage was defined as such by the reciprocal attitude of the *coniuges*.

It is important that the cohabitation of a man and a woman would normally be assumed to be marriage unless there was evidence to the contrary:

In liberae mulieris consuetudine non concubinatus sed nuptiae intel-legendae sunt, si non corpore quaestum fecerit. (*Digest* 23.2.24, Modestinus *i regularum*)

In intercourse with a free woman, marriage, not concubinage, is to be understood, unless she has been a prostitute.[75]

I have argued elsewhere that free-born and respectable women were both legally and morally eligible to be concubines. In law, women ineligible for marriage with any free-born citizen (such as prostitutes under the Augustan legislation) or with a particular class of free-born men (as were freedwomen with senators under the same statues) were eligible only for concubinage with such men. But women of free birth and impeccable morals might be socially more acceptable as concubines than as wives if there was a marked social disparity between them and a particular man. The general rule, however, can still be as Modestinus expresses it: if there was no fundamental or statutory legal disqualification (such as slavery or a profession which prevented marriage with an *ingenuus*) and (I add) no evidence that concubinage was intended, then a free woman cohabiting with a man is assumed to be his wife.[76]

The degree to which third parties could be ignorant of the nature of

---

[74] See Orestano, 'Sul matrimonio presunto in diritto romano', arguing strongly that the text is classical.

[75] *D* 25.7.4, Paul: 'Concubinam ex sola animi destinatione aestimari oportet'; Paul *S* 2.20.1: 'Concubina igitur ab uxore solo dilectu separatur.'

[76] Treggiari, '*Concubinae*' 71 ff. Superficial similarities between Roman concepts of marriage and US 'common-law marriage' are not to be pressed. See Longo, '"Common-law marriage" statunitense e matrimonio romano: prospettive di una comparazione'.

the union between two people who were eligible to be married to each other is strikingly illustrated by the scandalous stories which circulated about the emperor Gaius. All his marriages are said by Suetonius to have taken place irregularly. Livia Orestilla was snatched from her bridegroom C. Piso at the wedding and led off to the emperor's house instead. Lollia Paullina was summoned back from her husband's province and rapidly married and divorced. But his last wife Caesonia was not acknowledged as his wife until she bore him a daughter and Gaius announced on the same day that he was a husband and a father. Dio's version, which says that Gaius wanted to claim a child born thirty days after the marriage, suggests that the news of the marriage was announced on the day of the daughter's birth, but that Gaius wanted to date the marriage a month before, so that there was no doubt the child was born legitimately.[77] A child conceived outside wedlock took its status from the time of its birth: the infant would thus be legally his child.[78] Since no public ceremony or documentation was necessary, if a father acknowledged a child and claimed that he had regarded its mother as his wife before the child's birth and the mother confirmed that she regarded the man as her husband, the evidence that a marriage existed was irrefutable, as long as each had *conubium* with the other. And who would contradict the emperor? The testimony of seven witnesses might be demanded of a Junian Latin who wanted to prove marriage with a Roman or Latin in order to claim Roman status (and he had also to have a child who reached the age of a year).[79] But to make a marriage between eligible persons only their mutual consent was required, and to prove it their statements (when both were alive to make them) would, in normal circumstances, suffice. So the account of Gaius' third marriage is theoretically possible, though scandalous. It points up, on the one hand, the potentially privileged nature of information about the existence of the marital relationship between two individuals and, on the other, the need for openness once a child was involved.

II. INTERVENTION BY PUBLIC AUTHORITY

As we have seen, custom and statute regulated *conubium*, the right of marriage of near relations, the very young, and people of disparate citizen status. But there was scarcely any law dealing directly with *matrimonium*. Republican praetors regulated property-settlements on divorce; jurists discussed problems of dowry. Public authority

---

[77] Suet. *Cal.* 25; Dio 59.23.7.   [78] G 1.89.   [79] G 1.29 ff.

took notice of the fact of marriage. We are told that it was part of the censor's job to enquire of each man who presented himself at the census whether he was married. That the question took the form 'Have you a wife for the purpose of breeding children?' is suggested by the story that Carvilius Ruga (c.230 BC) could not in conscience take the oath that he had a wife to bear him children, since he knew her to be sterile.[80] But a slightly different formulation is directly quoted by Cicero and Gellius in a story of a joke inappropriately offered to Cato the Censor in 184 BC. The citizen was asked on oath whether to the best of his judgement he had a wife, that is whether, to the best of his knowledge and belief and by his own intention, he was living in valid marriage: 'Ex tui animi sententia tu uxorem habes?' Exploiting the ambiguity of 'ex tui animi sententia', which could also mean 'to your taste', L. Nasica replied, 'non hercule ex mei animi sententia', 'not to mine, on my honour'.[81] Unless the second formulation of the question was invented merely for the sake of the joke, it seems likely that the censors had a certain latitude in framing the question.[82] This sporadic registration of marriages and children enabled some check to be made on whether wives and husbands had *conubium* with each other and whether their children were Roman citizens. Much was accepted on faith by the censors, but a public declaration of a wife's name implied some degree of openness about her identity.

It also allowed censors to encourage marriage and procreation as means of strengthening the citizen body. The censors of 403 BC had allegedly fined old bachelors for failing to do their duty to the state.[83] This fine seems to be what Festus oddly calls the 'wife-tax', but it is quite unclear if censors regularly levied it.[84] Later censors seem to have resorted to exhortation in attempting to compel men to marriage as a duty to the gods and the state.[85] Manpower was a continuing preoccupation. But neither quinquennial censors nor the Senate were in a position to sustain a consistent policy. Laws aimed at improving the economic state of the poor were partly intended to encourage them to rear children. But only an emperor was in a position to

[80] Sulpicius ap. Gell. 4.3.2.: 'iurare a censoribus coactus erat uxorem se liberum quaerundum gratia habiturum'; DH *Ant.* 2.25.7.
[81] Cic. *de or.* 2.260; Gell. 4.20.3 ff. On the registration of wives and daughters see Brunt, *IM* 15–16, suggesting that the names of wives *in manu* and *sui iuris* were registered by husbands, those of wives who remained *in potestate* by fathers.
[82] On the risks of using them see Saller, 'Anecdotes as historical evidence for the Principate'.
[83] VM 2.9.1.
[84] 519L: 'Uxorium perpendisse dicitur, qui quod uxorem non habuerit, res populo dedit.'
[85] Perhaps both Q. Caecilius Metellus Macedonicus, censor 131–130, and Q. Caecilius Metellus Numidicus, censor 102–101. See M. McDonnell, 'The speech of Numidicus at Gellius, *N.A.* 1.6'.

confront the perceived problem directly and to introduce complex legislation on the subject of marriage.

When Caesar controlled the state, Cicero advised him to encourage the propagation of children. There is a possibility that he offered rewards to fathers of large families.[86] Once Octavian had consolidated his power, he claimed to be a new founder of the state, and such claims involved a set of expectations. Augustus must aspire to be a father of cities.[87] Around the same time, historians were reissuing or elaborating detailed accounts of earlier shapers of Roman society, particularly Romulus and Numa. Octavian might have adopted 'Romulus' as a title instead of the safer and more numinous 'Augustus', which itself was associated with the founding of Rome. Such accounts derive their inspiration from moralistic traditions about the Utopian social systems developed by mythical or idealized founders or lawgivers of Greek cities. The tradition typically includes repressive legislation designed to check conspicuous consumption and women's misbehaviour.[88] Alternatively, a founder might design a system which gave positive support to virtue.[89]

When Augustus restored temples in 28 BC[90] he may also have made an abortive effort to renovate sexual morality. A remark of Livy's on Roman intolerance of necessary remedies and an ode of Horace suggest that reaction was so unfavourable that Augustus dropped the proposal for the moment. Horace calls on an undefined man to restore old values of frugality and chastity to Rome: 'Oh let whoever wishes to take away impious slaughter and civil madness, if he seeks to have the words "Father of cities" inscribed beneath his statues, let him dare to curb unbroken licence. He will be glorious to posterity.' The benefactor will need courage, but a later generation will be grateful to him. The link is made between the vices of parents and the corruption of children: fathers are avaricious and unscrupulous, mothers, thanks to their rich dowries, can control their husbands or take lovers. Surplus wealth should be given to Capitoline Jove (or

---

[87] Hor. *O* 3.24.   [86] Cic. *pro Marcello* 23; Dio 43.25.2.
[88] Cf. Balsdon, 'Dionysius on Romulus: a political pamphlet?'
[89] The ideal was 'a city well founded on public law and customs' (Cic. *Rep.* 1.3). Cicero, in his theoretical writings, prefers centuries of development by many people to one lawgiver working in a hurry (*Rep.* 2.2). He therefore emphasizes the specific contributions of each king: Romulus lays the foundations, a senate and *auspices* (ibid. 17), Numa religion and clemency (ibid. 27), and so on. In proposing ideal religious laws, Cicero is keen to ban women's private celebration of nocturnal rites (*Legg.* 2.21, 35 ff.) but in private law prefers women to be controlled by their own self-restraint or by their husbands. (*Rep.* 4.6). He thinks that censors should forbid celibacy (*Legg.* 3.7). *Iustae nuptiae*, legitimate children, and the sanctities of the home were part of the recipe for a healthy state (*Rep.* 5.7), but the details have been lost. Cicero adopts Ennius' idea that Rome stood because of her ancient customs and her men, but these are dying out (*Rep.* 5.1 ff.).
[90] *RG* 19.2, 20.4, app. 2; Nep. *Att.* 20.3.

thrown away). The horse-breaking or pruning will not be pleasant:
penalties will be needed, but legislation is useless without a fundamental change in behaviour.[91] The underlying appeal is to a
mythical period of sound morality and plain living. Livy, Horace, and
Vergil constantly evoke the stern and self-denying fathers of the race.
Livy's Sabine women and Tanaquil or Lucretia, Horace's dour
peasant mothers, even Vergil's Lavinia, dynastic pawn that she is,
stand for the women who collaborated with such men to breed
warrior sons.

1. *The Augustan Legislation*

Augustus introduced radical legislation which modified rights to
marry, manipulated freedom to dispose of property, and attempted
to encourage marriage and reproduction, especially in sections of
society most susceptible to the type of rewards (*praemia*) and penalties (*poenae*) which the emperor had at his disposal. His first great
piece of legislation was the *Lex Julia de maritandis ordinibus* of 18 BC.
This met with praise and non-compliance, and had to be followed a
generation later by the *Lex Papia Poppaea* (sponsored by the suffect
consuls of AD 9), which relaxed some provisions of the earlier law.
The difference between the Julian and Papio-Poppaean Laws is
obscured because the law as it stood from AD 9 is normally cited as the
Julian and Papian Law. The laws were not brilliantly drafted, and
later emperors, the Senate, and the jurists therefore made even more
additional rulings, clarifications, and interpretations than they would
otherwise have done. A large body of law developed, which had a
considerable impact on the marital experience of at least the upper
classes for the rest of the pagan period.

Augustus' laws responded to a complex situation and shifting
political possibilities. They are themselves complex. We should not
seek for one simple motive. But the need to encourage nuptiality and
reproductivity in order to supply Rome with soldiers and administrators appears to have been prominent in the minds of Augustus and

---

[91] Livy *Praef.* 9; Hor. *O* 3.24, esp. 25 ff. Cf. Prop. 2.7; Flor. 2.34: [Octavian, after closing the
temple of Janus] 'Hinc conversus ad pacem pronum in omnia mala et in luxuriam fluens
saeculum gravibus severisque legibus multis coercuit' (given titles, including Augustus); Oros.
6.22.3: 'Clausis igitur Iani portis rempublicam, quam bello quaesiverat, pace enutrire atque
amplificare studens leges plurimas statuit, per quas humanum genus libera reverentia discipli-
nae morem gereret.' For the view that there was an abortive Augustan measure in 28 see esp.
Williams, 'Poetry in the moral climate of Augustan Rome'; *contra*, Badian, 'A phantom
marriage law'. I am unconvinced by F. Cairns's view ('Propertius on Augustus' marriage law')
that Propertius was arguing for the law.

his advisers.[92] Particular attention was paid to maintaining the dignity of the Senate.[93]

Although our chief interest in this chapter is in *conubium*, it will be convenient to look at the law as a whole. Many of its provisions affect the law of property, so we shall be looking ahead also to topics treated in Chapter 11.[94]

Direct quotations from the two laws are rare. (Passages which appear to be quoted verbatim are printed below in capitals.) They were omnibus laws. The *Lex Julia* is said to have contained at least thirty-five chapters; the topics into which the ·standard modern compilation is classified number slightly more.[95]

(a) Restrictions

The law forbade intermarriage of senators, their children, and their descendants in the male line with freed persons, actors, and actors' children.

Lege Iulia ita cavetur: QUI SENATOR EST, QUIVE FILIUS, NEPOSVE EX FILIO PRONEPOSVE EX FILIO NATO CUIUS EORUM EST ERIT, NE QUIS EORUM SPONSAM UXOREMVE SCIENS DOLO MALO HABETO LIBERTINAM AUT EAM, QUAE IPSA CUIUSVE PATER MATERVE ARTEM LUDICRAM FACIT FECERIT. NEVE SENATORIS FILIA NEP- TISVE EX FILIO PRONEPTISVE EX NEPOTE FILIO NATO NATA LIBERTINO EIVE, QUI IPSE CUIUSVE PATER MATERVE ARTEM LUDICRAM FACIT FECERIT, SPONSA NUPTAVE SCIENS DOLO MALO ESTO NEVE QUIS EORUM DOLO MALO SCIENS SPONSAM UXOREMVE EAM HABETO. (*Digest* 23.3.44 pr., Paul *i ad legem Iuliam et Papiam*)

It is laid down in the Julian Law: LET NO SENATOR, SENATOR'S SON, OR GRANDSON BY A SON, OR GREAT-GRANDSON BY A SON AND GRANDSON

---

[92] Suet. *Aug.* 34, 89.2. Schol. ad Hor. *Carm. saec.* 20 connects the Julian Law with losses of 80,000 men in the civil wars. Dio, on the other hand, thinking also of the adultery law, stresses the curbing of misbehaviour (54.16.3–4) Augustus himself makes the general claim for his laws that they revived old practices and left good examples for posterity (*RG* 8.5).

[93] Cf. Rawson, *FAR* 49 n. 51. Brunt (*IM* 104, 114) argues that Augustus' motive was demographic, but the law 'would at best have had little demographic effect' (p. 154). Galinsky, 'Augustus' legislation on marriage and morals', concentrates on the need to maintain the morality and moral prestige of the ruling class. Wallace-Hadrill, 'Family and inheritance in the Augustan marriage laws', stresses economic motives, des Bouvrie, 'Augustus' legislation on morals—which morals and what aims?', the strengthening of the empire and preservation of the social structure.

[94] There is a vast bibliography. See Csillag 24ff., Volterra, *Enciclopedia* 768ff., on the history of scholarship. The following other works may be cited: Astolfi, *IP*; Daube, *Duty of procreation* 23ff.; Dixon, *RM* 84ff.; Falcão, *Las prohibiciones matrimoniales de carácter social en el imperio romano*; Frank, 'Augustus' legislation on marriage and children' Furneaux, 'Excursus on the Lex Papia Poppaea'; Humbert, *Le remariage à Rome* 138ff.; Jörs, *Die Ehegesetze des Augustus*; Last, 'The social policy of Augustus'; Nardi, 'Sui divieti matrimoniali delle leggi augustee'; Nörr, 'The matrimonial legislation of Augustus: an early instance of social engineering'; Raditsa, 'Augustus' legislation concerning marriage, procreation, love affairs and adultery'. The most useful works in English are Brunt, *IM* appendix 9, and Cherry, 'Studies in the marriage legislation of Augustus'.   [95] *ADA* 28 pp. 166ff.

KNOWINGLY AND FRAUDULENTLY HAVE A BETROTHED OR WIFE A FREEDWOMAN
OR A WOMAN WHO HERSELF OR WHOSE FATHER OR MOTHER PRACTISES OR HAS
PRACTISED THE STAGE PROFESSION. AND LET NO DAUGHTER OF A SENATOR OR
GRANDDAUGHTER BY A SON OR GREAT-GRANDDAUGHTER BY A SON AND GRAND-
SON BE KNOWINGLY AND FRAUDULENTLY BETROTHED OR WIFE TO A FREEDMAN OR
TO A MAN WHO HIMSELF OR WHOSE FATHER OR MOTHER PRACTISES OR HAS
PRACTISED THE STAGE PROFESSION. AND LET NOT ANY OF SUCH PEOPLE
FRAUDULENTLY AND KNOWINGLY HAVE SUCH A WOMAN AS BETROTHED OR WIFE.[96]

It is interesting, in view of the ban on the children of actors, that
members of senatorial families were allowed to marry the children of
freed persons. Nor did social taboos inhibit intermarriage with
sufficiently distinguished persons of such slave descent.[97] We are
specifically told that free-born Roman citizens in general were permitted to marry freed persons.[98] They were presumably also allowed
to marry the children of actors and actresses. All free-born persons,
including senators, were forbidden to marry infamous persons. The
text which specifies categories of infamous people unfortunately
omits the most obvious class, so editors supplement it:[99]

Ingenui prohibentur ducere [corpore quaestum facientem] lenam et a
lenone lenave manumissam et in adulterio deprehensam et iudicio publico
damnatam et quae artem ludicram fecerit. (*Tituli Ulpiani* 13.2)

Free-born men are forbidden to marry [a woman who earns her living as a
prostitute], a procuress, a woman manumitted by a procurer or procuress, a
woman taken in adultery, a woman condemned in a public court, and any
woman who has formerly practised the stage profession.

That prostitutes must be inserted here is suggested by various other
references.[100] Of the detected adulteress, Ulpian notes that this law
made no qualification about by whom she was caught or where: it
sufficed that she was caught.[101] It is not clear how the corresponding

[96] This is the first indication that the *liberi* of senators were to be regarded as sharing and
affecting their status, although they are not yet called *senatorii*. Cf. Nicolet, 'Le cens sénatorial
sous la République et sous Auguste' 38. A senator's daughter who lost her honourable status by
prostitution *vel sim.* could, according to Paul's sensible interpretation, marry a freedman (*D*
23.2.47).   [97] e.g. *AE* 1954.171.
[98] *D* 23.2.23: 'Lege Papia cavetur omnibus ingenuis praeter senatores eorumque liberos
libertinam uxorem habere licere'; Dio 54.16.2.
[99] For criticism of the text see Astolfi, *IP* 36-7, and 'Femina probrosa, concubina, mater
solitaria' 37ff.
[100] *ADA* 170. There is a clear discussion by Ulpian of the definition of a woman who openly
practises prostitution (*D* 23.2.43 pr.–5). A procuress was no better, and an innkeeper who
prostituted her maidservants was to be regarded as a procuress (ibid. 6–9).
[101] *D* 23.2.43.12–13. A known adulteress suffers automatic *infamia*. There is naturally no
allusion to the later Julian Law on adultery, which took account of the specific circumstances of
detection in laying down how a husband or father should or might behave. Ulpian rightly shows
that the classes of women taken in adultery and women condemned on a criminal charge of
adultery overlap only partially. *D* 48.5.30.1 for contravention.

prohibition to free-born women would have run: presumably they were at least forbidden to marry pimps and actors. A person of higher rank was naturally barred from marriages forbidden to his inferiors.[102] Forbidden marriages seem not originally to have been null but not to have conferred the advantages provided by the law for people who married in accordance with it.[103]

Si ignominiosam libertam suam patronus uxorem duxerit, placet, quia contra legem maritus sit, non habere eum hoc legis beneficium. (*Digest* 23.2.48.1, Terentius Clemens *viii ad legem Iuliam et Papiam*)

If a patron marries his freedwoman who is disgraced, it is held that he does not have this advantage conferred by the law, because he is a husband in despite of the law.

The advantage referred to here is a specific one: that if a freedwoman was married to her patron and divorced him, she could not remarry without his consent.[104] Clemens regards the man who has married the *ignominiosa* as forfeiting the privilege he would have had as patron under the statute. But the marriage itself is regarded as existing. Another instance is given of a couple disqualified from a privilege offered by the law, and this text offers a clearer indication of the concept of marriages against the Julio-Papian Law:

Aliquando nihil inter se capiunt, id est si contra legem Iuliam Papiamque Poppaeam contraxerint matrimonium, verbi gratia si famosam quis uxorem duxerit, aut libertinam senator. (*Tituli Ulpiani* 16.2)

Sometimes [husband and wife] take nothing from each other's estate, that is, if they have contracted marriage against the Julian and Papio-Poppaean law, for instance if someone has married a wife who is infamous, or a senator has married a freedwoman.

A distinction seems to have been drawn between marriages which were valid in civil law and marriages valid according to the Augustan Law.[105] This helps account for the papyri in which people are concerned to emphasize that their marriage is in accordance with the law.[106] The law should be classified as *minus quam perfecta* (less than perfect), that is, one which inflicted penalties for non-compliance but

---

[102] *D* 23.2.49; cf. ht 44.8. It is disputed whether the laws mentioned concubinage as an alternative form of union which would be licit between, for instance, senators and freedwomen or any free-born citizen and an ex-prostitute. Cf. *D* 25.7.3. I see no reason for the law to have concerned itself with such extra-legal matters. On women ineligible for marriage Castello, *In tema di matrimonio e concubinato nel mondo romano*, is useful.

[103] M. Aurelius made the marriage of a senator's daughter and a freedman null: *D* 23.2.16 pr. See e.g. Corbett 35 ff.; Csillag 101 ff.; Falcão, *Prohibiciones* 24 ff.; Chastagnol 'Les femmes dans l'ordre sénatoriale'.

[104] Stated in this form by Ulpian (*D* 23.2.45 pr.). There is considerable discussion, e.g. ibid. 1 ff., ht 46, 48, 50–1.   [105] Cf. *FV* 168.   [106] *PSI* 730, *Pap. Mich.* 508.

did not invalidate an act. Marriages which contravened the law were not null.[107] The ban on soldiers being married may have been introduced as part of this statute. It is undated, but existed before Claudius conferred on them the privileges due to married men under the Julian Law.[108] The ban on soldiers' marriages would be inconsistent with the law's aim of increasing citizen manpower, but so were the bans on intermarriage between senators and *libertinae* or between any *ingenuus* and infamous persons. There is the difference that nothing stopped a *senatoria* or a prostitute bearing legitimate citizen children to a suitable citizen husband, while the procreative powers of a Roman soldier were made unproductive as far as the begetting of legitimate citizen children went. But the law is not notable for consistency, and perhaps here military discipline outweighed demographic purposes. The effect must have been to keep Roman women, on the whole, away from the army and frontiers and keep them in Italy as breeding-stock. If there was a genuine shortage of citizen women for breeding, to deny one large class of Roman men the right to marry may have seemed sensible.[109]

These were restrictions on the ability to make a fully valid marriage which enabled a person to qualify for various benefits of the law. The normal *conubium* of civil law was limited. The law may nevertheless have been so couched as to encourage marriage between all classes in society with two major exceptions. All free-born people were prohibited from marrying people in certain disgraced categories (a restriction which was tighter for senators and their descendants in the male line, *liberi*). Already in republican times such matches with infamous persons might have earned a censorial *nota*. Senators and their *liberi* were prohibited from intermarrying with ex-slaves. This in my view is a new restriction, for I do not believe that the law had previously prohibited marriage between *ingenui* and *libertini*.[110] But the emphasis in the complete text may have been on the permitted rather than the prohibited. Augustus was also concerned to invalidate restrictions which private individuals might want to make on the marriages of others. Clauses in wills which made a bequest, for instance, conditional on the beneficiary not marrying or not rearing children, 'si uxorem non duxeris' or 'si filios non susceperis', were ruled null.[111]

---

[107] Cf. Buckland, *Textbook* 6. For this view Corbett 35; Astolfii, *IP* 32 ff.; *contra*: Nardi, 'Sui divieti matrimoniali delle leggi augustee'.

[108] Dio 60.24.3. Cf. Suet. *DA* 24.1: Augustus discouraged even senior officers from visiting their wives. Cf. Corbett 39 ff. Whitehorne, 'Ovid *AA* 1.101–132 and soldiers' marriages', suggests 13 BC for the ban.

[109] Cf. on the shortage of women Saller, 'Slavery and the Roman family', 70–1, with recent bibliography.   [110] Corbett 31 ff., Watson, *Persons* 32 ff.

[111] Paul *S* 3.4b.2. Cf. *D* 35.1.74, ht 62.2, 63, 64, 72.4, 79.4.

Freed persons whose patrons imposed an oath that they would not marry were allowed to break their oaths.[112]

In chapter xxxv the law dealt with *patresfamilias* who failed to allow children to marry.

Capite trigesimo quinto legis Iuliae QUI LIBEROS QUOS HABENT IN POTESTATE INIURIA PROHIBUERINT DUCERE UXORES, VEL NUBERE, VEL QUI DOTEM DARE NON VOLUNT ex constitutione divorum Severi et Antonini per proconsules praesidesque provinciarum coguntur in matrimonium collocare et dotare. Prohibere autem videtur et qui condicionem non quaerit. (*Digest* 23.2.19, Marcianus *xvi institutionum*)

In the thirty-fifth chapter of the Julian Law THOSE WHO WRONGFULLY PREVENT THE CHILDREN WHOM THEY HAVE IN THEIR POWER FROM MARRYING OR WHO ARE NOT WILLING TO GIVE DOWRIES in accordance with the constitution of the Deified Severus and the Deified Antoninus are compelled through the proconsuls and governors of provinces to give them in marriage and give them dowries. For a man is interpreted as preventing if he does not look for a match.

It appears that the innovation of the Severan constitution was to empower provincial authorities to act: the original law probably mentioned only authorities in Rome. Other practical arrangements were made to facilitate marriage. For instance, if a woman who was required to marry was under the guardianship of a man who was under age and so could not create a dowry for her, the urban praetor was to give her a special guardian to fulfil this function.[113]

Engaged people were allowed to count as if married. (The law may have spoken of men as *maritorum numero*.) The Julian Law laid down no limit to the time of an engagement, so men abused the privilege by becoming engaged to very young children. The Papian Law therefore specified a limit of two years: it may more precisely have said that an engagement with a girl of 10 was allowed to count, up until the time when she became eligible to marry on her twelfth birthday. It may be relevant to remember that such girls might be cohabiting with their men, wives in all but name and legality. Suetonius tells us that Augustus shortened the time allowable for engagements to count under the law and Dio says the limit was two years. It is unclear whether Dio's inference that Augustus meant that the *sponsa* had to be at least 10 if the *sponsus* was to benefit is correct. Brunt argues that this represents a later tightening-up (perhaps rather a clarification) but that in Augustus' time the *sponsae* could still be infants.[114]

---

[112] *D* 37.14.6.4. Cf. *ADA* 178.   [113] *Tit. Ulp.* 11.20.

[114] Suet. *DA* 34; Dio 54.16.7 (not certainly dating the revision to 18 BC). See Volterra, *Enciclopedia* 771; *contra*, Astolfii, 'Il fidanzamento nella "Lex Iulia et Papia"' 682 ff, cf. *IP* 5 ff., most of whose arguments are fantastic. Cf. Brunt, *IM* 560.

The Julian Law seems to have laid down ages at which people were expected to be married. We do not know what these were. According to Tertullian, they were higher than the age before which the Papian Law demanded that people should have children.[115] The Papian ages, as we shall see, were between 20 and 50 for women and 25 and 60 for men.

(b) Praemia

By chapter vii the statute was deep into the question of the privileges which would be granted to those who had not only married but become parents in accordance with the terms of the law. Gellius tells us that the senior consul of each pair was not to be the older man (as before), but the one who had more children than his colleague. The children who counted were either alive and in his power or had died in war. But if both had equal numbers of children, the elder was senior. There was no regulation in the law to cover cases where both were unmarried but had equal numbers of children, or both were married but childless.[116]

It is clear that whether a man was married was also a relevant consideration in judging seniority.[117] Children were also taken into account when former magistrates drew lots for the governorships of senatorial provinces.[118] In standing for office, a man was allowed to subtract one year from the normal minimum age for each child.[119] Preference was also accorded to paternity in co-opting candidates to posts vacated by death.[120]

Children who died in war counted:

An bello amissi a tutela excusare debent? Nam et in fascibus sumendis et in iudicandi munere pro superstitibus habentur, ut lege Iulia de maritandis ordinibus de fascibus sumendis et publicorum kapite [xxvi], item privatorum kapite vicesimo vii de iudicandis cavetur. Et puto constituendum, ut et a tutelis excusent; proinde sive tres bello amiserit sive unum duosve, pro superstitibus cedent. (*Fragmenta Vaticana* 197, Ulpian *lib. de officio praetoris tutelaris*)

Ought those lost in war to exempt from *tutela*? For they are regarded as if surviving in the context of taking up the *fasces* and in that of adjudication, as

---

[115] *Apol.* 4.8: 'Nonne vanissimas Papias leges, quae ante liberos suscipi cogunt quam Iuliae matrimonium contrahi, post tantae auctoritatis senectutem heri Severus, constantissimus principum, exclusit?' Seneca also plays with the idea of the exemption of men over 60: why has Jupiter, in the poets, stopped fathering children (sc. on a variety of mythological heroines)? Has he reached 60 and had his foreskin fastened up by the Papian Law? Or has the emperor given him the *ius trium liberorum*? (fr. 119).

[116] s.15. Cf. *Decl. min.* 278.6.   [117] Dio 53.13.2.

[118] Tac. *A* 15.19; Fronto *Ep. ad Ant. Pium* 8.1 (Loeb i.236); Dio 53.13.2.

[119] *D* 4.4.2; Pliny *Epp.* 7.16.2.   [120] Tac. *A* 2.51.2.

is laid down in the Julian Law on the Marriage of the Orders on seniority in office and in chapter xxvi on public duties and also about acting as adjudicator in chapter xxvii on private duties. And I think we must decide that they also excuse from acting as guardian; accordingly, whether he has lost three in war, or one, or two, they will count as surviving.

Aristo held that only those killed in battle counted; others held that any child, of either sex or any age, who died in war, for instance in a siege, should count.[121]

In the Flavian period the constitutional law of the Latin town of Malaga expressed the rules for its own council as follows:

Qua in curia totidem suffragia duo pluresve habuerint, maritum, quive maritorum numero erit, caelibi liberos non habenti, qui maritorum numero non erit; habentem liberos non habenti; plures liberos habentem pauciores habenti praeferto prioremque nuntiato ita, ut bini liberi post nomen inpositum aut singuli puberes amissi virive potentes amissae pro singulis sospitibus numerentur. (*FIRA* i.23.56, AD 82–4)

In this senate, [if] two or more have the same number of votes, let [the presiding magistrate] give preference and announce as elected first a candidate who is married or in the category of married men over an unmarried man who has no children and is not in the category of married men, a man who has children over one who has none, a man who has more children over one who has fewer. The rule is that two children who died after they were named, or one child lost after he reached puberty or she reached marriageable age, should be counted to their fathers as equivalent to one surviving child.

If there was still a tie, the lot was used. The category of those who count as married, though they are not, includes men engaged to under-age girls and (in other contexts) soldiers after Claudius' ruling. The law made such categories necessary, for instance for women who counted as married for a certain time after divorce or the husband's death.

A similar set of rules from another part of the Flavian municipal law survives from the Municipium Irnitanum. It lays down the order of voting in the town council: first the member who has most children born in *iustae nuptiae* or counts (or would if he were a Roman citizen count) as being the father of as many children. If these criteria were insufficient to fix precedence, then preference was given to seniority as ex-duumvir or councillor.[122]

Children allowed a man to claim immunity from the onerous task of

---

121 *D* 27.1.18, *xx ad legem Iul. et Pap.*; *FV* 199.
122 González, 'The Lex Irnitana' 147ff., table VA and note ad loc.

acting as a guardian or curator. Three surviving children were required in Rome, four in Italy, five in the provinces.[123] We have just seen that children killed in war were allowed by the interpreters to count as if still alive. Ulpian discusses whether grandchildren counted:

Sed utrum soli filii an et nepotes debent prodesse? Subsistendum, quoniam lex quidem privatorum capite xxvii 'ex se natos' appellat, lex vero publicorum kapite xxvi liberorum facit mentionem. Puto tamen eandem esse aequitatem in nepotibus, qui in locum filiorum succedunt, quae est in filiis. (*Fragmenta Vaticana* 198)

But ought children alone to confer the privilege, or grandchildren too? One must hesitate, since the law in chapter xxvii on private duties calls them 'born from himself', but the law on public duties in chapter xxvi mentions *liberi*. I think that equity is the same for grandchildren, who succeed to the position of children, as for children.

His own view was clearly controversial. But by the time of Marcus Aurelius at least, it seems clear that it was held that *liberi* counted to exempt a man from the duty of guardianship. The word *liberi* is technical: it covers both sons and daughters and grandchildren and remoter descendants in the male line, the old *sui heredes* of a *paterfamilias*.[124] They are the descendants who might be *in patria potestate* and would continue the family line. Tradition might persuade Augustus to allow them to count. Ulpian in another passage shows that grandchildren through a daughter did not usually count, for Marcus Aurelius in AD 168 granted to fathers-in-law of veterans of the Praetorian Guard the privilege of counting their daughters' children. This indicates that by that date, whether or not it was clear in the original statute, grandchildren through a son did count. Ulpian is speaking specifically of release from *tutela* and claim on *caduca*.[125]

Similarly, a freedman would claim freedom from the duty of work he had promised to his former owner (to perform *operae*) if he had two or more children. This privilege was not given to freedmen who

[123] Just. *Inst.* 1.25 pr.; cf. *D* 27.1.2, 50.5.1 pr. Cf. *ADA* 175.

[124] *D* 50.16.220 pr.: '"Liberorum" appellatione nepotes et pronepotes ceterique qui ex his descendunt continentur: hos enim omnes suorum appellatione lex duodecim tabularum comprehendit.' Cf. 2.4.10.9, 26.2.1.1, ht 6 (distinguishing from *filii*) 27.1.2.7 (only grandchildren by sons counted and all the offspring of a dead son counted as one).

[125] *FV* 195: 'Ex filia nepotes non prodesse ad tutelae liberationem, sicut nec ad caducorum vindicationem, palam est, nisi mihi proponas ex veterano praetoriano genero socerum avum effectum; tunc enim secundum orationem divi Marci, quam in castris praetoris recitavit Paulo iterum et Aproniano conss. viii Id. Ian. (AD 168), id habebit avus, quod habet in nepotibus ex filio natis. Cuius orationis verba haec sunt: "et quo facilius veterani nostri soceros rint, illos quoquo novo privilegio sollicitabimus, ut avus nepotum ex veterano praetoriano natorum iisdem commodis nomine eorum fruatur, quibus frueretur, si eos haberet ex filio."'

had engaged in the disgraceful occupations of acting or fighting wild beasts in the arena.[126] It is not absolutely certain, but seems likely, that it was the original law which ruled that a freedwoman who was over 50 (and presumably a freedman over 60) and a freedwoman who had married with her male patron's consent were not bound to perform *operae.*[127]

Maternity was the only way for a woman to escape from the requirement that she be under lifelong guardianship. Free-born women qualified for freedom from guardianship if they had three children; freedwomen who were under the guardianship of their patron or his male descendants needed four children to escape, though three sufficed if they had guardians of another type.[128]

Other economic privileges concerned inheritance rights. The rights of husband and wife to inherit from each other were regulated and, to some extent, improved. The previous situation was that, by the Voconian Law of 169 BC, the right of a woman to inherit from a man registered in the top property class was limited. She could not be *heres* (heir and executor), but only a legatee, and could not receive more than the heir or joint heirs. At most, therefore, a wife could be left half her husband's property. There were, however, ways around this limitation. A wife could be left, for instance, a usufruct of the house she lived in, although ownership went to the son. Augustus (while leaving the Voconian Law in force) improved the position of the wife who bore her husband children.[129] But the basic maximum percentage allowed by the new law to either husband or wife from the other was only 10 per cent of the estate. This figure was famous enough for the law, or a woman who took one-tenth, to be called *decimaria.*[130]

Vir et uxor inter se matrimonii nomine decimam capere possunt. Quod si ex alio matrimonio liberos superstites habeant, praeter decimam, quam matrimonii nomine capiunt, totidem decimas pro numero liberorum accipiunt. Item communis filius filiave post nominum diem amissus amissave unam decimam adicit; duo autem post nominum diem amissi duas decimas adiciunt. Praeter decimam etiam usumfructum tertiae partis bonorum capere possunt, et quandoque liberos habuerint, eiusdem partis proprietatem. Hoc amplius mulier, praeter decimam, dotem capere potest legatam sibi. (*Tituli Ulpiani* 15.1–4)

---

[126] *D* 38.1.37 pr., Paul quoting the statute.

[127] *D* 38.1.35; *CJ* 6.6.2. Other sources in *ADA* 177.

[128] G 1.145, 194; cf. *Frag. Dos.* 15 (*ADA* 179). On *tutela* of women see Dixon, 'Infirmitas sexus: womanly weakness in Roman law', and *RM* 89–90.

[129] Brunt, *IM* 563–4; Dixon, 'Breaking the law to do the right thing: the Voconian law in ancient Rome'; Gardner 120 ff.

[130] *P. Ox.* 2089; *FV* 294. On capacity to inherit see Humbert, *Le remariage à Rome* 147 ff.

Husband and wife can take reciprocally one-tenth on account of their marriage. But if either has surviving children from another marriage, then, apart from the tenth which he or she takes on account of the marriage, he or she can take as many further tenths as there are children. In the same way, a common son or daughter whom they lost after the name-day adds one-tenth, but two lost after the name-day add two-tenths. Apart from the tenth, they can take a usufruct of one-third of the property, and if they subsequently have children, the ownership of this third. Furthermore, the wife can take a legacy of her dowry besides the tenth.

These provisions are seen in action in the writings of the jurists. The legacy of a usufruct to a widow was probably already a common practice, since it secured her the means of livelihood, while the capital belonged to an heir or other legatee, most often a child of the testator. The law encouraged this practice.[131] It must often have been likely that a surviving *coniunx* would be able to have children and so increase his or her qualification. It was particularly reasonable for husbands (who tended to be older than their wives) to make provision in their wills for the widow to obtain outright ownership if she had children by another husband. So the phrase 'in tempus liberorum' or 'cum liberos habuerit' ('at the time when she has children) is especially quoted from the wills of husbands.[132]

Aliquando vir et uxor inter se solidum capere possunt, velut si uterque vel alteruter eorum nondum eius aetatis sint, a qua lex liberos exigit, id est, si vir minor annorum XXV sit aut uxor annorum XX minor; item si utrique lege Papia finitos annos in matrimonio excesserint, id est vir LX annos, uxor L; item si cognati inter se coierint usque ad sextum gradum, aut si vir absit et donec abest, et intra annum, postquam abesse desierit. Libera inter eos testamenti factio est si ius liberorum a principe impetraverint; aut si filium filiamve communem habeant aut quattuordecim annorum filium vel filiam duodecim amiserint vel si duos trimos vel tres post nominum diem amiserint, ut intra annum tamen et sex menses etiam unus cuiuscumque aetatis impubes amissus solidi capiendi ius praestet. Item si post mortem viri intra decem menses uxor ex eo pepererit, solidum ex bonis eius capit. (*Tituli Ulpiani* 16.1)

In some instances, husband and wife can take the whole estate from each other, as for instance if both or one of them has not yet reached the age at which the law demands children, that is, if the husband is under 25 or the wife under 20, or if both have outlived the age prescribed by the Papian Law and are still married, that is, if the husband is over 60 and the wife over 50; or if the pair are related within the sixth degree, or if the husband is away (both while he is away and for the year following the end of his absence). They have unrestricted right of making their wills if they have been granted the

---

[131] *ADA* 182, citing *D* 19.5.10, 22.1.48, 33.2.43; *P. Ox.* 2089.
[132] *D* 22.1.48, 35.1.61, 31.51.1, 35.1.62; *CJ* 6.53.4.

right of children (*ius liberorum*) by the emperor, or if they have a common son or daughter, or if they have lost a son aged 14 or a daughter aged 12 or two children aged 3, or three children after their name-day. But even one child of whatever age lost before the age of puberty gives the right of inheriting the whole estate during the period of eighteen months from his death. A wife may also take the whole if she bears him a child within ten months of her husband's death.

It will be apparent that the making of a will must often have been complicated by the testator's inability to predict the make-up of his family at the time of his death. Only if a couple could prove they had reared one child to the age of puberty, or two to the age of three, or three who survived the first week or so of life, could they be sure they had qualified by reason of children. A couple who remained married after both had passed the upper ages mentioned in the law were also secure, as were those who were close kin. But a husband under 25 and a wife under 20 could not rely on being still of such a useful age when one of them died. A parent who made a will while he had one young child alive was in considerable uncertainty and a husband who hoped his wife was pregnant at the time of his death was gambling. If an estate was left to a survivor who failed to qualify, it would revert to the next heir.

Aliquando nihil inter se capiunt, id est, si contra legem Iuliam Papiamque Poppaeam contraxerint matrimonium, verbi gratia si famosam quis uxorem duxerit aut libertinam senator. (*Tituli Ulpiani* 16.2)

In some instances they take nothing from each other, that is, if they have contracted a marriage in defiance of the Julian and Papio-Poppaean Laws, for instance, if someone marries a woman who is disgraced or a senator marries a freedwoman.

The deterrent effect of this ruling must have been strong for the propertied classes. A senator could make a freedwoman his *iusta uxor* if he was granted a dispensation by the emperor.[133] Alternatively, if he lost his place in the Senate she began to be his legal wife.[134] Since the marriage between a senator and a freedwoman would not be valid according to the Augustan laws, and bequests between them would be nullified, it was to their advantage if the union were regarded as concubinage. For a man could at least make gifts to his concubine.[135] Whether she could receive a bequest is more doubtful, in view of the general regulations about capacity to take legacies or inheritances.

---

[133] *D* 23.2.31. Further, Nardi argued that all those whose marriage was *iniustum* counted as unmarried (*La reciproca posizione successoria dei coniuges privi di conubium*).

[134] *D* 23.2.27. A rescript of Pius took account of a freedwoman who deceived a senator about her status (ht 58).   [135] *D* 24.1.3.1.

Caelibes quoque qui lege Iulia HEREDITATES LEGATAQUE CAPERE vetantur,
item orbi, id est qui liberos non habent, quos lex [Papia plus quam dimidias
partes hereditatis legatorumque capere vetat] . . . (Gaius 2.111)

Unmarried persons too, who are forbidden by the Julian Law TO TAKE
INHERITANCES AND LEGACIES, and also *orbi*, that is, those who have no
children, whom the [Papian Law forbids to take more than half of an
inheritance or legacies] . . .

Item orbi, qui per legem Papiam ob id quod liberos non habent, dimidias
partes hereditatum legatorumque perdunt . . . (Gaius 2.286a)

In the same way *orbi*, who according to the Papian Law lose half
of inheritances and legacies on account of the fact that they have no
children . . .

The plain sense of *orbi* is 'those who do not have children'. As we
have seen, *liberi* occurred elsewhere in the law. We hear of Marcus
Aurelius ruling that a man who left his grandsom as heir was not
regarded as dying without children.[136] Conversely, if a man who had
liberi but not children was left an inheritance or bequest, he must
have qualified as not being *orbus*. We are specifically informed that
grandchildren by a daughter did not enable a man to claim as an
eligible kinsman property left ownerless because the person to whom
it was willed could not take it (*caduca*). This makes it clear that
grandchildren by a son enabled a man to claim *caduca* or what was
willed to him. (The existence of grandchildren implies that at least
one son had lived to puberty.) Since a woman's legal position in
regard to her children and descendants was very different from a
man's, it is probable that she could not count grandchildren, either in
inheritance matters or to free herself of guardianship.

In the original statute adoptive children counted to their adoptive
parents. There was thus no reason why a sterile couple could not obey
the spirit of the law. Later, by a Neronian senatusconsultum of AD 62,
children given in adoption were credited to their natural parents.[137] It
has been held that illegitimate children (but presumably not those
born in a stable relationship against the laws) counted to their
mothers.[138] Such a ruling would have affected those classes in society
which are neglected by the sources. But since the laws forbade *spurii*
to be registered, it seems impossible that mothers were allowed to
benefit from them.

Moderns have worried about whether one child sufficed to allow a
person to take an inheritance. But Gaius is quite explicit (and correct
in logic):

---

[136] *D* 50.16.220.2. Cf. *TLL* s.v. 926.
[137] Tac. *A* 15.19. Cf. *FV* 169, 196.   [138] Astolfii, *IP* 175–6.

Non est sine liberis, cui vel unus filius unave filia est: haec enim enuntiatio 'habet liberos', 'non habet liberos' semper plurativo numero profertur, sicut et pugillares et codicilli. (*Digest* 50.16.149, Gaius *viii ad legem Iuliam et Papiam*)

A person is not without children if he or she has one son or one daughter, for this expression 'he has children', 'he does not have children' is always used in the plural number, as are notebooks and writing-tablets.

nam quem sine liberis esse dicere non possumus, hunc necesse est dicamus liberos habere. (*Digest* 50.16.149, Gaius *x ad legem Iuliam et Papiam*)

For if we cannot say that a man is without children, we have to say he has children.

The provenance of these excerpts makes it perfectly clear that Gaius is discussing the marriage law and presumably *orbi*. This view of Gaius accords with a well-known Latin usage of *liberi* when one child was meant.[139] It seems that the number of children required varied in different contexts. Although three or more were required for some privileges (freedom from being, or being under, a *tutor*, for instance), two were enough to exempt the freedman from *operae*, and one to give some seniority for office and to increase the right of a wife or husband to benefit from each other's wills. So there is no reason to think it improbable a priori that the law demanded only one child to free a person from the incapacity to succeed. The reason why the emperors seem to have granted always the privilege of being the fictitious parent of *three* children must be that this sufficed to cover free-born residents of Rome against any disabilities created by the law and to give them all the privileges available under it.

Relatives within the sixth degree, including relatives by marriage, and also the son of a first cousin could inherit the whole inheritance or legacy, even if unmarried and childless.[140]

Feminis lex Iulia a morte viri anni tribuit vacationem, a divortio sex mensum, lex autem Papia a morte viri biennii, a repudio anni et sex mensum. (*Tituli Ulpiani* 14)

To women the Julian Law gave a grace-period of one year from the death of a husband and six months from a divorce, but the Papian Law gave two years from the death of a husband and one year and six months from a divorce.

Suetonius also mentions this extension of the grace-period by the second law, though he writes of a three-year period. Possibly the juristic text should be corrected to three years to agree with

---

[139] Cf. Juv. 9.82 ff., which shows that one child qualified a man to inherit, but three children were better than one. See further *TLL* s.v. *liberi* 1303.

[140] *FV* 214, 216–17.

Suetonius.[141] There are no other texts on this point. It is noteworthy that no *vacatio* was laid down for men. The ancient requirement of one year's formal mourning by widows provides a context for this discrimination.

The Papian Law offered privileges to the former owners of freed slaves who possessed a fortune of 100,000 sesterces or more. The tenor of the new rules is always to favour parents, though the details are complicated. A patron had a claim on the freedman's estate, whether he made a will or not. The situation before the Augustan Law was that a male patron could claim half the property if the freedman made a will or if he died intestate leaving as *sua/suus heres* a wife *in manu*, a daughter-in-law who had been in his son's *manus*, or an adopted child. If the freedman had natural children, he could exclude the patron and it did not matter if they had been emancipated or given in adoption. This rule was introduced by the praetor in the late Republic. He had not improved the rights of women, whether *patronae* or the female *liberi* of *patroni*, which remained as they had been under the Twelve Tables: that is, they could claim only if the freedman died intestate and did not leave a *suus heres*.[142] Under the Papian Law, unless the freedman had three *liberi* the patron was allowed to claim a child's share in the estate, which is hypothetically to be regarded as divided into three shares. If the freedman had three *liberi*, he could exclude the patron from any claim on his estate. If he left two children, the patron could claim one-third; if he left only one child the patron got half.[143] Before this law, since the freedwoman had no intestate heirs and needed her patron's consent to make a will, he could control what happened to her property. But from now on a freedwoman with four children escaped from her patron's guardianship. So the Papian Law granted him a share in the estate proportionate to the number of her *liberi* at the time of her death. If all four children survived, he could claim one-fifth; if all were dead, he claimed the whole. The same right was given to a patron's son, grandson by a son, and great-grandson by a grandson by a son.[144] The Papian Law also extended the right of the female descendants of a male patron. As long as the patron's daughter had three children, she had the same entitlement which the praetor had previously given to her brother. But what was the position of a patron's daughter in

---

[141] *DA* 34. I do not agree with Geiger, 'Tiberius and the Lex Papia Poppaea', in thinking Tiberius' personal motives important.

[142] G 3.40ff. Cf. Watson, *Persons* 231ff. An attempt by Verres as praetor to enhance the rights of a daughter of a *patronus* seems to have been abortive.

[143] G 3.42ff.; *D* 37.14.10–11, ht 17. These rights are very frequently mentioned by the jurists (*ADA* 189ff.).   [144] G 3.45–6.

relation to a freedwoman exempt from *tutela* because of four children, who left a will? The law on this point was carelessly drafted,
says Gaius, and jurists disputed the matter. But a *patrona* had a claim
if the freedwoman made no will.[145] A woman who had herself freed a
male slave also gained under the Papian Law the rights given by the
praetor to a man, as long as she had two children (if she was
free-born) or three (if she was herself a freedwoman). Further, if a
free-born *patrona* had three children, she had the same privileges as a
man under that law. But this did not apply to freed *patronae*. No new
rights were offered to *patronae* of intestate freed*women* (for the
patrona would normally inherit automatically under the Twelve
Tables). If a freedwoman died testate, a childless *patrona* had no
claim; if the *patrona* had children she had the same rights as a male
patron had under the edict against a freedman's will. The son of a
patrona, as long as he had one child, had roughly the same rights as a
patronus.[146]

It will be seen from these extremely complicated rules that the
number of children required varied in specific contexts and that the
required number was consistently higher for women.

Another specific privilege was conferred on male patrons. If a
patron married his freedwoman, restrictions were put on her power
to divorce. The original statute appears to have said, 'Let the
freedwoman who is married to her patron not have the power of
making a divorce, as long as her patron wants her to be his wife.'[147]
This was somewhat modified in practice. On the other hand, the
patron was not allowed to restrict the marriage of his or her freed
slaves in general.[148]

(c) Caduca

The importance of the section on property which could not be taken
by the heir or legatee and therefore fell to another eligible person or
to the imperial treasury is reflected in the frequency of reference in
the jurists.[149]

Quod quis sibi testamento relictum, ita ut iure civili capere possit, aliqua ex
causa non ceperit, caducum appellatur, veluti ceciderit ab eo: verbi gratia si
caelibi vel Latino Iuniano legatum fuerit, nec intra dies centum vel caelebs
legi paruerit vel Latinus ius Quiritium consecutus sit: aut si ex parte heres
scriptus vel legatarius ante apertas tabulas decesserit vel peregrinus factus
sit. (*Tituli Ulpiani* 17.1)

---

[145] G 3.46ff.; *Tit. Ulp.* 29.5.   [146] G 3.53; *Tit. Ulp.* 29.6–7.   [147] *D* 24.2.11 pr.–1.
[148] *D* 37.14.6.4.
[149] *ADA* 192ff. (But such excerpts are reworked, since Justinian abolished the law.)

What a person for some reason does not take, when it is left to him by will, although he could take it under civil law, is called *caducum*, as if it has fallen from him: for instance, if it is bequeathed to an unmarried person or to a Junian Latin, and the unmarried person does not obey the law within 100 days, or the Latin does not obtain the rights of a Roman citizen within 100 days, or if a person who is written down in a will as part-heir or legatee dies before the will is opened or becomes an alien.

The Papian Law allowed *caduca* to go to ascendants or *liberi* up to the third degree. Such beneficiaries had to be mentioned in the will and had themselves to be qualified by having at least one child. If it was a legatee who lost his legacy, a fellow legatee took precedence over an heir in claiming the *caduca*.[150] But Caracalla issued a constitution which claimed them for the fisc.[151] Previously the treasury had only taken *caduca* when qualified claimants were lacking.[152] Another disability, which was no doubt irksome, was that the Julian Law barred the unmarried from attending games. This ban was lifted on certain occasions, such as Augustus' own Secular Games. There is no evidence that this prohibition survived Augustus.[153]

In order to have at least the theoretical possibility of checking whether a person had children, it was necessary to introduce registration of births and of newly enfranchised citizens. This was done under the *Leges Aelia Sentia* and *Papia-Poppaea*.[154] A father registered a child, naming himself, the child, and his wife. Excerpts could be copied and sent, for instance, to the authorities in Egypt. Citizens in the provinces registered their children wtih the competent authority there.[155] Illegitimate children were not allowed to be registered on the official list, but the practice of making a public declaration of their birth grew up in imitation of the official procedure. A serving soldier might declare before witnesses that he was the father of a certain woman's child, or a woman, with the authority of her guardian, might declare that she had given birth to children by an unnamed father.[156]

Since Rome had no public prosecutor, infringements or alleged infringements of the law had to be prosecuted by private individuals. The law therefore established a reward for successful prosecutors. This was expressed as a percentage of the amount gained by the treasury, but we do not know the original figure. Nero reduced it to

---

[150] G 2.206–7. Cf. Juv. 9.88–9. Further references in *ADA* 194 n. 2.   [151] *Tit. Ulp.* 17.2.
[152] Tac. *A* 3.28.4; *Tit. Ulp.* 28.7.   [153] *FIRA* i.40.1 = EJ 30.A; Dio 54.30.5.
[154] *FIRA* iii.2, the earliest example, a wax tablet of AD 62.
[155] Cf. *FIRA* iii.1, 3; Apul. *Apol.* 89. See Bell, 'A Latin registration of birth' Schulz, 'Roman registers of births and birth certificates'; Lévy, 'Les actes d'état civil romains' and 'Nouvelles observations sur les *professiones liberorum*'; Gardner, 'Proofs of status in the Roman world'.
[156] *FIRA* iii.4 (on which see Gilliam, 'Some Roman elements in Roman Egypt', 115 ff.), 5.

25 percent.[157] The upper classes regarded themselves as terrorized by spies and informers.[158]

(d) Effects

There is a strong tradition that Augustus perceived that the Julian Law had little effect and was therefore compelled to rework it in AD 9 in the Papio-Poppaean Law, which made various concessions and remedied abuses.[159] After that, the law may have been more effective in encouraging the wealthy and office-seeking class to marry and have children. As Pliny points out, 'the rich are urged by huge rewards to raise children, but the only way for the poor to bring up children is to have a good emperor'. Trajan's alimentary schemes did more for the poorer classes than Augustan legislation.[160] Elsewhere Pliny joins the moralists in believing that it took not only rewards but constant preaching to make ordinary free-born Romans—and specifically his fellow citizens at Comum—want to take on the tedious task of child-rearing, and that, higher in the social scale, the rewards of *orbitas* (that is, the flattering attentions of fortune-seekers) made even one child unattractive.[161] Tacitus held that the laws did not prevent people limiting their families.[162] But there is some evidence that young men entering on a senatorial career chose to marry a little earlier, in the hope no doubt of benefiting from the concessions given to fathers.[163] Men may also have remarried rapidly for the same reason.[164] The tendency to marry about the time of the quaestorship had existed in the Republic, when a dowry and marriage connections were the only immediate rewards. But now a man stood for election earlier and the proper age for marriage was adjusted downwards.

The law received continual attention from emperors, the Senate, administrators, and jurists. For instance, some complexities in the administration of the law seem to have been sorted out by a senatorial committee under Tiberius in AD 20.[165] Conscientious emperors monitored the law. Trajan is praised for checking the sinister private prosecutors.[166] M. Aurelius tightened up the law on intermarriage

---

[157] Suet. *Nero* 10.1.
[158] Tac. *A* 3.25, 28.4. For later regulation of prosecutors by Senate and emperors, *D* 49.14.15. Those who informed against themselves might have some of the confiscated property restored: emperors encouraged wards and women to admit infringements (ht 13, 15.3, 16).
[159] Dio 56.1.2, 6.6, 10.1.   [160] *Pan.* 26.1 ff. at 5.
[161] *Epp.* 1.8.10–11, 4.15.3. Moralizing on childlessness is documented by Friedländer, *Sittengeschichte Roms* i.246 ff.   [162] G 19.5.
[163] Tac. *Ag.* 6.1, 3; Pliny *Epp.* 7.24.3, 8.23.7. Cf. Saller, 'Men's age at marriage and its consequences in the Roman family'.
[164] Pliny *Epp.* 4.2.6–7. For women 9.13.16 with Sherwin-White ad loc.
[165] Tac. *A.* 3.28.6.
[166] Pliny *Pan.* 34.1.

between senators' daughters and freedmen.[167] Refinements were constantly introduced by juristic interpretation. Monographs were written by Gaius, Marcellus, Mauricianus, Terentius Clemens, Paul, and Ulpian.[168] The Senate intervened repeatedly, under the emperor's guidance. A Tiberian senatusconsultum ruled that men and women who reached the upper ages of 60 and 50 without having conformed with the law would continue to be penalized.[169] Another decree, the *Senatusconsultum Claudianum* under Claudius, allowed men over 60 to remedy this by marrying women under 50.[170] An undated *Senatusconsultum Calvisianum* ruled, on the other hand, that the marriage of a man under 60 and a woman over 50 was *impar* (unequal) and severely penalized those who began a marriage at such ages. The couple could not take legacies, inheritances, or dowry. When the woman died the dowry was *caduca*.[171] The *Gnomon of the Idiologus*, a compilation of administrative rules begun under Augustus, which in the form in which we have it reflects the system in Egypt between 150 and 161, incorporates this decree. It says that a dowry given by a woman over 50 to a man under 60 was confiscated by the fisc (not passed on to other who were qualified). According to the *Gnomon*, a dowry given by a woman under 50 to a man over 60 was also confiscated. This conflicts with the *Senatusconsultum Claudianum*, which Ulpian recognizes as still in force. The other details it cites are as follows. Anything left to an unmarried childless man over 60 was confiscated. (Presumably all the property mentioned as forfeited is thought of as going directly to the fisc.) But a man with a wife but no children, if he denounced himself, was allowed to keep half. A woman of 50 could not succeed; a woman under 50 could, if she had three children (or four if a freedwoman). A free-born or freed Roman woman with property worth 20,000 sesterces was taxed 1 per cent per annum as long as she remained unmarried. Inheritances left to Roman women owning property worth 50,000 sesterces were confiscated if they had neither husband nor children. A Roman woman could receive one-tenth of her husband's estate; anything above that was confiscated. Roman men owning 100,000 sesterces could not succeed unless they had wife and children. Those with less property could succeed. There are various features in this which are not attested elsewhere. The most interesting is the exemption of the poorer classes. It is possible that the census qualification of HS100,000 for a man and HS50,000 for a woman below which penalties did not

---

[167] *D* 23.2.16 pr.
[168] *ADA* 168.   [169] Talbert no. 33.
[170] Talbert no. 50.
[171] *Tit. Ulp.* 16.4; Talbert no. 144.

apply was part of the original law.[172] But many of these detailed rules may be unique to Egypt.

The *Senatusconsultum Tertullianum* under Hadrian gave a woman with *ius liberorum* the right to succeed to her intestate children.[173]

Other new regulations expanded the law by introducing new prohibitions on intermarriage. A senatorial decree of the period 175–80 forbade a guardian or his son or grandson to marry his ward. This was to avoid risk to her fortune.[174] There was nothing, however, to prevent a guardian marrying his own daughter to a boy in his guardianship or marrying his ward if her father had previously sanctioned the match.[175] For similar reasons of the potential abuse of power, imperial *mandata* provided that an official should not marry a woman of the province in which he was serving.[176] Like a guardian, an official could bestow his own daughters in marriage in the province and could marry a woman to whom he was engaged before taking up the office.[177]

The effect of the Augustan Law is attested by attempts to evade it. As early as Seneca, moralists inveigh against men of modest means who were often hired to take the name of husband, in order to flout the laws against celibacy. It seems that he means that women 'hired' husbands, for he laments the lack of marital authority by a man who took the woman's role in marrying, 'qui nupsit'.[178] Suetonius mentions a man who married the day before the allotment of quaestorships and divorced the day after, and Tacitus attests fraudulent adoptions before elections or selection of governors.[179] It is possible that some free-born people adopted disreputable professions which put them outside the scope of the law.[180]

More respectable people were driven to ask the emperor for the right to be registered as the fictitious parents of three children. Augustus arranged for the *ius trium liberorum* to be given to Vestal Virgins and to Livia after the death of her second son. The emperor himself might not qualify under the law: Gaius is said to have

---

[172] *FIRA* i.99.24–33. Cf. Besnier, 'L'application des lois caducaires d'Auguste d'après le gnomon de l'idiologue'. Astolfi, 'Note per una valutazione storica della "Lex Iulia et Papia"' 203 ff., relates the census qualifications to the earlier *Leges Furia* and *Voconia*.

[173] Talbert no. 82.   [174] Talbert no. 130; Corbett 44.

[175] *D* 23.2.64.2, 66 pr.

[176] *D* 23.2.38, 57, 63, 65, 24.1.3.1, 34.9.2.1 (mentioning rescript of Severus and Caracalla); Corbett 42 ff. See for the general context and a bare list Duyvendak, 'Restraining regulations for Roman officials in the Roman provinces'; dell'Oro, 'Il divieto del matrimonio fra funzionario romano e donna della provincia' (for Severan date); Volterra, 'Sull'unione coniugale del funzionario della provincia'.   [177] *D* 23.2.38.

[178] Sen. fr. 7. For *nubere* with a man as subject cf. Pompon. *com.* 89; Mart. 12.42.1; Juv. 2.134; Tac. *A* 15.37.8.   [179] Suet. *Tib.* 35.2; Tac. *A* 15.19.

[180] Levick, 'The *senatus consultum* from Larinum' 104.

obtained a senatorial decree to enable him to take bequests originally willed to Tiberius, because he was unmarried and childless at his accession.[181] The grant appears to have been much prized.[182]

One effect which might have been expected to follow, but which as far as I am aware is unattested, is a revival of *manus*. For if a wife were *in manu mariti*, the reciprocal rights of wife and husband to succeed each other ought to have been much enhanced. If he had no child, the wife could succeed on intestacy to the whole of her husband's property. Conversely, her property was automatically transferred to him during her lifetime. It is possible that the law could have disqualified a childless wife *in manu* from intestate succession, but it cannot have attacked the ancient property-rights of husbands whose wives entered *manus*. But I can find no trace of increased resort to *manus*, so I take it that the institution continued to decay.

What difference did the Augustan legislation make? It may have persuaded upper-class men to marry earlier than they might otherwise have done. The incentives for the more prosperous freedmen should have had some impact. Women in both these classes were given new reason to want to be wives and prolific mothers, but the privileges they might win may have seemed less attractive to other members of their families who had moral or legal influence over them. What many Romans had henceforth to bear in mind was the effect of the law on disposal of property. Augustus had made the social and legal context of marriage much more complex than before. It is for this reason that his legislation marks a new era in the history of Roman marriage. If we had the letters of a Cicero to a Terentia, a Tiro, and an Atticus of the time of Tiberius or Vespasian, we might be able to produce a post-Augustan case-study to compare with the comparatively unregulated affairs of the late Republic. As it is, we can only speculate how far the thought of the Julio-Papian Laws dominated the minds of the wealthy when they planned to marry or make their wills.

---

[181] Dio 55.2.5, 56.10.2, 59.15.1. The grant to free-born women was *ius iii liberorum* (the number needed to avoid *tutela*: Paul. *S* 4.9.9). See Sherwin-White, *Pliny* 558; Dixon, *RM* 89 ff.

[182] e.g. Pliny *Epp.* 10.2; *CIL* 6.1877, 10247.

PART II
Sponsi

3

Choosing a *Coniunx*

It is a truth universally acknowledged, that a single man in possession of a good fortune, must be in want of a wife.

(Jane Austen, *Pride and prejudice*, chapter 1)

The Dromios came to England at the end of the sixteenth century, the precise date being probably 1592. There is no certainty on where they came from—Ephesus and Syracuse have both been suggested—but historians of the family admit that they seem to have been persons somewhat below the middle station of life, if not of actually servile condition. In England, however, they prospered, and already in the reign of James I were importing wines in a large way. On the strength of this they married first into the London citizenry—the Frugals, the Hoards, and the Moneytraps—then into the landed gentry—the Mammons, the Overreaches, the Clumseys, and the Greedys —and finally into the fringes of the aristocracy itself—the No-lands, the Littleworths, the Rakes, the Foppingtons, and the Whorehounds.

(Michael Innes, *A night of errors* [1948], prologue)

WHETHER the consent of the bride and even of the bridegroom was legally required may be academic if the pressure exerted by the family or by society was strong.[1] We may recollect at the outset that the wider society allowed few excuses for refusing to marry. Vocation to the priesthood of Vesta seems to have been imposed by family ambition rather than by a pre-pubertal girl's desire for celibacy, and in any case, since there were only six Vestals at a time and they could retire after thirty years, virginity was not a statistically significant career. Lifelong celibate women are otherwise practically un-exampled,[2] although nothing can be proved for the lower classes.

---

[1] An earlier version of this and the next chapter appeared in '*Digna condicio*: betrothals in the Roman upper class'. See now, on actual patterns of choice, Syme, 'Dynastic marriages in the Roman aristocracy'.

[2] The artist Iaia of Cyzicus, contemporary with Varro but probably not a Roman citizen, is described by Pliny (*NH* 35.147) as *perpetua virgo*.

Women owed the state children, young men had the additional duty of maintaining the male line and the family name, *nomen*. But even grandchildren in the female line might be valued for sentimental reasons, particularly if they were male. One consolation for the father of a daughter was that she was likely to produce grandchildren earlier than would a son.[3] The traditional idea that everyone should marry was further reinforced by the Augustan legislation, which made celibacy for men between 25 and 60 and for women between 20 and 50 socially and economically disadvantageous. A man who reached 60 without ever having married was a rarity in the propertied classes. Poets enjoyed more licence than most.[4] The consuls who passed Augustus' marriage legislation were unmarried and childless at that time.[5] But it is not certain that Q. Poppaeus Sabinus and M. Papius Mutilus never married, for evidence on them is extremely thin.[6] Men who had been married and produced heirs might, however, resist the pressures of family and friends, as did Q. Cicero.[7] Elderly and wealthy *caelibes* and and *orbi* were certainly available later to be satirized by Juvenal and Martial, despite the law, but we need not assume that they had never attempted matrimony.

A predisposition of society and of the individual family in favour of marriage in general does not mean that any match would do. A *digna condicio*, a suitable match, must be the aim.[8] Society would rank matches according to birth, wealth, position, and so on, on a scale which ran from lofty or first-class, rich or honourable, down to vulgar and low. All these judgments are relative. Plautus underlines this when he makes a man who is looking after the daughter of a friend say that he has a dowry to give her which will enable him to dispose of her in a match worthy of her: 'ut eam in se dignam condicionem conlocem'.[9] There should be no risk that she will have to marry

---

[3] VM 7.1.1; Stat. *S* 4.8.27; cf. Ov. *Tr.* 4.5.33–4, 5.10.75–6.

[4] e.g. Vergil and Horace, if the silence of Suetonius may be trusted. Vergil's heirs are said to have been a half-brother, Augustus, Maecenas, Varius, and Tucca, while Horace's was Augustus (Suet. *Verg.* 37, *Hor. fin.*).   [5] Dio 56.10.3.

[6] *PIR*[2] P628, P92.   [7] Cic. *A* 14.13.5.

[8] *Laud. Tur.* 2.35: 'tu ipsa mihi di[gnam et aptam con]dicionem quaereres.' Cicero speaks of *dignitas* when a marriage is based on suitability and results in harmony, a happy combination of eligibility and affection (*Clu.* 12: 'nuptiae plenae dignitatis, plenae concordiae'; cf. 35, where respectability of motive is emphasized: 'Quae nuptiae non diuturnae fuerunt; erant enim non matrimoni dignitate sed sceleris societate coniunctae'). Comparative material which I have found helpful includes Bourdieu, 'Marriage strategies and strategies of social reproduction'; Davidoff, *The best circles. Society, etiquette and the Season*; Slater, 'The weightiest business: marriage in an upper-gentry family in seventeenth century England'. Lawrence Stone in *The family, sex and marriage in England 1500–1800* 182–3 conveniently lists four basic motives in the choice of marriage partner in the 18th cent.: 'the economic or social or political consolidation or aggrandisement of the family'; personal affection, based on thorough acquaintance; physical attraction; and romantic love.   [9] *Trin.* 159.

beneath her social class because she lacks a proper fortune. Of course, it was even more desirable if a girl could get rather more than she had a right to expect in terms of social status, good birth, or wealth. In a rhetorical exercise the pirate-king's daughter who marries a well-born prisoner and goes back to his home with him is clearly getting a *honesta condicio*, a match with an upper-class husband, which would otherwise have been impossible.[10] *Condiciones* might be termed lofty, *altissimae*, rich or splendid, *luculentae*, or first-class, *primariae*,[11] depending on what type of qualification the speaker had in mind. A woman who looked down on a suitor might call his offer *sordida*: so Martial says of a woman of noble ancestry who rejects an *eques* and marries a police constable.[12] An unequal match would disgrace the better-born partner: it would be *turpis*.[13] More generally, a bad bargain might be *pessima*. One partner might be regarded by the other or by outsiders as *impar*: so, by a stretch of the imagination, Augustus' daughter Julia contrived to regard her aristocratic third husband, Tiberius.[14]

I. Conventional Criteria

Philosophers and moralists in attacking conventional behaviour show what criteria they thought were normally applied in choosing a husband or wife. So, in the first century AD, Musonius Rufus says:[15]

Therefore those who contemplate marriage ought to have regard neither for family, whether either one be of high-born parents, nor for wealth, whether on either side there be great possessions, nor for physical traits, whether one or the other have beauty. For neither wealth nor beauty nor high birth is effective in promoting partnership of interest or sympathy, nor again are they significant for producing children. But as for the body it is enough for marriage that it be healthy, of normal appearance and capable of hard work, such as would be less exposed to the snares of tempters, better adapted to

[10] Sen. *Contr.* 1.6.9.
[11] Pliny *Epp.* 1.10.8; Plaut. *Miles* 952, *Stich.* 138, *Trin.* 746; cf. Cic. *F* 4.5.3: 'cum aliquo adulescente primario coniuncta'; ibid. 5: 'adulescentibus primariis nuptam.' A mother may want to see her daughter make the most splendid match possible with a social superior, 'quam splendidissimis nuptiis iungi' (Livy 4.9.5). For the assumption that *genus* (birth) and *nobilitas* (rank) were prime criteria, cf. Curt. 9.1.26.   [12] Mart. 5.17.
[13] Cf. Ov. *Her.* 16.173–4: 'Non ego coniugium generosae degener opto, | nec mea, crede mihi, turpiter uxor eris.'
[14] Plaut. *Stich.* 138; Tac. *A* 1.53.2; cf. Livy 6.34.9. Cn. Calpurnius Piso (consul AD 7), proud of his own family and his wife Plancina's, held Tiberius barely his equal and Tiberius' children (sc. because of their grandfather the new man Agrippa and/or their great-grandfather the *eques* Atticus) as distinctly inferior (Tac. *A* 2.43.4). Apul. *M* 6.23 uses *nuptiae impares* of a misalliance between god and mortal' *matrimonium impar* usually means a disparity of age. *Impar* is used of one partner in relation to the other or one side of the family in relation to the other (Tac. *H* 2.50) to indicate social disparity.
[15] For Musonius' unusually 'liberated' attitude, see de Ste Croix, *The class struggle in the ancient Greek world* 110.

perform physical labour and not wanting in strength to beget or to bear
children. (13B, trans. Cora Lutz, *YCS* 10 [1947] 91)

He then insists that there should be virtue on both sides. Isidore of
Seville in the seventh century similarly lists four criteria for assessing
possible husbands, three for wives:

Apud veteres in eligendis maritis quatuor ista spectabantur, virtus, genus,
pulchritudo, oratio; in feminis tria: si generosa, si bene morata esset, si
pulchra. Nunc autem non genus ac mores, sed magis divitiae in uxoribus
placent; nec quaeritur quam sit femina pudica, sed potius quam formosa.
(PL 83.812, *de ecclesiasticis officiis* 2.20, *de coniugatis*)

In the old days, four qualifications were regarded in choosing husbands:
manliness, family, looks, speech; in choosing women, three: if she was
well-born, of good character, beautiful. But nowadays it is not family and
character, but rather wealth, which pleases us in a wife, and no one asks
how virtuous a woman is, but rather how beautiful she is.

In the *Etymologiae* he applies much the same formulation to his own
day: 'In choosing a husband, four qualifications are usually regarded:
manliness, family, looks, wisdom.' (In the example from the *Aeneid*
which follows, he makes it clear that wisdom is the same as 'speech'.)
'In the same way, in choosing a wife four things impel a man to love:
beauty, family, wealth, character. But it is better to look for character
than beauty. Nowadays, however, people seek wives qualified by
wealth or beauty rather than excellence of character.'[16]

The change from three to four is not inconsistent: in the good old
days wealth was not a criterion. Even in decadent modern times it is
not mentioned as a qualification for a man. Looks and birth figure for
both sexes; good character (chiefly chastity) in the woman are
balanced by a broader range of masculine virtues (*virtus*) and of
intellectual qualities (*oratio* or *sapientia*).

The list ultimately derives from a classification in Theophrastus'
lost work on marriage (*de nuptiis*) in which he asked the question
(which subsequently became commonplace)[17] whether the wise man
would marry. According to Jerome,

[16] *Etym.* 9.7.28–9: 'In eligendo marito quattuor spectari solent: virtus, genus, pulchritudo,
sapientia . . . Item in eligenda uxore quattuor res inpellunt hominem ad amorem: pulchritudo,
genus, divitiae, mores. Melius tamen si in ea mores quam pulchritudo quaeratur. Nunc autem
illae quaeruntur, quas aut divitiae aut forma, non quas probitas morum commendat.'

[17] Democritus and Epicurus held that he should not, lest the pleasures and pains of marriage
disturb him (Clem. Alex. *Strom.* 2.28.138). The Pythagoreans and Stoics held that he or she
should (Mus. pp. 38ff., 90ff. [Lutz]; Hierocles: Stob. 4.22.1.22). Cicero after the divorce from
Terentia is supposed to have said that he could not pay attention to a wife and philosophy (Jer.
adv. Iovin. 1.48 = 316 A). Whether any man, or a particular individual, should marry (or stand
for office) was also a question debated in the rhetorical schools (Quint. *Inst.* 2.4.25, 3.5.8, 12,
13; cf. 3.5.11, 3.8.4).

cum definisset, si pulcra esset, si bene morata, si honestis parentibus, si ipse sanus ac dives, sic sapientem inire aliquando matrimonium, statim intulit: 'haec autem raro in nuptiis universa concordant.' (Jerome *adversus Iovinianum* 1.47 = 313 C)

When he had laid down the conditions, that if she were beautiful, of good character, with honourable parents, and if he himself were rich and healthy, then sometimes the wise man would enter on marriage, he at once added the rider: 'But these things rarely all come together in a marriage.'

The criteria in Isidore's sermon correspond with those of Theophrastus. The philosophers' lists vary and all are overschematic and incomplete, but they fit well enough with classical formulations in non-philosophical writings. So Dido, perhaps already subconsciously meditating marriage, falls in love with Aeneas because of his *virtus*, birth, face, and words.[18] So Ovid, when he makes a mythological young man assure a girl of his qualifications, lists his *patria*, good birth, wealth, morals, and love for her. She replies that he is admittedly worth courting.[19] Juvenal adds up a complete list of looks, charm, wealth, birth, fertility, and chastity—a *rara avis*, but who would really want to marry such a paragon?[20] Statius pictures a bride who is not only highly educated and compatible in character with her bridegroom, but meets all other qualifications: 'forma, simplicitate, comitate, | censu, sanguine, gratia, decore'.[21] Pliny, in responding to Junius Mauricus, who had asked him to look out a husband for his niece, produces a short-list of one, Minicius Acilianus. He mentions the young man's *patria*, Brescia, 'in our own part of Italy', which retains the ancient virtues. As to his family, his father is a highly placed *eques* who could have had a senatorial career and was offered promotion by Vespasian; his maternal grandmother, from Padua, is a model of old-fashioned propriety even to the people of Padua; his uncle is also notably virtuous. He is himself a hard-working and modest young man, who has already held offices up to the praetorship (which would make him over 30). He is ruddy-complexioned and

---

[18] Verg. *A* 4.3 ff., cf. 11.336 ff. (not in a marital context); Hor. *O* 4.1 (see Bradshaw, 'Horace, *Odes* 4.1'; Habinek, 'The marriageability of Maximus: Horace, *Ode* 4.1.13–20', with further references to conventional criteria in poets); Jer. *adv. Iovin.* 1.47 = 313 c. Cf. Plut. *Ant.* 87.4, emphasizing the attraction of Antonia the younger as a bride because of her famous beauty and discretion.   [19] Ov. *Her.* 20.225–8, 21.131–2.

[20] 6.161 ff.: '"Nullane de tantis gregibus tibi digna videtur?" | Sit formosa decens dives fecunda, vetustos | porticibus disponat avos, intactior omni | crinibus effusis bellum dirimente Sabina | rara avis in terris nigroque simillima cycno: | quis feret uxorem cui constant omnia?' Cf. Courtney ad loc. for parallel lists of wifely virtues, particularly in the context of epitaphs rather than in pre-marital computation. Also Apul. *M* 8.1 (nobility, fame, money, qualifications outweighed by vices).

[21] *S* 2.7.85 ff.: 'figure, candour, charm, financial standing, blood, position, looks', a reference I owe to E. Courtney.

looks like a gentleman, indeed looks like a senator. These attractions must be mentioned, since they are proper compensation for a bride's virginity. Pliny is more bashful about adding that Acilianus' father is rich. But even Mauricus ought to take that into account, for the sake of the future children of the marriage.[22] At least three of Isidore's criteria appear here: much emphasis on the virtues of candidate and family; the family's social status and background; the man's looks. There is nothing specifically on his ability as a speaker, but Pliny describes instead his success so far in his public career. Apart from love (which could not be mentioned here), the list fits precisely that given by Ovid. It is a pity that the qualifications of the girl are alluded to only indirectly in Pliny's respectful remarks about her father and uncle. (Probably he did not know her.) It is a pity too that we cannot see Mauricus' complete file of candidates or Pliny's other similar letters of recommendation, and that we do not know if this *condicio* came off. Perhaps it did, since Pliny published the letter. The strength of the tradition which Pliny represents and which the publication of this letter reinforced is shown by the similarity of the points covered by a letter of recommendation written centuries later by Sidonius Apollinaris to Sagittarius, guardian of the daughter of a certain Optantius. Sidonius asks him to endorse the choice of husband already made by the woman's mother. The suitor, Proiectus, is a *vir clarissimus*, of noble family with a father and uncle *spectabiles* and a grandfather a priest, of good morals and wealth. Good looks are not explicitly mentioned, but he has the energy of youth, so his list of qualifications adds up to every fitting quality (*decus*).[23]

The basic qualities desired by aristocrats will hardly vary from Greece to Rome to Christian European nations, although other criteria, such as religious orthodoxy, might be added. But the conventional list is so general that it was only a guide to the categories which had to be considered. What degree of good birth was the minimum, or the maximum, to be hoped for? Patrician, plebeian noble, a family which claimed to be able to trace itself back to the kings, or the early Republic or the Punic Wars or the Augustan period? How much wealth might be held to compensate for comparatively un-distinguished family or disastrous close relatives? Not only would a man's comparative scores in the four conventional areas have to be taken into account, but also subtler points (not only the general prestige of his family but the effectiveness and helpfulness of his living kinsmen, for instance). And this was only a beginning. Calculations then had to be made about whether the woman and her family had

enough to offer him in exchange. It might be seen as a coup for the
inferior partner to win someone whose qualifications were greater,
but such a match might disgrace the superior. Moralists disapproved
of unequal matches for various reasons. A Pythagorean text attributed to Callicratidas of Sparta suggests that a wife who is richer and
better born will attempt to govern her husband. The domineering rich
wife became a stock character in Roman comedy and later Latin
literature.[24] Calculations of relative worth might appear quite differently to the two main interested groups or individuals. My remarks
perhaps suggest an over-schematic and over-rationalist approach. It
may be doubted whether actual Romans brought to the task of
choosing a wife or a husband quite the degree of cold objectivity
which a modern committee hopes to apply to choosing scholarship
candidates. Imponderable factors and gambles as well as personal
feelings weighted decisions. But the assumption of society was that
any specific pairing could be examined against objective, though
imprecise, criteria.

2. Birth

Disparity of birth in a husband or wife was something to be avoided
by all classes. One of the unlucky horoscopes given by Dorotheus of
Sidon involves a misalliance: 'One of them will be consoled with a
woman servant or a foreign woman or one who is worse in (her)
lineage than is he.'[25] The Calpurnius Piso who conspired against Nero
and who was not intelligent or brave, but had the bluest republican
blood in Rome, married a woman who was far less well born than he,
in fact *degener*, degenerate in the technical sense and also, as it
happened, in her sexual behaviour. Her one qualification, says
Tacitus, was her physical beauty.[26] The opposite of *degener* is
generosus or *generosa*. The quality of *generositas* is stressed in
considerations of the compatibility of potential marriage partners.
Having a partner who is less well born or positively *humilis* may
create difficulties for a husband or wife and be remembered against
the children.[27]

High birth, particularly patrician status or old plebeian *nobilitas*,
was a major attribute which could compensate for shortcomings
in other respects. Although the Julii Caesares had not been distinguishing themselves in public life in the second century, a Julia was
able to ally herself with the up-and-coming new man, Marius. The

[24] e.g., in the context of choice, Stob. 4.28.18; Plut. *libb. educ.* 13 F.
[25] *Carmen astrologicum* (Teubner trans.) 2.24.11.   [26] Tac. *A* 15.59.8.
[27] Cf. Hor. *S* 1.6.36; Ov. *M* 14.698–9, 9.491 ff.

advantage is held by modern scholars to have been on her side, which is true from the practical point of view, but that is not to say that old-fashioned aristocrats may not have thought she was lowering herself.[28] Both partners had something to gain from the alliance.

Patrician blood helps account for Lucullus' willingness to marry one of the Clodiae without a dowry.[29] The patrician group, even in the late Republic, was too small for them to marry only among themselves, but the presumption of their superiority remained strong among them and surfaces from time to time in the context of marriage. So Augustus' daughter Julia, who, if an anecdote in Macrobius may be trusted, was vividly aware of the dignity of her social position as the daughter of Caesar, appears to have attached importance to her father's lineage rather than his power. Ignoring the fact that her father was a Caesar only by adoption and through the female line, she despised her third husband, Tiberius, a descendant of distinguished lines of plebeian nobility, Claudii Nerones and Livii Drusi, as her social inferior.[30]

The position of an Ap. Claudius Pulcher, whose patrician ancestors had been in Rome at least since the early Republic, or of a Julius, who claimed kin with Romulus, was unassailable, but plebeians, even new men, could claim other glories and have family pride of their own. 'Crescit occulto velut arbor aevo | fama Marcelli.'[31] The deeds of a war hero, the conspicuous chastity of a great-grandmother, could add to the qualifications of a young man or woman. For the male line, achievements in public life create a kind of rank, important in politics, intertwined with more tenuous genealogical claims but logically separable.

3. Rank

Nobilitas, possession of at least one ancestor in the male line who had achieved curule rank, was the best status, and the more numerous, ancient, and eminent the magistrates the better. Antique smoke-blackened busts should ideally be reinforced by recent office-holders. Newer families could point only to recent achievement by father or grandfather, but at least the blood was scarcely diluted.[32] Although

[28] Cf. Wiseman, NMRS 55. The marriage had taken place by 111 BC.
[29] Varro RR 3.16.2.
[30] Macr. Sat. 2.5.8; Tac. A 1.53.2 (where Goodyear ad loc. takes a different view from mine). Her previous husband Agrippa, a new man, ignobilis loco (Tac. A 1.3.1), must have seemed worse: her grandson Gaius liked to think he was not his grandfather (Suet. Gaius 23.1).
[31] Hor. O 1.12 45–6.
[32] On the wider social and political context, Gelzer, RNob, and Wiseman, NMRS, are fundamental. I adopt P. A. Brunt's definition of nobiles ('Nobilitas and novitas'). For the self-assertion of novi against nobiles see D. C. Earl, Moral and political tradition of Rome ch. 2, and for snobbery affecting a whole society see the brief discussion by Balsdon, RA 18 ff.

technically it had no effect on a person's status, the mother's side of the stemma always had some importance. Often it would be more obscurely known, as Asconius warns us in a salutary note,[33] and it could therefore be used by a hostile orator to a person's discredit. Cicero attacked Piso's maternal ancestry and claimed that Antony attacked Octavian's mother for coming from Aricia, which was surprising as she was the daughter of Caesar's sister Julia, and Antony himself gloried in being the son of another Julia.[34] Both republican and early imperial authors refer to good or bad birth on the mother's side or to unequal parents.[35] The expression *materna nobilitas* is Vergil's, but the idea occurs in Propertius, when he describes the distinction of Cornelia's family on both sides, from the houses of the Scipiones and Libones, both propped on their ancestral honours.[36] Tacitus describes Galba's adopted son Piso as noble on both sides of his family.[37] Rubellius Plautus could be seen as a plausible threat to Nero because he was equally closely related to Augustus, though in the female line.[38] The importance of maternal descent had perhaps been increased by the accident whereby Octavian was related by

[33] *Pis.* 10C: 'Socrus Pisonis quae fuerit invenire non potui, videlicet quod auctores rerum non perinde in domibus ac familiis feminarum, nisi illustrium, ac virorum nomina tradiderunt' ('I have not been able to discover who was Piso's mother-in-law, because [I deduce] historians have not recorded the names of women in their houses and families equally with those of men, unless the women were illustrious'). For the meaning of *domus* and *familiae* see Saller, '*Familia, domus* and the Roman conception of the family'.

[34] *Pis.* frr. 13–14, 34, 53, 62; *Red. Sen.* 15; *Phil.* 3.17. The Sarakatsani may be compared: 'It is true that the prestige of paternal connexions is greater, but the quality of the mother's family of origin is also critical, for criticism of the mother, who contributes important moral qualities to the characters of her children, is a peculiarly effective method of denigrating a family' (Campbell 43).

[35] Sall. *BJ* 11.3: 'materno genere impar erat' ('by his mother's family he was unequal'); Hor. *S* 1.6.36: 'quo patre sit natus, num ignota matre inhonestus' ('who his father is, whether he is ignoble because of an unknown mother'), cf. 24; Stat. *S* 4.4.75: 'stemmate materno felix' ('happy in his maternal descent'); Tac. *A* 6.42.4; 'materna origine Arsacidem, cetera degenerem' ('on his mother's side an Arsacid, for the rest degenerate'). For consideration of the mother's side of the stemma, cf. Ov. *M* 13.146ff. (Ulysses on his divine descent): 'est quoque per matrem Cyllenius addita nobis | altera nobilitas: deus est in utroque parente. | Sed neque materno quod sum generosior ortu' ('On my mother's side too there is Mercury and a second nobility is added to us [sc. as well as his claim to be the great-grandson of Jupiter, in which he was the equal of his rival Ajax]: there is a god in the ancestry of both my parents. But not because I am more nobly born on my mother's side [sc. than is Ajax]'). Tac. *H* 1.48, on T. Vinius, notes that his father was of a family which had held the praetorship, but on his mother's side he had the distinction of a grandfather who had been one of the proscribed ('pater illi praetoria familia, maternus avus e proscriptis'). Tacitus may be mistaken (*PIR*[2] v450), but it does not affect my point. Brutus exploited the Servilii (for Ahala) as well as his paternal descent from the Bruti of legend (Cic. *A* 13.40.1).

[36] Verg. *A* 11.340–1; Prop. 4.11.30ff.

[37] *H* 1.14: 'nobilis utrimque'. Cf. Syme, *Tac.* ii.654.

[38] Tac. *A* 13.19.4: 'Rubellium Plautum, per maternam originem pari ac Nero gradu a divo Augusto' ('Rubellius Plautus, on his mother's side related to the deified Augustus in the same degree as Nero'). Cf. Odysseus' claim that his descent from Jupiter was as close as that of Ajax

blood to Caesar through his grandmother Julia, Caesar's sister, Tiberius was Augustus' stepson and son-in-law before he became his son by adoption, Gaius was the great-grandson of Augustus through his daughter Julia and granddaughter Agrippina, and so on. The female line had become vital to the imperial succession during the first two reigns. This situation did not alter. Since senatorial families had difficulty perpetuating themselves at that level in society,[39] descent through women became similarly important for them. Lesser magistracies already achieved by a family would confer lesser rank. What a man or a woman's father had achieved in his own career might well carry more weight with a prospective father-in-law or son-in-law. Better, perhaps, an energetic new man like Marius (who perhaps had been elected praetor before he won Julia) than a nonentity with a praetorian ancestor. But many factors had to be taken into account.

New achievements in politics tend to go along with new marriages. Pompey's effective self-defence in the courts in 86 BC led to his engagement to the judge's daughter Antistia, a marriage which ended when an even more advantageous match was offered by Sulla as a reward for Pompey's military success.[40] It may be postulated that as a man moves up the *cursus honorum*, he moves into successive 'brackets' as a potential husband or father-in-law. Tullia's engagement to her first husband comes at the end of 67 (the exact date is unfortunately unknown), just before Cicero enters upon his praetorship and probably at the outset of her fiancé's career. (Piso was a moneyer in c.64, quaestor in 58.[41]) Young men often seem to have provided themselves with a wife about the time when they first sought election. Financial motives were important here, which may have led some to settle for wealth if necessary, without birth or rank.[42] The girl's father, at the same time, will have looked for a promising son-in-law, who could perhaps be had cheaper before his quaestorship than later. So Ti. Gracchus (according to one version) was chosen by Ap. Claudius Pulcher as his son-in-law after his ability had been recognized by his early adlection as augur.[43] Cicero married the well-born and well-dowered Terentia after his brilliant defence of Roscius in 80 and in good time for his candidacy for the quaestorship in 76.[44] The first marriage of a *novus homo*, particularly if he won a

(Ov. *M* 13.141 ff.: 'sed enim, quia rettulit Aiax | esse Iovis pronepos, nostri quoque sanguinis auctor | Iuppiter est, totidemque gradus distamus ab illo' ('but, since Ajax has brought up the point that he is the great-grandson of Jupiter, I claim him as the beginner of our line too, and we are the same number of degrees removed from him').   [39] Hopkins, *DR* chs. 2 and 3.
[40] Plut. *Pomp.* 4, 9.   [41] Cic. *A* 1.3.3.   [42] See sect. 4.   [43] Plut. *Ti. Gr.* 4.1.
[44] Plut. *Cic.*, our main source on Cicero's early career, apart from his own occasional reminiscences, does not mention the marriage in his chronological account, but only indirectly when he includes Terentia's dowry (8.2) in a list of Cicero's assets (which follows his account of

woman whose family had an assured position in politics, provides the best evidence of how a woman's family might back a potential front-runner. But they might have to pay for it: a remark of Cicero's indicates that sons-in-law who had to seek election were likely to ask for money from their fathers-in-law. One advantage with Dolabella was that he was the only candidate for Tullia's hand, except for Atticus' nominee, who would not put Cicero into debt.[45]

In the Principate, Augustan legislation had the effect of making marriage and procreation attractive to those who might hope for inheritance from people outside their immediate family and to magistrates on whom a wife and children conferred seniority. So again, men are found marrying at about the time of candidacy for office and, conversely, the woman or her family would look for signs of probable success. Agricola is the classic example. Going to Rome to stand for office after his military service in Britain, he married the well-born Domitia Decidiana, a union which stood him in good stead as he faced the greater tests ahead.[46] A son born in late AD 62 or in 63 allowed Agricola to hold the quaestorship a year early, in 64, and a daughter born in 64 qualified him for his praetorship in 68, two years early. Marriage at about 22 seems to have been the ideal for aspiring politicians.[47]

Arranging a suitable match was the art of the possible. Rank and birth were not the only, or even paramount, considerations. Augustus, who had a wider choice than any other father, since he was not unduly particular about the age of candidates for his daughter Julia's hand and was ready and able to put pressure on men who were already suitably and happily married, undertook an exhaustive search for her third husband. He reviewed *equites* as well as senators: 'multis ac diu, etiam ex equestri ordine, circumspectis condicionibus'.[48]

Wiseman has shown that the grandest of republican noble families were prepared to intermarry with people of municipal origin. Only the Metelli, Ahenobarbi, and Caepiones are not known to have intermarried outside the charmed circle of the *nobiles*.[49] Nor did senators feel obliged to confine themselves to the daughters of

the prosecution of Verres in 70 and is to be taken as background for Cicero's work in the 60s). The marriage is usually conjecturally dated to 79 (and therefore immediately before Cicero's visit to Athens and the east; e.g. Bailey, *Cicero* 22, E. Rawson, *Cicero. A portrait* 25) or to shortly after his return in 77 (e.g. Mitchell, *Cicero. The ascending years* 99). I incline to the latter date.

[45] Cic. *A* 7.3.12.   [46] Tac. *Ag.* 6.1.   [47] See ch. 12.1(*a*).
[48] Suet. *DA* 63.2 ('having investigated many possible matches over a long time, even from the equestrian order'). Cf. Tac. *A* 4.39.5. Born in 39 BC, Julia had been married first at 14 to her cousin Marcellus, aged 17, in 25, widowed at 16, and remarried in 21 to Agrippa, who was approximately the same age as her father.   [49] Wiseman, *NMRS* 53 ff.

senators. The two *ordines*, distinct in status, were intermixed in their family lives: many senators had equestrian fathers, brothers, sons, and sons-in-law. Although in theory any senator outranked the most eminent *eques*, in fact the *gratia* and wealth of an Atticus or a Maecenas were greater than those of the undistinguished mass of senators, the *pedarii*. So when the *eques* Cornelius Nepos writes of the excellent match made by the daughter of the *eques* Atticus, he must be understood to be evoking a snobbish social consciousness which was slightly out of touch with reality:

His igitur rebus effecit ut M. Vipsanius Agrippa, intima familiaritate coniunctus adulescenti Caesari, cum propter suam gratiam et Caesaris potentiam nullius condiciones non haberet potestatem, potissimum eius deligeret affinitatem praeoptaretque equitis Romani filiam generosarum nuptiis. (Nepos *Atticus* 12.1–2)

It was these actions which persuaded M. Vipsanius Agrippa, who was linked in close friendship with the young Caesar, and because of his own influence and Caesar's power could have made any match he liked, to choose to ally himself with Atticus' family and to prefer marriage with the daughter of a Roman knight to union with an aristocrat.

However, the actions mentioned, Atticus' apparently disinterested protection of people who were temporarily in a weak position in a period of civil war, were another example of his ability to be a friend to all kinds of politicians and of his *gratia*, his ability to make himself useful to Agrippa. Atticus had brains, friends, connections, experience of the workings of politics. Besides, his daughter was his only child and would inherit a considerable property. Agrippa was undoubtedly powerful in 37 BC, but his family was equestrian, and some sticklers among aristocratic fathers might have cold-shouldered him. Nevertheless, the marriage was a coup for Atticus, the culmination of years of hard work.

Political connection is sometimes explicitly attested as the main motive for a particular marriage.[50] It is not our task here to list all the marriages which modern scholars have traced to such connection. Although their attribution of motive may well be right, it need not be the sole motive. The opposite procedure, to deduce political connection (even a fleeting one) from marriage alone, is illicit.[51]

---

[50] Plut. *Caes.* 14.4–5; Tac. *H* 3.78 (abortive bribe by Vitellius).

[51] Bailey, 'The Roman nobility in the second civil war' 267: 'Marriage in Rome as elsewhere, could be political . . . Yet, where political implications are not independently attested, μεμνᾶς' ἀπιστεῖν. Two of Cato's three nieces, daughters of Servilia, married Caesarians. Cato's (and Hortensius') Marcia belonged to the pro-Caesarian Philippi. Not all marriages were politically significant (Tullia's husbands seem to have been selected on purely social and personal grounds); not all that were have come to light. If we had the full particulars it is likely that nearly every member of the numerically small and inbred Roman aristocracy would be found in some

4. Wealth

High position and distinguished ancestors were an endowment: triumphs could be counted over like cash as a dowry.[52] Conversely, wealth might compensate for lack of birth. Wiseman instances a match mooted for Q. Cicero in 44 BC[53] and the engagement of Caesar as a boy to a certain Cossutia, of equestrian birth but considerable wealth.[54] Direct evidence that the Romans perceived that birth on one side could be balanced by wealth on the other is provided by Suetonius' account of the father of the emperor Galba, patrician and consul in AD 22 but short, hunch-backed, and only a mediocre orator, though an active advocate.

Uxores habuit Mummiam Achaicam, neptem Catuli proneptemque L. Mummi, qui Corinthum excidit; item Liviam Ocellinam, ditem admodum et pulchram, a qua tamen nobilitatis causa appetitus ultro existimatur et aliquanto enixius, postquam subinde instanti vitium corporis secreto posita veste detexit, ne quasi ignaram fallere videretur. (Suetonius *Galba* 3.4)

His wives were Mummia Achaica, the granddaughter of Catulus and the great-granddaughter of L. Mummius, the destroyer of Corinth, and then Livia Ocellina, who was very rich and beautiful and is said to have taken the initiative in courting him because of his noble birth. She pressed him even harder when, in response to her repeated advances, he took off his clothes in private and showed her his deformity, so that there could be no question that he had taken advantage of her ignorance of it.

Ocellina also had beauty, of which more later. The match came off successfully and she made Mummia's surviving son, the future emperor, her heir.[55]

The examples quoted so far are all of rich women. To some extent this reflects a bias in our sources towards explaining the advantage

sort of connexion with nearly every other.' See also Wiseman, 'Factions and family trees'; Brunt, *The Fall of the Roman Republic and related essays* 443 ff.

[52] Juv. 6.169. Tacitus makes Poppaea rank her *triumphalis avos* (grandfathers who had triumphed) as one of her attractions to Nero (along with her beauty, fecundity, and 'true heart', Tac. *A* 14.1.2). Her grandfather C. Poppaeus Sabinus won triumphal insignia for successes in Thrace (Tac. *A* 4.46ff., cf. 6.39.3, 13.45.2). Nothing is known of the father of her father T. Ollius (*PIR*[2] O62) or earlier ancestors.

[53] *NMRS* 56. The lady was the well-dowered Aquilia (Cic. *A* 14.13.5). Q. Cicero needed a dowry to pay back the divorced Pomponia's.   [54] Suet. *DJ* 1.1.

[55] Suet. *Galba* 4.1: 'adoptatusque a noverca sua Livia nomen et Ocellare cognomen assumpsit mutato praenomine; nam Lucium mox pro Servio usque ad tempus imperii usurpavit' ('And, having been adopted by his stepmother Livia, he took her family name and the surname of Ocella and changed his first name, for he took the name Lucius instead of Servius down to the time when he became emperor'). Since women could not legally adopt, this is really an instance of change of name. Cf. Syme, *RP* iii.1159. For an earlier traditional instance of birth allied with wealth, cf. the marriage of the only Fabius who survived the Cremera, 'inductus magnitudine divitiarum', with a lady of Maleventum, who insisted that their first son should take her father's *praenomen* (Fest. 174L; Incertus *de praenominibus* 6).

brought to men by marriage. It should also be linked with a difference
for the two sexes in the immediate economic results of marriage. A
man on marriage normally acquired a dowry, whether complete and
at once or by three annual instalments, or as a mixture of real estate
transferred at once and cash in instalments. The amount of the
dowry, and even of the wife's personal wealth, which would not
(unless she was *in manu* or under her husband's *tutela*) be under his
control but which might be used to help pay their joint expenses, was
therefore a major consideration. For the woman, the husband's
wealth would partly dictate their joint style of life,[56] but only came to
her if he died and left her an inheritance. To an upper-class man at
first marriage, particularly if he had not yet inherited family property,
his wife's dowry could be expected to bring essential capital at an
important moment in his career. Cicero discusses marriage for young
Quintus and young Marcus in 44 BC as an alternative to life supported
by an allowance from their fathers.[57] This consideration is likely to
have outweighed the topos, dearer perhaps to the 'middle classes',
that a well-dowered wife was likely to bully her husband because she
had too great a hold over him.[58]

Specific admission that a man aims at acquiring a *dotata uxor* (a
well-endowed wife) is easily found. A man would, as Soranus says,[59]
investigate the financial position of a potential bride carefully. If
negotiations proceeded successfully, her dowry would no doubt be an
important subject of discussion. A particularly striking instance of the
social acceptability of the motive is afforded by Plutarch's account of
the second marriage of Cicero. Terentia alleged that he was overcome by Publilia's youthful charms, a disreputable motive for marriage. But Tiro defended his patron by putting forward a more
laudable reason: Publilia's wealth.[60]

A substantial dowry could be used to attract suitors who would not
otherwise have come forward. Sidonius virtuously deplores the behaviour of the demagogue Paconius, who married his daughter into a
family of superior status by offering a splendid dowry.[61] A woman's
age and previous marital history might also make it necessary to offer
a larger dowry. A mother mentioned by Scaevola increased her
daughter's portion at her third marriage, and Apuleius is quite frank
(though tendentious): a beautiful virgin hardly needs a dowry at all,
but a widow or divorcee was expected to offer something besides
herself. It was normal for a *vidua*, no longer young and not particularly beautiful, who wished to attract a young man of ability, good

---

[56] Below, ch. 12.   [57] Cic. *A* 15.29.2, 16.1.5.   [58] See ch. 10.   [59] *Gyn.* 1.34.
[60] Plut. *Cic.* 41.3–4 Cf. Lyne, *The Latin love poets from Catullus to Horace* 6.
[61] *Epp.* 1.11.5.

looks, and fortune to offer him a 'long' dowry and favourable terms. Apuleius himself however, after having scorned many splendid offers, married his widow with a token dowry, counting nothing but herself and reckoning all the wealth and appurtenances as residing in the harmony and mutual love of their union. His appeal to the jurors to believe in his high-mindedness shows how the ideal of personal compatibility coexisted with considerations of personal advantage and how effective attacks on the self-interest of others were likely to be.[62] Plautus, writing in a genre in which the old woman who makes her husband's life a misery but cannot be divorced because of her dowry was a stock character, is even blunter: old women win husbands by means of their dowry.[63] An old woman has no other possible attraction.[64]

Moralists harped on the theme that too many of their contemporaries married for money. There was a topos that it was better to marry a man than money.[65] Seneca in his tract *de matrimonio*, quoted by Jerome, related an anecdote which he probably attributed to Porcia, daughter of Cato. 'When she was asked why she did not marry again after losing her husband, she replied that she could not find a husband who wanted her more than her property. In this remark she elegantly showed that wealth is chosen above virtue (*pudicitia*) in a wife, and that many marry wives with their fingers, not their eyes.'[66] This last expression, 'multos non oculis sed digitis uxores ducere', is confirmed and clarified by Plutarch, who, after arguing that men should not marry for beauty, goes on, 'One ought not to marry with the eyes nor with the fingers, as some men do, who reckon up how big a dowry they will get with their wives, but form no opinion about what they will be like to live with.'[67] Others might argue merely that disparity of wealth was a bad basis for marriage.[68]

[62] *D* 32.41.7; *Apol.* 92.

[63] *Most.* 281: 'quibus anus domi sunt uxores, quae vos dote meruerunt' ('who have old women as their wives at home, who earned you by their dowry').

[64] Pompon. *Atell.* 89: 'nupsit . . . dotatae, vetulae, varicosae, vafrae' ('he has married a little old varicose, wily wife with a dowry'). Cf. probably Plaut. fr. inc. 22. Note the handicaps of age and previous marriage alleged against Cornificia, who nevertheless rejected a suitor for his poverty (Cic. *A* 13.28.4). For the physical unattractiveness of old women, see Richlin, *The Garden of Priapus* 109–16.

[65] Plaut. *Stich.* 135; Cic. *Off.* 2.71: 'cum consuleretur [sc. Themistocles] utrum bono viro pauperi an minus probato diviti filiam collocaret: "Ego vero", inquit, "malo virum, quo pecunia egeat, quam pecuniam, quae viro." Sed corrupti mores depravatique sunt admiratione divitiarum.' Cf. Stob. 4.22.6, on the need to assess character rather than birth or dowry; ibid. 118: a poor good man is better than a bad rich one.

[66] *adv. Iovin.* 1.46 = 312C. But Frassinetti 187 edits the passage out.

[67] *Praec. conj.* 141C–D. Cf. Publilius 36: 'Animo virum pudicae non oculo eligunt.'

[68] Livy 1.34.4; *Decl. min.* 257.7–8, 301.20–1; Calp. *Decl.* 29: 'pauper et dives: iniquum est matrimonium. ne pecora quidem iugum nisi paria succedunt' ('A poor woman and a rich man: the marriage is unequal. Not even beasts take on the yoke unless they are equally matched').

Lack of dowry might ruin a woman's chances. It was particularly crucial when a girl reached marriageable age and needed to find a first husband. The highest-placed families might see a girl's brief years of maximum attractiveness as a crisis. Scipio Africanus, according to an anecdote in Valerius Maximus, asked to be recalled from campaigning in Spain in order to deal with his daughter's engagement and dowry. Happily, the Senate was able to solve the problem by finding her a dowry from the treasury. The story is certainly unhistorical, but significant for Roman mentality.[69] Girls who were dowerless would often have to marry men of lower social status[70] or might even seem unplaceable, *inlocabiles*.[71] Giving dowries to dowerless girls was a recognized charitable and public service.

Women, or their families, must also have needed the assurance that a suitor could maintain them at least in the style to which they were accustomed. So Pliny, recommending a prospective bridegroom, mentions delicately that his father has ample resources, a qualification which many of his contemporaries would have put first, to the neglect of the young man's education, background, morals, career, and looks, to all of which Pliny gives priority. Nevertheless, when the foundation of a family is planned, money is important.[72] In the fifth century the equally judicious and benevolent Sidonius Apollinaris, writing to a girl's guardian to support the suit of a young man already accepted by her mother, similarly attests the distinction of his family, excellence of his morals, ample patrimony, and youthful vigour.[73] We may take it for granted that, *ceteris paribus*, wealth was as much desired in a husband as in a wife. Horace says ironically that Queen Cash can give a man a wife with a dowry, as well as credit, friends, birth, and good looks—the first item on the list could perhaps be taken seriously.[74]

But, as in the nineteenth century it was acceptable for a young man with his way to make to admit, at least among friends, that he could only succeed by marrying a rich wife, whereas it was improper and potentially counter-productive for a girl to 'hang out for a rich

---

[69] 4.4.10. See ch. 10.4. For similar urgency (though dowry is not mentioned) for others threatened with foreign service abroad cf. Tac. *A* 3.35.2.

[70] Sen. *Contr.* 7.6.18.

[71] Plaut. *Aul.* 191.

[72] *Epp.* 1.14.9.

[73] *Epp.* 2.4.1.

[74] *Epp.* 1.6.36–7 Cf. Juv. 3.160–1: 'Quis gener hic placuit censu minor atque puellae | sarcinulis impar?' The richer the suitor, the bigger the dowry would need to be. Cf. Schaps 76; Bedford, *The legacy*, pt. 3 ch. 4, on 'a rich man's *dot* and a poor man's *dot*' (p. 119 of the Fontana edn.).

husband',[75] so in the Roman world a greater delicacy screened inquiry into the wealth of prospective husbands. Apuleius can embroider an attack on the whole family of his opponent by claiming that a girl has been over-exposed in the marriage-market to young men of fortune (a double slur).[76] It was nevertheless the duty of the woman's family to obtain reliable information about the financial standing of potential husbands. A fifth-century lady from Marseilles who allowed her daughter to marry an adventurer should have verified his account of extensive estates round Clermont. Not only were they not his, but he was still a *filiusfamilias* and had no property at all.[77] In the more tightly knit republican aristocracy, discreet inquiries might be expected to produce an accurate picture in time to avoid such disappointments, although reliable information was not always quickly or easily obtained. When Atticus in 45 BC, with Cicero's anxious collaboration, began looking out potential fiancés for the 6-year-old Attica, Cicero approved a possible suitor as a man and for his family and resources. Second-hand information on his character was promising.[78] But he also reported about a month earlier a disquieting conversation in which the scholarly man-about-town Curtius Nicias dropped the word that Talna had recently proposed to marry Cornificia, an 'old' woman with several marriages behind her, and had been rejected by the lady and her mother because his property was worth only 800,000 sesterces. Cicero found this worrying and worth passing on. The two passages show how cautiously a father might conduct his researches

[75] A successful example is the politician Laurence FitzGibbon in Trollope's *Phineas Redux* (ch. 74). Frank Gresham in *Dr Thorne* is encouraged by his aunt the Countess de Courcy to believe that it is his duty to marry money in order to preserve the family estates (ch. 8). But Trollope's heroes do not, in the end, yield to such economic imperatives. The contrast between FitzGibbon and Phineas is instructive, as is an ironic passage of *Dr Thorne*: 'There is no doubt but that the privilege of matrimony offers opportunities to money-loving young men which ought not to be lightly abused. Too many young men marry without giving any consideration to the matter whatever. It is not that they are indifferent to money, but that they recklessly miscalculate their own value, and omit to look around and see how much is done by those who are more careful. A man can be young but once, and, except in cases of a special interposition of Providence, can marry but once. The chance once thrown away may be said to be irrecoverable! How, in after-life, do men toil and turmoil through long years to attain some prospect of doubtful advancement! Half that trouble, half that care, a tithe of that circumspection would, in early youth, have probably secured to them the enduring comfort of a wife's wealth . . . There is no road to wealth so easy and respectable as matrimony; that is, of course, provided that the aspirant declines the slow course of honest work' (ch. 18). Cf. also *The Eustace Diamonds* chs. 4 and 13 (Frank Greystock) and 9 (Lord Fawn).
[76] *Apol.* 76: 'filia autem per adulescentulos ditiores invitamento matris suae nequicquam circumlata, quibusdam etiam procis ad experiundam permissa' ('the daughter was, at her mother's suggestion, passed around to all the rather rich young men and even left on approval with some of them—but to no avail').
[77] Sid. *Epp.* 7.2.7ff.
[78] Cic. *A* 13.21a.4.

into available men.[79] Cicero picked up opinions from Scrofa and other unnamed people, as well as Nicias, and Cicero will not have been Atticus' only confidant. We cannot tell if Cornificia and her mother showed less delicacy in making their inquiries and in breaking off negotiations.

5. Personal Qualities

Good looks in a woman were an obvious qualification[80] and figure on moralists' lists of what was desired in a marriage partner. Musonius thought it would be more sensible to look for health, strength, and normal appearance rather than beauty (which laid the possessor open to special temptations);[81] Isidore thought *pudicitia* or good character should be more important than beauty in the list of female qualifications. He claims that in his day women were married for their wealth or beauty.[82] Good looks in a woman were certainly an influential motive, although one which will usually be stressed by critics who want to suggest that the man was attracted by mere externals. So Octavian wanted Livia for her beauty according to Tacitus and took her from her husband with indecent haste.[83] On the other hand, the convention that all brides are lovely will naturally reign in *epithalamia*.[84] Beauty and virginity together, says the tendentious Apuleius, meant a dowry was hardly necessary.[85] Afranius claims that people who did not much care for real dowries thought a beautiful virgin had half her dowry already.[86] Metaphorically, beauty was a dower.[87] A widow could make a good marriage as long as she was still in her prime and had a good face.[88]

Good looks in the man also figure on Isidore's lists, and Musonius

[79] Cic. *A* 13.28.4. Juventius Talna was the son of a friend of Cicero. Cornificia, whose elderliness may be relative, was sister of Q. Cornificius (quaestor 48, praetor ? 45 BC). Cicero includes Nicias' remarks on Talna's character: not particularly bright, but unassuming and provident. The identification of the two young men is accepted by Bailey, but must rest chiefly on the fact that the unnamed nominee's father was a friend of Cicero. If the identification is right, then presumably the unreliable Nicias' gossip was disproved before the second letter was written. But Cicero was being deliberately discreet (writing *A* 13.28.4 in his own hand, omitting the name in 13.21a.4), and it is possible that two different men are described.

[80] Mart. 1.10.3.

[81] 13 B. Cf. *Epigrammata Bobiensia* 22.7–8. Among the Sarakatsani the kinsmen of the prospective bridegroom inquire not only about the prestige and quality of a girl's kin, but about her industry, virtue, health, and temperament. See Campbell 39 ff.

[82] PL 83.812, *Etym.* 9.7.29.

[83] *A* 5.1.3. It is not clear whether the patrician suitor of the Maid of Ardea, 'nulla re praeterquam forma captus' (Livy 4.9.4), was infatuated or disinterested.

[84] e.g. Cat. 61.185 ff.   [85] *Apol.* 92.

[86] *Com.* 156–7: 'formosa virgo est: dotis dimidium vocant | isti qui dotis neglegunt uxorias.'

[87] Ov. *M* 9.716–17, 11.301.

[88] Sen. *Matr.* ap. Jer. *adv. Iovin.* 1.46 = 312 E: 'aetatem integram et faciem bonam.'

appears to take the same view of them as he did for women.[89] The ancients were perfectly well aware of the uses of attractive looks in winning the affections of the bride, and Pliny says bluntly that they were a fair exchange for a girl's virginity.[90] The Romans took such an interest in people's faces, physiques, and deformities that they will hardly have ignored this variable in the context of marriage. Again, the bridegroom's looks will naturally be praised in *epithalamia*.

Ugliness in either sex was obviously a handicap. The sexagenarian Cicero vetoed one potential bride on the score of her looks: 'I've never seen anything uglier.'[91] But a couple of years later, after his second divorce, he suggested that he should be safe enough from susceptible and designing women, since old age made him ugly.[92] It is clear from Suetonius' account that Galba's physical deformity would have repelled some women.[93]

Face and physique shade into the less definable and more sub-jective quality of sexual attractiveness. Marrying because of physical attraction was irresponsible: it is attested therefore by a person's detractors, for instance a man's political enemies. So, for example, Gellius Publicola married beneath him, 'not, presumably, out of lust, but to demonstrate his democratic ideology', says Cicero, clearly meaning to hit him right and left.[94] The same accusation of sexual infatuation seems, inevitably, to have been brought against Cicero himself when he married a woman young enough to be his grand-daughter, and against Claudius when he married his niece.[95] It was less useful, perhaps less convincing, and more damaging to bring such a criticism against a woman. Cicero does not quite make it against Sassia, although she is alleged to have seduced her son-in-law before she married him.[96]

Since children were the object of marriage, health and good physique are properly emphasized by the moralists as qualifications for marriage. The point had probably been made early in the Helle-nistic period by the neo-Pythagoreans.[97] Musonius regarded it as more important than beauty. 'But as for the body, it is enough for marriage that it be healthy, of normal appearance, and capable of hard work, such as would be less exposed to the snares of tempters, better adapted to perform physical labour, and not wanting in strength to beget or bear children.'[98] A virgin could not demonstrate her fertility, but it seems highly likely that someone acting in the bridegroom's interest, if not the man himself, would inform

---

[89] Isid. PL 83.812, *Etym.* 9.7.28; Mus. 13B.   [90] Pliny *Epp.* 1.14.8.
[91] *A* 12.11 (? 29 Nov. 46).   [92] *A* 15.1.4.   [93] *Galba* 3.4.
[94] *Sest.* 110: 'ut credo, non libidinis causa, sed ut plebicola videretur.'
[95] Cf. n. 60; Tac. *A* 12.3.1.   [96] *Clu.* 12–13.   [97] Thesleff, *Texts* 58.   [98] 13B.

himself of the health and external physique of a potential bride.
The gynaecologist Soranus says roundly:

Since women usually are married for the sake of children and succession,
and not for mere enjoyment, and since it is utterly absurd to make inquiries
about the excellence of their lineage and the abundance of their means but to
leave unexamined whether they can conceive or not, and whether they are fit
for childbearing or not, it is only right for us to give an account of the matter
in question. One must judge the majority from the age of 15 to 40 to be fit for
conception, if they are not mannish, compact, and oversturdy, or too flabby
and very moist. (*Gynaecology* 1.9.34, trans. Temkin, p. 32)

    And both sides could find out something about the fertility of the
two families. Women who had produced, and ideally reared, children
in a previous marriage were in a stronger position.[99] Tacitus on Pallas
on Agrippina the Younger provides the *locus classicus*, misapplied
perhaps, since at the age of about 33 and after two marriages she had
only one son. Tacitus calls her 'a woman of proven fertility'.[100] Her
mother really was 'insigni fecunditate' and proved it in her one
marriage: it would have been an attraction if she had been allowed to
look for a second husband.[101] The Elder Agrippina's remarkable
record may lie behind Pallas' inflation of her daughter's capacity.
Poppaea too was allegedly a more desirable *parti* for Nero because
her son by Rufrius Crispinus showed her fecundity.[102]
    Lack of children (*orbitas*) could be an attraction, since the husband
could benefit from wealth obtained from a previous husband[103] or be
sure that the new wife would not be a jealous stepmother to his
existing children.[104]
    Considerations of compatibility in age are not emphasized in the
sources. Although Terentia apparently criticized Cicero for marrying
a young girl, the matching of a man with a woman young enough to be
his daughter or even granddaughter was generally accepted. One has
only to think of Caesar's daughter Julia and Pompey, Marcella and
Agrippa, Augustus' daughter Julia and Agrippa, Calpurnia and

[99] e.g. Lucan 2.330ff.
[100] *A* 12.2.3: 'at Pallas id maxime in Agrippina laudare quod Germanici nepotem secum
traheret, dignum prorsus imperatoria fortuna: stirpem nobilem et familiae [Iuliae] Claudiae
posteros coniungeret, ne femina expertae fecunditatis, integra iuventa, claritudinem Caesarum
aliam in domum ferret' ('What Pallas picked out for praise in Agrippina was that she would
bring with her the grandson of Germanicus, who deserved an imperial future. Claudius ought to
join a noble stock [sc. the Domitii] and its descendants to the Julio-Claudian family and refuse
to allow a woman of tested fecundity, in the prime of life, to take the glory of the Caesars into
another house'). Note also the mention of her youth. Vitellius also stresses her fertility (Tac. *A*
12.6.1–2). The rival candidate Aelia Paetina had the advantage of a daughter whom she shared
with Claudius already (Tac. *A* 12.2.1).
[101] Tac. *A* 1.41.3, cf. 2.43.7, 2.75.1, 4.12.5.   [102] Tac. *A* 14.1.2.
[103] Tac. *A* 13.19.2.   [104] Tac. *A* 12.2.2.

Pliny.[105] For a man to marry a woman who was much older than himself was discreditable. A couple who were both old might also be criticized.[106]

6. *Character*

The moralists naturally put *pudicitia* and good character at the head of their lists:

Above all a woman must be chaste and self-controlled; she must, I mean, be pure in respect of unlawful love, exercise restraint in other pleasures, not be a slave to desire, not be contentious, not lavish in expense, nor extravagant in dress. Such are the works of a virtuous woman, and to them I would add yet these: to control her temper, not to be overcome by grief, and to be superior to uncontrolled emotion of every kind. (Musonius 3, trans. Lutz, *YCS* 10 [1947] 41)[107]

This sort of thing was a topos. Excerpts from Greek drama assembled by Stobaeus under the rubric 'That in marriage one must examine character, not good birth or wealth' include the sage remark of the comic writer Diodorus that it is better to take a well-brought-up girl without a dowry than a badly brought-up one with money, and quotations from Euripides to show that discretion is to be priced above birth or wealth or beauty.[108] The philosophers insisted on this idea. Antipater the Stoic in the second century BC thought that a happy home life was not to be achieved by choosing a wife by worldly criteria: birth, which would make her puffed up, wealth, beauty, or anything else which impresses people. Such things make her proud and domineering. A wife should be chosen for her virtues and those of her father and, particularly, her mother, who would have had more influence on her. The suitor should determine whether she imitated her parents and had not been over-indulged. The philosopher authorized him to search out all sources of information, slaves and free people from both inside and outside her household, neighbours, guests and other visitors, cooks, seamstresses, and other craftsmen and craftswomen.[109] Ocellus Lucanus (*c.*150 BC) also argued that to choose a wife for her birth or wealth instead of her compatibility and 'sympathy' led to the unnatural domination of the wife over her husband and to disharmony and conflicting aims.[110] Nicostratus (of

---

[105] Cf. Stob. 4.22.5 on inequality of age. Fantham, 'Women in antiquity: a selective (and subjective) survey 1979–84' 14–15, has useful remarks on the family structures resulting from discrepancy in the age of *coniuges*.   [106] e.g. Pliny *Epp.* 8.18.8.

[107] Cf. 4.   [108] Stob. 4.22.6, 118, 122 = *El.* 1097–9, 127 = Eur. fr. 212 N².

[109] Stob. 4.22.4.103, cf. 4.22.1.25, and, for Hierocles, 4.22.1.24.

[110] ed. Harder p. 48.

uncertain date) chose a more direct check, which he said was practised by Indian sages, that of judging from a girl's face whether she was good-tempered, cheerful, and intelligent.[111]

The moral quality most desired by Greek philosophical writers seems to have been a kindly disposition and the ability to sympathize with the husband. The ideal was for the wife to be *sympathēs*, so that the husband and wife would achieve harmony (*symphōnia*). 'We could find nothing more sympathetic than a wife, or closer kin to our children.'[112] The Greeks dreaded a bad-tempered and quarrelsome woman, one who betrayed the interests of the family into which she had married or one who tried to usurp the husband's dominant position.[113] The Romans could also isolate bad temper and arrogance as failings.[114]

The layman agreed with the moralist:

Ubi vero quaeret uxorem, videat an nuptias suas amet, an nil pluris faciat marito, an misericors sit, an fortis sit, an possit, si quid viro inciderit, mala una tolerare: si his bonis fuerit instructa, dotata est. (Seneca *Controversiae* 1.6.6)

But when he seeks a wife, let him see if she wants to marry him, if she values nothing above her husband, if she is compassionate, if she is brave, if she is capable of bearing misfortunes together with him, if anything happens to her husband; if she is equipped with these good qualities, she has a dowry.

The virtuous wife was kind, compliant, loving, steady, faithful, and subordinate, but the lack of vices receives more emphasis than positive qualities. As Plutarch sensibly points out, it is very much more important to find a wife you can live with comfortably than to go for a rich dowry.[115] Unfortunately, forecasts about an agreeable character must have been even more difficult in Roman marriages than in modern ones, which usually follow a longer and more intense acquaintance. Since Plutarch's advice about how to be a congenial and sympathetic helpmate is largely addressed to the woman, and after her wedding, rather than to the suitor negotiating for a wife, consideration of the characteristics seen to make a partnership more successful may be postponed until a later chapter.

Little is said of the moral character desired in young men. Pliny of course gave a testimonial to the energy, industry, and modesty of Acilianus as a candidate. Similarly, he congratulates Servianus (the husband of Hadrian's sister) on the selection of Fuscus Salinator for their daughter. Personal qualities appear on the list of advantages:

---

[111] Stob. 4.22.4.102.   [112] Stob. 4.22.1 = Eur. fr. 164 N²; Ocellus p. 48.
[113] Hes. *Theog.* 590ff.; Stob. 4.23.7 (Naumachius), cf. Mus. 3; Stob. 4.22.7.
[114] Jer. *adv. Iovin.* 1.48 = 316D, but if this goes back to Seneca it was muddled after he wrote it.   [115] Plut. *Praec. conj.* 141C–D.

Domus patricia, pater honestissimus, mater pari laude; ipse studiosus
litteratus etiam disertus, puer simplicitate comitate iuvenis senex gravitate.
(*Epistulae* 6.26.1)

His house is patrician, his father of the highest standing, his mother of equal
repute; he himself is a literary scholar and eloquent, a boy for innocence, a
young man for charm, and an old man for seriousness.

Fronto commends his chosen son-in-law Aufidius Victorinus (to the
council of his home city of Cirta) for *mores* and eloquence (both
qualities intended to be attractive to them).[116] In general terms,
fathers and others no doubt considered the personal character of their
daughters' future husbands. Cicero puts the man himself first in his
list of the qualifications of a potential husband for the child Caecilia
Attica, before his family and wealth and (unless the text is corrupt)
the fact that he is better born than his own father (sc. because of his
mother's family).[117]

7. Pudicitia

Evidence for a girl's pre-marital chastity was thought to be more
reliable than physiognomical diagnosis, and of all the virtues chastity
was most emphasized in Roman literature. The point is repeatedly
made in the literary sources. *Pudicitia* is a more valuable dowry;
brides should take good character as a dowry; brides give ancestral
valour and chastity as dowry; virginity is a second dowry and the only
part of the dowry which a husband cannot give back; a wife of good
character is well enough endowed.[118]

Chastity, or at least unblemished repute, was expected of girls.
Because, in the middle and upper classes, they led sheltered lives
before marriage, it is unusual to find an enemy alleging over-
familiarity with potential suitors, as Apuleius does.[119] Rather, a kiss
or more given to a family slave or freedman,[120] or an incestuous
relationship with a brother,[121] allegations no doubt often picturesque
rather than veridical. Wild fears might be entertained about seaside

---

[116] *ad amicos* 2.11 (Loeb i.292). Intellect and eloquence are also conventional criteria.
[117] Cic. *A* 13.21a.4. If this is Juventius Talna (cf. n. 79), then 13.28.4 gives Curtius Nicias'
notions about his character. In contrast, Cicero belatedly praises the natural gifts and
cultivation, along with admitted faults of character, of his unexpected son-in-law, Dolabella (*A*
7.3.12).
[118] Plaut. *Amph.* 839ff.; ps.-Sen. *Mon.* 105; Plaut. *Aul.* 239, 492–3; Hor. *O* 3.24.21ff.; Ter.
Ad. 345–6; Sen. *Contr.* 1.6.6; Apul. *Apol.* 92.
[119] Apul. *Apol.* 76.   [120] VM 6.1.3–4.
[121] For the three sisters of Clodius see allegations made at his trial for sacrilege that he
committed incest with Clodia Luculli during her marriage (Plut. *Cic.* 29.3, cf. *Luc.* 34.1, *Caes.*
10.5), general gossip about all the sisters (Plut. *Cic.* 29.4), and the specific claim by Cicero that
his incest with Clodia Metelli went back to his childhood (*Cael.* 36), antedating her marriage.
For the sisters of Gaius Suet. *Gaius* 24.

holidays.[122] Ordinarily, virginity was an attraction and *pudicitia* an endowment which might make up for lack of dowry. So Livy makes Ligustinus say that his cousin brought him only her chastity and her free status, and, as it turned out, fertility.[123]

Pudicitia, to be assumed in a cloistered girl (unless there was evidence to the contrary), was tested in marriage, as was fertility (merely an embarrassment if unaccompanied by fidelity). So Q. Metellus, an example of undiluted good luck, won a wife distinguished for chastity and fecundity;[124] the Elder Agrippina also stood out.[125] Tried chastity in a woman who had been married could be a qualification for remarriage. Hard to substantiate for a divorcee, it could be proved by a widow's initial determination to remain single and *univira*. To overcome the reluctance of a Violentilla[126] might be seen as a coup and the bridegroom might expect continuance of fidelity in the second marriage. *Pudicitia* will not be numbered among the attractions of an Agrippina Minor or a Poppaea Sabina.[127]

Unchastity is alleged as a disqualification.[128] According to Tacitus, Agrippina dissuaded the young Sextius Africanus from marrying Junia Silana, on the grounds of her age and immorality.[129] Perverse suitors are occasionally said to have found promiscuity an attraction: a republican husband who married a woman with the intention of divorcing her for adultery and keeping part of her large dowry[130] and Vestinus, who in marrying Statilia Messallina had it firmly in mind that she had Nero among her lovers.[131]

The sexual morality which conventional views expected in a man is more difficult to define. Upper-class society drew the line at passive homosexuality and incest, frowned on notorious and habitual adultery. But all the most demanding wife was entitled to expect in a husband was *pudor*, which covers not only a certain sexual restraint and sobriety but modest demeanour (particularly towards male elders and betters), indeed little more than good manners.[132] Only rarely will one find allusion to a man's ability to restrain his passions in order not to frighten a virgin bride,[133] a consideration which might

---

[122] Varro *Men.* 44. Cf. Griffin, *Latin poets and Roman life* 90–1.
[123] 42.34.3.	[124] VM 7.1.1.	[125] Above, n. 102.
[126] Stat. *S* 1.2.138ff.; cf. 3.5.	[127] Tac. *A* 12.2.3, 13.45, 14.1.2.
[128] e.g. Cic. *A* 15.29.2.	[129] Tac. *A* 13.19.2.
[130] VM 8.2.3; Plut. *Mar.* 38. Cf. Watson, *Persons* 68–9.	[131] Tac. *A* 15.68.5.
[132] The views put forward by Cicero in *Cael.* are particularly revealing (though not his own). Allegations are made by the prosecution against Caelius' chastity (*pudicitia*: Cic. *Cael.* 6, cf. 30) but his *pudor* defended him from homosexual affairs when he was younger (ibid. 9). In his famous passage on the licence which must be allowed to youth, Cicero implies that a man who has not been a passive homosexual or seduced others (probably men) or corrupted chaste women is free from accusations of loose living: 'Parcat iuventus pudicitiae suae, ne spoliet alienam . . . ne probrum castis . . . inferat' (42).	[133] Cf. *Decl. min.* 251.6.

have been important to considerate parents. There were, however, two schools of thought on the degree of violence to be used on the wedding-night.[134] Since authoritative male opinion held that girls were precociously passionate,[135] there were grounds for the view that a bridegroom should overpower his bride, since her reluctance was mere pretence. But there is a strong literary tradition about the trauma of marriage for a virgin[136] that may be supposed to have some roots in fact, so that we could wish to see in the literature some allusion to parents' concern to find a kind and considerate husband for their girl.

Views on the husband having a mistress might well vary. In comedy, some characters see a young man's affair with a courtesan as making it impossible for a girl's parents to consent to her marriage with him.[137] But other parents might regard such a tie as trivial.[138] In real life, we find Augustine giving up his concubine in order to become engaged.[139] Papinian regarded it as valid for a wife to make an agreement with her husband that he would pay her a fine if he re-engaged in sexual relations with the woman who had been his concubine before his marriage.[140]

8. Affinitas

Not just high birth, or comparably high birth, but the appropriate type of family connections might be seen as important. Cicero, in considering Talna for Attica, took some account of his acquaintance with his father. In picking candidates for Tullia's hand a few years earlier, he had given great weight to the advantage of having someone from 'his old gang', as Atticus suggested, an allusion probably to a suitor from Arpinum.[141] Pliny commends his nominee Minicius Acilianus to Junius Mauricus, a senator and uncle of a prospective bride, on the strength of an equestrian father 'from our part of Italy' ('illa nostra Italia') which had preserved the old-fashioned virtues, and of a maternal grandmother whose austerity furnished a model even to the proverbially austere people of Padua.[142] 'Mogli e buoi dei paesi tuoi.' A known background and the assumption of compatibility

[134] Claudian *Carm. min.* 25.132 ff., *contra Fesc.* 4.
[135] Hopkins, 'The age of Roman girls at marriage' 314.
[136] Cat. 62.20 ff., 45 ff.; Mart. 4.22; Plut. *QR* 29.
[137] Ter. *And.* 822, *Heaut.* 713–14, *Hec.* 538–9.
[138] Ter. *Hec.* 541–2. [139] Aug. *Conf.* 6.15. [140] *D* 45.1.121.1.
[141] *A* 6.1.10: 'tu enim ad me iam ante scripseras "ac vellem te in tuum veterem gregem rettulisses".' Arpinate connections are conjectured because the man referred to seems to be Pontidia's candidate and she seems to have Arpinate connections. See SB on *A* 115 and on *A* 5.21 (SB 114) 14.
[142] *Epp.* 1.14.4 ff. For Minicius Acilianus cf. perhaps 2.16.1. He is otherwise unknown.

(of the families, not just of the couple) and the strengthening of local ties (sometimes perhaps the joining of adjacent estates) were important to republican nobles and new men and remained important to the expanded governing class of the early Empire.[143] Conversely, strangers might be dangerous, like the plausible young man who deceived the two Marseillaises, or Apuleius, who came from out of town and won a rich widow of Oea, a success which resulted in his prosecution. At least some elementary checking of parentage and background was normal when a marriage with an outsider (*extrarius/ extraria* or *alienus/aliena*) was planned.[144]

A particular form of marriage with people of similar background is intermarriage with close relatives, whether blood relations (*cognati*) or relations by marriage (*affines*), of which more in a moment.

Marriage may consolidate existing ties; it also creates *affinitas*, not only between the partners but between the families. To the male-monopolized literary tradition, it often seems that the creation of *affinitas* between males was one of the most important results of a match, and even its chief object. A *locus classicus* is given by the (clearly Roman)[145] negotiations in Plautus' *Trinummus*. Young Lysiteles wants to redeem his prodigal friend Lesbonicus by marrying his sister. Lysiteles obtains the consent of his father Philto and sends him to negotiate:

> PHILTO. Meu' natus me ad te misit, inter te atque nos
> *adfinitatem ut conciliarem* et gratiam.
> Tuam volt sororem ducere uxorem; et mihi
> sententia eademst et volo. (442–5)

PHILTO. My son has sent me to you, to arrange a marriage-tie and good feeling between you and us. He wants to marry your sister; my decision is the same and I want it too.

This theme recurs several times,[146] and Lesbonicus in his formal expression of thanks says

> LESBONICUS. Quom *adfinitate vostra* me arbitramini
> dignum, habeo vobis, Philto, magnam gratiam. (505–6)

LESBONICUS. Because you think me worthy of a marriage-tie with you, I am very grateful to you, Philto.

[143] Wiseman, *NMRS* 60–1. Syme, *Tac.* ii.601 ff., on 'successive alliances' (p. 605) between Baetica and Narbonensis in the antecedents of the 2nd-cent. imperial family.

[144] Ter. *Ph.* 579 ff., cf. *Ad.* 672; Ov. *Her.* 14.62 for *externi generi*.

[145] The plot is Greek, but the detail is often Plautine. As a general hypothesis, I postulate that Greek and Roman views on marriage were similar and that ideas dressed by Plautus in Roman technical vocabulary were recognizably Roman (though they may also have been Greek and present in his Greek source). For a prudent analysis of how to exploit Plautus as a source for Roman *mores* see McDonnell, 'Divorce initiated by women in Rome' 54–5. For defence of the Roman nature of Plautus' handling here see Watson, *Persons* 3 ff. [146] 453, 699 ff.

When the arrangement is concluded, a message of congratulation is sent to the girl, who is otherwise a dramatic necessity of no interest as a character. The male network is completed when Lesbonicus' father returns and is at once greeted as father-in-law by Lysiteles, and further reinforced when a second marriage is arranged between Lesbonicus and the daughter of his father's faithful friend Callicles.[147]

The securing or strengthening of *affinitas* between father-in-law and son-in-law is naturally stressed. Caesar and Pompey provide a classic example,[148] a relationship which Caesar proposed to reverse after the death of Julia by marrying a daughter of Pompey.[149] Accius in a fragment from his tragedy *Oenomaus* makes Pelops tell Oenomaus that he had wanted to be his son-in-law.[150] Agrippa chose Atticus rather than Attica (if we can trust Nepos).[151] The ideal of close co-operation between father-in-law and son-in-law is vividly illustrated by Catullus' attempt to express his unusually close relationship with Lesbia in terms of the love a father bears to sons and sons-in-law.[152] So P. Crassus bound to himself the orator Ser. Sulpicius Galba by giving his daughter in marriage to Galba's son.[153] Cicero cemented his friendship with Atticus by arranging a match between his brother and Atticus' sister.[154] Augustus admitted Iullus Antonius to his close kinship by marrying him to his niece.[155] Atticus reached *affinitas* with the son of the deified Julius when his granddaughter, the child of Agrippa and Attica, was betrothed by Octavian to his stepson Tiberius when she was scarcely a year old.[156]

The creation of *affinitas* was one motive: its converse was marriage within the family.[157] Two different economic motives may be perceived: one is that the dowry of a comparatively rich woman is directed to helping a kinsman, the money is kept in the family.[158] The other is to ensure that a poor woman, with little or no dowry to attract

---

[147] 571 ff., 1151–2, 1183–4. Cf. Ter. *Hec.* 637, 723.

[148] e.g. Cat. 29.24; Vell. 2.44.3, Suet. *DJ* 21.   [149] Suet. *DJ* 27.1.

[150] *Trag.* 502–3: 'Ego ut essem adfinis tibi, non ut te extinguerem | tuam petii gnatam' ('I sought your daughter's hand so that I would be your kinsman, not your slayer').

[151] Nep. *Att.* 12.1. Cf. Hortensius' motive in marrying into Cato's family (Plut. *Cato* 25).

[152] 72.4. Cf. Cic. *Sest.* 6–7.; VM 7.1.1; Tac. *A* 1.55.5.

[153] Cic. *Brut.* 98. Cf. the pleasure given through new *affinitas* to L. Aemilius Paullus (consul 50) by the engagement of his nephew and Antony's daughter in 44 (*F* 12.2.2, with Bailey, 'Who is Junia?').   [154] Nep. *Att.* 5.3.   [155] Vell. 2.100.4.

[156] Nep. *Att.* 19.2 ff.

[157] But marrying a cousin will strengthen blood-relationship: Plaut. *Poen.* 1158: 'mi patrue, salve. nam nunc es plane meus' ('Hail, my uncle, for now you are really mine').

[158] Thomas, 'Mariages endogamiques à Rome: patrimoine, pouvoir et parenté depuis l'époque archaïque' 348, citing *D* 28.7.23.24. Cf. Moreau, 'Structures de parenté et alliance à Larinum d'après le *Pro Cluentio*' 120 ff. For 'Mediterranean endogamy' outside Rome see Pitt-Rivers, *The fate of Shechem or the politics of sex. Essays in the anthropology of the Mediterranean* 163–4.

an outsider, is not left unmarried or forced into a misalliance. The first type may be represented by the marriages with cousins which are attested in certain aristocratic families in the late Republic.[159] A striking instance is provided by M. Brutus' second marriage, to his cousin Porcia. After the death of her husband Bibulus and her father Cato, he divorced Claudia, the daughter of Ap. Claudius Pulcher, in order, says Sir Ronald Syme,[160] to strengthen 'the family tie and obligation of vengeance yet further' by marrying her. These motives may well have preponderated, but a widow with only one brother may have had a financial qualification as well.

Cousin-marriages by Ap. Claudius' sisters may have been partly motivated by the notorious shortcomings of their dowries. One was taken off her brother's hands by L. Lucullus, her mother's second cousin, with no dowry at all. Another married a first cousin, again on the side of her mother Metella, Q. Metellus Celer.[161]

The economic motive of providing a husband for a dowerless girl could probably be recognized as right and proper by the Roman audience who went to see Terence's *Phormio*.[162] The plot turns on a clever dodge by the parasite Phormio, who, when Antipho falls in love with a respectable but dowerless girl, cast on the world by the death of her mother, kindly offers to pose as a friend of her father's and bring evidence in court to show that Antipho is her nearest male relative and must marry her.[163] This apparent legal compulsion does not appeal to Antipho's father, when he returns from abroad and finds out about it: he would have preferred Antipho to exercise the other legal option and give the girl a dowry:

> DEMIPHO. . . . verum si cognata est maxume,
>   non fuit necessum habere; sed id quod lex iubet,
>   dotem dareti', quaereret alium virum.
>   Qua ratione inopem potiu' ducebat domum?   (295–8)

DEMIPHO. But however much of a relative she is, it wasn't necessary to marry her; but as the law says, you could have given her a dowry and let her look for another husband. Why did he choose instead to take a pauper to his home as his wife?

Since this is comedy, the bride he has taken will naturally turn out to be the child of his father's brother.

---

[159] Cf. Tac. *A* 12.6.5 (the Senate's debate on Claudius' marriage to his niece): 'sobrinarum [sc. coniugia] diu ignorata tempore addito percrebuisse.'

[160] *RR* 58; cf. stemma II. See also Münzer, *Römische Adelsparteien und Adelsfamilien* 340 ff.

[161] Syme, *RR* stemma I, revised by Wiseman, *Catullus and his world. A reappraisal* 16–17. For Clodia Metelli, ibid. 23–4 (no direct evidence on initiation of marriage). For Clodia Luculli see Varro *RR* 3.16.2.

[162] The Andrian woman was forced to emigrate *cognatorum neglegentia* and became first a spinster and then a hetaera (Ter. *And.* 69 ff.).   [163] 91 ff., esp. 114–15, 120, 125 ff.

A clear indication of the validity of the motive—rescuing a kins-woman from a dowerless state which would have forced her to be an oppressed wife or no wife at all—is given in the speech which Livy puts in the mouth of Sp. Ligustinus:

Cum primum in aetatem veni, pater mihi uxorem fratris sui filiam dedit, quae secum nihil adtulit praeter libertatem pudicitiamque, et cum his fecunditatem, quanta vel in diti domo satis esset. Sex filii nobis, duae filiae sunt, utraeque iam nuptae. Filii quattuor togas viriles habent, duo prae-textati sunt. (42.34.3–4)

As soon as I reached the right age, my father gave me his brother's daughter as my wife, who brought with her nothing except her free status and her chastity, and with them her fecundity, which would be enough even in a rich household. We have six sons and two daughters, both now married. Four of the sons are grown up, two are boys.

Sentimental reasons also come into play, if we can take comedy as evidence for less aristocratic circles at least. The father in *Cistellaria* compels a young man, in love with his mistress, to marry a relation (*cognata*).[164] In *Rudens*, as soon as old Daemones discovers his long-lost daughter, Palaestra, his first thought is that he will arrange a match for her:

> DAEMONES. Is improviso filiam inveni tamen;
> et eam de genere summo adulescenti dabo
> ingenuo, Atheniensi et cognato meo.   (1196–8)[165]

DAEMONES. Yet I have unexpectedly found my daughter, and I will give her to a young man of excellent family, free-born, an Athenian citizen and my kinsman.

In real life, Paulus cites an instance of a husband and wife agreeing that her son by a previous marriage and his daughter by a previous marriage should be betrothed, and drawing up a legal document which penalized anyone who stopped the marriage. But on the father's death the daughter refused to marry her stepbrother. A case against the father's heirs for damages was rejected by the jurist, on the grounds that the stipulation was immoral and that it was dis-honourable to tie up with penalties any marriage, whether future or already contracted.[166] In this example the parents' motive is not indicated.

Unsentimental reasons of state or dynastic politics might sway Lucullus, whose cousin-marriage is mentioned above,[167] or Augustus, who organized multiple and permutated endogamy, aiming at the

---

[164] 97–8, 195, 498.   [165] Cf. 1214.
[166] *D* 45.1.134 pr., *lib. xv resp.* Y. Thomas, 'Mariages endogamiques' 349, takes the motive to be the consolidation of inheritance from both parents.   [167] n. 29.

perpetuation of his line through his only daughter and the maximum concentration of Julian blood in possible successors. Tiberius kept his two daughters-in-law, the elder Agrippina and Livia Julia, as widows, for lack of suitable Julio-Claudian husbands.[168] A generation later, it was (according to Tacitus) the view of the minister Pallas, whose experience in the households of the long-widowed Antonia and of the uxorious Claudius must have made him an authority on the subject, that the emperor could not afford to let his niece the younger Agrippina go off and marry outside the family, because she took with her the blood of Germanicus. Better the shocking uncle–niece marriage.[169]

There were possible disadvantages which went with marriage with close kin. Plutarch, presumably thinking of the comparatively late introduction of marriage with first cousins and the absence of marriage with full sisters or half-sisters, seems to believe that the Romans avoided marriage between close relatives and asks why they did not marry close kinswomen. Was it so that they could enlarge their relationships by marrying outsiders or because they were afraid of quarrels within the family or so that a woman would have more protectors (since her husband would not be wearing the second hat of a kinsman)?[170]

We have so far concentrated on attested motive. More general information may now be sought about the practice of endogamy within families. But first we need to clarify Roman concepts of cousinship. The Romans divided cousins as follows:

Quarto gradu sunt . . . ex transverso . . . fratres patrueles sorores patrueles (id est qui quaeve ex duobus fratribus progenerantur), item consobrini consobrinaeque (id est qui quaeve ex duabus sororibus nascuntur, quasi consororini), item amitini amitinae (id est qui quaeve ex fratre et sorore

---

[168] Cf. Tac. *A.* 4.12, 39–40, 52–3.   [169] *A* 12.2.

[170] Plut. *QR* 289 D–E. According to *QR* 265 D, marriage with first cousins became legal at Rome after scandal had been caused by the marriage of a poor man with a cousin who was an heiress. The people acquitted him, thus setting a precedent. Cf. for second cousins Livy fr. of bk. 20 (edited by Krueger, 'Anekdoton Livianum'), which is a précis rather than a direct quotation: 'Livius libro vicesimo. P. Celius [? *read* Cloelius] patricius primus adversus veterem morem intra septimum cognationis gradum duxit uxorem. Ob hoc M. Rutilius plebeius sponsam sibi praeripi novo exemplo nuptiarum dicens seditionem populi concitavit adeo ut patres territi in Capitolium perfugerent' (241–219 BC). Cf. Weiss, 'Endogamie und Exogamie im römischen Kaiserreich' 355, Y. Thomas, 'Mariages endogamiques' 351–2. It is not certain that the alleged custom of not marrying cousins is historical. There is no word in the ancient sources to indicate that only *fratres patrueles* and *consobrini* in the strict sense were forbidden to marry, as is held for instance by Franciosi, *Clan gentilizio e strutture monogamiche. Contributo alla storia della famiglia romana* i.168. Some accounts—e.g. DH *Ant.* 1.64.2–3 with Serv. ad *A* 7.366; 3.13.4—suggest that cousin-marriage was held to have been possible in legendary times. I do not understand why Gratwick holds that 'First-cousin marriages do not appear in Plautus or Terence at all, yet marriages of this degree of kin were commonplace in . . . New Comedy' (*CHCL* ii.113).

propagantur). Sed fere vulgus omnes istos communi appellatione consobrinos vocant. (*Digest* 38.10.1.6, Gaius *viii ad edictum provinciale*)

In the fourth degree there are . . . laterally . . . *fratres patrueles* and *sorores patrueles* (that is, male and female children of two brothers), and also *consobrini* and *consobrinae* (that is, male and female children of two sisters) and *amitini* and *amitinae* (that is, male and female children of a brother and of a sister). But ordinary people usually call all these by the common appellation of *consobrini*.[171]

The first are respectively 'the child of one's paternal uncle', 'the child of one's maternal aunt'. The viewpoints vary: while *patruelis* is the child of my *patruus*, *consobrini* looks at the relationship from the point of view of the older generation: the children of two sisters. *Amitinus/a* (rarely used) is formed from *amita*, which is a paternal aunt, but is made to cover the child of a maternal uncle (*avunculus*). *Patrueles* and *consobrini* coincide with the sociologist's classification of 'parallel cousins', which in French at least may be more helpfully called patrilineal and matrilineal parallel cousins. *Consobrinus* is then extended to cover, not only *patrueles* but also 'cross cousins', the children of a brother and a sister, who again subdivide into ego's mother's brother's child and ego's father's sister's child. The Romans may initially have attached more importance to *patrueles*, the only type of cousin who were agnates and bore the same name, but this distinction had been thoroughly obscured by the time of Trebatius, even though it had some relevance still for intestate succession.

Augustine picked up Plutarch's point in a discussion of kindred and affinity which goes back to Adam and Eve, whose children necessarily and whose grandchildren unnecessarily contracted brother–sister matches. Such unions then became taboo, even among pagans.

Experti autem sumus in conubiis consobrinarum etiam nostris temporibus propter gradum propinquitatis fraterno gradui proximum quam raro per mores fiebat, quod fieri per leges licebat, quia id nec divina prohibuit et nondum prohibuerat lex humana . . . Fuit autem antiquis patribus religiosae curae, ne ipsa propinquitas se paulatim propaginum ordinibus dirimens longius abiret et propinquitas esse desisteret, eam nondum longe positam rursus matrimonii vinculo colligere et quodam modo revocare fugientem. Unde iam pleno hominibus orbe terrarum, non quidem sorores ex patre vel matre vel ex ambobus suis parentibus natas, sed tamen amabant de suo genere ducere uxores. Verum quis dubitet honestius hoc tempore etiam consobrinorum prohibita esse coniugia, non solum secundum ea, quae

---

[171] Cf. G 3.10: 'fratres patrueles . . . qui ex duobus fratribus progenerati sunt, quos plerique etiam consobrinos vocant.' *D* 38.10.10.15 lists all three types, adding that e.g. Trebatius calls them all *consobrini*, and pointing out that the parents may only be half-siblings. There are therefore sixteen types of first cousin, those in the fourth degree.

disputavimus, propter multiplicandas adfinitates, ne habeat duas necessitu-
dines una persona, cum duae possint eas habere et numerus propinquitatis
augeri; sed etiam quia nescio quo modo inest humanae verecundiae quid-
dam naturale atque laudabile. (*de Civitate Dei* 15.16)

We are aware that even in our own time intermarriage with *consobrinae* has
rarely occurred in practice, because the degree of kinship is next to the
degree of brother and sister. This was so although law allowed it, since it was
not prohibited by divine law and had not yet been prohibited by human law
. . . For our fathers of old took solemn care that relationship should not cut
itself off gradually by setting out rows of slips and cease to be relationship,
but that before it was planted too far away they fastened it up and made it
turn back by the bond of matrimony. So when the earth was now full of
people, they did not take wives who were their sisters born from the same
father or mother or both parents, but they still loved to take wives from their
own kind. Does anyone doubt that it is more honourable that the marriage of
cousins is now forbidden? The reason is not only the one we discussed, that
relationships by marriage should be multiplied, so that one person should
not have a double connection when two persons could have it, and that the
number of relations should be increased, but also because somehow there is
something natural and praiseworthy in human modesty.

The chronology of all this is vague, and when he talks of our fathers of
old he is more likely to be thinking of the patriarchs and the marriages
of Isaac and Jacob (a favourite theme among Church fathers) than of
the Romans. The prohibition of cousin-marriage to which he refers is
attributed to Theodosius.[172] But the second conjecture of Plutarch
and the North African bishop's opinion on multiplying *affinitates* both
seem to reflect a Roman view.[173]

   Although marriage with first cousins was an option which in certain
circumstances families would choose to exercise, the evidence is
against the conclusion that such alliances were habitually preferred.
Augustine specifically states that his experience disproved it, but we
may doubt his breadth of observation. Saller and Shaw have argued
effectively that the inscriptions of the western Roman world indicate
that marriage of brothers' children cannot have been practised on a
significant scale.[174] Unfortunately the epigraphic evidence normally
reveals only *coniuges* who might be children of brothers who had the
same *nomen*, so the figures only give us the maximum number of

---

[172] Ps.-Aur. Victor *Epit. de Caes.* 48.10, Ambrose *Epp.* 60.8. See Y. Thomas, 'Mariages
endogamiques' 348, on the ineffectiveness of the prohibitions.
[173] The Spaniard Isidore (*Etym.* 9.6.29) takes over Augustine's viticultural sentence almost
verbatim. I have not seen Ph. Moreau, 'Plutarque, Augustin, Lévy-Strauss', *Rev. belge de phil.
et d'hist.* 56 (1978) 41 ff. See Y. Thomas, 'Mariages endogamiques' 380, who argues that
Augustine borrowed from an antiquarian.
[174] Saller and Shaw, 'Close-kin marriage in Roman society?'. The fact that many of the
inscriptions in the sample come from the military might distort.

theoretically possible cousins linked through two brothers. We have no way of identifying cousins whose mothers were sisters, or children of a brother and a sister. Further, Saller and Shaw also surveyed marriages in a sample of six well-attested senatorial families during the Principate, the Acilii Glabriones, Aemilii Lepidi, Annii Veri, Arrii Antonini, Aurelii, and Calpurnii Pisones, which reveal 'not one between cousins related within a legally recognized degree'. A sample of 110 consuls from the early second century AD confirms. But here again they appear to have focused only on cousins through brothers. The stemma of the Aemilii Lepidi, to take one example, may not show any Aemilia Lepida married to an Aemilius Lepidus, but it contains good examples of other sorts of cousin-marriages. The triumvir M. Aemilius Lepidus had a son, M. Aemilius Lepidus, who married Servilia. Young Lepidus and Servilia were first cousins through their mothers, the two Juniae. The triumvir's great nephew, L. Aemilius Paullus, consul in AD 1, was married to Julia, the granddaughter of Augustus. His parents were Paullus Aemilius Lepidus and Cornelia, daughter of Augustus' ex-wife Scribonia by a previous marriage, which was not in itself a recommendation except that this made her half-sister of Augustus' daughter Julia. The couple were half-cousins on their mothers' sides.[175]

The immediate family of Augustus is the extreme case. His daughter Julia married his sister Octavia's son, Marcellus. Octavia's daughter Marcella the younger had a son, Messalla Barbatus, who married Domitia Lepida, daughter of Antonia the elder, another daughter of Octavia. Marcella and Antonia were half-sisters, which makes their children half-*consobrini*. In the same generation, Lepida's full *consobrinus*, Germanicus, son of the younger Antonia and grandson of Octavia, married Agrippina the elder, granddaughter of Augustus and therefore his second cousin. His sister, Livia Julia, another grandchild of Octavia, married Augustus' grandson C. Caesar, her second cousin and Agrippina's brother. Later she married Drusus Caesar, the only son of her father's brother, her first cousin. The youngest of the family, Claudius, married Valeria Messallina, daughter of Domitia Lepida: his mother and both her grandmothers were daughters of Octavia, so they were first cousins once removed. In the next generation, of Germanicus' children, his son Nero Caesar married Julia, daughter of the first-cousin marriage between Drusus

---

[175] *PIR²* i.57 and Syme, *RR* stemma IV. Later intermarriage with the imperial family was ill-starred. Paullus' cousin Aemilia Lepida was engaged to the younger Julia's brother L. Caesar, who died before they could marry. In the next generation a brother and sister married Germanicus' children Drusilla and Drusus. But they produced no children to give us cousin-marriages.

and Livia Julia and herself his first cousin, through his father and her mother. Counting through her father, they were merely second cousins. Germanicus' daughter Agrippina the younger married Cn. Domitius Ahenobarbus, son of her mother's sister the elder Antonia, her first cousin. By the time we get to the final flower of this policy, the marriage of the future emperor Nero and his former adoptive sister Octavia, the multiplicity of their ties has got out of hand. They were first cousins once removed, since his grandfather and her father were brothers. They were second cousins, since their fathers were sons of the Antoniae. They were also third cousins, by her descent from Messallina, daughter of Domitia daughter of Antonia the elder, and his from Agrippina daughter of Germanicus son of Antonia the younger. Again tracing Messallina's line, Octavia was a great-granddaughter of Antonia the elder, and Nero was a grandson: which makes them first cousins once removed. So much for the more prominent members of the family. There is no indication in any of the sources that this dynastic policy inspired revulsion, though, largely beginning with the difficult circumstances of Augustus, it carried close-cousin marriage to apparently quite unprecedented lengths.

Augustus' family also reinforced links established by marriage. His niece Marcella the elder married her mother's second husband's son, Iullus Antonius. He eventually chose to arrange a match between his own daughter and his wife's son. Livia's other son had previously been married to Augustus' niece.

Saller and Shaw's researches are sufficient to show that the marriage of the children of two brothers was not *the* preferred or even a common pattern either for the upper classes or the inhabitants of the Romanized West as a whole. Such marriages did occur and were not, in the classical period, contemned, or Livy would not attribute such a match to Ligustinus and Cicero would condemn Antony's marriage to Antonia. Others have argued that marriages of the children of two sisters or of a brother and a sister, that is, marriages across agnatic boundaries, were always more acceptable. Without going into conjectural reconstructions of ancient taboos, it seems possible to find practical reasons which might make such matches more common in historical times.

In a peasant society, if two brothers inherited property from their *paterfamilias* and wanted to keep it together or reunite it (for one generation) after their own deaths, and if they only had one child each but of opposite sex, then the simple solution of matching the cousins will easily have presented itself. The grandfather's estate was kept together; no dowry went out of the immediate family, but no new dowry came in. The father of the only daughter saw himself succeeded in due course by grandsons of the same *nomen*. If the brothers each had a son, this expedient immediately became less attractive. By the second century BC, although ancestral property might be kept in the family as long as possible, the main family house and land could easily be passed on as a unit to one member, perhaps the eldest son, as happened in Cicero's family, and the younger compensated with other property. The specific economic motive for marriage of *fratres patrueles*, of avoiding fragmentation of land, no longer applied. Diversification of holdings, complicated testamentary dispositions, and dotal contracts offered more flexibility. Perpetuation of the name may have continued to be a motive. On the other hand, if there were two brothers both intent on maximizing their *affinitates* for the sake of political careers, it made good sense for them to deploy their children to make new connections. We would scarcely expect M. Cicero to have considered young Q. Cicero a useful match for his daughter, even if their ages had been suitable.

The marriage of a brother's daughter and a sister's son may also be useful if the brother has no son. Brothers quite frequently adopted their sister's sons in order to perpetuate their names.[176] An alternative is that perhaps chosen by Augustus for Marcellus: did he design to adopt the grandsons which Julia might bear to her cousin, as he in fact adopted her two eldest sons by Agrippa?

But where the brother has a son of his own, the main feature of such a marriage is that it doubles the bond between two patrilineal families. The same is true of marriages between a brother's son and sister's daughter, which also restores the woman to her mother's natal family. Better still, the marriage of children of two sisters makes a marriage-tie between two patrilineal families previously linked only by the blood-tie of the sisters. So, for instance, of Octavia's daughters Marcella the younger married into the Valerii Messallae and Antonia the elder married into the Domitii Ahenobarbi: the marriage of their children plants a Domitia among the Valerii.

But by this period it is important not to concentrate attention on the male line. The links between and through women, though frequently hidden because the women themselves are unmentioned in the sources and because nomenclature does not, until the time of Augustus, begin to tell us about maternal lineage, seem often to have been strong. One would like to guess that affection between sisters, married into different families, resulted in close contact between their children, as the etymology of *consobrini* might suggest, and that, since matchmaking was at least as much a pursuit of a network of

---

[176] See Hallett, *Fathers and daughters in Roman society* 163–4, for a recent statement.

matrons as of thoughtful *patresfamilias*, cousin-marriage sometimes resulted. We can call the motive family affection or family solidarity, in the broad sense of family.

In a society in which remarriage was common, renewal of family ties between step-relations and descendants of half-siblings seems to have worked in much the same way as marriage with cousins, as examples already cited from the Augustan period have suggested.

The Romans were, as Augustine says, concerned to make new bonds in their families. As the jurists' discussions of kindred show, they counted the lineages in both male and female lines. They intermarried not only with first cousins, but with those whose blood relationship was quite distant, as when Clodia married L. Lucullus, her mother's second cousin through his mother. They counted kin up to the seventh degree, which could theoretically include 1,024 types of relative. The sixth degree, important for succession in Augustan legislation, contained a mere 448 types of relative, which takes us up to grandchildren of first cousins, grandchildren of great uncles and aunts or of parents' nieces and nephews, and various others. As Modestinus sensibly says, it was not easy to go beyond the sixth grade.[177] He goes on to discuss relationship by marriage, which did not have degrees.[178]

Apuleius, in the cosmopolitan Graeco-Roman world of the second century, gives a charmingly sentimental portrayal of a projected match between cousins in a Greek town. Charite breathlessly tells her own story:

Speciosus adolescens inter suos principalis, quem filium publicum omnis sibi civitas cooptavit, meus alioquin consobrinus, tantulo triennio maior in aetate, qui mecum primis ab annis nutritus et adultus individuo contubernio domusculae, immo vero cubiculi torique, sanctae caritatis adfectione mutuo mihi pigneratus votisque nuptialibus pacto iugali pridem destinatus, consensu parentum tabulis etiam maritus nuncupatus, ad nuptias officio frequenti cognatorum et adfinium stipatus templis et aedibus publicis victimas immolabat . . . (*Metamorphoses* 4.26)

A handsome youth, of the first rank among his fellow citizens, whom the whole city claimed as a son of the community, and, besides, my cousin, just three short years older than me, who was bred and brought up with me from our earliest years in inseparable companionship in our home, practically in the same bedchamber and couch, pledged to me by the shared sentiment of holy love and long since destined for a pact of marriage by vows to marry,

[177] *D* 38.10.10.18, Paul, ibid. 17, ht 3, G, 4 pr., Mod.
[178] But there were names for relations by marriage in the vertical line as far up as grandparents-in-law and as far down as grandchildren-in-law and across to brother- and sister-in-law. There was even a name for the women who were wives of two brothers in relation to each other: *ianitrices* (*D* 38.10.3–6; cf. Isid. *Etym.* 9.7.17).

announced also as my husband by a written contract with the consent of our parents, was on his way to the wedding, surrounded by a great crowd of kinsmen and connections and sacrificing in the temples and public shrines . . .

9. *Motives of Affection*

This charming vignette, typical of the romantic novel, allows us to pass to another possible set of motives, masked in our sources. Charite is allowed to love her future husband because he is a cousin. In marriage within the family group, the original affection of young people who knew each other well gave a practical basis for a new relationship. I suspect that the engagement of Drusus and Antonia, which led to a marriage idealized as affectionate and exclusive and the long widowhood of the *univira*, was rooted in an original liking between them, as well as in the affection Augustus and Livia had for them. They had been brought up in the closely linked households of Livia and Octavia, were close in age, and must have felt like cousins.

Without an 'excuse' such as a shared childhood, the beginning and growth of affection was more difficult to justify. The story of Sulla and Valeria fits the traditional portrayal of his character, while his careful checking of her background before he gave rein to his feelings fits the gravity of a Roman senator. His enemies claimed that Catiline had fallen in love with Orestilla (with the extreme consequence that he murdered his son). Terentia (or those who circulated the story about her—but the account may be reliable, since it presumably goes back to Tiro) thought people might believe that Cicero had fallen in love with Publilia. Although she was a young girl at her first marriage, Cicero had been her guardian and so presumably knew her fairly well.[179]

If we may trust Dio's account, prior affection was a familiar enough motive for Augustus to take it into account. In his speech on the Papio-Poppaean Law of AD 9, his second attempt at legislating men into matrimony, Dio makes him point out the concessions he had made (in the previous Julian Law): 'I allowed men outside the Senate to marry freedwomen, so that if anyone was inclined to such a marriage by love (*erōs*) or familiarity (*synētheia*: cf. *consuetudo*) he might do it lawfully.'[180] Augustus' 'concession' seems in fact only to have been a restatement of what was previously allowed: his innovation is to deny such marriages to *senatorii*. Dio is right in remarking that the law made room for emotional motivation in making a

[179] Plut. *Sulla* 35.3 ff., *Cic.* 41.3–4; Sall. *BC* 15.2–3. Cf. Tac. *A* 12.3.1.
[180] 56.7.2.

marriage. A remarkable instance of this is furnished by the new laws which aimed at regulating manumission of slaves. The general rule was that owners under the age of 20 could not free slaves and slaves under 30 could not be freed, unless a special case was made to a council. Among reasons for freeing a slave which were recognized as valid was a young man's wish to marry his slavewoman.[181] It appears then to be the lawmakers' perception that men were reluctant to marry and that one way to encourage them was to allow them to follow their own feelings.

Falling in love at sight is what young men in comedy do (without always intending marriage): it remains more acceptable for men than for women. Statius portrays Arruntius Stella as falling in love with the widowed Violentilla and Violentilla (through the intervention of Venus) as in turn falling in love with him.[182] This is all thoroughly acceptable, although Violentilla's resolve to remain faithful to her dead husband must not be broken lightly. When the long-widowed Pudentilla married Apuleius, her kinsmen charged him with having used magic to make her besotted with him. They avoided claiming that she had fallen in love naturally, which would not have allowed any case against Apuleius. But he is able to claim that she loved him, justifying this by the encouragement she had previously been given by her son to marry him.[183]

It may be postulated, though not proved, that a growth in individualism and an increased tendency to seek for personal happiness in private life had led to heightened expectations of emotional rewards in marriage around the time of Cicero. Such a trend cannot be quantified or precisely dated. But I shall argue in Chapter 8 that in the mid-first century BC, when our sources are much richer than earlier, we have vivid portrayals, sometimes idealized, sometimes as 'realistic' as we can expect, of the joys of life in the close family circle of husband, wife, and children. When there is friction between husband and wife, the whole household is upset.[184] When harmony is lost between Cicero and Terentia, instead of continuing to avoid each other (which was comparatively simple, given the number of houses they owned), they considered divorce and remarriage (probably for both of them) the best solution. Similarly, Octavian claimed that he divorced Scribonia for incompatibility.[185]

Three elements come together. First, the idealization of marriage as a mutual support, involving fidelity, self-sacrifice, mutual respect, public displays of closeness and trust (iconographically, the handclasp; the ritual kiss on greeting and farewell, the normal gesture

[181] G 1.18–19; *Tit. Ulp.* 1.12 ff. [182] *S* 1.2. [183] Apul. *Apol.* e.g. 84–5.
[184] Cic. *A* 5.1.3–4. [185] Suet. *DA* 62.2.

between equals). This is attested as early as Plautus.[186] Second, perhaps increased expectations of personal happiness, in career satisfaction (most confidently diagnosed in the behaviour of politicians in the late Republic) and private life.[187] Third, a romanticism spreading from the literary portrayal and the actuality of erotic relationships with social equals and inferiors.

If this reconstruction is accepted, then it is hard to deny that such views of the ideal nature of marriage itself and of the possibility of individual gratification or happiness must have had some impact on the selection of a husband or wife. In societies where first marriages are usually arranged by parents or other kin and where the couple are very young (and perhaps do not meet until the wedding), it is hoped that proper sentiments will develop after the marriage begins. Traditional Hindu society is an obvious example. Rome is not. It is likely that in society at large most girls married in their late teens. For those who married younger, it is likely that parents were responsible for the choice, but that does not mean that parents failed to consider the potential affective relationship between their daughter and the suitor. Moreover, the man was normally fully adult. He would have some freedom to decide whether he felt he could live happily with a particular woman. At a woman's second marriage, she would also be able to consider personal feelings. The gamut of such feelings could run from a lack of revulsion in an obedient daughter through mild liking to affection and expectations of marital happiness to the romantic passion which the moralists deprecated. Tullia might properly reject a suitor because she disliked him; she was also allowed to feel liking when she accepted Dolabella. The conventions have some points of contact with those of the English eighteenth century.

But the writings attributed to Rome's one female erotic poet, which circulated in her high aristocratic circle, would have shocked an English papa. Sulpicia was the granddaughter of Servius Sulpicius Rufus, the jurist and friend of Cicero and of Postumia, who advised Cicero on Tullia's third marriage. Her father was the younger Servius Sulpicius Rufus, her mother a Valeria. Her mother's brother, who looked after her, was Messalla Corvinus, who had been a student at Athens with young M. Cicero, fought for Brutus at Philippi, and later stood high in the counsels of Octavian. This patrician lady ranked as high as any woman outside Augustus' family in the 20s. She moved in the circle of poets her uncle had collected; like them, she was educated and sophisticated, *docta puella*, and wrote charming and passionate elegies. She appears to be not yet married; she is

---

[186] *Amph.* 711 ff.   [187] Hopkins, *DR* 79 ff.

surrounded by anxious friends, particularly her uncle, who worry that she will marry beneath her; she is not allowed to do what she wants; the man she is in love with (who is concealed under the Greek name Cerinthus) may prefer some common whore to her, 'Servius' daughter Sulpicia', and she has to be careful to preserve her reputation, but she is passionately in love. She exults in her passion's consummation and asserts the appropriateness of the match. What does her repute matter? 'But it delights me to have sinned, I am sick of wearing a calm face to deceive rumour: let it be said that I have been a worthy woman with a worthy man.'[188]

I have little doubt that these are the preliminaries to a marriage which was socially a *digna condicio*. What is striking is that now a marriage for which the groundwork may well have been laid by Messalla, Valeria, and numerous well-meaning elders is presented by a protagonist in the guise of a romantic affair. The subject is, I think, the private preliminaries to marriage, the kisses once concealed and the subject of rumour, which then become licit.[189] In her verses Sulpicia explores the same themes of romance and eroticism as do her male contemporaries, always leaving us in doubt about what is real and what imagined. But unlike the men she can play with the tension between her claim to freedom and the anxious concern of her family, between the danger of making a silly mistake and passion, between reputation and love.[190] It could be argued that all this is the fantasy of an extra-marital affair, an adulterous fling with a man ineligible for matrimony, the obverse of the liaisons of Horace with various insubstantial hetaerae. But it makes better sense as an assertion of the claim of a high-born woman to experience love, before marriage, with a future husband.

Choice may always in practice be relatively restricted, but it was not restricted in the Roman upper classes in quite the way that the schemata of the moralists would lead us to expect. The Romans did not choose *coniuges* simply by reference to objective criteria: both opportunities and limitations imposed by circumstances and individual choice were the most important factors in determining selection.

10. The Lower Classes

Since literary and juristic sources are lacking, little is known specifically about selection of marriage partners among the lower classes. Professor Brunt has suggested that economic calculations should

---

[188] [Tib.] 3.13–18. See esp. 3.14.5, 16 5–6, 14.8, 16.3–4, 13.2, 18.6, 13.9–10. Cf. Lowe, 'Sulpicia's syntax'.   [189] Stat. *S* 1.2.30.   [190] 13.16.2.

have discouraged the free-born poor from marrying. Others have credited them with more courage and less prudence. The sort of popular literature which might tell us what poor citizens thought has almost disappeared, though a stray line from a farce called *Condiciones* gives a hint that they sometimes felt they could not afford to marry.[191]

It can be suggested that endogamy within trades or related jobs was not uncommon. In the late Empire, in some occupations which were vital to the state, such as baking, women who inherited a business were compelled by law to marry men who could carry on the work.[192] But earlier the reasons for such marriages will have been purely economic and practical: people involved in such work are likely to know each other and need each other.

The major consideration of social status at this level will have been free birth or at least free status.[193] Ligustinus emphasizes the free (and no doubt free-born) position of his cousin-wife. As Maecenas admitted men to his friendship as long as they were free-born, so in less aristocratic circles, where intermarriage with ex-slaves was acceptable to some, others would prefer to keep their family free from the taint of servile origin. Since freedmen themselves on their monuments are often concerned to draw attention to the free birth of at least some of their children,[194] since Horace implicitly ranks himself above his father,[195] it is understandable that Livy (though anachronistically) makes the peasant soldier Ligustinus draw attention to the social status of his wife.

On the other hand, intermarriage between free-born and freed was fairly common among the *opifices* and *tabernarii* (craftsmen and shopkeepers) of the late Republic and early Empire. At this point we may draw attention to the republican inscription of Larcia Horaea, who was freed on account of her virtues by her owners, a husband and wife who were themselves freed, and married to one of their two sons. The epitaph gives some idea of the avowed motives for the elevation of a slave-girl to freedwoman and wife.[196]

For the slave class itself, evidence on the motives for the formation of *contubernia* is naturally sparse. The reasons which led owners to arrange, encourage, or endorse matings were child-breeding (as in

[191] Brunt, *IM* 136–40; den Boer, 'Demography in Roman history: facts and impressions'; Pomponius Bononiensis *Com*. 34: 'Vix nunc quod edim invenio: quid nam fiet, si quam duxero?' Stobaeus in 'That it is not good to marry' has only one passage making the specific point that it is bad for a poor man to marry and have children (4.22.2.29).

[192] Waltzing *Étude historique sur les corporations professionnelles chez les Romains jusqu'à la chute de l'empire de l'occident* ii ch.2.   [193] Cf. Ter. *Ph*. 168–9.

[194] e.g. *AE* 1939.10.   [195] Hor. *S* 1.6.8.   [196] *ILLRP* 977.

the free population) and morale. Meritorious slaves would be re-
warded with a mate.[197] How far slaves were able to choose for
themselves is unclear. If they were, the same sort of criteria which
operated for free people no doubt had their effect: social standing in
slave society, career prospects (especially likelihood of manumission), the size of the slave's *peculium* (pocket-money and private
property, which might be considerable), physical attractiveness. As it
happens, the tomb inscriptions of slaves and ex-slaves so often stress
affection in their married lives that it is hard not to think that this
sometimes preceded the initiation of *contubernium*. For instance,
Aurelia Philematium met her future husband when they were both
slaves and she was 7 years old. We do not know when their *contubernium* and when their legal marriage began, but the epitaph suggests
that they were fond of each other from their first meeting.[198]

11. Conclusions

Consideration of what the ancients say about the criteria for the
selection of a husband or wife has suggested variety and multiplicity
of motive. In individual instances, outsiders might see one motive as
dominant or select one for praise or blame. Modern writers also tend
to attribute one overriding reason to each marriage which they
discuss. Reconstructions of political history naturally tend to give a
privileged place to considerations of political advantage, that is, the
aggrandizement of individual politicians rather than the securing of a
majority for a particular measure. But even the rather general
accounts of motivation which we have discussed suggest that calculations of the characteristics of a potential *coniunx* were intricate. It is a
pity that we do not have accounts of the thought-processes of all the
parties to even one Roman marriage. But something can be learnt
both of private calculations and of overtly stated reasons if we
examine the etiquette and practical steps which led to formal
betrothal.

[197] Cato *Ag.* 143.   [198] *ILLRP* 793.

4

From Negotiation to Engagement

When you become engaged to someone, I, or your father, should
his health permit him, will inform you of the fact. An engagement should come on a young girl as a surprise, pleasant or
unpleasant, as the case may be. It is hardly a matter that she
could be allowed to arrange for herself.

> (Lady Bracknell in Oscar Wilde, *The Importance of Being
> Earnest* Act I)

I. Actors and Agents

PASSAGES dealing with the creation of *affinitas* and the motive for
marriage which it constitutes often give some indication of who took
the initiative. The senior male was often regarded as the main
agent—so, for instance, Augustus or P. Crassus.[1] But this may reflect
chiefly his power of taking the final decision and does not exclude an
initial approach by the junior man or the suitor. So Lysiteles offers
for Lesbonicus' sister, although he uses his own father as his intermediary and acts in the absence of Lesbonicus' father.

An abortive attempt is described in some detail by Tacitus. The
powerful *eques* Sejanus, who had allegedly begun an affair with
Tiberius' daughter-in-law before the death of her second husband
Drusus, was prompted by her to fulfil his promise to marry her. He
therefore wrote to the emperor as head of her family, suggesting that
his services were enough to merit a close connection (*coniunctio*) with
the imperial house and presenting himself as a candidate for Livia
Julia's hand, if a husband was required. Tiberius replied that princes
did not have the freedom of choice allowed to other mortals, but had
to put their fair fame first. So he would not give the easy answer, that
Livia herself could decide whether to marry again, or that she could
consult her mother and grandmother, who were more closely related
to her than himself (her uncle and father-in-law) and better fitted to
advise her (that is, had she not been a member of the imperial family).

---

[1] ch. 3 nn. 154ff.; *HA Sev.* 14.9 etc.

He drew attention to the exacerbation of the feud between Livia and Agrippina and the difficulties between their sons (his grandsons) which would follow such a marriage, and the improbability of Livia allowing her husband to remain a modest *eques*. However (he deceitfully concluded), he would not oppose Sejanus' and Livia's plans.[2] For our purposes, it does not matter if Tacitus is an accurate reporter here. The account shows how he thought such delicate negotiation might be handled between a suitor who combined impudence with diplomacy and long experience in dealing with Tiberius and an emperor who in a sense stood *in loco parentis* to the woman and was noted for his caution in bestowing imperial brides, his deviousness, and guile. Not, perhaps, a typical case of negotiation initiated by a junior, but one which would not seem altogether aberrant to an upper-class readership.

Though the scheming Sejanus is hardly a typical case of a man in seach of a bride, it is clear that bachelors were often on the hunt for eligible wives. The younger Q. Cicero was fairly precocious. Agricola seems to have gone to Rome with the firm intention of finding a wife, and M. Cicero was certainly on the look-out after his divorce from Terentia.[3] The initiative must often have come from the bridegroom.

An example of initial approach by the woman's father may be culled from Terence's *Andria*, where the virtuous reputation of young Pamphilus is such that Chremes comes to his father to suggest a match:

> SIMO. . . . Hac fama impulsus Chremes
> ultro ad me venit, unicam gnatam suam
> cum dote summa filio uxorem ut daret.
> Placuit: despondi . . .   (99–102)

SIMO. . . . influenced by this reputation, Chremes on his own initiative came to me and suggested giving his only daughter with an excellent dowry in marriage to my son. I agreed. I made the engagement . . .

When a woman reached marriageable age or was divorced or widowed while still reasonably young, it was natural and usual that suitors would present themselves, as King Latinus' heiress Lavinia in more heroic times was sought in marriage by many men from mighty Latium and the whole of Italy.[4] The word for suitor, *procus*, is used chiefly in mythological contexts, but the verb *petere* is used regularly

---

[2] *A* 4.39–40.   [3] Cic. *A* 15.29.2; Tac. *Ag*. 6.1; Cic. *A* 12.11.
[4] Verg. *A* 7.52 ff.: 'Sola domum et tantas servabat filia sedes | iam matura viro, iam plenis nubilis annis. | Multi illam magno e Latio totaque petebant | Ausonia; petit ante alios pulcherrimus omnis | Turnus, avis atavisque potens, quem regia coniunx | adiungi generum miro properabat amore' ('There was only a daughter to preserve that mighty house. She was now ready for a husband, marriageable and of full years. Many men courted her from mighty

for seeking in marriage.[5] The long-widowed Aemilia Pudentilla was sought by the chief men at Oea after the death of her father-in-law, who had made it his business to scare off suitors (the part Tiberius had in effect probably played for Livia Julia and Agrippina the Elder).[6] But the same verb could be used of the bride's family making approaches to possible bridegrooms: so Statius describes Arruntius Stella, as an eligible bachelor, being sought by many mothers as a son-in-law.[7]

In any case, the search by both parties or their families will often have been tedious and complicated. For the girl's family, it was important to have a husband ready to marry her at that short-lived and not precisely predictable moment when she was 'ripe'. A family's anxiety is neatly illustrated by Cicero's story of one Caecilia, who was eager to make a match for her sister's daughter. She took the girl to visit a shrine and obtain an omen, and succeeded in uttering ominous words which meant that, after her own unexpected death, the girl would marry her widower.[8] We have already seen how Atticus began reviewing the field by the time Attica was 6, and how Cicero got himself involved. He assured the anxious father that a good match for Attica was as dear to his heart as to Atticus' own.[9]

(a) Cicero and Tullia

The mechanics of the search are also revealed a few years earlier when Atticus performed similar services for Cicero. In 51 BC Cicero, who was away governing Cilicia, had asked Atticus to help in the arrangement of Tullia's third marriage, his 'top domestic priority'.[10] Others also took a close interest: we hear of P. Sestius (the tribune of 57), who discussed Tullia with Atticus; M. Caelius Rufus (another of Cicero's forensic clients, who was keeping Cicero up to date with the inner workings of politics during his absence in 51–50 BC), who may have had only a general commission, but briefed Cicero about Dolabella's separation from his wife; the famous Servilia (Cato's half-sister), who supported Servius Sulpicius Rufus (son of a man with whom Cicero had a close connection and who was to write him an undeservedly celebrated letter of condolence on Tullia's death a few years later) and was ready to negotiate with him;[11] an obscure

Latium and the whole of Italy, but above all the handsome Turnus courted her, powerful because of his grandfathers and great-grandfathers, whom the king's wife longed with marvellous love to have joined to her as son-in-law'). Cf. Apul. *M* 8.1, 8, 9.

[5] *Procatio*, courting by suitors, occurs once (Apul. *Apol.* 72).   [6] Apul. *Apol.* 68–9.
[7] *S* 1.2.70ff. Cf. n. 4 above for enthusiastic co-operation by a girl's mother. Ov. *Her.* 21.129–30 uses *petere* of each side in turn.   [8] *Div.* 1.104.
[9] *A* 13.21a.4.   [10] *A* 5.17.4.   [11] *A* 5.17.4; *F* 8.6.2; *A* 5.4.1, 6.1.10.

Pontidia (perhaps a woman of Arpinate connections), who at one point seemed to be trifling, but whose candidate (never clearly identified) Cicero eventually preferred to Servilia's, because he belonged to Cicero's 'old gang'.[12] There was rather a shortage of good candidates (*inopia*)[13] and the whole procedure was long drawn out. It presumably began before Cicero left Rome in early May of 51. The formal engagement (*sponsalia*) to Dolabella, which was achieved by Tullia and her mother, did not take place (probably) until late May or early June of 50.[14] The experience of both Cicero and Atticus illustrates the difficulty a father might find in choosing the right man and in catching him when he was available. All that we know of Tullia's two previous engagements, to a rising politician and a wealthy patrician, is that Cicero was clearly pleased with himself when he announced them.[15] The absence of information about the preceding negotiations, at least in 56 when the letters are comparatively rich, may reflect the discretion with which negotiations were conducted until the engagement was firm. It is striking that in 51, when Cicero's position as a consular and Tullia's good repute were assured, she did not have a wide choice. Restrictions may have been imposed by her own tastes (which we know her father intended to consult),[16] by her age (she was in her mid-twenties), by her record of infertility,[17] by political uncertainties and hostilities, by the amount of dowry which Cicero would offer, and the financial standing he wanted in a son-in-law. Cicero knew well that he never had a wide-open choice, *omnium potestas*.[18] There were two sequels to all the discreet enquiries and negotiations through third parties. If we can trust at all what Cicero wrote to Ap. Claudius in early August of 50, when he had the embarrassing task of explaining how he had become the father-in-law of the man who was prosecuting Claudius, Cicero told 'his people'

---

[12] *A* 5.21.14, 6.1.10, with SB's notes.

[13] *A* 5.4.1. (I would not refer *inopia* to Cicero's shortage of funds.) Cf. 7.3.12.

[14] SB *A* iii.244. SB's commentary on all the passages cited below is essential. TP contribute nothing. Collins, 'Tullia's engagement and marriage to Dolabella', is useful.

[15] *A* 1.3.3; *QF* 2.4.2, 6(5).1–2. Cf. *Pis*. fr. 13 = Asc. 4c.   [16] *A* 5.4.1.

[17] Modern conjectures put Tullia's birth as early as 79 BC (Balsdon, *RW* 179) and as late as 76/75 (Sumner, 'The *lex annalis* under Caesar' 258 n. 30, whom I would follow). Betrothed to C. Calpurnius Piso Frugi in 67 (*A*. 1.3.3), she was married to him perhaps by late 63 (*Cat*. 4.3, not conclusive since engagement created 'in-law' relationships), widowed in 57. It is assumed (because a long period of celibacy is unlikely) that marriage to Furius Crassipes followed soon after the engagement celebrated in spring 56 and lasted until about 53 (TP iii.146; SB *A* ii.186 and *Cicero* 95, 125, is less definite). I think it likely that divorce took place in 52 or 51, shortly before the search for a new husband. We hear of no pregnancies or births during these years; there were certainly no surviving children.

[18] *Pis*. fr. 13 = Asc. 4c: 'Ei (Pisoni) enim filiam meam conlocavi quem ego, si mihi potestas tum omnium fuisset, unum potissimum delegissem.' For the thought and expression cf. Nep. *A* 12: 'Agrippa . . . cum . . . nullius condicionis non haberet potestatem, potissimum eius deligeret affinitatem.'

(which must mean principally Tullia and her mother) that, since he was going to be abroad for such a long time, they need not refer the decision to him, but do what they thought fit.[19] However, as we have seen, he went on investigating possibilities from a distance. In at least one instance he was advised to keep in the background and not to commit himself—as it happens, to Dolabella.[20] He made his preferences clear in letters to Terentia.[21] Eventually (some time in the spring of 50), the young and extremely promising patrician Ti. Claudius Nero, 'a nobly born, talented, and self-controlled young man',[22] who had been visiting Asia and had probably called in person on Cicero, negotiated with him and obtained his consent to a match. Cicero at once sent trustworthy messengers off to Terentia and Tullia to inform them that Nero had his backing, but the men arrived after the engagement party had been held.[23] Both in ancestry and in solidity of morals, he would have been distinctly preferable to the flashy Dolabella. He served under Caesar and became quaestor in 48, praetor in 42, marrying his cousin Livia Drusilla in the late 40s.[24] Dolabella, on the other hand, made more of a mark as a Caesarian, getting to the consulship, by an unorthodox route, in 44.

The details of the negotiations with Dolabella elude us. In February of 50 Caelius had thought it worth while to report from Rome that Dolabella's wife had left him, but, in connection with Dolabella's prosecution of Cicero's predecessor as governor of Cilicia, had urged Cicero to keep his nose clean: 'de Dolabella integrum tibi reserves suadeo', that is, I think, not to make any overtures about a possible marriage alliance until after the trial.[25] In early April Cicero was able to write caustically to Appius about Dolabella's rashness in attacking such an influential man and about the childish and stupid remarks he had made (reported to Cicero by Caelius). Cicero claimed that, far from being likely to form a new alliance with Dolabella ('coniunctionem . . . novam', Tacitus' word), he would have broken off any

---

[19] *F* 3.12.2: 'ego vero velim mihi Tulliaeque meae, sicut tu amicissime et suavissime optas, prospere evenire ea quae me insciente facta sunt a *meis* . . . in quo unum non vereor, ne tu parum perspicias ea quae gesta sint ab aliis esse gesta; *quibus ego ita mandaram ut, cum tam longe afuturus essem, ad me ne referrent, agerent quod probassent.* In hoc autem mihi illud occurrit: "quid tu igitur si adfuisses?" rem probassem, de tempore nihil te invito, nihil sine consilio egissem tuo.'

[20] *F* 8.6 (SB 88) 5. SB interprets differently.   [21] *A* 6.1.10, 6.4.2.

[22] *F* 13.64.2. The whole letter is significant for Nero's *clientelae* in the east and Cicero's friendly feelings towards him.   [23] *A* 6.6.1.

[24] Livia was born 30 Jan. 58, which will give 46 as the earliest legal date for her marriage. But Nero was in Gaul settling veterans 46–45 (Suet. *Tib.* 4.1), so the marriage is likely to have followed his return. Her first (or first surviving) child, Tiberius, was born 16 Nov. 42, which gives early 42 as the latest possible date of marriage. Nero could have had another wife before Livia, but the civil-war period was not a propitious time.   [25] *F* 8.6.1, 5.

pre-existing friendship because of the attack on Appius.[26] This makes it clear that there was speculation in Rome about a possible marriage alliance between Cicero and Dolabella, but that Cicero was in a position to deny it, either because he was as yet uncommitted or, more likely, because negotiations were so far tentative and undertaken by others, perhaps thought by Cicero at the time of writing to be no longer in progress or unlikely to produce results. A letter to Atticus written shortly after 5 June shows that Cicero believed that the situation was still open:

Tu quando Roman salvus (ut spero) venisti, videbis, ut soles, omnia quae intelleges nostra interesse, in primis de Tullia mea, cuius de condicione quid mihi placeret scripsi ad Terentiam cum tu in Graecia esses . . . (ad Atticum 6.4.2)

When you get safely (I hope) back to Rome, please see to everything which you see concerns my interests, as you always do, especially my dear Tullia. I wrote to tell Terentia what I would like concerning a match for her while you were in Greece . . .

In his previous mention of this subject to Atticus, in February, Cicero had come down in favour of Pontidia's candidate (of whom he knew Atticus would approve) and asked Atticus (although he was in Greece) to help. Cicero had also informed Terentia.[27] No mention of that suitor or any other here. Instead, Atticus gets a general commission to act as the situation dictates. Cicero does not know how negotiations have been developing in Rome. Does his description of his recent instructions to Terentia suggest a similar general commission, a balance sheet of what Cicero would ideally like (which does not imply that there had been no similar discussion before Cicero left for Cilicia) and of the candidates who he thought were still in the running, or endorsement of any specific candidate? Either explanation would fit Cicero's wording. But the sequel suggests that this letter to Terentia, unfortunately so vaguely dated,[28] which Cicero seems to

---

[26] F 3.10.5.   [27] A 6.1.10.

[28] Atticus left Rome for Epirus in late Aug. or early Sept. 51 (A 5.19.1) and presumably arrived back in late May or early June 50 (A 6.4.1). The letter to Terentia must post-date A 6.1.10 of 20 Feb. and, since Tullia is not mentioned in the intervening letters, A 6.2 (? late Apr.) and 6.3 (SB 117) (which para. 1 shows is the next letter which Cicero wrote to Atticus, dated by SB to May or the beginning of June), it might be suggested that new developments and the letter to Terentia just antedate A 6.4 and Atticus' departure from Greece. I conjecture that Cicero did not write to Atticus at once because he was still in Greece and could do nothing useful there, but was about to leave. 'Cum tu in Graecia esses' (ibid. 2) would then be more informative, meaning 'when you were still in Greece' or 'since you were in Greece'. The slowness of communication between Rome and Cilicia meant that about three months were needed for an exchange of letters. A fast courier is known to have travelled from Rome to Cybistra, in the eastern part of Cicero's province, in 46 days in late summer 51 (A 5.19.1).

have expected would be communicated to Atticus on his arrival, accompanied the trustworthy messengers who informed Terentia of Cicero's approval of a match with Ti. Nero. Three considerations can be adduced to explain Cicero's lack of explicitness to Atticus. First, Cicero's information was not as up to date as he expected Atticus' to be as soon as he arrived in Rome and before he received the letter. Secondly, the letter was written in haste, on the march. It may also be suggested that Cicero considered discretion necessary. We do not know how the letter was sent, but in the third paragraph, in order to mystify an unauthorized reader, Cicero resorts to Greek and pseudonyms. The sense would only be obscure to someone who could not read Greek, so presumably Cicero is protecting himself against an unreliable professional letter-carrier. Considering how delicate a matter Tullia's *condicio* was, it would be desirable for Nero's name not to be bandied about among gossiping couriers on the main routes of the Empire.

That was early June. At the end of July Cicero shook off the cares of his province and set sail for Side in Pamphylia, from where, having received his own mail, which had probably been a little delayed by his changes of itinerary, he wrote three letters of varying tone, to Caelius, Ap. Claudius, and Atticus. For in his post-bag (along, no doubt, with letters from Terentia, Tullia, and others, which do not survive) was a letter from Caelius:

Gratulor tibi affinitatem viri me dius fidius optimi; nam hoc ego de illo existimo. Cetera porro, quibus adhuc ille sibi parum utilis fuit, et aetate iam sunt decussa et consuetudine atque auctoritate tua, pudore Tulliae, si qua restabunt, confido celeriter sublatum iri. Non est enim pugnax in vitiis neque hebes ad id quod melius sit intellegendum, deinde, quod maximum est, ego illum valde amo. (*ad Familiares* 8.13.1)

I congratulate you on your marriage alliance with a definitely first-class man—that's what I think of him. As for the other things, which up to now have let him down, they have been shaken off as he has grown older, and any which remain will, I am sure, swiftly be removed by your company and moral authority and by Tullia's goodness. For he is not aggressive in his vices nor slow to understand what is better. And then, the most important thing, I am very fond of him.

An interesting recommendation of a newly accepted bridegroom. Dolabella's acknowledged vices were no doubt those which Cicero had excused in Caelius a few years earlier and which were to reappear in Dolabella within a short time of his second marriage.[29] We do not know the motives for the recent divorce between him and his previous

---

[29] *Cael.* 27ff., 37ff.; *A* 11.17.1, 25.3.

wife, but she had left him. The only other piece of information we
have about her is that Cicero made a joke about Fabia Dolabellae, we
do not know when. He had to believe it when she said she was 30, as
she had been telling him so for twenty years. Perhaps, then,
Dolabella's senior and married for her money, some conclude—with
perhaps undue faith in the realism of Cicero's jokes.[30]

Cicero replied to Caelius appropriately:

Dolabellam a te gaudeo primum laudari, deinde etiam amari. Nam ea quae
speras Tulliae meae prudentia temperari posse, scio cui tuae epistulae
respondeant. Quid si meam legas quam ego tum ex tuis litteris misi ad
Appium? sed quid agas? sic vivitur. Quod actum est di approbent! Spero
fore iucundum generum nobis, multumque in eo tua nos humanitas adiuva-
bit. (*ad Familiares* 2.15.2)

I am delighted that you express approval of Dolabella and are fond of him.
As for those things which you hope will be moderated by my dear Tullia's
good sense, I know what they correspond to in your (earlier) letter. What
would you think if you read the one I sent to Appius at that time, after
reading yours? Oh well, that's life. May the gods approve of what has been
done! I hope I shall find him a pleasant son-in-law—your social skills will be
a great help in bringing that about.

Cicero had a taste for pleasant and not necessarily dependable young
men, and in writing to one of them, and a friend of Dolabella's at that,
he was obliged to be tactful. Nevertheless, he was, to say the least,
apprehensive about his daughter marrying such a man, and he
delicately hints that he will welcome Caelius' help in keeping
Dolabella on the right track. Cicero's good manners in picking up
Caelius' reference to Tullia's morality (*pudor*) by mentioning her
good sense but omitting any reply to the compliment about his own
auctoritas[31] show how carefully he phrased his rejoinder to a con-
gratulatory letter which Caelius must have realized might not be a
wholly welcome surprise.

The letter which Cicero wrote to Ap. Claudius, still under prosecution by Dolabella, was masterly. He thanks him for his kind wishes for
Tullia and himself and points out that (as he is sure Appius realizes)
the engagement was made by others: he did not know what was
happening, but he had given 'his people' a commission to do whatever
they thought fit, as communication with him would be too difficult.
But he says firmly that if he had been in Rome he would have
approved of the match, although he would have deferred to Appius in

<hr>

[30] *F* 8.6.2; Quint. *Inst.* 6.3.73, unless, as seems less likely, this refers to a successor to Tullia
rather than her predecessor, or to another Dolabella.

[31] See SB on *F* 2.15 (SB 96) 2.

arranging the timing of it[32] (that is, he would have been willing to postpone the announcement of the engagement of the daughter of Appius' successor to Appius' prosecutor until after the trial was over). Cicero is committed to supporting the marriage: he will smooth the ruffled feathers of the dangerous aristocrat as tactfully as possible, but he will not compromise his own *dignitas* by showing anything other than satisfaction in his new marriage alliance. To Atticus, Cicero could express himself frankly:

Ego dum in provincia omnibus rebus Appium orno, subito sum factus accusatoris eius socer. 'Id quidem' inquis 'di adprobent!' Ita velim, teque ita cupere certo scio. Sed crede mihi, nihil minus putaram ego, qui de Ti. Nerone, qui mecum egerat, certos homines ad mulieres miseram; qui Romam venerunt factis sponsalibus. Sed hoc spero melius. Mulieres quidem valde intellego delectari obsequio ét comitate adulescentis. Cetera noli ἐξακανθίζειν. (*ad Atticum* 6.6.1)

While I'm in my province polishing up Appius' record as governor, all of a sudden I've been turned into his prosecutor's father-in-law. 'May the gods approve it,' say you. Amen, and I'm sure you hope so. But believe me, it's the last thing I expected. I had sent the women reliable messengers to tell them about Tiberius Nero, who had negotiated with me direct. They reached Rome after the engagement had been celebrated. But I hope this match is better. I understand that the women are really delighted with the young man's attentiveness and charm. Spare your criticism of other things.

Both the conventional pious prayer (unusual in the letters and surely inspired by a realistic estimate of the chances of this marriage) and the allusion to 'other things' are recurrent features.[33] It is this letter in particular which suggests that Terentia and Tullia herself were the chief agents in arranging the match, on the side of the Cicerones. But Dolabella's charm is mentioned as a redeeming feature of the match rather than as the motive for it. Cicero is not accusing his womenfolk of falling for mere sex appeal.[34]

Finally Cicero reached Brindisi on 24 November and was met there by Terentia.[35] By the time he had covered the Appian Way as far as Trebula (between Beneventum and Capua) Cicero had also seen Tullia and Dolabella.[36] Presumably they were married by now. Cicero

[32] Text cited at n. 19. For an even more delicate case of timing an announcement of a forthcoming marriage, compare the defendant Pompey's engagement to the daughter of his judge (Plut. *P* 4.2–3).   [33] *F* 2.15.2, 8.13.1, *A* 7.3.12.

[34] Cicero also received congratulations from Atticus' wife Pilia (*A* 6.8.1). From Athens on 15 Oct. he wrote asking Atticus for news about Tullia, 'that is, about Dolabella' (*A* 6.9.5).

[35] *A* 7.2.1–3.

[36] *A* 7.3.12. Cicero pretends that reporting on Dolabella is an afterthought. Although he calls him *gener* (son-in-law), this does not prove that the marriage had taken place, since the word was also applied to a *sponsus*. But the evidence that instalments of dowry fell due on 1 July (11.2.2, 3.1) makes that the wedding anniversary.

found him talented and cultivated, but his faults could not be denied: 'The other things (*reliqua*) you know—we shall have to put up with them.' But, says Cicero, perhaps forgetting Nero, Dolabella is much better than any of the other suitors, any of whom (except Atticus' candidate) would have made Cicero go into debt.

This is our most detailed account from antiquity of the motives, hopes, methods, and reactions of one of the principal actors in the arrangement of a marriage. The gaps in our knowledge are only too evident. There is much more we would like to know of Cicero's role; still more is completely lacking: the part played by Tullia and Dolabella themselves, or Terentia, or other interested parties. We have concentrated on the mechanics, on the realistic estimate and the hard bargaining. But we should remember that it was also a matter in which a father was emotionally involved. Cicero looked forward to mulling the whole matter over in conversation with Atticus. And it can hardly be accidental that, on his arrival in Brindisi, when he wrote about the pleasures Atticus had discovered in his baby daughter, he devotes a paragraph to the philosophical doctrine that love of children is instinctive and fundamental to human society.[37] In denying that self-interest alone motivates mankind, Cicero is surely thinking of his own affection for Tullia and arguing that her happiness might be one of his objectives. Nowhere does this motive emerge explicitly, but neither does Cicero claim that the advancement of the Cicerones is his chief object. It was necessary to his *dignitas* that Tullia be matched with young men of the first rank (*adulescentes primarii*), but not, as he was to demonstrate, that she remain married if she was unhappy, even though political advantage might dictate it.[38]

(b) The participants

Marcianus assumes that matchmaking is a paternal responsibility, though passages in other authors demonstrate it was also a mother's.[39] The mother of a son, particularly if she was widowed, would look out for a suitable wife for him and be approached by other *matronae* about plans for his marriage.[40] It was appropriate that, where possible, women should deal with women and men with men.

Although young girls were not encouraged to be forward, they must have been encouraged to accept marriage as their career and they must have had some interest in the choice of husband. A father might concede that in the choice of a son-in-law he was concerned with grandchildren, but for his daughter the choice affected the whole of her life.[41] It can be argued that they were allowed some social contact with potential husbands under responsible chaperonage and that their thoughts were turned in a suitable direction, so that they gave some encouragement to eligible men. Aunts, married elder sisters, matrons who were friends of the family could help a virtuous adolescent to be noticed by other women and recommended to suitable *partis* or to appear where they might attract suitors.[42]

The greater freedom allowed to matrons and *viduae* (divorced women and widows) meant that they could take some initiative in finding new husbands. A few examples are described, neutrally or for censure.[43] Cicero claims that not only did Sassia seduce her son-in-law but she married him without taking advice from anyone.[44] Soon after Sulla's wife Metella died in 81 BC, he was the object of a neat approach by Valeria, who was well-born, good-looking, and recently divorced. After he informed himself about her family and her past, a passionate flirtation and marriage at once followed.[45] After the death of her first husband Domitius Ahenobarbus in AD 40, Agrippina the Younger pursued Sulpicius Galba, 'omnibus sollicitaverat modis', despite the fact that he was still married to Lepida—so blatantly that Lepida's mother slapped her at a gathering of married women. Galba could not be tempted, even after Lepida's death.[46] It is the context which makes the first and third of these initiatives deplorable; the provocative behaviour of Valeria is comparatively innocent.

The other examples are not shocking at all. That Livia Ocellina took the initiative, 'ultro appetisse', does not disturb Suetonius.[47] Nor was Cicero, who may be suspected of having more delicacy of mind, scandalized by a woman making the first advance, even to a cadet of his own family. In July 44 young Quintus told Cicero that a certain lady, probably called Tutia, was proposing marriage to him. The story probably turned out to be wishful thinking on young Quintus' part, as Cicero had thought. But it is interesting that the elder Q. Cicero thought it credible that a woman on the point of a divorce from

[41] Fronto *ad amicos* 2.11 (Loeb i.292): 'filiam meam despondi ei nec melius aut mihi in posteritatem aut meae filiae in omnem vitam consulere potui quam quom talem mihi generum cum illis moribus tantaque eloquentia elegi.'
[42] Thoughts: Epict. *Ench.* 40; matrons: e.g. Cic. *Div.* 1.104; *Laud. Tur.* ii.34–5. The comparative difficulty of knowing much about young women was, *mutatis mutandis*, to persist. *The Times* in 1923 said of Lady Elizabeth Bowes-Lyon at the time of her wedding to the Duke of York 'people know very little about her, as of necessity they know very little about well-bred young ladies living quietly at home' (quoted in the *Sunday Times Magazine*, 4 Aug. 1985, p. 22).
[43] On both girls and older women see 'Iam proterva fronte: matrimonial advances by Roman women'.
[44] Cic. *Clu.* 12, 14. Cf. *Cael.* 68, where Clodia acts for once 'de suorum propinquorum . . . sententia atque auctoritate'.
[45] Plut. *Sulla* 35.3 ff.   [46] Suet. *Galba* 5.1.   [47] Suet. *Galba* 3.4.

her previous husband should be offering a match to his son, who was
aged 22. He checked up on her reputation and family, as was usual,
but did not think that there was anything disgraceful or even worthy
of comment in the fact that she had allegedly made the offer. (M.
Cicero may be hinting that young Quintus prided himself on the
impression he apparently thought he had made on her.)[48] Finally, I
think Apuleius may have disguised the amount of initiative shown by
the widow who married him. By his account Aemilia Pudentilla of
Oea long resisted her father-in-law's blackmailing attempt to make
her marry his other son. She was then sought in marriage by the chief
men of the town and made up her mind to marry again, partly on
medical advice and partly on that of relations. Her son invited
Apuleius to marry her and, though he later turned against him, the
engagement had been made and Pudentilla kept to it. Apuleius
wishes to suggest that he had not taken the initiative and that
Pudentilla had had the backing of her family. The prosecution
claimed that she had been bewitched, that is, she had fallen in love. It
seems likely that she had at least acted more independently than he
says.[49]

While the letters about Attica's betrothal show the gleaning of
information from friends or acquaintances, the correspondence on
Tullia highlights the intervention of friends in support of one or other
nominee. It would be interesting to have, not just Pliny's recommendation of Acilianus, his response to a request for suggestions,[50]
but Iunius Mauricus' complete file of testimonials to possible husbands for his niece. As so often in Roman social relations, the tactful
intervention of a friend to smooth the way, an indirect approach by a
third party, which spared the principal loss of face if his application
was refused (*agere per aliquem*),[51] would be preferred to more direct
methods. So Balbus prepares the political coalition of 59 BC; Vergil
and Varius arrange a preliminary interview between Horace and
Maecenas; a cultivated Greekling, enjoying the entrée to both
houses, goes between Cicero and Clodia, or so it is alleged, giving rise
to gossip about marriage negotiations, although both were married
already.[52] The thing was customary and recognized. The word was
conciliare, used for the arrangement of a match, particularly the

---

[48] Cic. *A* 15.29.2, 16.2.5.

[49] Apul. *Apol.* 68ff. *HA Marcus* 29.10 also credits Fabia with wooing Marcus after Faustina's
death.   [50] *Epp.* 1.14. See pp. 87–8.

[51] *A* 7.3.12. Cf. 5.4.1 ('agente Servilia'); Suet. *DA* 69.1: 'condiciones [*admittedly extra-
marital*] quaesitas per amicos.' One reason for indirect methods may be the need to guard
against losing face or giving offence. Among the Sarakatsani a refusal may lead to violent feud:
Campbell 39 and ch. 6.

[52] Balbus: Cic. *A* 2.3.3; Vergil: Hor. *S* 1.6.55; Clodia: Plut. *Cic.* 29.2–3, Wiseman, *Cinna the
poet and other Roman essays* 138ff.; Syme, *RR* 407–8.

bringing about of an initial meeting, not only by family members such as a father or father-in-law,[53] but by unrelated parties, as when the trickster Palaestrio in comedy undertakes to arrange a meeting between the braggart warrior and a rich matron who is supposed to be in love with him.[54] There is a well-attested historical example:

Erat nupta soror Attici Q. Tullio Ciceroni, easque nuptias M. Cicero conciliarat, cum quo a condiscipulatu vivebat coniunctissime, multo enim familiarius quam cum Quinto; ut iudicari possit plus in amicitia valere similitudinem morum quam adfinitatem. (Nepos *Atticus* 5.3)

Atticus' sister was married to Q. Tullius Cicero, and the marriage had been negotiated by M. Cicero, with whom Atticus lived in close friendship from the time they were at school together, much more intimately in fact that with Quintus, which proves that similarity of character is much more important to friendship than relationship by marriage.

The friend who eventually negotiated a match for Caecilia Attica in 37 BC was the great M. Antonius, who arranged for her to marry Agrippa, the friend of his triumviral colleague: 'harum nuptiarum concilator fuit (non est enim celandum) M. Antonius, triumvir rei publicae constituendae'.[55] The proper noun *conciliator* also describes Pallas, chief proponent of Claudius' marriage with his niece.[56]

Marriage-agents could aspire to professional status, and the vocabulary also covers disreputable procurement.[57] For a broker in financial matters, Seneca and later Latin sources use the Greek word *proxeneta*.[58] Later, *proxenos* is used specifically for a marriage-broker who expected to make money by the transaction. In the late Empire the emperor would have preferred the broker to take nothing for his pains, but set a limit of a fee equal to 5 per cent of what the bride brought as dowry or what the bridegroom gave as *donatio* before the wedding.[59] But already Ulpian, in a corrupt passage, mentions a man acting as 'condicionis vel amicitiae proxeneta', a function he apparently regards as made necessary by the size of the Roman state.[60]

---

[53] Plaut. *Trin.* 386; Apul. *Apol.* 68.   [54] Plaut. *Miles* 801, 1212.

[55] 'The negotiator of this marriage (it is no secret) was M. Antonius, triumvir to set up the Republic' (Nep. *Att.* 12.2). Octavian asked Maecenas by letter to arrange a marriage for him with Scribonia (cvvθέcθαι) (App. *BC* 5.53).

[56] Tac. *A* 12.25.1: 'obstrictus Agrippinae ut conciliator nuptiarum.' According to Plut. *Cato min.* 30.2, Pompey approached Cato's confidant Munatius in 62 about a possible marriage alliance with Cato's daughter or niece.

[57] Fest. 54L: '*Conciliatrix* dicitur, quae viris conciliat uxores et uxoribus viros.' The feminine again, of a bawd: Lucil. 271; cf. Plaut. *Miles* 1410. Dio Prusias mentions προμνήcτριαι as used by the richer classes in Greece (*Eub.* 80). See Noy, 'Matchmakers and marriage-markets in antiquity'.   [58] Sen. *Epp.* 119.1; Mart. 10.3.4; etc.

[59] *CJ* 5.1.6, an anonymous and undated imperial *constitutio*.

[60] *D* 50.14.3 ('a broker for a match or friendship').

In earlier days advising on the weighty business of disposing of a daughter in marriage had been one of the functions of the orator as a man of practical wisdom. The subject was on a par with buying or cultivating land.[61] Presumably it was also a courtesy for the client to consult his patron, or for friends to consult friends, even if they did not in the end take their advice.[62] We have seen the intervention of matrons in the discussion of candidates for Tullia and how the *laudata* offered to find a suitable new bride for her husband. Women were in an ideal position to know about unmarried girls and to advise prospective brides and their mothers, but they could also offer advice to fathers and bridegrooms. It is said to have been Octavia who, on the death of Marcellus, proposed first to her brother Augustus and then to Agrippa that he should divorce her own daughter Marcella and marry her widowed niece Julia. Octavia then bestowed Marcella on her stepson Iullus Antonius.[63] In imperial times the *princeps* as the fountain-head of patronage might expect to be consulted and informed by members of the senatorial class. An indiscreet marriage could provoke displeasure. Advice from the emperor might be enough to convince even reluctant parents.[64]

Negotiation at various stages could be conducted by the principals, their parents and other relatives, friends of comparable higher or lower social status, and even servants.[65]

2. Procedure

According to Servius, commenting on Vergil's phrase 'pactae coniugis', 'hic ordo est, conciliata primo, dein conventa, dein pacta, dein sponsa.'[66] So even if the first hurdle had been successfully leapt and a woman was *conciliata*, perhaps through a mediator, there were still other stages through which the families had to pass. Servius is probably over-precise, but he is partly confirmed by Juvenal, who, in dissuading a man from entering upon the degraded married state of

[61] Cic. *de or.* 3.133.
[62] See e.g. Plut. *Pomp.* 4.2–3. For consultation of a *consilium* on a variety of topics see Wiseman's remarks, *RPL* 15.
[63] Plut. *Ant.* 87.2–3.   [64] Tac. *A* 6.30.4.
[65] Antony was alleged to have sent his trusted freedman Callias to Lepidus in Africa in 37 to arrange for the marriage of his daughter and Lepidus' son, who had been engaged since 44 (App. *BC* 5.93).
[66] Ad *A* 10.722: '"Of his promised wife": the order of events is *conciliari, conveniri, pacisci, sponderi*.' Vergil is describing a man who fled into exile, leaving his marriage incomplete. (Servius would say precisely at the third stage leading to engagement.) She had got as far as giving him a guerdon. On *A* 10.79 Servius specifies two even earlier stages, *sperare* and *petere* (hoping for and seeking). Cf. Arnob. *adv. Gent.* 4.20. On archaic procedure see further Kupiszewski, 'Das Verlöbnis im altrömischen Recht'.

modern times, lists the tiresome preliminaries: 'conventum tamen et pactum et sponsalia nostra | tempestate paras' ('You prepare an agreement, a pact, and a betrothal in our time').[67] What exactly was meant by *conventa* is partially explained by a note in Festus: 'conventae [sc. coniugis] condicio dicitur cum primus sermo de nuptiis . . . habebatur.'[68] *Concilio* then seems to refer to the initial overtures from one side and the agreement in principle, *convenio* to a more definite agreement of both sides, perhaps involving a meeting.[69] *Pacta* (the passive participle from *pacisco*, which is used only of a woman) means 'promised'. In Plautus, Philto gets to this stage within a hundred lines of having accosted the girl's brother Lesbonicus, after being commissioned by his son Lysiteles to win his consent. Philto makes the first approach. But he meets nothing but polite and grateful refusal, so perhaps he is jumping Servius' second stage when he goes on:[70]

> PHILTO. . . . sine dote *posco* tuam sororem filio.
>   Quae res bene vortat—*habeone pactam*? Quid taces?
> STASIMUS. Pro di inmortales, condicionem
>   quoiusmodi!
> PHILTO. Quin fabulare—Vin? 'Bene vortat, spondeo'?

> (*Trinummus* 499–502)

> PHILTO. . . . *I ask for* your sister for my son without a dowry. May it turn out well. *Do I have her promised*? Why do you say nothing?
> STASIMUS. Ye gods, what a match!
> PHILTO. Why don't you talk? Won't you say 'May it turn out well, I engage her'?

He tries to get Lesbonicus to proceed at once to the final step of the *sponsio*. After further discussion about the dowry, Philto persuades Lesbonicus that that side of the question must be discussed with his son, and once again makes his formal proposal, this time getting Lesbonicus to make the right response.

> PHILTO. De dote mecum convenire nihil potest:
>   quid tibi lubet tute agito cum nato meo.
>   Nunc tuam sororem filio posco meo.
>   Quae res bene vortat! Quid nunc? Etiam consulis?
> LESBONICUS. Quid istic? Quando ita vis; di bene vortant! Spondeo.

> (Ibid. 569–73)

---

[67] 6.25–6, with Courtney ad loc. See also Fordyce on Cat. 62.27.
[68] 'The expression "conventa coniunx" is used when talk of marriage and its terms first takes place', 54L, cf. *TLL* 844 17ff. *OLD*: 'to bring a woman to a man as a wife, match' splits fewer hairs than Servius and so does not help us here. Cf. Apul. *M* 8.8.
[69] Dictionaries do not decide between the two senses, both of which occur in the passive. Agreement is probably uppermost. Cf. Livy 4.4.10 for the impersonal verb and Cic. *Caec.* 51, *A* 6.3.1, for the legal phrase *pactum et conventum*.   [70] *Trin.* 442ff. (quoted above), 451ff.

PHILTO. No agreement about dowry can be made with me: do what you like about it with my son. Now I ask for your sister for my son. May it turn out well! What now? Are you still thinking about it?

LESBONICUS. Very well then. Since that is what you want: may the gods make it turn out well. I promise [her].

Making the *pactio* is less formal than the legal *sponsio*, but the literary sources usually treat *pactio* as roughly equivalent. It is a solemn agreement[71] and may usually have involved specific terms. The *Oxford Latin Dictionary* translation, 'a marriage settlement', seems, however, too specific.[72] The passive participle *pacta* is used quite frequently to mean 'betrothed'.[73] The deponent verb *pacisci* is used of the male partner, whose role is active.[74] The woman is the object of a *pactio* made between her parents and the intended bridegroom.[75]

The woman was also the object of the *sponsio*. The traditional question-and-answer formula of demand and promise of a bride is attested only between males, although women could accomplish this form of contract when they themselves were not its object. The male monopoly is presumably a matter of etiquette rather than law. Ulpian, explaining that in his time consent was enough to constitute betrothal, *sponsalia*, explains that the word derives from the ancient custom of *stipulatio* and *sponsio*.[76] The form is clear from Plautus, for example, the more correct engagement between Lysiteles and Lesbonicus' father which eventually ratifies the agreement between Lysiteles' father and Lesbonicus discussed above:

CHARMIDES. Filiam meam tibi desponsatam audio.
LYSITELES.   Nisi tu nevis.
CHARMIDES. Immo hau nolo.
LYSITELES.   Sponden ergo tuam gnatam uxorem mihi?
CHARMIDES. Spondeo et mille auri Philippum dotis.

(*Trinummus* 1156–58)

---

[71] Cicero (*Balb.* 29) in a list of agreements between states may even rank it above *sponsio*. In Ov. *Her.* 20.151 ff. there is constant play on *pactum*.

[72] Cf. esp. Plaut. *Aul.* 201–2; Livy 4.4.8; for *pactum matrimonii* Tac. *A* 6.45.5. The early Empire saw the introduction of *tabulae nuptiales*, sealed at the wedding ceremony by witnesses: the first attested example is of Messalina and Silius (Tac. *A* 11.30.4; Juv. 10.336; cf. *RE* iv A/2.1949–55 (Kübler) s.v.). *Tabellae sponsalium* are indirectly attested by Tertullian (*de virg. vel.* 12.1: 'hae sunt tabellae . . . naturalium sponsalium et nuptiarum'), but although some documented arrangement would be a natural accompaniment to a betrothal, Roman marriage itself was not validated even in later classical law by *tabulae* and the whole emphasis in republican betrothal is on the oral *sponsio* or informal consent.

[73] e.g. Cic. *A* 5.21.2; Livy 1.2.1.

[74] Livy 4.4.10, 44.30.4; ps.-Sen. *Oct.* 141; *Decl. min.* 343.   [75] Cat. 62.28; cf. 57 ff.

[76] *D* 23.1.2, *sg de sponsalibus*: 'sponsalia autem dicta sunt a spondendo: nam moris fuit veteribus stipulari et spondere sibi uxores futuras.' Cf. ibid. 4: 'sufficit nudus consensus ad constituenda sponsalia.'

CHARMIDES. I hear my daughter has been betrothed to you.
LYSITELES. Unless you do not wish it.
CHARMIDES. No, I am not unwilling.
LYSITELES. Then do you promise your daughter to me as my wife?
CHARMIDES. I promise, and 1,000 gold Philippi as dowry.

It is essential that the question *spondesne?* and the specific promise
spondeo be used, as is shown clearly in another Plautine passage:

MEGADORUS. Quid nunc? Etiam mihi despondes filiam?
EUCLIO.   Illis legibus,
    cum illa dote quam tibi dixi.
MEGADORUS.   Sponden ergo?
EUCLIO.   Spondeo.
MEGADORUS. Istuc di bene [vortant]—
EUCLIO.   Ita di faxint. Illud facito ut
                                                          memineris,
    convenisse ut ne quid dotis mea ad te adferret filia.

(*Aulularia* 255–8)

MEGADORUS. Well then. Now do you betroth your daughter to me?
EUCLIO. On those conditions, with the dowry which I told you.
MEGADORUS. Then do you promise her?
EUCLIO. I promise her.
MEGADORUS. May the gods make it turn out well—
EUCLIO. May the gods do so! Do you remember this, that we agreed that my
    daughter will bring you no dowry.

Convenisse is formally correct here.
A final Plautine extract shows the suitor checking that there is a
pactio before proceeding to the formal *sponsio*:

AGORASTOCLES. . . . tuam mihi maiorem filiam despondeas.
HANNO. Pactam rem habeto.
AGORASTOCLES.   Spondesne igitur?
HANNO.   Spondeo.

(*Poenulus* 1156–7)

AGORASTOCLES. . . . Please promise your elder daughter to me.
HANNO. Take the matter as agreed.
AGORASTOCLES. Do you promise her then?
HANNO. I promise her.

The one-word question and answer are invariable, words which were
also used in other business contracts. Dowry may be brought in as
another element of the contract. Two Plautine fathers specify at the
sponsio what they will give, the miserly Euclio securing an agreement
that he is to pay no dowry at all, the gentlemanly Charmides

compelling Lysiteles to accept his condition (*lex*) of a generous dowry.[77]

The precision with which Plautus uses the verbal contract to emphasize the moment when a formal engagement is made, marking it in some instances as a dramatic climax, suggests that in his day the *sponsio* was still a vital custom. It is accompanied too by invocations of the gods which seem semi-automatic and which we have seen come naturally to the lips of Cicero or Caelius well over a century later.[78] But the formal *sponsio* occurs in only a small proportion of the available betrothals in Plautus and is absent from the plays of Terence, although this might be accounted for by his lack of interest in legal forms and vocabulary.[79] When the antiquarian Varro in the mid-first century BC wants to illustrate the 'promising away' by a father of his daughter, he quotes an anonymous play.[80] In his exhaustive treatment of *spondere* and cognate words, Varro treats the engagement-*sponsio* as obsolete, although *sponsus* and *sponsa* for the engaged persons were still in current use.[81] It seems likely that the verbal contract had gone out of use during the second century.

The old custom had put the woman on a par with other pieces of property: she could be promised as her dowry could be promised, by the father in whose power she was. At an earlier stage, the mercantile nature of the contract may have been still more overt. Scholars argue from the word *cosponsi* (used by Naevius to describe the two parties to the contract)[82] and the use of *sponsus* for the fiancé that originally he too was bound by a second *sponsio*. Perhaps the fiancé or his *paterfamilias* in early times promised a bride-price, or later promised that he would marry the woman.[83] Further support is found in the evidence of the jurist Servius Sulpicius Rufus that in Latin cities other than Rome actions for breach of promise to marry were still possible down to the grant of Roman citizenship in 90 BC. Suit could be brought by either side and damages granted. Gellius' account of what Sulpicius wrote makes it perfectly clear that both parties said *spondeo*: the prospective bridegroom stipulated from the man responsible

---

[77] *Trin.* 1157ff., where the contract is repeated.

[78] *Di bene vortant*: Plaut. *Aul.* 257, cf. 272; *Trin.* 573, cf. 1155; *di approbent*: Cic. *F* 2.15.2; Atticus ap. *A* 6.6.1.

[79] *Spondeo* is said of daughter and dowry in the spurious alternative closing scene of *Andria*, without a preceding *spondesne?* (20–1; cf. Watson, *Persons* 15 n. 5). McGlynn, *Lexicon Terentianum*, indicates no other instance of *spondeo*; *pactio/pacisci* are also absent. *Spondeo* does not occur in the index of Ribbeck, *Comicorum Romanorum fragmenta*.

[80] *LL* 6.71: 'Sponden tuam gnatam filio uxorem meo?' (*Com.* p. 134).

[81] *LL* 6.69ff.   [82] *LL* 6.70.

[83] Cf. Donatus on Ter. *And.* 102: 'Despondi: ex vetere more quo spondebat etiam petitoris pater' ('I engaged [him]: in accordance with the ancient custom by which the suitor's father also promised').

for the woman that she would be given in marriage and the bridegroom made a similar promise, that he would marry her.[84] Sulpicius is a contemporary and authoritative source. It is argued convincingly that both the dual promise and actionability originally held good of Roman law too, but Servius 'gives the impression that in Rome they had long ceased to be double or actionable'.[85]

No double promises occur in Plautus. There is one *spondeo* without a preceding *spondesne?*, the promise extracted from the girl's brother Lesbonicus, who was not her guardian, a promise which her father later treats as constituting a valid engagement, although the fiancé courteously suggests that it depends on his retroactive approval and formal *sponsio*.[86] The lonely *spondeo* is elicited by *posco* and impatient questions. Watson regards this as showing that informal means of ratifying an engagement, which could not be enforced because there had been no legal contract, had already become usual in the time of Plautus: he regards the four Plautine question-and-answer contracts as the survival in common use of a form which had ceased to make engagements actionable.

The comic representation of a betrothal in Plautus must correspond to a form actually in use, and hence if the full form for an enforceable *sponsio* is not given the implication must be that *sponsalia* had ceased to be actionable. Naturally, the original form of question and answer would continue to be employed long after *sponsalia* had ceased to be actionable and it is not surprising that in four other places Plautus has *spondesne* (or *sponden*)?, *spondeo*. The text which departs from the old form is more revealing than the four which keep to it. (*RPL* 15)[87]

But this may be too schematic. There is no obvious reason why, when the question and answer were still used to make enforceable contracts of other types, parties who had ratified an engagement to marry in this ancient form should be exempt from suit if they failed to carry out their promise. I prefer to imagine the actionable *sponsio* and the informal agreement (expressed by *spondeo* without a preceding *spondesne?* or by another verb such as *despondeo* on the part of the woman's guardian) existing for a while, in the time of Plautus and perhaps later, side by side, until the oral contract is dropped,

---

[84] Gell. *NA* 4.4.
[85] Watson, *Persons* 12.
[86] *Trin.* 569ff., 1156ff. Cf. Watson, *Persons* 14ff., and *RPL* 14–15.
[87] Cf. *Persons* 16. There is a further example of *spondesne? spondeo* at *Curc.* 674, where the brother promises his long-lost sister.

probably in the second century but certainly well before the time of Sulpicius and Varro.[88]

The words used in informal engagements are not clearly attested. The usual word which describes ratification of a betrothal is *despondere*. Very often a woman is described as *desponsa* (betrothed) without any indication of who was responsible for the ratification.[89] Varro suggests the unconvincing etymology from *de sponte*, because the person who betrothes the girl is allowing her to go outside his control.[90] This usefully demonstrates that Varro took it for granted that it would be the woman's *paterfamilias* or, if she were independent of the control of a male ascendant, perhaps someone with a moral right to impose his wishes on her, a guardian or close relative, who betrothed her. This is borne out by the attested examples. Fathers routinely say that they have betrothed their daughters, whether in comedy or in real letters.[91] But the verb may also be used of the father of the bridegroom: Chremes comes to Simo to ask that the latter's virtuous son marry his daughter, with a large dowry. Simo accepts: 'despondi' ('I made the engagement').[92] What is more striking is that the father of the man is said to engage the woman.[93] A brother seems also to have had some moral right to betroth his sister. The woman's father in *Trinummus* accepts this as not improper.[94] When the soldier in *Curculio* discovers his long-lost sister, it is naturally his social and dramatic duty to bestow her in marriage at once, particularly as a candidate is at hand. Since she is present and a lady of some worldly experience, he takes the course which is so unusual in comedy, of asking her if she wants the marriage.[95] This little scene highlights the etiquette, which Watson has pointed out, that a woman should not be seen to act directly in making her own engagement.[96] This theory and form long survived the extinction of the all-male formal contract and

---

[88] I agree with Watson, *Persons* 13, that Varro *LL* 6.72 should not be taken to imply that engagements were *sometimes* actionable in his day. Gaudemet, 'Origine et destin du mariage romain', shows that classical law is unusual in making a sharp distinction between marriage and engagement and in keeping engagement non-actionable.

[89] With indication of the person to whom she is engaged (in the dative): Plaut. *Mil.* 1007, *Trin.* 1156; Livy 1.26.2; Apul. 4.32.

[90] *LL* 6.71.

[91] Plaut. *Aul.* 271; Cic. *A* 1.3.3. Cf. for requests to fathers Plaut. *Aul.* 238, 241, 255, *Poen.* 1157; for reports on fathers Plaut. *Aul.* 205, *Cist.* 601; Pacuv. *trag.* 115; Livy 38.57.6; VM 4.2.3; Tac. *Ag.* 9, *A* 12.3.2; Suet. *DA* 63.2, *Otho* 1.3. *Destinare* of the father's action: Pliny *Epp.* 6.16.1.

[92] Ter. *And.* 102.

[93] Plaut. *Cist.* 498; Ter. *Ad.* 734, *Hec.* 124. Only in *Ad.* is the girl apparently without a protector (and moreover the young man has already had a child by her). For real life see Suet. *Claud.* 27.1.   [94] Plaut. *Trin.* 603–4, 1133, 1156.

[95] 671 ff. For a father's wish to marry off a newly discovered daughter, even when no suitor is known to him, cf. *Rud.* 1196 ff.   [96] *Persons* 18.

the obsolescence of strict patriarchalism, continuing when at least some women exercised freedom of choice.

By extension, other persons of some moral authority might also be seen as main agents in making an engagement. An alleged kinsman in *Phormio* redisposes of his son's bride elsewhere.[97] The formidable woman Sassia betrothes her daughter to her stepson.[98] Octavian betrothed his friend Agrippa's daughter when she was a baby to his stepson Tiberius.[99] Finally, a piquant variation: when Hortensius persuaded Cato to divorce Marcia so that he could marry her, her father Philippus, according to Plutarch, refused to betroth her unless Cato acted with him. They betrothed her jointly. Similarly, when Livia married Octavian, the betrothal had been performed by her previous husband. Gaius compelled Memmius Regulus to betroth his ex-wife Lollia Paullina to him.[100]

Although it was not improper for a young man to negotiate with a prospective father-in-law on his own behalf, there seems to be only one example of a classical writer using *despondeo* to describe the action of the prospective bridegroom. Caelius, whose style is notoriously colloquial and whose love of gossip matched Cicero's own, wrote to him, 'Cornificius adulescens Orestillae filiam sibi despondit' ('Young Cornificius has engaged Orestilla's daughter to himself').[101] But the young man's willingness to engage a woman to himself was implied by his initial suit (*poscere* or *petere*). A suitor might be expected to attempt to win the good opinion of a girl's parents by gifts.[102]

Our accounts of Roman engagements are so discreet that we rarely hear of unsuccessful proposals. Stories about heroines with droves of suitors naturally include rejection of all but one. The fictional Thrasyllus, rejected on account of his bad character, burns with indignation at the insult of a *repulsa*.[103]

3. Sponsalia

The father may report success in arranging an engagement in informal language, as Cicero writes to his brother that he thinks he has

[97] Ter. *Ph.* 924–5, where the legal context is meant to be Athenian.

[98] Cic. *Clu.* 179. I have not found *despondere* with female subject elsewhere. Note, however, that Cicero wants to stress Sassia's unusual influence and that the other near kin of the couple were dead.

[99] Nep. *A* 19.3. Cf. Plut. *Caes.* 14.4 on Pompeia (*Pomp.* 47.6 is more accurate).

[100] Marcia: Plut. *Cato min.* 25.5; Livia: Vell. 2.79.2: 'cum prius despondente ei Nerone, cui ante nupta fuerat Liviam . . . duxisset eam uxorem' ('after he had married Livia, who was betrothed to him by Nero, to whom she had previously been married'). This should not be taken to imply that the marriage had been *cum manu*. Lollia: Dio 59.12.1.

[101] *F* 8.7.2. Cf. Vulg. Deut. 22.23.   [102] Apul. *M* 8.2.

[103] Apul. *M* 8.2: 'morum tamen improbatus repulsae contumelia fuerat aspersus.'

fixed things up with Furius Crassipes.[104] But the formalities were still to come, postponed because, first, two days were unpropitious according to the religious calendar, and then a period during which Crassipes had to be out of town followed the agreement. It was some days later that the engagement was actually made:

Dederam ad te litteras antea quibus erat scriptum Tulliam nostram Crassipedi prid. Non. Apr. esse desponsam. (*ad Quintum fratrem* 2.6 (5)1)

I have previously written to you a letter in which I said that my dear Tullia was betrothed to Crassipes on 4 April.

The previous letter has been lost. Here an agreement which Cicero hoped was firm has clearly been put on a formal footing: presumably Cicero used a word such as *despondeo* and Crassipes promised to marry Tullia. Some formality may be suggested by Cicero's unusual use of Tullia's formal name, instead of the diminutive Tulliola which he commonly preferred. Such ritual as there was could, it seems, be improvised on the spot if necessary. When Livy describes the sudden engagement of the Elder Gracchus to the daughter of Scipio Africanus, the whole procedure progresses rapidly from a mass request from the Senate assembled at a banquet to ratification by formal *sponsalia* in the middle of this public occasion.[105]

(a) Consent

All that was legally necessary was the giving of consent by the parties and their *patresfamilias*, if any.[106]

Sufficit nudus consensus ad constituenda sponsalia. Denique constat et absenti absentem desponderi posse, et hoc cotidie fieri. (*Digest* 23.1.4, Ulpian *xxxv ad Sabinum*)

Bare consent is sufficient to make a betrothal. In fact it is agreed that an absent person may be betrothed to another absent person, and this is a daily occurrence.

A written document might be drawn up, but need not be. The betrothal could be ratified equally well in person, in each other's presence, or by a messenger or letter sent by either, or by proxy.

---

[104] *QF* 2.4.2, mid-Mar. 56.

[105] 38.57.5–6: 'Senatum eo die forte in Capitolio cenantem consurrexisse et petisse, ut inter epulas Graccho filiam Africanus desponderet, quibus ita inter publicum sollemne sponsalibus rite factis cum se domum recepisset, Scipionem Aemiliae uxori dixisse filiam se minorem despondisse' ('[It is said that] the Senate, which happened to be dining on the Capitoline that day, rose *en masse* and asked Africanus to betroth his daughter to Gracchus during the feast. This betrothal was formally celebrated at the public function and when he returned home Scipio told his wife Aemilia that he had betrothed their younger daughter'). This is one of two variant versions of how the marriage was arranged.

[106] *D* 23.1.7.1, Paul, 11, Iul.

Ulpian insists that it was perfectly usual for the *sponsi* not to be present at the ratification of their betrothal.[107]

But in classical law the woman's consent, both to engagement and marriage, is essential.[108] We are told by Julian, quoted with approval by Paul, that a *filiafamilias* could make her own engagement. The consent of the father would be assumed unless he gave clear indication that he disapproved.[109] We must note that such a daughter could be acting under her father's orders and that she need not be a girl at her first marriage.[110] But the old patriarchalism was eroded. The Augustan marriage laws forbade a *paterfamilias* to prevent the marriage of his daughter[111] or to refuse to give her a dowry. Severus and Caracalla ordered provincial governors to enforce this rule, and Marcianus comments that the law seemed to cover fathers who did not look for a match for their children.[112] A daughter who compelled her *paterfamilias* to consent to her marriage need not have been acting alone: her mother may well have taken the initiative in making a match for her.

(b) Celebrations

So much for what was legally necessary in the classical period. Etiquette demanded that the family and friends be informed of the happy event and that they should reciprocate with congratulations. What survives for us is correspondence to and from the father of the bride.[113] By the time of Cicero if not before, a party was the normal concomitant of an upper-class engagement. *Sponsalia* describes both the formal betrothal and the party: there is no abstract noun corresponding to *despondeo*.[114] Cicero, in the same letter to Quintus, goes on to say that he held a party for Crassipes two days afterwards (unlike Africanus, who conflated the two events):

A.d. viii Id. Apr. sponsalia Crassipedi praebui. Huic convivio puer optimus, Quintus tuus meusque, quod perleviter commotus fuerat, defuit. (*ad Quintum fratrem* 2.6 [5] 2)

---

[107] *D* 23.1.18, Ulp.: 'In sponsalibus constituendis parvi refert, per se (et coram an per internuntium vel per epistulam) an per alium hoc factum est: et fere plerumque condiciones interpositis personis expediuntur.'

[108] 'Consent to Roman marriage: some aspects of law and reality' 37, 40.

[109] *D* 23.1.7.1: 'In sponsalibus etiam consensus eorum exigendus est, quorum in nuptiis desideratur. intellegi tamen semper filiae patrem consentire nisi evidenter dissentiat, Iulianus scribit.' Cf. ht 12; Gaudemet, 'La conclusion des fiançailles à Rome à l'époque préclassique'.

[110] Cf. *D* 23.3.24, which shows a *filiafamilias* giving a dowry from her *peculium*.

[111] As of his son.   [112] *D* 23.2.19.

[113] e.g. Cic. *F* 3.12.2, 8.13.1; Pliny *Epp.* 6.26.

[114] *TLL* shows that *desponsalia*, *desponsatio*, and *desponsio* are late. *Sponsio* is not used to mean betrothal.

On 6 April I gave a betrothal party for Crassipes. That nice boy, your Quintus and mine, missed this feast because he was slightly unwell.

It seems that such parties were given by the woman's father[115] and that the fiancé was the guest of honour. Relatives, probably on both sides, would be invited, including children. (Young Quintus was ten years old.) These affairs could be large and grand, since fathers would seize the chance to celebrate an important new alliance as well as a happy family event. So a wide circle of acquaintances might be bidden to attend. Going to engagement parties was a social duty which might become a bore and an imposition, on a par with attending weddings and coming-of-age parties. It could eat up the time of the busy politician, who would be invited as a courtesy by *amici* (whose daughters, no doubt, were often unknown to him). Attendance was part of the politeness of princes.[116] Emperors would usually, it seems, make a major celebration of the betrothal parties of their daughters (three times, presumably, for Augustus' daughter Julia). Claudius was eccentric in treating the day of Octavia's betrothal as an ordinary working-day.[117] Other people's parties went off with more or less éclat: the notoriety of a certain modest affair was secured when Lollia Paullina turned up improperly dressed in her impressive collection of pearls and emeralds.[118]

The *sponsus* sent his betrothed a ring, which Tertullian calls *anulus pronubus*.[119] The Elder Pliny claims that even in his day the custom persisted of using an iron ring, the type which had been generally worn by Romans of all classes before the advent of luxury: 'etiam nunc sponsae muneris vice ferreus anulus mittitur, isque sine gemma' ('Even now an engaged woman is sent an iron ring as a present, not even one with a stone in it').[120] It seems doubtful if all *sponsi* kept up this tradition even in Pliny's time. Tertullian a century later speaks of a gold ring even in the good old days. Pliny's text suggests that it was sent rather than given in person at the *sponsalia*, but this again need not be inviolable custom. These are the only two certain references to

[115] Or by other family members in his absence. It is quite likely that Tullia's *sponsalia* with Dolabella included a party.
[116] Pliny *Epp.* 1.9.2; Sen. *Tranq.* 12.4 (to make it worse, the woman might be one who kept getting married); Suet. *DA* 53.3.
[117] Suet. *Cl.* 12.1.
[118] Pliny *NH* 9.117. They were worth 40m. sesterces and were (Pliny thinks) part of spoils seized by her grandfather M. Lollius. The text suggests that she was Gaius' wife at the time. (*Contra*, Balsdon, *RW* 264.)
[119] *Apol.* 6.4, claiming that old-fashioned women wore gold only on one finger, the one on which the *sponsus* had put the engagement ring, or (literally) 'the finger which the fiancé had pawned by means of the *anulus pronubus*'.   [120] *NH* 33.12.

an engagement ring in the classical period.[121] Both Greeks and Romans who wore rings for any reason would choose first to wear one on the finger next to the little finger of the left hand, from which a tiny nerve was thought to run straight to the heart, but no connection was made with engagement or wedding rings in particular.[122] Neither surviving Roman rings, which often have motifs of marriage, but cannot certainly be identified with those given by *sponsi*, nor representations in art help to give us further information on the engagement ring, although it seems likely that the woman continued to wear the same ring when married. It was a present, as Pliny says, just like other presents which might be exchanged by an engaged couple. Paul too talks of a particular fiancé sending his fiancée a ring as a present, one which did not belong to him (borrowed or stolen?), which he replaced with one which was his property after the wedding.[123] The symbolic value of this ring seems minor, but rings given by *sponsi* were no doubt usually not only presents but pledges of love and fidelity (*pignora*).[124] Such pledges were customary also in extra-marital love-affairs and in commercial transactions.[125]

The giving of the ring does not seem to have been a normal or necessary part of the celebration of the engagement. We have also to consider whether the giving of a kiss or the joining of right hands was ritually performed at the ceremony. The main evidence is a tendentious passage of Tertullian's tract on the veiling of virgins:

Si congressio viri mulierem facit, non tegantur, nisi post ipsam nuptiarum passionem. Atquin etiam apud ethnicos velatae ad virum ducuntur. Si autem ad desponsationem velantur, quia et corpore et spiritu masculo mixtae sunt per osculum et dexteras, per quae primum resignaverunt pudorem spiritus, per commune conscientiae pignus, quo totam condixerunt confusionem, quanto magis tempus illas velabit, sine quo sponsari non possunt, et quo urgente sine sponsalibus virgines desinunt esse. (Tertullian *de virginibus velandis* 11.4–5)

If it is sexual intercourse with a man which makes them women, they would not be veiled, except after they have undergone marriage. But even among the pagans women are led to their husbands veiled [sc. at the wedding]. But if they are veiled for their betrothal, because they are mingled with the male body and spirit through a kiss and their right hands, through which for the first time they give up the modesty of their spirit, through the shared pledge

---

[121] But there is a strong probability that Ter. *Ad.* 347 contains mention of a ring sent as earnest of intention to marry. Cf. Fantham, 'Sex, status and survival in Hellenistic Athens: a study of women in New Comedy' 55.

[122] Gell. 10.10.   [123] *D* 24.1.36.1.   [124] Cf. Juv. 6.27.

[125] Anné, *Les rites de fiançailles et la donation pour cause de mariage sous le bas-empire* 26 ff., 34 ff. The whole of the following discussion on rings and ceremonies is much indebted to Anné.

of their awareness, by which they contracted their complete fusion, how much more will time veil them, without which they cannot be engaged, and under pressure of which they cease to be virgins even without betrothal.

It is Tertullian's aim to encourage the wearing of veils by African girls from the beginning of puberty, not from marriage, the day of the wedding or engagement, because as soon as they become sexually aware they endanger both themselves and men. In arguing, fairly enough, that St Paul, when he told Corinthian women to cover their heads at Christian prayer-meetings, meant to include virgins,[126] he adds the opinion that nature, not marriage and parental decision, makes a girl adult. He makes the same point in his treatise on prayer:

De illis tamen quae sponsis dicantur constanter super meum modulum pronuntiare contestarique possum: velandas ex ea die esse qua primum viri corpus osculo et dextera expaverint. Omnia enim in his praenupserunt . . . et spiritus per conscientiam et pudor per osculi experimentum . . . et mens per voluntatem. (Tertullian *de oratione* 22.10)

I can firmly pronounce and argue in accordance with my prescription about those who are dedicated to *sponsi*: they ought to be veiled from the day on which they first trembled at the body of a man in the kiss and right hand. For in these things everything made an advance marriage . . . both their spirit through their awareness and their modesty through the trial of a kiss . . . and their mind through their will.

Tertullian clearly means that at the *desponsatio*, which made the girl *sponsa*, she and her *sponsus* joined hands and exchanged a kiss. He interprets this as signifying the couple's intention to consummate a physical union in marriage, and the consciousness of this intention and promise means that the girl has given up her maiden modesty. The physical contact with a male body and the mental awareness make her to all intents and purposes a married woman already. It may perhaps be accepted that Tertullian had observed that girls wore a veil at the *sponsalia*. His interpretation of the formal kiss would hardly have been recognized by his pagan contemporaries. To take a person by the hand and greet him with a kiss was common practice in Roman society.[127] In particular, it was customary between male and female relatives and between husbands and wives and to mark an agreement.[128] Since engagement was held to mark the beginning of new relationships (*affinitates*), it would be natural for these to be marked by a formal kiss of greeting, which might also symbolize a

[126] I Cor. 11.5ff. Cf. Anné, *Rites de fiançailles* 63–85, Barnes, *Tertullian* 140–1.
[127] Anné, *Rites de fiançailles* 65 (inadequately documented).
[128] *Ius osculi*: Plut. *QR* 6 = *Mor.* 265 B–C. Cf. *RE* x/2.1284–5 (Schneider); Plaut. *Amph.* 711 ff.; Anné, *Rites de fiançailles* 82–3.

promise (*pignus*) and prefigure the joining of hands at the wedding ceremony. It has also been argued that Tertullian might be referring, not to a recognized part of the ritual at the *sponsalia*, but to intimacies which might naturally be permitted between an engaged couple.[129] Not only the precise dating of the exchange and the insistence on its significance in both passages, but the usage of the kiss and the taking of the hand in non-erotic contexts are against this. But Tertullian can only be taken as evidence for North Africa. No other classical author takes any interest in a betrothal kiss. But in a constitution addressed to a *vicarius* in Spain Constantine refers to a kiss as if it were a normal and recognized part of a betrothal ceremony:

Imp. Constantinus ad Tiberianum vicarium Hispaniarum. Si ab sponso rebus sponsae donatis interveniente osculo ante nuptias hunc vel illam mori contigerit, dimidiam partem rerum donatarum ad superstitem pertinere praecipimus, dimidiam ad defuncti vel defunctae heredes, cuiuslibet gradus sint et quocumque iure successerint, ut donatio stare pro parte media et solvi pro parte media videatur: osculo vero non interveniente, sive sponsus sive sponsa obierit, totam infirmari donationem et donatori sponso vel heredibus eius restitui. Quod si sponsa interveniente vel non interveniente osculo sponsaliorum titulo (quod raro accidit) fuerit aliquid sponso largita et ante nuptias hunc vel illam mori contigerit, omni donatione infirmata ad donatricem sponsam sive eius successores donatarum rerum dominium transferatur. (*Codex Theodosianus* 3.5.6 = *Codex Justiniani* 5.3.16, AD 319)

The Emperor Constantine to Tiberianus, Governor of the Spains. If when things have been given by the *sponsus* to the *sponsa* when a kiss takes place, it happens that he or she dies before the marriage, we advise you that a half part of the things given belongs to the survivor and half to the heirs of the dead man or woman, of whatever degree of kinship they are and by whatever right they succeeded, so that the gift appears half to stand and half fall. But if the kiss has not taken place, whether the *sponsus* or the *sponsa* dies, the whole gift is invalidated and is restored to the *sponsus*, the giver, or to his heirs. But if the *sponsa*, whether or not a kiss occurs, bestows something on her *sponsus* as a betrothal present[130] (which rarely happens) and it happens that he or she dies before the marriage, then the whole gift is invalidated and the ownership of the things given must be transferred to the *sponsa*, the giver, or to her successors.

Here the kiss clearly marks the conclusion of a formal betrothal. We cannot be sure whether it was Constantine who introduced the point about whether the betrothal was formal or not into the correspondence, but it sounds very much as if his mention of the kiss is a routine way of describing a formal engagement, familiar to the central

---

[129] Anné, *Rites de fiançailles* 68.
[130] Not 'on the strength of her engagement', since *CJ* reads *donationis*.

bureaucracy and not limited to Spain. Anné has argued convincingly from the evidence that a kiss was later part of the betrothal ceremony all over the Latin West as well as in the eastern Empire and that it had its origin in pagan Roman custom, general in the western provinces, rather than in eastern or Christian practices.[131]

Classical betrothal, then, lacked legal forms, although the exchange of a kiss seems to have been a normal part of the ceremony in the western Empire before the early fourth century AD, and the giving of a ring by the *sponsus* was accepted custom, though not necessarily associated with the actual *sponsalia*. Since in the classical period of Roman law an engagement was not actionable, it was not accompanied by the giving of sureties, an eastern practice which seems to have been introduced by Constantine and his successors.[132] But it was usual for *sponsi* and their families to give valuable gifts about the time of the engagement. By the *Lex Cincia* of *c.* 200 BC, gifts between *sponsi* and between parent-in-law and son- or daughter-in-law, as between blood relations, were exempt from the limits on the value of gifts set by the law.[133] The praetorian edict distinguished between gifts given out of liberality and munificence and those given with a purpose. The classical jurists applied this distinction to gifts between *sponsi*. If the *sponsus* or *sponsa* gave the other a gift out of liberality, *liberalitatis gratia*, the gift immediately became the recipient's property and could not be reclaimed.[134] If the *sponsus* gave a gift *liberalitatis causa* and was then killed by the enemy, the gift remained valid.[135] If the *sponsus* gave the *sponsa* a slave and her father gave him a baggage-animal, and then no marriage followed, the *sponsus* was not entitled to take back the slave and could be sued if he did.[136] But if a gift were given *affinitatis contrahendae causa*, for the sake of contracting a marriage relationship, then it could be reclaimed if no marriage followed, unless it were the donor who broke the engagement.[137] The gift, to be valid, had to be made before the marriage and could not be given on condition that it took effect on marriage.[138] Apart from slaves and livestock, we hear of gifts such as a farm and a silver vessel.[139] Gifts were made by the parents as well as by the parties themselves[140] and

---

[131] pp. 71–85. I do not think we need add to the evidence on kissing the passage about Corduban custom quoted by Frassinetti 182.

[132] Anné, *Rites de fiançailles* 87–135, with earlier bibliography, Corbett 18–23.

[133] *FV* 302, Paul. The maximum amount of the value of the gifts is not stated.

[134] *D* 39.5.1.1, Iul.

[135] *CJ* 5.3.11, Diocletian and Maximian. Cf. *FV* 262, Pap., on *res simpliciter donatae*.

[136] *CJ* 5.3.10, Diocletian and Maximian.

[137] *FV* 262. Cf. *CJ* 5.3.7, Carus and Numerian, 15, Constantine. This is the beginning of what in the 4th cent. became *donatio ante nuptias*.

[138] *FV* 96; Paul; *CJ* 5.3.6, Aurelian; *D* 24.1.5 pr., etc.; *CJ* 3.5.4, Gordian, AD 239.

[139] *CJ* 5.3.10, 14, 8, 12; *FV* 96.   [140] *CJ* 5.3.10, 12.

were also given to the parents.[141] The *sponsa* might receive gifts on the day of the *sponsalia* or after: this sounds as if other relatives and friends might want to mark the occasion.[142] A gift from the *sponsus* might become part of the dowry which the *sponsa* brought to him on marriage.[143] Constantine erased the distinction between free and conditional gifts between *sponsi*. According to his ruling of AD 319, if the *sponsus* or his parent failed to fulfil his engagement, then the *sponsa* could keep his gifts. If it was the fault of the *sponsa* or her *paterfamilias*, then the *sponsus* could sue for restitution of his gifts. Similarly, the *sponsa* lost her gifts to the *sponsus* if she broke the engagement and could sue for them if he broke it. Heirs of either had the same rights.[144] This ruling about engagements voluntarily broken by either party was followed in 336 by a ruling on engagements broken by death which allowed each party or his or her heirs to keep half of the gifts of the *sponsus* to the *sponsa* if the other party died (as long as the betrothal was formal), but returned the whole gift given by the *sponsa* to the *sponsus* to her or her heirs if she or her *sponsus* died.[145]

The development of such gifts into *donatio ante nuptias*, an endowment of the wife by the future husband, is outside our scope, since, although roots can be found, for the West, in Celtic custom and in Roman gifts from the *sponsus*, and, for the East, in widespread customs of non-Greek peoples, it only became accepted by imperial legislators from Constantine onwards.[146]

(c) Age of sponsi and length of betrothals

Sponsi were supposed to be of an age to understand what they were promising. Post-classical jurists set a minimum age of 7.[147] Non-jurists did not always think understanding so important. Octavian and Antony betrothed their daughters Julia and Antonia, both born in 39 BC, to the young M. Antonius Antyllus and to L. Domitius Ahenobarbus respectively in 37.[148] Through Octavian, Agrippa's daughter Vipsania Agrippina was betrothed to Tiberius when she was scarcely a year old. Since her mother Caecilia Attica was born in 51 and

---

[141] *CJ* 5.3.2.   [142] *D* 16.3.25 pr.
[143] *CJ* 5.3.1, Severus and Caracalla, 14, Diocletian and Maximian.   [144] *CJ* 5.3.15.
[145] *CJ* 5.3.16. Gifts for the *sponsa* might be received on her behalf by her father or mother (*D* 3.5.31[32].1, 16.3.25 pr.).   [146] See Anné, *Rites de fiançailles* 239–486, esp. 395–460.
[147] *D* 23.1.14: 'In sponsalibus contrahendis aetas contrahentium definita non est ut in matrimoniis. Quapropter et a primordio aetatis sponsalia effici possunt, si modo id fieri ab utraque persona intellegatur, id est, si non sint minores quam septem annis' ('The age for contracting engagements is not laid down like that for marriages, so engagements can be made from the earliest age, as long as both persons understand what is happening, that is, if they are not younger than seven'). The text could well be interpolated from 'si modo' or from the gloss, 'id est', to the end.   [148] Dio 48.54, 51.15.5; Suet. *DA* 63.

married perhaps in 37,[149] if we put her birth in 36 and betrothal in 35, then her *sponsus* was himself only about 7.[150] It seems to have been considered unusual for a boy to be engaged before he took the *toga virilis*.[151] Claudius' daughter Octavia was betrothed in infancy to L. Iunius Silanus.[152] Considerations of advantage on both sides led to the provisional establishment of such heiresses early in life. But often, perhaps because good matches failed to materialize, or because it was more advantageous to keep a number of suitors hopeful or to wait and see how possible *sponsi* turned out—or perhaps simply because the sources fail to inform us of failed early engagements or the early date of successful ones—we hear of engagements either a short time before a marriage or when a girl was barely marriageable (i.e. reached puberty or the age of 12) or because they happened unusually late.[153] It must also be remembered that many men evaded the purpose of the *Lex Julia de maritandis ordinibus* by making engagements with immature girls and still claiming the privileges of married men.[154]

Apart from such artificial limits, engagements could be of varying duration.

Saepe iustae et necessariae causae non solum annum vel biennium, sed etiam triennium et quadriennium et ulterius trahunt sponsalia, veluti valetudo sponsi sponsaeve vel mortes parentium aut capitalia crimina aut longiores peregrinationes quae ex necessitate fiunt. (*Digest* 23.1.17, Gaius *i ad legem Iuliam et Papiam*)

Often just and necessary reasons draw out an engagement not only for a year or two, but even for three or four years or longer, for instance the ill health of the *sponsus* or *sponsa* or the deaths of parents or capital charges or unusually long trips abroad which must be undertaken.

Gaius was presumably commenting on Augustus' two-year limit. It is a pity that the extract is so brief. We should expect him to mention the incapacity of the girl by reason of age, and perhaps the occupation of the *sponsus* in a public career, though that is partly covered by

---

[149] *RE* suppl. i.268 (Münzer). She first appears in Cic. *A* 6.2 (SB 116) 10 (? late Apr. 50 BC) as of an age to receive messages of affection.

[150] The betrothal of Vipsania antedated Atticus' death in 32 (Nep. *A* 19.4).

[151] Attention is drawn to Caesar and Quinctilius Varus as *praetextati* (Suet. *DJ* 1.1; Sen. *Contr.* 1.3.10), to Claudius as *admodum adulescens* (Suet. *Cl.* 26.1), and to his son Drusus as almost sexually mature, *prope iam puberem* (Suet. *Cl.* 27.2).

[152] Dio 60.5.7, AD 41. Agrippina destroyed the engagement in 48 and Octavia was betrothed to Nero in 49 (Tac. *A* 12.3–4, 9; Suet. *Cl.* 27.2).

[153] e.g. Tac. *Ag.* 9.7; *vixdum nubilis*: Otho's daughter at the time of her betrothal to Drusus, son of Germanicus (Suet. *Otho* 1.3); Tac. *A* 6.15.1. The long but abortive engagement between an Antonia and a son of Lepidus (n. 65) exemplifies early arrangements made for political advantage and remembered, or broken, when politics dictated.

[154] Suet. *DA* 34.2; Dio 54.16.7, 56.7.2.

peregrinationes, if the word may be taken to include foreign service. Nor is it clear whether one or two years might be considered a normal desirable maximum in the absence of considerations of the Julio-Papian Law, which would only affect men over 25. Later emperors ruled that it was permissible for girls to break engagements if the young man had failed to marry them within two years or had gone abroad for three. Girls could not be expected to lose the opportunity for marriage at the right age.[155] Augustine suggests—tendentiously, but there may be something in it—that engagements were prolonged in order to ensure that the frustrated *sponsus* valued his bride.[156]

Tacitus' engagement may indicate the norm. Agricola engaged his daughter to him in AD 77. Agricola was then suffect consul and the girl very promising, 'egregiae tum spei': she had been born in AD 64, so she was about 13. Tacitus himself was at least 19. The exact date of Agricola's consulship, which probably lasted two months, is not known. After his consulship Agricola bestowed Julia on Tacitus in marriage, was immediately appointed to the governorship of Britain, and probably left for his province in early 78. So the length of the engagement is vague, but must be well under a year and could be as short as two months. There was clearly an appreciable interval.[157] Delay imposed or justified by the provincial command of a *sponsus* is exemplified in Tiberius' engagement to Julia, pregnant by her previous husband, in 12 BC. He was sent off to Pannonia after the betrothal and returned to marry her in 11.[158] Tullia's third engagement casts little light on the question. She seems to have been betrothed to Dolabella in late May or in June of 50 BC and married soon after, probably on 1 July.[159] There is no indication that anyone thought of postponing the wedding until Cicero returned in November or that he thought of speeding up his slow journey.

The interval between formal betrothal and wedding could be no more than a few days, and a formal betrothal could be omitted altogether, though the eastern Dio (at the end of our period) thinks that would be illegal.[160]

4. Breaking an Engagement

Either party or a *paterfamilias* could break an engagement, either in person or by messenger or letter (*repudiare, repudium mittere*,

---

[155] *CJ* 5.1.2, Constantine, 5.17.2, Valerian and Gallienus.
[156] *Conf.* 8.3.7. [157] Tac. *Ag.* 9.7. [158] Dio 54.31.2, 35.4.
[159] Since Cicero paid the second instalment of the dowry on 1 July 48 (*A* 11.3.1, cf. 4a), this will have been the wedding anniversary.
[160] Suet. *Gaius* 25.1; *D* 23.1.9; Dio 59.12.1.

repudium renuntiare, nuntium remittere).[161] No especial difficulty attached to a *repudium*, although valuable gifts which had been given on condition that a marriage would follow, or dowry which had already been transferred to the *sponsus*, might have to be returned.[162] In earlier times censors and praetors had penalized fathers who broke an engagement by giving a woman to another man.[163] But in the late Republic there were no constraints.

The Julian and Claudian families may be used to illustrate the incidence of broken engagements, although they provide an extreme case. At 16, Julius Caesar broke off his match with the wealthy Cossutia (which had probably been approved by his father, who died the year before), apparently having already planned the marriage with Cornelia which soon followed.[164] As a father, he brought about the breaking of his daughter Julia's engagement to Caepio.[165] The young Octavian similarly jettisoned the daughter of P. Servilius Isauricus when a more advantageous alliance offered with Antony's stepdaughter Clodia.[166] In 39, the short-lived agreement reached at Puteoli was marked by the engagement of the infant daughter of Sextus Pompey and Scribonia to Octavian's nephew and Antony's stepson, the 3-year-old Marcellus.[167] Two abortive engagements, one dubious, are recorded for Octavian's daughter Julia in early childhood.[168] Claudius, Livia's grandson, was engaged to Aemilia Lepida, daughter of Augustus' granddaughter Julia, but he had to break off the engagement because her parents, the younger Julia and L. Aemilius Paullus, had offended Augustus. It is difficult to conjecture any cause of offence except the fatal scandal which ruined Julia in AD 8.[169] Similarly, in AD 48 Claudius broke the engagement between his daughter Octavia and L. Junius Silanus, son of the same Aemilia Lepida, which had stood since AD 41, since, allegedly because of the plotting of Agrippina (his mother's first cousin), the young praetor

---

[161] Plaut. *Aul.* 783, *Truc.* 848; Ter. *Ph.* 928; *D* 23.1.6 (a girl's tutors did not have authority to break her engagement by themselves, any more than they could ratify it), ht 10 (a girl's *paterfamilias* could break her engagement, but if she was emancipated he could not, nor reclaim any dowry which he had already paid), 50.16.101.1, 191 (vocabulary).

[162] Gifts: Corbett 18–19; *dos*: *D* 22.1.38.1.

[163] Varro *LL* 6.71. Several excerpts on engagements come from commentaries on edicts (*D* 23.1.7–9, 13, 18).   [164] Suet. *DJ* 1.1.

[165] Suet. *DJ* 21. For detailed discussion see B.A. Marshall 'The engagement of Faustus Sulla and Pompeia' 91 ff.

[166] Suet. *DA* 62.1.   [167] App. *BC* 5.73; Dio 48.38.3.

[168] Suet. *DA* 63.2: Antony's son Antyllus (cf. Dio 48.54, 51.15.5) and, according to Antony, the Getan king, Cotiso.

[169] Suet. *Cl.* 26.1. Aemilia Lepida was born *c*.3 BC and eventually married M. Junius Silanus (consul AD 19), as demonstrated by Pliny *NH* 7.58 (*PIR²* A419). Syme (*RR* 432) conjectured that she was betrothed to Silanus in AD 8, but now connects the breaking of the engagement to Claudius with her parents' disgrace that year (*History in Ovid* 208).

had been accused of incest with his sister Junia Calvina, daughter-in-law of the prosecutor Vitellius.[170] An engagement between Quinctilius Varus, a grandson of the younger Marcella and great-grandson of Octavia, and one of the daughters of Germanicus, which was of long standing, seems to have come to nothing, perhaps because of the condemnation of his mother Claudia Pulchra and the unsuccessful accusation brought against him in AD 27.[171] Nothing is heard of the sequel to the betrothal of Germanicus' son Drusus and the barely marriageable daughter of Otho.[172]

We hear of some betrothals broken by the death of one of the couple, natural or not. Augustus' adoptive son, L. Caesar, at the time of his death in AD 2 was betrothed to another Aemilia Lepida, who carried in her veins the blood of Pompey and Sulla.[173] Claudius' second fiancée, Livia Medullina, is said to have died on the day chosen for the wedding.[174] Claudius' elder son, Drusus, died by a bizarre accident a few days after he had been betrothed to Sejanus' daughter.[175] His cousin, Germanicus' son Nero, had been betrothed in AD 17 to Junia, daughter of Q. Caecilius Metellus Creticus Silanus, but she died fairly soon after, and he married Julia, daughter of Tiberius' son Drusus, in AD 20.[176] One of the daughters of Germanicus also lost a *sponsus* in AD 22, Asinius Saloninus, son of Gallus and Vipsania Agrippina.[177]

Removal by execution of a person betrothed to a member of the imperial house must have been repellent. It was proper for the connection to be broken first. When Silanus committed suicide on the day Claudius married Agrippina, odium attached to Claudius, whom the author of the *Apocolocyntosis* accuses of killing his son-in-law. The engagement between Julia and Antyllus must have been obsolete for some time if Antony taunted Octavian with having betrothed her to Cotiso, and Octavian will certainly have renounced it before the campaign of Actium, but still Dio is shocked at the murder of Antyllus, because he had been betrothed to Caesar's daughter.[178] Similarly, the execution of Sejanus was more horrifying because of his connections with the imperial house, not only the betrothal of his daughter to the ill-fated son of Claudius, but because he himself was, if we can trust our sources, at the time betrothed to someone who

[170] Tac. *A* 12.3–4, cf. 8.1–2; Suet. *Cl.* 27.2; Dio 60.5.7, 61.31.7–8, cf. 21.5.
[171] Sen. *Contr.* 1.3.10; Tac. *A* 4.66.1. See Humphrey, 'The three daughters of Agrippina maior' 131.   [172] Suet. *Otho* 1.3.
[173] Tac. *A* 3.23.1; *PIR*[2] A420.   [174] Suet. *Cl.* 26.1; *PIR*[2] L213.
[175] Suet. *Cl.* 27.1; cf. Tac. *A* 6.8.6.
[176] Tac. *A* 2.43.3; *CIL* 6.914: 'Iunia Silani [f. spon]sa Neronis Caesaris.' Julia: Tac. *A* 3.29.4.
[177] Tac. *A* 3.75.1. Cf. Humphrey, 'The three daughters of Agrippina maior' 131.
[178] *Apoc.* 10.4, 11.2; cf. Suet. *Cl.* 27.2, Dio 60.31.8, 51.15.5.

stood in the relation of a daughter to the emperor. Tacitus makes two orators in the aftermath of the fall of Sejanus stress his *affinitas* to the imperial house and call him the *gener* (son-in-law) of Tiberius. Zonaras, following Dio, states categorically that Tiberius in AD 30 made Sejanus a kinsman through Julia, the daughter of his son Drusus. But it seems likely that he has confused Julia with her mother Livia Julia and that the engagement considered in AD 25 had been ratified.[179]

Fathers in the governing class often broke engagements for reasons of political advantage. However, it is clear that they might also do so if they discovered that the marriage was likely to be unhappy. The charge against Silanus, of incest with his sister, was calculated to upset an affectionate father. As Tacitus says, 'Caesar listened, because out of love for his daughter he was readier to entertain suspicions against his son-in-law.'[180] *Sponsi* seem to have been often rejected (whether honestly or not) for moral reasons, and a man who suffered several broken engagements would get a bad name.[181] The morals of *sponsae* might come under severer attack, since they could, under the developed Augustan Law as interpreted by Septimius Severus, be accused of adultery.[182]

Other reasons might be discovered which made a projected marriage ineligible. For instance, Seneca imagines a father discovering that a daughter's fiancé is a non-citizen. The impossibility of the pair forming a valid marriage gives him a proper pretext to break off the match.[183] The example suggests that it was correct for an engagement to be broken only for strong reasons. Nevertheless, either party was legally free to break it at any time[184] and there was little social disadvantage attached, unless one was often repudiated or excessively inconsiderate in repudiating. A father in comedy is naturally prepared to be incensed when he receives a message of *repudium* precisely as he has just completed preparations for his daughter's wedding, but instantly placated by the substitution of a new bridegroom.[185] Cato took offence when he lost Aemilia Lepida to Metellus Scipio, who had been engaged to her before but repudiated her. Cato attacked Scipio in the manner of Archilochus.[186] On the other hand, the Caepio whose engagement to Caesar's daughter Julia was broken when her father gave her to Pompey in 59 was apparently willing to be mollified by an alliance with Pompey's own daughter,

---

[179] Tac. *A* 5.6.2, 6.8.6; Dio 58.3.9 (Zonaras), cf. 58.7.5; Suet. *Tib.* 65.1. See E. Meise, *Untersuchungen zur Geschichte der Julisch-Claudischen Dynastie* 57–60.
[180] Tac. *A* 12.4.3.   [181] Sen. *Ben.* 4.27.5, unless this refers to divorce.
[182] *D* 48.5.14.3.   [183] Sen. *Ben.* 4.35.1.
[184] e.g. *CJ* 5.1.1, Diocletian and Maximian.   [185] Plaut. *Aul.* 783–4.
[186] Plut. *Cato min.* 7.1–2.

which indeed offered him a more eminent father-in-law. She was already engaged to Faustus Sulla, and eventually married him, not Caepio.[187]

The concern of family members in an engagement is well represented by one of the formulae for rupture, *affinitatem renuntiare* (to renounce a relationship).[188] For an engagement created the same ties as marriage. The vocabulary of relationship by marriage was used from the time of betrothal,[189] as has become sufficiently clear from the preceding discussion. Silanus, as Claudius' son-in-law elect, had carried out many of the functions and enjoyed the promotions proper to an actual son-in-law.[190]

5. The Engaged Couple

There is unfortunately very little evidence which might cast light on how the relationship of an engaged couple was expected to develop before the marriage. Were even young *sponsi* allowed time together, so that they might get to know each other? What were the standards of chaperonage? It is a pity that we so rarely know dates of betrothal and marriage, even in the relatively well documented imperial family. If it was known well in advance, for instance, that Drusus and Antonia were to marry, as they eventually did at the relatively advanced ages of 21 or 22 and 19 or 20, then they certainly had some opportunity to get to know each other in the closely linked households of their childhood, those of Livia and Octavia. The same can be said for Julia and Marcellus, brought up again by Livia and Octavia. They married at 14 and 17. Examples could be multiplied for the Julio-Claudian family, which became more and more intertwined with itself. The well-bred girl of comedy, who is not normally given the chance to speak to her *sponsus* before the wedding, is not a type who can be found in literature from the first century BC on. Romance instead idealizes the heroine who is already in love with her affianced husband, even if their affection needs to be explained by blood-relationship and a shared upbringing.[191] The virgin certainly needed to be protected from seducers, but the phobia of pre-marital sex with a *sponsus* does not seem to occur until the empire becomes Christian.[192] Rather, the maiden is to warm to her future husband. Ovid's *Amores*, he claims, were not for puritans, but highly suitable reading for the engaged girl or the inexperienced boy: 'Me legat in sponsi facie non frigida virgo' ('Let me be read by the maiden who

[187] Plut. *Pomp.* 47.6, cf. *Caes.* 14.4; App. *BC* 2.14; Suet. *DJ* 21.
[188] D 22.1.38.1.   [189] D 22.5.5, 38.10.6.1. Cf. 23.2.12.2, ht 14.4.
[190] *PIR²* 1829.   [191] Apul. *M* 4.26.   [192] Tert. *de virg. vel.* 11.3.

warms to see her betrothed').[193] Ovid paints a picture of the degree of
physical intimacy which a *sponsus* might expect when Cydippe, who is
pining away, writes to Acontius of her frustrated and anxious
affianced husband:

> Et minus audacter blanditur et oscula rara
> appetit et timido me vocat ore suam.
>
> (*Heroides* 21.195–6)

He woos me less boldly and seeks few kisses and calls me his own in a
frightened voice.

Even St Augustine allowed kisses between an engaged couple as a
sign of love (unless he refers to the ritual kiss of the *sponsalia*) and
Ambrose in his commentary on the Song of Solomon (where the
passionate girl was taken as an allegory for the Church awaiting
Christ) has some practical remarks on the desirability of encouraging
love by gentle wooing, and in his explanation of Psalm 118 sympathet-
ically portrays the aroused passions of the engaged girl.[194] A discreet
display of passion in courtship during the engagement is also allowed
for in Statius' epithalamium for Stella and Violentilla.[195] But she had
been married before.

---

[193] *Am.* 2.1.3 ff.

[194] Aug. *de amicitia* 6 = PL 83.811; Ambrose *Comm. in cant. cant.* 1.2 = PL 15.1853–4,
Expositio in Ps. cxviii = PL 15.1201: 'Constitue ergo virginem desponsatam multo tempore et
iusto ferventem amore, quae multa probata opera dilecti probabilium testium adsertione
cognoverit desideriis suspensis dilatam frequenter, iam non ferentem moras, quae omnia
fecisset, ut sponsum videret, aliquando votis potitam suis, ad improvisum sponsi adventum
gaudio turbatam, non quaerere primordia salutationis, non verborum vices, sed statim quod
desiderasset exigere.' Aug. *Enarratio in Psalm.* 122.5 = PL 36.1633 counselled postponement
of love until the girl was safely married.

[195] *S* 1.2.26 ff.

5

Nova Nupta and *Novus Coniunx*

Every woman should marry—and no man.
(Disraeli, *Lothair*, chapter 30)

A MARRIAGE is initiated, in law, by an exchange of consent. The beginning, as an important event, was also often marked by ritual and celebration. The legal, religious, and social features of *nuptiae* were often almost inextricably intertwined. Such complexity is after all appropriate to an action which makes a transition for both bride and bridegroom, changes the composition of two families, and brings with it the hope of children and new dispositions of property.

1. Ceremony and Celebration

Much information about quaint rituals is collected in the handbooks, and the more striking customs tend to be known only from classical antiquarians.[1] We must be careful not to assume that every upper-class wedding incorporated all the small religious rites which are attested, any more than that every individual English family at Christmas clings to all the customs which have clustered round that festival from the Middle Ages to the twentieth century. Wassail-bowls and Christmas trees come and go. So may the parting and braiding of a Roman bride's hair or the carrying of a coin in her shoe. Such details are preserved by antiquarians. A writer who mentions a wedding incidentally or wants to pick out a few salient features of a normal wedding will concentrate on such features as the dinner, the sealing of the dotal tablets by witnesses, the passage of the bride to the bridegroom's house. These were all normal components of an upper-class wedding in the early Principate.

The expense of the wedding seems normally to have been under-taken by the bride's family.[2] Occasionally the bridegroom had to pay,

---

[1] Balsdon, *RW* 180ff., gives a refreshingly judicious account.
[2] Plaut. *Aul.* 294–5; Varro *Men.* 40–1; *D* 26.7.52: 'Curator pro minore non tantum dotem dare debet, sed etiam impendia, quae ad nuptias facienda sunt.'

if for some reason the festivities took place at his house.[3] From time to time sumptuary laws attempted to check expenditure on wedding-feasts. It seems that they might be seen as a very special celebration, for a second-century *Lex Licinia* set limits of 200 *asses* for a wedding, but only 30 for ordinary dinners. Similarly, Augustus put weddings and the drinking-parties which followed at the top rate: 200 sesterces for ordinary days, 300 for festivals, but 1,000 for weddings.[4] These limits were no doubt often exceeded.

We often hear of weddings which begin in the town house of the bride's family. Scaevola mentions one which was to take place in a suburban house in a park which belonged to her future husband. The bride was taken there three days before and given separate apart-ments, and the move to his quarters (which corresponded with the usual procession through the streets from one house to another) was carefully distinguished. Messallina also found a spacious suburban house attractive.[5] There was nothing to stop a marriage taking place quietly on a country estate or in the husband's province.[6] The day of the wedding was supposed to be carefully chosen. A number of days were to be avoided for religious reasons: various sacred periods, *dies religiosi* (when battles and judicial activity were also avoided), *dies festi* (religious festivals), except that widows could remarry then because they would have fewer guests, the Kalends, Nones, and Ides of each month.[7] It may have been reassuring for bride and bridegroom to know that in classical law they could not be summoned to appear in court on their wedding-day.[8] The day was set and the guests summoned.[9] It was a duty (*officium*) to accept wedding-invitations and both the wedding and the group of guests who attended it were also called the *officium*.[10] Well-attended weddings were *celebres*: the crowds, the noise, and the public splendour all made an impact on the neighbours and others who were not invited.[11] The wedding of Marcus Aurelius was made *celeberrimae* when Pius even gave a donative to the troops to mark the occasion.[12] Grand guests added éclat: so Claudius and Agrippina graced the weddings of

[3] e.g. Juv. 6.202–3. Cf. Rage-Brocard '*Deductio in domum mariti*' 19–20.

[4] Gell. 2.24.7ff.

[5] *D* 24.1.66.1; Juv. 10.334 (sc. her *horti*, which had previously belonged to Lucullus and Asiaticus).   [6] Apul. *Apol.* 87; *HA Marc.* 9.4.

[7] Marquardt, *PL* 43 = *VP* 51–2; Balsdon, *RW* 180–1. The taboo times are 18–21 Feb., Mar., esp. 1, 9, 23, May, the first two weeks of June, 24 Aug., 5 Oct., 8 Nov. On the primitive calendar for marriage, Torelli, *LR* 19ff.

[8] *D* 2.4.2.   [9] *Adhibere*: Tac. *A* 11.27.1; Juv. 2.135.

[10] Suet. *Cl.* 26.3, *Nero* 28.1; Juv. 6.203; Apul. *M* 4.26.

[11] Phaedr. 1.6.1; Stat. *S* 1.2.230ff. *Celebrare nuptias* is the usual phrase for holding a wedding: Verg. *A* 7.555; Tac. *A* 4.75.1.

[12] *HA Pius* 10.2. Cf. for other donatives on the occasion of imperial weddings *HA Marc.* 27.8.

a freedman and of a chief centurion who followed the emperor's example and married their nieces.[13] The bridegroom would come attended by a throng of his relations, making offerings at temples en route.[14] At Larinum it was said to be the custom to invite a great crowd to the dinner.[15] People of higher social class might be asked. Some Roman aristocrats had a taste for attending the weddings of such disreputable people as mimes and clowns.[16]

The bride's toilette was part of the festivities for the women of the family. The dress prescribed by the antiquarians was a woollen tunic woven on an archaic upright loom (*tunica recta*), fastened by a girdle (*cingulum*) knotted with a complicated 'Herculean' knot (which the bridegroom would have to untie).[17] On her feet she wore orange slippers, *lutei socci*.[18] Her hair was parted and plaited into six braids. For this a spear should be used, the *hasta caelibaris*.[19] The coiffure was fastened with woollen fillets, crowned with a garland and then a flame-coloured veil.[20] This *flammeum* is undoubtedly archaic, since it was also the daily ceremonial garment of the wife of the priest of Jupiter. It continued as one of the main symbols and components of the wedding ceremony, routinely mentioned by many authors.[21] Indeed, the verb used of the woman marrying, *nubo*, is related to *nubes*, a cloud, and means literally 'I veil myself'. From this come *nupta*, a married woman, *nova nupta*, a bride, and *nuptiae*, the wedding. The event turns on the bride and on her veiling.[22] In classical times rich brides would wear jewels.[23] The ceremony of dressing provided an opportunity for emotion, advice, and good wishes. Apuleius draws a pathetic picture of a mother adorning her daughter, with kisses and prayers for grandchildren.[24] The bridegroom was also expected to make a careful toilette, unlike Cato, who turned up in his horrific whiskers.[25] The houses of bride and bridegroom would have doorway and vestibule garlanded with green boughs and flowers, the façade decorated with hangings.[26] The house and even the crossroads on the processional route might also be illuminated with torches.[27]

[13] Suet. *Cl.* 26.3: 'nuptiarum officium et ipse cum Agrippina celebravit.'
[14] Apul. *M* 4.26.   [15] Cic. *Clu.* 166.
[16] Plut. *Ant.* 9.3–4 (Antony got drunk at the wedding of Hippias).
[17] Fest. 55L, 342L, 364L; Isid. *Orig.* 19.22.18.   [18] Cat. 61.9–10.
[19] Ov. *F* 2.560; Plut. *Rom.* 15.5, *QR* 87; Fest. 55L, 454L; Arnob. 2.67. Torelli, *LR* 33 ff., has treated this topic in detail and helpfully compares modern 'Afro' styles.
[20] Prop. 4.11.34; Serv. ad *A* 7.403; Fest. 56L.
[21] e.g. Caecil. *com.* 198; Cat. 61.8; Stat. *Theb.* 2.341; Juv. 6.225. Cf. Rage-Brocard, '*Deductio in domum mariti*' 22.
[22] *OLD* s.v.   [23] Lucan 2.360ff.   [24] Apul. *M* 4.26.
[25] Lucan 2.372ff. For the well-groomed man, perfumed and garlanded, see Apul. *M* 4.27.
[26] Cat. 64.293; Lucan 2.354–5; Stat. *S* 1.2.231; Juv. 6.51–2 (with Courtney ad loc.), 79, 227–8; Apul. *M* 4.26.   [27] Stat. *S* 1.2.231; Apul. *M* 4.26.

Omens must be sought and recorded.[28] Originally real diviners, *auspices* skilled in interpreting the flight of birds, had attended weddings. But by Cicero's time a friend of the family who attended bore the title of *auspex*.[29] Like the veil, the *auspices* were part of a proper formal wedding, signifying the public approval of the couple's friends. It was shocking to do without them.[30] Although bird-watching had gone out of fashion, mention is made of favourable omens, which were no doubt secured from examining the entrails at the sacrifice.[31] It is not certain to which deities sacrifice was made. The sources are usually vague, mentioning 'gods', but Tellus and Ceres are sometimes specified. In the Principate an offering might be made to the emperor.[32] If the sacrifice were omitted, bad luck might be expected to follow. Even Cato and Marcia did not omit that element.[33] The *auspex* 'was a cross between a family priest and a best man'.[34] But it was usual to have more than one: Cato and Marcia, at their second wedding, are said to have displayed Stoic restraint by having only one, Cato's nephew Brutus.[35] The *auspices* pronounced some solemn words to the couple, or at least the bride.[36]

Some verbal exchange may have taken place between bride and bridegroom. But the consent of the man could also be signified in his absence by letter or a messenger. If parents or other responsible relatives participated, they handed over the bride, but it is not clear that this was a formal part of the ceremony. Tiberius handed his niece Agrippina over to Cn. Domitius on Capri and ordered the wedding to be held in Rome.[37] The important thing was that a marriage was more respectable *tradentibus parentibus*.[38] A married woman (married only once and with a living husband) called the *pronuba* had the role of joining the bride to her husband.[39] In art, the moment in which the couple joined their right hands had immense significance. Pledging faith by clasping hands is commonly mentioned in many contexts in literature, but is not particularly emphasized in relation to

[28] Cic. *Clu.* 14; Verg. *A* 4.45; Vell. 2.79.2. Cf. Humbert, *Remariage à Rome* 12 ff.

[29] *Div.* 1.28: 'Nihil fere quondam maioris rei nisi auspicato ne privatim quidem gerebatur, quod etiam nunc nuptiarum auspices declarant, qui re omissa nomen tantum tenent.' Cf. Varro ap. Serv. ad *A* 4.45; VM 2.1.1: 'Apud antiquos non solum publice, sed etiam privatim nihil gerebatur nisi auspicio prius sumpto. Quo ex more nuptiis etiam nunc auspices interponuntur, qui, quamvis auspicia petere desierint, ipso tamen nomine veteris consuetudinis vestigia usurpantur.' Humbert, *Remariage à Rome* 14.

[30] Plaut. *Cas.* 86; Cic. *Clu.* 14.

[31] Cf. Vell. 2.79.2; Stat. *S* 1.2.229–30; Serv. ad *A* 3.136; Humbert, *Remariage à Rome* 12 ff.

[32] Corbett 72–3; Humbert, *Remariage à Rome* 16; Price, *Rituals and power. The Roman imperial cult in Asia Minor* 119.

[33] See Williams, *Figures of thought in Roman poetry* 54–5, on Cat. 68.75–6; Lucan 2.353.

[34] Balsdon, *RW* 183. [35] Lucan 2.371. [36] Tac. *A* 11.27.1.

[37] Tac. *A* 4.75.1. [38] *Decl. min.* 251.3. Cf. Cat. 62.60–1.

[39] Isid. *Etym.* 9.7.8–9.

weddings.[40] The dotal contract, an important legal concomitant of marriage, was often ratified at the wedding. This is described in the literary sources of the Principate as *tabulae* or *tabulae nuptiales*, by jurists as *tabulae dotales*, or similar names.[41] Its sealing by the witnesses was normally an important moment.[42] Obviously the contract was drawn up carefully in advance of the wedding. It contained a statement of the contents of the dowry and agreements about what would happen to the dowry at the end of the marriage.[43] The earliest reference to such a document is in later descriptions of the marriage of Messallina and Silius in AD 48,[44] but the contract had no doubt long been normal. To act as witness was a friend's duty and privilege and added to the solemnity and sentiment of the occasion. According to Augustine, the contract was read aloud in the presence of the guests.[45] The witnesses took it in turns to attach their seals to the dotal tablets.[46] The contract, like other items of the wedding, was seen as joining the couple.[47] But it was not essential to the legality of the marriage.[48] The *auspex* was the first to congratulate the couple, followed by the guests, who wished them good fortune, 'feliciter'.[49]

Presents were given to the *coniuges*, by family, friends, and slaves.[50] We also hear of bride and groom giving each other substantial presents of money before the wedding (when such gifts were valid).[51] Juvenal mocks at the custom of the bridegroom giving the bride a precious dish full of gold coins as a compensation for the wedding-night. This gift is a precursor of the *donatio ante nuptias*

[40] See Kötting, in *Reallexikon f. A. u. C.* 881 ff.; Reekmans, 'La "dextrarum iunctio" dans l'iconographie romaine et paléochrétienne'; Kleiner, *Roman group portraiture. The funerary reliefs of the late Republic and early Empire* 23 ff.; Kampen, 'Biographical narration' 51–2. The joining of hands was also Jewish and Greek. The convenient expression *dextrarum iunctio* is not classical. The symbolic gesture may be described by Lucan: 'iunguntur taciti' (2.371).

[41] *Tabulae*: Juv. 2.119, 9.75, etc.; Quint. *Inst.* 5.11.32. *Tabulae dotales*: D 23.4.29 pr., 33.4.12, cf. 31.89.5. *Tabulae nuptiales*: Tac. *A* 11.30.4; *Dotale/ia instrumentum/a*: D 24.3.48, 33.4.17.1, 38.16.16. Kübler in *RE* iva (1932) 1949 ff. s.v. *tabulae nuptiales* distinguishes nuptial from dotal contract (as does *CJ* 5.27.10 pr., but that has nothing to do with a formal wedding). It seems that dotal contracts, drawn up and even implemented before the marriage, were normally publicized and witnessed at the wedding. On oral *dotis dictio* as part of the wedding ritual see Kupiszewski, 'Das Verlöbnis im altrömischen Recht' 144.

[42] Apul. *Apol.* 67, 88. Post-classical references in Rasi, *Consensus facit nuptias* 65.

[43] Apul. *M* 4.26, *Apol.* 91. It might be left pending, no wedding taking place: ibid. 68. Surviving examples are *PSI* vi.730 and *Pap. Mich.* 508, 2217, 4703 = *FIRA* iii.17, which shows seven witnesses. (Cf. the number for divorce. But ten were needed for *confarreatio*: G 1.112.) Cf. Sanders, 'A Latin marriage contract'; Levy, 'Les actes d'état civil romains' 468 ff.

[44] Tac. *A* 11.30.4; Suet. *Cl.* 26.2, 29.3; cf. Juv. 10.336.

[45] *Serm.* 51.22.   [46] Juv. 2.119, 3.81–2; cf. Suet. *Cl.* 29.3.

[47] Juv. 6.200 ff.: 'si tibi legitimis pactam iunctamque tabellis | non es amaturus, ducendi nulla videtur | causa.' Cf. 9.75.

[48] Quint. *Inst.* 5.11.32; D 39.5.31 pr.; *CJ* 5.4.9, Probus.

[49] Schol. ad Lucan 2.371; Juv. 2.119. Wishes for a long and harmonious marriage were also appropriate (Cat. 66.87–8; *Decl. min.* 291.5).

[50] Ter. *Ph.* 39–40; Livy 42.12.4.   [51] D 24.1.66. Cf. Cic. *Clu.* 28.

which became customary in post-classical law.[52] Juvenal thinks it
nearly as bad that the host was also expected to hand out cakes to the
departing guests, who had already eaten too much.[53] The local people
might also expect largesse: Apuleius claims that Pudentilla avoided
this at her second marriage by holding the wedding in the country.
She had recently spent HS50,000 on *sportulae* for her son's wedding.[54]

The bride was taken to her new home (usually the husband's
house) in a merry procession, which did not include the bridegroom.
This *deductio in domum mariti* (also more generally called a *pompa*)
was one of the most prominent features of the ceremony. It took
place by torchlight, and these torches are mentioned as symbols of the
whole wedding.[55] After the bride was persuaded to leave her mother
and come out, she went accompanied by a flautist and torch-bearers.
Everyone shouted 'hymen hymenaee'.[56] An alternative cry was
'Talasio'.[57] Traditionally the bride was attended by three boys whose
parents were still alive, *patrimi et matrimi*, one of whom carried a
special torch of a wood called *spina alba* while the others held her
hands.[58] According to Varro, the torch was lit from the bride's
hearth.[59] Others threw nuts to the crowd.[60] Obscene songs and jokes
were a vital feature of this stage of the proceedings.[61] Either the bride
or an attendant carried a spindle and distaff.[62] It seems that the
bridegroom was involved in the singing of the Fescennine verses and
in lighting the torches.[63] Though we hear little of his part in the
proceedings, it is clear that he went ahead of the bride's procession
and, since it would be a melancholy business to sing solo, he too must
have been accompanied by a noisy crowd of friends and attendants.
He needed to be at his house in time to receive his wife. These
separate processions form the procedure called *uxorem ducere* or
deducere. According to one antiquarian, tradition had in the distant
past dictated that the bride take three coins, *asses*, to the husband.
One was held in her hand and then given to the husband, as if to make

---

[52] Juv. 6.203 ff.   [53] 6.202–3.

[54] *Apol.* 87. Cf. Pliny *Epp.* 10. 116–17.

[55] e.g. Verg. *A* 4.339–40, Ov. *Her.* 14.10. See for a complete account Rage-Brocard,
'Deductio ad domum mariti' 19 ff.

[56] Ter. *Ad.* 905 ff.; Cat. 61.56 ff., 92 ff.; Plaut. *Cas.* 798 ff. According to Fest. 364L, a virgin
bride was removed from her mother's arms with simulated force, in imitation of the seizure of
the Sabines.

[57] Livy 1.9.12; Plut. *Rom.* 15.2 ff., *QR* 31; Mart. 1.35.6–7, 3.93.25, 12.42.4; Plut. *Pomp.* 4.3.

[58] Fest. 77L, 283L; Pliny *NH* 1.16, 30.18.

[59] *De vita populi Romani* 2.78 (Riposati), ap. Non. 161L. (It was enough for the boy to be
ingenuus.)

[60] Cat. 61.121; Verg. *E* 8.30; Fest. 178–9L.

[61] Varro *Men.* 10; Cat. 61.120 (exemplified in 122 ff.); Pliny *NH* 15.86; Fest. 76L.

[62] Varro *LL* 5.61; Plut. *QR* 1.   [63] Calp. Flacc. *Decl.* 46.

a purchase; one was kept in her shoe and deposited on the hearth of the household gods, the *lares*; the third, kept in a purse, was dedicated at the shrine of the gods of the district, the *lares compitales*, at the crossroads.[64] The importance of the removal of the bride to the bridegroom's house is reflected in the phrase *ducere uxorem*, literally 'to lead a wife', used of the husband when he marries. The bride is taken from her original family by the bridegroom.

Mulierem absenti per litteras eius vel per nuntium posse nubere placet, si in domum eius deduceretur: eam vero quae abesset ex litteris vel nuntio suo duci a marito non posse: deductione enim opus esse in mariti, non in uxoris domum, quasi in domicilium matrimonii. (*Digest* 23.2.5, Pomponius *iv ad Sabinum*)

A woman can, it is agreed, marry a man who is absent either by means of a letter from him or by means of a messenger, if she is led to his house. But a woman who is absent cannot be married by a husband either through a letter or by a messenger from her. For *deductio* is necessary to the house of the husband, not of the wife, for the former is the domicile of the marriage.

Denique Cinna scribit: eum, qui absentem accepit uxorem, deinde rediens a cena iuxta Tiberim perisset, ab uxore lugendum responsum est. (*Digest* 23.2.6, Ulpian *xxxv ad Sabinum*)

Then Cinna writes as follows: he gave the opinion that when a man who had married a wife *in absentia* then died on his way back from dinner in the vicinity of the Tiber, he had to be mourned by his wife.[65]

Cui fuerit sub hac condicione legatum 'si in familia nupsisset', videtur impleta condicio statim atque ducta est uxor, quamvis nondum in cubiculum mariti venerit. Nuptias enim non concubitus sed consensus facit. (*Digest* 35.1.15., Ulpian *xxxv ad Sabinum*)

When a woman is left a legacy on this condition 'if she marries in the family', the condition seems to be fulfilled as soon as she is taken as a wife, even if she has not come to her husband's bedroom. For it is not sexual intercourse but consent which makes a marriage.[66]

The *deductio* was a normal part of the ceremony, modified sometimes, as when the wedding took place in the husband's *horti* and only one house was involved, but it does not seem to have been legally necessary.[67] It fulfilled the useful purpose of publicizing the marriage.

When the bride reached the bridegroom's house, she ritually anointed the doorposts with oil or fat (according to Pliny, in the old

---

[64] Varro *de vita populi Romani* 1.25 (Riposati) ap. Non. 531M s.v. *nubentes* = Bruns ii.65. Cf. Rage-Brocard, '*Deductio in domum mariti*' 26–7; Watson, *XII Tables* 14.

[65] Cf. Paul *S* 2.19.8: 'Vir absens uxorem ducere potest: femina absens nubere non potest.'

[66] Cf. *CJ* 5.3.6, Aurelian.

[67] Cf. *CJ* 5.4.22, AD 428; Rage-Brocard, '*Deductio in domum mariti*' 101.

days wolf-fat) and adorned them with woollen fillets.[68] She was then lifted over the threshold, not by the bridegroom, but by her attendants.[69] The ritual words 'Ubi tu Gaius, ego Gaia' may have been uttered at this point, at least in a *coemptio* ceremony. Still at the entrance, she was offered fire (another torch) and water (in a water-vessel) by the bridegroom.[70] This sharing of fire and water, *aquae et ignis communicatio*, was because these elements are essential to human life, most obviously cooking and washing. It has deep roots in the Roman idea of home and of rights between citizens, host and guest, and family members. A banished man was not to be harboured by a fellow citizen: he was denied fire and water. Again, this part of the ritual is seen as important: 'by these a new wife is made', says Ovid.[71]

The house and especially the symbolic marriage-bed, which for the first time now stood in the atrium, were decorated as lavishly as possible.[72] But the consummation of the marriage took place in the bedroom and, according to Plutarch, in the dark.[73] Christian critics mocked at the number of minor deities needed for this part of the ceremony. A shocking ritual is mentioned in which the *pronuba* ordered the bride to sit on the phallus of a statue of Priapus or Mutunus Tutunus: it is not clear how much research was needed to unearth this item of archaic ritual.[74] Pagans could be equally indecent in their imaginings.[75] Gentleness in wooing a timid bride could be seen as the norm, but a man might also argue that resistance was feigned.[76] In Ovid's description of the wedding of the Danaids, from the point of view of one of them, the fifty brides arrive soberly at their father-in-law's house and are received by him in an atmosphere of incense and artificial light. But the fifty bridegrooms needed friends and alcohol to support them in the ordeal: they arrive with their friends, drunk

[68] Pliny *NH* 28.142, 29.30; Plut. *QR* 31; Donat. ad Ter. *Hec.* 1.2.60 (135); Isid. *Orig.* 9.7.12; Serv. ad *A* 4.458; Arnob. 3.25; Mart. Cap. 2.149.

[69] Plut. *QR* 29, *Rom.* 15.5; Lucan 2.359.

[70] Varro *LL* 5.61 (with philosophic argument that the fire represents the male reproductive powers and the water the female), *de vita populi Romani* 2.79 (Riposati) = Non. 268L. See Corbett 73–4; Humbert, *Remariage à Rome* 19ff.

[71] Ov. *F* 4.791–2; Fest. 3L; Plut. *QR* 1; Cf. Serv. ad *A* 4.103, 339 (associating the rite especially with *confarreatio*).   [72] Cat. 64.47ff.; Lucan 2.356–7; Juv. 10.334–5.

[73] *QR* 65; cf. Tac. *A* 15.37.9. For an odd remark on the need for two pillows for a virgin see Varro *de vita populi Romani* (Riposati) 1.26 = Non. 122L.

[74] Aug. *Civ. dei* 6.9.3, 7.24.2; Arnob. 4.7; Lactant. *Inst.* 1.20.36. Cf. Rage-Brocard, '*Deductio in domum mariti*' 31–2. For Dea Pertunda see Arnob. loc. cit.; Aug. *Civ. dei* 6.9; Tert. *ad nat.* 2.11.12–13; Skinner, 'Pertundo tunicamque palliumque'.

[75] e.g. Sen. *Contr.* 1.2.22; *Priapea* 3.7–8.

[76] Ambrose *Comm. in cant. cant. prologus* 3 = PL 15.1853: 'etiam in his coniugiis temporalibus nubenti prius plauditur quam imperatur; ne ante dura offendant imperia quam blanditiis amor fotus inolescat'; Cat. 66.11ff. and, on eager brides, 79ff.

and garlanded, and go directly to the bedchambers to find their brides and their deaths.[77]

On the day after the wedding it was customary to hold a dinner and drinking-party at the bridegroom's house: this was called the *repotia*.[78] At this party the bride made her first offering to the household gods of her new home.[79] The newly married couple were expected to go to further parties in the days which followed, something which Apuleius and Pudentilla wanted to avoid.[80]

Tacitus lists the routine components of a formal wedding twice. In the mock wedding of Nero and Pythagoras they are the veil, the *auspices*, dowry, the marriage-bed, and nuptial torches. When he wants to emphasize the openness of the equally scandalous wedding of Silius and Messallina, he mentions the advance notice of the date, invitations to witnesses, the formality of the ceremony, the bride listening to the words of the *auspices*, the sacrifice, the bride reclining among the guests and kissing and embracing the bridegroom, the consummation of the match. Juvenal, on the same event, selects for mention the veil, the *lectus genialis* decked in purple, dowry, *auspex*, witnesses. In another mock marriage Juvenal emphasizes the sealing of the dotal contract, the congratulations of the guests, the bride reclining against her husband's chest.[81]

The individual weddings of which we hear in the sources vary considerably in their extravagance and publicity. We know that on 12 February 56 Cicero intended to attend a dinner at Atticus' house in Rome on the occasion of his wedding to Pilia. Perhaps the whole ceremony took place there and there was no *deductio*. Cicero also felt obliged to go from Tusculum to Rome for Milo's wedding on 18 November 55. But when his own daughter married for the third time, nobody seems to have thought he should hurry home from Cilicia.[82] Similarly, Augustus made little of the occasions of his daughter's weddings. In 25 BC illness prevented him celebrating her first wedding to Marcellus, so he put Agrippa in charge. In 21 Augustus was out of Rome: he summoned Agrippa and ordered him to divorce Marcella, go back to Rome, and marry Julia.[83] Similarly, Tiberius in AD 28 handed over Agrippina to Cn. Domitius (presumably on Capri) and ordered the wedding to be celebrated in Rome. Her sisters' weddings (in 33, after the ruin of their mother and two brothers) seem to have taken place quietly on Capri, although Tiberius wrote to inform the

[77] Ov. *Her.* 14.21 ff. For lack of sobriety in bridegrooms cf. Ter. *Hec.* 138–40.

[78] Varro *LL* 6.84; Hor. *S* 2.2.59ff., with Acron; Gell. 2.24.14; Fest. 351L. Cf. Humbert, *Remariage à Rome* 6.   [79] Macrob. *S* 1.15.22; Fest. 187L.

[80] Apul. *Apol.* 87.   [81] Tac. *A* 11.27.1, 15.37.9; Juv. 10.333ff., 2.119–20.

[82] Cic. *QF* 2.3.7, *A* 4.13.1; above, ch. 4.1(*a*).   [83] Dio 53.27.5, 54.6.4–5.

Senate.[84] In the Julio-Claudian period an emperor could choose to make a wedding of a member of his family a big public event or not, rather as protocol dictates which British royal weddings are state occasions and which merely private ceremonies. Later emperors might make their daughters' weddings *celeberrimae*, but the wedding of Marcus' son was like that of a private citizen, though accompanied by a donative. Marcus had to send one daughter abroad to marry Verus.[85] Apuleius and Pudentilla, by marrying in the country, avoided not only giving *sportulae* to the neighbours but also dining at her brother-in-law's house or in his company: it appears that they did not even invite close kin.[86]

2. Legal Consent

As we saw in Chapter 2, it was continuing consent of the partners (and their *patresfamilias* if any) which made a potentially legal marriage an actual one. The giving of consent gave rise to a marriage. But there was no legal prescription about how this consent was signified. The legal texts on consent at the beginning of a marriage are few. The classical doctrine is expressed most clearly in the following passage:

Nuptiae consistere non possunt, nisi consentiant omnes, id est qui coeunt quorumque in potestate sunt. (*Digest* 23.2.2, Paul *xxxv ad edictum*)

A marriage cannot exist unless everyone consents, that is, those who come together and those under whose power they are.

A later source confirms this:

Iustum matrimonium est, si . . . utrique consentiant, si sui iuris sunt, aut etiam parentes eorum, si in potestate sunt. (*Tituli Ulpiani* 5.2)

A marriage is valid if . . . both parties consent, if they are independent, or their parents too, if they are in power.

It has been held that the second text means that the consent of *patresfamilias* sufficed, without that of the couple.[87] But this cannot be true for contemporary law, and the Ulpianic text is not giving a history of what once may have been true. It is merely a poorly phrased version of what Paul says. It may originally have been true that only the consent of the *patresfamilias* was legally necessary and that their consent bound their children.[88] But there is no satisfactory evidence

[84] Tac. *A* 4.75.1, 6.15.4.   [85] *HA Ant.* 10.2, *Marc.* 27.8; 9.4.
[86] Apul. *Apol.* 87–8. Cf. Pliny *Epp.* 10.116–17.   [87] See Corbett 54.
[88] For what it is worth, Dionysius' understanding of the situation is that the father agrees to his son's marriage, i.e. the son's consent is prior (*Ant.* 2.27.4). According to Rasi, everyone is agreed at least that the consent of the *paterfamilias* of the woman sufficed on her side (*Consensus facit nuptias* 60). He cites comedy to prove that only *patresfamilias* needed to consent (p. 95).

on the archaic period. In the middle Republic the praetors penalized those responsible for allowing a widow to remarry without having mourned her husband for ten months. The people concerned are the woman's *paterfamilias*, if he knew his son-in-law was dead and if he bestowed his daughter on a new husband; the new husband if he knew the circumstances and *unless* he was acting on the order of his own *paterfamilias*; the new husband's *paterfamilias* if he allowed the marriage; a woman who did not complete her mourning for a husband, parent, or child and (more specifically) a *sui iuris* woman who knowingly remarried before her mourning for a previous husband was over. Watson has argued that it is implied that the consent of a *filiafamilias* was not needed and therefore the praetors did not proceed against her. It seems to me that a *filiafamilias* who cut short her mourning to remarry is included in the broad fourth class, which covers all women who did not carry out their ritual duties. But it is not clear that it is *consent* which is really at issue here. A broader responsibility seems to be meant. The man's father 'allows' his marriage, which covers formal consent when the son has arranged the marriage or a more active role. But the woman's father actively bestows her: his having taken a leading part, when he knew the circumstances, is what makes him culpable, which he apparently would not have been had he, for instance, signified formal consent by letter because he was too far away to know that his daughter was a widow rather than a divorcee. The woman is culpable in any case, because the duty to mourn is applicable only to women and she is supposed to know about it. Perhaps if she had a *paterfamilias* the praetor would proceed against him first. Naturally if she is *sui iuris* she is fully responsible. The same must apply to a *sui iuris* bridegroom. In short, the passage does not certainly yield the information that the consent of a daughter in power was not needed in about 200 BC.[89]

Lawyers down to Justinian consistently stated the necessity of the consent of the *paterfamilias*. Naturally, they emphasize the marriage of the son, since that brought the possibility of new *sui heredes*.[90] If a

[89] Lenel, *Edictum Perpetuum* 78. See Watson, *Persons* 41 ff.; Treggiari, 'Consent to Roman marriage: some aspects of law and reality', 37–8.

[90] *D* 23.2.35, Pap.: 'filius familias miles matrimonium sine patris voluntate non contrahit'; *CJ* 5.4.12; Just. *Inst.* 1.10 pr.: 'Iustas autem nuptias inter se cives Romani contrahunt, qui secundum praecepta legum coeunt . . . sive patres familias sint sive filii familias, dum tamen filii familias et consensum habeant parentum, quorum in potestate sunt. Nam hoc fieri debere et civilis et naturalis ratio suadet in tantum, ut iussum parentis praecedere debeat. Unde quaesitum est, an furiosi filia nubere aut furiosi filius uxorem ducere possit?' On *sui* see Corbett 57–8. On the role of the father see Volterra, 'Quelques observations sur le mariage des filii familias', distinguishing initial consent by the father from continuing consent by the *coniunx*, and attacking the views of Solazzi and Rasi. I find his view over-schematic but preferable to those of his opponents.

person was free of paternal power because his *paterfamilias* was dead or had emancipated him, no formal consent from a third party was necessary. If an emancipated son married without his father's approval, this did not affect the claim of an eventual son of the marriage on the grandfather's estate (unless he was disinherited).[91]

A father who did not know a marriage was being made or who expressed his opposition to it was clearly not a consenting party. Nor did a generic commission to a friend to find a husband for one's daughter imply consent.[92] There is debate about how positively the father's consent needed to be expressed. Was it enough if he knew about the marriage and did not refuse consent? Could positive consent be tacit? Corbett decides that, 'Probably the true conclusion is that there was in all cases a presumption of consent, even an irrebuttable presumption, where a parent acquainted with the facts did not take the opportunity to protest; for it is difficult to draw any substantial distinction between a positive consent which may be tacit and an absence of opposition which must be accompanied by knowledge.'[93]

If a daughter was passing out of the power of her father by entering *manus*, it is clear that his direct authorization, normally his participation in ritual, was needed. Often, the presence of the father at the wedding in his house would sufficiently indicate consent. Or he could make arrangements for dowry, even without being present, which would imply his agreement. Papinian in one passage seems to be thinking of the verbal giving of consent by the bride's father to the intended bridegroom, before the wedding, and this is enough: the father did not have to express consent at the wedding as well.[94] We have seen that Augustus, as father of Julia, and Tiberius, as *paterfamilias* of the daughters of his adoptive son, authorized marriages without being present at the wedding. Normally, a father would have expressed his consent well in advance, before arrangements for dowry and wedding were made. But it is clear that there was no set form for him to do so during the ceremonies.[95] Moreover, the mother (whose consent was not legally required) is regarded as having a share in the handing over of the bride.

The part of the bridegroom's father is even less clear, though he might have a share in welcoming the bride to her new home and he would presumably often be a guest at her parents' house. We shall see in Chapter 13 that a *paterfamilias* could unilaterally produce the divorce of his son or daughter, but that this power was whittled away until in classical law it was held that his action merely destroyed his

---

[91] *D* 37.4.3.5.   [92] *D* 23.2.34 pr.   [93] p. 60.   [94] *D* 23.2.34 pr.
[95] Note that the father's consent to the engagement of a *filiafamilias* was, in Julian's view, to be taken for granted unless he explicitly denied it (*D* 23.1.7.1).

relationship with his child's *coniunx*. It may be helpful, therefore, if we regard the initial consent of the *paterfamilias* as establishing a relationship between him and his son- or daughter-in-law. By consenting to the marriage of his son, he accepts the grandchildren as *sui heredes*. By allowing his daughter to pass into *manus*, he cuts his legal tie to her. If the daughter remains a *filiafamilias*, a tension is set up between her legal and economic relationship with her father and a socio-moral and economic relationship with her husband. In either case a web of obligation and interest binds father- and son-in-law, as long as each wills the continuance of the marriage. But a man cannot be compelled against his will to fill the role of father-in-law.

What happened if a *paterfamilias* was mad or a prisoner of war?

Si furiosi parentis liberi, in cuius potestate constituti sunt, nuptias possunt contrahere, apud veteres agitabatur. Et filiam quidem furiosi marito posse copulari omnes paene iuris antiqui conditores admiserunt: sufficere enim putaverunt, si pater non contradicat. In filio autem familias dubitabatur. et Ulpianus quidem rettulit constitutionem imperatoris Marci, quae non de furioso loquitur, sed generaliter de filiis mente capti, sive masculi sive feminae sint qui nuptias contrahunt, ut hoc facere possint etiam non adito principe. (*Codex Iustiniani* 5.4.25 pr.–2, Justinian, AD 530)

It was a question among the ancients whether the children in the power of a madman can contract marriage. It was admitted by almost all authorities on ancient law that the daughter of a madman could be joined to a husband: for they held it sufficient if he did not refuse. But there was a doubt about a *filiusfamilias*. Ulpian, however, cites a constitution of the emperor Marcus, which does not mention a madman, but speaks generally about the children of someone whose mind was afflicted, whether those contracting a marriage are male or female. This rules that they can do this even without petitioning the emperor.

To resolve any remaining doubt, Justinian eventually ruled that this permission applied to children of *furiosi*:

Si nepos uxorem velit ducere avo furente, omnimodo patris auctoritas erit necessaria: sed si pater furit, avus sapiat, sufficit avi voluntas. Is cuius pater ab hostibus captus est . . . uxorem ducere potest. (*Digest* 23.2.9. pr.–1, Ulpian *xxvi ad Sabinum*)

If a grandson wishes to marry a wife when his grandfather is mad, his father's authorization will be necessary; but if it is the father who is mad and the grandfather sane, the grandfather's will is sufficient. A man whose father is captured by the enemy . . . can marry a wife.[96]

---

[96] Cf. *D* 23.2.10 (if the father is missing), ht 11: 'Si filius eius qui apud hostes est vel absit . . . uxorem duxit vel si filia nupserit, puto recte matrimonium vel nuptias contrahi'; 23.4.8: 'Quotiens patre furente vel ab hostibus capto filius familias ducit uxorem filiaque familias nubit, necessario etiam pactio cum ipsis dumtaxat dotis nomine fieri poterit.'

This was because the position of those who were in the power of a captive was in suspense. If he died in captivity, jurists argued about whether his children's freedom was backdated to the moment of his capture or took effect on his death. By the time of Papinian and Tryphoninus, the former view (which was more convenient for the survivors) prevailed. If he returned to his native land, he recovered *patria potestas* by *postliminium* and it was as if his power had never been suspended.[97]

Medio tempore filius, quem habuit in potestate captivus, uxorem ducere potest, quamvis consentire nuptiis pater eius non posset: nam utique nec dissentire. Susceptus ergo nepos in reversi captivi potestate ut avi erit suusque heres ei quodammodo invito, cum nuptiis non consenserit. Non mirum, quia illius temporis condicio necessitasque faciebat et publica nuptiarum utilitas exigebat. (*Digest* 49.15.12.3, Tryphoninus *iv disputationum*)

In the mean time a son, who was in the power of a prisoner, can marry a wife, although his father cannot consent to his marriage, for at all events he cannot dissent. Therefore a grandson who is acknowledged will be in the power of the captive as his grandfather if he returns and will be an intestate heir to him as it were against his will, since he did not consent to the marriage. This is not surprising, because it was the circumstances of that time and necessity which produced this effect and the public utility of marriages demanded it.

A marriage made without his consent would be *iniustum*.[98]

Eorum qui in potestate patris sunt sine voluntate eius matrimonia iure non contrahuntur, sed contracta non solvuntur: contemplatio enim publicae utilitatis privatorum commodis praefertur. (Paul *Sententiae* 2.19.2)

The marriages of those who are in their father's power are not rightly contracted without his will, but once contracted they are not dissolved: for consideration of public utility is put before the interests of private citizens.[99]

We hear of fathers who subsequently gave their implicit consent.[100] This would make the marriage fully *iustum*. The Augustan Law

[97] G 1.129; *D* 49.15.12.1, Tryph., cf. ht 8, Paul, 10 pr., Pap., 16, Ulp., 22.2, 23, Jul.; *Tit. Ulp.* 10.4; Buckland, *Textbook* 67–8.

[98] See *D* 1.5.11, Paul, arguing that a child born to a woman whose *paterfamilias* did not know of her marriage would not be *iustus filius* to his father, even though the grandfather had died during the pregnancy. It is implied that children conceived after their mother ceased to be *filiafamilias* would be *iusti*: 23.2.18: 'Nuptiae inter easdem personas nisi volentibus parentibus renovatae iustae non habentur.' Corbett 62 regards such marriages as null.

[99] *Pace* Corbett 62, who interprets 'once contracted' as 'with his consent': the father may not withdraw consent once given, i.e. may not compel divorce (a right which he had once enjoyed but which was restricted in the Antonine period). Cf. Solazzi, 'Studi sul divorzio I: il divorzio della filiafamilias' 6–7; Matringe, 'La puissance paternelle et le mariage des fils et filles de famille en droit romain' 215.

[100] *FV* 102, where a *filiusfamilias* marries and accepts a dowry in his father's absence. After the father's return, he acquiesces in the marriage and becomes liable for the dowry. *CJ* 5.4.5, Alex.

allowed a *paterfamilias* to be compelled to consent to the marriage of his child.[101]

Theoretically, neither a dependent son nor anyone else could be forced into marriage.[102]

Non cogitur filius familias uxorem ducere. (*Digest* 23.2.21, Terentius Clemens *iii ad legem Iuliam & Papiam*)

A *filiusfamilias* is not compelled to marry a wife.

But moral suasion could be successfully exerted.

Si patre cogente ducit uxorem, quam non duceret, si sui arbitrii esset, contraxit tamen matrimonium, quod inter invitos non contrahitur: maluisse hoc videtur. (*Digest* 23.2.22, Celsus *xv digestorum*)

If, because his father compels him, he [sc. the *filiusfamilias*] marries a wife whom he would not have married if he had been acting of his own volition, he has still contracted a marriage, although marriage cannot be contracted by unwilling parties. It is held that he has preferred this course of action.

The son in this instance may morally not have consented, but since he chose not to disobey his father he is seen as legally consenting, and the marriage is valid.[103] The *filiafamilias* may, as in engagements, have been presumed to consent unless she made her dissent clear.[104] But she might not be present at an engagement, whereas she had to be present at her own wedding and her presence would imply consent. Matringe puts the situation well:

Peut-on penser qu'un mariage célébré au milieu de la liesse des parents et des amis, donnant lieu à des fêtes qui parfois duraient plusieurs jours, pouvait avoir lieu, alors qu'un des époux protestait énergiquement contre son accomplissement? Peut-on imaginer l'exécution des rites religieux sans la collaboration des époux? Si une contrainte pouvait peser sur eux pour leur faire accepter le marriage projeté par le père, elle était surtout d'ordre familial, social et moral. Dans ce cas, même si l'union ne réalisait pas leurs vœux intimes, ils étaient mariés bon gré, mal gré. De nos jours, il arrive encore que des parents marient leurs enfants sans tenir compte de leurs désirs et en effectuant au besoin une pression sur leur volonté. Mais le consentement des époux reste une condition de fond essentielle pour la validité du mariage.[105]

---

[101] *D* 23.2.19.

[102] *CJ* 5.4.14, Diocletian and Maximinian: 'Neque ab initio matrimonium contrahere neque dissociatum reconciliare quisquam cogi potest. Unde intellegis liberam facultatem contrahendi atque distrahendi matrimonii transferri ad necessitatem non oportere'; *CJ* 5.4.12, Diocletian and Maximian, AD 285: 'Ne filium quidem familias invitum ad ducendam uxorem cogi legum disciplina permittit. Igitur, sicut desideras, observatis iuris praeceptis sociare coniugio tuo quam volueris non impediris, ita tamen, ut in contrahendis nuptiis patris tui consensus accedat.' Cf. Matringe, 'La puissance paternelle' 199.

[103] Bibliography: Rasi, *Consensus facit nuptias* 63–4.

[104] *D* 23.1.12. Cf. Gaudemet, 'Justum matrimonium' 319ff.

[105] 'La puissance paternelle' 199.

The unsubstantiated remark about conditions in France in the late 1960s or earlier throws into high relief the essential fact that whether a person gives legal consent may be independent of his or her independent will. It is unfortunately true that children have in the past been starved and beaten into submission to their father's will and gone through long and elaborate religious ceremonies and given legal consent. But there are also subtler ways of exerting pressure. Upbringing and social expectations may make it almost impossible for a young person, especially a daughter, to refuse to consent.[106]

3. Real Consent

Although the legal consent of both bride and bridegroom was essential throughout (at least) the classical period of Roman law, this requirement is consistent with a high degree of variation in independence of choice, approval of a match, and commitment to a specific partner. The same may be said of the position of the *paterfamilias*. The legal requirements (deriving originally from folk customs) are important in setting the social context for long periods of time. But, though the rules may remain the same, the way they operate may change radically. It has been vigorously argued that sons and daughters in England were much freer than those in continental Europe to choose their own marriage partners because from the end of the twelfth century until the middle of the eighteenth English law did not require parental consent for the valid marriage of women over 12 and men over 14.[107] Social, moral, religious, and economic expectations might run counter to this, but the law's insistence on the consent of the bride and bridegroom alone must have remained 'a deep and ultimately unbridgeable obstacle to arranged marriage',[108] to the automatic assumption that parents disposed of children at will.

Similarly, the necessity for the legal consent of *filiifamilias* must also have modified the freedom of a Roman father to decide his child's marriage autonomously. Social expectations also reduced his monopoly. From earliest times, the model *paterfamilias* operated

[106] On compulsion see Stone, *Family, sex and marriage* 130 (Elizabeth Paston); Fraser, *The weaker vessel. Woman's lot in seventeenth-century England* 14. On English disapproval of forced marriages from the 14th cent. on see MacFarlane 133 ff.; Fraser, op. cit. 307 ff., Stone, op. cit. 185 ff. On conditioning of children, Stone 128.

[107] Macfarlane 119 ff., esp. 124 ff. I would not accept, as he does, that this tendency in English law derives from Germanic law and that the 'patriarchal' tendency in the countries affected by the reception of Roman law simply derives from Rome. In Rome there was a tension between *patria potestas* and the principle that marriage depended on free consent. The medieval English principle that 'marriages should be free', which Macfarlane quotes from Maitland (p. 126), is in fact Roman (*CJ* 8.38.2).

[108] Macfarlane 131.

through careful consultation of friends and kinsmen, not as an autocrat. The expectation gradually grew that his mother, aunt, sister, or wife might advise and influence him, though women were not formal members of an advisory council. Although conventional morality preached the duty of son to father, it balanced it with the duty of father to son. The father was to strike a balance between severity and indulgence, prudence and affection.

How far it was proper for a father to order a son to marry or to marry a specific wife was debatable. The philosophers argued that some actions, such as going to serve in the army, farming, entering a political career, acting as a defence counsel, or marrying a wife, were in themselves morally neutral.

Propterea in eiusmodi omnium rerum generibus patri parendum esse censent, veluti si uxorem ducere imperet aut causas pro reis dicere. Quod enim utrumque in genere ipso per sese neque honestum neque turpe est, idcirco si pater iubeat, obsequendum est. Sed enim si imperet uxorem ducere infamem, propudiosam, criminosam aut pro reo Catilina aliquo aut Tubulo aut P. Clodio causam dicere, non scilicet parendum, quoniam accedente aliquo turpitudinis numero desinunt esse per sese haec media atque indifferentia. (Gellius 2.7.18–20)

Accordingly, in all those kinds of things they hold that one ought to obey a father, for instance if he orders you to marry a wife or be advocate for the defence. For both these actions are in themselves as a category neither honourable nor dishonourable. So if your father orders you, you should oblige him. But if he orders you to marry a wife who is infamous, shameful, or criminal, or to defend some Catiline, Tubulus, or P. Clodius, then of course you should not obey him, because when an element of dishonour enters in, then these things cease to be morally neutral and indifferent.

But, as we have seen, the approval of a mother was also morally desirable. The mother was on display, handing over the bride, at a daughter's wedding. Catullus, in his hellenizing epithalamium, gives equal rights to father, mother, and the daughter herself in disposing of her virginity.[109]

On the other hand, the consent of a father was regarded as morally, as well as legally, necessary:

Nam nec in terris filii sine consensu patrum rite et iure nubunt. (Tertullian *ad uxorem* 2.8.6)

For even on earth children do not marry righteously and legally without the consent of their fathers.

Again, the approval of a mother for a child's choice was important. Terentia supported Tullia in her choice of Dolabella; all Cicero could

[109] 62.20ff.

supply, apparently, was written authorization after the engagement
had been announced. It was also desirable that a son's choice of wife
should please his mother. When Brutus in 45, after divorcing
Claudia, married his widowed cousin Porcia, his mother Servilia
disapproved. This was regrettable, as was the fact that the two ladies
treated each other with hostility after the wedding. But Brutus,
according to Cicero (who had wanted to see the marriage made),
balanced his duty to each.[110] Brutus at this time was about 40.

The extreme scenarios which may occur are that a father orders his
son to marry a certain wife, without taking the son's own wishes into
account, and that a son chooses to marry a certain wife, ignoring the
express disapproval of his father. A less extreme scenario occurs
when the son marries a woman without the knowledge or explicit
consent of his father. (The logically parallel instance to this, of a son
being married because his *paterfamilias* expressed consent for him,
although he did not know about it, seems unlikely to happen in real
life.) The most pacific possibilities are that the father succeeds in
persuading the son to marry the wife of the father's choice or that the
son persuades the father to approve of his choice. Rhetorical literature makes play with these themes in the relationship of father and
son, but takes no interest in the dilemmas of fathers and daughters,
which were to provide such rich material for later drama and novel.
Nor are mothers and other kin of much concern. The orators
maintain the virtue of filial choice:

Quod si licet aliquando etiam contra patris voluntatem ea quae alioquin
reprehensionem non merentur filio facere, nusquam tamen libertas tam
necessaria quam in matrimonio est. (*Declamationes minores* 257.5)

But if it is ever permissible for a son to do anything against his father's wishes
(as long as it is something which does not deserve moral obloquy), then such
freedom is never so necessary as it is in marriage.

Equally, they can justify the advantage of well-informed paternal
choice in which a son acquiesces:

Habui patrem sanae mentis nec tam severum ut crudelis esset, nec tam
indulgentem ut incautus. Duxi uxorem quam pater iusserat, nec tamen
nuptiarum mearum me paenitet. Fili, nonne saepe excandui, saepe recon-
ciliatus sum, saepe quod negaveram dedi? (Seneca *Controversiae* 2.3.2)

I had a father who was sane and neither so severe as to be cruel nor so
indulgent as to be imprudent. I married the wife whom my father told me to
marry. But I am not sorry I married. My son, have I not often lost my temper
and often made it up, often granted you something after first saying no?

[110] *A* 13.22.4.

Such well-worn arguments about feelings on both sides suggest that potential conflict between fathers and sons was a familiar theme. Either side might give in. By the time of Cicero or the Elder Seneca, there was no orthodoxy holding that the father's rights were superior. In earlier times *patria potestas* had perhaps originally made a father a despot in such matters; at the end of our period Church teaching was adding to his strength. But in the classical period moral obligations were reciprocal between father and son, or, for that matter, mother and daughter.[111]

Apart from law and morality, other factors influenced choice. It has been shown that children of marriageable age were often father-less and motherless.[112] The moral influence of other kin was likely to be weaker than that of a parent. Economic circumstances might also weaken a surviving parent's clout. If there was no inheritance to be expected and the son was already making his own way in the world, he could perhaps shake off the influence even of a *paterfamilias*. Young people in England who went away to work at young ages early established independence in their choice of marital partner.[113] The same must have been true of Rome's landless workers and soldiers. But no comparable employment opportunities offered for Roman girls, who presumably therefore remained in their natal family and were more subject to influence when they married.

Stone has defined four basic options in matchmaking:

The first is that the choice is made entirely by parents, kin and family 'friends', without the advice or consent of the bride or groom. The second option is that the choice is made as before, but the children are granted a right of veto, to be exercised on the basis of one or two formal interviews which take place after the two sets of parents and kin have agreed on the match. It is a right which can only be exercised once or twice, and tends to be more readily conceded to the groom than to the bride. The principle that underlies this concession is that mutual compatibility is desirable to hold a marriage together, and that this will slowly develop between any couple who do not demonstrate an immediate antipathy towards each other on first sight. In a deferential society, this is a reasonable assumption. The third option, made necessary by the rise of individualism, is that choice is made by the children themselves, on the understanding that it will be made from a family of more or less equal financial and status position, with the parents retaining the right of veto. The fourth option, which has only emerged in this century, is that the children make their own choice and merely inform their parents of what they have decided.[114]

[111] Saller, '*Pietas*, obligation and authority in the Roman family'.
[112] Saller, '*Patria potestas* and the stereotype of the Roman family'.
[113] Stone, *Family, sex and marriage* 182 ff.
[114] Stone, *Family, sex and marriage* 181–2.

He holds that English society has shifted through all these options. I suggest that the Romans arrived at the second option by the second century at latest. If we can trust comedy as a reflection of social assumptions, young men were already arriving at the third stage. In the upper classes a growth of individualism was in full swing by the early first century, though the absence of sources does not allow us to assert that it did not exist earlier. By the time young Q. Cicero reached marriageable age, though no doubt he looked only for brides of a social status his father and mother would have approved and of a financial standing that he himself approved, he was close to the final stage, of regarding parents as having merely a right to be informed, which Stone attributes to the twentieth century (though I would put it earlier in England).

The process which led to the formation of a Roman marriage could therefore be sophisticated and complex. The wedding itself acted as a *rite de passage* for the bride, who set aside childish things when she dedicated her toys to the household gods and became a *matrona*. The ritual retained its sacramental character even when *confarreatio* was not involved. The veil and the torches had resonances for the Romans which they scarcely have for us. The bride, through outward and visible signs, perhaps through ritual words and through the giving of consent, implied dedication to a particular role of wifely virtue. The ideal of the good wife and the proper relationship between the *coniuges* will be the subject of the next chapters.

PART III

Coniuges: Ideals and Reality in the
Relationship of Husband and Wife

PART II

6
The Greek Philosophical Background

And whereas 'tis observed by Aristotle in his Politicks (and it is a proof of his being as wise as he was a learned Man) that the Estate of Republicks entirely hangs on private Families, the little Monarchies both composing and giving Law unto the great; 'tis evident that the disposal of Families and all domestic concerns therein lies chiefly on the Wife.

(Allestree, *The Ladies Calling*, Preface)

SOME components of the Romans' ideology of marriage have emerged from consideration of legal structures, choice of *coniunx*, and wedding ritual. In Part III we shall examine popular morality, moving from the formal teachings of philosophers to the ideas expressed by poets, rhetoricians, and the authors of epitaphs. Because all Latin literature, but especially philosophical writings, was inescapably influenced by Greek tradition, it will be necessary to go back to classical Athens to disentangle some of the main themes and place Roman conventional theories in a cultural context.

The ancient philosophical and rhetorical tradition concerning the practical advantages and disadvantages of the married state and the virtues and vices of wives was pervasive, if not rich. The authors of Graeco-Roman literature, being male, were less acute in their observation of husbands. Roman literary expression on such topics cannot be dissociated from Greek theory, which goes back at least to Plato, from Greek characterization of good and bad marriages, which goes back to Homer, from the fertile Greek tradition of misogynist satire, and from Greek lists of good and bad wives. Latin authors may utter Greek views because they have made them their own or merely because it suits their literary purposes. There is an amusing instance in Plautus *Miles gloriosus* 672 ff., where the old man Periplecto-menus, a *senex lepidus*, describes his happy bachelor life to the lover Pleusicles and the slave Palaestrio. The old man wants to spend his money on himself and his friends and have his house to himself, free from the nagging and greed of a rich and well-born wife. The others put the counter-argument that begetting children is a pleasure and that a man who can bring them up in a rich and noble household is securing his own memorial and the continuity of his family. Note that the direct counter-argument, that a good wife is a pleasure, is not made. A man's object in marrying a wife is the children she should produce. It has been shown that the theme of the expenditure caused by a wife or mistress (*sumptus*) was one of which Plautus was fond and that the whole passage here has been expanded and reworked from his Greek model.[1] But the arguments concerning the advantages and disadvantages of marriage, and the qualities of wives, are standard in both Greek and Roman contexts. Here and elsewhere[2] Plautus uses with enthusiasm the Greek topos on *sumptus* and gives it a highly Roman colour. It must surely have appealed to the Roman audience. The *senex lepidus* holds centre-stage and secures a walk-over with his arguments.

The points briefly touched on in this scene belong to a series of routine arguments which were rapidly acclimatized into Roman literature. Marriage alone can provide a man with legitimate children, his family with posterity, and the state with free-born and legitimate citizens. But children are not an unmixed blessing: they may be bad—in which case they are undesirable—or good—in which case we worry about what will happen to them. A good wife is also a blessing, but they are few compared with bad wives, who are expensive to support and nag their husbands. Rich wives, the *epiklēroi* of Greek comedy and the well-dowered wives (*dotatae*) of Roman, attempt to dominate their husbands.[3]

These ideas belong to a common stock familiar to both Greek and Roman by the time of Plautus. Just as we and our contemporaries have been exposed through the press and general conversation, if not through serious study, to the ideas of Freud or Masters and Johnson, so a Roman writer of satire or comedy must have been at least vaguely aware of a whole literary and philosophic tradition. His audience were in touch with the same stock of ideas through the theatre and through street culture, if not through written literature. A Roman author might not consciously attribute the idea which he expressed

---

[1] Fraenkel, *Elementi plautini in Plauto* 133–4; Williams, 'Evidence for Plautus' workmanship in the *Miles Gloriosus*' 86–95, arguing particularly against Leo, *Plautinische Forschungen* (2nd edn.) 180, who holds 612–764 to be 'echt attische'. But Fantham ('Sex, status and survival in Hellenistic Athens' 73) finds Periplectomenus' speech 'indisputably Greek in tone'.

[2] *Aul.* III.v, *Epid.* 223–35, *Trin.* 250 (the two latter on courtesans).

[3] Fantham, 'Sex, status and survival in Hellenistic Athens' 73.

to Semonides or Hesiod, Xenophon or a shadowy Pythagorean. Still less should we expect adherence to a consistent doctrine or a preference for Greek theorizing over the ancient Roman tradition.

1. Greek Popular Philosophy concerning Marriage

But the Greek background is relevant to Roman ideas of the classical period on the nature of marriage. Greek ideas shaped the categories in which people automatically thought. I shall discuss the Greek philosophical contribution in approximate chronological order, without necessarily implying that each writer was acquainted with his predecessors. It is not necessary here to describe Hesiod's account of the creation of woman as a curse rather than a helpmate, or Semonides' catalogue of the nine types of bad wife and the one type of good wife. But the Romans might be inclined to take seriously the views of philosophers (if they knew them), and the Greek moral philosophers found in Homer the marriage of Odysseus and Penelope as a recipe for perfection and the marriage of Paris and Helen as the recipe for failure. Their views on marriage depended on their opinion about the moral nature of men and women.[4] Plato held that virtues were the same for both sexes, therefore women were not intrinsically inferior to men.[5]

(a) Xenophon

Xenophon's Socratic dialogue on estate management, the *Oeconomicus* (? 362/361 BC), in which he makes Ischomachus, representative of an older generation, the mouthpiece of his own ideas, bases Ischomachus' success as a farmer and outdoor man on the fact that he is able to delegate all the indoor work to his wife.[6] The division of tasks between the sexes is divinely ordained: since man has on the whole more physical endurance, he works out of doors, but the woman, because she must feed babies under cover and is more timid and therefore adapted to protecting produce indoors, is suited to working in the house.[7] Their abilities and deficiencies balance each other's and their work is of equal importance and value. In memory and the ability to apply their minds to work, and in self-control, both sexes have equal potential.[8] The wife's tasks are compared with those of the queen bee[9] and her husband claims that she is just as much a

---

[4] The Greek philosophical tradition is conveniently surveyed by Vatin 17–40.

[5] *Meno* 72–3, *Rep.* 451 Dff. See also Foucault, *L'Histoire de la sexualité* iii. *Le souci de soi* ch. 5.

[6] *Oec.* 7.3.   [7] Cf. Arist. *Pol.* 1277[b]24–5.

[8] *Oec.* 7.26ff.

[9] 7.32 ff.: a female in this text, as in Semonides 7 (*PLG* ii.446ff.), though not in the *Georgics*.

leader as he is.[10] Her duties—supervising servants and stores; making clothes; nursing sick slaves; teaching the maids to spin; training, disciplining, and rewarding the staff; keeping supplies, tools, kitchen and dining utensils, clothing, and footwear in good order—are thoroughly discussed with an insistence on precision, discipline, and tidiness which deliberately reflects the best practice of the army or the merchant marine.[11] Xenophon digresses from his theme to tell the moral tale of how a husband should discourage his young wife from falsifying her natural beauty by wearing rouge, powder, or high heels, since husband and wife share each other's bodies as partners and owe each other the genuine attractions of good health (produced by healthy exercise, for the wife such useful pursuits as kneading dough and shaking blankets).[12] Only now does Ischomachus at last turn to the husband's outdoor duties on the farm.

The most remarkable feature of this detailed and, if we accept its premiss, sympathetic study of the duties of the chatelaine is its insistence on the equal partnership (*koinōnia*) of husband and wife, in their sexual relationship and in their property.[13] He put all his property, she all her dowry, into the marriage, but the better contribution would be made by whichever turned out to be the better partner.[14] The focus of the book is intended to be economic, so that Xenophon defines the usefulness of the marriage partnership as lying in (1) the production of children, so that (a) the species may not become extinct (a purpose common to all animals) and (b) the parents may be fed in their old age (peculiar to humans); (2) the provision of a shelter for protection from the elements, stocked with food and supplies. But his characterization of partnership only just falls short of specifically naming a bond of affection between husband and wife. Unlike later writers, he makes husband and wife equal partners. Since the wife has equal moral potential, she may emerge as the moral superior and leader.

At the least, she is to grow into her role as the leader responsible for indoor administration, as her husband's colleague.

The pleasantest experience of all is to prove yourself better than I am, to make me your servant; and, so far from having cause to fear that as you grow older you may be less honoured in the household, to feel confident that, with advancing years, the better partner you prove to me and the better house-wife to our children, the greater will be the honour paid to you in our home. For it is not through outward comeliness that the sum of things good and beautiful is increased in the world, but by the daily practice of the virtues. (7.42–3, Loeb trans.)

---

[10] 7.39–40.   [11] 7.35–9.19.   [12] 10.4ff., 12.2ff.
[13] 10.3–4.   [14] 7.13.

In insisting that the wife serves the joint interests rather than the husband's, and vice-versa, Xenophon is far more generous to the dignity of the married woman than most classical theorists. The reservation to the husband of the power to delegate and the slightly patronizing tone natural to a man who married an ignorant 14-year-old girl should not be allowed to diminish his achievement, though modern women may wince when they read Socrates' approving remark that Ischomachus' wife must have had a masculine mind.[15]

(b) Aristotle

Plato had made Meno argue that woman's virtue consists in 'organizing her house well, safeguarding its contents, and being subject to her husband'.[16] It is this view which Aristotle adopted and developed. In the *Politics* he argued that women's moral qualities are different in kind, not only in degree, from men's: they have a kind of *sōphrosynē*, courage, and justice, but these are not equivalent to the corresponding virtues in men because their faculty of deliberation is weak.[17] Their virtues fit them to be ruled but not to rule.[18] Women are therefore controlled like fellow citizens politically, but, unlike male citizens in a democratic state, they never take a turn at ruling their husbands. Their status is, however, better than that of the other constituent elements of the household—slaves, who are ruled despotically, and children, who are governed like subjects of a king[19] —except that male slaves might in practice become superior free men, who were 'naturally more able to lead' than females, and that sons might grow up and become rulers.[20] Aristotle also held that male and female need each other, that is, for reproduction.[21] He is unusual in arguing here that the city is prior to the family, though both are natural.[22]

A rather more detailed and interesting discussion occurs in the *Nicomachean Ethics* in the section on *philia*, 'friendship', book 8.

[15] 9.16, 7.5, 10.1. For piquant recent work on her identity, with comments on the priggishness of Ischomachus (which I do not find remarkable in a didactic work: the tone of a Shirley Conran or a Peg Bracken can be equally infuriating), see Harvey, 'The wicked wife of Ischomachus', MacKenzie, 'The wicked wife of Ischomachus—again'. Discussion of Xenophon by Foucault, *L'histoire de la sexualité* ii. *L'usage des plaisirs* 169–83.
[16] *Meno* 71 E.
[17] The Platonic view of women's moral equality was later adopted by the Stoics (*SVF* iii. 58–9, nos. 245–54) and Epicurus (Lact. *Inst.* 3.25). On *sōphrosynē* see Helen North, *Sophrosyne. Self-knowledge and self-restraint in Greek literature*. She points out that 'feminine *sophrosyne* (chastity, modesty, obedience, inconspicuous behavior) remains the same throughout Greek history' (p. 1). The Latin equivalent is *pudicitia* (p. 307). For the reason for Aristotle's view see Smith. 'Plato and Aristotle on the nature of women'.
[18] *Pol.* 1259ᵇ–1260ᵃ.
[19] 1252ᵇ–1259ᵃ; cf. *MM* 1194ᵇ23–9.   [20] Cf. *MM* 1194ᵇ15–18.   [21] 1252ᵃ.
[22] 1253ᵃ; contrast *EN* 1162ᵃ17–19 and Plato *Legg.* 721 A.

Communities of friends live under various constitutions: monarchy, which in its corrupt form is tyranny, aristocracy, which may become oligarchy, and, the worst of the three, timocracy, which may deteriorate into democracy. The rule of father over son is monarchic, power-sharing by brothers is timocratic.

The association of man and wife seems to be aristocratic; for the man rules in accordance with his worth, and in those matters in which a man should rule, but the matters which befit a woman he hands over to her. If the man rules in everything, the relation passes over into oligarchy; for in doing so he is not acting in accordance with their respective worth, and not ruling in virtue of his superiority. Sometimes, however, women rule, because they are heiresses; so their rule is not in virtue of excellence but due to wealth and power, as in oligarchies. (1160ᵇ32–1161ᵃ3, trans. Ross)

The friendship of man and wife, again, is the same that is found in an aristocracy; for it is in accordance with virtue—the better gets more of what is good, and each gets what befits him; and so too with the justice in these relations. (1161ᵃ22–5, trans. Ross)

Between man and wife, friendship seems to exist by nature, for man is naturally inclined to form couples—even more than to form cities, inasmuch as the household is earlier and more necessary than the city, and reproduction is more common to man with the animals. With the other animals, the union extends only to this point, but human beings live together not only for the sake of reproduction but also for the various purposes of life; for from the start the functions are divided, and those of man and woman are different; so they help each other by throwing their peculiar gifts into the common stock. It is for these reasons that both utility and pleasure seem to be found in this kind of friendship. But this friendship may be based also on virtue, if the parties are good, for each has its own virtue and they will delight in the fact. And children seem to be a bond of union (*syndesmos*) (which is the reason why childless people part more easily); for children are a good common to both and what is common holds them together. How man and wife and in general friend and friend ought mutually to behave seems to be the same question as how it is just for them to behave; for a man does not seem to have the same duties to a friend, a stranger, a comrade, and a schoolfellow. (1162ᵃ16–33, trans. Ross)

(c) Peripatetics

Three short books on economics are also attributed to Aristotle. Of these *Oeconomica* 2 need not detain us, since, after dividing the subject into financial administration by kings, provincial governors, cities, and individuals, the author discusses a set of examples which include nothing on domestic management. The work is assigned by scholars to the late third century BC.

Oeconomica 1, however, is assigned to an unknown Peripatetic, a pupil or pupil of a pupil of Aristotle. Philodemus attributes it to Theophrastus himself. The author is indebted both to Xenophon and to Aristotle. He makes economics prior to politics, since the city is an aggregate of households, land, and property. The components of a household are human beings (which include the wife) and property.[23] As Hesiod put it, a man needs 'first and foremost, a house, a woman, and an ox for the plough'.[24] So economics include rules for the association of husband and wife, and this involves specifying what sort of woman she ought to be.[25] The association between husband and wife is natural; each needs the other and they co-operate for their mutual good.[26] They have children, both to satisfy the reproductive instinct and to ensure that they will be cared for in their old age. Some of the functions of husband and wife are opposite and complement each other. The physically stronger man is adapted to defending and acquiring property, to working out of doors, and to educating children, the weaker woman to showing caution, guarding possessions, working indoors, and nurturing children.[27]

A section on the husband's duties claims to reflect Pythagorean ideals. The husband is not to do wrong to his wife: then she will be less likely to wrong him. Injury to the wife is defined as associations outside the house, that is, with other women. The Pythagoreans say that a wife is like a suppliant sitting at the hearth.[28] Like Xenophon, the author holds that a man should choose a young bride and train her to administer her domestic sphere and organize the slaves.[29] Like Xenophon, he rules out artificial aids to attractiveness. Like Aristotle in *Nicomachean Ethics* on friends, he thinks that a man will find most congenial a wife whose character resembles his own.[30]

The third book of *Oeconomica* attributed to Aristotle is a monograph on the reciprocal duties of husband and wife. It hardly refers to household management at all, but treats in unusual detail the moral duties of each, giving an emphasis to the husband's duty which goes beyond that of Xenophon or the surviving fragments of Pythagorean

---

[23] Arist. *Oec.* 1343^a, 1343^b. For recent discussion see Laurenti, *Studi sull'Economico attribuito ad Aristotele.*

[24] *WD* 405.   [25] Arist. *Oec.* 1343^a.   [26] Cf. *EN* 1162^{a}19 ff.

[27] *Oec.* 1343^b.

[28] 1344^a; Cf. Iambl. *VP* 48, 84, etc. The most idiosyncratic remark in the monograph concerns *homilia*, intercourse, and is probably not to be taken in the restricted sense of sexual relations, but of companionship in general. Cf. Victor ad loc. But since it comes immediately after the discussion of a husband's extra-marital relationships, it seems likely that marital rights to coitus are prominent. This may be related to a theme in *Oeconomica* 3 (p. 145) that a good and loving wife can be depended on to be faithful in her husband's absence and, on the other hand, to Solon's ruling that a wife is entitled to coitus at least three times a month (Plut. *Am.* 769 A, *Solon* 89 c).

[29] 1344^a, 1345^a.   [30] 1159^{b}2 ff., 1344.

handbooks. Most unfortunately, the work exists only in Latin versions and it is therefore hazardous to conjecture whether it is identical with or derives from the *Rules for husband and wife* which Hesychius of Miletus (sixth century AD) lists among works which were attributed to Aristotle or the book on marriage mentioned by Jerome[31] and whether it should be dated before or after the Pythagorean works to be discussed below. *Rules for husband and wife* would be an appropriate title for *Oeconomica* 3, but this evidence does not suffice to date it among pre-Stoic Peripatetic works.

The main text is a Latin translation made by Guillaume Durand, Bishop of Mende, who died in 1296. Fragments of another version appear in the margin of one of the manuscripts of Durand, and there is also another Latin translation of *Oeconomica* 1–3. These can be used occasionally to correct Durand.[32]

The book begins so abruptly that one might think that something has been lost. But the first words at least make it clear that the first topic is the good wife. She is to take care of everything inside the house, avoiding the dangers of gossiping women outside; she is to control expenditure and avoid fine dress and gold ornaments, since modesty and a well-ordered life are preferable. The husband is to leave domestic matters to her, since it is not fitting that he should know about them. But 'in all other matters let her be careful to obey him and not try to meddle with any public business or with anything concerning the marriage of their children'.[33] The second is an unusual prohibition. The author continues with a statement which partly corresponds with a dictum of the Pythagorean text ascribed to Melissa. A woman ought to think that her husband's tastes and wishes (*mores*) are a law for her life, imposed by God, linked with their marriage and fortune. If she tolerates them patiently and humbly, she will easily be able to rule the household, but if not, it will be difficult. She is to share in all his adversities, forgive all his offences (regarding these as mistakes or accidents or aberrations caused by illness), and always obey him.[34] This is very much what another Pythagorean, Perictione, says. The wife should in fact serve her husband even more than a slave, since she is bought for a great price, to share his life and to have his children begotten on her.[35] Besides, sharing his misfortunes gives her a great chance to show her virtues and to win good repute, as did Penelope and Alcestis.[36]

[31] *Adv. Iovin.* 1.49 = 318B.
[32] The Loeb trans. by C. Armstrong is the most accessible text. I use Rose's pagination, which Armstrong gives.
[33] Rose p. 140, my trans.   [34] p. 141.
[35] 'Magno enim pretio empta fuit, societate namque vitae et procreatione liberorum, quibus nil maius et sanctius fieret.'   [36] p. 141.

After this idealization of the strict subordination of the wife, it is a relief to find that the husband is to deduce his rules of conduct from the rules prescribed for the wife. He is to regard her as a suppliant who has come into his family from outside and therefore someone whom it would be sin to injure. Moreover, she will leave in his family children who will take their name from both parents and who will support them in their old age. The husband is to train his wife so that she will be a good mother, and is required by religion to honour her after his own parents.[37] He is therefore to be physically faithful to her. 'For it is the greatest honour for a virtuous woman, if she sees her husband maintaining chastity towards her and not paying attention to any other woman rather than her, but holding her his own above all others and faithful and loving towards him. This makes her yet more concerned to be so.'[38] He should give due share of honour to parents, wife, and children, giving her his honourable and faithful society (*homilia*). A wise man must not scatter his genes, breeding degenerate children to compete with his legitimate heirs and bringing dishonour on them and their mother. In his manner towards her, he is enjoined to avoid reproof and to treat her with more politeness than he would a mistress. The proper attitude for both husband and wife is a mixture of love and respect (literally, 'fear').[39] He must first master himself in order to set her a good example. By his proper conduct towards her he will get a loyal and agreeable wife. The author then takes Odysseus as the outstanding example of a faithful husband and gives an interesting discussion of the episodes of Calypso and Nausicaa.[40] To sum up, if husband and wife do their duty to their parents and parents-in-law, their children, friends, and the house and property which they have in common, then they will be happy and supported in their old age by their own children. This book could not, with any pretence of consistency, have been written by either Aristotle or Theophrastus, and is probably comparatively late. I have discussed it with the Aristotelian works in order not to prejudice the issue.

Aristotle's successor Theophrastus apparently took an even harder line than his master, concluding in his 'golden book on marriage'[41] that the philosopher should hardly ever marry. A wife was a distraction and an expense:

There are many things which married women must have, expensive clothes, gold, jewels, outlays, slave women, various articles of furniture, litters, and a gilded chariot. Then all night long you will hear chatter and complaints:

---

[37] pp. 142–3.   [38] pp. 143–44.   [39] pp. 144–5.
[40] p. 146.   [41] Jer. *adv. Iovin.* 1.47 = 313 c.

'So-and-so goes out better dressed than I do', 'This woman is honoured by everyone, but poor little me, the other women are rude to me at women's get-togethers', 'Why were you looking at the woman next door?', 'What were you talking about to the slave-girl?', 'What have you brought back from the forum?' We can't have a man-friend or a companion without her thinking that we love someone else and hate her . . . It is difficult to support a poor wife and torture to put up with a rich one. (Jerome *adversus Iovinianum* 1.47 = 313C)

Jerome here seems to have introduced a Roman flavour, but the line of argument is probably original. Theophrastus apparently went on to say that it was hard to find a perfectly qualified wife and if a man found a good one he would have to worry about her when she was in childbed. A philosopher had no need of a wife as a companion. It was stupid to marry in order to breed children, as a defence in old age or in order to have heirs, since it was better to choose friends as heirs.[42]

(d) Pythagoreans

High ideals on the sanctity of family life were attributed to Pythagoras. In the speech which the Neoplatonist Iamblichus (c. AD 250–325) makes him give at Croton,[43] he insists that there should be order and *sōphrosynē* in the household and lays down a single standard of marital fidelity for both husband and wife. The leaders of Croton were so moved that they at once dismissed their mistresses. Although the exactness of this account in the context of sixth-century Italy must be doubted (especially since Pythagoras left no writings), the Pythagorean order which flourished in Croton in the fifth century and was revived in mainland Greece and in the towns of southern Italy, especially Tarentum, in the fourth century was generally agreed to insist on purity. Since the order admitted women, it was essential that non-members should be assured of its high sexual standards.[44] When interest in Pythagorean ideas revived, probably chiefly in Magna Graecia and especially in Tarentum in the third and early second centuries BC,[45] various works were attributed to people claimed as Pythagoreans. The great and semi-legendary lawgivers of Greek colonies in Sicily and southern Italy, Zaleucus (traditionally seventh century) and Charondas of Catane (traditionally sixth century), were adopted, as was Theano, the wife or daughter of Pythagoras, and Perictione, presumably identified with the mother of Plato. Because

---

[42] Periplectomenus makes almost the same point in the *Miles*: he will leave his money to his *cognati*: 705 ff. The whole scene is very close to Theophrastus.

[43] *VP* 45–50.

[44] See for a brief account Pomeroy, *GWWS* 134 ff.

[45] I follow Thesleff, *Introduction* 99 ff.

it was accepted that women had been members of the earlier Pythagorean order, moralizing works about women's capacity to be philosophers and their moral duties were naturally often attributed to
women writers. Sermons on wifely duty would have more impact on
women when they were thought to have been uttered by a female
saint.[46]

If we follow Holger Thesleff's tentative dating,[47] a number of
Pythagorean works known from fragments can be put in the third
century BC. There seems to be no good reason to attribute them to a
Pythagorean revival in the second century AD.[48] He suggests that the
laws of Zaleucus and Charondas were composed probably in the
eastern Greek lands in about the third century BC. Pythagorean ideals
percolated to Rome perhaps as early as the fourth century and
certainly by 181 BC.[49] Some Doric prose texts of Pythagorean pseudepigrapha had probably been collected by the second century BC and
survived (Thesleff conjectures in Roman libraries) to be used eventually by John of Stobi in his anthology in the early fifth century AD.
As far as the present study is concerned, the apocryphal Pythagorean
works on household management would fit appropriately into the
Western cultural context of the third and second centuries. Romans
of the age of Cato may well have been receptive to handbooks which
dealt with successful partnership between husband and wife, which
promised maximum profits not only in family harmony but also in the
efficient running of the household. The Hellenistic reconstruction of
the severe laws of early Greek colonies, in which sumptuary laws on
female dress and luxury hold a conspicuous place, also fits well into
the climate of ideas in which the debate on the repeal of the Oppian
Law was held at Rome after the end of the second Punic War. That

[46] Cf. for later women philosophers Vatin 35–6; Pomeroy, 'Technikai kai mousikai', 57–8,
Women in hellenistic Egypt from Alexander to Cleopatra 61 ff. I have not seen Meunier, *Femmes
pythagoriciennes: Fragments et lettres de Théano, Perictioné, Phintys, Mélissa et Myia.*

[47] Thesleff, *Introduction*, esp. pp. 96–116. At a subsequent Fondation Hardt colloquium, in
response to Walter Burkert, Thesleff was prepared to entertain the possibility that he should
bring the dating of the Doric pseudepigrapha down to the 2nd cent. rather than the 3rd. See
Burkert, 'Zur geistesgeschichtlichen Einordnung einiger Pseudopythagorica'; Thesleff, 'On
the problem of the Doric pseudo-Pythagorica: an alternative theory of date and purpose'.
Thesleff remained sceptical about the hypothesis of an Augustan or later date for the extant
tracts (pp. 82–3). He argued for the existence of a corpus of Doric pseudo-Pythagorean writings
in the early 1st cent. BC (p. 73). 'If the 3rd century is too early—and as the Hadrianic age is
definitely too late for the majority of the Pythagorean tracts—a Hellenistic date and a
(formerly) Doric environment seem preferable to an early Imperial date and a completely
non-Doric environment' (p. 72). The tracts in which I am interested here were barely
mentioned at the colloquium. It is sufficient for my argument if they were written and circulated
and available to influence Roman thinking before the age of Cicero.

[48] As did Wilhelm, 'Die Oeconomica der Neupythagoreer Bryson, Kallikratidas, Periktione,
Phintys'.

[49] Thesleff, *Introduction* 52–3.

these laws continued to attract interest in Graeco-Roman society down to the time of the triumvirs is shown by the account of Diodorus the Sicilian.

Zaleucus is supposed to have introduced at Locri a clever law that a free-born woman was not to go out with more than one maid in attendance, unless she was drunk, or leave the city at night, unless she was going to commit adultery, or wear gold ornaments or purple-bordered clothes, unless she was a courtesan.[50] Pythagorean ideals were also perceived in the laws of Thurii attributed to Charondas but probably to be dated to the fourth or third century. Men were forbidden to father children outside marriage and strongly discouraged from marrying again on the death of first wives who had borne them children. Women were to be *sōphrones* (self-controlled) and not commit adultery, for fear of divine retribution.[51]

A book attributed to Perictione on the harmony to be achieved by a woman urges a woman to attain the virtues of justice, courage, and *phronēsis* (prudence) for her own sake and that of her husband, children, and house.[52] Thanks to these qualities, she will not follow unlawful love-affairs, but love her husband, children, and home. For adultery makes women hostile to both free and slave people in their own houses, making them lie to their husbands and destroy their joint property. A good woman shows moderation in her way of life, in clothes, baths, perfumes, hairdressing, gold, and jewels, which lead to sexual licence and all sorts of vice. The body may be allowed food and drink and clothes to keep it warm and decent (goatskin and sheepskin, if she is poor), but fashionable clothes and purple dye and gold or Indian and other imported stones or elaborate hairstyles or perfume of Arabia or white face-powder, rouge, mascara, eye-liner, hair-dye, or frequent baths are all forbidden. True beauty comes from wisdom. She is not to think high birth, wealth, a powerful city, repute, and the friendship of famous and powerful men essential to her happiness. She will honour the gods and the laws, revere her husband, and act agreeably to him, never thinking selfishly and 'preserving her bed. For everything depends on this.' She must endure everything which affects her husband, whether he is unfortunate or makes mistakes (through ignorance, illness, or drunkenness)[53] or whether he keeps mistresses—adultery being a common failing of men but not venial in a wife. She is to tolerate all his failings: anger, stinginess, carping, jealousy, unjustified accusation, and anything else which is natural to him. She will do everything quietly and discreetly as he likes it. If she loves her husband and pleases him, she

[50] Diod. 12.21; cf. Ath. 12.521 B.   [51] Stob. 4.2.24; cf. Diod. 12.12.1.
[52] Thesleff, *Texts* 142 ff. = Stob. 4.25.50, 4.28.19.   [53] Cf. [Arist] *Oec.* 3 p. 141.

is herself in harmony and loves her whole household and makes others outside it benevolent to it. But if she hates him, she destroys the whole household and its possessions and longs for her husband's death and for other lovers. A wife is harmonious if she is full of wisdom and *sōphrosynē*. She helps her husband, children, kin, slaves, and whole household. She follows her husband's ideas on their shared life, likes his friends and relations, agrees with all his tastes, and so achieves harmony.[54] A second, shorter fragment returns to the insistence on honouring and obeying parents in all the changes and chances of life, in health and sickness, for richer for poorer, and so on, but does not return to the subject of marital virtue.[55]

This uplifting tract, probably from the eastern Mediterranean, is followed by a Western group of handbooks, which Thesleff puts in the following order: Bryson's *Oeconomicus*, Callicratides' *On the happiness of the household*, Melissa's *Letter to Cleareta*, Phintys' *On the sōphrosynē of women*. Bryson survives in Arabic and Hebrew versions, some indication of the appeal his work has had for husbands in different cultures over the centuries.[56] In true Pythagorean and Aristotelian style, Bryson found four things necessary to make housekeeping complete: money, slaves, a housewife who could deputize for the husband, and children.[57] The wife should be submissive, but sexual fidelity should be reciprocal. She was not to be chosen for her rank, beauty, or money, but for the sake of the home and children, for her physical and mental health and her virtues, reason, sagacity, strength, self-control, submissiveness, and righteousness. But the husband should also be good, because successful housekeeping brought everything into play.

The book on domestic happiness attributed to Callicratidas formulated the matter more theoretically. He held that the household, like a choir or a body, was a system (*systama*) of opposites. The chief parts of it were classified as humans and possessions, as in *Oeconomica* I. 'There is an entity which rules and one which is ruled and one which helps the house and the kindred. The ruling one is the husband, the ruled the wife, and the helping one is their children.'[58] The type of rule exercised by a husband is political. For there are three sorts of power (*archē*), despotic, epistatic, and political. The first is for the benefit of

[54] Thesleff, *Texts* 142 ff. = Stob. 4.25.50; full trans. in Pomeroy, *GWWS* 134–6 or *Women in hellenistic Egypt* 8–70.
[55] Thesleff, *Texts* 145 = Stob. 4.25.50.
[56] A full modern German trans. is available: Plessner, 'Der Οἰκονομικὸς des Neupythagoreers "Bryson" und sein Einfluß auf die islamische Wissenschaft'. Thesleff, *Texts* 57–8, gives a useful summary. For commentary, Wilhelm, 'Die Oeconomica der Neupythagoreer'.
[57] Cf. Arist. *Pol.* 1253[b] 6ff.
[58] Thesleff, *Texts* 102 ff. = Stob. 4.28.16.

the ruler, like that of a master over his slaves, the second is for the sake of the ruled, like that of trainers over athletes or of teachers over pupils. But political power aims at the advantage of ruler and ruled and is to be seen in the household, the city, and the universe.[59] The wife is to be subordinate to her husband. If it happens that a man marries above him, the couple will struggle for dominance. For a wife who is richer or better born prefers to rule her husband, which is unnatural. They should aim at imitating music. The husband should be guardian, *kyrios*, and teacher and therefore should choose a malleable but sufficiently mature child of good parents, whom he can train to love and fear him.[60] A man who rules like a master is hated by his wife; a man who rules epistatically is despised; but a man who rules politically is honoured and loved.[61]

The letter of Melissa to Cleareta (which may be next chronologically) is on the theme of avoidance of luxury, which we have already seen in Perictione. A good wife should wear plain white, should aim to look beautiful to her husband and not to the neighbours, should have virtues and not jewels for ornament, should seek to have a good reputation for running her house well and pleasing her husband, by fulfilling his wishes. 'For the wishes of the husband ought to be an unwritten law for a well-conducted (*kosmia*) wife.' Orderliness (*eutaxia*) is the best dowry she can bring and she should trust in the beauty and richness of her soul rather than in physical beauty or money to attract a husband.[62]

A manual on female discretion (*sōphrosynē*) attributed to another woman, Phintys, called it the greatest female virtue, since it enabled her to love and honour her husband. Women ought to have a philosophical training as much as men. 'I think that some things are peculiar to women, some to men, and others common to men and women, others more men's than women's, and others more women's than men's.' Leading armies, taking part in politics, and addressing the people are peculiar to men. It is peculiar to women to 'keep house, stay indoors, welcome and care for the husband'. Courage, justice, and thought (*phronēsis*) are common to both sexes, but thought is more especially for men and *sōphrosynē* for women. This comes from holiness in sexual conduct, especially avoiding strange men because of the risk of bearing bastards, which would be a

---

[59] Thesleff, *Texts* 105–6 = Stob. 4.28.17.

[60] Stob. 4.28.18.

[61] Thesleff, *Texts* 106 = Stob. 4.28.17.

[62] Thesleff, *Texts* 115–16 = Herscher, *Epistolographi graeci* 607–8. Städele, *Die Briefe des Pythagoras und der Pythagoreer*, comments (pp. 253–66) and dates (p. 256) to between the 2nd cent. BC and the 2nd cent. AD, probably towards the end of this period. I incline to the earlier dating.

betrayal of the oath to come into a family to share the husband's life and bear his children, and from decency and self-restraint in dress, going out, sacrifices, and women's rites.[63]

Apophthegms, *Advice to women* (both lost), and a number of letters to women were attributed to the famous Theano, said by some to be the wife or daughter of Pythagoras. Their date and provenance is obscure. She was a popular peg on whom various moral sayings suitable to a virtuous wife were hung.[64] Two letters deal with the conduct proper to a wife whose husband is having an affair with a hetaera. Theano advises Nicostrata not to be jealous and vengeful, but to tolerate it in silence as a passing phase. Being his partner for life (while he frequents his mistress merely for pleasure), she is to continue to show how different she is from a hetaera, by caring for the house and showing love for the children, rather than trying to rival a woman who is too dangerous to fight. If she punishes her husband, she will suffer herself. If she leaves him and remarries, she may repeat the experience and end up alone and husbandless. If she fights him, it will not improve his behaviour.[65] A letter to Eurydice is similar: the husband only goes to a hetaera for a change.[66]

Such ideas long remained commonplace. Naumachios, an epic poet of the second century AD, who may be mentioned here for convenience, is quoted with approval by Stobaeus in his chapter on advice to married people. He is still preaching to women that they must marry as their parents choose, put up with a bad husband, forbear from quarrelling with him if he misbehaves, cultivate discretion themselves, run the house efficiently and humanely, leaving outside work to him, avoid corruption by not encouraging old women to call, eschew fine clothes and jewellery and eye make-up.[67]

A work on the universe attributed to a certain Ocellus, who allegedly lived in Lucania before the time of Plato, and which is probably to be dated around 150 BC, treats sexual and marital relations in the context of procreation and displays ideas similar to those of the Pythagoreans and Stoics. Sexuality is god-given, 'necessary and fine', but intercourse is not for pleasure but for the procreation of children. Wives should be selected not for wealth or family, but for their compatibility and 'sympathy'. Choosing a wife for the

---

[63] Thesleff, *Texts* 151 ff. = Stob. 4.23.61.

[64] Thesleff, *Texts* 194. Cf. W. Burkert, *Gnomon* 39 (1967) 550. Thesleff ('On the problem of the Doric pseudo-Pythagorica' 68) compares form and subject-matter with the letters of Melissa and Myia, but Theano's letters 'probably existed in Attic versions only'.

[65] Thesleff, *Texts* 198 ff. = Herscher, *Epistolographi graeci* 604. Städele, *Briefe* 308, thinks not before the 1st cent. BC but probably 2nd cent. AD.

[66] Thesleff, *Texts* 197 = Herscher *Epistolographi graeci* 606. Städele, *Briefe* 337, 351, puts this text after Synesius, presumably in the 5th cent. AD.   [67] Stob. 4.23.7.

wrong reasons leads to disharmony and disagreement instead of harmony and unity, for the wife who excels her husband in wealth or birth seems to rule him against the natural law and he is unable to get the leadership, which is bad for the household and the city.[68]

By the second century BC Romans were increasingly in contact with less middle-brow philosophical ideas coming from the thinkers of mainland Greece, the established schools of Athens, and other centres further afield than southern Italy and Sicily. Some of the ideas of Plato and Aristotle fit happily with the Pythagorean tradition.[69] Epicureans seem to have avoided discussing marital ethics, since Epicurus held that the wise man would not usually marry.[70] Aristo the Stoic (*fl.* 250 BC) could with some justification hold that household ethics were trivial, consisting of old women's saws, beneath the dignity of philosophy. If a man knew how to live aright, he also knew how to live with a wife. But Cleanthes opposed this view successfully.[71] The later Stoics held that marriage and procreation were natural and right for philosophers.[72] Only the wise man was a real householder and money-maker.[73] Their theoretical focus was on the completeness of the household rather than on Pythagorean harmony, and they emphasized the connection with the state.

Antipater of Tarsus in the second century BC pointed out in *On marriage* that if young people (particularly of the upper class) did not marry and produce children, the state and the worship of the gods could not survive.[74] There are a number of important communities, *koinōniai*, in human culture, but only the pair of husband and wife shares property and children (everyone's dearest possession), soul and body. At this point he begins to draw practical conclusions similar to those of the Pythagoreans. For the partnership of husband and wife looks towards the husband's soul. The wife's purpose in life is to please him. Antipater parts company with the Pythagoreans when he argues that the relationship between husband and wife is more important than that with parents. Those who find married life disagreeable do so because they married for the wrong reason: beauty or dowry. It is their fault if they have not trained their wives to organize things as they want them. For a wife can make life easier: two pairs of

[68] Ocellus Lucanus, ed. Harder 43 ff.

[69] Vatin 32, citing DL 10.118 and modern bibliography.

[70] Jer. *adv. Iovin.* 1.48 = 317 D. This has been denied. For bibliography see Laurenti, *Filodemo e il pensiero economico degli epicurei* 65.

[71] Sen. *Epp.* 94.2 ff. Chrysippus also wrote on marriage. Cf. Bickel, ed. Jer. *adv. Iovin.*

[72] Jer. *adv. Iovin.* 318 A (Chrysippus) = *SVF* iii.727; *SVF* i.270 (Zeno), iii.611, 616 = Stob. 2.94.7, Cic. *Fin.* 3.68.

[73] *SVF* iii.159, 623 = Stob. 2.95.9.

[74] Cf. Dio 56.3.6–7, 5.2–3 (speech of Augustus).

hands and two pairs of eyes are better than one.[75] Antipater also wrote a book on *Living with a wife* in which he again recommended men not to marry for worldly reasons, since a rich or well-born wife might be proud or domineering.[76]

Romans who picked up Greek ideas of this sort in southern Italy, Sicily, Greece, or the Near East, or from Greeks who came to Rome, need not have been serious students of philosophy. Greek ideas about marriage were also floating around in tags from poetry, especially tragedy and new comedy, like the quotations from Euripides and Menander which were anthologized and appear in Stobaeus' collection. For instance, the topos that a rich or noble wife dominates her husband, which we have seen in the handbooks, occurs already in Euripides.[77]

This, then, is some of the material which was theoretically available to the hellenized Romans of the late Republic. It will be useful to disengage some of the main themes.

2. *Sexuality: The Double Standard and the Ascetic Impulse*

Which came first, the city or the family? The general view was that the family was more ancient, since the city was made up of family groups. Marriage was intended for the procreation and upbringing of children.[78] Sexual intercourse was both a natural animal instinct and divinely ordained.[79] Marriage was divinely sanctioned, accompanied by sacrifice to the gods.[80]

It was universally agreed that extra-marital intercourse was forbidden to women. The possibility of pre-marital intercourse by girls or extra-marital intercourse by widows and divorcees does not seem to have constituted a problem for philosophers. Nor are the sexual morals of non-citizens or slave-women of any interest to them: prostitutes or hetaerae are outside their purview except when they impinge on the lives of citizens. They preach to male citizens and to women who have entered into a quasi-contractual relationship with them, not just to share their beds, as Xenophon says, but to be partners of home and children.[81] The reason which underlies the insistence on wifely fidelity is the constant one, that the husband must

---

[75] *SVF* iii.254, 63 = Stob. 4.22.1.25. Other authorities attribute these writings to Antipater of Tyre, who had contacts with Cato Uticensis.

[76] *SVF* iii.254, 62 = Stob. 4.22.4.103.

[77] Stob. 4.22.1.1, 4.22.3.71, 75, 4.22.4.94, 95. Fraenkel finds it a favourite theme which appears in Menander, Diphilus, Philemon, Demophilus: *Elementi plautini* 416. On men dominated by women cf. Griffin, 'Propertius and Antony' 24 n. 79.

[78] Xen. *Oec.* 7.19, Antipater, Ocellus (see above).

[79] See above on Arist., Ocellus.

[80] [Arist.] *Oec.* 3 p. 143.   [81] Xen. *Oec.* 7.11.

be sure that the children he is bringing up are his own, though this is not directly stated. The reason is rather put in the form that the woman must not introduce bastards into the family which she has joined.[82] Adultery might also be held to anger the gods.[83] On the human level, Perictione points out that it turns a woman against her husband and family and thus undermines the whole relationship.

It is far more striking that so many philosophers forbade adultery and even extra-marital sexual intercourse to men. It may be worth recalling as the presumably standard Athenian view pseudo-Demosthenes' famous remark on the three kinds of heterosexual sexual relationship open to Athenian men—with courtesans, concubines, and wives.[84] But Plato in his severest legislative mood in the *Laws* makes the Athenian stranger rule out homosexuality and sex with any woman from whom the man does not want children. This rule would make men fonder of their own wives. Men are to go into training like athletes. No man is to dare to touch any well-born or free person except his own wedded wife, he is not to plant his seed in mistresses because that is unholy and produces bastards, nor yet in males, because that is unfruitful and unnatural. These novel rules are somehow to be imposed by public opinion or enforced by disqualifying from citizenship any man who has intercourse with anyone except his wife. Although at least once it seems that Plato is interested only in outlawing illicit sexual relations with respectable citizens of either sex, his more general and extreme utterances also cover intercourse with hetaerae or slave-boys. He obliterates the usual distinction between free citizens, who are violated or corrupted by illicit sexual relations, and persons of inferior status, who are not regarded as moral beings, so that sexual connection with them is only of interest in the context of its possible relevance to the self-control of the 'superior' partner.

According to Iamblichus, Pythagoras forbade fornication to husbands. The Pythagoreans are supposed to have held, like Plato, that it was wrong for a man to father bastards.[85] This idea was shared by the author of *Oeconomica* 3, who held that bastards would be degenerate, that is, in the view of Nicostratus, would be tainted by the immorality of their parents,[86] a view which has had a long history,

---

[82] Phintys.   [83] Charondas says this (p. 194), but the belief is no doubt general.

[84] 59.118–22. Cf. Lacey, *The family in classical Greece* 113, for the correct interpretation that in 'we have courtesans for pleasure, concubines to look after the day-to-day needs of the body, wives that we may breed legitimate children and have a trusty warden of what we have in the house' the services listed are cumulative: only the wife performs all of them. Note that adultery with other men's wives is not an option.   [85] See on Charondas.

[86] [Arist.] *Oec.* 3 above. On the legal position of bastards at Athens, a very different matter, see Lacey, *The family in classical Greece* 103–5.

finding vivid expression in *King Lear*. There is also a strong tradition that the Pythagoreans early developed the idea that a wife was to be regarded as a suppliant sitting at the hearth and to be treated with particular respect because of her helplessness.[87] Wronging the wife is defined by *Oeconomica* 1 as keeping company with other women, outside the house. The author of *Oeconomica* 3 reflects on the satisfaction and moral support which a wife derives from seeing that her husband is faithful and cares more for her than for any other woman.[88] It had also occurred to the author of *Oeconomica* 1 that a wife was less likely to commit adultery if the husband did not.[89] There is also the general consideration that virtue was the same for both sexes[90] and that a man should be *sōphrōn*.[91] When the bride's mother and the bridegroom's father told each to be discreet, sexual restraint was certainly in the forefront of their minds for the bride, but a measure of it was part of their recipe for Ischomachus too.[92] The strongest call to fidelity comes in *Oeconomica* 3 and the eloquent sermon on Odysseus.

The severest view comes from Ocellus. Others had held that it was wrong to have intercourse with a woman from whom a man did not want children, that is, sex for pleasure outside marriage was wrong. Ocellus held that the sexual act should never be undertaken for pleasure but only for reproduction, within marriage.[93] A man should not indulge his appetites until he reached the age of 20, and then not often.[94] Sobriety, forethought, and decency in the specific sexual act were essential in order to engender virtuous children.[95]

A less idealistic tradition also existed. Even Plato had recognized that he was building castles in the air. The handbooks addressed to wives took an earthier view, advising them to tolerate their husbands' infidelities with hetaerae, since they visited them only for pleasure and relaxation. (Homosexuality and affairs with married women are not mentioned in this context.) Men were prone to this failing and it meant very little. The wife was to show how different she was from the hetaera and not seek to compete. We may here see the beginning of the sharp distinction between the sexual roles of wife and mistress which has provided such useful support to the double standard.[96]

---

[87] This is quoted by the author of *Oeconomica* 1, probably in the late 4th cent; 1344ª; cf. 3 pp. 142–3; Iambl. *VP* 48, 84, etc.

[88] pp. 143–44.

[89] [Arist.] *Oec.* 1344ª.

[90] Cf. Plato, the Stoics, but not Aristotle.

[91] Plato, Aristotle, Phintys.   [92] Xen. *Oec.* 7.14–15.

[93] Ocellus 45.   [94] Ocellus 54.   [95] Ocellus 45, 55 ff.

[96] Below, ch. 9.II.1.

3. The Household Unit

Aristotle in the *Politics* had defined three relationships in which a man functions within the family as those of master of his slaves, husband to his wife, father to his children. The three roles are despotic, gametic, and teknopoietic. (To these is added the art of making money, *chrēmatistikē*.)[97] These three pairs, as David Balch has shown, remain central to the philosophic analysis.[98] The social and economic unit consists of the married pair, their servants, and their eventual children. A three-generation household is not envisaged, despite the insistence on the respect due to parents[99] or the fact that Ischomachus and his bride had parents alive at the time of their wedding.[100] Other relations must be treated dutifully but are regarded as outside the immediate household. Bryson sees the husband in control of money, slaves, his wife, and his children. Callicratidas has the husband and wife as the primary pair of opposites and their children as their helpers, those who will eventually look after them in their old age.[101] He does, however also stress the fact that marriage creates new kinsmen—father, brothers, mother's father, father's father, on the side of the spouse—as well as friends who increase the house.[102] Neither Melissa nor Phintys nor Theano speaks of duties of the wife which extend outside her household (apart from going out to sacrifices). Antipater insists that the partnership of husband and wife is uniquely important to the community, sharing both property and children. The complete household requires a wife and children. The adult male is seen as living separately from parents (who may indeed be assumed to be dead) and in need of a wife.

4. The Subordination of the Wife

The subordination of the wife to the control and interests of the husband and to the well-being of the household is a constant theme. Aristotle had founded it on the moral inferiority of women, arguing, as he did for slaves, from observation of current Greek practice. Despite the views of Plato, Xenophon, and the Pythagoreans and Stoics on the moral perfectibility of women, their recipes for harmony or good order rest on the headship of the husband. Partnership and community (*koinōnia*) are constantly emphasized, but only

---

[97] 1253[b].

[98] *Let wives be submissive.* 'The Neopythagorean moralists and the New Testament' is to appear in *ANRW* ii/26.

[99] Perictione; *Oec.* 3 pp. 143–4, *SVF* iii.731 (Chrysippus).

[100] Xen. *Oec.* 7.10.7.14–15.

[101] Cf. Xen. *Oec.* 7.12, 19; *contra*, Theophr. ap. Jer. *adv. Iovin.* 1.47 = 315 D.

[102] Thesleff, *Texts* 104 = Stob. 4.28.16.

Xenophon comes near to recognizing the wife's equal responsibility and privileges. The idea of division of tasks[103] theoretically gives the wife a province in which she is supreme, so that even Aristotle insists that the husband must delegate suitable jobs to her, for if he takes charge of everything himself his power deteriorates from aristocracy to oligarchy, just as a rich or powerful wife who trespasses on his prerogatives creates the same corruption. But it is very clear that the household is to be run to suit the husband, not the wife.

It was perhaps left to Antipater to state clearly that the partnership was organized for the benefit of the husband's soul, a view which was to be given fresh currency by Plutarch. The wife was to subordinate herself as well as her work. She must share his misfortunes'[104] tolerate all his vices and failings,[105] do everything according to his wishes,[106] avoid having any social contacts which exclude him and cut to the minimum her activities outside the house,[107] run an efficient household,[108] be strictly chaste,[109] dress economically and plainly:[110] in short, suppress her personality and depend entirely on him. Submissiveness is the keynote.[111] Opposition only made the wife suffer worse.[112] She really won when her husband defeated her.[113]

The theory of division of labour is implicit in the frequent insistence on the wife's role as housewife and custodian and on the propriety of her keeping within doors as far as possible. Although the Greek and especially Athenian practice of secluding their women may well appear to have been more thorough-going and more strictly sanctioned by morality than anything current in Rome at any period, it will be worth keeping in mind the common Mediterranean idea that a woman's place is in the home.[114] The logical consequence of Xenophon's view is that while all outdoor life is open to the husband and honourable for him—work in his own fields, hunting, the agora, foreign campaigns, travel, the whole world—and while he can retire to his own fireside when work is done and be cared for and welcomed by his wife, his wife is almost confined to one place. The favourite example of Penelope and Odysseus makes this restriction even clearer.

[103] Xen. (pp. 185–6); Arist. *EN* 1160ᵇ32; *OEC.* 1, 3, Phintys.
[104] See *Oec.* 3, Perictione.
[105] *Oec.* 3, Perictione, Theano, Naumachius.
[106] *Oec.* 3, Perictione, Melissa.
[107] *Oec.* 3, Perictione, Phintys, Naumachius.
[108] Xen., Perictione, Melissa (p. 196), Theano, Naumachius.
[109] Perictione, Phintys, Naumachius.
[110] Xen., *Oec.* 1, Theophrastus, Perictione, Meliisa, Naumachius.
[111] Bryson.   [112] Theano.   [113] Iambl. *VP* 11.54.
[114] Schaps, 'The women least mentioned'; Lacey, *The family in classical Greece* 167 ff.

5. Affection

A relationship of affection between husband and wife is very little stressed in the tradition, though wives are told to love their husbands and children. Callicratidas says that the husband's rule, being political, should inspire respect and love; it is a mixture of pleasure and righteousness. The former comes from loving, the latter from abstention from unworthy action. The author of *Oeconomica* 3 stands out for his view that the attitude of both husband and wife towards each other should be compounded of love and respect.

We have so far discussed Greek theorists whose ideas might have percolated into Roman culture by the time of Cicero. In so doing, we may have obscured the continuity which exists between Antipater's *On marriage* in the second century BC and the Stoic Hierocles' book of the same title in the late first or early second century AD. But well before the time of Hierocles Latin writers had entered the debate, and we cannot ignore the possibility that Greek philosophers knew of their views. By 167 many of the ideas of Greek philosophers and moralists were 'in the air', so it would be foolish to attempt to trace the transmission into Latin literature and thought, especially as so many of the ideas are merely based on traditional practices. But, to change the metaphor, occasional links may represent the spider's web which existed. From now on, Roman theorizing is bound to be affected by Greek categories and instances.

7

Graeco-Roman Theories of Marriage

Martial, the things for to attain
The happy life be these, I find:
The riches left, not got with pain;
The fruitful ground, the quiet mind;
The equal friend; no grudge nor strife;
No charge of rule nor governance;
Without disease the healthful life;
The household of continuance;
The mean diet, no delicate fare;
Wisdom joined with simplicity;
The night dischargèd of all care
Where wine may bear no sovereignty;
The chaste wife wise, without debate;
Such sleeps as may beguile the night;
Contented with thine own estate;
Neither wish death, nor fear his might.

(Henry Howard, Earl of Surrey,
'The Happy Life': *The New
Oxford Book of English Verse
1250–1950* [1972] 44)

1. The Reception of Greek Ideas in the Second and First Centuries BC

Let us take as an initial example the *sententia* of a censor of the late second century BC on the mixed advantages and disadvantages of marriage: 'If we could manage without wives . . . we would all do without the annoyance (*molestia*), but since nature has taught us that we cannot live comfortably with them, nor live at all without them, we must take thought for our eternal welfare rather than our temporary pleasure.'[1] Stobaeus gives a list of quotations on this precise topic of

---

[1] Gell. 1.6. The orthodox view is that Gellius is mistaken in attributing the fragment to Q. Caecilius Metellus Numidicus, the censor of 102–1: it is credited instead to Q. Caecilius Metellus Macedonicus, censor in 131, whose speech on this topic was read to the Senate by Augustus (Livy *Per.* 59, cf. Suet. *DA* 89.2). The question has recently been thoroughly

the mixture of advantages and disadvantages. His topoi-headings
derive from much earlier sources. The anthology here includes tags to
show that you cannot have a household without evil, that although
the rich wife stops her husband doing what he wants she produces one
good result, children, and that marrying is an evil but a necessary
evil.[2] All of these, but especially the last, are part of the climate of
opinion which produced Metellus' remark.

Lucilius, in his two satires on wives, *de mulierum ingenio et moribus*
and *de nuptiarum et matrimonii molestiis*, took up the debate. It has
been held that he was attacking Metellus by satirizing all the draw-
backs of marriage and the vices of wives.[3] Certainly the fragment
which begins 'homines ipsi hanc sibi molestiam ultro atque aerum-
nam offerunt, | ducunt uxores' ('human beings of their own free will
bring themselves this annoyance: they marry wives') suggests that
Lucilius may have remembered Metellus (or vice versa).[4] The attack
on women's unchastity and neglect of wool-work, the camouflaging
of assignations by pretended visits to goldsmith, mother, kinswoman,
and female friend, extravagant staffs including eunuchs, shows
commonplaces already familiar.[5] Since we only have fragments of
each author and dating is controversial, close connections cannot be
explored.

Varro in his *Menippean Satires* exploited the same moralizing
tradition, though he argued theoretically in favour of marriage: the
sane man would marry, he said, contradicting Menander.[6] In another
piece, 'On the duty of a husband' (*de officio mariti*), he apparently
took an ironical view of the husband's role. This contrasts nicely with
the complete lack of irony in the tract ascribed to Perictione on the
wife's duty to tolerate a husband's failings. 'A fault in a wife must
either be removed or tolerated. If a man removes it, he makes his wife
more agreeable; if he tolerates it, he makes himself more virtuous.'[7]

---

re-examined by Myles McDonnell ('The speech of Numidicus at Gellius, *N.A.* 1.6'), who
argues attractively that there were two Metellan censorial speeches on increasing the birth-rate,
but that the Gellian fragment comes from Numidicus.

[2] 4.22.3.68, Susarion; ibid. 71, ? Menander; ibid. 77, Menander. See further McDonnell,
'The speech of Numidicus' 84.

[3] Marx ii. 247 ad Lucil. 678–9; Raschke, 'The early books of Lucilius' 83, and earlier
discussions cited there. The titles are not original.

[4] 678–9; cf. 68c (Marx). But both *molestia* and *molesta* are common words. See now
McDonnell, 'The speech of Numidicus' 84.

[5] 26.680; ? 996ff.; 995; 993–4; 1056ff.

[6] *Men.* 167, from 'The pot found its lid'; cf. Men. fr. 59 and Courtney on Juv. 6.28.

[7] 83 = Gell. 1.17.4: 'Vitium uxoris aut tollendum aut ferendum est. Qui tollit vitium uxorem
commodiorem praestat; qui fert sese meliorem facit' ('A fault in a wife must either be removed
or tolerated. A man who removes it makes his wife more congenial, one who tolerates it makes
himself better').

Philodemus, the Epicurean philosopher and poet who was a pro-tégé of Piso (consul 58), compiled for private circulation the equivalent of 'sloppy academic textbooks',[8] which include a work 'On vices and the corresponding virtues'. The surviving sections of the papyrus roll of book 9 which was kept in the villa which probably belonged to Piso at Herculaneum include a critical account of Xenophon's *Oeconomicus*, the part on the duties of a wife.[9] Philodemus, who was presumably chiefly resident in this luxurious and cultured house, which his patron would visit for philosophical house parties in spring vacations from the Senate, could well afford to follow the Epicurean line that marriage was unprofitable for a philosopher. Though in one of his poems he pretends to be ready to marry,[10] he claims that Xenophon does not show that marriage was necessary or profitable for philosophic housekeeping in a peaceful life. Were all wives capable of learning as well as Ischomachus'? Was the husband to be blamed for all that went wrong? Some wives collaborated in enriching their family, but others caused positive damage.[11] A wife could waste what she was supposed to guard. In short, a man could live happily without a wife.[12]

The copy-book headings which Roman schoolmasters drew from the mimes of Publilius the Syrian in the late Republic yield a dozen lines on women and marriage. They are similar to the brief epigrams which Stobaeus or earlier anthologists took from Euripides or Menander. They may be taken to represent both the common coin of the hellenized world and the sort of quip which society thought would not corrupt the morals of schoolboys. Some are misogynist: 'A woman is only good when her wickedness is overt'. Others take the conventional line on the reclamation of straying husbands ('A wife's complaisance soon makes a mistress hated'), or state a paradox or wifely submission ('A chaste wife, by obeying her husband, commands')[13]

The more serious and deliberate adaptation of Greek moralizing ideas will be sought in Cicero's philosophical works. Two passages in particular concern us.

---

[8] A. A. Long in *CHCL* i.630.
[9] Balch 39–40 points out Philodemus' dependence on *Oec.* 1 and on Zeno.
[10] *AP* 11.34. See Sider, 'The love poetry of Philodemus', arguing that Philodemus was married.
[11] To refrain from wasting a husband's fortune is called 'negative thrift' in Richard Allestree (1619–81) *The ladies calling* 189.
[12] Jensen ed. περὶ κακιῶν καὶ τῶν ἀντικειμένων ἀρετῶν . . . col. II, IX. For discussion see Laurenti, *Filodemo e il pensiero economico degli epicurei* 39–46 and 55–66 on similar arguments against [Arist.] *Oec.* 1.
[13] Publilius *Sententiae* 20, 445, 93, cf. Iambl. *VP* 11.54.

Nam cum sit hoc natura commune animantium, ut habeant libidinem procreandi, prima societas in ipso coniugio est, proxima in liberis, deinde una domus, communia omnia, id autem est principium urbis et quasi seminarium rei publicae (*de officiis* 1.54)

Because the urge to reproduce is an instinct common to all animals, society originally consists of the pair, next of the pair with their children, then one house and all things in common. This is the beginning of the city and the seed-bed of the state.

In omni autem honesto de quo loquimur nihil est tam illustre nec quod latius pateat quam coniunctio inter homines hominum et quasi quaedam societas et communicatio utilitatum et ipsa caritas generis humani, quae nata a primo satu, quod a procreatoribus nati diliguntur et tota domus coniugio et stirpe coniungitur, serpit sensim foras, cognationibus primum, tum affinitatibus, deinde amicitiis, post vicinitatibus, tum civibus et iis qui publice socii atque amici sunt, deinde totius complexu gentis humanae; quae animi affectio suum cuique tribuens atque hanc quam dico societatem coniunctionis humanae munifice et aeque tuens iustitia dicitur, cui sunt adiunctae pietas, bonitas, liberalitas, benignitas, comitas, quaeque sunt generis eiusdem. (*de finibus* 5.65)

In the whole area of what is morally right of which we are speaking, there is nothing so glorious or wide-ranging as the unity of human beings with each other and the partnership and sharing in advantages and love of the human race, which springs from our first begetting, since children are loved by their parents and the whole household is joined together by marriage and offspring. Then it gradually spreads outside the house, first to blood-relatives, then to relatives by marriage, then to friends, neighbours, fellow citizens, and the allies of the state, and eventually embraces the whole human race. This attitude of mind, which gives each his own and which generously and fairly protects that partnership of human unity, is called justice. To it are linked dutifulness, goodness, liberality, kindness, courtesy, and similar virtues.[14]

If we can take these passages as describing his own position, Cicero, in common with Peripatetics and Stoics, regards the pair as the original animal group, from which we derive all larger groups. The couple and children are the basic unit.[15] The keynote is *societas* and the common ownership of goods, the Greek *koinōnia*. From the love of children and wife, like a stone in a pond, come concentric rings of affection for others. The instinct to provide for the family is also

[14] From the speech of M. Piso, explaining the position of Antiochus, the contemporary head of the Academy.

[15] Cf. *Fin.* 4.17, *Tusc.* 5.5, *Off.* 1.12; *D* 1.1.1.3, Ulp.: 'Ius naturale est, quod natura omnia animalia docuit: nam ius istud non humani generis proprium, sed omnium animalium, quae in terra, quae in mari nascuntur, avium quoque commune est. Hinc descendit maris atque feminae coniunctio, quam nos matrimonium appellamus, hinc liberorum procreatio, hinc educatio: videmus etenim cetera quoque animalia, feras etiam istius iuris peritia censeri.'

natural.[16] The virtues required in family life are the same as those needed in friendships and in social life in general. Unfortunately, Cicero gives no extended discussion of the family, although in the *Laws* he legislated that the censors should register the children of citizens, prevent celibacy, and control morals.[17] He naturally held that the good conduct of homes was directly linked to discipline in public life. He mentions as properly Roman the idea that censors should teach men to control their wives (which avoided direct state intervention) and the social sanctions imposed on women by the ancient prohibition of wine and the custom that kinsmen stopped kissing women who lost their reputation.[18] If there was too much freedom in the state, licence would spread so that there would be no proper control (*dominatio*) in the household. This would cause a breakdown in relations between father and son. 'Even slaves will behave more freely, wives will have the same rights as husbands, amid such freedom dogs, horses, and donkeys will run around so freely that men have to yield the road to them.'[19]

In Cicero's philosophy, then, the ideas of the origin of the family, its economic purpose, the community of interest between husband and wife, and the subordination of women are in the mainstream of Greek orthodoxy. He is naturally inclined to exalt Roman practice and to appeal to Roman traditions. The idea of the division of functions between husband and wife does not seem to be specifically mentioned in the extant works, but Cicero was familiar with it, since in his youth he had translated the *Oeconomicus*. In fact his translation and Philodemus' critique suggest that the accessible and pragmatic Xenophon had maintained an important place in thinking on this subject in the Roman upper class of the first century. The topicality of consideration of proper conduct in family life is also illustrated by M. Brutus' book of advice to parents, children, and brothers, which unfortunately did not survive.[20]

The rule of husband over wife which Greek philosophers posited had been embodied (independently) in the original Roman marriage with *manus*. But, while Greek philosophical writers use words like *archein* and *kratein* without hesitation, Roman parallels such as *imperare* seem to be used with more nuances. Thus, although a late grammarian[21] can state bluntly that by right of marriage a bride is subjugated to the *imperium* of her husband, earlier Latin writers seem conscious that by their time such usage would be old-fashioned

[16] *ND* 2.157, *Off.* 1.12.   [17] *Legg.* 3.7.   [18] *Rep.* 4.6.
[19] *Rep.* 1.67. As Balch points out (p. 49), this is a paraphrase of Plato *Rep.* 562 c–563 E.
[20] Sen. *Epp.* 95.45; cf. Rawson, *ILRR* 286–7.
[21] Fest. 55L: 'nuptiali iure imperio viri subicitur nubens.'

and unrealistic. The husband of the *dotata uxor* may lament that he sold his control for a dowry. In parody, a bride may be told to hold sway over her husband.[22] Cicero, looking back to Appius Claudius Caecus in the late fourth century BC, will think him unusual in holding, not just *auctoritas*, but even *imperium* over his family of four grown sons, five daughters, slaves, and clients. Even for that period, he does not mention the wife. It seems a fair deduction that Cicero did not think contemporary husbands had the ability to order their wives—perhaps not even their children *in potestate*, though they had the legal right. He is not merely making the distinction Aristotle would make between despotic power and political or aristocratic power depending on consent.[23] There is a tendency to use the invidious *imperium* when the wife takes it over.[24] That is tyranny. A feeling that there were serious cracks in husbands' supremacy may lie behind the neat joke attributed to Cato (the only one dealing with women out of twenty-nine to which his name is attached by Plutarch in the *Apophthegms of kings and generals*) that 'All men rule their wives, we rule all men, our wives rule us.'[25]

Greek topoi on women's extravagance and on the domineering rich wife were naturalized with enthusiasm by the time of Plautus. It is hard to say that the Romans could not have invented these hackneyed themes for themselves. The *dotata uxor* required some adaptation from the Greek model, the *epiklēros*, who accompanied the family property. As Roman dowry and divorce evolved, the rich wife was in a position to exert pressure on her husband.

It is worth asking why some phenomena, equally probable in a social context, do not become topoi. The dowerless girl, though frequently a figure in comedy and occasionally mentioned in other literature, does not become a topos in the same way as the *dotata*, though her unprotected state gave her a certain dramatic pathos which might have attracted rhetoricians. The theme would not, however, have enabled them to expatiate on the wrongs of husbands. Similarly, tight-fisted husbands cut no figure beside extravagant wives or misers in general.

---

[22] Plaut. *As.* 87, *Cas.* 818–19; cf. Williams, 'Some aspects of Roman marriage ceremonies and ideals' 17.

[23] *Sen.* 37.

[24] Plaut. *Cas.* 409, *As. Arg.* 2; Cic. *Par.* 36; cf. VM 3.5.3; Tac. *A* 12.1.

[25] 198 D 3. 'Wife jokes', like mother-in-law jokes, are only funny if there is some degree of male insecurity. When a man lamented that his wife had hanged herself from a fig-tree, Cicero is supposed to have asked for a cutting (Quint. *Inst.* 6.3.88). For the topos of women enslaving men see Griffin, 'Propertius and Antony' 24 = *Latin poets and Roman life* 43 n. 79.

2. *Crisis, Reform, and Tradition: The Triumviral Period and the Early Principate*

The civil wars of the late Republic caused introspection and a fairly general belief that a decline in the standards of family life was one of the causes of fratricidal strife. Sallust saw an ill-defined link between sexual licence, extravagance, unscrupulous money-grabbing, and conspiracy. Horace measured the difference between the thrifty peasant mothers who kept their sons hard at work out of doors and the flighty young modern wives who cared more for dancing, lovers, and bribes than for bearing and rearing children. It was not surprising that their sons were degenerate. The blame was put particularly on the women.[26] Augustus' legislation followed.

Areius Didymus chose at about the time of the Julian Laws to restate Aristotle's position: 'A first community (*politeia*) is the coming together of a man and woman according to law for the procreation of children and community of life.'[27] The words seem to echo or prefigure the new legislation. Compare the formula in a contract of AD 100: '[——]s Nomissianus filiam suam virginem . . . secundum le[gem Iulia]m quae de maritandis ordinibus lat[a est liberorum procreando]rum causa in matrimonio(m) eam collo[cavit, uxorem eam duxit] M. Petronius Servillius . . .' ('[——] Nomissianus gave his virgin daughter in marriage in accordance with the Julian Law on the marriage of the orders for the sake of breeding children; M. Petronius Servillius married her . . .)'.[28] But the debate continued on philosophical lines with no obvious allusion to the changes produced by the Augustan reform.

Dionysius of Halicarnassus, also writing under Augustus, took the traditional view of the relationship of the household to the state. The conduct of families was important: the lawgiver should start by regulating marriages and sexual conduct. Some have suppressed some forms of misbehaviour, e.g. animal promiscuity, but have done nothing to safeguard marriages and ensure female chastity. Romulus was an effective lawgiver. He did not, like some Greeks, appoint a supervisor of women (Cicero's point) or pass specific laws allowing a husband to sue for adultery or desertion or a wife for ill-usage or desertion or in order to recover her dowry. Instead he secured the good behaviour of wives by making confarreate marriage indissoluble (and Dionysius points out that this remains in force, ignoring its rarity in his time) and giving her shared rights within it. She was to be a

---

[26] Sall. *BC* 10–13, 25; Hor. *O* 3.6, 24.
[27] Stob. 2.7.26. For Areius see Bowersock, *AGW* 33–4, 39–41; Balch 40 ff.
[28] *FIRA* iii.17.

partner in all her husband's property and religious rights. 'This law compelled married women, since they had no other recourse, to live according to the wishes of the husband and it compelled the husbands to control their wives, since they were a necessary and inalienable possession.' If the wife was virtuous and obedient, she was as much mistress of the house as he was master and when he died she had the same rights of succession as his children. Some offences on her part were judged by the husband, but serious ones like adultery or drinking wine (which the Greeks thought trivial) by a council of the husband and her kinsmen. Punishments were severe down to the time of the divorce of Carvilius Ruga in 231. These laws, he concludes, secured the good conduct of women.[29] Dionysius is conscious that he is describing a situation which, apart from the survival of *confarreatio*, no longer exists. Divorce has removed the need for family punishment of offending wives; the wife can divorce a cruel or absconding husband and can reclaim her dowry. It is, however, worth noting that he picks out the indissolubility of Roman marriage as a praiseworthy characteristic and that he agrees with the philosophers and Cicero in idealizing community of property and the consequent absorption of the wife into her new family. He published his work at a time when the new Romulus had imposed state controls on marriage, attempting both to regulate and encourage marriage and to check adultery. Romulus, theoretically, was starting from nothing and could create institutions good in themselves. Augustus, finding a corrupt system, in which, for instance, indissolubility of marriage and community of property had ceased to be the norm, could only tinker with it and hedge the family about with regulations and penalties.

Dionysius' contemporary Livy deliberately set out to portray the good old traditional morality of Rome. His early books are full of memorable virtuous wives and daughters, with a few undutiful ones. He presumably means to include domestic virtue among those he regards as in decline in his own time, when Romans could no longer tolerate either their vices or the cure for them.[30] But the set piece on the repeal of the Oppian Law in 195 BC which opens book 34 suggests that, although Livy gives a rattling good speech to the die-hard Cato, who wanted to keep the emergency wartime ban on women owning more than half an ounce of gold, or wearing coloured clothes or riding in a wheeled vehicle within a mile of the city, his own sympathies were

[29] *Ant.* 2.24–26.1, which began to be published in 7 BC. Cf. Balsdon, 'Dionysius on Romulus: a political pamphlet?' Among earlier scholars who argued that Dionysius followed a political pamphlet, Gabba, 'Studi su Dionigi di Alicarnasso I: la costituzione di Romolo', suggests that the hypothetical source was Roman and incorporated a list of laws of Romulus in the style of Bruns or Riccobono (199). His remarks on how Dionysius will have pondered and remodelled his ideas are perceptive.   [30] *Pref.* 9.

with Valerius, the reforming tribune.[31] Cato is shocked because the women are out on the streets, protesting, and cannot be kept indoors by order of their husbands. He appeals to senators to keep their women under better control and suppress an incipient revolt. Modesty ought to keep women at home, within the boundaries of their own sphere.[32] Women have traditionally been made subject to their husbands, in the hope of containing their licence, but there is a constant danger that they will break out. If they are allowed equality with men, they will immediately be superior.[33] Imperialism brings new risks of luxury, expenditure, and avarice. Repeal of the law will lead to bitter competition between rich and poor, and husbands will not be able to escape from nagging.[34] Valerius proves out of Cato's own *Origines* that it was not unprecedented for women to take part in public events. He shows that the law was an emergency measure and argues that it is unfair that Roman women should be the only ones not to enjoy the pleasures of the peace, that men and horses should wear purple, and that women from Latin cities should flaunt luxuries which are denied to the women of Rome. Women enjoy none of the insignia and distinctions which men can win—magistracies, priesthoods, triumphs, military decorations, and booty: their only joy and glory is in dress and ornaments, which are called the *mundus muliebris*.[35] Women are always under the control of men, except when they are unlucky enough to see their loved ones die. It is the duty of men to make their dominion tolerable.[36] The law was unanimously repealed by all the tribes.

If Valerius represents Livy's view of what enlightened Roman husbands believed in the early second century, that view cannot be seen as liberal towards women by the standards or practice of the late Republic. But it may well be what Livy himself would have approved for his own day. Valerius' optimistic picture of the wise and gentle control of wives by their husbands is reminiscent of the recipe which Augustus, according to Cassius Dio, gave the senators in 18 BC

---

[31] Is this debate coloured by Hortensia's protest about the taxation of rich women in 42 BC? (VM 8.3.3; App. *BC* 4.32–4; Quint. *Inst.* 1.1.6.)

[32] 34.2.10: 'si sui iuris finibus matronas contineret pudor.'

[33] 34.4.3ff.   [34] 34.2–4.

[35] 34.7.9. For this topos cf. Sen. *Matr.* ap. Jer. *adv. Iovin.* 320 A–B. Valerius Maximus gives a more hostile version: 'quas [sc. feminas] et inbecillitas mentis et graviorum operum negata adfectatio omne studium ad curiosiorem sui cultum hortatur conferre' ('women whom the weakness of their mind and the fact that the undertaking of more serious business is denied to them urge to bestow all their interest on a more elaborate adornment of themselves)'. But this is only part of the growth of luxury, to which men have been as prone (9.1.3). For women's exclusion from public life see Sen. *Cons. ad Helv.* 14.2 (mothers, themselves excluded from office, push their sons in public life); App. *BC* 4.32–3. Cf. n. 69.

[36] 34.5–7.

—although they did not believe him when he claimed that he gave
advice and orders to Livia on such subjects as dress, jewellery,
propriety, and deportment in public.[37]

Heightened interest in wifely morality and in the re-creation of the
old Roman virtues is also indicated by the collection of *Apophtheg-
mata matronarum* by Maecenas' freedman Melissus, who was employed by Augustus to organize the library in the Portico of Octavia.
In his 150-volume collection of wise and witty sayings, Melissus
included not only the virtuous remarks of matrons but also the salty
jokes of Augustus' daughter Julia. It has reasonably been argued that
the latter (which reach us through Macrobius, who perhaps knew
them through a third-century epitome) could not have been circulated by Melissus during the lifetime of Augustus.[38] But it is also hard
to think that it would have been diplomatic to publish them immediately after his death, when Julia's ex-husband was *princeps*. Nor
would they fit particularly happily into the period of disgrace of Julia's
daughter Agrippina in the late 20s AD. So the date of publication must
be left obscure. The apophthegms of *univirae*, which were used by
Seneca and are preserved by Jerome, fit in nicely with Augustus'
moral revival and badly with his encouragement of remarriage.
Melissus' older contemporary, the Palatine librarian C. Julius
Hyginus, also compiled moral exempla of virtuous wives, which were
mined by Seneca and Valerius Maximus.[39]

The views of Philo, the Alexandrian Jew, are of intrinsic interest,
but cannot be shown to have directly influenced Roman thinking. He
deduces detailed rulings from the Sixth Commandment, against
adultery, which, he points out, was placed at the head of the second
tablet of Jewish Law because pleasure is such a strong motive. His
text stresses Jewish penalties and ideas, but much of it also reflects
Greek philosophical doctrine and is aimed at a wide audience. A
relatively long attack on unions forbidden to Jews as incestuous (not
only mothers but also stepmothers, not only full sisters but also
stepsisters and wife's sister, or foreigners) must be to the address of
Alexandrian Greeks.[40] It is more interesting that he approves of
intermarriage with non-kin because it strengthens fellow feeling
outside kin-groups.[41] He preaches against sexual relations with one's
own wife for the sake of pleasure, not procreation.[42] For this reason
intercourse with menstruating women is forbidden, because they are
infertile, and a man is not to marry a woman known to be barren since
incontinence is the only possible motive for such a match, although he

---

[37] 54.16.4–5.   [38] Bickel ed. Jer. *adv. Iovin.* 309 ff.   [39] Ibid. 329 ff.
[40] *Special laws* 3.13–29.
[41] Ibid. 25; cf. Plut. *QR* 108, Aug. *Civ. dei* 15.16.   [42] 9.

may keep a virgin bride who turns out to be barren, since living together creates affection.[43] Pederasty, effeminacy, bestiality, prostitution, adultery (on the ground that it destroys a man's hope of children and brings falsity into his family), rape, seduction of virgins or engaged women or widows are all prohibited.[44]

When he presents rules of female conduct, Philo's dependence on previous Greek teaching is clear. Men govern states and women households.[45] The market, council-chamber, lawcourt, and open-air life in general are for men; for women there is only the life of the house and indoors.[46] A woman must not be a busybody or wander around in sight of strange men; if she has to go out to perform religious duties, she should go when the agora is not full.[47] In a passage which departs from the usual Greek themes, he argues that a good woman does not get involved in verbal or physical quarrels, she should not unsex herself by hearing, let alone uttering, abuse, and she should not get into fights, even to protect her husband. If she does, she must especially avoid grabbing his opponent's genitals. For similar reasons, she is barred from watching men compete naked in the gymnasium.[48] Finally, he states that in each human soul there are two elements, a male element which clings to God and a female element which clings to the created world. This concept, in a twisted form, was to pass into Christian doctrine. 'He for God only, she for God in him.'

3. Seneca and after

Seneca gave little attention to women in his philosophical works apart from his treatise *On marriage*. A philosopher should marry, not because he needs a wife or children (for he is self-sufficient) but because it is a natural instinct.[49] He stated vigorously the Stoic view that women are the moral equals of men: nature did not create them any less adequate to choose honourable courses, and they can, with practice, tolerate pain and effort as well as men.[50] The roles of husband and wife were equal, a point about which he is vague.[51] He combats the view that a son, wife, or relative cannot confer benefits but only perform duties, and a slave only services. Since he argues that a slave can confer benefits, it follows that Seneca must have believed that a wife could do the same.[52] A husband should take

---

[43] 33 ff.   [44] 37 ff.; cf. 12 and, later, Clem. Alex. *Paed.* 2.83 ff.
[45] 170.   [46] 169.
[47] 171, the opposite in Phintys (Thesleff, *Texts* 153–4).   [48] 172 ff.
[49] *Epp.* 9.17–18. *Libido* is given for procreation, not pleasure (*Cons. ad Helv.* 13.3).
[50] *Ad Marciam* 16.1.
[51] *Ben.* 2.18: 'sunt aliquae partes mariti, sed non minores uxoris', in the context of how to receive favours.   [52] *Ben.* 3.18.1.

Odysseus as his model and a wife Penelope (supposing that she was as chaste as Homer thought and did not merely fool people).⁵³ It was wicked for a husband to demand chastity from his wife and keep a mistress: having a mistress was a serious injury to a wife.⁵⁴ His own wife Paullina appears in the *Moral epistles* to warn him to take better care of his health. This wifely concern proves to him that their breath is intermingled.⁵⁵

Seneca's purpose in *On marriage* was to recommend the institution and a type of marital conduct which pleased him. Fragments of this survive in a work by Jerome in which he attacks marriage. Most of the more pointed remarks which can convincingly be identified as Senecan tend to the extreme position Jerome espoused. Thus, Jerome quotes some Senecan anecdotes about a man who went too far in love of his own wife, drinking from the same cup and even wearing her breast-band. 'A wise man ought to love his wife with judgment, not passion (*affectu*). He controls the impulses of pleasure and does not rush headlong into intercourse; nothing is more shameful than to love your wife as if she was your mistress.'⁵⁶ It was also shameful to marry a woman who had previously been your mistress—and unsatisfactory, 'since fear which panders to lust goes away, what is permitted becomes cheap'.⁵⁷

Jerome starts from the position that virginity is superior to wifely chastity and from the startling claim that Greek, Latin, and barbarian history agreed.⁵⁸ After virgins, his second class of admirable pagan women who might serve as models for the decadent Christians of his own day is formed of a first division of *univirae* who committed suicide rather than accept the embraces of other men, whether as husbands or not, and a second division of *univirae* who lived as chaste widows. The women who are named in Frassinetti's reconstruction of the fragments which he judges securely Senecan are Lucretia, Bilia, Claudia, 'Marcia, Cato's younger daughter',⁵⁹ Annia, the younger Porcia, Marcella the Elder, Valeria and Artemisia, Hindu suttees, Alcibiades' mistress, who risked death in order to bury him, Alcestis and Laodamia, Penelope (by extension).⁶⁰ But the argument of

⁵³ *Epp.* 88.7–8. For Penelope as model cf. [Arist.] *Oec.* 3 p. 142; Prop. 3.12.22; Jer. *adv. Iovin.* 1.45 = 312A.
⁵⁴ *Ira* 2.28.7, *Epp.* 94.26, 95.37, cf. *Ben.* 1.9.3.
⁵⁵ *Epp.* 104.1–2: 'spiritum illius in meo verti.'
⁵⁶ *Adv. Iovin.* 1.49 = 318D, 319A.
⁵⁷ Ibid. 1.49 = 319B; cf. *Ben.* 1.9.4; Dio 54.16.6.
⁵⁸ Ibid. 1.41 = 306B–C.
⁵⁹ There is a confusion in the name and identification: Cato's daughter was Porcia, his wife Marcia.
⁶⁰ Of these, Lucretia, suttees, Alcibiades' mistress, Alcestis, and Laodamia are at the top half of the second class.

Seneca was probably rather different from the exaltation of virginity or physical fidelity intended by Jerome, in short, his emphasis on sexuality. Seneca's emphasis seems rather to have been on loyalty to the husband. The fragment which especially suggests this is a corrupt text:

Brutus Porciam virginem duxit uxorem, Marciam Cato non virginem; sed Marcia inter Hortensium Catonemque discurrit et sine Catone vivere potuit, Porcia sine Bruto non potuit. (*Adversus Iovinianum* 1.46 = 312 D–E)

Brutus married Porcia as a virgin, Cato married Marcia, who was not a virgin. But Marcia ran around between Hortensius and Cato and was able to live without Cato, Porcia could not live without Brutus.

Jerome is presumably making the point that virgin brides become more devoted wives. There are two indications that he has altered Seneca's text and his argument. The more striking one is that as it stands the text is historically incorrect. Porcia was the widow of Bibulus when she married her cousin Brutus. Marcia (as far as we know) had no husband before Cato,[61] although after she had given him children he arranged for her to marry his friend Hortensius. Later, after Hortensius died, they remarried. The traditional account does not make Marcia responsible for these transfers. Since Cato's eccentric marital behaviour was well known, and defended by Stoics (it was dramatically narrated by Seneca's nephew Lucan), all this, and the allegedly heroic suicide of Porcia, must have been familiar to Seneca. It is generally recognized that the 'non' should be transposed to describe Porcia:[62]

Brutus Porciam non virginem duxit uxorem, Marciam Cato virginem; sed Marcia inter Hortensium Catonemque discurrit et sine Catone vivere potuit, Porcia sine Bruto non potuit.

Brutus married Porcia not as a virgin, Cato married Marcia, who was a virgin. But Marcia ran back and forth between Hortensius and Cato and was able to live without Cato, Porcia could not live without Brutus.

The second oddity about Jerome's transmitted text now disappears. The 'sed' now makes sense, because the second half of the fragment expresses the surprising fact that the result was the opposite of what general beliefs might have suggested. Jerome's fixation with virginity naturally led him to suppose that the noble Porcia was virgin at the time of her marriage to Brutus. Seneca's point was more subtle. In the

---

[61] *RE* xiv.1602 no. 115.

[62] Bickel ed. *adv. Iovin.* 297–8. Cf. Plut. *Cato* 25.1 ff. That the morality of Cato's handing over of his wife to Hortensius was a debating-topic in the rhetorical schools is shown by Quint. *Inst.* 3.5.11, 10.5.13. Tertullian attacked Cato (*Apol.* 39.12). Plutarch emphasizes that Porcia was not a virgin (*Brut.* 13.3).

other examples he cites, he is interested in women who have loved one husband and out of loyalty to him refuse to marry again. The text does not emphasize their status as *univirae* except for 'the Younger Porcia'. There is a concentration on quotable remarks, for instance, the Elder Marcella's reply to her mother's question whether she was glad she had married: 'So much so that I would not do it again.' Since Marcella married twice, this is piquant.[63] The point Seneca seems to be making about Marcia and Porcia is that, contrary to the usual assumption,[64] virgin brides do not necessarily become more closely tied to their husbands than widows. But something else may be wrong with the text. The contemptuous tone of 'discurrit', so unfairly applied to Marcia, is very like that which Jerome uses for Christian women who married again and perhaps for Terentia.[65]

The text of *On marriage*, as reconstructed and ordered by Frassinetti, makes Seneca pass from remarks on the ideas of Epicurus and Chrysippus on whether the sage should marry to criticism of wrong reasons for marrying (women who in order to benefit from the Augustan laws 'buy poor husbands and control them', adulterers who marry each other for transient lust). Presumably the original work argued also that philosophers should marry and that there were sound reasons for marrying. Seneca goes on to the example of the Younger Porcia (Marcia in Jerome), who attacked mercenary motives. A wife should be chosen for *pudicitia* (chastity). Perhaps at this point Seneca launched into the series of examples of women who showed this virtue. These are Lucretia; the wife of Duillius, who had bad breath: she proved her chastity by remarking that she had assumed that all men suffered from it; the Claudia who towed Cybele's ship off a mud-bank. Then there may have been an easy transition to wifely fidelity, illustrated by further examples from Greek and Roman history and by witty remarks of married women, probably drawn chiefly from Hyginus and Melissus. There was a section attacking sensuality and excessive love in marriage and two examples of husbandly tolerance of wifely bad temper, which Jerome deploys in a list of bad wives.[66] These themes may have formed part of a more comprehensive treatment of reciprocal duties.

Frassinetti convincingly reserves for the peroration a eulogy of female chastity, which he considers very fine.[67]

---

[63] *Adv. Iovin.* 1.46 = 313A. Bickel (ed. 290) thinks she is unidentified, but it is hard to imagine how Seneca or his source, probably Maecenas Melissus, could mean anyone other than the eldest daughter of Octavia.

[64] For which see VM 2.1.3, quoted below in sect. 3, and Stat. S 5.1.45 ff.

[65] *Adv. Iovin.* 1.48 = 316A, which Bickel but not Frassinetti regards as Senecan. I think 'Illa . . . est' was rehandled by Jerome.   [66] 1.48 = 316A–E.   [67] p. 186: 'bellissima.'

Pudicitia inprimis est retinenda, qua amissa omnis virtus ruit. In hac muliebrium virtutum principatus est. Haec pauperem commendat, divitem extollit, deformem redimit, exornat pulchram; bene meretur de maioribus, quorum sanguinem furtiva subole non vitiat; bene de liberis, quibus nec de matre erubescendum nec de patre dubitandum est; bene inprimis de se, quam a contumelia externi corporis vindicat.[68] Captivitatis nulla maior calamitas est quam aliena libidine trahi. Viros consulatus inlustrat, eloquentia in nomen aeternum effert, militaris gloria triumphusque novae gentis consecrat; multa sunt quae per se clara ingenia nobilitent; mulieris propria virtus pudicitia est. Haec Lucretiam Bruto aequavit, nescias an et praetulerit, quoniam Brutus non posse servire a femina didicit. Haec aequavit Corneliam Gracco, haec Porciam alteri Bruto. Notior est marito suo Tanaquil: illum inter multa regum nomina iam abscondit antiquitas, hanc rara inter feminas virtus altius saeculorum omnium memoriae, quam ut excidere possit, infixit. (Jerome *adversus Iovinianum* 1.49 = 319C–320)

First of all, *pudicitia* must be kept, for when that is lost all virtue collapses. This is the chief virtue of women. This recommends a poor woman, extols a rich one, redeems an ugly one, adorns a lovely one; [a chaste woman] deserves well of her ancestors, since she does not pollute their blood with illegitimate offspring; she deserves well of her children, who have no need to blush for their mother or doubt their father, and well especially of herself, because she defends herself from the insult of another man's body. The worst disaster in being a prisoner of war is to be prey to a stranger's lust. Men are made illustrious by consulships, eloquence raises them to immortal fame, military glory and the triumph of a new family [or 'over a new tribe'] hallow them; there are many things which in themselves ennoble glorious abilities. The peculiar virtue of women is *pudicitia*. This made Lucretia the equal of Brutus or perhaps put her above him, since it was from a woman that Brutus learnt to be incapable of being a slave. This made Cornelia the equal of Gracchus, and Porcia of the second Brutus. Tanaquil is more famous than her husband: he, among the many names of kings, has been hidden by antiquity, she, by her rare virtue among women, has been enshrined so deep in the memory of all the ages that she cannot be shaken loose.[69]

Here again the sense of *pudicitia* is wider than mere sexual fidelity. Tanaquil was more noted for her devotion to her husband's interests than for her chastity.[70] It seems likely that Seneca explored other aspects of wifely duty, as Phintys did in her exploration of *sōphrosynē*.[71] Seneca lacks Jerome's fixation on sex. One of his *Moral*

---

[68] Cf. Tac. *A.* 4.3.4: 'seque ac maiores et posteros municipali adultero foedabat.'

[69] For the idea of feminine triumphs see Prop. 4.11.71–2. For Lucretia cf. Sen. *Cons. ad Marciam* 16.2: 'Bruto libertatem debemus, Lucretiae Brutum' ('We owe our liberty to Brutus but our Brutus to Lucretia'). For competition in *pudicitia* compared with men's in courage, see Livy 10.23.8.   [70] Cf. Bickel ed. *adv. Iovin.* 365–6.

[71] For Tanaquil as a paradigmatic good wife, cf. Juv. 6.566 and Courtney ad loc., citing Auson. *Parentalia* 30.5. She recurs in Allestree, *The ladies calling*, preface, along with Theano, Aspasia, Diotime, Cornelia, and Livia, in the context of the need to educate women.

epistles shows that he had thought a little about how a husband's treatment of his wife ought to be adapted to her individual situation, not in order to suit her personality but in order to make the marriage work. Ideally, the philosopher would vary his advice to a husband married to a virgin bride, a woman previously married, a rich one, a dowerless one, barren or fertile, old or young, a mother or a stepmother.[72]

The rhetoric of the praise of *pudicitia* and the promise to women of glory and moral equality with men must not blind us to the narrowness of the sphere to which Seneca confined women—virtuous conduct towards husband and children and probably the wise governance of the household. Cornelia, Porcia, and Tanaquil are not exalted for acting as politicians independently of their husbands or sons. And in his writings Seneca shows that although he might think highly of exemplary women and of some of his own kinswomen, he is as prone as, for instance, Tacitus to regard vice and weakness as typical of the whole sex.[73]

Columella in his handbook on farming looks back nostalgically to Xenophon's views of family life. Marriage, according to Xenophon, was a delightful and useful partnership in life (*vitae societas*), created, as Cicero said (sc. in his *Oeconomicus*), so that the human race should not die out and so that parents should have defences in their old age (*propugnacula*). He repeats the doctrine of division of labour and Xenophon's reasons for it and claims that until recently this system was followed in Rome. 'The work of the household was carried out by the *matrona*. For there was the highest reverence, mixed with harmony (*concordia*) and diligence.' Wives were keen to increase their husband's prosperity, there was no division of property and no delegation to stewards. But in Columella's own time wives shirk spinning and have handed over their duties to the steward's wife.[74]

C. Musonius Rufus, a Roman *eques* from Volsinii (*c.*AD 30–100), who was admired by many cultivated members of the upper class, was a Roman steeped in Stoic theory but also a staunch representative of Roman values, or a rather more 'liberal' type than Seneca. In his surviving diatribes he treats women and marriage seriously. He naturally held that marriage was in accordance with nature, since male and female had a strong yearning for each other. Marriage allowed life in common and legitimate children, which ensured the survival of the city and of humanity. It was no handicap for the philosopher, but a patriotic duty which applied to him as much as

---

[72] *Epp.* 94.15.
[73] See Manning, 'Seneca and the Stoics on the equality of the sexes'. A survey of Tacitus' use of the word *muliebris* indicates his preconceptions.   [74] *RR* 12 pr.

anyone.[75] The woman too should be a philosopher, for she ought to be good.

In the first place a woman must be a good housekeeper; that is, a careful accountant of all that pertains to the welfare of the house and capable of directing the household slaves . . . But above all a woman must be chaste and self-controlled; she must, I mean, be pure in respect of unlawful love, exercise restraint in other pleasures, not be a slave to desire, not be contentious, not lavish in expense nor extravagant in dress. Such are the works of a virtuous woman, and to them I would add these: to control her temper, not to be overcome by grief, and to be superior to uncontrolled emotion of every kind . . . As for justice, would not the woman who studies philosophy be just, would she not be a blameless life-partner, would she not be a sympathetic helpmate, would she not be an untiring defender of her children, and would she not be entirely free of greed and arrogance? (3: 'That women too should study philosophy' = Lutz pp. 38–43)

He goes on to say that this paragon will also be brave and will put her philosophy to practical application, suckling her children and work-ing alongside her slaves. There is nothing original here, but Musonius expresses it with unusual force. He explains the division of labour and spheres in the conventional way. Women will not usually do gym-nastics nor men spin, but there may be some exceptions.[76] A daughter should receive the same education as boys, because the virtues, including *sōphrosynē*, are the same for both sexes. 'Again, it is recognized as right for a woman in wedlock to be chaste, and so is it likewise for a man. The law, at all events, decrees the same punish-ment for committing adultery as for being taken in adultery.'[77] The note on penalties is inaccurate for the Julian Law since the fines were different, but both sexes might suffer exile. Musonius is clearly thinking of his own time.

Musonius came out unusually strongly against the double standard:

Men who are not wanton or immoral are bound to consider sexual inter-course justified only when it occurs in marriage and is indulged in for the purpose of begetting children (ἐπὶ γενέσει παίδων), since that is lawful, but unjust and unlawful when it is mere pleasure-seeking, even in marriage. But of all sexual relations those involving adultery are most unlawful, and no more tolerable are those of men with men, because it is a monstrous thing and contrary to nature. But, furthermore, leaving out of consideration adultery, all intercourse with women which is without lawful character is shameful and is practised from lack of self-restraint. So no one with any self-control would think of having relations with a courtesan or a free woman apart from marriage, no, nor even with his own maid-servant. The fact that

---

[75] 14: 'Is marriage a handicap to the pursuit of philosophy?', trans. Lutz, 'Musonius Rufus' 90–7.   [76] 4 = Lutz p. 47.   [77] 4 = Lutz p. 45.

those relationships are not lawful or seemly makes them a disgrace and a reproach to those seeking them; whence it is that no one dares to do any of these things openly, not even if he has all but lost the ability to blush, and those who are not completely degenerate dare to do these things only in hiding and in secret. And yet to attempt to cover up what one is doing is equivalent to a confession of guilt. 'That's all very well,' you say, 'but unlike the adulterer who wrongs the husband of the woman whom he corrupts, the man who has relations with a courtesan or a woman who has no husband wrongs no one for he does not destroy anyone's hope of children.' I continue to maintain that everyone who sins and does wrong, even if it affects none of the people about him, yet immediately reveals himself as a worse and a less honourable person, for the wrong-doer by the very fact of doing wrong is worse and less honorable. Not to mention the injustice of the thing, there must be sheer wantonness in anyone yielding to the temptation of shameful pleasure and like swine rejoicing in his own vileness. In this category belongs the man who has relations with his own slave-maid, a thing which some people consider quite without blame, since every master is held to have it in his power to use his slave as he wishes. In reply to this I have just one thing to say: if it seems neither shameful nor out of place for a master to have relations with his own slave, particularly if she happens to be unmarried, let him consider how he would like it if his wife had relations with a male slave. Would it not seem completely intolerable not only if the woman who had a lawful husband had relations with a slave, but even if a woman without a husband should have? And yet surely one will not expect men to be less moral than women, nor less capable of disciplining their desires, thereby revealing the stronger in judgment inferior to the weaker, the rulers to the ruled. In fact, it behooves men to be much better if they expect to be superior to women, for surely if they appear to be less self-controlled they will also be baser characters. What need is there to say that it is an act of licentiousness and nothing else for a master to have relations with a slave? Everyone knows that. (12: 'On sexual indulgence' = Lutz pp. 84–9 at 87–9)

Musonius also emphasizes more strongly than any of the writers we have met so far the affective content of marriage. He argues that children may be produced in any sexual union, so the aim of replacing the population could be achieved without marriage. (He ignores, justifiably in this theoretical context, man-made requirements of legitimacy.) So marriage must be something more than a tool of reproduction. Now we have a full philosophic statement of the sharing of love as a motive for marriage. This had certainly been present in Roman idealization of marriage, on tombstones for example, as we shall see later, but the philosophers had neglected the topic.

But in marriage there must above all be perfect companionship (*symbiōsis*) and mutal love (*kēdemonia*) of husband and wife, both in health and sickness and under all conditions, since it was with desire for this as well as for having children that both entered upon marriage. Where, then, this love for each other is perfect and the two share it completely, each striving to outdo the other in devotion,[78] the marriage is ideal and worthy of envy, for such a union is beautiful. But where each looks only to his own interests and neglects the other, or, what is worse, when one is so minded and lives in the same house but fixes his attention elsewhere and is not willing to pull together with his yoke-mate nor to agree, then the union is doomed to disaster and though they live together, yet their common interests fare badly; eventually they separate entirely, or they remain together and suffer what is worse than loneliness. (13A: 'What is the chief end of marriage?' = Lutz pp. 88–9)

Dio Chrysostom (c.AD 40–after 112), a pupil of Musonius, wrote an *Oeconomicus* of which the six surviving fragments concentrate on slaves and children. He produced the remark that piety in a woman is physical love for her husband.[79] He identified *homonoia* (concord) with the good marriage, a conventional view.[80]

Epictetus, (c.AD 55–c.135), another pupil of Musonius, has little to say specifically on marriage, though he inveighs against adultery as a contradiction of nature, since human beings are born to fidelity.[81] He argued, against Epicureans and Cynics, that marriage and child-rearing were duties.[82]

The anti-marriage tradition comes to full flower in Juvenal's notorious sixth satire, which exploits the whole range of philosophical and popular topoi against women and marriage. Primitive matrimonial virtues are long gone. It is ridiculous for Juvenal's friend Postumus, an established rake, to think of taking a wife for the sake of an heir, when his sexual urges would be better satisfied by adultery or homosexuality, and to hope to find a virtuous wife, when chaste girls and faithful wives no longer exist. Much space is devoted to women's lustfulness, unattractiveness, greed, cruelty, fickleness, deceit, quarrelsomeness, the dominance of rich wives, the disagreeableness of the paragon and the bluestocking, the disgust aroused by the female athlete, the hard drinker, and the gossip, the shocking conduct of society women at religious rites or with their various hangers-on, the impudence of the adulteress, upper-class wives' reluctance to bear children (they resort to abortions) or the likelihood that they will palm off bastards on the husband, their eagerness to murder stepchild or husband. Martial also trounces wives—women who marry their previous lovers or have affairs with slaves or practise serial marriage

[78] Lutz compares Tac. *Ag.* 6 and Rom. 12.10.
[79] Loeb v. 348 ff., frr. 1–6, esp. 3 = Stob. 3.42.12, 4.19.46, 4.23.60, 4.28.12, 4.28.13, and esp. 4.23.59.
[80] 38.15.   [81] 2.4; cf. 3.7.16, 21.
[82] 3.7.16 ff., 3.22.67 ff.

or domineer over their husbands.[83] But he is severe on men for similar reasons.[84] He is, however, chiefly interested in jokes, not moralizing.

4. Plutarch and Others

The pro-marriage tradition culminates in Plutarch (slightly older than Juvenal, slightly younger than Martial). Plutarch's *Advice to bride and groom* on how to be amiable partners is overtly Greek, but Roman readers would have had no difficulty in adopting his general ideas. The young couple are not to be put off by early difficulties in bed or by early quarrels, nor rely on initial sexual passion lasting.[85] Husbands must not try to humiliate rich or noble wives, but respect their status.[86] Wives must stay at home.[87] When a good woman undresses, she puts on modesty (*aidōs*). Both must show their love through respect for each other, *aidōs*.[88] The concord of the house is based on the husband's leadership and choices.[89] Women can be kept sweet if their husbands persuade them to give up luxury and extravagance instead of trying to compel them.[90] Neither caresses nor quarrels should be indulged in in the presence of others.[91] A wife must make herself agreeable to her husband's every mood, 'and the wife ought to have no feeling of her own, but she should join with her husband in seriousness and sportiveness and in soberness and laughter'.[92] But the husband is also to adjust to his wife and share her amusements.[93] This should not extend to inviting wives to be present at licentious parties. It shows respect for his wife if a man shares his drunkenness, debauchery, and lust with a courtesan or a maidservant rather than with her.[94] A man should not be too fond of his appearance and so make his wife dress like a whore, but should show her a good example in discretion and orderliness.[95] A wife should welcome her husband's advances but not take the initiative (again, like a hetaera).[96] She is to have his friends and follow his gods, not her own.[97] The pair should share their good and bad fortune, their children, and their property, and put their resources together: 'as we call a mixture "wine", although the larger of the component parts is water, so the property and the estate ought to be said to belong to the

[83] 1.74, 6.22, 6.39, 9.15, 8.12, 10.69. Highet, *Juvenal the satirist* 264–5, and Courtney ad loc. set Juvenal in context.
[84] For dowry-hunting: 2.65; for adultery with a former wife: 3.70; for marrying only in order to escape the penalties of the Julian Law: 5.75; etc.
[85] 2–4 = 138D–F.   [86] 8 = 139B.   [87] 9 = 139C.
[88] 10 = 139C.   [89] 11 = 139D.   [90] 12 = 139D–E.
[91] 13 = 139E–F.   [92] Loeb trans. 14 = 139F–140A.
[93] 15 = 140A.   [94] 16 = 140B.
[95] 17 = 140C. Cf. *Quaest. conv.* 6.7.2 = 693B, ruling out make-up but recommending cleanliness.   [96] 18 = 140C–D.   [97] 19 = 140D.

husband, even though the wife contribute the larger share'.[98] It is not beauty, birth, wealth, or even discretion (*sōphrosynē*) that makes a wife agreeable but 'conversation, character, and comradeship'.[99] There should be no bitterness or gloominess in a wife's manner to her husband, though a husband may have to tolerate an austere and ungracious wife if she finds other manners incompatible with her high moral standards.[100] Good women keep at home as much as possible, talking to and through their husbands.[101] Women must subordinate themselves to their husband, to avoid looking ridiculous; the husband must control his wife 'as the soul controls the body, by entering into her feelings and being knit to her though goodwill. As, therefore, it is possible to exercise care over the body without being a slave to its pleasures and desires, so it is possible to govern a wife, and at the same time to delight and gratify her.'[102]

A marriage of a couple who love each other is like a mixture of liquids: they amalgamate their bodies, property, friends, and relations. Plutarch approves of the Roman law against gifts between husband and wife because it shows that they really share everything. The marriage of 'those who marry for dowry or children is of persons joined together; and that of those who merely sleep in the same bed is of separate persons who may be regarded as cohabiting, but not really living together'.[103]

A wife can expect hostility from her mother-in-law but can win her over by making her husband love her and by not turning him from his mother.[104] Mothers are especially attached to sons and fathers to daughters. It is civil for the wife to show especial deference and trust to her husband's parents.[105] Women should keep quiet when their husbands are angry but comfort them when they are silent.[106] Sex is a good cure for quarrels,[107] but they should avoid quarrels in bed, which are hard to make up elsewhere.[108] The wife must avoid confidantes who stir her up against her husband and should not divorce him for infidelity (which is playing into his mistress's hands).[109] But both should keep clear of unholy intercourse with others from whom they do not want children.[110] A man should not be like Gorgias, who preached harmony to the Greeks, but failed to have concord in his own household of three because his wife was jealous of his affair with the maid. Women's adulteries are more easily concealed than men's

---

[98] Loeb trans. 20 = 140 F.
[99] Loeb trans. 22–26 = 141 A–F.   [100] 28–9 = 141 F–142 C.
[101] 30–2 = 142 C–D.   [102] Loeb trans. 33 = 142 E.
[103] Loeb trans. 34 = 142 F–143 A.
[104] 35 = 143 A–B. Plutarch here cites a folk-custom of Lepcis Magna.
[105] 36 = 143 B–C.   [106] 37 = 143 C.   [107] 38 = 143 D.
[108] 39 = 143 E.   [109] 41 = 144 A.   [110] 42 = 144 B.

offences against their wives—a remarkable statement.[111] Men should
not give pain to their wives by having sexual relations with other
women, a trivial pleasure.[112] Similarly, wives must not do anything to
irritate their husbands.[113] In bed the wife must be unlike all other
women to her husband, because of her chastity and exclusive affection for him.[114] The husband is to show her respect and not teach
her wantonness by his behaviour.[115] The bride, Eurydice, is to eschew
extravagant dress, but the husband is not to indulge in gold cups,
wall-paintings, mule-trappings, or horses' neck-bands, a refreshing
variant on the usual theme of wives' *sumptus*.[116] He must study
philosophy and discuss it with her, so that she can scorn magic and
laugh at superstition.[117] She is to follow godly matrons like Theano,
Claudia, and Cornelia and various Greek ladies, and so find
happiness.[118]

This hotchpotch of Greek and Roman, because of its accessibility
has had a lasting influence. Although as usual the wife's duties are
more clearly explained than the husband's, Plutarch's basic humanity
gleams through his commandments.

In his dialogue on whether the preference should be given to
homosexual or heterosexual love, the *Amatorius*, Plutarch makes the
homosexual Pisias attack heterosexual intercourse as sordid, because
it takes place in brothels. 'For it is obviously not fitting for virtuous
women to love or be loved.'[119] Plutarch's father argues that the sexual
relationship is a tie which holds marriage together. Love ought to go
with sex;[120] sexual intercourse is the beginning of love (*philia*) for
wives, since, although the pleasure is short-lived, honour, delight,
affection, and loyalty spring from it and increase daily. So it is a duty
for men to keep alive the sexual bond with their wives and Solon was
right to legislate that men should make love to their wives at least
three times a month, not just for pleasure but to renew the marriage
treaty and to wipe out grievances. It follows that husbands should be
physically faithful, for in marriage it is better to love than to be
loved.[121]

Another author quoted by Stobaeus is Nicostratus, who may be
dated to the Antonine period.[122] In his book *On marriage* he main-

---

[111] 43 = 144C.   [112] 44 = 144D.   [113] 45 = 144E.
[114] 46 = 144F.   [115] 47 = 145A.   [116] 48 = 145A–B.   [117] 48 = 145C–E.
[118] 48 = 145F–146; cf. Jer. *adv. Iovin.* 49 = 320B.
[119] 753C: ἐρᾶν/ἐρᾶσθαι. A similar debate is the subject of ps.-Lucian *Erotes*, probably to be
dated to the early 4th cent. AD, where the arguments in favour of homosexuality win. The
narrator decides that all men should marry but only philosophers enjoy the privilege of
pederasty (51).
[120] 756E.   [121] 769A–E.
[122] Bickel ed. *adv. Iovin.* 337.

tained that neither husband nor wife should commit adultery, since it may entail ill repute and engender bastards begotten from selfish and undisciplined lust. The ideal for a man is a kind wife who knows how to look after him. He can relax with her and confide all his secrets, even public business, to her, since it is like confiding in himself. She is the human being closest to him, who gives most pleasure and least pain, who gives him children and mourns him most sincerely on his death.[123] Husbands should choose brides whose physical beauty is a true reflection of the soul and who show good temper, intelligence, and cheerfulness.[124] Nicostratus also criticized extravagant dress.[125] The vivid vignette of the husband's happy home life is his most striking contribution.

We may end this selective survey of Graeco-Roman theorists with the highly conventional but comprehensive catalogue of the benefits of marriage which the Severan historian Cassius Dio puts into the mouth of Augustus as part of his speech on the Papio-Poppaean Law in AD 9:

For is there anything better than a wife who is chaste, domestic, a good house-keeper, a rearer of children; one to gladden you in health, to tend you in sickness, to be your partner in good fortune, to console you in misfortune; to restrain the mad passion of youth and to temper the unseasonable harshness of old age? And is it not a delight to acknowledge a child who shows the endowments of both parents? (56.3.3–4, Loeb trans.)

5. *Christians*

While hellenized Romans and Greeks with some experience of Roman culture were engaged in their well-worn debate, a new fusion of Greek and Jewish ideas was being created by early Christian thinkers. Paul and the author of 1 Peter were much influenced by the Aristotelian tradition and perhaps by a need to convince non-Christians that their views of marriage and the position of women were not revolutionary.[126] Later authors, for instance Tertullian and Clement of Alexandria, adopted the extreme ascetic views which we have seen in Philo.[127] The Aristotelian subjection of women becomes entrenched in Church doctrine, justified by appeals to observation of nature or God's will. So does the distinction of spheres: 'Affaires abroad do most appertaine to the man . . . That which the wife is

---

[123] Stob. 4.23.65.   [124] Stob. 4.22.4.102.   [125] 4.23.62–3.
[126] Cf. Balch.
[127] See esp. *Strom.* 3.3, 71 ff., *Paed.* 2.83 ff. A wife's function is to produce children and keep house: ibid. 82, 108. Cf. Broudéhoux, *Mariage et famille chez Clément d'Alexandrie*, esp. pp. 129 ff.

especially to care for, is the businesse of the house.'[128] Paul's preference for celibacy combines with Tertullian's advocacy of avoidance of
remarriage to produce an extreme ascetic theory that virginity was
best, chaste widowhood second, chaste marriage third, often with
sexual intercourse allowed for reproduction only and abandoned
after the birth of children. Protestant theologians, often taking
inspiration from Latin sources and from Plutarch, were to revise
these views. But the idea that marriage was indissoluble except by
death, an idea which had its roots in Roman ideals but not in Roman
practice, remained strong.[129]

   The transmission of pagan theory into Christian doctrine is outside
our scope. We turn now to the aspirations of Romans who were not
writing as moralists and to the attitudes and practice which members
of the upper class claimed as their own.

---

[128] William Gouge, *Of domesticall duties* (1626) 148. On Gouge and other Puritan conduct-
books see Davies, 'Continuity and change in literary advice on marriage'.
[129] The fascinating topic of the development of Christian theory from the 1st to the 20th cent.
is irrelevant to the study of the pagan authors, though not vice versa. See Gaudemet, 'Les
transformations de la vie familiale au bas empire et l'influence du christianisme' and 'Tendances
nouvelles de la legislation familiale au ivme siècle'; Wicker, 'First century marriage ethics: a
comparative study of the household codes and Plutarch's conjugal precepts'; Peter Brown, *The
Body and Society*.

8

Coniugalis Amor

O quam multarum egregia opera in obscuro iacent!
How many women's noble deeds go unacknowledged.

(Seneca *Consolatio ad Helviam* 19.5)

A woman may achieve greatness, or at any rate great renown, by
merely being a wonderful wife and mother, like the mother of the
Gracchi; whereas the men who have achieved great renown by
being devoted husbands and fathers might be counted on the
fingers of one hand.

(Dorothy L. Sayers, *Gaudy Night*, chapter 3)

IN a seminal article in 1958, Gordon Williams traced specifically
Roman ideas of marriage, drawing particularly on Plautus and
Catullus.[1] He suggested that the poets who insist on the wife's duty to
be *morigera* or *morem gerere* to her husband—or (in comedy) a
mistress' to her lover[2]—are drawing on a formula from the ancient
marriage ceremony, perhaps spoken by the *pronuba* at the moment
of the joining of hands. A wife who is *morigera* accommodates her
wishes to her husband's. The word is archaic and drops out of use.[3]
Williams proceeds from this convincing argument to draw some wider
conclusions about the original ideals of Roman marriage. Taking his
cue from Plautus' *Mostellaria*,[4] he postulates three important

---

[1] 'Some aspects of Roman marriage ceremonies and ideals'.
[2] Naev. *com.* 90–1; Plaut. *Cist.* 175, *Men.* 202, 787–8, *Most.* 188–9, 224ff.; Ter. *And.* 294;
Lucr. 4.1281.
[3] In a detailed analysis of *morem gerere*, *morigera*, and *morigerari*, Williams argues that the
verb 'will originally have meant something like "to regulate one's own individual behaviour
(being the expression of one's character) in the interest of another". Therefore its original
application will have been to the peculiarly intimate sort of dutiful submission required of a
person who lives in close daily contact with the object of his obedience. It was consequently
appropriate for (and probably confined to) wifely and filial obedience' (p. 29).
[4] 204ff., esp. 204–5: '*Philematium*: illi me *soli* esse oportere *obsequentem*: | solam ille me *soli*
sibi suo ⟨sumptu⟩ liberavit'; 224ff. '*Scapha*: Si tibi sat acceptum est fore tibi victum *sempiternum*
| atque illum amatorem tibi proprium futurum in vita, | *soli gerundum censeo morem* et
capiundas crines' (my emphasis).

features: '(i) the ideal of faithfulness to one man . . . (ii) the ideal of wifely obedience to a husband . . . and (iii) the marriage-bond conceived of as eternal'.[5] Williams holds that this trio of ideas is recognizably Roman and, originating in the upper classes, spread to the middle and lower classes, of whom we know from the epitaphs, and that they had as ideals, though not necessarily as practice, a long history. This reconstruction, with which I broadly agree, suggests a way of carrying the discussion further and of relating theory to practice and to a wide cross-section of society over a long time-span.[6]

Of all Latin writers, apart from the scribbler of graffiti, the supplier or purchaser of a modest tomb inscription will be least suspected of being a deep student of Greek philosophy. In trying to isolate ideas which are especially, if not peculiarly, Roman, it seems sensible to pick out some attitudes which are emphasized in tomb inscriptions and then to relate them to literary sources.[7] The interpenetration of highly sophisticated literature and the norms of epigraphic sentiment is clear: not only does Tacitus in his memoir on his father-in-law echo inscriptions in the epithet he gives to Domitia Decidiana, *amantissima uxor*, but similar expressions occur in less funereal literature. Conversely, the more elaborate epitaphs have literary pretensions.[8] There is a risk and indeed probability that, in picking scattered inscriptions from Rome, Italy, and the Latin West, I may be including the sentiments of authors of non-Roman descent. Rome itself, for instance, had a large population of enfranchised slaves. But my premiss is that people who expressed themselves in Latin epitaphs were Romanized and that the ideas and feelings claimed by freedmen whose names and, at least in part, education may be Greek are indistinguishable from those of pure Roman blood. We can rarely tell which individual belongs to which race. Similarly, Latin epitaphs in

[5] 'Some aspects of Roman marriage ceremonies and ideals' 23.

[6] On norm and practice see Chafe, *Women and Equality. Changing patterns in American culture* 21.

[7] The following study is selective, based on a directed search through *Carmina epigraphica* and the indices of *CIL*, especially Jory's index to vol. 6. Richmond Lattimore's stimulating *Themes in Greek and Latin epitaphs* suggested lines of enquiry. Among more technical works, Harrod, *Latin terms of endearment and of family relationship. A lexicographical study based on Volume VI of the* Corpus inscriptionum latinarum, remains useful. Hesberg-Tonn covers a wide range and makes valuable points. See too Griffin, *Latin Poets and Roman life* 156ff.; Krummrey, 'Zu dem Grabgedicht für Aelia in Nikopoli a.d. Donau (*CLE* 492)'; Pitkäranta, 'Formule sepolcrali'. I am much indebted to projects on *coniuges* and *uxores* registered in inscriptions from the city of Rome in *CIL* 6 which were carried out by Susan E. Dorken, the second with Marie Laurence, thanks to grants from the Social Sciences and Humanities Research Council of Canada.

[8] Tac. *Ag.* 45.5: *amantissima uxore*; cf. Lucr. 3.894–5: *uxor optima*; Cic. *F* 14.4.6: *fidissima atque optima uxor*; Ov. *Tr.* 3.3.55: *optima coniunx*; Pliny *Epp.* 8.18.8: *uxor optima*. For *Laud. Tur.* see esp. Wistrand's edition and Horsfall, 'Some problems in the "Laudatio Turiae"'.

the provinces rarely attest native culture. The Greek epitaphs of the West, on the other hand, could not be used with any confidence to illustrate Roman attitudes.

Most of the more specific descriptions of the qualities of a *coniunx* are naturally inscribed on the orders of the other *coniunx*. Certain adjectives were such common coin that they could be used without much distinction whenever some expansion of the bare mention of names and relationship was required. An unpublished study by Susan Dorken of *coniuges* and *uxores* in the *CIL* inscriptions of Rome and northern Italy shows that in Rome the combination of noun plus adjective outnumbers the noun alone by about three to one. Of the adjectives and adjectival phrases, *bene merens* ('well-deserving') is overwhelmingly the commonest in Rome and *carissima/carissimus* ('very dear') in the north. Next most common in Rome is *carissima/carissimus*. To select only the adjectives used for 3,728 wives (women specifically commemorated as *coniuges* or *uxores*) in Rome, *bene merens* is well ahead of the competition, but quite often used in conjunction with other adjectives (1,305 instances); *carissima* comes next (576), then *sanctissima* ('very holy', 208), *optima* ('excellent', 156), *dulcissima* ('very sweet', 144) *pientissima* etc. ('very dutiful', 107), *incomparabilis* ('incomparable', 103), *rarissima* ('very rare', 35), *castissima* ('very chaste') surprisingly uncommon (23), *fidelissima* ('very loyal', 24), *amantissima* ('very loving', 14). The comparable list of 1,241 husbands (*coniuges* only, not *mariti*) is *bene merens* (932), *carissimus* (265), *optimus* (70), *pientissimus* etc. (46), *dulcissimus* (35), *sanctissimus* (9), *incomparabilis* (8), *rarissimus* and *amantissimus* (2), *castissimus* and *fidelissimus* (1). There are a handful of other adjectives for each sex.[9] These findings do not quite square with the frequency of the same adjectives in contexts where the marital relationship is not specified but may be convincingly conjectured. The most striking result is that while generally deserving (*bene merens*) or moral (*sanctissima* or *optima*) conduct is stressed for wives, the affection which they inspire or in which they are held

---

[9] Cf. Harrod, *Latin terms of endearment*, who examines adjectives in *CIL* 6 and classifies them according to specific relationships. His totals are (after *merens*) *carissimus* 1,713 (especially between *coniuges*), *dulcissimus* 1,634 (especially children), *pientissimus* 907, *piissimus* 737 (of parents towards children rather than vice versa), *optimus* 679, *sanctissimus* 386 (distinctively of wives and virgins), *incomparabilis* 283, *pius* 116, *rarissimus* 83, *fidelissimus* 78, *dignissimus* 62, *amantissimus* 61, *indulgentissimus* 56, *carus* 51, *bonus* 50, *dulcis* 46, *castissimus* 40 (especially wives), *sanctus* 36, *innocentissimus* 35, *castus* 34 (wives), *praestantissimus* 21. For descriptions of slave-mates cf. Treggiari, 'Contubernales in *CIL* 6' 59; Günther, *Frauenarbeit-Frauenbindung. Untersuchungen zu unfreien und freigelassenen Frauen in den stadtrömischen Inschriften* 311. Curchin, 'Familial epithets in the epigraphy of Roman Spain', finds *carissimus*, *optimus*, or *bene merens* commoner than *pientissimus* for husbands and wives.

(*carissima*, *dulcissima*) is more important than specific virtues such as chastity or faithfulness.[10] But our task here is to attempt to isolate specific virtues.

1. Virtues Related to Sexual Fidelity

Chastity in women, expressed by *castissima* or occasionally *pudica*, is quite often praised.[11] This is fairly often given a prominent place in the longer eulogies, many of which are in verse and therefore conveniently assembled in *Carmina epigraphica*. These give some impression of individual wives. Veratia C.l. Eleutheris, for instance, married to another ex-slave, kept the flower of her youth chastely (a rare reference to pre-marital restraint?), not plucking the joys of shame, lived content with the husband she had approved, and behaved in everything as a good wife should.[12] This could be spelt out: 'chaste and loyal, she always loved her husband's couch, sober, no adulteress, simple and kind-hearted, devoted only to her husband, ignorant of the husbands of others.'[13] Reference to the marital bed, the shared couch, which the wife keeps as she keeps the house,[14] is made elsewhere.[15] Keeping away from other men or just avoiding outside contacts is also associated with sexual fidelity in the eulogy of Aurelia Philematium.[16]

Chastity on the husband's part might imply a slightly wider gamut of behaviour.[17] It is claimed by a grieving husband from Galeata, who mourned a wife of 20, one of twin daughters of virtuous parents. He puts into his wife's mouth a description of her background and the thought: 'I was beloved, a modest and happy wife joined to a chaste husband, but the envious law of fate rendered our vows fruitless and left me, poor loving wretch, only the consolation of being allowed to

[10] Curchin, on a small sample, notes 'the supremacy of affection over piety' ('Familial epithets' 180). But see the reservations of M. Beard in 'Roman inscriptions 1981–5' 142.

[11] There are roughly three pages on *casta* etc. in Jory. See Lattimore's list, *Themes in Greek and Latin epitaphs* 296. *Pudica* is sometimes used alone (8.7156 = *CE* 512.7) or in conjunction with *casta* in the epitaphs (e.g. 6.11252). Among others, Graxia Alexandria is commended for her *pudicitia* (6.19128). Iiro Kajanto, *Classical and Christian. Studies in the Latin epitaphs of medieval and Renaissance Rome* 132, notes 15 instances of *pudica*, 3 of *pudicissima*, and 13 of *pudicitia* in Jory's index. Both virtues continue to be praised in early Christian epitaphs (Kajanto, loc. cit.). (Subsequent references to *CIL* in this chapter will be given by number alone.)

[12] 6.19838 = *CE* 968.

[13] 6.12853 = *CE* 548.

[14] 6.15346 = *ILLRP* 973.

[15] 6.4763 = *CE* 448: 'quae commune torum servavit casta mariti | et fidei plena pietate nobili vixit'; 6.30127: 'castum servare cubile.' Cf. Verg. *A* 8.412, Sen. *Herc. F.* 309.

[16] 6.9499 = *ILLRP* 793.

[17] In Spain 'adjectives of propriety such as *castissima* or *pudicissima* are naturally confined to females' (Curchin, 'Familial epithets' 181). Mrs Dorken finds one male instance in Rome.

yield up my life in my husband's arms.' It is hard to deny that this is the language of romantic love.[18]

Literary sources abundantly confirm the central position of wifely chastity, *castitas* and *pudicitia*, sexual integrity and scrupulousness. *Castitas*, stainless purity, has cult associations and relates to physical and mental integrity; *pudicitia* connotes rather the conscience which keeps a person from shameful actions.[19] The technical loss of *pudicitia* through rape was a disaster to the virtuous and seduction a lapse which inevitably led to further crimes.[20] Indiscreet behaviour damaged the wife's reputation. But the idea that a man's honour was involved in the chastity of his womenfolk does not seem to have been as developed among the Romans as it was later to become.

The *pudica* was often *univira*.[21] Tacitus attributes to certain German tribes the custom that only virgins married. They regarded the one husband as their one chance of matrimony, one body and one life with their own. Women divorced for adultery, he claims, had no hope of remarriage, but he appears to think that this also applied to widows and women divorced for any other reason (if any such existed).[22] In the inscriptions the woman who, at the time of her death, had been married only once may be entitled to the epithet *univira*,[23] or *univiria*[24] or *unicuba*, *uniiuga*[25] or *unimarita*.[26] Such praise was linked to ritual, for only *univirae* were originally allowed to sacrifice to the goddess Pudicitia or to act as *pronubae* at weddings.[27] The latter custom shows that it was hoped that the bride would also have only one husband.

[18] 11.6606 = *CE* 386.

[19] The *Glossarium* (450.58, cf. 403.37) regards them as interchangeable and gives *castus* as the equivalent of *sōphrōn*.

[20] Livy 1.58.7; Tac. *A* 4.3.3; cf. Sen. ap. Jer. *adv. Iovin.* 1.49 = 319 C.

[21] VM 2.1.3: 'Quae uno contentae matrimonio fuerant corona pudicitiae honorabantur: existimabant enim eum praecipue matronae sincera fide incorruptum esse animum, qui depositae virginitatis cubile <in publicum> egredi nesciret, multorum matrimoniorum experientiam quasi legitimae cuiusdam intemperantiae signum esse credentes' ('Women who were content with one marriage used to be honoured with a garland of *pudicitia*. For they thought that a woman's loyalty was undiluted and her heart was pure if she was incapable of leaving the bed in which she had laid aside her virginity. They held that experience of several marriages indicated intemperance, although it was a lawful one').

[22] G 19.2ff. Cf. Sen. ap. Jer. *adv. Iovin.* 44 = 310 D, 311 B, 46 = 312 C, 313 A, etc. Cf. Wistrand, *Laud. Tur.* 37.

[23] e.g. *CE* 1306.4; 6.25392, 31711, 14.418, 913 (Ostia). Kötting, '"Univira" in Inschriften', counts only about 80 examples of the adjective and its cognates, including μόνανδρος, in all the pagan, Jewish, and Christian inscriptions. He rightly points out that the word is used in pagan inscriptions to describe either a woman who dies in her first marriage or a widow who does not remarry after the death of a first husband. He claims that there are only about 20 (citing 19) pagan *univirae*: 3.2667, 5.7763, 6.2318, 12405, 13299, 13303, 25392, 26268, 31711, 8.7384, 11294, 19470, 9.5142, 10.3058, 3351, 11.6281, 14.418, 839, 963.

[24] 3.3572 = *CE* 558, 6.3604, 13299, 23183, 26268, 8.11294.   [25] 3.3572: *unicuba uniiuga*.

[26] 6.30428. For further bibliography see Courtney on Juv. 6.230.

[27] Livy 10.23.5, with the definition 'ut uni nuptam ad quem virgo deducta sit'; Serv. ad *A* 4.166; Tert. *de exhort. cast.* 13.1.

The poets, as Williams shows, also paid due honour to women who married only once. Imaginative prose follows suit.[28]

Occasional inscriptions, usually of substantial length, use *virginia* to describe the wife who was a virgin when she married and *virginius* of the man who married such a wife. The pair may be called *virginii*, but more often the wife dedicates *virginio meo* or the husband calls the wife *coniunx sua virginia*.[29] The relationship is emphatically celebrated by Aurelia Maura, who laments that she, the *virginia*, had to carry out for her husband the duty of commemoration which a *virginius* should do for his *virginia*.[30] Such inscriptions often mention the length of the marriage: again the emphasis is on the good fortune and compatibility of a pair whose union lasted from the wife's girlhood.[31] Marriages lasting thirty-five, forty-eight, or fifty years are typical.[32]

Epitaphs also describe more vaguely a woman who contented herself with her husband alone. This might theoretically connote the serially monogamous as well as the *univira*, but it probably again means the woman who only married once. The phrases are *solo contenta marito* (content with her husband alone) *vel sim.*[33] or *uno contenta marito* (content with her one husband).[34] Catullus appropriates the language of epitaphs to describe Lesbia's failure to achieve monogamy—'uno non est contenta Catullo'—or to give conventional praise to a wife—'viro contentam vivere solo'.[35] The Roman ideal

[28] Williams, 'Some aspects of Roman marriage ceremonies and ideals' 23–4, citing Hor. *O* 3.14.5; Verg. *A* 1.343 ff., 4.550 ff.; Prop. 4.11.36, 68. Add Tac. *G* 19.3–4; Apul. *M* 8 on Charite.

[29] Cf. *OLD* s.v. *virgineus* 1c, Lattimore, *Themes in Greek and Latin epitaphs* 278, Humbert, *Remariage à Rome* 63, 346–7. Plut. *Pomp.* 74.3 has Παρθένιος ἀνήρ of Cornelia's first husband, when she wishes she had died before hearing of his death, rather than surviving his death and her second husband's fall.   [30] 5.1880.

[31] e.g. 3.2217: 'Aur. Glycon et Valentia virginI [sc. virginii] vivi sibi posuerunt'; 3.14524: 'virginio meo, cum [q]uem [*sic*] quinquaginta annis ben[e] laboravi adqu[e] inculpatim covixi'; 6.10219: 'virgine[ae suae] . . . libertae idem coniugi carissimae'; 6.12389: 'coniugi virginiae q.v. annis xxxxv'; 6.34728: 'coniugi dulcissimae . . . maritus virginiae pudicae fideli'; 11.4483: 'D.M. C. Lusio Lucifero Valeria Iustina virginio et coiugi carissimo cum quo convixit annis xlviii mens x qui vixit annis lxx coiugi incomparabili b.m.'; 13.2000 'qui vixit . . . sine ulla lesione animi cum coiuge sua virginia cum qua vixit annis xxxxviii ex qua creavit filios iii et eiliam [sc. filiam]'. See also 3.14292, 6.2736, 16872; Engström, *CLE* 378, 457.

[32] 5.1880, 11.4483, 13.2000, 3.14524.

[33] 3.1537 = *CE* 597: 'mihi solus coniunx Aelius'; 6.12853 = *CE* 548: 'dedita coniugi soli suo'; 13.5383; *CE* 455, 652 (AD 368): 'omne bonum soli servasse marito'; 1872; all in Williams, 'Some aspects of Roman marriage ceremonies and ideals' 23; Engström, *CLE* 204.

[34] 3.2667 = *CE* 643: 'uno contenta marito'; 6.19838 = *CE* 968: 'coniuge namque uno vixit contenta probato'; cf. Williams, loc. cit. (last n.).

[35] 68.135: 'she is not content with Catullus alone'; 111.1: 'content to live with her husband alone'; cf. Afran. *com.* 117: 'uno ut simus contentae viro'; Plaut. *Merc.* 824: 'uxor contenta est quae bona est uno viro'; Mart. 10.63.8: 'una pudicitiae mentula nota meae'. Cf. Williams, 'Some aspects of Roman marriage ceremonies and ideals' 25, Bömer on Ov. *F* 6.231. Note that this phrase includes avoidance of adultery in marriage, while the use of *univira* stresses the fact that the woman either had had no previous husband or did not remarry when widowed.

of lifelong monogamy for women was given further currency by Tertullian.[36]

For a husband to claim that he had married only once is rare in the inscriptions. One woman is allowed the claim that she was her husband's only wife.[37] But we shall see later that husbands may regard themselves as inconsolable. While Propertius makes Cornelia boast that her tombstone will show her to have been married only once and tell her daughters to imitate her, she balances the two possibilities —that her widower may wish to marry again or that he might stay celibate, content with her ghost.[38] In the Republic the continuance of the line, in the Principate Augustus' legislation, demanded remarriage, unless a man had enough heirs already. No doubt too men were expected to need a bedmate, companion, and chatelaine, although some found that a concubine sufficed to fill these roles. But it was good fortune if a man only married once. Laelius, Germanicus, and Statius' father are selected for mention.[39] Statius himself was happy in not having been married before he married Claudia.[40] Germanicus' father Drusus was remarkable in being physically faithful to his wife, and Cato in confining himself to his two wives.[41] It was, naturally, rare for non-philosophers to claim that they had sexual intercourse only in order to breed children, but it is attested, though it need not be believed. The claim is made for some Christians, along with the claim that Christian men avoided remarriage.[42] It is even rare for a man to be praised for being satisfied with one woman at a time, *una contentus*.[43]

But, despite the ideal of monogamy for women, Roman practice was mostly against it. Society expected widows and divorcees to marry, unless perhaps they were beyond child-bearing. It was good fortune for Cornelia that she died before her husband and so could claim to be *univira*. Many of the women who win this title on their inscriptions also died comparatively young. Of the *univirae* on Seneca's list, where we have any facts to go on, Porcia probably predeceased Brutus (and in any case he was her second husband), we do not know what happened to Marcia after Cato's suicide, and

[36] Williams, 'Some aspects of Roman marriage ceremonies and ideals' 24, citing *pud.* 16, *de virg. vel.* 9, *de monogamia* 8.13.17, etc.

[37] 6.14404 = *CE* 1038: 'diceris coniunxs una fuisse viri.'

[38] 4.11.36, 67–8ff, 85ff. In fact, Paullus in 12 or later married the younger Marcella (Syme, 'Marriage ages of Roman senators' 329).

[39] Plut. *Cato min.* 7.3; Tac. *A* 2.73.3; Stat. *S* 5.3.240–1.

[40] *S* 3.5.24ff., cf. 1.2.

[41] VM 4.3.3; *Cons. ad Liviam* 305; Plut. *Cato min.* 7.1.3.

[42] *SHA Pesc.* 6.7; Min. *Oct.* 31.5.

[43] Ovid taunts Catullus with a variant (*Tr.* 2.429: 'nec contentus ea [sc. Lesbia]'). The exact phrase is used in Sen. *Contr.* 1.5.1—of a rapist. Cf. Cato *Ag.* 143; Calp. Sic. 3.24.

Marcella the Elder married twice. Antonia the Younger, who is praised by Valerius Maximus but not by Jerome, is unusual among the women of Augustus' family in being permitted to remain a widow. Remarriage was not morally objectionable to pagan writers, except when they wanted to take a particularly high moral line, although lifelong monogamy for women was morally better and luckier.[44]

Valerius Maximus' section on *pudicitia*[45] concentrates on severe punishment of homosexuals, of unmarried girls who were compromised, and of seducers. Several foreign married women who defended or avenged their honour are also attested. It is of some interest that he invokes *Pudicitia* as the chief support (*firmamentum*) of both men and women: he is probably thinking that it protected boys against homosexual advances and discouraged attempted seduction of other men's wives and daughters.

Regulus, according to Horace, refused the kiss of his virtuous wife: she, because she was *pudica*, regarded him as her husband, he, as a legal purist, remembered that he was a prisoner of war and so no longer her husband.[46] *Pudicitia* broadened out into loyalty, love, and dutifulness.[47] Already in Plautus it is connected with safeguarding the husband's reputation. The young wife whose *paterfamilias* wants her to desert her absent husband and who, like her sister in the same circumstances, behaves just as if he were still with her, tells her father:

> Pudicitiast, pater,
> eos nos magnuficare qui nos socias sumpserunt sibi.
>
> (*Stichus* 100–1, cf. 99)

It's a matter of *pudicitia*, father, for us to esteem those who have taken us as their partners.

The author of *The ladies calling*, preaching to English gentlewomen of the Civil War period, neatly divided a wife's duty to her husband into duty to his Person, his Reputation, and his Fortune. The first two are closely linked, for if fidelity and especially sexual fidelity are owed to his Person, it is also true that her sexual misconduct would reflect on his Reputation.[48] Plautus' heroines are loyal to both. They love and respect their husbands. Affection for the husband and open display of affection were the obverse of *pudicitia*. Regulus' wife can

[44] Humbert, *Remariage à Rome*, esp. pp. 42 ff.
[45] 6.1.　　[46] Hor. *O* 3.5.41 ff.
[47] See Wistrand, *Laud. Tur.* 36–7.
[48] Allestree, *The ladies calling* 175 ff.

offer a kiss and Postumus' Galla, as loyal as Penelope, can hang on his neck when he comes home.[49]

2. Faith

Fides (faith) is often associated with sexual loyalty. Philematium was 'casta, pudens, volgei nescia, feida viro' ('chaste, modest, ignorant of the mob, faithful to her husband').[50] *Fides* may be *pudica*.[51] A seducer tries to shake a wife's lawful *fides*.[52] *Fides* also means the wider loyalty which a wife promised to her husband on marriage and vice versa.[53] It could be described as *fides uxoria*, or *maritalis* or *coniugalis*.[54] This reciprocal loyalty and trust must be seen against the background of the general concept of *fides* so important in Roman life and thought. Reciprocal relationships such as those of patron and client or patron and freedman depended on good faith and moral obligation. The informal contract of marriage—only in a very loose sense a *foedus* (treaty)—was similarly based.[55] The reciprocity of *fides* is neatly expressed in the phrase the butcher Aurelius Hermia applies to his wife: 'fida fido viro' ('faithful to her faithful husband').[56] The whole of the *Laudatio 'Turiae'* is a commentary on conjugal faith, both hers to him and his to her.[57]

Valerius Maximus makes *fides* cover the courage and self-sacrifice shown by Turia and Sulpicia when their husbands were proscribed by the triumvirs and also Aemilia's magnanimous treatment of Scipio Africanus when he had an affair with her maid.[58] The protection extended to husbands could thus cover a considerable range. Conversely, when Carvilius Ruga divorced his sterile wife, this would be seen as a failure in loyalty: not even the desire for children should have priority over marital faith, precisely as 'Turia''s husband said.[59]

[49] Prop. 3.12.22–3. Cf. Plin. *Epp.* 4.19.2: 'amat me, quod castitatis indicium est.'

[50] 6.9499 = *ILLRP* 793.

[51] Ov. *M* 7.720–1.

[52] Ov. *Her.* 17.4; cf. Stat. *S* 3.5.3.

[53] *Pacta*: Ov. *Her.* 6.41 etc.; *promissa*: Val. Flacc. 8.221–2, 249.

[54] VM 4.6 pr.: 'valenter inter coniuges stabilitae fidei'; 4.6 ext. 3: 'uxoriae fidei'; 6.7: 'de fide uxorum erga viros'; Quint. *Decl. min.* 335.16, of the husband; VM 2.1.4: 'coniugali fidei', again of the loyalty owed by the husband to the wife.

[55] See, for general connotations, Schulz, *Principles of Roman law* 223 ff., and Fraenkel, 'Zur Geschichte des Wortes *Fides*'. There is a very long article in *TLL*, of which cols. 679–80 are especially relevant.

[56] 1.1221 = 6.9499 = *ILS* 7472 = *ILLRP* 793. Cf. 6.6208: 'coniunx fida viro'; 6.37454: 'fida amator coniugis sui'. *Fidelis* (e.g. 6.34728) and *fidelissima* (e.g. 6.19753) occur occasionally of wives. *Fidelissimus* occurs for husbands (e.g. 6.8154, 15996) but is much commoner of dependants such as slaves and, like *fidus/fidissimus*, is relatively rare.

[57] *Laud. Tur.* 1.26: 'fide[i] in nos', 2.43: 'fidissuma' 2.45: 'fidem exuerem'.

[58] 6.7.

[59] VM 2.1.4; *Laud. Tur.* 2.45.

Good faith was especially necessary in marriage because of the economic interdependence of husband and wife. The wife was guardian of the husband's property, especially of the house, but sometimes of his business interests, whether the husband was the exiled Cicero or a small shopkeeper, and the husband held the dowry as it were in trust for the wife or their children. Because the relationship was one of trust, strict accounting might be neither practicable nor proper.[60]

The good wife was a trustworthy confidante, like the anonymous *laudata* who used to be identified with the Turia praised by Valerius Maximus. A famous fourth-century pagan eulogy picks up this theme.[61] Both Brutus' Porcia in legend and the conspirator's wife in rhetoric exemplify the *fides* of the staunch wife who could keep dangerous secrets.[62]

3. Respect and Co-operation

Reverentia is also used in this sort of legal context for the respect due to a *coniunx* because of the nature of the bond.[63] Pliny praises this quality in a wife, who deserved it in return,[64] but it is not applied to wives in inscriptions as much as it is between children and parents.[65]

Obsequium is a more prominent virtue and more characteristically Roman. It is less an attitude of mind than a manner of behaving obligingly. Gordon Williams glosses it as wifely obedience or dutifulness and regards it as particularly Roman. The verb *obsequi* and its derivatives are so frequent in this use that the word seems almost to be a technical term and arouses the suspicion that it may have been pleonastically linked with *morigera* as part of a formula spoken at weddings, but survived that word's disappearance. At any rate, obedience in wives is praised as a virtue on the epitaphs from early times to late.[66] *Obsequium* was owed by son to parent or freedman to patron,[67] but was thought particularly appropriate to a wife. So the freedwoman Larcia Horaea is made to say that she showed obedience to her ex-owners and parents-in-law but *obsequium* to their son, her husband.[68] Epitaphs link this quality with chastity, with being con-

---

[60] *D* 24.1.31 pr.–1; *Laud. Tur.* 1.37ff.; cf. 6.37965.8. Cf. Pearce, 'The role of the wife as *custos* in ancient Rome'.

[61] *Laud. Tur.* 2.4; 6.1779 c 6.

[62] Plut. *Brut.* 13.4ff.; Sen. *Contr.* 2.5.19; Tac. *A* 12.5.5.

[63] *D* 25.2.3.2, ? 24.3.14.1; *CJ* 5.13.1.7. Cf. Corbett 125–6.

[64] *Epp.* 8.5.1. Cf. Col. 12 pr. 7.

[65] e.g. 6.3150, 10853, 10620, 28888.

[66] Williams, 'Some aspects of Roman marriage ceremonies and ideals' 24–5.

[67] e.g. 6.27556; *D* 38.2.1.1. Donatus on Ter. *Andr.* 64 says it was appropriate towards a superior.

[68] 1.1570 = *ILLRP* 977, time of Caesar.

tented with the husband alone and with pleasing him,[69] and with
holiness and reverence and all the virtues attributed to our anonymous heroine.[70] One woman is dedicated to marital *obsequium*.[71]
Obsequium may be almost the same as *officium* and used to describe
the last duty of burial.[72] It is still a virtue in Christian epitaphs:
'castitas, fides, caritas, pietas, obsequium' and all the virtues God
has taught women.[73]

But there is one problem with identifying it with wifely obedience.
One of our earliest epitaphs applies the adjective equally to wife and
husband. Both Q. Pompeius Bithynici l. Sosus and his wife Satriena
P.l. Salvia were 'opsequentes et concordes'.[74] The conjugal *obsequium* mentioned by the freedwoman Firma in connection with her
happiness with her husband (perhaps of slave status) seems to be his
towards her.[75] The adjective does not seem to indicate any precise
relationship of inferior to superior as between *coniuges*, but rather to
be a vague term of approval, almost always superlative like *castissima* and *piissima*.[76] Lysiponus, whose two happy marriages were
interrupted by death, the first after fifteen years and the second after
twenty-eight, says that both wives were *obsequentissimae* to him, but
still calls the second wife his lady, *domina*.[77] The term is only
occasionally used of men, for instance to a beloved and 'obsequentis-
simus contubernalis'.[78] Co-operation rather than obedience seems to
be the key meaning in usage. One husband, to praise his wife, laments
that he could not match her in *obsequium*, another that his wife
surpassed him *obsequio pietatis*.[79] There may, however, be a
strengthening in the idea of subordination in Christian usage.[80]

In literature, the disguised Jupiter could be *obsequens* in bed with
Alcmena.[81] There is a strong element of obedience in the verb:
Plautus links the adjective with *oboediens* and Seneca with obedience
to parents and submissiveness.[82] But, although *obsequium* is a very
proper attitude in a son, a parent can also be *obsequens* and mild to
children, and an agreeable man is *obsequens*, cheerful, agreeable,

[69] 6.3150, 28888; 8.2756 = *CE* 1604, Lambaesis, 21179 = *CE* 429, Caes. Maur.; 13.5383 = *CE* 455, Vesontio.
[70] 6.10853; *Laud. Tur.* 1.30.
[71] 6.26642: 'in castitate omniq(ue) obsequio maritali deditae.'
[72] 6.23004 = *CE* 1258; cf. *TLL* s.v. I 3b col. 183.
[73] 12.2143 = *CE* 765, Vienne; cf. 11.4631 = *CE* 1846, Umbria.
[74] 6.33087 = *ILLRP* 365.
[75] 2.1399 = *CE* 1140.   [76] *TLL* s.v.   [77] 6.20116.   [78] 6.23001.
[79] 6.13300: 'impar obsequis'; 8.5804; cf. *NS* 1899 p. 149; 'ob obsequium omnem [*sic*] erga ipsam.'
[80] 11.4631 = *CE* 1846. See Aug. *de bono coniugali* 1.1, where marriage is defined as 'alterius regentis alterius obsequentis amicalis quaedam et germana coniunctio'.
[81] Plaut. *Amph.* 290.
[82] Plaut. *Bacc.* 459; Sen. *Ben.* 3.38.2.

outgoing, and a good mixer.[83] Friendships are made pleasurable and are maintained by the polite attentions implied by *obsequium*.[84]

In short, compliance, complaisance, obligingness seem more prominent in the *obsequium* of a wife than the strict obedience which might be demanded of a soldier or a slave or freedman.[85] Even when a wife is urged to conciliate her murderous husband by turning herself into a doormat or when Trajan's wife toes his line on civil behaviour, 'obedience' will not do as a translation.[86]

Nor is the lack normally supplied by more specific words such as *oboedire* or *parere*.[87] A wife who accommodated herself to her husband's wishes was not simply obeying: her attitude might be more subtle, reasoned, and gracious, and the 'superior' party in a relationship might also permit himself to practise *obsequium* without obsequiousness and loss of face. *Obsequium* on the part of a husband could be contemptible, enforced on men who were debarred by circumstances from freedom of action.[88] But it may also be avowed as proof of self-sacrifice and devotion, and Tullia and Terentia were delighted, when the bridegroom Dolabella showed it, and *comitas*, to them both.[89]

Inscriptions sometimes use the verb *placere* to describe relationships between friend and friend and freedman or freedwoman and patron, for instance *placuit patrono suo*, 'she pleased her patron'.[90] It is occasionally used to describe a wife pleasing her husband.[91] The usual usage is to describe a dependant giving satisfaction to a superior. But when Horace uses the participle, without a dative, *placens uxor*, I doubt if this implies inequality. 'Congenial' or *simpatica* or *conveniens* would render the idea.

Womanly subjection is a Catonian ideal,[92] but not the norm then or

---

[83] Cic. *QF* 1.3.3; Ter. *Haut.* 152; Caec. *com.* 108–9: 'modo fit obsequens, hilarus, comis, communis, concordis, dum id quod petit potitur.'

[84] Cic. *Cael.* 13, *A* 6.6.1.   [85] e.g. Tac. *H* 1.82; Col. 12.1.6; Pliny *Pan.* 42.2.

[86] Ps.-Sen. *Oct.* 84–5, 177, 213; Pliny *Pan.* 83.7.

[87] In 8.13134 (Carthage) 'hobes caro sponso' has been interpreted as *hob(oedi)e(n)s*, but I doubt this. I find no use of *parere* or *(h)oboedire* in Jory.

[88] Sen. *Contr.* 7.6.17, 7.8.4.

[89] *Decl. min.* 280.14; Apul. *Apol.* 100; Cic. *A* 6.6.1.

[90] e.g. 6.6548, 7981, 37454.

[91] 5.1071 = *CE* 66 (Aquileia): 'Anicia P.l. Glycera fui, dixi de vita mea | satis. Fui probata | quae viro placui bo|no qui me ab imo ordine ad summum | perduxit honorem'; 6.5254 = *CE* 86: 'viro et patrono placui et decessi prior'; 6.6593 = *CE* 1030: 'viva viro placui prima et carissuma coniunx.' Cf. *ILLRP* 802 (probably wife): 'Brutia Q. l. Rufa pia patrono dum vixsit placuit.' For *liberti/ae* cf. 6.37454; for friends, 6.6548. For literary parallels cf. Sen. *Contr.* 2.7.8: 'At hercules adversus externorum quondam opiniones speciosissimum patrocinium erat: ego viro placeo.' Plut. *Praec. conj.* 141 A–B, *Aem. P.* 5.2–3 (comparing Aemilius Paullus' inexplicable divorce of Papiria); Jer. *adv. Iovin.* 1.48 = 317B.

[92] Livy 34.3.1; Cato *Ag.* 143.

later. A woman, however, needed to do her duty to her husband. It was therefore improper for her to be under the obligation to obey another man. Hence, a freedwoman who married with her patron's consent could no longer be compelled to perform services for him, though she might for a *patrona*. A wife ought to be *in officio mariti* (literally 'in the duty of her husband').[93] The concept does not imply subordination. *Officium* is defined as 'mutual serviceableness between status-equals'.[94] For the husband to be subordinate to the wife was of course never acceptable.[95]

4. Kindness

Dolabella's two qualities again appear together in the *Laudatio 'Turiae'*: 'Domestica bona pudicitiae, opsequi, comitatis, facilitatis.'[96] *Comis* (courteous, kind, obliging, etc.) seems not elsewhere to be used of a wife in *CIL* 6, but is used of the delightful Rhodanthion by his wife. She calls him *comis*, *dulcis* (sweet), and *amoenus* (lovely). Literary writers connect it with being pleasant, kind, or easy-going.[97]

It was regarded as a virtue for a man to be kind and courteous to his wife and children.[98] The model wife Fannia was praised by Pliny for managing to be pleasant and *comis* and for managing the rare combination of amiability and venerability.[99] *Comitas* relieved what might otherwise have been the excessive austerity of a virtuous wife: Valerius Maximus thought that the ancient Romans, while forbidding their wives wine, had allowed them the indulgence of gold, purple, and hair-colour so that their *pudicitia* should not be gloomy and horrid.[100] But the line between affability and dangerous charm might be difficult to draw. Tacitus criticizes Livia for not keeping to the old austerity:

Sanctitas domus priscum ad morem, comis ultra quam antiquis feminis probatum, mater impotens, uxor facilis et cum artibus mariti simulatione filii bene composita. (*Annals* 5.1)

She ran her household with old-fashioned morality, she was more gracious than women in the old days thought proper, she was an ambitious mother, an easy-going wife and one compatible with her husband's craft and her son's hypocrisy.

---

[93] *D* 38.1.48 pr.   [94] Crook 94.   [95] Mart. 8.12, 10.69.
[96] 1.30; cf. Caec. *com.* 108 (above, n. 83).
[97] Enn. ap. Cic. *Off.* 1.51; Fest. 55L s.v. *comptus* associates it with κόσμιος.
[98] Hor. *Epp.* 2.2.133; Livy 33.21.4.
[99] *Epp.* 7.19.7.   [100] 2.1.5.

The adjective *facilis* in praise of a *coniunx* is, apart from the unusually full and literary eulogy already cited, rare in the epitaphs of Rome.[101] *Facilitas*, which is often linked with *comitas*,[102] was a desirable quality in a friend, and therefore usually in a *coniunx*, but could shade into an over-tolerance comfortable for the wife or husband whose shortcomings were forgiven, but discreditable in the eyes of outsiders.[103] It was particularly likely to proceed from conjugal affection.[104] It is almost synonymous with *indulgentia*, a quality for which the 'inferior' party in various relationships often expresses gratitude on tombstones: child to father or mother, freed slave to patron, wife to husband, especially freedwoman to patron and husband, but occasionally also husband to wife or parent to child.[105] The literary sources again show plenty of *indulgentia* from parent to child, but no peculiar usage of the word to describe the husband's attitude to his wife. It occurs both of the husband's attitude and the wife's or of a mistress's to her lover.[106]

Indulgent kindness was repaid by dutifulness, but the inscriptions do not show any preponderance of *pietas* on the wife's side.[107] The superlatives *pientissimus/a* and *piissimus/a* (occasionally *pius/a*) are about equally common of husband and wife in *CIL* 6, and this is one of the most usual terms of approval.

But adjectives which have nothing to do with duty are as common or more common. *Coniugi dulcissimo/ae* roughly rivals *coniugi piissimo* and synonyms in these epitaphs.[108] *Coniugi carissimo/ae* (beloved) is extremely popular, while *amantissimo/ae* (loving) is surprisingly rare.[109] It is usual for adjectives to be more generously applied to wives when husbands commemorate than to husbands by wives, but this is linked presumably to the socio-economic causes which make commemoration by husbands more common, rather than to any lack of appreciation of husbands' merits or affection.

The inscriptions, then, show a mixture between emphasis on

---

[101] 6.9693.4–5 seems to be the only example: 'nobilis Euphrosyne facilis formosa puella | docta opulenta pia casta pudica proba.' It occurs as a *cognomen*.

[102] e.g. by Cic. *Am.* 66; Sen. *Clem.* 5.8.1.

[103] Cf. Ov. *Am.* 2.19.57, ironically.

[104] *D* 24.1.1.

[105] 6.21921, 21518, 11617, 9177, 1860, 28954, 22404, 20277.

[106] *Decl. min.* 280.14, 300.7, 376.4, 385.5. See Cotton, 'The concept of *indulgentia* under Trajan' 261–2, for parental indulgence.

[107] LS finds *pietas* raré from wife to husband, Curchin ('Familial epithets' 180) proportionately rarer than from husband to wife. Richard P. Saller, '*Pietas*, obligation and authority in the Roman family', 399 ff., shows that *pietas* is expected reciprocally of all family members.

[108] *Dulcis* of a husband: Cat. 66.33, 67.1.

[109] 6.9987 = 33819, 12473, 19743. Cf. Tac. *Ag.* 45.6. Harrod points out that it sometimes has a passive sense.

fulfilment of duty—deserving behaviour, dutifulness, chastity—and on affection between the *coniuges*, the love which the dead partner inspired, or the sweetness of his or her nature.

5. Husbands and Wives in the Inscriptions

The more detailed epitaphs, particularly those in verse, show a marked tendency to praise wives for their virtues as wives (and mothers) and husbands for virtues displayed in a wider sphere. Women are, as has often been pointed out, praised for their attentiveness to housework, summed up particularly by spinning, *lanificium*. In an idealized archaic time, matronly industry was in perfect balance with the husband's activity in the forum. Claudia in the Gracchan period 'kept house, made wool'.[110] The catalogue of the virtues of Amymone in the time of Hadrian runs 'very good and very beautiful, a wool-maker, pious, righteous, thrifty, chaste, staying at home' ('optima et pulcherrima, lanifica, pia, pudica, frugi, casta, domiseda').[111] The theme was still alive in the second century, and Lattimore has collected seven examples, to which several others might be added.[112] But the idea of wool-working was already so conventional by the triumviral period that it could be taken as read, since it was the common characteristic of all virtuous wives.[113] *Lanificium* had been important as the wife's major contribution to household economy, the manufacture of raw materials produced by the husband outside on the farm and the provision of warm clothing for family and workers. When the better-off Roman woman ceased to cook or clean, spinning remained a task which she could properly continue while supervising her slaves or entertaining guests, on the model of Lucretia or the Homeric Arete. Spinning also had a moral function. Like embroidery in the nineteenth century or knitting in the twentieth, it provided employment for hands which might have been idle. It was incompatible with adultery or riotous living and it provided a guarantee that the wife was home-loving, *domiseda*[114] or *nescia vulgi*, and not a gadabout. The theory has had a long life, for as recently as the 1960s matrons and girls in Apennine villages used to sit knitting or sewing outside—for the sake of air and light—with their

---

[110] 1.1211 = 6.15346 = *ILLRP* 973 = *CE* 52; Col. 12 pr. 8–9.
[111] 6.11602, cf. 34045 = *ILS* 8402 = *CE* 237. Phaedrus (4.5.5) links 'lanificam et frugi rusticam'.
[112] Lattimore, *Themes in Greek and Latin epitaphs* 297; 3.754 = *CE* 492: I do not see why the editors date to the 3rd cent.; 6.23852 = *CE* 471, 11.3276 = *CE* 552.
[113] *Laud. Tur.* 1.30, 33.
[114] Cf. 6.11602 = 34045.

chairs turned to face their front doors.[115] Apart from specific *lani-ficium*, women are praised for housekeeping (especially when thrifty) and for industry.[116] But some husbands felt that other activities or qualities deserved commemoration. This is clearest in the exceptional *Laudatio 'Turiae'*, where the wife's involvement in all family business, administration of property, and support to kin and husband is described in detail. Training and education are occasionally selected for praise.[117] The craftswomen, shopkeepers, market-women, and midwives who often worked alongside their husbands are not usually praised for their efforts directly (though something is implied by the mention of the trade). But there is one striking example from Capsa where a well-to-do businessman commemorated his wife (probably in the late second or early third century AD):

Here lies my wife Urbanilla, full of modesty, at Rome companion and partner in my business, rooted in parsimony. When all our business had been successfully completed and she was returning to our country with me, ah, Carthage snatched my unhappy partner from me. I have no hope of living without such a wife. She kept my house, she helped me with counsel.[118] Deprived of light, unhappy, she rests closed in marble. I your husband Lucius have covered you in marble here. This is the fate which fate has given us when we are brought into the world. (*CIL* 8.152 = *CE* 516)

In general, wives may be praised for their thrift, which conserved the household's resources, or their industry, which augmented wealth. 'Everything we have was won by your hard work.'[119] Another African eulogy is less specific, piling up adjectives: 'Postumia Matronilla, incomparable wife, good mother, most dutiful grandmother, *pudica*, religious, hard-working, thrifty, efficient (*efficax*), vigilant, careful, a woman of one husband and one bed, a matron of all industry and faith. She lived fifty-three years, five months, and three days.'[120]

Husband's virtues tend to be seen outside the house. 'Deserving

---

[115] The *locus classicus* is Livy 1.57.9. Cf. Varro *Men.* 190; Ov. *AA* 2.686; Asc. 43c. Pliny incidentally informs us that Italian women did not twirl their spindles as they walked along country roads (*NH* 28.28). For spindles (held, not used) in monumental art see Kampen 92. Expressions such as 'Gli piace lavorare' (she likes working), used by modern but old-fashioned women about good wives, imply that they are interested in sewing and knitting. I have not observed that Italian husbands place the same value on these skills.

[116] 3.754 = *CE* 492; 8.152 = *CE* 516; 6.29580.

[117] 6.9693 = *CE* 1136, 12652 = *CE* 995A. De Marchi, 'Le virtù della donna nelle iscrizioni sepolcrali latine', collects praise of the wife as helpmate. His most interesting examples are *bona conservatrix* (8.4067), *conservatrix* (6.7579), *iutrix optima* (10.354).

[118] For *consilio vel sim.* see 3.754 = *CE* 492, 6.9275, 19000, 8.152 = *CE* 516.6; *Laud. Tur.* 2.6, 8, cf. 4, 44, 56.

[119] 8.5804, 5834 = *CE* 636, 635.

[120] 8.11294, between Capsa and Sufetula.

conduct and good deeds are helpful and hard work and loyalty. These things made the freedman approved by his masters.' Thus Alexandria about Ursus, to whom she had been married for twenty-six years.[121] Or 'trading for many years on the Appian Way, a most faithful man above all men, whose fame is known for eternity, who lived more or less 68 years without stain, Statia Crescentina his wife to a very worthy and deserving husband'.[122] Faith, truthfulness, accessibility, compassion are credited to himself by Praecilius of Cirta.[123] Just occasionally, something more relevant to marital happiness occurs: 'I returned deposits, I always united friends, I disturbed no man's marriage-bed, no one will complain [of me], my dear wife lived happily and always honourably with me, I did what good I could, I always went away without a quarrel.'[124] A husband from Baetica claims that other husbands could scarcely match him for affection and goodness.[125]

Wives are praised for their lack of guile, for their dedication to their families, and for putting their husband first.[126] Perfect harmony was secured by the wife appropriating her husband's wishes—'et vellet, quod vellem, nollet quoque ac si ego nollem'[127]—and having no secrets from him: 'intima nulla ei quae non mihi nota fuere.'[128]

Agreement between husband and wife resulting from trust and sympathy may be called *concordia*, a happy state occasionally claimed on tombstones, especially in conjunction with long length of marriage.[129] Despite some suggestion in the evidence above and in the theorists that *concordia* is achieved by the subordination of the wife, the epitaphs also associate it with equality, as in 'concordes pari viximus ingenio' ('we lived harmonious with equal character').[130] Prima of Faventia is made by her husband to say that she was worthy of her companion (*sodalis*): 'one love remained and also equal,

[121] 3 suppl. 9623 = *CE* 627, Salonae.

[122] 6.9663.

[123] 8.7156 = *CE* 512.

[124] 14.2605 = *CE* 477, a freedman from Tusculum.

[125] 2.1399 = *CE* 1140.

[126] 6.28753 = *CE* 108: 'innocua simplex quae numquam serbabit dolum'; 11.3276 = *CE* 552, Sutri: 'intenta rebus, suis dedita vixit'; 6.1779 (a late epitaph): 'sibi maritum praeferens, Romam viro.'

[127] 3.754, cf. p. 992 and suppl. 7436 = *CE* 492 (the husband is the speaker). Cf. Sall. *BC* 20.4 and perhaps Cat. 8.7–9.

[128] 3.754. Cf. for the husband confiding in the wife 6.1779: 'arcana mentis cui reclusa credidi'; for joint secrets *Laud. Tur.* 2.4: 'Quid ego nunc interiora [no]stra et recondita consilia . . . eruam?'

[129] *CIL* 1.1220 = 6.33087 = *ILS* 8401 = *ILLRP* 365 = *CE* 1563; 2.3596, 6.9663, 10215, 13300, 18414, 21165, 26926 = *CE* 461, 37556, 9.1837 = *CE* 960, 3158. Cf. von Hesberg-Tonn 174–7. On the marital *Concordia Augustorum* paraded on Antonine coins see Kampen, 'Biographical narration and Roman funerary art' 52.

[130] 9.1837.

faithful life. If he grieved for anything, I joined myself too to his grief. I was equal, while I could be.'[131] Equality was essential for yoke-mates if they were to pull equally, and it is often evoked.[132]

Love joined the pair: they are therefore joined also in death.[133] The sharing of a tomb, or the expectation that the tomb will be shared when the surviving partner dies, is sometimes expressed as the sharing of a marriage-bed, a poignant comparison familiar from literature. The shared bed then becomes eternal and the partner who dies first may wait for the other there.[134] *Coniuges* express grief by regretting that they survive their partner, especially when they might have been expected to die first.[135] They wish they had died with or instead of him or her.[136] One wife is said to have vowed to die instead of her husband, and did so.[137] The surviving husband may want to remain unmarried and a widow may vow to preserve her bed inviolate.[138] Like the wife praised by Jerome[139] who said her dead husband was still alive for her, wives and husbands claim that their dead live on: 'hic aliis obiit, vivit libertae suavis patronus.'[140] A dead wife remains a wife for ever, *coniunx perpetua*.[141] A wife who dies first may be made to express satisfaction: 'viro et patrono placui et decessi prior' ('I pleased my husband and patron and died before him').[142] Grief often sounds deep and real.[143]

A striking example is provided by the virtuous silversmith from Cirta. A jolly man, who claims to have lived to 100, he says, 'Laughter and luxury I always delighted in, in the company of my dear friends, but such a life after the death of my chaste lady Valeria I did not find; while I could I had an enjoyable life with my holy wife.'[144]

---

[131] 11.654 = *CE* 491; Engström, *CLE* 218.1–3: 'Concordes animae quondam, cum vita maneret. | Moribus eximi(i)s pariles et amore iugali | sedibus his iunctae per saecula longa quiescunt.'

[132] e.g. 1.1217 = 6.30105 = *CE* 68, 11.1122 = *CE* 1273. *Compar* is used as a synonym for *coniunx* in a few epitaphs, e.g. 3.1895, 4185, 5.914, 6.10867, 25578, 36431.

[133] 11.1122 = *CE* 1273, Parma, 6.19008 = *CE* 1571.

[134] 11.1122, 6.11252, 12.5193.

[135] *Laud. Tur.* 2.51–3, 13.1597 = Engström, *CLE* 35, and see ch. 14 n. 94.

[136] 2.4427 = *CE* 542, 13.2205 = *CE* 444, 6.12652 = *CE* 995B.

[137] To be commemorated by him: 10.7563ff. = *CE* 1551.

[138] 6.25427, 35050, 8.16737a = *CE* 634, 11.1491; an idea remarkable by its absence from *Laud. Tur.*

[139] *Adv. Iovin.* 46 = 313B.

[140] 11.1273 = *CE* 1009: 'for others he has died, but for his freedwoman he lives, my delightful patron'; cf. 6.11082 = *CE* 1298, 19049 = *CE* 545.

[141] 6.19008 = *CE* 1571; cf. Apul. *M* 8.14.

[142] 6.5254. Cf. Tac. *Ag.* 44.4 on Agricola's fortune in leaving wife and daughter to survive him and other references cited by Ogilvie ad loc.

[143] e.g. 6.18817, 30127 = *CE* 490, 9.3968 = *CE* 498. For comparison, Henry Wotton's epigram 'On the death of Sir Albertus and Lady Morton' has the right lapidary quality: 'He first deceas'd—she, for a little, try'd | To live without him, lik'd it not and dy'd.' Cf. Hesberg-Tonn 163. [144] 8.7156 = *CE* 512.

A Roman husband who commemorates a wife he lost in the eighth month of pregnancy with their fourth child and who spelt out her name in the initials of a dozen lines of *senarii*; the painter whose wife had been the *educatrix* of a *clarus vir* and who was left to weep and lead a life of mourning (*vitam sordidam*) when she preceded him into the underworld after forty years of marriage; the wife who says that she and her husband were united equally in love as boy and girl and prematurely separated, so that she prays she may see him in her dreams and be allowed to rejoin him gently and swiftly: it is hard to see these as merely conventional expressions of grief.[145] When a survivor makes standard claims that they lived without a single quarrel[146] or says that the dead never gave him cause for grief except by dying,[147] then we may certainly doubt his accuracy in the specific instance, but we cannot doubt that *concordia* was the ideal and that many people were happy enough to look back on their own marriages as markedly successful and loving.

Plenty of inscriptions insist not so much on performance of duties as on love. Pleasantness, simplicity, and hard work are combined with *adfectio coniugalis*, which must mean affection here.[148] Survivors claim reciprocated love ('she blamelessly loved husband and home') and advertise their success: a freedwoman is praised for the love and devotion with which she ran her mistress's household and for having been lovable to her husbands; a mother is made to pray that her daughter will learn by her example to love her husband; a husband boasts 'This is to have loved one another.' Love is the sweet solace of life.[149]

Sometimes the language must be classified as romantic. A wife may be 'once upon a time my home, my hope, my only life' or 'the cause of my life'.[150] A widower is tormented by love like any elegiac poet.[151] From early times it was clearly part of the wife's role to become attached to her husband. Claudia's virtues begin with that—'suom maritum corde deilexit suo' ('she loved her husband with her heart') —before the mention of her successful child-bearing.[152] But even then the affectionate tone is present.

---

[145] 6.28753 = *CE* 108, 9792, 18817; Lattimore, *Themes in Greek and Latin epitaphs* 277.

[146] Examples listed by Lattimore, *Themes in Greek and Latin epitaphs* 279 n. 107.

[147] There are various formulae on the lines of *de quo/qua nihil (umquam) dolui nisi cum decessit/nisi mors/mortis/morte*: 6.5767, 8628, 8827, 9141, 9438, 9810, 15126, 26467a, 29054.

[148] 6.29580.

[149] 6.29580, 11252; Paci, 'Nuovi documenti epigrafici dalla necropoli romana di Corfinio' 46–64; 8.8123 = *CE* 1287, 10.1951, 8.7427 = *CE* 1288.

[150] 3.754 = *CE* 492, 6.14211 = *CE* 964, if I have rightly interpreted the shaky grammar.

[151] 6.17050 = *CE* 1301.

[152] 1.1211 = 6.15346 = *ILLRP* 973 = *CE* 52, Gracchan period.

Can this scattered evidence be taken as representative of ideas in the Roman West from about the time of the Gracchi to the early third century AD? More detailed studies could usefully be done. It must always be borne in mind that only a fraction of the epitaphs which were set up have reached us (and of those published I have here concentrated on those in the *Corpus inscriptionum latinarum* and have not undertaken a comprehensive survey) and that only a fraction of the population, even of the Roman citizen population, adopted the epigraphic habit and could afford to commemorate itself. Many epitaphs omit to specify marital relationship. Of those that do, most are composed in the briefest form, without epithets, not to mention verse eulogies. From this preliminary review, I venture the following hypotheses:

1. The passer-by who read an inscription was expected to accept as normal and desirable close family ties and a particularly close relationship between husband and wife, which make the married pair the basic unit of commemoration among the civilian population (except when children who died young were commemorated by parents or with a dead parent).[153]

2. The epithets given by either *coniunx* to the other tend to refer to his or her conduct in the relationship, though in the vaguest terms, or to the affection in which he was held. More specific descriptions of the wife's good qualities may concentrate on her household role and her conduct towards the family, while those of the husband may set him in the context of his peers (fellow merchants etc.).

3. Although some epithets suggest the subordinate status of the wife, these are balanced by similar usage about husbands. Most of the qualities praised are reciprocal. Wives are often thought of as partners (*sociae*),[154] which might but need not imply equality, and (like the occasional husband) as *compares*, which must imply equality, at least of love or effort.[155] As Lattimore puts it:

It is of course impossible to determine just what proportion of these decorous sayings express conviction, but at least we can conclude that they outline an ideal, and that this ideal concedes considerable importance to the position of women in the household. They are thought of not as subservient, but as free partners, and the success of the family is thought of as dependent in large measure on their qualities. Were this not generally the case, no

---

[153] See Saller and Shaw, 'Tombstones and family relations in the Principate: civilians, soldiers and slaves'.

[154] 2.3596; 6.30115: 'sociam tumulis', 38733 = *CLE* 323: 'uxsor sociata amore', 12845 'unanimi . . . sociata marito.' I have not found *socius* used of husbands.

[155] e.g. 5.1250, 1628, 1642, 2065, 6.10867, 38788.

Roman widower would have taken the trouble to write even false encomia on the gravestones.[156]

4. Despite the dignified language of tombs, which naturally leads to an emphasis on moral qualities which may impress the reader, there is also an insistence on the love which deserved the dedication and the love which inspired the dedicator to pay for it. This again is entirely consistent with the tradition observable in, say, English tombstones.

5. The expression of passionate grief and romantic love was not avoided by either sex.

6. Faithfulness to death was an accepted ideal. Some *coniuges* express revulsion at the idea of marrying again. But others clearly regard remarriage of widows and widowers as normal, and praise a woman for her virtuous love for first and second husband.[157] The former sentiment is inscribed when the survivor has not remarried, though he or she may have done so subsequently; the latter when remarriage had occurred.

The ideal of a monogamous union lasting until the death of one of the partners which Gordon Williams found important to the Romans is certainly there. The idea of wifely subordination which he discerned in the early evidence is there too. It continued as a thread in a rather more complex pattern later, but is modified by ideas about reciprocity and an almost equal partnership of husband and wife. This is seen very clearly in the *Laudatio 'Turiae'* which gives priority to love between husband and wife as the keystone of their lives.

How far does the literary evidence support this suggested web of ideas? There is plenty of evidence, so the following discussion must be selective. But I have deliberately looked for counter-evidence which would disprove my reconstruction. The series of interlacing hypotheses suggested by the epigraphic evidence may be reduced to two general questions. How far was there in Latin literature, 'contaminated' as it was from the beginning by Greek ideas, an inclination not to adopt the Aristotelian view of the necessary subordination of wives and even to go beyond the enlightened arguments of Pythagorean or Stoic philosophers on the moral equality of women? How far was Roman marriage ideally viewed as lifelong and based on love, which could be romantic?

6. Partnership

One of the key ideas in Latin literature on the relationship of husband and wife seems to be *societas*. Community of property and

---

[156] *Themes in Greek and Latin epitaphs*, 180.   [157] 6.7873 = *CE* 1024 is a good example.

partnership in life (*koinōnia biou*) had been a philosophical point, but the Romans give it more emphasis.[158] Sallust was contemptuous of polygamous societies in which no wife had the position of equal partner, but all were held equally cheap.[159] Ovid frequently uses the idea of partnership. *Socius* is a favourite adjective, applicable to any sexual union but especially to the marriage-bed.[160] Wife and husband are joined by *socialia foedera*.[161] The wife is *socia* and the husband *socius* or *socius tori*[162] and they enjoy *socialia iura* and *socialis amor*.[163] Their years together are *sociales* or *socii anni*.[164]

Societas was the appropriate word to describe the position of a wife who entered her husband's family and took his status: 'a wife is a woman who is bestowed on a man in marriage and comes into partnership of life.'[165] The wife was to share all her husband's goods.[166] She was a partner in his good fortune or bad: she could share his anxieties and labours.[167] Partnership might be far-reaching: just as a wife in the Principate took her husband's rank and might arrange *societas omnium bonorum* (community of property) with him, so she might be considered to arrogate to herself a share in his social status and political power.[168]

Sharing and partnership are often linked with the philosophers' idea that *coniuges* should hold their property in common.[169] We have already looked at the husband endowing the wife with his goods. But it was logically also held that the wife should share her property with

---

[158] Cf. Stob. 4.22.1.18, quoting Gaius *On behalf of Lucilla*, for the view that *koinōnia* increases love.

[159] *BJ* 80.6–7; cf. Tac. *G* 18.1.

[160] *Am.* 3.6.82, *AA* 1.566, *F* 2.729; cf. *sociare cubilia*: *M* 10.635, *Her.* 3.109; 'mihi sociatam foedere lecti': *Ibis* 15.

[161] *Her.* 4.17; *M* 14.380.

[162] *M* 1.620, 8.521, 10.268, 14.678, *P* 2.8.29.

[163] *Am.* 3.11.45, *M* 7.800, *Tr.* 5.14.28, *P* 3.1.73.

[164] *Am.* 1.9.6, *Tr.* 2.161, *Her.* 2.33.

[165] *Decl. min.* 247.2: 'Uxor est quae femina viro nuptiis collocata in societatem vitae venit.' Cf. *CJ* 9.32.4 pr., Gordian, AD 242: 'Adversus uxorem, quae socia rei humanae atque divinae domum suscipitur, mariti diem suum functi successores expilatae hereditatis crimen intendere non possunt.'

[166] *Decl. min.* 247.

[167] Livy 1.9.14: 'in societate fortunarum omnium civitatisque et . . . liberorum'; Lucan 2.346–7, Marcia to Cato: 'Non me laetorum sociam rebusque secundis | accipis: in curas venio partemque laborum'; Tac. *G* 18: 'mulier . . . admonetur venire se laborum periculorumque sociam', *A* 3.15.2, Plancina to Piso: 'sociam se cuiuscumque fortunae et si ita ferret comitem exitii promittebat', ibid. 12.5.5, speech of Claudius: 'coniugem prosperis dubiisque sociam, cui cogitationes intimas, cui parvos liberos tradat.' Cf. Plut. *Brut.* 13.4, *QR* 1.

[168] *D* 34.1.16.3; Tac. *A* 12.37.6 (hostile, of Agrippina the Younger); cf. Polyb. 31.26.3 (of Aemilia Scipionis); Dio 55.16.2 (of Livia).

[169] Cic. *Off.* 1.54: 'una domus, communia omnia', etc. Clear distinction of property might be impracticable even for lawyers (*D* 29.5.1.5).

her husband, as she had done when *in manu*. Martial praises Nigrina for such old-fashioned generosity.[170]

A similar idea is expressed by *consors*. Quintilian combines *socia tori, vitae consors*.[171] The word was originally used for equal sharers in an inheritance. Quintilian's phrase is echoed by Modestinus' definition of marriage as 'coniunctio maris et feminae et consortium omnis vitae, divini et humani iuris communicatio'.[172] The idea must have been common. Tacitus had already expanded it in the phrase 'consortia rerum secundarum adversarumque'.[173] *Consortium* in late and Christian writers becomes a synonym for *matrimonium*; *consors* retains more of its specific sense.

The idea of comradeship or companionship, evoked by Tacitus in his ironical account of Plancina, is sometimes associated with these ideas. In a passionate defence of his right to choose a wife to his own taste, whose soul will be joined to his, a young man in a rhetorical exercise refers to her as a companion in toils, anxieties, and cares ('comitem laborum, sollicitudinum, curarum').[174] A good wife accompanied her husband wherever he went, heroically braving Arctic conditions.[175]

7. Agreement

An ideal marriage was ensured by harmony, *concordia*, or even identified with it.[176] Concord was the result of a balance of forces, and it took two to produce it.[177] The husband of the anonymous *laudata* thought that theirs was well known.[178] Tacitus attributes it to his parents-in-law and links it with their mutual affection and habit of each putting the other first, though even more credit was due to

[170] 4.75: 'O felix animo, felix, Nigrina marito | atque inter Latias gloria prima nurus: | te patrios miscere iuvat cum coniuge census, | gaudentem socio participique viro.'

[171] *Decl. min.* 376.2. Cf. Aug. *de bono coniugali* 3.3 on 'naturalem in diverso sexu societatem', referring chiefly to sexual intercourse.

[172] *D* 23.2.1. For the huge modern bibliography on this passage see Robleda, *El matrimonio en derecho romano* 66 ff.

[173] *A* 3.34.8.

[174] *Decl. min.* 257.5.

[175] Stat. *S* 5.1.127 ff.; Ov. *Tr.* 1.3.79 ff. For soft lovers to brave the cold is a topos: e.g. Cic. *Cat.* 2.23; Verg. *E* 10.23.

[176] e.g. Plaut. *Amph.* 475; Cic. *Clu.* 12; Cat. 64.336, 66.87; VM 2.1.6; Stat. *S* 1.2.240, 5.1.44; Pliny *Epp.* 4.19.5; Mart. 4.13; Juv. 6.231 with Courtney ad loc.; *CJ* 6.25.5.1, AD 257; Isid. *Etym.* 9.7.9; cf. Apul. *M* 9.27; Dio Prusias 38.15: 'What is a good marriage but the *homonoia* of the husband to his wife?' Conversely, a bad marriage involved discord (*Decl. min.* 301.20). For the building of a Temple of Concord by Livia, 'sola toro magni digna reperta Iovis', (Ov. *F* 1.650), see Flory, 'Sic exempla parantur: Livia's Shrine to Concordia and the Porticus Liviae', with extensive bibliography.

[177] Plaut. *Amph.* 962; Cic. *A* 8.6.4; Mart. 4.13.7–8: 'Candida perpetuo reside, Concordia, lecto, | tamque pari semper sit Venus aequa iugo.'

[178] *Laud. Tur.* 2.34.

Domitia Decidiana than to Agricola.[179] A harmonious marriage was
not lightly to be broken up by outsiders. Antoninus Pius forbade a
paterfamilias to impose a divorce on a harmonious couple.[180] *Concordia* seems to be demonstrated by outward signs that a couple are
getting on well together and to be strongly linked with affection.
Suetonius points out that Tiberius at first lived harmoniously and with
mutual love with Julia: his later alienation was marked by his ceasing
to share her bed.[181] An agreeable wife may be termed *concors*,
concordans, or *bene conveniens*, which seems to have much the same
sense.[182] An alienated *coniunx* was *discors*.[183] *Longa concordia* was
what you wished a bridal couple.[184]

A cognate idea is expressed by describing the couple as *unanimi*, of
one mind. One inscription describes a couple as 'loving in marriage
and equal in unanimity'. Catullus used the word to evoke the
harmony proper in bride and bridegroom consummating their licit
passion.[185]

The ideal expressed by *societas*, *concordia*, and related concepts is
that of a close and harmonious partnership based on affection and
co-operation. Once a couple achieves it, they are closely bound and
others should not come between them. There may be some tendency
to put more responsibility on the wife, for accommodating herself to
her husband, but there is also, as in the inscriptions, an insistence on
reciprocity. Romans recognized that the marital relationship may
become more firmly established with time.[186] Or discord may supplant

---

[179] Tac. *Ag.* 6.1: 'Vixeruntque mira concordia, per mutuam caritatem et in vicem se
anteponendo, nisi quod in bona uxore tanto maior laus, quanto in mala plus culpae est.'
[180] *D* 24.1.32.19, 43.30.1.5; Paul *S* 5.6.15.   [181] *Tib.* 7.3.
[182] Tac. *A* 3.33.1; Afran. *com.* 53; Suet. *Tib.* 7.2; *D* 24.1.32.19: 'concordantibus viro et
uxore.'
[183] Cat. 64.379–80 (of a girl who has stopped sleeping with her husband); Aug. *c. Faust.* (of a
husband).   [184] *Decl. min.* 291.5; Cat. 66.87; Mart. 11.53.7–8: 'Sic placeat superis ut
coniuge gaudeat uno | et semper natis gaudeat illa tribus.'
[185] 6.12845: 'unanimi Calpurniano sociata marito, 31711: 'Celsino nupta univira unanimis',
10.7643: 'coniugio amantes et unanimitate pares'; Cat. 66.80.
[186] The most memorable expression of this is Lucr. 4.1278ff., following straight on his
discussion of sexual desire and reproduction, though he is not talking only of conjugal love:
'Nec divinitus interdum Venerisque sagittis | deteriore fit ut forma muliercula ametur. | Nam
facit ipsa suis interdum femina factis | morigerisque modis et munde corpore culto, | ut facile
insuescat [te] secum degere vitam. | Quod superest, consuetudo concinnat amorem'; VM 4.6
pr.: 'A placido et leni adfectu ad aeque honestum, verum aliquanto ardentiorem et concita-
tiorem pergam legitimique amoris quasi quasdam imagines non sine maxima veneratione
contemplandas lectoris oculis subiciam, valenter inter coniuges stabilitae fidei opera percur-
rens, ardua imitatu, ceterum cognosci utilia, quia excellentissima animadvertenti ne mediocria
quidem praestare ruburi oportet esse'; *Decl. min.* 257.6: 'copulatos iam diu diducis animos.' Cf.
for the difficulty of late bonding Pliny *Epp.* 8.18.8, on the wife of Domitius Tullus: 'parum
decore secuta matrimonium videbatur divitis senis ita perditi morbo, ut esse taedio posset
uxori, quam iuvenis sanusque duxisset.' Children might strengthen a harmonious relationship (*D* 43.30.1.5).

concord. Supposing that concord is maintained, the hope traditional
at weddings that the couple may live happily until old age and the
death of one or the other can be restated with even more force, as in
Statius' poem to his wife.[187]

8. Romantic Feelings

Is there a romantic quality in the conjugal love expressed in literature? The love of two people who are already married cannot fulfil
all the features which have been defined by Niall Rudd in a convincing
article as characteristically romantic.[188] These are love at first sight,
accompanied by physical symptoms, idealization of the beloved, the
effect of love on the rest of the lover's character, the desire for
marriage and for love which lasts to the grave or beyond, the
postponement or interruption of physical consummation, which is the
ultimate aim. Rudd finds enough examples in fiction to show that
these ideas were attractive to the Romans. He points out that poets
occasionally permit romantic love to married people and that
Plutarch's *Amatorius* is a defence of romantic love in marriage. If we
take his position as our starting-point, I believe that it will be possible
to show a romantic element in some Romans' treatment of actual
marriages, particularly their own. We may expect, to judge from the
ideas which emerge from the inscriptions, that Romans were capable
of idealizing their partners, that they could desire a lifelong love, and
that the sexual relationship was an important part of their union.

It will be useful at this point to turn to several specific examples and
to direct our attention both to the subordinate or other position of the
wife in the relationship and to the romantic or unromantic quality of
the feelings expressed.

9. Husbands and Wives in Literature

Let us first look at some of the few remaining documents which
illustrate a marriage in action—letters between husband and wife.
Our best literary examples of letters between husband and wife are
the twenty-four letters from Cicero to Terentia, full of affectionate
phrases and often discussing practical matters, on which she was to
make up her own mind.

Take as an example the series of four letters from Cicero to

---

[187] e.g. Mart. 4.13.9–10: 'diligat illa senem quondam, sed et ipsa marito | tum quoque, cum
fuerit, non videatur anus.' Stat. *S* 3.5.22 ff.: 'Etenim tua (nempe benigna | quam mihi sorte
Venus iunctam florentibus annis | servat et in senium) tua quae me vulnere primo | intactum
thalamis et adhuc iuvenile vagantem | fixisti, tua frena libens docilisque recepi, 106 ff.: '[sc.
tellus] creavit | me tibi, me socium longos astrinxit in annos.'
[188] 'Romantic love in classical times?'.

Terentia in 58 BC.[189] Writing just before he left Italy for exile at Thessalonica, Cicero explained that his letters were not as frequent as they could have been, because he became upset when he wrote to her or read her letters. If his fate is unalterable, he wants only to die in her arms. Ought he to ask her to join him? No, because she is not well enough for the journey. But how can he manage without her? She must look after his interests in Rome, but if things get hopeless, then she had better come to him. 'One thing I do know, if I have you I won't feel that everything is over for me.' She must decide what to do about their children. Then he goes on to discuss finances: has she been able to protect her property? She has been encouraging him in her letters to be brave and hope for the best. He in return encourages her to bear up and to remember that their honour is uncompromised. He suffers more for her wretchedness than for his own.

In his next surviving letter, five months later, he is still weeping when he writes to Terentia and his daughter, whom he wanted always to be happy, and whom he tried to make happy. He knows that Terentia is managing everything with love and courage, which does not surprise him, but he is sorry that she has to relieve his suffering by such suffering of her own. 'Alas, my light, my longing, to whom everyone always went for help, to think that you now are so harassed, brought so low in tears and mourning, and that this is happening through my fault, since I saved others so that we might perish!'[190] Then he goes on to discuss their house (which had been demolished) and to tell Terentia she should not be spending her own money on his behalf. She is carrying the whole load, and must be careful of her health. He will do what she asks and will stay put where he is.

A few weeks later, he again writes about the reports he is receiving from all sides about her courage and praises her for her bravery, loyalty, goodness, and kindness.[191] He is now hoping to be recalled, and looks forward to her embrace and to 'getting back' her and himself. Again, he begs her not to raise money by selling her own property: it might be all that their son has to depend on.[192]

In the last letter, he has heard from her and nearly ruined her letter by crying over it, because although their calamity is shared, it is all his

[189] F 14.4, 2, 1, 3.

[190] F 14.2, esp. 2: 'A te quidem omnia fieri fortissime et amantissime video, nec miror, sed maereo casum eius modi ut tantis tuis miseriis meae miseriae subleventur. Nam ad me P. Valerius, homo officiosus, scripsit, id quod ego maximo cum fletu legi, quem ad modum a Vestae ad Tabulam Valeriam ducta esses. Hem, mea lux, meum desiderium, unde omnes opem petere solebant, te nunc, mea Terentia, sic vexari, sic iacere in lacrimis et sordibus, idque fieri mea culpa, qui ceteros servavi ut nos periremus.' Ovid has *lux mea* in a similar context (*Tr.* 3.3.52).

[191] F 14.1.1: 'Te ista virtute, fide, probitate, humanitate.'   [192] 14.1.5.

fault.[193] He is ashamed of having let his good wife and adorable children down. He keeps calling up a mental picture of them.[194] Yet again, he is following her advice about how to approach other people.[195] He hopes she will be able to join him if she achieves his recall, but he does not want her to come at once.[196] She is dearer than anything in the world to him.

Now, Cicero had an ulterior motive: it was very much to his own advantage to keep Terentia working for him. But it is impossible to feel that these letters are insincere, though the old orator cannot help writing beautifully about his griefs. He scarcely puts a foot wrong. Only once did Terentia apparently think he had criticized her—about her co-operation with his brother Quintus.[197] He manages the emotional side of the relationship much better than with Quintus, who was hurt because Cicero, in his misery, had avoided meeting him.[198] The Roman ideal of partnership (which is not explicitly mentioned) comes out in Cicero's careful identification of their interests.[199] When he blames himself he uses the first-person singular, otherwise he usually insists on the first-person plural.

Letters to other people at about this time mention Terentia with great respect and affection. She is his unfortunate and faithful wife, whom he wanted to take with him, his unhappy wife, who has to bear more than woman ever did.[200] Later letters to her continue to address her in a lover's language, to sympathize with her, to praise her, confide in her.[201] The abrupt notes of 47 BC, about the time when he begins to complain about her to Atticus, can to some extent be excused as a possibly partial selection of hasty communications. They still express concern for her health.[202] But the long-standing marriage was about to end in divorce, and the tone of the final grudging and lifeless notes is in sad contrast with his earlier effusions. It is apparent from these letters that Cicero treats Terentia as an equal partner, with her own talents and responsibilities, and that he was capable from time to time of romantic emotion.

We have three letters from Augustus to Livia, all dealing with her grandson Claudius, quoted by Suetonius.[203] They make it clear that extensive family consultation took place on all important matters.

[193] 14.3.1.   [194] 14.3.2, cf. 2.3, 3.5.
[195] 14.3.3.   [196] 14.3.5.   [197] 14.1.4.
[198] QF 1.3.
[199] Cf. SHA Avid. 9–11 (alleged letters between M. Aurelius and Faustina).
[200] QF 1.3.3, A 3.19.2, 23.5.
[201] F 14.5.1, 7, 8, 12, 14, 16, 18.
[202] E 14.20–4. On 14.20 (449) TP quote Long's observation that 'a gentleman would write a more civil letter to his housekeeper'.
[203] Cl. 4.

Augustus, who from time to time in these extracts addresses his wife as *mea Livia*, carries out a commission from her to talk to her son Tiberius about what line they should all take about public appearances by Claudius. Is he to be allowed to follow a public career or is he unfit? Livia is to show the letter to 'our Antonia'—her daughter-in-law and Augustus' niece, the boy's mother. The first-person plural is used frequently. The letters are tactful, since Livia was more closely related to Claudius than her husband was, but Augustus makes it clear that he is involved and concerned, as a kinsman and as emperor. The letters fit in with what we know from other sources about Livia's influence. When he was going to have an important conversation with his wife, Augustus followed a practice he had adopted for administrative business in general: he wrote down what he wanted to say.[204] The affectionate tone of these letters is striking, although it is less emotional than that which Cicero used to Terentia under the stress of his exile.

We must also add Ovid's verse epistles to his wife from exile, which come close to those of Cicero.[205] Although, since they were meant for publication, he was more guarded than Cicero needed to be, his poems show that it was acceptable to express intense emotion towards a wife and dependence on her loyalty, judgment, and help. She is his light, his excellent or dear or dutiful or loving wife.[206] Although they are both still alive, he is deprived of her for ever.[207] She is enshrined in his heart, he thinks of her daily.[208] He pictures their grief at their parting, he thinks of her burying his ashes just outside Rome, he thinks of her sufferings as the wife of an exile, and he tortures himself with the thought that she may be ashamed to be married to him.[209] She shows true piety and *socialis amor*.[210] Like Terentia, she worked hard in his interests.[211]

Pliny's letters about and to his wife, like Ovid's, were meant for publication. What we have is an edited version of the letter originally sent, with strict excision of 'extraneous' material, so that each letter is

---

[204] Suet. *DA* 84.2: 'Sermones quoque cum singulis atque etiam cum Livia sua graviores non nisi scriptos et e libello habebat, ne plus minusve loqueretur ex tempore.'

[205] Nagle, *The poetics of exile. Program and polemic in the* Tristia *and* Epistulae ex Ponto *of Ovid*, draws up a list of parallel passages from Ovid's and Cicero's letters from exile. I am not convinced that Ovid is modelling himself closely on Cicero. But the romantic treatment of his wife is similar. Nagle also (pp. 43–54) shows that Ovid adapts traditional elegiac motifs previously used to mistresses.

[206] *Tr.* 3.3.52, 55, 3.4B.53, 1.2.37, 1.3.17.

[207] *Tr.* 1.3.63.

[208] *Tr.* 1.6.1 ff., 3.3.15 ff., cf. 3.4B.59 ff.

[209] *Tr.* 1.3.17 ff., 3.3.65 ff., 4.10.73–4, 4.3, 5.11.

[210] *Tr.* 5.14.29–30.

[211] *Tr.* 1.6.5 ff.; 3.1.

an essay on one topic. This makes it difficult to tell, for instance, whether the letters to Calpurnia's aunt and grandfather announcing her miscarriage, which appear to us unsympathetic towards her, though much concerned about the disappointment and worry caused to her relations, may not have included in their original form more sorrow for her pain and disappointment. But cutting may not be the cause. Pliny often adopts poses which would appear proper to his readers (and, as Sherwin-White points out, to his grandfather-in-law). Here the self-controlled *paterfamilias* seems uppermost. For our purposes of investigating general mores rather than an individual's character, the evidence of the letters that this was a creditable attitude must be taken seriously.[212] Early in the marriage, Pliny had reported to the aunt on her niece's progress in warm terms. Calpurnia was intelligent and a careful housekeeper; she loved Pliny, which proved her chastity. Because she loved him, she had taken up the study of literature. He thought there was an excellent prospect of perpetual and increasing *concordia* between them. Pliny shows that he was very well aware of the great age difference between himself and his third wife. But in the earliest letter of all, promising a joint visit to her grandfather, he speaks of himself and Calpurnia very much as a couple, using always the first-person plural.[213] When we reach the letters to Calpurnia herself, we find him worried about her health. He has sent her to Campania to convalesce, while business keeps him in Rome. He asks for at least one letter a day, for it is an anxious business to have no news of someone you love ardently. She replies that only his letters comfort her for his absence. He says that he keeps rereading hers, but that is torture as well as pleasure and makes him burn with the desire to be with her and hear her conversation.[214] Finally, in his third letter, during an extension of their unaccustomed separation Pliny echoes the theme of the excluded lover. He tells his wife how he spends the night awake imagining her; he cannot stop himself going into her room, at the times he usually visits her, though he knows he will not find her there and he has to go away sick at heart, like a man forbidden the door.[215]

There is also a less illuminating verse letter from Statius to his wife. He praises her for her unshakeable faithfulness, her concern for him, her pride in his achievements, her care for her daughter, and talks in

---

[212] *Epp.* 8.10, 11; Sherwin-White, *Pliny* 459.   [213] *Epp.* 4.1.   [214] *Epp.* 6.4, 6.7.

[215] *Epp.* 7.5. Cf. Lucr. 4.1061–2: 'Nam si abest quod ames, praesto simulacra tamen sunt | illius et nomen dulce observatur ad auris'; Ov. *Tr.* 3.3.17ff. See Sherwin-White's comments (*Pliny* 407): 'The three letters are a valuable document for social history: they blend together, for the first time in European literature, the role of husband and lover, and like other letters of Pliny cast a favourable light on the attitude of his social equals to marriage.' I agree, except that I think something of the same attitude is already present in Cicero.

romantic terms of how she is his first love and he was made for her and
bound to her for long years. In the most remarkable passage he
rejoices that she has broken him in like a horse (a reversal of the usual
procedure).[216]

It is impossible in any of these letters from husbands to wives to find
the domineering tone that Rome's original patriarchal institutions
might lead us to expect. Cicero and Ovid appeal to their wives for
moral courage. Augustus, despite his constitutional position, treats
Livia as a close colleague and trusted adviser.[217] Pliny, who, unlike
Cicero and Augustus in their genuinely private letters, does not
discuss business with his wife[218] (but this might be literary propriety,
not a reflection of his practice), is overtly romantic, though his
attitude is conditioned by the great difference in age between him and
his child bride.

We may add Quintilian, who lost his wife, mother of two sons,
before her nineteenth birthday. 'I was so cast down by this misfortune
that now no good luck can make me happy. For, because she
possessed every virtue a woman can have, she brought [sc. by her
death] to her husband an incurable grief, and because she died at such
a youthful age, particularly compared with mine, this too can be
counted among the griefs of childlessness.'[219] Or there is an outsider's
evidence on the bereavement of Macrinus, who lost a wife of old-
fashioned virtue, who lived with him thirty-nine years without quarrel
or offence, showing him all the reverence which she herself deserved.
All her assortment of virtues made her loss worse, though Macrinus
had the consolation of a long marriage, which Quintilian lacked.[220]
We should not linger on the effusions of Statius, except to note that he
could say that it was a pleasure to love a wife while she was alive, but a
religion to love her when dead. Abascantus' passionate mourning for
Priscilla was approved by Domitian and the public.[221]

Among poetic treatments of marital interaction we might cite a
letter composed by Propertius from a wife to her soldier husband (in
which she promises a chastity which, like Penelope's, will make all his
hardships worth while).[222] A more striking example is Lucan's
reconstruction of the last anguished conversations between Pompey

---

[216] S 3.5, esp. 22–8.

[217] I note in passing that Augustus used to get annoyed when his children or grandchildren
called him 'Lord' (Suet. DA 53.1). The feminine equivalent, domina, was the formal way for a
husband to address his wife, for instance in legal documents, though he might equally well call
her 'my dear wife'. (D 32.41 pr.: 'domina uxor', 36.1.59.2: 'uxor carissima'; 6.11458: 'Aliae
Pyriliae dominae uxori Iulius Hercules'; cf. 11252: 'domine Oppi marite.')

[218] Sherwin-White, Pliny 359.

[219] Inst. 6 pr. 4–11. The two boys died at 5 and 9.

[220] Pliny Epp. 8.5.

[221] Stat. S 5 pr. and 1.37 ff.   [222] Prop. 3.12.

and his young wife Cornelia before Pharsalus. She woos him with caresses and kisses until he tells her of his forebodings and his plan to ensure, by sending her away, that the best part of himself survives. She then faints with the promptitude of a heroine in *Love and freindship*, but recovers to upbraid him for not understanding her *fides* and her willingness to take her chance with him. She becomes frenzied, she cannot bear to embrace him or say farewell. Finally, she faints again and is taken away. Lucan then describes in detail her feelings and memories in her newly widowed bed. The scene makes a dramatic ending to a book. After Pompey's defeat, the last interview is equally harrowing. When he is murdered, she regrets that she cannot perform his funeral, she wants to die of grief. But she carries Pompey in her heart and instead of her husband she loves her grief.[223] Lucan attributes intense emotion and its physical expression to a man in his late fifties at his fifth marriage and his much younger but still twice-married wife. The treatment is not to be sharply distinguished from that of star-crossed lovers elsewhere in poetry, though Pompey and Cornelia display less self-control than Dido and Aeneas.

Even prose authors relate circumstantial details illustrating conjugal romanticism. Suetonius tells a sad story of Tiberius encountering the wife he had been compelled to divorce and following her like any disconsolate lover.[224] Examples could no doubt be multiplied, but these should suffice to prove our hypothesis.

Two other features of the Roman tradition must be mentioned. Falling in love is (at least from the time of Augustus) proper for a couple who are to marry each other. Arruntius Stella has recourse to gifts, prayers, tears, and the complaints of an excluded lover before he wins Violentilla.[225] Rhetoricians take account of the passionate love of the newly married.[226] Immature people are particularly inclined to fall violently in love when they are legitimately married.[227] Marriage would only last if both desired it from the start: 'Matrimonium vero tum perpetuum est si mutua voluntate iungitur.' Quintilian here comes close to saying that falling in love is a prerequisite. Conversely, people who are forced into marriage rapidly tire of each other. Worse still if there is a disparity of age.[228] Rhetoricians could argue the opposite: the statements collected here will represent *an* acceptable view of things, not the only one. But 'all love is great, still greater for an acknowledged *coniunx*'.[229]

---

[223] 5.725 ff., 8.40 ff., 577 ff., 9.55 ff. Cf. Plut. *Pomp.* 74–5 (where fainting is again a motif), 78.4, 80.6.
[224] *Tib.* 7.3. The melodramatic scenario involving a suicide pact on which Ovid declaimed (Sen. *Contr.* 2.2, esp. 9 ff.) is based on the idea of romantic love between husband and wife.
[225] Stat. *S* 1.2.   [226] Sen. *Contr.* 2.2.
[227] *Decl. min.* 286.10.   [228] *Decl. min.* 376.2, 306.18–19.   [229] Prop. 4.3.49.

The second feature is the desired permanence of the marriage. In the declamation just quoted, the young husband links mutual love with 'eternity'. A marriage which the couple wants will be *perpetuum*. Catullus, in equating his affair with marriage, had prayed that his relationship with Lesbia might be *perpetuum*, 'that we may be allowed to perpetuate for the whole of life this eternal treaty of hallowed love'. Cicero hoped to die in the arms of his wife.[230]

Not all the features which occur in later romantic literature are prominent or present in Roman descriptions of conjugal affection. Romans had long enjoyed comedies in which young men fell in love at first sight and sometimes wished to marry the object of their passion. But reciprocal feelings in the breasts of young ladies could not be represented on the comic stage. Epithalamia, produced by outsiders, will describe attractiveness rather than personal feelings. Autobiographical accounts of pre-marital states of mind are simply lacking. So we can only guess about whether Romans fell in love before marriage, pined for sight of the beloved, or chafed at the postponement of consummation with the romantic fervour described in some later literature. But there is some indication that personal liking, even between young people at a first marriage, was sometimes thought desirable. It may be that individualism had grown stronger in the first century BC,[231] that the search for satisfaction in a passionate sexual relationship had consequently become more common, and that the romantic ideas associated with extra-marital affairs had been transferred to *iustae coniuges*. The hypothesis about the growth of individualism is based on the introduction of new literary genres, so that its implied statement about the second century and earlier is an *e silentio* argument. But the behaviour of politicians in self-aggrandizement, display, and competition supports it. The interplay between ideals in marital and extra-marital love is complex. There is reason to suppose that marital ideals had an impact on the conception of a grand passion or of a faithful mistress or a good-hearted courtesan, as we can see in Plautus, Terence, Catullus, and the elegists. The romanticism of star-crossed illicit lovers was then transferred back to marriage partners. The essential Roman theme was that marriage was perpetual until death. It demanded loyalty, sexual fidelity (at least from the wife), respect, and consideration for each other. The well-spring of these was love. A successful marriage was happy; its interruption by death caused grief. The expression of passion for an idealized *coniunx* is not confined to epitaphs or epic, but is a theme in all types of literature.

---

[230] Cat. 109.5–6; Cic. *F* 14.4.1; cf. Ov. *Tr.* 3.3.37ff.; Tac. *Ag.* 45.5.
[231] Hopkins, *DR* 79ff.

Romantic love in literature is traditionally linked with Alexandrian poetry and especially the narrative of the love of Jason and Medea by Apollonius (which led to marriage of a sort). But it is hard to rule out a romantic tinge in Homer's loving Andromache with her controlled and factual statement of what Hector means to her, or his faithful and prudent Penelope, to whom Odysseus struggles to return despite the attractions of Calypso, Circe, or Nausicaa. The Romans were not the first to romanticize marriage. But the tendency appears among them more strongly than among the classical Greeks.

A recent study of marriage in England has, with attractive argument, pushed back the Anglo-American idea of romantic love, the primary importance of the emotional relationship between man and wife, to at least the early thirteenth century.[232] The bases of conjugal love are found in two principles, that the conjugal relationship replaced all others and that husband and wife were companions and equal partners. The first is put in a form which echoes biblical language: 'a man hath so great a love to his wife that for her sake he adventureth himself to all perils; and setteth her afore his mother's love; for he dwelleth with his wife, and forsaketh father and mother.'[233] The second is close to what has been argued for Roman *societas*. Much of the more formal expression in medieval and early modern English thinking on this subject could be paralleled in the classical texts which I have discussed. This is not to argue for an unbroken transmission from pagan Rome to the encyclopaedia of Bartholomaeus Anglicus. Yet scholars and gentlemen read Ovid and (in the sixteenth century) Plutarch.

In conclusion, Rome's particular (though not entirely original) contribution to the ideology of marriage was the ideal of the wife's faithfulness to one man, the eternity of the bond, and the partnership of the couple. Subordination of the wife, I would argue, was not essential or important by the time of Cicero.[234]

---

[232] MacFarlane 174–208. His chapter adopts much the same approach as mine, arguing from moralists and philosophers, literature and letters. The hypothesis, like mine, is controversial.
[233] Bartholomaeus Anglicus, quoted by Macfarlane 159, 183.
[234] See also Bradley, 'Ideals of marriage in Suetonius' *Caesares*'.

9
Sexual Relations

Casta est quam nemo rogavit.

The chaste woman is the one nobody has asked.

(Ovid *Amores* 1.8.43)

And the wildest dreams of Kew are the facts of Khatmandhu,
And the crimes of Clapham chaste in Martaban.

(Kipling, 'In the Neolithic Age')

I. REGULATION

We have already discussed the positive theories of conjugal virtues and the prominence given to wifely fidelity. It has also been suggested that the marital relationship was expected by ordinary Romans to give scope for both love and sexual expression. The task of this chapter is to explore attitudes to the extra-marital sexual activity of either partner during a marriage. The object is to cast light on sexual relations between husband and wife.

1. Terminology

Something about attitudes may be deduced from vocabulary and construction. The technical language is more robustly native and more sharply defined when it describes the infidelity of a wife. The verb *adulterare* seems to have been prior to the abstract noun *adulterium* and the nouns which describe the agents, *adulter* and *adultera*. The active verb is generally used with the man as subject, either absolutely or with the woman as object.[1] But the man may be passive or the woman active.[2] The transitive verb, however, seems

---

[1] The verb is not common in ordinary prose, though, especially in a metaphorical sense, it became a favourite with Christian writers. Absolutely: Cato ap. Gell. 10.23.5; Cic. *Off.* 1.128; transitive: Suet. *DA* 67; *D* 48.9.5; woman subject of passive: Suet. *DJ* 6; *Decl. min.* 325 arg.; *D* 48.5.30.4. Tert. *de pudic.* 4.4: 'semet ipsum adulterat' extends the range.

[2] Man subject of passive verb: Cato ap. Gell. 10.23.5. Woman subject, verb absolute: Sen. *Contr.* 7.6.2; Caper ap. Keil, *Grammatici latini* vii.107.10: 'adultera quae adulterat.'

not to occur with the man as object in classical usage. The effect of the relationship on the man is of little concern to anyone apart from the moral philosopher, except on interesting occasions when he is caught in the act and risks injurious treatment.

'Adulterium (est) cum aliena uxore domi coire: an et in lupanari?' ('It is adultery to have sexual intercourse with somebody else's wife at home: can the word also be applied to sex [with her] in a brothel?') Quintilian is talking of agreed definitions and possible extensions. He has already denied that *adulterium* is the correct word for what goes on in a brothel.[3] The word was derived from *alter* or *altera* (another of two), since the adulterer took himself to another woman and the adulteress to another man.[4] This etymology means that adultery is strictly only committed by a person who has a prior bond to someone else. While the grammarians identify the *adulter* with the married man, the word is more generally used of any illicit lover and especially of the lover of a married woman. Papinian points out that the Julian Law on adultery used the words *stuprum* (illicit intercourse) and *adulterium* indifferently, but he says that strictly *adulterium* is committed with a married woman and that the word comes from the fact that she conceives a child by a man other than her husband. *Stuprum* is committed with a virgin, widow, or divorcee.[5] It is interesting that he stresses the production of a bastard, not the sexual infidelity of the wife. *Adulterare* was early used to mean 'to practise counterfeiting'[6] so perhaps the risk of counterfeit children was an idea present from early on together with the idea, suggested by the transitive use of the verb, that the wife was corrupted, adulterated, or made false.[7]

Comedy, satire and colloquial writing used the convenient and less portentous Greek words *moechus/a* for adulterers, along with several associated verbs.[8]

Despite the grammarians' definition, the juristic usage is closer to

[3] *Inst.* 7.3.10, cf. 7.3.9.

[4] Festus 20L: 'adulter et adultera dicuntur, quia et ille ad alteram et haec ad alterum se conferunt.' Cf. Aug. *Serm.* 51.22: 'non eat ille ad alteram et illa ad alterum: unde appellatum est adulterium quasi ad alterum.' The fact that the lovers did not belong to each other, were *alieni*, is often alluded to (e.g. Plaut. *Mil.* 1168, 1402; Hor. *S.* 1.2.57, 2.7.46; *D* 48.5.9 pr.; Aug. *Civ. dei* 4.25).

[5] *D* 48.5.6.1: 'proprie adulterium in nupta committitur, propter partum ex altero conceptum composito nomine: stuprum vero in virginem viduamve committitur.' Cf. 50.16.101, Mod.: 'Inter stuprum et adulterium hoc interesse quidam putant, quod adulterium in nuptam, stuprum in viduam committitur. Sed lex Iulia de adulteriis hoc verbo indifferenter utitur.'

[6] Plaut. *Bac.* 268. Cf. *OLD* s.v. *adulter* (adj.) 2 (used in the Vulgate to mean bastard, Hebr. 12.8), *adulterinus* 2: 'forged' (cf. Plaut. *Bac.* 266; Cic. *Clu.* 41), *adulteratio*, *adulterator*, *adulteratus* esp. 2: 'produced by cross-breeding.' [7] See *OLD* s.v. *adultero* 2, 3.

[8] e.g. *moechus*: Plaut. *Bac.* 918; Ter. *Eun.* 960; Cael. ap. Cic. *F* 8.7.2; soldiers' song in Suet. *DJ* 51; Hor. *S* 1.2.38, 1.4.4; Juv. 6.100. *Moecha*: Hor. *S* 1.4.113; Mart. 2.47.1. *Moechor* (intrans.): Hor. *S* 1.2.49; Mart. 6.91.2; commoner in Christian writers.

the norm in making *adulterium* an extra-marital sexual relationship of a married woman. Adultery was therefore a triangular, not a bilateral, relationship. The lover is *adulter* towards both wife and husband.[9] The married woman is *adultera* of her lover; in relation to her husband she remains a wife, though an adulterous one, *adultera coniunx*. To call, for instance, Messallina *adultera Claudi* would lead to confusion.[10] The female parallel to the *adulter* in relation to the married pair is *paelex*, a word also used with a dependent genitive denoting the husband or the wife.[11] The nouns thus stress the third party's relationship to each member of the married couple and the position of the married delinquent in regard to the third party rather than in regard to the wronged *coniunx*.

Normal usage does not define as *adulter* the married man who has a *paelex*. As long as the mistress was not herself married or was of low social status, her existence has no impact on the terminology applied to him. It was etymology which led scholars to take a different view, and morality which led some philosophers and later the Christian theologian to try to make linguistic usage symmetrical. Augustine has an eloquent redefinition of adultery.[12]

The Augustan Law defined all sexual intercourse with people of either sex who fell under the law as *stuprum*, a word which was in general use for any irregular or promiscuous sexual acts, especially rape or homosexuality.[13]

2. Law

Adultery, according to Juvenal,[14] came in during the Silver Age. Adultery by a wife was undoubtedly always grounds for divorce. It is also said that kinsmen, together with the husband, could sentence an adulterous wife to death. Dionysius, after his tendentious description of indissoluble marriage as established by Romulus, which encour-

---

[9] With genitive of mistress: Cic. *Sest.* 39; Juv. 10.318; Suet. *DJ* 74; Tac. *A* 15.50.4, 68.5; cf. *moechus*: Plaut. *Mil.* 775; Suet. *Otho* 3.2; *Decl. min.* 291 tit. *Adulter* with gen. of husband: Sen. *Contr.* 4.7; *Decl. min.* 279 tit., 286 tit.

[10] Ov. *Ars* 1.295, *M* 10.347; Sen. *Contr.* 6.6 exc. But 'adulteram viri fortis uxorem' is possible (Sen. *Contr.* 1.4.6) and 'adultera coniunx' (Ov. *Am.* 3.4.37). But rhetorical husbands call the guilty pair *adulteri mei* (Sen. *Contr.* 1.4.1, 2, 10, 12; *Decl. min.* 347.4), striving for an unusually strong effect.

[11] Gen. of wife: Cic. *Clu.* 199; *Inv. in Cic.* 2; Sen. *Contr.* 6.6 exc.; Ov. *M* 6.537; cf. Ov. *AA* 2.377.

[12] *Quaest. Exodi* 71.4 = *Corpus Christianorum, series latina* xxxiii.104: 'si femina moecha est habens virum concumbendo cum eo, qui vir eius non est, etiam si ille non habeat uxorem, profecto moechus est et vir habens uxorem concumbendo cum ea, quae uxor eius non est, etiam si illa non habeat virum.'

[13] Cf. *stuprator, stuprare*. Vaguer nouns often have sexual connotations (*facinus, dedecus, flagitium*, etc.). *Iniuria* to wife, husband, and house: Sen. *Contr.* 2.7.5.   [14] 6.24.

aged the wife to identify her interests with the husband's, goes on to say that if the wife transgressed, she was judged by the wronged husband. But certain offences were judged by the kinsmen with the husband. In the context, this has to mean her kinsmen.[15] But since he is speaking of marriage with *manus*, Dionysius might mean by that her husband's kin, her new agnates. Among these offences were adultery and drinking wine (an offence which seems trivial to the Greeks). Romulus allowed both to be punished by death, since they were the worst offences which could be committed by a woman, because adultery led to folly and drunkenness to adultery. It is by no means clear what further folly was possible, but perhaps he means neglect of all duties. Since he thinks divorce was not originally practised, he presumably thought the death penalty the only way of disposing of faithless wives.[16]

Dionysius is not a source to be followed with confidence on such matters. But he has some weight as evidence for what people in the Augustan period wanted to believe. He clings to the idea of the self-regulating family. Like Cicero, he deplores direct state interference.[17] The principle that the *paterfamilias* should take no serious action without consulting a council (*consilium*) was well established in Roman practice, though not in law. Dionysius' reference to kinsmen (*syggeneis*) is therefore fairly convincing. Whatever Dionysius thought this meant, modern scholars are divided on whether we should take it to mean that the husband of the monarchic period called in his wife's relations or his own.[18] Support for the view that the wife's blood-relations would appropriately be called upon to hear the evidence which would justify her punishment is found in the account which Dionysius' contemporary Livy gives of the action taken by Lucretia. She summoned her father and her husband to tell them she had been raped. Since she is about to impose on herself the penalty which would (according to the Augustan Law) have been appropriate for adultery, her procedure is entirely correct if her father was among those who would have judged her.[19] In such legendary times she must have been transferred from his power to her husband's control. Some support for the retention of rights over her

---

[15] Cf. Watson, *XII Tables* 34 n. 18.

[16] DH *Ant.* 2.25.6 See Kunkel, 'Das Konsilium im Hausgericht' 233; MacCormack, 'Wine drinking and the Romulan law of divorce'; Watson, *XII Tables* 34–5; Pomeroy, 'The relationship of the married woman to her blood relatives in Rome'. On wine see further pp. 268–9, 461–2.   [17] Cf. Cic. *Rep.* 4.6.

[18] For recent discussions see Volterra, 'Il preteso tribunale domestico' 113; Cantarella, 'Adulterio, omicidio legittimo e causa d'onore in diritto romano', both of whom argue that the husband's kin acted, and, for the opposite view, Watson, *XII Tables* 34–6. Gide 130–2 is still worth reading.

[19] Livy 1.58, cf. DH *Ant.* 4.66ff. See Watson, *XII Tables* 35.

by her former *paterfamilias* may be found in the fact that Augustus
later allowed a father who had transferred a daughter in this way to
kill her if he caught her in adultery. The question about whose kin
acted is important if Dionysius is right in giving priority to the kin,
that is, in denying full powers to the husband. In disciplining *filiifamilias* a *paterfamilias* had full power, extending to the death penalty.
Although custom demanded that he consult a *consilium*, there was
probably no compulsion on him to abide by a majority vote. The
membership of such a council was fluid: it consisted of whomever the
paterfamilias summoned on a particular occasion, people whom he
considered appropriate and who were available. It was right to invite
respected *amici*, as a father who tried his son for plotting to kill him
invited Augustus, and kinsmen would hardly include those in the
father's own power. Probably everyone present would be
paterfamilias.[20]

Watson argues that

In one case and one case only did the family council have legal recognition
and that was where a woman who was no longer in the *potestas* of her *pater*
was thought to have misbehaved . . . Very reasonably the right of inflicting
the supreme penalty was not simply entrusted to the husband even when the
wife was in his *manus*. For later times, moreover, there is evidence that the
family had the right to punish and put to death a woman who was *sui iuris*,
and this is unlikely to have been an innovation posterior to the fifth century.[21]

The argument is attractive, but the evidence seems insufficient to
prove that the woman's family had always had the right, in conjunction with the husband, to put her to death. By the Livian tradition we
are informed that after the consul L. Postumius Albinus was taken ill
on his way to his province and came back to Rome to die, his wife
Publilia was accused of poisoning him. Licinia, the wife of Claudius
Asellus, was also accused about the same time. Their guilt being
proved, both were strangled by the decree of their kinsmen (*cognati,
propinqui*). It is not clear whether Valerius Maximus is right in
hinting that no public trial took place, since the family thought that
would be too slow, or whether, as the text of the *epitome* suggests, a
public trial was in process and the family pre-empted execution.[22]

[20] Sen. *Clem.* 1.15; VM 2.9.2. There is also the interesting example of L. Gellius (consul 72,
censor 70), who invited almost the whole Senate to investigate charges against his son of
attempted parricide and adultery with his stepmother. Both father and advisers agreed to acquit
(VM 5.9.1). Gruen, *LGRR* 527, dates this to 70. For the domestic tribunal see Greenidge,
Legal procedure of Cicero's time 367–73; Wesener, *RE suppl.* ix (1962) 373–6; Watson, *XII
Tables* 43–4; Kunkel, 'Das Konsilium im Hausgericht'; Guarino, 'Tagliacarte' (reviewing
Kunkel); J. A. C. Thomas, '*Lex Julia de adulteriis coercendis*' 637–8.   [21] *XII Tables* 44.
[22] Livy *Per.* 48 (*c.*154 BC): 'Publilia et Licinia, nobiles feminae, quae viros suos consulares
necasse insimulabantur, cognita causa, cum praetori praedes vades dedissent, cognatorum

Private execution by the family, after public condemnation, is reported to have been used against women implicated in the Bacchanalian scandal of 186 BC.[23]

There is rather better evidence in Tiberius' reversion to *mos maiorum* in encouraging *propinqui* to take disciplinary action against unchaste women when no public prosecution was launched.[24] Even when a trial had been held before the Senate, that of Appuleia Varilla in AD 17, Tiberius was able to ask that the penalties of the Julian Law (relegation and confiscation) not be imposed but that it should be left to her relations to punish her according to the precedent established by their ancestors. He suggested banishment 200 miles from Rome.[25] Finally, there is the conscious archaism of the trial of Pomponia Graecina for superstition, turned over by the Senate in AD 57 to her husband and *propinqui*. The husband, Aulus Plautius, seems to have taken the leading role, for it was he who pronounced her innocent. This investigation is explicitly linked by Tacitus with the ancient custom of trials affecting a wife's life or citizen status and good repute. This suggests that conviction could have entailed death (or in more civilized times exile) and *infamia*.[26]

Only one husband is directly said to have taken part in trying his wife. Two husbands, *ex hypothesi*, were dead when their widows were accused of murder. None of the known private trials of individuals deals with adultery, although the charge against Graecina has been seen as connected.[27]

The words *cognati* and *propinqui* (usually) refer to blood-relations,

---

decreto necatae sunt'; VM 6.3.8: 'Publicia [*sic*] autem, quae Postumium Albinum [consul. 154] consulem, item Licinia, quae Claudium Asellum viros suos veneno necaverant, propinquorum decreto strangulatae sunt: non enim putaverunt severissimi viri in tam evidenti scelere longum publicae quaestionis tempus exspectandum. Itaque quarum innocentium defensores fuissent, sontium mature vindices extiterunt'; Obseq. 17: 'In provinciam proficiscens Postumius consul . . . profectusve post diem septimum aeger Romam relatus expiravit.' L. Postumius Albinus had been *flamen Martialis* since 168, so she was *flaminica* and the marriage confarreate. See further Strachan-Davidson, *Problems of the Roman criminal law* i.34–5 (suggesting that these women were still *in patria potestate* and that this is the only certain instance where the family carried out executions without state authorization); Kunkel, 'Das Konsilium im Hausgericht' 223.

[23] VM 6.3.7 (186 BC), Bacchanals: 'a quibus cum multae essent damnatae, in omnes cognati intra domos animadverterunt . . .'

[24] Suet. *Tib.* 35: 'matronas prostratae pudicitiae, quibus accusator publicus deesset, ut propinqui more maiorum de communi sententia coercerent auctor fuit.'

[25] Tac. *A* 2.50.4: 'Liberavitque Appuleiam lege maiestatis: adulterii graviorem poenam deprecatus, ut exemplo maiorum propinquis suis ultra ducentesimum lapidem removerentur suasit.'

[26] Tac. *A* 13.32.3: 'Et Pomponia Graecina insignis femina, A. Plautio . . . nupta ac superstitionis externae rea, mariti iudicio permissa; isque prisco instituto propinquis coram de capite famaque coniugis cognovit et insontem nuntiavit.'   [27] Furneaux ad loc.

but *propinqui* (which may be contrasted with *adfines*),[28] the word used in most of these texts, has no legal connotation. They are the kinsmen whom it was proper for a woman to consult before she acted.[29]

The evidence so far cited supports the view that custom allowed a family council consisting of the woman's *propinqui* to take disciplinary action against her, even when she was *sui iuris*. It was more decent for women to be dealt with privately than by public trial. Since a council was by definition a body consulted by an individual, it is reasonable to suppose that her husband or *paterfamilias* would normally summon the *consilium*, put the matter to it, and pronounce the decision or take action afterwards. But the evidence does not prove that consultation of a council was prescribed by a given statute. Introduction of such a rule by Romulus must be legend: the patriarchal system had been there from the beginning, although refinements (of which this might be one) could grow up gradually. *Mos* evolves and commands more loyalty than legislation. It is hard to see how the execution of women, like that of *filiifamilias*, could have been other than a primitive survival of custom. But since none of the evidence is earlier than the time of Augustus, it is likely to be contaminated by the debate on state intervention which began in Cicero's day and was prominent in the mind of Livy. Some apologists thought domestic jurisdiction should have existed as they described it. But they were unclear about the details of its workings and they produced few examples. This might mean that the antiquarians were inventing. Unfortunately, it is also precisely what we should expect if household jurisdiction was informal, extra-legal, effective, and taken for granted.

There is also evidence for husbands alone taking action against wives. Many scholars hold that it may be taken for granted that a husband could legally kill his wife in certain circumstances.[30] A certain Egnatius Metennius under Romulus is alleged to have beaten his wife to death for drinking wine. Valerius Maximus claims that he was neither brought to trial nor criticized. Slightly better authorities relate that he was tried but acquitted by Romulus. If they are right, the story is irrelevant to our discussion.[31] More cogent is Cato's

[28] *OLD* s.v. *propinquitas* 3a.

[29] Cic. *Cael.* 68: 'de cognatorum sententia . . . de suorum propinquorum . . . sententia atque auctoritate'; cf. *Caec.* 14, 15. When Sassia investigated her husband's death and tortured slaves (who belonged to his son and herself) she called in friends and guests of the dead man and friends of her own (*Clu.* 176–7).

[30] Cantarella, 'Adulterio, omicidio legittimo e causa d'onore in diritto romano' 255.

[31] VM 6.3.9. Pliny *NH* 14.89: 'Invenimus inter exempla Egnati Maetenni uxorem, quod vinum bibisset a dolio, interfectam fusti a marito, eumque caedis a Romulo absolutum'; Serv. ad *A* 1.737: '*libato summo tenus attigit ore*: et verecundiam reginae ostendit et morem. Nam apud maiores nostros feminae non utebantur vino nisi sacrorum causa certis diebus. Denique

notorious statement, quoted by Gellius to show that wine-drinking by wives was as heavily punished as adultery:

Atque haec quidem [*the abstinence of women*] in his, quibus dixi, libris pervulgata sunt; sed Marcus Cato non solum existimatas, set et multatas quoque a iudice mulieres refert non minus, si vinum in se, quam si probrum et adulterium admisissent:

Verba Marci Catonis adscripsi ex oratione quae inscribitur De dote, in qua id quoque scriptum est, in adulterio uxores deprehensas ius fuisse maritis necare: 'Vir,' inquit 'cum divortium fecit, mulieri iudex pro censore est, imperium quod videtur habet, si quid perverse taetreque factum est a muliere: multatur si vinum bibit; si cum alieno viro probri quid fecit, condemnatur.' De iure autem occidendi ita scriptum est: 'in adulterio uxorem tuam si prehendisses, sine iudicio impune necares; illa te, si adulterares sive tu adulterare, digito non audet contingere, neque ius est. (Gellius 10.23.2–5)

And these matters are commonly stated in the books I have mentioned, but M. Cato says that women were not only assessed [*as bad*[32] *or perhaps as justly divorced*] but also penalized by the judge just as much for wine-drinking as for committing shameful acts and adultery.

I have added the words of M. Cato from the speech entitled 'On dowry', in which he also writes that husbands had had the right to kill wives taken in adultery. 'When a husband has made a divorce,' he says, 'he is to the woman a judge like a censor; he has, it seems, magisterial power, if she has done anything aberrant or shameful; she is fined, if she drank wine; if she did anything wicked with a man who did not belong to her, she is condemned.' About the right to kill he writes as follows: 'If you took your wife in adultery, you might kill her with impunity without trial; but if you committed adultery or were adulterated, she would not dare to lay a finger on you, nor has she the right to do so.'

Cato is highly tendentious. No other evidence confirms that the husband had the power of decision over deductions from the dowry of a divorced wife in the second century. Gellius himself thought that a third person acted as judge.[33] Presumably Cato means that the husband could retain fractions if he charged his wife with moral fault, but ignores the sequel that his 'decision' could be reversed by the judge if an *actio rei uxoriae* were brought. Cato himself would have liked the husband's dispositions to be final. Cato does not say that a husband could condemn a divorced wife to death.[34] But he claims that

---

femina quae sub Romulo vinum bibit occisa est a marito. Metennius absolutus. Id enim nomen marito. Sic Granius Licinianus Cenae Suae'; Tert. *Apol.* 6: '. . . sub Romulo vero quae vinum attigerat inpune a Metennio marito trucidata sit.' The source is probably Varro. See Murray, 'Symposium and genre in the poetry of Horace' 48.

[32] Cf. Friedrich, *TLL* s.v. *existimo* 1518.82.

[33] Cato has been translated in this sense, e.g. by Gide 151–2.

[34] *Pace* Watson, *RPL* 23.

a husband who killed an adulterous wife in the heat of the moment would go scot-free, while a wife had no right to attack her husband if he committed adultery.[35] In saying that a wife had no *ius* he implies that a husband has such a right. *Ius* is a pervasive word for the legally minded Romans. It can describe law itself, or a man-made law-code, or a specific enactment. It may be contrasted with *fas* (what is morally right) or linked with customary practice.[36] It can refer to a right granted by a specific law. But it also has wider senses: what is right, the obligations and claims arising out of a particular relationship, the prerogative of an individual.[37] Although the word always has a legalistic flavour, it often has no juristic content. It is often used in argument where the speaker could not appeal to a specific law, recognized legal right, or even established custom. The adverbial use, *iure* ('legally', 'justifiably', 'rightly'), has a similar extension. Although the Twelve Tables prescribed that a thief in the night might justifiably be killed, describing him as *iure caesus*, not all verdicts of justified homicide rested on a law which permitted it in advance.[38] Cato's *impune* suggests that the husband would be able to persuade a court that he was not guilty of murder. Some might hold that he had acted *iure*, with justification. 'As everybody knows, the defence in a murder trial must either argue that the defendant did not do the deed, or that he acted rightly and *iure*.'[39]

The Romans were quite clear that marriage imposed obligations. Cicero uses 'ius illud matrimoni castum atque legitimum' ('that chaste and legal right of marriage') for the obligation to chastity from which, he claims, Sassia held herself dispensed by the condemnation of her husband.[40] But adultery was not at that date a crime in public law. The obligations and rights of *coniuges* were a matter of consensus and equity. But it is a big step from such a right to claiming for the husband the prerogative of killing an offending wife, and denying the wife any similar redress. Not all rights which a man may claim for himself are universally admitted.[41] The other texts cited in support of the view that husbands had, down to the Augustan Law, a legal right

---

[35] *Adulterari* seems to refer to passive homosexuality.

[36] e.g. *ius* linked with *fas* (Cic. *Att.* 1.16.6); with *consuetudo* (Cic. *2Verr.* 5.76); with *mos* (Cic. *Caec.* 2), with *mos maiorum* (Cic. *Mil.* 71).

[37] e.g. *iura necessitudinis* (Cic. *F* 13.14.1), *familiaria iura* (Livy 24.5.9), *coniugalia iura* (Ov. *M* 6.536).

[38] *FIRA* i.8.12.

[39] Cic. *Mil.* 8. He specifically cites Scipio's response that Ti. Gracchus was *iure caesum*, the law that a thief in the night may be killed *impune*, the unwritten law that we may kill *iure* in self-defence (8–10). Cf. Quint. *Inst.* 3.6.83.

[40] *Clu.* 175.

[41] e.g. Plaut. *Merc.* 985–6: 'si istuc ius est, senecta aetate scortari senes, | ubi locist res summa nostra puplica?'

to kill a wife taken in adultery are open to the same doubts. We must at the same time consider the claim that a husband could kill the adulterer whom he surprised in the act.

Horace, like other satirists, exploits the dramatic possibilities of disgrace, pain, and humiliation which await the seducer of a married woman. The vivid details of Falstaffian discomforts are drawn from the mime. Unless he escapes via the roof and *en déshabillé*, he may face death by beating or anal rape or castration or temporary indignities at the hands of servants. He may have to buy himself off or his reputation may be ruined.[42] Horace implies that at least one husband had been brought to trial for assault and that the verdict had been that he acted *iure*. Only one man dissented, Galba.[43] But although the verdict is interesting, Horace does not even mention the possibility that the husband might kill the adulterer with his own hand. But that is the right which scholars postulate, along with the right to kill the wife if he took them together in the act. The wife in Horace, however, is not frightened for her life, but only for her dowry.[44]

Beating and the threat of castration are already the apt penalty for adulterers in Plautus.[45] According to the moralistic tradition, various painful indignities actually were inflicted on adulterers by husbands who took the law into their own hands to avenge their pain. Either they were not brought to trial for taking private vengeance rather than bringing a prosecution, or they were acquitted.[46] What the soldier threatens in *Bacchides* is not evidence of what a Roman husband could legally do. He speaks of killing wife and lover, to make her admit that he is not contemptible.[47] This seems to be the only passage in comedy which even mentions killing both. Plautus wants to make a joke, not to illustrate law.

[42] On the mime see R. W. Reynolds, 'The adultery mime'. *Infamia* is the risk which provides least drama in farce and may therefore be considered the most realistic on the list.

[43] *S* 1.2.46. Ps.-Acro ad loc. claims that he was a lawyer and a chaser of matrons. Cantarella ('Adulterio, omicidio legittimo e causa d'onore in diritto romano' 257) tentatively identifies him with Ser. Sulpicius Galba, consul 144, and compares Cic. *de or.* 1.240 for his interest in equity.

[44] *S.* 1.2.131. The slave-girl is afraid of physical punishment (ibid., cf. 2.7.60 for her collaboration).

[45] *Mil.* 1394–427; cf. *Curc.* 25–38, *Poen.* 862–3.

[46] VM 6.1.13: flogging, castration, rape by servants. Again, the husbands delegate the punishment. The pairs of men cited are (husbands first) Sempronius Musca and C. Gellius; C. Memmius and L. Octavius; Vibienus and Carbo Attienus; P. Cerennius and Pontius; anon. and Cn. Furius Brocchus. See Wiseman, *NMRS* 113, for a Cerinnius (? Terrinius). One L. Furius Brocchus was *monetalis* c.63. In a rhetorical exercise, blinding might be permitted (*Decl. min.* 357) but this is not known to have happened.

[47] Esp. 864, taken seriously by Watson, *RPL* 23. For the possibility of exacting retribution by *flagitatio* see Veyne, 'Le folklore à Rome'; C. G. Brown, 'Ares, Aphrodite and the laughter of the gods' 292–3, citing Cat. 42 and charivari in various cultures.

The rhetorical schools used as a premiss for *controversiae* a law which permitted adulterers to be killed. Although the topic was a favourite one, it is comparatively rare for husbands to be specified as the killers. The law is stated by the elder Seneca as:

Adulterum cum adultera qui deprehenderit, dum utrumque corpus interficiat, sine fraude sit. (Seneca *Controversiae* 1.4)

Whoever catches an adulterer with an adulteress, as long as he kills both bodies, let him be without risk of punishment.

This theme was used in the late Republic, for Seneca says that Cicero gave a speech on the variant which postulated a further rule that a son was allowed to kill his mother if she was taken in adultery.[48] There are other Senecan *controversiae* in which the killing of an *adulter* or of both lovers by a husband is part of the story and is not said to be illegal (or legal either).[49]

Writing under Domitian, Quintilian uses as a routine example the defence of a killer who claims the victims were adulterers. The legal situation which he postulates has been adduced as evidence for actual law before Augustus' reform, so it needs to be clearly stated here.[50] Unlike Seneca, he alludes to a law, but does not quote it. If the defendant admitted he had killed, he might defend himself by claiming that his victims were adulterers: 'It is allowed to kill an adulterer with the adulteress. That is certainly law.'[51] The defence might argue that it is permissible to kill *adulteri*. But, prosecution would retort, if they are killed in a brothel it is murder.[52] It was illegal to kill the adulteress without the adulterer.[53] It could be argued that if the law permits an adulterer to be killed, *a fortiori* he may be flogged, but if he may be flogged to death it may be more doubtful whether he may be starved to death or poisoned.[54] Apart from one Senecan text which he quotes, Quintilian never tells us that the defendant on the murder charge is the husband. He could just as well have in mind the

---

[48] *Contr.* 1.4.7. Cf. Calp. Flacc. *Decl.* 23, 31 (sisters too). The phrasing of the law quoted at the head of the declamation is repeated at 1.4.6, as used by 'new declaimers'. This has led Riccobono, *ADA* 114, to ask if it reflects the wording of the Julian Law. If so, *qui* would not be indefinite but would have the antecedent *pater*. For views on the partial connection of rhetorical themes with Roman law see Lanfranchi, *Il diritto nei retori romani. Contributo alla storia dello sviluppo del diritto romano*, esp. pp. 439 ff.; Bonner, *Declamation*, esp. pp. 119 ff.

[49] 1.7, 7.5, fr. 1 = Quint. *Inst.* 9.2.42. Cf. *Decl. min.* 286 (husband kills *adulter*), 291 with Calp. Flacc. 48 (husband kills both). There are no killings by third parties in Seneca. For incidental killing of *adulteri* by undefined agents as part of the story see Calp. Flacc. 11, 17.

[50] Corbett 128.

[51] 7.1.7. Cf. 3.6.17; *Decl. min.* 277.1: 'Occidere adulterum licet cum adultera'; 347 pr.: 'Adulterum cum adultera liceat occidere' (same wording in Calp. Flacc. 49 pr.), for statement of law, but here the killer is the husband.

[52] *Inst* 5.10.39: 'Occidisti adulteros, quod lex permittit, sed quia in lupanari, caedes est.'

[53] 5.10.104, cf. 3.11.7; Calp. Flacc. 49.   [54] 5.10.88, 3.6.27, 5.10.52.

woman's father, who in the actual law in effect in his time was allowed, in certain defined circumstances, to kill both lovers, and forbidden to kill the man without at least attempting to kill his own daughter. (Quintilian formulates this the other way round. Such a clause could conceivably also have occurred in the *Lex Julia*.) In one instance at least, Quintilian makes it clear that the defendant he is thinking of is the father. In the story involving the brothel, the advocate is to rebut the prosecution point by saying, 'I was allowed, because I was the father.'[55] I am inclined to think that the Augustan Law, which was topical under Domitian and the complexities of which young advocates would need to study, forms a substratum to his examples, though the favourite point about the brothel probably comes from rhetorical embroidery rather than juristic scholarship.[56] His point about inflicting injury on the adulterer agrees with a later comment by Papinian.[57] Quintilian is of course capable of combining fact and fiction.[58] But he held that the scenarios used in the schools should be as close as possible to real life and that declamations should reflect the procedure of the courts for which they were the training.[59]

The evidence from the rhetorical school exercise proves too much (if it is thought to reflect pre-Augustan law) or too little (if it is fiction). The rule used by Cicero and Seneca apparently permitted anyone who caught *adulteri* in a compromising situation to kill them. The rule as referred to by Quintilian omits the requirement that they be caught in the act, but hints at limitations about place (not in a brothel) and enforces the killing of both. While Seneca reflects the exciting fictions of the schools, where a mutilated warrior without hands begs his son to kill his wife and her lover and then disowns him for sparing them, or a husband kills his brother despite their father's pleas, events which result in a case to contest the disowning and in a suit for maintenance,[60] Quintilian envisages a world closer to reality, in which a man charged with double murder might defend himself by

[55] 5.10.40: 'Vel contra: "Licuit, quia pater eram . . .".'
[56] A father could kill adulterers only if he caught them in the matrimonial home or his own residence.
[57] Quint. *Inst.* 5.10.88: 'Iuris confirmatio est eius modi: ex maiore: "si adulterum occidere licet, et loris caedere".' Cf. *D* 48.5.23.3: 'Sed qui occidere potest adulterum, multo magis contumelia poterit iure adficere.'
[58] e.g. he combines the scenario of the priest who is allowed to save the life of one criminal (a common school motif, which I take to be non-Roman) with the rule that forbade killing the adulteress without killing the adulterer (which could be at least based on the Augustan Law): 5.10.104. This situation also occurs in *Decl. min.* 284, which may be Quintilian's. The two laws are there quoted as 'Sacerdos unius supplicio liberandi habeat potestatem. Adulteros liceat occidere.'
[59] *Inst.* 2.9.4.
[60] *Contr.* 1.4, 7; cf. 9.1: all cases which narrate impassioned negotiation in the bedroom.

claiming to have found the couple in adultery. This is precisely the situation which exercised the juristic commentators on the Augustan Law. But the scenario from which he starts is probably that developed in rhetorical exercises by the time of Cicero: that anyone catching adulterers in the act could kill them with impunity. This is a far more extreme custom than anything claimed for actual law in the pre-Augustan period. It does not seem logical to argue from the rhetoricians that statute or custom conferred on husbands or fathers the right to kill without trial the adulteress, adulterer, or both when taken in the act.

One further piece of evidence remains. The Augustan law on adultery is known to have abrogated several previous laws.[61] It might still be expected that jurists discussing the rules on killing would use words which imply what the previous legal situation had been. So when Paul says that the husband taking his wife in adultery is able to kill only certain types of man, 'except his wife, whom he is forbidden to kill', it might be thought that the law introduced a new prohibition.[62] But other references to this chapter phrase the matter neutrally or suggest that the law gave a new permission.[63]

No text, therefore, demonstrates without doubt that a husband had the legal right to kill a wife out of hand if he took her in adultery. But Cato shows that he might be expected to be acquitted of murder if he did. The regulations of the Augustan Law suggest a society in which it was accepted as natural that either a woman's father or her husband might attempt to kill her in the heat of the moment. If we attempt to imagine such a scene, as the rhetoricians did, it will be apparent that it might be dangerous for a man, even with the advantage of surprise, to attend to the lady without dealing with the lover first. So an attempt to kill both *adulteri* is likely. Papinian held that the power of life and death which the *paterfamilias* had over children (by a law of the regal period) applied to killing an adulterous *filiafamilias*.[64] Doubt could focus only on his right to kill her out of hand. It is arguable that *manus* would have given a husband a similar right.[65] But Cato hedges his statement with no qualifications about *manus*. By Cato's time, many wives will not have been legally in their husbands' power. The 'right' seems to depend on a man's status as husband rather than as holder of

---

[61] *Coll.* 4.2.2, Paul *lib. sg. de adult.*

[62] Paul *S* 2.26.4: 'excepta uxore quam prohibetur.' Cf. Csillag 185, 267.

[63] *D* 48.5.25 pr., Macer: 'Marito quoque adulterum uxoris suae occidere permittitur'; *Coll.* 4.3.1: 'Certae autem enumerantur personae, quas viro liceat occidere in adulterio deprehensa uxore, quamvis uxorem non liceat', 4.10.1: 'nulla parte legis marito uxorem occidere conceditur'; cf. 4.3.2.   [64] *Coll.* 4.8.1.

[65] Esmein, 'La délit d'adultère à Rome et la loi *Julia de adulteriis*' 89. Contra Gide 133–6, arguing that *manus* gave power over a wife's property but not her person.

manus. The rough justice handed out to adulterers according to tradition depended on the husband's domestic resources rather than his domestic jurisdiction. (Slaves were in his power and other dependents living in the household could be disciplined, but the adulterers of literature are usually outsiders.)

The justification for violence must have been the indignation felt by the husband against the wife who had betrayed her duty and the marauder from outside, rather than a theoretical power of life and death over the wife. Livy makes Sextus Tarquin threaten Lucretia that he will say he caught and killed her in adultery with a slave, but Tarquin was only a guest and a kinsman.[66] We would indeed expect to hear of stern husbands who killed guilty wives caught *flagrante delicto*. It is striking that even Valerius Maximus produces no example. Actual killings of wives and adulterers are absent from the Roman record, and we have seen that comedy, farce, and satire dwell on the savage bullying but not the killing of the adulterer and scarcely touch on violence to the woman.[67] A husband who killed his wife in the late Republic would probably have to answer to her kinsmen and defend himself on a murder charge. Adultery might not be easy to prove unless he could display the adulterer's corpse, which might involve him in further enmities. The upper class at least seems to have found divorce (with the option of retaining a fraction of the dowry) a more convenient solution for dealing with the wife. It was alleged that money might be extorted from the lover by way of revenge.[68]

In his description of the mores of the Gauls, Caesar praises their strict marital customs. The men have power of life and death over their wives as well as over their children. The implication must be that Romans have no such right over wives. If a highly placed man dies, his kinsmen determine whether his death is suspicious: if it is, they torture his wives and if they are proved guilty, burn them to death. This tells us more about moralists' views on the laxity of contemporary Rome than about Celtic customs.[69]

3. *Public Repression of Adultery*

Adultery was also repressed by public methods. On several occasions in the middle Republic the aediles are said to have taken action

[66] 1.58.4.
[67] Beating a wife to death for drinking (accidental?) is not comparable with killing *adulterae* on the spur of the moment.
[68] Gell. 17.18 (Sallust); Hor. *S* 1.2.133; *Decl. min.* 279: 'Adulterum aut occidere aut accepta pecunia dimittere liceat.' Ps.-Acro on Hor. *S* 1.2.46 asserts that a money penalty had been normal and legal. The rhetoricians postulated a law that the husband could seize all the adulterer's property (*Decl. min.* 273), but also one which made *ignominiosus* anyone who took money on account of adultery (ibid. 275). [69] Caes. *BG* 6.19.3.

against adulterers as they did against homosexual seducers.[70] In 328 BC M. Flavius (tribune 327, 323) was prosecuted unsuccessfully by the aediles for having seduced a *materfamilias*.[71] In 295 Q. Fabius Gurges, presumably as aedile, fined certain matrons who had been convicted of *stuprum* by the people. A temple to Venus was built with the proceeds.[72] The plebeian aediles of 213 also accused a number of matrons before the people; some of them were condemned and exiled.[73] In the first century BC the procedure could still be invoked, for a Metellus Celer summoned Cn. Sergius Silus for an unsuccessful attempt to bribe a *materfamilias*. This Metellus is probably the tribune of 90, who was probably aedile in about 88.[74]

The aediles in such instances initiate action to punish behaviour generally accepted as anti-social. The person charged may appeal to the people and the case may then be argued and a verdict given by the assembly, with the aedile presiding. The magistrate asks for a certain penalty during the hearing and imposes it if the defendant is condemned.[75] If the charge succeeds, a magistrate may later define the offence in an edict. Eventually a specific law may be passed by the people. This is what happened for counterfeiting.[76]

The censors also acted sporadically to penalize men for private misbehaviour. They sometimes punished husbands for unjust or procedurally incorrect divorce. Since they dealt directly with husbands and fathers and only indirectly with women (apart from independent single women), censorial discipline was expected to affect women through an intermediary *paterfamilias*, although Cato

[70] Homosexuals: VM 6.1.7–8; Plut. *Marcellus* 2.3–4. (In general see Lilja, *Homosexuality in republican and Augustan Rome* 106ff.) The aediles' jurisdiction with appeal to a *iudicium populi* dates from 367 BC. See Jones, *Criminal courts of the Roman Republic and Principate* 37. On tribunician repression of homosexual *stuprum* see ibid. 30. That women were tried before the plebeian assembly indicates that they were allowed to appeal from the decision of a magistrate (Strachan-Davidson, *Problems of the Roman criminal law* i.141–4). See Marshall, 'Maesia of Sentinum' 52–6.
[71] Livy 8.22.2–3; VM 8.1 Absol. 7; cf. Jones, *Criminal courts of the Roman Republic and Principate* 30.
[72] Livy 10.31.9.
[73] Livy 25.2.9. On all these trials see Hartmann in *RE* i.432–5 s.v. *adulterium*. Bauman, 'Criminal prosecution by the aediles' 254, argues that the women went into exile to avoid execution.
[74] VM 6.1.8. The consul of 60, who was probably aedile in about 67, is less likely. See Sumner, *Orators* 132–3; *MRR* ii.41. The undated trial of Calidius of Bononia (VM 8.1 Absol. 12), who was charged with adultery after being found in a married woman's bedroom but got off when he said he had gone there to meet a slave-boy, may be aedilician.
[75] Jones, *Criminal courts of the Roman Republic and Principate* 2–13 at 3: 'The magistrate pronounced judgment, the condemned appealed, and the people decided by their vote.'
[76] Strachan-Davidson, *Problems of the Roman criminal law* i.108–10; Kunkel, *Untersuchungen zur Entwicklung des römischen Kriminalverfahrens in vorsullanischer Zeit* 121ff.
[77] Cic. *Rep.* 4.6; Gell. 10.23.4.

also apparently saw the judge who adjudicated on the fate of the dowry after divorce as parallel to a censor.[77] We would expect that censors might have affixed a censorial *nota* on men who notoriously tolerated the sexual misconduct of their wives. But there is no evidence. Measures taken by censors against citizens, and especially senators, for alleged homosexuality or adultery are rarely attested. Adultery seems, however, to have been the pretext for the expulsion of Sallust from the Senate.[78]

4. Legislation

No general law on adultery is attested in the Republic. But since the Augustan Law is said to have abrogated several previous statutes it is worth asking if there were any.[79] Some people thought that Sulla, a notorious rake himself, must have done something.[80] Cicero hoped that Caesar would repress illicit sexual behaviour (*libidines*) when he was dictator.[81] Caesar in fact achieved a reputation for severity, by imposing a capital penalty on a freedman of his own who committed adultery with the wife of an *eques*. But although he interested himself in sumptuary measures and the encouragement of the birth-rate, there is no evidence that he interfered in sexual morality by any general measure. Nor can anything be discovered in the triumviral period or between 28 and 18.[82] The Scantinian Law of 149 BC on homosexual behaviour might have been among those abrogated, but we have evidence of its survival alongside the adultery law.[83] We must conclude that it is not clear whether Augustus abolished actual statutes.

(a) The Julian Law on adultery

The Julian Law was proposed by Augustus himself, and is logically linked with the marriage law of 18 BC.[84] Cassius Dio, after describing

---

[78] Pieri, *L'histoire du cens jusqu'à la fin de la République romaine* 99 ff., esp. pp. 100, 105 on archaic punishment of husbands. For Ap. Claudius see *MRR* s. 50 BC; for Sallust, Dio 40.63.4, cf. ps.-Cic. *Inv. in Sall.* 16.

[79] *Coll.* 4.2.2, Paul. Gardner, perhaps rightly, rejects this (p. 123).

[80] Plut. *Comp. Lys. et Sullae* 3. Sulla's intervention in private morality is shown not only in his sumptuary law but in a measure against gaming (*D* 11.5.3). But see Gardner 127.

[81] Cic. *Marc.* 23.

[82] Suet. *DJ* 48. Suetonius regards his jurisdiction as domestic, but the incident may date to his dictatorship. See Watson, *Persons* 227.

[83] Suet. *Dom.* 8.3; Juv. 2.43–4.

[84] Sources on the context and contents of the law are most conveniently collected in *ADA* i.112–28, which I have used as a basis for the account which follows. Only a few verbatim extracts survive. The copious scholarship of the jurists, surviving in *D* 48.5 and elsewhere, is directed to problems of interpretation and clusters around a few clauses, e.g. the right to kill, the judicial procedure, and the evidence of slaves. Modern scholarship is extensive and also often focuses on technical legal matters. A select list of some of the more recent and useful

the marriage law, says that the Senate brought pressure on Augustus to make marriage more attractive by disciplining women and that he, put out by their ironical allusions to his own amours and their cynical reaction to his claim that every man could control his own wife as he did, made some vague statements about female dress, deportment, and chastity. If any credence can be given to this lively and entertaining account, then Dio cannot have thought that the adultery law was passed immediately after the marriage law. But it must have come into effect by 16, when Augustus went to Gaul and Horace praises its impact.[85] The law is variously referred to as the Julian Law on adulteries, on repressing adulteries, on adulteries and fornication, on chastity, on adulteries and chastity.[86] It had nine chapters or more: our information comes from at least five of these.[87] The first chapter defined the crime as deliberate adultery (*adulterium*) or fornication (*stuprum*) with a married woman or a virgin, widow, or divorced woman of respectable station, or a male. But as far as we know it did not define what acts constituted this prohibited sexual activity. Definition should at least have been attempted, however unsatisfactory it might have been. Attempted seduction or incitement was also covered.[88] The offence could only be committed with a person of

works follows: Andréev, 'La lex Iulia de adulteriis coercendis'; Bauman, 'Some remarks on the structure and survival of the *quaestio de adulteriis*'; Biondi, 'La *poena adulterii* da Augusto a Giustiniano'; des Bouvrie, 'Augustus' legislation on morals: which morals and what aims?'; Cantarella, 'Adulterio, omicidio legittimo e causa d'onore in diritto romano'; Castelli, 'Il concubinato e la legislazione augustea'; della Corte, 'Le *leges Iuliae* e l'elegia romana'; Csillag 175–99; Daube, 'The *Lex Julia* concerning adultery'; id., 'The accuser under the *Lex Julia de adulteriis*'; id., 'Fraud no. 3'; Dorey, 'Adultery and propaganda in the early Roman empire'; Esmein, 'Le délit d'adultère à Rome et la loi *Julia de adulteriis*'; Galinsky, 'Augustus' legislation on morals and marriage'; Garnsey, 'Adultery trials and the survival of the quaestiones in the Severan age'; Raditsa, 'Augustus' legislation concerning marriage, procreation, love affairs and adultery'; Richlin, 'Approaches to the sources on adultery at Rome'; J. A. C. Thomas, '*Lex Julia de adulteriis coercendis*'; Townend, *The Augustan poets and the permissive society*; Volterra, 'In tema di accusatio adulterii'.

[85] Dio 54.16; Hor. *O* 4.5.20–4; Dio 54.19.1. If Hor. *Carm. saec.* 57ff. refers to this law, it cannot be later than early 17.

[86] *Lex Julia de adulteriis/adulteris* (*D* 48.5.18, 20, 26; *CTh* 9.7), *de adulteriis coercendis* (rubr. *D* 48.5; *Coll.* 4.2.1, 14.3.3; Just. *Inst.* 4.18.4), *de adulteriis et de stupro* (*CJ* 9.9), *de pudicitia* (*CJ* 9.9.8), *de adulteriis et de pudicitia* (Suet. *DA* 34). [87] I, II, V, VII, IX (*ADA* 112).

[88] *D* 48.5.13, Ulp. 1 *de adult.*, with Daube, 'The *Lex Julia* concerning adultery' 378–9; Just. *Inst.* 4.18.4. On males see also *D* ht 9 (8) pr.; Paul *S* 2.26.12; Just. *Inst.* 4.18.4. The subject of homosexual *stuprum* is not known to have been mentioned in ch. 1, but it is logical to suppose that it was. However, see *ADA* 124 n. 3. There were questions about the status of the wife, husband, father, and marriage: *D* 48.5.25.3. On the definition of respectable station the law may have been hazy. It was early established that the law did not apply to prostitutes (unless married), procuresses, and actresses (Tac. *A* 2.85.1–4; Suet. *Tib.* 35; *D* ht 11 pr., 14.2). Jurists argued that shop- and tavern-keepers (Paul *S* 2.26.11, cf. *CTh* 9.7.1 = *CJ* 9.9.28 (29), Constantine, AD 326) and women already condemned for adultery (*D* 25.7.1.2) were exempt. Castelli ('Il concubinato e la legislazione augustea' 149) would add the other categories whom the Papio-Poppaean Law forbade free-born men to marry, i.e. freedwomen of procurers and women condemned in the courts (*Tit. Ulp.* 13.2).

free status.[89] Papinian points out that the law used the words *adulterium* and *stuprum* indiscriminately.[90]

It is to the legislator's credit that he defined the offence as committed only if the offender knew what he was doing and had malicious intent, *sciens dolo malo*. A woman or boy who was raped was innocent before the law. This applied, on Ulpian's view, even when a woman had concealed the rape from her husband, although others would have argued that she had been seduced.[91] The definition also protected the innocent second wife of a bigamist: he was guilty of fornication, but she was completely innocent, because she believed herself to be his wife.[92]

The law seems to have used the terms *matrona* or *materfamilias*. The phrase *aliena materfamilias* appears to have occurred for 'another man's wife'.[93] In Cicero's time the word *materfamilias* had, in juristic contexts, been strictly restricted to the wife *in manu*.[94] In literary texts, whether or not the strict usage is consciously present, the word resounded with dignity and sanctity.[95] Marriage with *manus* was rare by the time of Augustus. It is highly unlikely that he restricted the crime of adultery to wives under the control of their husbands. That he did not is suggested by the fact that wives who were transferred by their fathers to the control of husbands were put in a special category in chapter 2. If only wives *in manu* were liable to the adultery law, the old form of marriage would have been effectively discouraged. It seems necessary to assume that the drafter of the law extended the definition of *materfamilias* to cover all women validly married in Roman law. It would therefore become interchangeable with *matrona* and it is quite likely that the text dithered between these words as it did between *adulterium* and *stuprum*. Women whose extra-marital activity was fornication rather than adultery ought to have been referred to consistently as *virgines* (with some qualification) or *viduae* (divorcees or widows). But if the law was as loosely drafted as it seems, then perhaps there were clauses which appeared to apply to single women but where they were not specifically mentioned.

Interpretation of the law steadily extended the connotation of

---

[89] *D* 48.5.6 pr. and other texts cited in *ADA* 113. Paul *S* 2.26.16 says that the seduction of a slave-woman did not come under the law unless it was part of a plan to corrupt the mistress.

[90] *D* 48.5.6.1; cf. ht 13; 50.16.101 pr.

[91] *D* 48.5.40 pr.; *Coll.* 5.2.2; *CJ* 9.9.7, 20.

[92] *CJ* 9.9.18, AD 258.   [93] *D* 48.5.9 (8) pr.

[94] Cic. *Top.* 14, cf. Fest. 125M; Gell. 18.6.9, discarding a ridiculous contemporary conjecture about the difference between *materfamilias* and *matrona* and arguing that *matrona* had been used for any married woman even before she bore children (ibid. 4ff.).

[95] e.g. *Rhet. ad Her.* 4.12; Cic. *2Verr.* 5.137; Livy 8.22.3.

materfamilias. Papinian argues that the word also covered the *vidua*.[96] Ulpian goes further. In a passage which is not related explicitly to the adultery law but is surely derived from the need to redefine the term in order to extend the effects of the law, he claims that *materfamilias* ought to be taken to include any woman of respectable morals:

'Matrem familias' accipere debemus eam, quae non inhoneste vixit: matrem enim familias a ceteris feminis mores discernunt atque separant. Proinde nihil intererit, nupta sit an vidua, ingenua sit an libertina: nam neque nuptiae neque natales faciunt matrem familas, sed boni mores. (*Digest* 50.16.46.1, *lix ad edictum*)

We ought to take *materfamilias* to mean a woman who does not live dishonourably: it is morals which distinguish and separate the *materfamilias* from all other women. So it will make no difference whether she is married or widowed or divorced, free-born, or a freedwoman: for it is not marriage or birth which makes a *materfamilias* but good morals.

He protests too much. It was Ulpian's own opinion that a freedwoman who was her patron's concubine also qualified as a matron (and therefore could be sued by him for adultery, though not *qua* husband).[97] Such protection of an extra-legal relationship which did not produce legitimate children is far from the Augustan concept of what needed to be done. But it is understandable when we consider how second- and third-century emperors and jurists had extended the scope of the statute.

After the senatusconsultum of AD 175–80 which prohibited marriage between a guardian and his ward under the age of 25 (except in certain circumstances), not only was such a marriage null, but the guardian liable to be charged with adultery.[98] Severus and Caracalla extended the adultery charge to fiancées, although the offended man was not to sue as if he were a husband. A hopeful litigant asked Papinian if he could use a husband's privilege to sue for adultery a former fiancée whose father had given her in marriage to someone else. The reply was that the innovation was too bold.[99] Sex. Caecilius Africanus, who wrote under Marcus, held, with Ulpian's warm approval, that husbands could charge wives to whom they were not united in valid Roman marriage.[100] Ulpian thought that a husband could also accuse a wife who had been a prostitute, though if she had been single she would have been outside the scope of the law.[101] There was a tendency to bring concubines within the rules. Ulpian held that

[96] *D* 48.5.11 pr. [97] *D* 48.5.14 pr. [98] *D* 48.5.7.
[99] *D* 48.5.14.3; cf. *Coll.* 4.6.1, 12.7. But Alexander stretched the husband's right to allow him to accuse the man who raped his betrothed during their engagement (*CJ* 9.9.6 pr., AD 223).
[100] *D* 48.5.14.1, 6, 8; *Coll* 4.5.1 (if the marriage has become valid, he could not charge her *qua* husband with offences committed while it was invalid). [101] *D* 48.5.14.2.

only freedwomen who were concubines to their patrons should be regarded as quasi-wives.[102] People might exploit the law for their own ends. A senatusconsultum ruled that if a husband suborned a man to commit adultery with his wife, so that he could ruin her by taking her in the act, he, as well as his wife, could be charged with adultery.[103]

Incest is confusingly treated by the jurists. A clear distinction needs to be made between extra-marital incest and incestuous marriages. The former clearly fell under the law. If the woman was married and had an incestuous relationship outside the marriage she was guilty of adultery, if she was unmarried she was (usually) guilty of *stuprum*. But there is evidence that incest was handled under a different law, except when it involved adultery, and that the procedures were different.[104] On the other hand, incestuous marriage might be equated with adultery. If a man seduced his sister's daughter, that was a double crime: incest and fornication. He deserved more than the penalty under the adultery law, that is, presumably, he should be punished for fornication and under another law on incest. If he married her, she might be excused because such a marriage was not forbidden by general human law (which prohibited only the mating of ascendant and descendant), but he might be prosecuted as for adultery. However, men too were often leniently treated, if they had acted in error.[105]

Slaves were liable as the active partners in adultery, although as passive partners in fornication they were outside the scope of the law. This is typical of the double standard which applied to sexual relationships with slaves and also of the ingrained Roman belief in the active/passive dichotomy in sexual behaviour. Minors under 25 could also be charged with adultery.[106]

---

[102] *D* 48.5.14 pr., 6.   [103] *D* 48.5.15.1; Talbert p. 455 no. 183.

[104] *D* 48.5.18.4, ht 40.5, 7, 8; Paul *S* 2.26.15; *ADA* 125. De Martino, 'L'ignorantia iuris nel diritto penale romano'.

[105] *D* 48.5.39—pr.–7, Pap. *xxxvi quaest.* esp. pr.–3: 'Si adulterium cum incesto committitur, ut puta cum privigna nuru noverca, mulier similiter quoque punietur: id enim remoto etiam adulterio eveniret. Stuprum in sororis filiam si committatur, an adulterii poena sufficiat mari, considerandum est. Occurrit, quod hic duplex admissum est, quia multum interest, errore matrimonium illicite contrahatur an contumacia iuris et sanguinis contumelia concurrant. Quare mulier tunc demum eam poenam, quam mares, sustinebit, cum incestum iure gentium prohibitum admiserit: nam si sola iuris nostri observatio interveniet, mulier ab incesti crimine erit excusata. Nonnumquam tamen et in maribus incesti crimina, quamquam natura graviora sunt, humanius quam adulterii tractari solent: si modo incestum per matrimonium illicitum contractum sit.' The *Philadelphia Digest* prefers the conjecture *mulieri* for *mari*. I cannot make sense of this, nor is it in accord with Paul *S* 2.19.5 = *Coll.* 6.3.2–3: 'Nec socrum nec nurum nec privignam nec novercam aliquando citra poenam incesti uxorem ducere licet, sicut nec amitam aut materteram. Sed qui vel cognatam contra interdictum duxerit, remisso mulieri iuris errore ipse poenam adulterii lege Iulia patitur, non etiam ducta.' Cf. 48.5.39.7, Paul, 23.2.68, Paul, on leniency to those who married collaterals because of ignorance of the law.

[106] *D* 48.5.37.

The second chapter dealt with the father's right to take summary vengeance. The wording appears to have been as follows (quotation from the text of the law in capital letters), though the order may have been different:[107]

Secundo vero capite permittit PATRI, SI IN FILIA SUA, QUAM IN POTESTATE HABET, AUT IN EA, QUAE EO AUCTORE, CUM IN POTESTATE ESSET, VIRO IN MANUM CONVENERIT, ADULTERUM DOMI SUAE GENERIVE SUI DEPREHENDERIT ISVE IN EAM REM SOCERUM ADHIBUERIT, UT IS PATER EUM ADULTERUM SINE FRAUDE OCCIDAT, ITA UT FILIAM IN CONTINENTI OCCIDAT. (*Collatio* 4.2.3, Paul *libro singulari de adulteriis*)

But in the second chapter it allows A FATHER, IF IN [THE CASE OF] HIS DAUGHTER, WHOM HE HAS IN HIS POWER, OR OF ONE WHO WITH HIS AUTHORITY WHEN SHE WAS IN HIS POWER HAS COME INTO THE CONTROL OF HER HUSBAND, HE CATCHES AN ADULTERER IN HIS HOUSE OR THE HOUSE OF HIS SON-IN-LAW, OR THE LATTER CALLS IN HIS FATHER-IN-LAW, THAT THAT FATHER MAY WITHOUT RISK TO HIMSELF KILL THAT ADULTERER, PROVIDED THAT HE KILL THE DAUGHTER AT THE SAME TIME.

The father had the privilege even if he were adoptive.[108] But he had to be *paterfamilias*. He could not kill her if he had previously emancipated her. If the father was *filiusfamilias*, he could not kill his daughter, since he did not have direct power over her, nor could her grandfather, who, although he was her *paterfamilias*, was not her father.[109] It is interesting that if the father had authorized his daughter's transition from his own power to the control of her husband that also granted him the privilege.[110] The law may also have specified, as later jurists did, that the father's right was unaffected by the rank of the adulterer.[111]

Jurists argued that this meant that he could kill even an ex-consul or his own patron.[112] The rule about place was strict.[113] The woman did not have to live in her father's house.[114] But if he had more than one house, he could only kill her in the house in which he actually lived.[115] Ulpian suggests the reason for this was that the daughter had committed a graver injury by bringing her lover into the home of her father or husband.[116] The father had to catch his daughter in the act of making

---

[107] *ADA* 113–14.   [108] Paul *S* 2.26.1; *D* 48.5.23 pr.

[109] *Coll.* 4.7.1; *D* 48.5.21, 22 (Ulpian, approving), 24.1. Paul thought that a father who was *filiusfamilias* ought to be allowed to kill his daughter, though it was against the letter of the law (*S* 2.26.2; *Coll.* 4.12.2 says it is allowed). Similarly, Marcellus had argued that a father ought to be allowed to kill an independent daughter (*Coll.* 4.2.4).

[110] Cf. also *Coll.* 4.7.1.

[111] Paul *S* 2.26.1: 'Capite secundo legis Iuliae de adulteriis permittitur patri tam adoptivo quam naturali adulterum cum filia cuiuscumque dignitatis domi suae vel generi sui deprehensum sua manu occidere'; *Coll.* 4.2.5.

[112] *Coll.* 4.2.5, Paul quoting Marcellus; *D* 48.5.25.3.   [113] *D* 23.2.43.13.

[114] *D* 48.5.23.2.   [115] *D* 48.5.24.3.   [116] *D* 48.5.24.2.

love. This was underlined as early as Labeo.[117] It must mean that merely finding a daughter with a man in a possibly compromising situation would not do: there had to be no doubt about their turpitude. The father had to kill both in one immediate and uninter-rupted act: this meant, according to Ulpian, that he could not kill the *adulter* today and keep his daughter to be killed several days later. They had to be killed almost with one blow and in one onslaught, with equal anger against both. But if the daughter ran away while he was killing the lover and he only caught her and killed her several hours later, that would count as an unbroken sequence.[118] It did not matter which he killed first, but if he only killed one he would be accused of murder, under the Sullan *Lex Cornelia*. Nor did he fulfil the letter of the law if he killed one and only succeeded in wounding the other, although the emperors Marcus Aurelius and Commodus granted impunity to a father who had killed the man and seriously wounded the woman, on the grounds that he had, as required, shown equal indignation and severity against both, and fate rather than he had willed her recovery.[119] The father had to kill with his own hand.[120] Papinian regards the Augustan Law as merely reiterating a right to kill the daughter which had existed since the alleged law of the regal period: the novelty was in ordaining that both should be killed.[121]

The right of a husband in similar circumstances is formulated in much the same pattern, but is strictly limited.

Marito quoque adulterum uxoris suae occidere permittitur, sed non quem-libet, ut patri: nam hac lege cavetur, ut liceat viro deprehensum domi suae (non etiam soceri) in adulterio uxoris occidere eum, qui leno fuerit quive artem ludicram ante fecerit in scaenam saltandi cantandive causa prodierit iudiciove publico damnatus neque in integrum restitutus erit, quive libertus eius mariti uxorisve, patris matris, filii filiae utrius eorum fuerit (nec interest, proprius cuius eorum an cum alio communis fuerit) quive servus erit. (*Digest* 48.5.25 [24] pr., Macer 1 *publicorum*)

A husband is also permitted to kill the adulterer of his wife, but not any adulterer at all (as a father is allowed): for the law lays down that it is allowed to a husband, if he catches a man in adultery with his wife in his own house (but not his father-in-law's as well), if he has been a pimp or one who was previously an actor or went on the stage as a dancer or singer, or was condemned in a public court and not restored to his former status, or was a

---

[117] *D* 48.5.24 pr., Ulp. *lib. i de adult.*: 'Quod ait lex, "in filia adulterum deprehenderit", non otiosum videtur: voluit enim ita demum hanc potestatem patri competere, si in ipsa turpitudine filiam de adulterio deprehendat. Labeo quoque ita probat, et Pomponius scripsit in ipsis rebus Veneris deprehensum occidi.' [118] *D* 48.5.24.4; cf. *Coll.* 4.2.6–7, 8.1, 9.1.

[119] *D* 48.5.33 pr., Macer. The father who killed only the man would be arraigned under the *Lex Cornelia de sicariis*. His defence would be helped if his daughter had escaped despite his efforts (*Coll.* 4.9.1, Pap. *lib. sg. de adult.*). [120] Paul *S* 2.26.1. [121] *Coll.* 4.8.1.

freedman of the husband or wife or the father, mother, son, or daughter of either of them (and it makes no difference if he belonged wholly to either, or was shared with somebody else) or who is a slave.

The jurists insist on the vital difference in the privilege of the husband and the father that the husband could only kill the *adulter* with impunity if he belonged to a number of prescribed classes. We are also told by Paul that these included prostitutes, *infames*, gladiators, and those who fought wild animals in the arena.[122]

Alexander Severus wrote to the governor of Narbonese Gaul that a husband who killed an adulterer who belonged to the permitted categories was exempt from punishment, along with his sons who assisted him. But if the adulterer was not in this category, he had committed homicide, although, because it was night and his emotion was justified, he might be let off lightly, with exile.[123]

The other major limitation on the husband, omitted in this passage, is that he had no right to kill his wife.[124] This need not have been explicitly stated in the law. But, according to most jurists, his rights were not affected if he was a *filiusfamilias*.[125] A husband who killed an adulterer had to report the homicide to the responsible magistrate.[126] The killing would then be investigated and the husband would have to prove that the dead man had been caught in adultery in his house and that he belonged to one of the categories mentioned in the law. Only then would the killing be unpunished.[127] It is clear that calculations about the status of the *adulter* would be difficult to make in the heat of the moment. They were useful as retrospective justification if the husband had killed an unidentified man whom he found in bed with his wife, or they might be an element in planning a homicide if the husband had prior information that his wife had a lover.[128]

Although the law did not allow the husband to kill his wife, the crime might be treated with relative leniency. The penalty of the Sullan murder law seemed too harsh to Pius and Marcus, if a husband had acted in reaction to a painful shock. The sentence might be hard

---

[122] *Coll.* 4.3.1–5, 4.12.3. The victim could be a Roman citizen as well as a Latin or a *dediticius*. It could be argued that a freedman who had been given the right to wear gold rings counted as *libertus* for this law (*D* 48.5.43 [42], Tryph.). Cf. *D* 48.5.23.4, Pap. (pointing out that the father could kill any *adulter*); *CJ* 9.9.4 (on status). On the location: *Coll.* 4.12.6.

[123] *CJ* 9.9.4, Alex.

[124] *Coll.* 4.3.1, Paul *lib. sg. de adult.*: 'quamvis uxorem non liceat'; 4.10.1, Pap. *lib. sg. de adult.*: 'nulla parte legis marito uxorem occidere conceditur.'

[125] *D* 48.5.6.2, ht 25.2; *Coll.* 4.3.2.

[126] *Coll.* 4.3.5: 'Debet autem profiteri apud eum, cuius iurisdictio est eo loco, ubi occidit, et uxorem dimittere. Quod si non fecerit, inpune non interficit.' Cf. Paul *S* 2.26.6: within three days.

[127] *D* 48.5.43: 'an inpune occidatur?'; *CJ* 9.9.4 pr.: 'ut . . . impune occidi potuerit.'

[128] Corbett 136–7.

labour for a lower-class uxoricide and relegation for an upper-class man, instead of death and exile.[129]

If the husband killed the *adulter*, he was compelled at once to divorce his wife.[130] The fifth chapter of the law allowed the husband to detain the *adulter*, if he did not wish or was not allowed to kill him, for twenty hours, with the object of securing evidence to prove the adultery.[131]

The law then seems to have gone on to prescribe procedures for prosecution. Certain people, such as minors, were forbidden to prosecute.[132] A wife could not prosecute her husband for adultery.[133] A clause which belonged to chapter 7 prohibited the prosecution for adultery of a man who was abroad on public service.[134]

Procedural matters attracted juristic scholarship. A Roman husband could not *qua* husband prosecute a woman who was *iniusta uxor* because she did not have *conubium* with him. This must be a late accretion.[135] It was obvious that a husband could not prosecute his wife without divorcing her.[136] He could prosecute two (but not more) of his wife's alleged lovers at one time.[137] There was a great deal of discussion on the rules about timing, priority of accusers, and the dropping of charges.[138] It is of some interest that Gordian had to answer three enquiries which turn on the geographical mobility of wives and husbands. His replies make the following points. A wife should normally be prosecuted in the province in which adultery was alleged to have been committed. If a woman left a province after an accusation had been made against her, she could clearly be tried in absence. But if she left the province without being charged, then she could not be tried in absence, nor could the case be transferred to the

---

[129] *D* 48.5.39.8, Pap. *xxxvi quaest.*: 'Imperator Marcus Antoninus et Commodus filius rescripserunt: "Si maritus uxorem in adulterio deprehensam impetu tractus doloris interfecerit, non utique legis Corneliae de sicariis poenam excipiet." Nam et divus Pius in haec verba rescripsit Apollonio: "Ei, qui uxorem suam in adulterio deprehensam occidisse se non negat, ultimum supplicium remitti potest, cum sit difficillimum iustum dolorem temperare et quia plus fecerit, quam quia vindicare se non debuerit, puniendus sit. Sufficiet igitur, si humilis loci sit, in opus perpetuum eum tradi, si qui honestior, in insulam relegari."' Cf. *Coll.* 4.3.5, 12.4 = Paul *S* 2.26.5. *Coll.* 4.10.1 has exile as the maximum.   [130] *D* 48.5.25.1, cf. ht 44 (43); *Coll.* 4.3.5.
[131] *D* 48.5.26 pr., Ulp. *ii ad l. Iuliam de adult.*, quoting the text. The husband was to find witnesses to testify that he had caught the man in adultery: ibid. 5. Ulpian comments that the rule ought also to apply to the father (though the law did not say so), that the husband could arrest a man found in a house other than his own, that a man who was let go could not be brought back, but that one who escaped could be brought back and detained (ibid. 1–4). Paul adds that the witnesses might be neighbours (*S* 2.26.3).
[132] *D* 48.5.16.6, Ulp. *ii ad l. Iuliam de adult.*; cf. 23.2.43.10, 48.2.5. Minors could be sued for adultery: 4.4.37.1.   [133] *CJ* 9.9.1.
[134] *D* 48.5.16 (15) 1, Ulp. Tiberius ruled that if a magistrate or governor was accused of adultery he might be summoned but not tried and was to give sureties for his appearance after he left office. (ht 39 [38] 10).   [135] *Coll.* 4.5.1, Pap.   [136] *CJ* 9.9.11, AD 226.
[137] Paul *S* 2.26.10.   [138] *D* 48.5.12.4–11, 12.3, 16–20, 30.5–32, 36.

province where the husband, a soldier, was serving. He must postpone the accusation until he was free of military duties.[139]

The most important point of procedure is that a married woman
cannot normally be accused of adultery. A woman whose husband
had not divorced her, or died, could not be prosecuted for an alleged
adultery committed during that marriage. 'As long as a marriage lasts
. . . a woman cannot be accused of adultery: for a third party ought
not to disturb and trouble a wife approved by her husband and a
tranquil marriage, unless he has first accused the husband of pandering.' She was also protected from prosecution if that marriage had
ended and she had married again without notice of prosecution (of
her or her adulterer) being given. A prosecutor could bring charges
against her alleged adulterer. If he was acquitted, the woman could
not be charged. She was at risk if she was unmarried, or if the accused
adulterer died during the trial procedure or was condemned on
another charge. If the man was convicted of adultery, a case could be
brought against the woman (even though married), but the previous
verdict did not mean that she would necessarily also be condemned.
All this is Ulpian, some of it controversial.[140]

The ninth chapter laid down that if a slave were accused of adultery
and the prosecution wished to have him cross-examined under torture, he was to be valued and a sum equivalent to double the
valuation was to be paid to his owner.[141] The general rule was that
such compensation for loss was paid to the owner if a slave was
accused of a crime, tortured, and subsequently acquitted.[142]

There were also elaborate rules on obtaining evidence from other
slaves, who were likely to be the most important witnesses in a case of
this nature.[143] Both male and female slaves belonging to a man or
woman accused of adultery, or belonging to a parent who had turned
the slave over to the defendant's use, might be put to the torture. The
prosecutor and the accused and his or her advocate were to be present
at the interrogation and the latter might cross-examine.[144] If slave

---

[139] *CJ* 9.9.12, 14, 15.   [140] *D* 48.5.18, 28. Cf. *CJ* 9.9.13, AD 240.

[141] *D* 48.5.28 pr.–5, 16, Ulp. *iii ad l. Iuliam de adult.* The person to whom the compensation
was paid is defined in the law as 'the person to whom the matter shall pertain', a phrase which
required glossing. Riccobono (*ADA*) lists the material on torture of slaves under ch. VII, but
that on compensation under IX. Material on the compensation paid to the owner of the slave
defendant certainly belonged to IX (ht 28.16). I have for convenience put the rules on torture
and manumission here too.

[142] *D* 3.6.9, Pap.? Cf. *CJ* 9.46.6.   [143] *Coll.* 4.11.1, Pap.

[144] 48.5.28.6–7, Ulp. Various glosses on who is the slave of the accused: ibid. 8–10. Extension
by Hadrian to slaves outside the household: ibid. 6. Slaves of defendant or prosecutor were
confiscated by the state after torture (if they survived): ibid. 11–16. The wife's grandparents'
slaves, if employed by her, were included: *D* 40.9.12.5, Ulp. *iv de adult.* For comment see
Brunt, 'Evidence given under torture' 256–8. Such torture may have been specifically allowed
in the original law only if the prosecutor was the father or husband: Marcus extended it to cases

witnesses were tortured and the defendant acquitted, the judges assessed the compensation payable to the owner for death or injury: this was for the amount of the loss, not double.[145] Augustus prohibited manumission within a certain period of any slaves who might be needed as witnesses. After a divorce a woman (since she might be charged with adultery by her husband or father within sixty days) was not allowed in the sixty days subsequent to the divorce to manumit or alienate any of her slaves. The same rule applied to any slaves owned by her parent or grandparent and given over to her use: this includes manumission by will if the owner died within the period. This rule was not carefully drafted and caused considerable juristic comment. Ulpian, for instance, following Sex. Caecilius, argued that, since a trial would hardly be completed within sixty days, the rule should be held to apply to the time of the trial too.[146]

In practice the scope of the statute was widened to allow, for instance, the torture of slaves in whom the defendant had a usufruct. Jurists explored the intentions of the law: Ulpian explains the rule about confiscation, for instance, by claiming that it is so that the slave of prosecutor or defendant shall have no interest in testifying what his owner wants.[147]

The remaining provisions of the law are not assigned to particular chapters. The husband and father enjoyed priority in bringing a prosecution. They had sixty days to accuse *iure mariti* or *iure patris*.[148] After them, outsiders (*extranei*) were allowed to prosecute within the next four months. The time ran, for a married woman, from the date of divorce, for a single woman from the commission of the offence.[149] If several *extranei* presented themselves, the competent judge was to

where an outsider prosecuted. Cf. *D* 48.18.17 pr. Pap.; *Coll.* 4.11.1; *CJ* 9.9.3, 6.1; *ADA* 118; Brunt, art. cit. 256. This fits in with the 60-day ban on manumissions.

[145] *D* 48.5.28.15–16, 48.18.6 pr.

[146] *D* 40.9.12–14. Sex. Caecilius seems to have taken a strong line on problems in the law and may have dedicated a book to it (Honoré, *Ulpian* 222). Ulpian held that the prohibition did not apply after consensual divorce (ht 14.4, cf. Solazzi, 'Divortium bona gratia'). Cf. *CJ* 9.9.3, 9.9.35 pr.–1.

[147] *D* 48.5.28 (27) 8, 11–14. Brunt, 'Evidence given under torture', argues convincingly that the law originally required the slaves to be confiscated before torture, not after, as in Ulpian's day.

[148] *D* 48.5.2.8, 14, 12.7–13, 15.2; *Coll.* 4.4.1, Paul; *CTh* 9.19.4; *CJ* 9.9.1. Some texts say that they need not fear prosecution for false accusation if the defendant was acquitted (*D* 4.4.37.1; *Coll.* 4.4.1). Those which contradict are emended by moderns: *D* 48.5.31 pr., 15.3. The father qualified as for the right to kill (*D* 48.5.15.2, 25.3). Later the father of an emancipated daughter was allowed to sue *iure patris* (*Coll.* 4.7.1, Pap.). Esmein, 'La délit d'adultère à Rome' 118ff., has a full discussion of procedure.

[149] *D* 48.5.4.1, ht 30.5–6; cf. ht 16.5, 31.1. A man charged with adultery could be prosecuted up to five years from the date of the crime, even though the woman was dead (ht 12 [11] 4, 32 [31]), but not later (*CJ* 9.9.5, AD 223). The limit did not apply to incest (ht 40.5). The rules were altered in AD 295 (*CJ* 9.9.27).

decide who should act.[150] The order in which the *adulteri* should be prosecuted was also regulated. The law forbade simultaneous prosecution of both.[151] If the woman were *vidua* (no longer married), the accuser might choose; if she were still married or had remarried, he must start with the man.[152] But if a husband had divorced his wife and given her notice of accusation so that she would not remarry, he could prosecute even though she had married again.[153] Rules about the dropping of an adultery charge and the possibility of renewing it may have appeared in the adultery law itself, but are of no great interest.[154]

The law also introduced a charge of pandering or procuring (*lenocinium*), which covered various activities and was stretched to cover others.[155] A husband who caught his wife in adultery and kept her as his wife, letting the man go, was liable for pandering.[156] The jurists argued that he was not liable unless he had 'caught the adulterer in his house' and that this must mean in the act. If he could claim not to know or not to believe it, he could defend himself.[157] It was also procuring if the husband profited from his wife's adultery.[158] Daube has argued convincingly that what the legislator had in mind was the husband who, on discovering adultery, waived his right to kill the adulterer or prosecute him or divorce and prosecute his wife, either gratuitously or in return for some consideration. He was not simply receiving hush-money.[159] The late republican practice of a quiet divorce or of mulcting the other man was excluded. The law seems also to have envisaged a husband who arranged in advance to take profit from his wife's adultery. If he ignored it through carelessness or over-trustfulness, that was not held to be an offence.[160] Conniving husbands are part of the contemporary portrayal of moral decadence.[161] Anyone who maliciously brought it about that a man or woman taken in adultery bought himself or herself off by money or any other means was liable as for procuring.[162] This much seems to have been in the original text.[163]

Daube doubts whether certain other categories of accessories were specifically described in the original statute. Those who provided

[150] *D* 48.5.2.9. The jurists debated whether husband or father should have priority, normally preferring the husband (ht 2.8, 3, 4 pr., 16 [15] pr.). For other sources see *ADA* 121 n. 2.
[151] *CJ* 9.9.8; cf. *D* 48.5.16.9, ht 18.6.   [152] *D* 48.5.5; cf. ht 2 pr.
[153] *D* 48.5.17; cf. ht 18 pr.   [154] See *ADA* 126-7.
[155] *D* 48.5.11.1, on providing accommodation and profiting from the discovery of an affair. On this see Daube, 'The *Lex Julia* concerning adultery' 373-7. Cf. ht 9 (specifying an assignation with someone else's wife or a male), 10, 30.6; 4.4.37.1; *CJ* 9.9.10.
[156] *D* 48.5.30 pr.; cf. ht 2.2, 12.13, 34.1, 4.4.37.1; *Coll.* 4.12.7; *CJ* 9.9.25 (26).
[157] *D* 48.5.30 pr., Ulp.; *CJ* 9.9.2, Severus and Caracalla (AD 199).
[158] *D* 48.5.2.2, ht 9 pr., ht 30.3-4.
[159] 'The *Lex Julia* concerning adultery' 374.   [160] *D* 48.5.30.4.
[161] Hor. *O* 3.6.25-32 etc. Cf. Tracy, 'The *leno-maritus*'.   [162] 48.5.15(14) pr.
[163] *D* 48.5, 2.2, ht 30.3. Cf. ht 9 pr., 30.4; 4.4.37.1.

accommodation to adulterers or took bribes to conceal fornication were liable: the similarity of the jurists' language suggests a common source. Papinian says that this applied to women too, which suggests that they were not explicitly mentioned in this clause.[164] But why should they be, if the prohibition was expressed generally, as usual, with the masculine pronoun *qui*? I am inclined to think that the rule against the person who provided accommodation appeared in the law. Adultery in the house of father or husband had been to some extent discouraged. It is unlikely to have escaped the notice of lovers that the safest rendezvous was not in a house belonging to either of themselves (since their slaves might be examined) nor in a common inn (not favoured by the upper classes) but in the house of a friend. Catullus had immortalized Allius, who lent a house in which he and his lady could consummate their love.[165] The jurists defined 'house' as any residence, or even a bath-house, and found that if someone provided a place in which the couple could discuss a future act of adultery, he was certainly liable.[166] Taking bribes to conceal adultery is not subsumed under helping adulterers to buy immunity. There would be room for this offence of third parties in the statute. At some point this subcategory of accessories was subdivided to make wives a subgroup. If the wife took a reward for conniving in her husband's adultery, she counted as a quasi-adulteress, as pandering was equated with adultery.[167] This may arise from an actual case. On the other hand, if Augustus was really concerned about connivance between *coniuges* in the upper classes, he would have done well to pay some attention to the wife, who was among those most likely to become aware of her husband's affair with a married woman. We might expect her to divorce him and claim that he was responsible for the divorce. He, if he wished to keep her, or prevent her from talking to others who might prosecute, had a motive to offer financial considerations, or the *adultera* might offer social advantages or indirect benefit to a child: the possibilities of discreet profit are manifold.

It is noteworthy that merely knowing about adultery and doing nothing was not an offence, except for the husband who took his wife *in flagrante delicto*. There seems to have been a loophole here.

Tryphoninus gives a useful check-list of many of the offences which were punished as if they were adultery, *pro adulterio*: knowingly marrying a woman condemned for adultery, not divorcing a wife taken in adultery, making a profit from one's wife's adultery, taking a

---

[164] *D* 48.5.11.1. [165] 68.68–9. [166] *D* 48.5.9–10.

[167] *D* 48.5.34.2. Equation: 4.4.37.1. But, as Daube points out ('The *Lex Julia* concerning adultery' 373), it was more correct to say that the statute made a person liable to a penalty as if he had committed a crime such as adultery or theft (G 3.194).

reward for concealing fornication one had discovered, providing a
house for the commission of adultery or fornication.[168]

The law prescribed fixed penalties: for adulteresses confiscation of
half their dowries and one third of their property and relegation to an
island, for male adulterers confiscation of half their property and
relegation to a different island.[169] The male who allowed himself to be
seduced by another man had half his property confiscated.[170] Marrying a woman condemned for adultery was punishable as adultery.[171]
The law forbade a condemned adulteress to give evidence. Paul used
this point in order to prove that women normally had the right to
testify in court. We may deduce that men condemned under the law
were also disqualified.[172]

The woman found in adultery by anyone and anywhere, even
though not accused, was disqualified, according to Ulpian, from
marriage with a senator.[173]

The penalties laid down by the law were already exceeded by
Augustus.[174] Under the later procedure which replaced the *quaestio*,
the penalty could be made either harsher or more lenient. Constantine probably increased the statutory penalty for both *adulteri* to
execution, as, in an obscure but hysterical rescript, Constans and
Constantius did for homosexuality, 'the crime which it is not
profitable to know'.[175]

The important innovation that a husband could not, without the
wife's permission, alienate an estate in Italy which was part of dowry
belongs to the adultery law.[176]

[168] *D* 4.4.37.1.
[169] Paul *S* 2.26.14: 'Adulterii convictas mulieres dimidia parte dotis et tertia parte bonorum
ac relegatione in insulam placuit coerceri: adulteris vero viris pari in insulam relegatione
dimidiam bonorum partem auferri, dummodo in diversas insulas relegentur.' Since it would
usually be the husband who had to pay over the dowry, concessions had in practice to be made if
he could not produce the whole amount, 'so that the punishment of the wife should not ruin the
husband'. He could make the usual deductions from the dowry (*D* 24.3.36; 48.20.4). Riccobono
(*ADA* 126 n. 2) has a useful list of individuals punished by relegation. Just. *Inst.* 4.18.4 claims
that the Julian Law punished both adulterers and homosexuals with execution. Augustus
himself went beyond his law in imposing a death penalty (Tac. *A* 3.24.2–3) and it is frequently
attested from the 3rd cent. onwards (*ADA* 126 n. 3).
[170] *Coll.* 5.2.2 (also mentioning that they usually lost the right to make a will). Just. *Inst.*
4.18.4 (which might apply to the seducer too, and which mentions the later penalty of flogging
and relegation for *humiliores*) confirms that confiscation was prescribed by the Julian Law.
[171] *D* 48.5.30.1; cf. 4.4.37.1, 23.2.26, 25.7.1.2; *CJ* 9.9.17 pr., 9.9.9.
[172] *D* 22.5.18. Riccobono (*ADA* 128 n. 2) draws attention to Papinian's question whether
those convicted under the adultery law could witness wills. It seems then that the law imposed
specific disqualifications and did not explicitly make those convicted generally *intestabiles*. We
may note again the incapacity of the condemned homosexual to make a will.
[173] *D* 23.2.43.10–13.
[174] See Biondi, 'La *poena adulterii* da Augusto a Giustiniano'; *ADA* 126.
[175] Corbett 146; *CJ* 9.9.30, AD 342.
[176] Paul *S* 2.21b.2, with supporting evidence in *ADA* 127 n. 3. For the limitation to Italy cf. *CJ*

(b) Ancient and modern reactions to the Julian Law

The law has been variously assessed. Augustus claimed that his legislation revived exemplary ancestral customs and set standards for posterity.[177] Horace modified his earlier view that laws without morality were doomed to failure and praised the sudden chastity of his contemporaries. Perhaps their hearts were changed.[178] Ovid mocked, too overtly.[179] Tacitus later endorsed Horace's pessimism.[180] Moderns have taken opposing views of the law's aims and methods. Gide sums up as follows:

Telles furent ces lois qu'Auguste intitulait lois sur la pudeur, et par lesquelles il se vantait d'avoir restauré les mœurs antiques. Jamais la morale et la pudeur publiques n'ont été plus insolemment outragées, même au siècle honteux d'Octave et de Tibère, que le jour où ces princes s'avisèrent de les prendre sous leur protection.[181]

But later writers often praise Augustus' efforts. As Raditsa has pointed out, it appealed to the conscience of moralists in the post-war era of the 1920s and 1930s, a time in which Mussolini and Hitler tried similar experiments.[182] Hugh Last, for instance, found much to praise:

This Lex Julia de adulteriis coercendis was an outstanding piece of legislation, and one which endured as the basis of Roman law on the subjects with which it was concerned. By bringing the family as an institution under public protection it marked a notable advance in the conception of the proper functions of the State and, by penalizing the practices of an age when men and women had begun to seek their own pleasure alone, it opened the way for a return to the ancient view of marriage as a union 'liberorum quaerundorum caussa'.[183]

P. E. Corbett is betrayed by the sources' emphasis on 'the peccant wife' (Last's phrase) into a one-sided assertion that the law 'would . . . provide a very necessary check up on the growing independence and recklessness of women'.[184] John Buchan in 1937 took a more measured view of the marriage and adultery laws as a package:

5.13.1.15; Just. *Inst.* 2.8 pr. But G 2.63 mentions doubt as to whether the rule should also apply to provincial land, Gaius also shows that the law provided that the husband could not encumber dotal land (*D* 23.5.4).

[177] *RG* 8.5.   [178] *O* 3.24.35 ff., 4.5.20 ff., 4.15.9 ff.; *Carm. saec.* 17 ff.

[179] e.g. *AA* 3.611 ff. *F* 2.139 ff. contrasts Romulus' violent rape of the Sabines and protection of outlaws with Augustus' preference for law and prescription of chastity to wives under his leadership. Lyne, *The Latin love poets from Catullus to Horace* ch. 10, gives a succinct statement of the tendency of the *Amores* to undermine the law.

[180] *A* 3.27.5, *H* 1.2.   [181] p. 171.

[182] See esp. *ANRW* ii/13.286 ff.

[183] *CAH* x.447. *Contra*, Balsdon, *RW* 78.

[184] p. 130. This echoes Dio 54.16.3, who speaks of the *akosmia* of women and young men.

Such legislation . . . was, indeed, wholly consistent with Roman tradition and with the best Roman habit of mind. But means of evasion were soon found, and beyond question his laws were in advance of general public opinion, an opinion which grew laxer as the years passed. Law should be regarded as an elastic tissue which clothes a growing body. That tissue, that garment, must fit exactly; if it is too tight, it will split and there will be lawlessness; if it is too loose, it will impede movement. It should not be too far behind, or too far ahead of, the growth of society, but should, as nearly as possible, coincide with that growth. Augustus's experiments were in advance of Rome's wishes, and though they might remain on the statute-book they suffered the fate of recent prohibition laws in the United States.

> Quid leges sine moribus
> vanae proficiunt?

. . . Yet the purpose did not wholly fail. Morality by acts of Parliament is an unattainable ideal, but such acts may do something to create a 'climate of opinion'. They acted as a brake, though a feeble one, upon one sort of ethical decline.[185]

The son of the manse, colonial administrator, lawyer, and Member of Parliament who, at the time he wrote that, had as Governor-General the prerogative of signing Canadian legislation, had every right to form such an opinion. But the conclusion reads like wishful thinking. There is little evidence that Augustus changed opinions or standards of behaviour in his own time.

Well before 1939 some eyes were open.

That there was a certain duplicity in the social programme of the Princeps is evident enough. More than that, the whole conception of the Roman past upon which he sought to erect the moral and spiritual basis of the New State was in a large measure imaginary or spurious, the creation conscious or unconscious of patriotic historians or publicists who adapted to Roman language Greek theories about primitive virtue and about the social degeneration that comes from wealth and empire.[186]

Anti-authoritarianism, the loosening of the coercive power of the churches, 'women's liberation', the sexual revolution, and the growing individualism of the 1960s and 1970s have enabled us in the 1980s and 1990s to see the law as repressive, cruel, hypocritical, counter-productive. Our conception is as much shaped by our own times and personalities as is that of nineteenth-century liberals or paternal conservatives who grew up in the 1880s and 1890s.[187]

Augustus was certainly far from the truth in claiming he had revived old customs. Although there had been some public control of

---

[185] *Augustus* 225–6.

[186] Syme, *RR* 452–3, cf. 444–5. The moral legislation is dismissively treated.

[187] Raditsa ('Augustus' legislation concerning marriage, procreation, love affairs and adultery') is an excellent example of the new-style interpreter.

sexual morality, Cicero prescribed the republican norm that the state should keep out of the homes of its citizens. Marauding men who sacked other men's houses by seducing their women might draw the disapproval of censors, but the task of keeping women in order was mostly delegated to their husbands and menfolk. Two of Augustus' innovations suggest that he thought that neither husbands nor fathers were doing their job. Both sets of elaborate rules involve a woman caught in the act: those concerning the conniving husband and those which compel a father to kill his daughter as well as her lover. Both would involve the man in such a painful or expensive situation that they might be expected to deter him from the hasty opening of any bedroom door. It has often been suggested that the rules about killing were intended to discourage killing: Augustus removed from husbands the privilege of killing a wife with impunity and severely restricted the rights of fathers. But if the hypothetical right to kill out of hand had in fact rarely been exercised in the late Republic, then one may ask if such rules were necessary. I lean rather to the view that Augustus was trying to deter potential adulterers by reviving alleged ancient custom. There were good reasons why he should not give the husband power to kill the wife, a right which might play into the hands of murderers.[188] Use of the 'privilege' of killing seems to have been rare.[189]

Where women are oppressed behind the closed doors of their homes, then legislation which brings domestic matters into the open court ought to be to their advantage.[190] If Augustus stopped the quiet murder of wives and daughters and slaves, it would be much to his credit. But no evidence suggests that this is the truth of the matter. Rather he kept alive, revived, or invented a custom which would later grow and on to which would be grafted new ideas of family honour. The Julian Law is at the root of the justification of the *delitto di onore* which has encroached so successfully in the law and court practice of Mediterranean countries.[191]

The law offered some encouragement to women to stay married.

[188] A husband might stand to benefit financially if his wife died; if he accused her successfully he stood to lose, since the state would take half her dowry and he would presumably only get one-sixth. See Pap. (*D* 48.5.23.4) on the wisdom of checking the husband's anger.

[189] Traces in rescripts of Marcus and Commodus on a father who wounded but did not kill his daughter (*D* 48.5.33 pr., Macer), of Pius and of Marcus and Commodus on husbands who killed wives (*D* 48.5.39.8, Pap.), and of Alexander on a husband and his sons killing an *adulter* (*CJ* 9.9.4).

[190] Cf. Daube, 'Fraud no. 3' 3–4: 'Augustus' ordinance, oppressive and male-chauvinist as it was, by bringing her before a public tribunal, did inch towards her treatment as a person rather than as an object.'

[191] Cantarella, 'Adulterio, omicidio legittimo e causa d'onore in diritto romano'; Campbell 193 ff.

They could not be sued as long as they did. On the other hand, if a woman divorced one husband to marry another or to remain single, she might lay herself open to charges of adultery in the first marriage.[192] The law must have made it considerably more dangerous than before for a woman to divorce a husband unilaterally and to form a successful new marriage, especially if there was an emotional motive or even a previous acquaintance with the new husband.

If we look at things from the point of view of the husband, we can see that his wife's reputation needed to be above suspicion. If it were not, and in particular if he could be shown to have had knowledge of her adultery with another man, he could be prosecuted by a third party. If he were rich, he might well tempt a prosecutor. The only way out of a risky situation might be to divorce and prosecute his wife himself, in order to prove her innocence. Then she could remarry him or another. The jurists were familiar with collusive prosecutions.[193] The courts also met husbands who suborned men to seduce their wives, a trick which was apparently common enough to necessitate a senatorial decree. The wife's fault was not condoned. If a husband was prosecuting his wife or her lover, neither of them would be exculpated by a countercharge of *lenocinium*.[194] Caracalla demanded that a husband set his wife an example of virtuous life, but again, says Ulpian, his misconduct did not lighten her punishment, but meant that he should be charged too.[195] By introducing such a structure of charge and countercharge, Augustus can hardly be thought to have raised the tone of conjugal life. He had merely made wife, husband, and their slaves and friends more insecure.

(c) Effectiveness of the Julian Law

Did the law repress adultery? To answer that question we would need statistics on the situation before and after. Such statistics are by nature unobtainable. Even now anonymous respondents to a questionnaire would conceal or exaggerate their own affairs and over- (or perhaps under-)estimate those of others. For the Roman period we have, outside love poetry, no autobiographical confessions of adultery. Genres which purport to describe the adulteries of others are difficult to use. Allegations of adultery were part of the republican orator's stock, although less damaging than pathic homosexuality or incest.[196] Such slurs, inspired by advocacy or politics, were easily invented. They pass into the biographies of Suetonius and Plutarch. Salacious gossip about the great seems to have continued after the

---

[192] *D* 48.5.12.10–11, Pap., 27, Ulp., 40.1, Pap. Cf. Esmein, 'Le délit d'adultère à Rome' 132.
[193] *D* 48.5.3, Ulp.   [194] *D* 48.5.15.1, Scaev., ht 2.4–6, Ulp.   [195] *D* 48.5.14.5, Ulp.
[196] e.g. Cic. *Cat.* 2.23, *Pro Flacco* 34, *Sest.* 20, *Pis.* 70, *Cael.* 29, 35.

passage of the Julian Law. Emperors, like republican *principes*, were favourite targets and malicious stories did them little damage. Allegations about ordinary senators, which in Cicero's day had been part of the cut and thrust of debate, might now turn into deliberate attempts to ruin them. But the contemporary sources which would reflect frivolous gossip (such as the letters of Caelius) are now absent, so we cannot say that people refrained from spreading rumours. The existence of scandalous allegations in the historiographical tradition suggests that they did not. Motive is often sought in illicit liaisons. Some instances are collected in Appendix 1. The moralists and satirists claimed that sexual excesses were rife. Again, it is hard to judge how much they relied on observation and counting, and how much on literary tradition.[197] Tacitus' declaration that, despite the law, there were scandalous adulteries and the islands were filled up with banished men and women sounds more convincing, but he too is arguing a case, against the law.[198]

The later history of the law ought to shed light on its effectiveness. But the attestation of adultery trials, our best available evidence, raises problems (cf. Appendix 2). Garnsey puts the matter clearly:

Finally, the relative absence of reference to simple adultery indictments against ordinary members of the senatorial order deserves comment. Perhaps the sources were selective and passed over the more routine senatorial investigations. Even allowing for a few such indictments, it still seems likely that there was no even enforcement of the adultery law within the senatorial order—if 'enforcement' is the word, for Tiberius launched no 'crusade' against adultery in the higher orders, and the private prosecutors, who alone could have carried out such a project, were already fully employed in a more lofty mission, that of protecting the Emperor against challenges to his *maiestas*.[199]

Enforcement was difficult from the start. Dio claims that before 16 BC Augustus failed to enforce his laws by even-handed treatment of the accused.[200] Tacitus accuses him of imposing severer penalties than those he had prescribed.[201] Tiberius returned on occasion to domestic jurisdiction. Other emperors reinforced the law and applied

---

[197] See Sen. *Ben.* 1.9.3–4, 3.16.2–3, *Cons. ad Helviam* 16.3 ('maximum saeculi malum, impudicitia'); Juv. 2 (homosexuality), 6 (adultery, *passim*), 14.25–33 (the adulteress an example to her daughter). But Seneca also argues that all generations always have complained of the immorality of their age, and always will. Men are always wicked, vice fluctuates: though sometimes adultery is more popular than other sins, the increase is relatively slight (*Ben.* 1.10.1–2). Moderns are knowledgeable: there was 'une véritable épidémie de séparations conjugales qui, ayant son origine dans l'habituelle infidélité des époux, tend, sous l'Empire, à devenir endémique' (Salvatore, 'L'immoralité des femmes et la décadence de l'empire selon Tacite' 261; cf. Carcopino 107ff.). [198] *H* 1.2. [199] *Social status* 24. [200] 54.19.2, 55.10.16. [201] *A* 2.50.

it strictly. Some might think the law slept.[202] Others hated and feared
the law and found it ironical when the noted adulterer Domitian
revived it.[203] Trajan is known to have gone out of his way to clear up
one case of adultery in order to set a precedent and avoid having
similar cases referred to him. A military tribune designed for a
senatorial career had complained to his commanding officer of his
wife's adultery with a centurion. The legate reported the matter to
Trajan, who cashiered and relegated the centurion. He then put
pressure on the husband, who in the mean time had become reconciled to his wife, to divorce her and continue with his accusation. The
case was heard at Centumcellae before the emperor and his council,
which on this occasion included Pliny. Trajan sentenced the wife
according to the statutory penalties, but put on record remarks about
military discipline.[204] Later, Septimius Severus passed measures
against adultery, including a constitution about slaves accused of
adultery with their mistresses. If a woman was accused of adultery
with her slave and subsequently died, Septimius disallowed her
attempt by will to free the man and make him her heir until after
sentence had been passed on him. This sounds like a general ruling
produced by a specific case. Cassius Dio found 3,000 cases pending
when he was consul—but the prosecutors usually did not follow them
through, and the emperor himself lost interest.[205] Caracalla enforced
the law unevenly, increasing the penalty to death.[206] Constantine
considered that outsiders brought false and vexatious charges, dis-
honouring marriage. He therefore reserved the right of accusation for
the husband and the wife's father, brother, or uncle.[207] Unlike the
Augustan marriage law, the adultery law remained on the statute-
book, though its provisions continued to be modified.[208]

The Senate also concerned itself with the operation of the law.
Senatorial decrees on the matter need not have been inspired by the

---

[202] Juv. 2.37: 'ubi nunc lex Iulia? dormis?', the words of a homosexual attacking women.

[203] Juv. 2.29ff.; Mart. 6.2.4, 6.4.5, 6.7.1–2, 6.91 (bk 6 is of AD 90), 9.5; Suet. *Dom.* 8.3. Mart.
1.74, 6.22, cf. 45, play with the idea that the Julian Law compels illicit lovers to marry.

[204] Pliny *Epp.* 6.31.4, with Sherwin-White ad loc, and Williams, *Change and decline* 154. For
Hadrian, *D* 29.1.41.1.

[205] *D* 28.5.49.2 and Just. *Inst.* 2.14 pr.; Dio 77.16.4 (Teubner 76.16.4). Cf. Mommsen,
Römisches Strafrecht 220 n. 5, 696 n. 2; Millar, *A Study of Cassius Dio* 17, 204ff.; Barnes,
'Cassius Dio's *Roman History*' 243, for this interpretation of what the list represents, *not* the
total for Dio's consular year or the whole reign of Severus. See also Wiedemann, *JRS* 71 (1981)
202. The passage shows that imperial encouragement might cause a steep increase in accusations, without ensuring that they were followed through.

[206] Dio 78.16.4 (Teubner 77.16.4).

[207] *CTh* 9.7.2; *CJ* 9.9.29: 'ne volentibus temere liceat foedare conubia . . . Extraneos . . .
procul arceri ab accusatione censemus: nam . . . nonnulli . . . proterve id faciunt et falsis
contumeliis matrimonia deformant.'

[208] For the changes made by Constantine and later emperors see Corbett 145–6.

emperor: often they are a reaction to scandals in the higher orders or to the perception of administrative problems.[209]

There were attempts to evade the law. Some upper-class women early on registered as prostitutes or engaged in activities which could technically define them as procuresses or actresses or professionals of the arena in order to escape the law. The scandalous case of Vistilia, a lady of praetorian family, who registered with the aediles as a prostitute, led to the closing of this loophole by a senatorial decree (or perhaps two) in AD 19. This measure prohibited descendants of senators of either sex down to great grandchildren, men or women whose father, either grandfather, or brother, and women whose husband had at any time possessed the right to sit in the fourteen rows reserved for the *equites*, from engaging in such professions.[210]

All this suggests that the law did not command assent and that the governing class as a whole did not encourage delation. Professional prosecutors who wanted to make big profits might find the risks even greater than in treason or extortion trials, because witnesses would be fewer and of lower status. Sporadically both Senate and emperors saw a need to tighten up: with imperial encouragement, prosecutors might at least lay charges. When eminent women were charged, treason was often also alleged and the case came before the Senate. Routine—and perhaps more genuine—prosecutions will have come before the standing court or, later, before curule magistrates or the prefect of the city in Rome and before governors in the provinces.[211]

The continuous interest of jurists in the law suggests that their concerns were not merely theoretical and that there was a critical mass of prosecutions.[212] While most people below the senatorial order and the wealthier *equites* were not worth the attentions of the senatorial advocates who are notorious in the sources as frequent *delatores*, modest fortunes combined with mild scandal may have been enough to tempt impecunious outside prosecutors. A woman's indignant relatives, whether 'outsiders' or father and husband, may

[209] Above, p. 281. For a conspectus, Talbert ch. 15, especially SCC nos. 22, 140, 183, 221; 60, 224 would also be relevant.

[210] Suet. *Tib.* 35.3; Tac. *A* 2.85.1; *D* 48.5.11.2. A copy of the decree has now come to light at Larinum: *AE* 1978.145. C. Ateius Capito was among the witnesses. See the edition and commentary by Levick, 'The *senatus consultum* from Larinum', and discussion of self-disqualification by Daube, 'Fraud no. 3' 2ff. For Vistilia's eminent family connections see Syme, 'Domitius Corbulo'.

[211] See Garnsey, 'Adultery trials and the survival of the quaestiones in the Severan age', and *Social status* 21ff.; Bauman, 'Some remarks on the structure and survival of the *quaestio de adulteriis*'; Talbert 466. For governors see *D* 48.2.3 pr., 48.8.2; for prefect 48.8.2.

[212] Papinian, Paul, and Ulpian all wrote monographs on the law. Cf. *ADA* 112; Bauman, 'Some remarks on the structure and survival of the *quaestio de adulteriis*', for the unusual prominence of this crime in the jurists.

also have prosecuted for personal revenge rather than profit. There may be a considerable number of prosecutions of alleged *adulteri* by husbands, without the expected follow-up in prosecutions of wives, since the lover may be acquitted or the prosecutor relent. In making adultery a crime, Augustus gave scope to two kinds of prosecutors: people closely related to the accused and motivated by a spirit of revenge, and outside *delatores*, champions of morality or seekers after gain. Prosecutions for extortion might be initiated by injured provincials and carried through by senatorial advocates, but the pool of potential prosecutors in extortion cases was tiny by comparison with those in adultery trials. The number of possible defendants was also infinitely larger. It was chiefly senators and administrators who risked accusations of treason, extortion, or electoral bribery, though upper-class women were occasionally involved in the first two. Ordinary citizens were not at risk, and if law-abiding had no cause to fear the laws on forgery, assassination, violence, or slave-stealing. But almost anyone, of any class and either sex, could be charged with adultery or *stuprum*.

Augustus had invented an odd crime. The extent and complexity of writing on this law are in striking contrast with Roman treatment of offences against clearly identified victims, such as rape and theft. In the Roman context, the Julian Law is surely anomalous. English law, in refusing to make adultery or lesbianism a crime and, more recently, in 'decriminalizing' homosexual relations in private between two consenting males over 21, has shown more sense. The inequities of the operation of the adultery law in twentieth-century Italy, for instance, are instructive: it affected only women and chiefly the under-privileged, and was often an instrument of revenge. For Rome, I suggest that the penalties fell heaviest on prominent and rich *adulteri*, prosecuted by outsiders, and perhaps on the less eminent against whom husbands, kin, and neighbours bore a grudge. The solidarity of the classes at risk may at times have softened the severity of the deterrent, just as discreet homosexuality often flourished in England although it was illegal.

The need for discretion if not rectitude was brought home to the aristocracy by the public disgrace of Augustus' own daughter in 2 BC. After Ovid's *Art of love* was published that year or soon after, poets eschewed overt encouragement of *la vie galante*. But a criminal law does not usually render the crime obsolete. The Julian Law probably deterred some; an example was made of some transgressors when opportunity arose.

II. ATTITUDES

We have discussed law and the repression of sexual activity which was seen as illicit. Earlier, we reviewed the teaching of moralists, which reached its highest expression in the attempt of Musonius and others to demand the same standard of sexual fidelity from husband and wife.[214] Here, I shall try to get to grips with the ideas which Romans expressed about sexual behaviour when they were not writing as philosophers or attributing ideal virtue to dead *coniuges*. An approach to their mentality can be made through the delicate and perennially disputed area of the 'double standard'.[215]

1. The Double Standard

In a seminal article on the double standard in England in the modern period, especially the seventeenth to nineteenth centuries, Keith Thomas defined it as follows: 'Stated simply, it is the view that unchastity, in the sense of sexual relations before marriage or outside marriage, is for a man, if an offense, none the less a mild and pardonable one, but for a woman a matter of the utmost gravity.'[216] Where a double standard exists, society as a whole permits, and often encourages, young men to gain sexual experience, but demands that unmarried girls preserve their virginity. It condones extra-marital encounters, if not long-term affairs, for married men, but condemns adulterous wives. Such attitudes can coexist with attempts by theologians to set higher standards. An extreme double standard occurs when the rake sets the example of virile behaviour, when the ruining of virgins and wives becomes an object. In its more moderate form, the inconsistent demands of continence for women and conquest for men are resolved by the presence of a class of women who are treated as 'fair game', women of another class or social group than a man's own or women designated as prostitutes. These two groups may of course overlap.[217] Thomas traces the operation of a double standard in English law. I shall begin with a search for literary expression of the idea.

[214] pp. 199–201, 211–28, esp. pp. 221–2, and Appendix 3.

[215] Anyone working on this theme must be indebted especially to Williams, *Tradition and originality in Roman poetry* ch. 8, and Griffin, 'Augustan poetry and the life of luxury'. Lyne, *The Latin love poets from Catullus to Horace*, esp. ch. 1, is also useful, particularly on the *demi-monde* (pp. 8 ff.).   [216] 'The double standard' 194.

[217] For unprotected women being classified as available and often forced into the class of prostitutes, the essay of Rossiaud, 'Prostitution, sex and society in French towns in the fifteenth century', and for preying on girls outside the group Lafont, 'Changing sexual behavior in French youth gangs', are suggestive. A belief allegedly current in a small group of young Englishmen in the 1950s is neatly and satirically summed up by Alan Coren: 'It was a general

The most striking example is Cicero's argument in the *pro Caelio*, a
speech which should never have been set to generations of schoolboys. The argument goes against the grain of what we know of his
own nature,[218] but was demanded by the case. The lines of it are very
well known: a young man can give free rein to his sexual instincts and
may well grow into a thoroughly respectable statesman, as long as he
follows certain ground rules. He must not be the *erōmenos* in a
homosexual affair, nor seduce a respectable boy; he must not raid the
households of his equals—either their wives, daughters, or slaves.[219]
But the *meretrix* is fair game. So, I assume, are his own slaves of either
sex. But Cicero concentrates on the prostitute, because he wants to
argue that Clodia, as a widow who has adopted an openly immoral
way of life, has put herself on the same level. In arguing that it is
permissible for young men to sow their wild oats, Cicero is using the
locus de indulgentia. A famous anecdote made the Elder Cato praise
a young man for occasionally visiting a brothel, but not for continual
resort to it. Horace in his version of this makes Cato justify whoring as
a safe outlet for a physical urge, which removes the danger that the
young man will chase married women.[220] But at least one school of
thought held that affairs with prostitutes ought to be conducted with
discretion, moderation, and economy: otherwise the young man's
reputation would suffer.[221] The *locus*, like much of the speech on
behalf of Caelius, is redolent of the comic stage. It is presented by
indulgent elders, who remember their own youth and suggest that
affairs with prostitutes are a passing phase. The young men will marry
and settle down as responsible citizens.[222] Both indulgence and condemnation were familiar from drama, the courts, and the rhetorical
schools. What we lack are personal records of what Roman fathers

principle among privately educated male undergraduates that one walked about holding hands
with well-born gels whom one planned eventually to marry, but screwed nurses; whereas the
rest of us walked about holding hands with nurses whom we planned eventually to marry, and
screwed well-born gels' (*My Oxford* [London 1977] 195).

[218] If we can trust *F* 9.26.2.

[219] Horace gives similar advice: *Epp.* 1.18.72ff.; cf. Plaut. *Curc.* 33ff.; *Decl. min.* 301.17–18;
Lyne, *The Latin love poets from Catullus to Horace* 1 ff.; Baldwin 'Horace on sex'.

[220] *S* 1.2.31ff.

[221] Cf. Hor. *S* 1.2.61; Livy 39.9.6: '[Hispalae] consuetudo iuxta vicinitatem cum Aebutio fuit,
minime adulescentis aut rei aut famae damnosa'; Sen. *Contr.* 2.1.14, 15, 2.3.5; *Decl. min.*
275.6, 356.1: 'filium fuisse luxuriosum et non sine maximo patrimonii et famae damno.' Cic.
Cael. 42: 'ne effundat patrimonium, ne faenore trucidetur' probably belongs here too.

[222] Cf. Plaut. *Bacch.* 409–10, 1079–80; Ter. *Ad.* 100ff.; Sen. *Contr.* 2.4.10: 'Nihil peccaverat;
amat meretricem; solet fieri; adulescens est, expecta, emendabitur, ducet uxorem . . . Nullum
illius vitium: aetatis est, amoris est', 2.6.11: 'Concessis aetati iocis utor et iuvenali lege
defungor: id facio quod pater meus fecit cum iuvenis esset . . . Bona ego aetate coepi; simul
primum hoc tirocinium adulescentiae quasi debitum ac sollemne persolvero, revertar ad bonos
mores'; Juv. 8.163–4: 'defensor culpae dicet mihi "fecimus et nos | haec iuvenes".' For the
opposite topos, attacks on the immorality of the younger generation, see e.g. Cic. *A* 1.16.1.

might really have felt when their sons entangled themselves with the Roman *demi-monde* or the hetaerae of Athens, a fate which one would willingly attribute to the idle son of Cicero.

Unlike Cicero, Horace cannot be accused of advocating a double standard. But he makes two assumptions which belong with the double standard: that it is normal for men to satisfy physical desire (and even dangerous for them to suppress it) and that women can be divided into two groups: those of one's own class, and those who are either slaves or belong to disreputable and lower-class professions. I shall refer to the second assumption as the 'dual classification'.[223] But he is not using the *locus de indulgentia*, for he is satirically analysing the possibilities open to any man, not just an immature youth. The extremes of adultery (dangerous) and recourse to street-walkers (sordid) might (according to a doctrine which he plays with for a moment) be avoided by the golden mean of affairs with a middle class of freedwomen. But although they represent a mean, men have been known to fall into excess in their passion for such women, courtesans, and actresses. Fewer problems are caused by purely physical encounters with slaves of either sex. There is no need here to ask whether the man is married or not.[224] Such explicit claims that men have an automatic right to sexual satisfaction, as long as the partner belongs to a certain category, are rare. But the assumption seems implicit in Roman society that intercourse with a slave, who had no moral responsibility and no choice, was morally neutral for the free initiator, as long as he was not trespassing on the owner's rights. It might, however, be prudent to abstain from exercising such rights of possession even over slaves in one's own household.[225] Objections to intercourse with a common prostitute were aesthetic rather than moral or prudential.[226] Upper-class Romans were unlikely to frequent women who openly prostituted themselves in brothels or taverns,

---

[223] Jerome makes the point (*Epp.* 77.3): 'Aliae sunt leges Caesarum, aliae Christi, aliud Papinianus aliud Paulus noster praecipit. Apud illos in viris pudicitiae frena laxantur et solo stupro atque adulterio condemnato passim per lupanaria et ancillulas libido permittitur, quasi culpam dignitas faciat, non voluptas. Apud nos quod non licet feminis, aeque non licet viris' ('The laws of the Caesars are different from those of Christ, and the teaching of Papinian differs from that of our Paul. They ride with a slack rein on male sexual behaviour and only homosexuality and adultery are condemned. Indiscriminate lust is allowed in brothels and with slave-girls, as if it was social rank and not sensuality which produced the immorality. But among us whatever is illicit for women is also illicit for men').

[224] *S* 1.2.   [225] Cf. 'Questions on women domestics in the Roman West' 192–3.

[226] On prostitutes see H. Herter in *Reallexikon f. Ant. u. Christ.* iii. 1154–213; Krenkel, 'Prostitution'; McGinn, 'The taxation of Roman prostitutes'. For a rare attack on the degradation inflicted by brothel-keepers on women and children see Dio Prusias *Eub.* 133–8. He also argues that corruption spread to attacks on women and boys of good station (139–52). For the contrary idea that prostitution is a safety-valve see Aug. *de ordine* 2.4.12: 'aufer meretrices de rebus humanis, turbaveris omnia libidinibus.'

without choosing their clients. They would more probably keep, or occasionally visit, courtesans, who profited from a sexual relationship with one or two men, the type personified by Volumnia Cytheris.[227] When Cicero met her at a delightful dinner party at the house of her patron (and no doubt quondam and sporadic lover) Eutrapelus in 46 BC, the rest of the company was male, and included at least two married men, Cicero himself and Atticus. She had, moreover, been the mistress of Antony during the early part of his marriage to Fulvia. Cicero makes the most of the impropriety of being unexpectedly in her company, but his mock horror is based on his reputation as a philosopher, not as a husband.[228]

The society of *demi-mondaines* impinges on the little world of Horace's Sabine farm along with visits from Faun, just as it does on the drinking-parties of old friends.[229] Neither love nor loyalty nor attraction is excluded from such relationships, though fickleness and cruelty and the traditional greed and availability of the harlot are also themes.[230] Barine, by her ascendancy over the young men, threatens the tranquillity of their parents and their brides. Phyllis is warned that she has lost Telephus to a rich girl of a higher social class, apparently a woman whom he could marry.[231] This joyful society of young courtesans and their lovers, both masked by Greek names, is not allowed contact with senior addressees such as Maecenas or men of high rank. It would be wrong to see individual reality in a Lydia or an Asterie. But that there were attractive music-girls, actresses, and high-class prostitutes available for drinking-parties seems beyond dispute. Slaves and freedwomen also figure.[232] Horace and his readers saw nothing shocking and much that was charming in a theme that not only reminded them of Greek literature but also gave them a prettified version of contemporary society.[233]

In texts which purport to be more realistic, it is not mixed parties with *meretrices* which shocked, but parties at which married women of high status were seduced or behaved as prostitutes.[234]

It is ironic that in order to portray wives or potential wives in a more romantic light, it was necessary to echo the themes of erotic poetry which had originally been used in an extra-marital context. So it is sometimes difficult to guess whether Horace intends us to think of wives or faithful mistresses and their lovers.[235] The affair of Sulpicia 'Servius' daughter' with 'Cerinthus', described by herself and another

---

[227] *D* 23.2.43.pr.–3.   [228] *F* 9.26, *A* 10.10.5, *Phil.* 2.58ff., 69, 77.
[229] Hor. *O* 1.17, 2.11, 3.14, 3.28, 4.11.
[230] *O* 1.8, 1.13, 1.27, 1.33, 3.7, 3.9, 1.25, 3.10, 3.15, 4.13.   [231] *O* 2.8, 4.11.
[232] *O* 1.33, 2.4.   [233] See Griffin 'Augustan poetry and the life of luxury' 96ff.
[234] Cic. *Phil.* 2.105; Suet. *DA* 69.1, *Gaius* 36.2, *Nero* 27.3.
[235] e.g. *O* 1.13, 3.9; cf. Cat. 45.

poet in the vein the elegists used for their affairs with pseudonymous women, is a literary version of pre-marital courtship with a young man who was no doubt highly eligible.[236] Near the beginning of the tradition of autobiographical or apparently autobiographical Latin love poetry, Catullus had neatly set the pattern for confusion of categories of relationships when he demanded the quasi-contractual loyalty of Roman friendship and played with the idea of fidelity in a relationship which was clearly extra-marital and, at least for a time, adulterous.[237] We must not expect legalistic definitions from erotic poets. They can, theoretically, be describing a relationship or potential relationship which involves the 'I' of the poem, a man approximating in age, social class, and perhaps experience and character to the poet himself, and another, who may be a boy, a woman, or a girl. The 'I' may be married or not: this does not usually matter. The object of his affections could theoretically, if female, be (1) his own wife,[238] (2) a woman of his own class or higher, who could be (*a*) a virgin, (*b*) married to another, or (*c*) *vidua*, or (3) a free woman of lower social class, married or not, *meretrix* or not, ex-slave or not, or (4) a slavewoman, his own or another's. The women of elegy who have a *vir* to impede, grieve, or excite the poet (or his persona) may be upper-class married women, lower-class married women, courtesans, or kept women with an acknowledged lover.

According to Apuleius in a famous passage, Catullus used the name Lesbia for a woman who was really named Clodia, Ticidas Perilla for Metella, Propertius Cynthia for Hostia, Tibullus Delia for Plania.[239] His reason for introducing this learned item of information is personal. His accusers, not confining themselves to the charge of magic, attacked his character because he had written erotic verses to the two young sons of Scribonius Laetus, concealing them under pseudonyms. He needs to dispose of the minor charge, that using pseudonyms was improper. (I do not guarantee that Apuleius is representing the prosecutor's criticisms fairly.) He therefore appeals to the practice of famous poets in masking women, and goes on to regret that Lucilius damaged the reputation of two boys by giving their real names and to approve Vergil for using the pseudonym

---

[236] [Tib.] 3.8–18. Another Sulpicia, contemporary with Martial, wrote chaste but sensuous love-poems which were edifying reading for husbands and wives who wanted to be faithful (Mart. 10.35, 38).

[237] Fidelity: 87, 109, cf. 82, 86; see Lyne, *The Latin love poets from Catullus to Horace* 36–7, 291–2; infidelity: 11, 58; cf. Wiseman, *Cinna the poet and other Roman essays* 114ff.; adultery: Wiseman, ibid. 111, citing Cat. 68.146, 83.

[238] A view put forward by Peter Green, arguing that 'Corinna was based, at least in part, on Ovid's mysterious first wife' (*Ovid: the erotic poems* 23). I cannot accept this view of Corinna.

[239] The Metella identification is also given by Ov. *Tr.* 2.433ff.

Alexis for 'Pollio's boy' in the *Eclogues*. He then disposes of the major charge, arguing that there is a complete divide between lascivious poems addressed to boys and the practice of the poets who wrote them. As Catullus said, the poet must be chaste, but his verses need not be. Apuleius appeals to the example of Plato and, even more audaciously, to Hadrian.[240] It could be held, then, with some plausibility, that the poets of the late Republic and early Augustan period had written erotic poems to and about ladies of high status. Metella must be a Caecilia Metella, nor would plain *gentilicia* be used for freedwomen (who had *cognomina* as well): all are likely to be of at least relatively high social status, and this will best suit Apuleius' argument.[241]

Lesbia must be one of the three notorious Clodiae Pulchrae. The balance of evidence slightly favours the sister most closely linked in the popular mind with her brother, P. Clodius, during the 50s, who had been widowed by the death of Metellus Celer in 59.[242] She seems to have remained unmarried, at least until after the trial of M. Caelius in 56.[243] Another sister had been divorced by L. Lucullus in about 66, and the third was widowed by the death of Q. Marcius Rex in about 61. We might think more kindly of Lucullus' allegations in 61 about his ex-wife's incest with Clodius if she had died in the mean time, but there is evidence to suggest that she was still alive and in the company of her daughter by Lucullus in 49.[244] We would expect all three to have remarried. But the scandal of 61 may have affected their chances (although Lucullus' ex-wife might have remarried before). A widow with children (all three sisters were mothers) could decline re-marriage, as Servilia did, even though still of child-bearing age. So remarriage and date of remarriage remain hypothetical for each of the three. All that is indicated with some certainty is that at the time of the consummation of Catullus' affair Lesbia was married. It is even more important that she was socially far above him.

In considering why poets and their mistresses were debarred from marrying each other, we have tended to ask whether the woman was

[240] *Apol.* 10ff. There are similar excuses for erotic verse in Ov. *Tr.* 2.345ff.; Pliny *Epp.* 4.14 (quoting Cat. 16.5–8), 5.3, 7.4. For further examples see Sherwin-White, *Pliny* 289ff.
[241] Apuleius is not concerned to give us a complete list of pseudonyms: he does not identify Gallus' Lycoris, who was Volumnia Cytheris (perhaps because she was only a freedwoman), Tibullus' Nemesis (portrayed as a courtesan, perhaps not identifiable), or Ovid's Corinna (although Ovid imagined people trying to identify her). See on this esp. Williams, *Tradition and originality in Roman poetry* 533ff.
[242] Cat. 79.1 for Clodius, on which see Skinner, 'Pretty Lesbius'. I am much indebted to Wiseman, *Cinna the poet and other Roman essays* 104ff., but do not follow his dating or his preference for *not* identifying Lesbia with Clodia Metelli. There is a large and largely unrewarding modern bibliography on the Clodiae.
[243] Wiseman, *Cinna the poet and other Roman essays* 111.   [244] Ibid. 112ff.

debarred because she was a courtesan. Perhaps we should be wondering instead whether Hostia was too high-born to marry a Propertius from Assisi, as Clodia or Metella would not have condescended to marry Catullus or Ticidas.

To write of love affairs with women of the upper class offered several advantages. They were, up to a point, free agents who, if they chose to love, conferred distinction on the poet. On the other hand, since the possibility of marriage between the lovers was *ex hypothesi* ruled out, the affair had all the romance and difficulties of the illicit. New rules could be developed: the mistress's duty to cheat her husband but not her lover, the woman's dominance over the man, her fickleness offset by his devotion. If she cheats him, she assumes the characteristics of the courtesan, always on the look-out for new lovers, or is even assimilated to a sex-hungry street-walker. Although Apuleius hints that erotic poetry might be meant purely as a compliment, it is impossible to think of Catullus' affair with Lesbia as entirely literary. Attacks on her infidelity and promiscuity cannot be read as the praises of a courtly poet worshipping from afar. I do not imply that each incident he describes or each interpretation of the nature of the relationship which he gives is to be accepted as historical. Once Catullus sets the fashion, a further degree of fictionalizing may be detected in his successors, until we suspect that no real individual inspired Ovid's clever variations on the theme of the course of an affair.

On the other hand, the elegists also immortalized their passions for their social inferiors, women like Lycoris and (probably) Nemesis. Lycoris, the lady sung by Cornelius Gallus in the late 40s and the 30s, had as the mime-actress Cytheris been launched on to the stage and into society by her patron P. Volumnius Eutrapelus. She became the mistress of his friend M. Antonius, who is said to have insisted on her being treated with respect, almost as if she were his wife, and to have taken her on official tours in company with his mother. She was loved by Brutus and then by Gallus.[245] These relationships can be taken to have been officially serial, a succession of 'love-affairs' which approximate quite closely to the experience of semi-professional kept women of a later age, such as Harriette Wilson. After becoming, at the age of 15, the mistress of the Earl of Craven, Harriette progressed rapidly to Frederick Lamb and then the Marquess of Lorne. She credits herself with honesty enough to warn her lovers before transferring her affections. Being kept by a man means that she is 'engaged' to him, but does not stop her seeing other men. New

---

[245] Cic. *Phil.* 2.58; Serv. on *E* 10; *Vir. ill.* 82.2.

candidates are introduced, sometimes by the current lover or by a
friend and sometimes by a professional *entremetteuse*, like the Mrs
Porter on whom the Duke of Wellington is said to have called in order
to ask for a meeting with Harriette, promising them a hundred
guineas each. On a later occasion, Harriette claims to have turned the
Duke away on a rainy night, just after his triumphant return from the
Peninsula.[246] All this is reminiscent of the ancient set-up, in which
the attractive courtesan picks and chooses among those who besiege
her door, admitting one and for the moment dismissing others, with a
mercenary *lena* to give her advice. As an object of the poet's
affections, professional or semi-professional courtesans (who must
not be given such a label in verse) have the advantage of being
necessarily attractive and charming, but not predictably accommodating. Their cruelty or deceitfulness or infidelity provides obstacles
and reactions. The poet can claim all the pangs of romantic love. The
world of elegy is part make-believe formulated from literature, and
part make-believe in real life, the erotic fantasies which women in the
business of love knew how to encourage. Poets and their readers
enjoy exploring both fantasies.

Ovid's Corinna slips most easily from one persona to another. It is
hardly surprising that contemporaries failed to agree on an identification with any known woman. I agree with the orthodox modern view
that they were wrong to try: of all those we have been considering,
this lady and this love-affair seem most likely to be fictitious.[247] In any
case, the mistress mentioned in separate poems in the *Amores* is not
always identified as Corinna. Ovid alludes quite often to the married
status of his beloved.[248] On the other hand, the poem which attacks
the wicked old confidante who wants to persuade his mistress to sell
herself to rich lovers or the one which describes how disillusioned
Ovid is when his girl asks him for presents have more the flavour of
the courtesan.[249]

Since the second edition of the *Amores* post-dates the Augustan
law on adultery, Ovid was prudent to create this shot-silk effect in his
portrayal of his mistress or mistresses. In the *Ars amatoria* (*c.*1 BC) he
carefully denies any reference to women who were covered by the
law. So the quarry is usually a *meretrix*.[250] But there is sometimes 'a

[246] *Harriette Wilson's Memoirs* 21, 27, 51 ff., 146 ff. I am indebted to J. Griffin for the
introduction.
[247] Ov. *Am.* 2.17.29, *AA* 3.538. See Williams, *Tradition and originality in Roman poetry*
538–9.
[248] *Am.* 1.4, 2.2 esp. 51, 2.12, 3.8.63. Cf. Williams, *Tradition and originality in Roman poetry*
539–40.
[249] 1.8 (though such *lenae* could corrupt married women, 19), esp. 34, 63 ff., 87 ff.; 1.10,
although this draws an explicit contrast between the behaviour desired in his mistress and that
of a prostitute (21 ff.).   [250] *AA* 1.31 ff., 435 3.615; cf. *Tr.* 2.303.

vestigial trace of a situation in which she is thought of as a married woman'.[251] It is hardly surprising that Ovid was accused of writing a handbook on adultery.[252]

This review of the evidence of love poetry suggests that, apart from encounters with boys, music-girls, and such, the poets portray the ups and downs of relatively long-term affairs with two classes of women, citizens of relatively high status who are married, and semi-professional women for whom 'courtesan' is a convenient term. Their lovers called them their *amicae* or *puellae*, avoiding the legalistic and derogatory word *meretrix*. The poets do not imply that an affair with an aristocrat was distinct in its nature from an affair with a courtesan, though the former, if unfaithful, may be equated with a courtesan and the latter, if loving, with a woman who could bestow her affection without thought of gain.

Catullus and his successors portray a world in which the poet and his friends can regard extra-marital affairs with women of the upper class as a romantic ideal. The reality of such a world is confirmed by the gossip of Cicero and Caelius, the slanted attacks of Cicero in his speeches or Sallust in his history, the moralizing of Horace, the gibes of Antony and Octavian, and the reaction of Augustus the legislator. It is possible to believe that the Roman upper classes of the late Republic were able to absorb and tolerate a degree of sexual licence for married women as well as married men. This is not to suggest that all wives claimed such licence. In such a malicious society, if no scandal is attached to a particular wife we can probably list her as above reproach: Terentia Ciceronis is perhaps such a one. Conversely, where scandal exists, we need not believe it. But contemporaries were prepared to believe that the widowed Clodia Metelli took a succession of lovers or that Caesar seduced the wives of a number of his fellow senators. The remarkable thing is that such allegations circulated freely but rarely produced any result. We shall see that adultery was rarely the formal grounds for divorce and was not very often alleged by outsiders as the underlying cause. The other most important effect which we would expect is bastards. But allegations that a certain lady's children were not her husband's are extremely rare. 'Pater . . . is est quem nuptiae demonstrant' ('The father is identified by the marriage').[253] What were the ground rules?

Certain circles of the aristocracy in Georgian and Edwardian England, in which divorce was difficult and infrequent, tolerated adultery by wives as long as certain conventions were observed. It was

[251] Hollis on *AA* 1.365; cf. 579–80, 2.551–2, 3.602.
[252] *Tr.* 2.212. See the useful discussion of Lyne, *The Latin love poets from Catullus to Horace* ch. 10.   [253] *D* 2.4.5, Paul.

the wife's duty to bear a legitimate successor to the husband's title and entailed property; if younger children were fathered by her lovers, that was relatively unimportant and they might even be acknowledged and supported by her husband despite tittle-tattle. Although adultery was 'criminal conversation' it might be lightly regarded. As long as the marriage appeared to function normally and the wife played her part as hostess and chatelaine, conducting *affaires* with a certain discretion and not running away with a lover, she could enjoy a good deal of freedom. People in society conspired to keep infidelity secret from servants and outsiders. Such mores were peculiar to a small group in either period, although tolerance for men having mistresses of a lower class and bastards was more widespread.[254]

If this sort of pattern existed in the Roman upper class in the period running roughly from Sulla to the Augustan legislation, it ran counter to conventional ideology as the habits of the fifth Duke of Devonshire and his Duchess, Georgiana, or of Edward VII, ran counter to the Christian morality of their times. Catullus builds a new morality of fidelity in adultery.[255] A basic class solidarity, underlying all the feuds, seems to play a role in both societies. A wife's adultery was most shameful when her lover was of a lower class. Three features seem to make the Roman situation different: the availability of divorce, the husband's right to refuse to rear children, and the separation of property. A husband who suspected his wife of adultery could, if he chose, divorce her, or expose any child which he thought was not his. A wife who preferred her lover to her husband could, if she chose, divorce. There was nothing to prevent her remarrying rapidly if she divorced when already carrying the lover's child: the appearance of legitimacy could therefore be maintained.[256] Or, supposing that the marriage was unbroken, husband and wife could dispose of their property in such a way that he did not support her bastard. In any case, the wife's adultery, even the production of a child, did not threaten the husband's property as it did in later societies. This argument is highly conjectural and is only adduced here in an attempt to see why allegations of bastardy are so rare in a society in which the infidelity of wives was allegedly comparatively frequent.[257] The question had occurred in antiquity: in an anecdote told about Augustus' daughter Julia an impertinent friend asked her why, in spite of her

[254] For the period c.1670–1810 see e.g. Stone, *The family, sex and marriage in England 1500–1800* 326ff.
[255] For the idea of a counter-cultural trend cf. Hallett, 'The role of women in Roman elegy: counter-cultural feminism'.   [256] See Gardner 52–3.
[257] Syme, 'Bastards in the Roman aristocracy' 514, puts the question: 'Transgression being so common, and language so free, one looks for allegations that a man is not the true son of his ostensible father. And one looks in vain.' See too 'No son for Caesar?'.

notorious promiscuity, all her children looked so like her husband. Her answer, that she only took lovers when legitimately pregnant, cannot be held to reflect an accepted practice.[258]

Inside the 'counter-culture' represented by Catullus and the elegists, there seems to be no double standard imposing stricter behaviour on women. The poets had an interest in omitting it. In rejecting such freedom, Cicero produces the full artillery of the double standard and dual classification: the woman who pleases herself in love is behaving like the most blatant kind of *meretrix*. Men of conventional morality like Cicero had no other means open to them of defending a young man who had a love affair with a woman of his own or a higher social class.

The rule for a young man's behaviour, as Cicero expresses it, was that he should not attack another man's family and household or inflict disgrace on the chaste, ruin on the innocent, and infamy on the respectable.[259] It was a topos that tyrants and wicked governors violated chaste daughters and wives.[260] Seduction was worse, since it alienated the wife's affection. The defence of the chastity of women is built into Roman law. Take, for example, the civil law of damages.

2. *Defending and Avenging Chastity*

Seduction, attempted seduction, or rape could be the subject of a suit. The Aquilian Law, which covered all sorts of damages, allowed actions for *iniuria*, insult or outrage, both to the person insulted and to members of the family. Insult to a slave is really insult to his or her owner. In the case of a free person, rather similar considerations apply and these show an asymmetry rooted in patriarchalism rather than in specifically sexual attitudes.[261] Buckland puts it succinctly:

An *iniuria* to a wife gave an action not only to her but to her husband. [47.10.1.3] An insult to a *filius* was an insult to the *paterfamilias* as well, who might sue for himself and for his son. . . . Where a married *filiafamilias* was insulted there might be three actions, or more, her own, her husband's, her father's and even her husband's father's. A *sponsus* might have an action on

[258] Macr. *S* 2.5.9.

[259] 42: 'Detur aliqui ludus aetati; sit adulescentia liberior; non omnia voluptatibus denegentur; non semper superet vera illa et derecta ratio; vincat aliquando cupiditas voluptasque rationem, dum modo illa in hoc genere praescriptio moderatioque teneatur. Parcat iuventus pudicitiae suae, ne spoliet alienam, ne effundat patrimonium, ne faenore trucidetur, ne incurrat in alterius domum atque familiam, ne probrum castis, labem integris, infamiam bonis inferat'; cf. 28.

[260] e.g. Cic. *Prov. cons.* 5, *QF* 1.1.8. For the attractiveness of provincial women see Varro *Men.* 176. For the abstinence of the good ruler: Tac. *A.* 12.6.3; cf. Isoc. *Nicocles* 36; Foucault, *L'histoire de la sexualité* ii.24.

[261] The law is of uncertain but republican date and earlier than the law of mandate: Buckland, *Textbook* 585 ff.

an insult to his *sponsa*. The penalty would not necessarily be the same in these cases: in each the personality of the plaintiff was considered. And though insult to wife or child was insult to *paterfamilias*, the converse was not true.[262]

The effect of this is that a *paterfamilias* or a husband can avenge an insult to child or wife to which that person consented, for instance seduction. That is related to a double standard, for, in offering protection, it makes the chastity of wife or daughter a commodity on which a price could be put. It also tends to assume that the person seduced is passive, an object or a victim. There is also a clear indication of the dual classification in a passage on attempted pick-ups, which is reminiscent of Cicero on the deportment of Clodia:

Si quis virgines appellasset, si tamen ancillari veste vestitas, minus peccare videtur: multo minus, si meretricia veste feminae, non matrum familiarum vestitae fuissent. Si igitur non matronali habitu femina fuerit et quis eam appellavit vel ei comitem abduxit, iniuriarum tenetur. (*Digest* 47.10.15.15, Ulpian *lxxvii ad edictum*)

If someone accosted virgins, but they were dressed like slave-girls, his offence seems lessened, and it is much less if women were not dressed as matrons but as prostitutes. So if a woman was not wearing the clothes of a respectable married woman and someone accosted her or lured her escort away, he is liable for damages.

This is elliptical, but the sense is clear that damages would be smaller if the man was under a misapprehension about the status of the women involved, because they were wearing the wrong sort of clothes.[263]

The Julian Law on violence also covered abduction. One lawyer in discussing this distinguishes married and unmarried victims and mentions that if the woman's father failed to prosecute, an outsider could do so.[264]

The duty of fathers and husbands to resent the extra-marital sexual activity of their women is illustrated by the regulations on killing in the Augustan law on adultery. It is the Augustan legislation which imposes a dual classification, so that women who are not *meretrices* or otherwise outside the scope of the law are now off limits. On the other hand, the law did not endorse a general distinction between the sexes.

---

[262] Buckland, *Textbook* 591. See too for related material of great interest Birks, 'Other men's meat: Aquilian liability for proper user'.

[263] Cf. Sen. *Contr.* 2.7.3–4 on correct clothes, demeanour, and attendants for a woman who wants to avoid unwelcome attentions in public.

[264] 48.6.5.2, *Marcianus xiv inst.*: 'Qui vacantem mulierem rapuit vel nuptam, ultimo supplico punitur et, si pater iniuriam suam precibus exoratus remiserit, tamen extraneus sine quinquennii praescriptione reum postulare poterit, cum raptus crimen legis Iuliae de adulteris potestatem excedit.' See Evans-Grubbs, 'Abduction marriage in antiquity'.

Both were liable to be charged with *stuprum*, although adultery was by definition a crime of married women. As Beryl Rawson puts it, 'There was . . . some discrimination against women . . . they could be punished for affairs with slaves and low-class persons while men could not be. But the area of discrimination was much narrower than is sometimes suggested.'[265]

One important loophole remained in the Augustan Law. Men might live in *concubinatus* without being charged with *stuprum*, under certain conditions. The details are highly controversial.[266] It was clear that if a man kept as concubine a woman who could not be charged with *stuprum* at all, he was exempt.[267]

3. Honour

If the link with a male relative or husband is one of the qualifications which ought to protect a woman, then it is natural for us to look for the idea that a man's honour is bound up with the chastity of his womenfolk, whether daughter, sister, wife, or even mother, which has been strong in Mediterranean cultures in recent times.[268] It is easy to find examples of a keen sense of women's honour, bound up with their sexuality. Lucretia is the paradigm for us as she was for the Romans. She commits suicide in front of her husband and father, because her honour has been tarnished by rape.[269] Women's repute could be irremediably damaged through no fault of their own.[270] Fathers and brothers were expected to defend the *pudicitia* and *fama* of their daughters and sisters.[271] The wife's adultery causes *dolor* to her husband and damages her *fama*.[272] But I cannot find that the woman's honour and that of her father or brother are identified.

The same applies to husbands. Caesar may say that his wife should be above suspicion. Pompey may call his wife a Clytaemnestra for betraying him while he was on campaign.[273] But they did not regard themselves as dishonoured by their wives' misconduct. The only texts I have found which suggest that blots on the woman's reputation directly affected her relatives or husband refer to Livia Julia's adultery with Sejanus and a military tribune's wife's adultery with a

---

[265] *FAR* 34.   [266] Cf. my '*Concubinae*'.   [267] *D* 25.7.1.1; cf. 3 pr.
[268] For mothers cf. Sen. *Contr.* 1.4. For modern cultures see e.g. Campbell, esp. pp. 152 ff., 187, 193 ff.; Peristiany (ed.), *Honour and shame. The values of Mediterranean society*, and *Mediterranean family structures*, *passim*. Note that all the cultures chosen for discussion have been exposed to strong Muslim influence.
[269] Lucretia: Livy 1.57.6–59.8; Verginia: Livy 3.44.2–50.10; VM 6.1.2. Both: Cic. *Fin.* 2.66, 5.64; VM 6.1.1–2.   [270] e.g. Sen. *Contr.* 1.2; *Decl. min.* 276.11, 280.7.
[271] Cic. *2Verr.* 1.67, 76, Lampsacenes: 'ille quod pudicitiam liberorum, hic quod vitam patris famamque sororis defenderat.' Roman fathers: VM 6.1.3–4, 6.   [272] Ov. *Am.* 2.2.50.
[273] See Appendix 1. Cf. Sen. *Contr.* 1.2.10: 'Nulla satis pudica est de qua quaeritur.'

centurion. But they both seem to be about social transgressions which aggravated adultery.[274] The third parties who are really affected by a woman's bad reputation are her children.[275]

This is not to suggest that a husband was supposed to feel nothing on discovering his wife's adultery. The proper reaction was *dolor*, grief, pain, and resentment.[276] Anger was justified and passion, *calor*, which might lead him to violence, was understandable.[277] He ought to take the lead in bringing the offenders to justice, for they had injured and harmed his *domus*. Adultery was a contamination; it violated marriage.[278] But there is no suggestion that the husband's own honour was ruined. There is no classical Latin word for 'cuckold', the 'word of fear' which terrorized Elizabethan husbands. That concept, so fertile for Mediterranean thought, gesture, insult, and comedy, seems not to have been invented until later.[279] It is even difficult to find sober texts which attest the concept of 'the wronged husband'.

Violence against the wife or lover was understood, killing of lower-class lovers allowed by Augustus. But the way to get redress, *vindicta*, was in the courts.[280] Again, there is no precise equivalent of the later concept of revenge as imperative if honour is to be preserved. The traditional literary punishments inflicted on adulterers are closer to primitive *talio*. Nor had Romans invented the duel.[281]

It is clear that society expected husbands (and fathers) to resent the misbehaviour of their women. What was the effect on wives of the infidelity of their husbands? This too was recognized as *iniuria* and the wife was expected to feel resentment of a mistress. But authors usually concern themselves with the moral status of the husband rather than with the effect of his behaviour.[282] Attacks on the double standard are fairly common. Appendix 3 collects texts on the topic. Pythagoreans and Stoics concerned themselves particularly with the fidelity of husbands. Roman Stoics took up this theme, and we find Seneca particularly exercised about the tendency of men to apply different standards to their wives and themselves. He thinks especially of adultery with other men's wives. Musonius, the author of the

[274] Tac. *A* 4.3: 'seque et maiores ac posteros municipali adultero foedabat'; Pliny *Epp.* 6.31.4: 'Nupta haec tribuno militum, honores petituro, et suam et mariti dignitatem centurionis amore maculaverat.'
[275] Sen. *Matr.* ap. Jer. *adv. Iovin.* 49 = 319c–320a; Tac. *A* 4.3.4.
[276] Ov. *Am.* 2.2.50; *D* 48.5.39.8; *Coll.* 4.11.
[277] *D* 48.5.23.4, ht 30 pr.; *Coll.* 4.10.1. A husband may weep and feel bereaved because his wife loved and preferred another (*Decl. min.* 319.6).
[278] *Coll.* 4.11; *D* 48.5.2.8, ht 30 pr. Cf. Apul. *M* 9.26.
[279] Cuckold: *Cornuto, cabrón, cocu*. See Pitt-Rivers, *The fate of Shechem or the politics of sex. Essays in the anthropology of the Mediterranean* ch. 2, 'Honour and social status in Andalusia', at pp. 23–4.   [280] *Decl. min.* 355.8, 257.3.
[281] Syme, 'Bastards in the Roman aristocracy' 323 = *RP* ii.511.
[282] A point made by Foucault, *L'histoire de la sexualité* ii.184ff.

Minor declamations, and Plutarch think of prostitutes and slaves. Musonius gives the clearest discussion of the question about harm to a third party. The lover of a married woman injures her husband because he destroys his hope of children, either by destroying the marriage or by casting doubt on the paternity of any children she bears.[283] But what harm is done by a relationship with a courtesan or unmarried woman? Musonius here is thinking of bachelors, for otherwise harm would be done to the wife. His answer is that it is still wrong. We would expect a moralist to consider damage to the woman, but Musonius' answer is simply that it is immoral, revealing lack of self-control in the man.

In contrast with later Mediterranean societies, admiration for the successful adulterer (except the self-congratulation of a love-poet) is almost absent from Roman literature.[284] Romantic old men get their come-uppance in comedy and so does the pretty lover of the miller's wife in the novel.[285] Public speakers unite in condemnation of the adulterer.[286]

The development of the Mediterranean ideas of male honour in connection with women's sexuality and chastity deserves further scrutiny. These ideas gave rise to a complicated etiquette and to such extremes as the duel, and in a diluted form spread to northern Europe. Other scholars derive them from Rome. To my mind it seems likely that the elements in the double standard which we have just discussed are of Muslim origin.

Pragmatists, even some writers of tracts, advised wives to turn a blind eye to their husbands' infidelities, with social equals as well as with inferiors.[287] This is a theme which is an important feature of the preaching of the double standard in English writings, but seems much less prominent among the Romans, perhaps because Roman wives acquiesced more easily and writers were less inclined to address women. Usually, such passages refer to trivial affairs with prostitutes. One rhetorical scenario is unusual, because the husband is having a serious affair with a married woman, which ends in his being blinded by the angry husband. Nevertheless, the wife's father uses the *locus de indulgentia*, which usually excuses youthful whoring.[288]

[283] *Spes liberorum* is vague and appears quite often, e.g. Vell. 2.103.5; Sen. *Cons. ad Helv.* 16.3.   [284] Campbell 199.

[285] Fantham, 'Sex, status and survival in Hellenistic Athens' 71; Apul. *M* 9.14ff.

[286] Cic. *Cat.* 2.23, *Sest.* 20, *Pis.* 28, *Mil.* 72, cf. *Sen.* 40, *Fin.* 2.73, *Off.* 1.128; *Decl. min.* 275.6.

[287] [Arist.] *Oec.* 3 p. 141; Theano *Letter to Nicostrate* (Thesleff, *Texts* p. 197 no. 3); Plut. *Praec. conj.* 16 = 140 B; Publilius Syrus *Sententiae* 445: 'Obsequium nuptae cito fit odium paelicis' (cf. Ov. *Her.* 5.133: 'manet Oenone fallenti casta marito'); *VM* 6.7.1; *Decl. min.* 357.2, wife's father on husband's adultery: 'respondisse illum esse quaedam aetati concessa, nec reprehendi lusus in eiusmodi iuventa debere.' For later teaching see e.g. Allestree, *The ladies calling* iii.177–8; Halifax, quoted by Thomas 196.   [288] *Decl. min.* 357.2.

There is one ancillary argument here, that wives, while pretending to be unaware of their husbands' adulteries with courtesans, since these are largely sensuous and frivolous, must distinguish themselves sharply from such women by fulfilling their role as wives and mothers and by chaste behaviour in bed. Plutarch was very well aware of the importance of sexual intercourse in binding the married pair together. He rejects the argument that heterosexual love is confined to prostitutes because it is improper for chaste women to love or be loved.[289] He exhorts the husband to faithfulness and advises the wife to avoid jealousy.[290] But on the proper etiquette in the bedroom he writes:

Herodotus was not right in saying that a woman lays aside her modesty along with her under-garment. On the contrary, a virtuous woman puts on modesty in its stead, and husband and wife bring into their mutual relations the greatest modesty as a token of the greatest love. (*Praecepta conjugalia* 10 = 139 c, Loeb trans.)

and later:

The wedded wife ought especially when the light is out not to be the same as ordinary women, but when her body is invisible, her virtue, her exclusive devotion to her husband, her constancy and her affection, ought to be most in evidence. (Ibid. 46 = 144 F)

So Plutarch could approve a Persian custom that the kings had their wives with them at dinner but sent them away and called for their concubines when they wanted to get drunk afterwards:

In so far they are right in what they do, because they do not concede any share in their licentiousness and debauchery to their wedded wives. If therefore a man in private life, who is incontinent and dissolute in regard to his pleasures, commit some peccadillo with a paramour or a maid-servant, his wedded wife ought not to be indignant or angry, but she should reason that it is respect for her which leads him to share his debauchery, licentiousness and wantonness with another woman. (Ibid. 16 = 140 B)

This ancillary argument, which might be called the 'ladies don't' precept, existed also in Roman consciousness. It is implied by contrasting portrayals of matronly and meretricious deportment outside the bedroom and by a poem in which Martial advises a wife to be a Lucretia all day, if she likes, but a Lais at night. When L. Aelius Caesar was criticized by his wife for his amours, he is said to have asked her to let him exercise his lust on other women: a wife was for *dignitas*, not sensuality.[291] Roman writers at least did not make the

---

[289] *Am.* 752 C–D, 756 E; *Praec. conj.* 4 = 138 F, 39 = 143 F; *Am.* 752 C, Pisias.

[290] *Praec. conj.* 44 = 144 C–D, 40 = 143 F.

[291] 11.104. 'Ladies don't move' is attributed to a husband of Cora, Lady Strafford, by Rupert Hart-Davis, *The Lyttelton Hart-Davis Letters . . . 1955–6* (London, 1978) 178.

mistake of denying sensuality to women, even respectable ones. That is clear in Lucretius' description of intercourse, and Ovid can argue that women are more sensuous than men.[292] But it was still good form for the man to be the pursuer, and one of the worst criticisms which can be made against even a promiscuous woman is that she made the first advance to her lovers.[293]

Implicit in the advice to wives to ignore the philandering of their husbands is the idea that it meant little. We may picture a continuum which runs roughly from brief encounters with a man's own slaves or prostitutes and music-girls through other people's slaves (where negotiation or poaching was involved) to respectable but unmarried women of a lower social class, and then to wives and women of his own class and long-standing affairs.[294] The last was the most serious transgression: an offence against the husband, the mistress's virtue, social ideals, and the man's own wife, especially since marriage with the mistress became a possibility (though one endangered by the Augustan Law). Where the mistress was of lower status, the greatest offence to the wife was caused when the husband kept her or introduced her into the home.[295]

It should now be possible to sum up. It is undeniable that the Romans, like the Greeks before them, demanded different standards of chastity from women and men. The preservation of virginity before marriage was essential. A few cautionary tales were handed down as a deterrent,[296] but the offence was more effectively avoided by the practice of marrying girls off soon after they reached puberty and by the strict upbringing of the daughters of the upper classes. To assert that a man debauched Roman virgins was almost too bad a charge even for blackening a political enemy.[297] (Allegations of incest with sister or daughter are the exception, and only made when the woman was already married. Allegations about the ruin of unmarried girls by

---

[292] Lucr. 4.1192 ff.; Ov. *AA* 1.271 ff. Lyne, *The Latin love poets from Catullus to Horace* 10, cites Lucr. 4.1274 ff. for the 'ladies don't move' precept. The section at 1233 ff. is concerned primarily with fertility and the sexual behaviour which favours reproduction. While he observes that prostitutes behave differently, Lucretius does not say that wives are, or ought to be, inert. His emphasis is that wives do not *need* to move as *scorta* do (1268, 1277), either to minimize the risk of conception (for, it is assumed, they want to conceive) or to please their partners (because even an unattractive wife is endeared to her husband by habit).

[293] Sempronia (Sall. *BC* 25.2; Hor. *O* 3.15). Cf. Plut. *Am.* 753 B.

[294] Tac. *A* 13.12.2 says that Nero's advisers did not interfere with his affair with the freedwoman Acte, because it did no one any harm, since he was already alienated from his wife, and would perhaps keep him from *stupra* with high-born women. For a simple version (slave, freedwoman, free-born woman) of this continuum, from the point of view of desirability to a man, see Hor. *S* 1.2; Mart. 3.33. Cf. [Dem.] *contra Neaeram* 122.

[295] Ter. *Ad.* 747; Tac. *A* 14.64.4.

[296] e.g. VM 6.1.2, 3, 4. For a girl to be spoilt (*vitiari*) is serious in the rhetoricians, but the offence is mended by love and intention to marry (e.g. *Decl. min.* 270.16, 18; cf. on marriage as a happy ending in comedy: Plut. *Mor.* 712 C). [297] Cf. Juv. 4.105.

men from another household were too serious for the girls to be permissible.) Discretion, if not virtue, prevails. Chastity was also demanded of married women and *viduae*.[298]

If respectable women were expected to abstain from sexual intercourse when unmarried and to reserve their bodies for their husbands during marriage, this was not because sexual activity was in general sinful.[299] The close association of sexuality and guilt develops with the Christian doctrine of original sin and redemption. The story of Eve is interpreted to show that woman first yields to temptation and then ensnares man, bringing about their joint fall from a state of grace. It was easy to move from that to the belief that her influence over Adam was due to her sensuality and therefore she was punished by the pains of childbirth. Fallen and seductive Eve is contrasted with Mary, the mother of the Redeemer, who must therefore be virgin. Such views of female sexuality have had a long history. Women must be controlled because they are both more sensuous than men and able to overcome male self-control.[300]

It would be more logical to justify a double standard by arguing that women are less sensuous than men and therefore are better able to live up to a higher standard.[301] This argument seems rare. The Romans in real life do not seem to have been concerned to distinguish different levels of libido in male and female. Women's passionate nature and tendency to lose control is, however, frequently castigated in phrases such as *impotentia muliebris*.[302] But the trait was not confined to women.

It can also be argued that women can live up to a higher standard because they are more moral than men. But then prescription becomes redundant. Such placing of women on a pedestal is more characteristic of Victorians than of Romans. For Roman ideology, virtuous virgins and matrons operate within a female sphere and are not set above men in general. But unusually brave women are rated on a masculine scale of *virtus* and may excel some men.[303]

Let us move to a different psychological area. Why should men object to women having the same sexual freedom as themselves? Ideas of the impact of a woman's sexual behaviour on male honour seem to have little weight for the Romans. Male possessiveness is a less convincing explanation than in more recent eras. What of the idea that a woman's procreative role is at the root of a double

[298] For an extreme definition of *vidua* see *D* 50.16.242.3, Lab.
[299] Jeremy Taylor (1613–67) makes a useful, though unorthodox, distinction: 'Chastity is either abstinence or continence: abstinence is that of virgins or widows, continence of married persons' (*SOED*).
[300] e.g. Campbell 199ff.   [301] Cf. Thomas 215.   [302] Livy 34.2.2.
[303] e.g. Epicharis (Tac. *A* 15.57).

standard? If the avoidance of bastards who usurp the place of a man's legitimate children is the reason for the double standard, then it is illogical to deny widows and divorced women or wives who avoid bearing bastards the right to do whatever they like.[304] The Romans might take the view that unmarried women who bore children were illicitly introducing children into their own families. Illegitimate children claimed kinship only with the mother and her kindred. A woman who was in her father's power would be palming off a bastard on him in much the same way as an unfaithful wife who cheated her husband. But the act would be overt, and the remedies for the *paterfamilias* easy: *emancipatio* or *exheredatio*. A woman who was already *sui iuris*, for instance one whose father had died or who had passed into a husband's control and then been widowed, would be more likely to divert wealth away from her kin to a bastard child. As far as I know, there is no evidence of concern that bastards would divert property away from legal heirs, except where the woman had, or might have, conceived during marriage.[305] The whole context of Roman thinking about the status of children must be borne in mind. Children born outside valid marriage were *iniusti* and their status depended on that of their mother. They would normally be slave if she was slave and citizen if she were citizen. All children of slave mothers were by definition illegitimate, since she was incapable of marriage, but they would scarcely be illicit in the eyes of her owner if they were fathered by himself or her *contubernalis*. Similar considerations would apply to any children borne by a recognized *concubina*. They would take her status, so if she was a free or freed Roman citizen they were free-born and Roman. But they had no automatic legal claim on her partner. Many people living in *iniustum matrimonium* would similarly be reasonably certain about the paternity of the children. They were illegitimate and followed their mother, but the father would regard them as his *filii iniusti*. None of these are really to be equated with bastards and no derogatory connotations attach to the words or phrases which the Romans normally use to describe them, such as *iniustus filius* or *filius naturalis*. They were often recognized by their father and treated accordingly. Children born to a mother who was not living in a stable relationship with one man are likely to have been viewed rather differently. But the evidence on the by-blows of lower-class women, for instance prostitutes, is sparse.

[304] Cf. Thomas 209, 216.

[305] On the risk of wives fraudulently introducing other men's children into the husband's family: Cic. *ND* 3.68; Mart. 6.2.3–4; *D* 48.5.6.1. Bastards of wives: Calp. Flaccus 2. Rules on acknowledgement of children and checks on pregnancies: *D* 25.3, 4; cf. 40.4.29. Other children fraudulently introduced into families: VM 9.15; Juv. 6.77; *D* 37.10 *passim*, 48.10.19.1, ht 30.1; 48.18.17.2.

Lawyers erase the distinction and call the children of no known
father, as well as those of *pater iniustus, vulgo quaesiti* or *spurii*. The
filiation *Sp. f.* which on tombstones acknowledges the lack of a legal
father can refer to any type of illegitimate child and demonstrates the
absence of a marked stigma attaching to him. Concern about legal
paternity seems insufficient as the root cause for the Romans'
relatively undeveloped form of double standard.

The suspicion grows that the double standard begins to arise in a far
earlier period of human history. It grows out of the female mammal's
instinct to rear young with the co-operation and protection of a male.
Male biological instinct is to implant genes in as many females
as possible; female instinct is also to breed, but for the production of
one child only one mating is necessary. A succession of mates for
successive pregnancies is possible but not advantageous unless she
changes to a healthier and stronger mate. If the pair remain together
after mating, the male is more likely to help rear the young. The
better the bonding between them and their offspring, the more
likelihood there is that the young will survive to maturity. Such a
pattern is not inconsistent with multiple female partners for a dominant male, or with a pack. Some theorists would go further back than
early mammals or animals and look for the beginnings of biological
instincts in genes themselves. I suggest only that we should look, not
at a psychological possessiveness or concern for purity of blood-lines
which is taken to be common to all males through all periods of
history (for there seems to be considerable variance here), but at
biological factors in the human condition, which might account for
different and complementary attitudes in men and women.[306] The
double standard then becomes a dominant, though not omnipotent,
pattern of behaviour. It pre-dates morality. Morality is invoked,
when society finds it necessary, to sustain the pattern. If conditions of
human life change, there is no moral reason for the perpetuation of
the double standard.

Such a conjecture must be left to be rejected or supported by
competent zoologists and anthropologists. It seems to fit in with the
thesis explored by Desmond Morris in a number of influential
popularizing works about the genesis of pair-bonding among the
ancestors of *Homo sapiens*. He argues that when the ancestors of
humans began to hunt in male groups on the plains and leave the
females behind with the young, it became necessary to secure sexual
loyalty from the females. 'Male and female apes had to fall in love and
remain faithful to one another.' Marked physical changes evolved

---

[306] *Contra*, Thomas 205.

which distinguish us from other apes and which can be explained by
the new need for relatively stable pairs, bound together by long-
lasting mutual attraction. Monogamy becomes the usual pattern,
with resort to polygamy when necessary, for instance when males are
scarce. The pattern remains remarkably general and constant, despite the strains which occur. 'It is the biological nature of the beast
which has moulded the social structure of civilization, rather than the
other way around.'[307] On my tentative hypothesis, casual sexual
encounters by males would be a survival from the period of ape-life in
the trees, when the group was less vulnerable and less organized. In
the phase during which the naked ape evolved away from other apes,
such activity with females outside the group (the double classification) during hunting-trips with males of the pack would not threaten
pair-bonds with females of the pack. We can arrive therefore at the
attractive conclusion which was expressed by the scholarly ladies of
Princess Ida, that the human male is still at an earlier stage of
evolution than the human female. The double standard has its roots
in biology, as does monogamy. Neither classical theory nor Roman
social structures can be blamed for its invention. Its ramifications
were less extensive in Roman society than they have been at other
and more recent periods. Although the Augustan adultery law
adopted a double classification of women, it was not until Constantine that the double standard was ratified, when he refused
to allow the husband's womanizing as justification for unilateral
divorce.[308]

[307] See Morris, *The illustrated Naked Ape* 30–39 ff.   [308] *CTh* 3.16.

PART IV
Paterfamilias and *Materfamilias*

10

Dos

His designs were strictly honourable, as the phrase is, that is, to
rob a lady of her fortune by way of marriage.

(Fielding, *Tom Jones* XI.4)

MARRIAGE had legal implications in two important areas: in the
production of legitimate children who were in the father's *patria
potestas* and took his status, and in property. (Between the spouses
themselves, it produced obligations of mutual respect, a theme not
given much prominence by the jurists.) Although in marriage without
manus the wife might have substantial property of her own, the
property which we shall examine here is that which was transferred to
the husband for at least the duration of the marriage, the *dos*. *Dos*
cannot exist without marriage.[1] It is not true, however, that marriage
cannot exist without *dos*. But Plautus attests the feeling, probably
familiar to his audience, that marriage without dowry was undesirable and disreputable and that the transfer and acceptance of *dos*
indicated that legal marriage rather than concubinage was intended
by both parties.[2] How far the poorest members of the population
could afford this sentiment, or afford to get married at all, is
uncertain. Documents from Egypt later attest quite small dowries,
and the jurists speak of relatively poor women who put all their
property into their dowry and of slave-women, precluded from legal
marriage, who nevertheless transferred a quasi-*dos* to their mates.[3] In
short, there are indications that dowry was firmly entrenched among
all classes.

Almost everything about Roman dowry is ambivalent. It is meant
to help secure the maintenance of the wife during a marriage or it is
her insurance policy in case the marriage ends. It is transferred to the
husband but may be recoverable by the wife's family. It can be cash or

---

[1] *D* 23.3.3, cf. ht 39.1, 59.2; *CJ* 5.3.20.2.
[2] *Trin.* 691. In Athens, marriage was invalid without dowry.
[3] *FIRA* iii.17, *PSI* 6.730; *D* 23.3.39 pr., ht 67; cf. Cic. *pro Flacco* 86.

moveable or immoveable property or a combination of all these. It may stay with the husband's family or the wife's or with their joint offspring. Husbands may see a large dowry as an attraction or a liability—and their attitudes may be different before and after the wedding. These remarks can be made with some confidence about the period from about 200 BC to about AD 200. But the sources from which we could construct a full account of chronological development are lacking.

1. Historical Development

If she entered *manus*, the wife passed into the power of husband or his *paterfamilias*, and all the property which she took with her was under the control of her new *paterfamilias*. If the woman had previously been *in patria potestate* she would have had no property of her own, except perhaps a *peculium* which her father allowed her to keep. On marriage, she lost her right to succeed her father automatically on intestacy, but gained a similar right in her husband's family. The portion which her *paterfamilias* therefore presumably bestowed on her might be the last claim she had on her original family. She left her family of birth, her husband's family absorbed her and was hence-forth solely responsible for her. If her *paterfamilias* had previously died or emancipated her, however, she was alone and independent. She will have had property which, when she entered *manus*, was transferred to her husband and passed entirely from her own control.

In early marriage in which the wife did not enter her husband's control, which developed before the Twelve Tables of the mid-fifth century, it seems likely that brides still took a portion, though they did not formally enter their new family. But there is no mention of *dos* in the Tables. Watson argues therefore that there were no legal rules about it at this early date: dowry went to the husband once and for all, although he had to pay a fine to her if he divorced a wife guilty of no fault.[4] When the wife was not *in manu*, her own property remained at her own disposal or that of her *paterfamilias*, if any. There is more scope for negotiation about the dowry which goes to the husband.

Evidence on what happened about dowry in these various legal circumstances is fragmentary for the pre-Ciceronian period, except for the evolving rules on what should happen on divorce. Plautine evidence suggests that the suitor asked a father for his daughter in marriage; the father agreed and at the same time promised a certain dowry. Etiquette did not allow the suitor to ask for a

[4] Watson, 'The divorce of Carvilius Ruga' 44–6, *XII Tables* 38–9; cf. Corbett 148.

particular amount of dowry: the contract rested on a one-sided *dotis dictio*.[5]

When Sp. Carvilius Ruga divorced his wife *c.* 230, it was for sterility rather than for a fault for which she deserved to lose her right to support. It seems that normally he would have been penalized. But he was able to argue that he could not, in conscience, say that he was married for the sake of breeding children, if he knew his wife was sterile. The state, through the question which the censors asked him, compelled him to divorce. Why, then, should he be punished? An answer was found. Gellius specifically states that Servius Sulpicius Rufus, Cicero's contemporary, in his book on dowry said that Ruga's divorce showed that *cautiones rei uxoriae* (guarantees for wife's property) were needed. Sulpicius is decisive on such a point.[6] It is significant that the property guaranteed as recoverable in the event of a divorce is called the wife's. During the marriage, it was presumably called *dos*, as it certainly is from now on. Gradually the praetors developed a system by which the wife could reclaim all or part of her dowry in the event of a divorce or the death of the husband, by the *actio rei uxoriae*.[7] Whereas before the husband had had a right to retain the dowry, subject to certain sanctions, by the second century the wife had a right to have the dowry restored to her, although if the matter came before a judge she might be penalized for bad behaviour, as Cato unctuously explained.[8] The details will be discussed later.

The property which a wife *in manu* brought to her husband was by the time of Cicero equated with the dowry of a woman not *in manu*. 'When a woman enters the *manus* of a man, everything which belonged to her becomes the husband's and is called dowry.'[9] It seems therefore to have been similarly recoverable, though it is not clear when and exactly how women in their husband's power became able to initiate a divorce.

During the marriage, as Cicero said, dowry belonged to the husband. This remains the view of the classical jurists.[10] Late classical

[5] Watson, *Persons* 57–63.   [6] Watson, 'The divorce of Carvilius Ruga'; Gell. 4.3.1–2.
[7] Corbett 148–51 (the action in use by the 2nd cent. BC, 182–3; Watson, *Persons* 67–76; Kaser, 'Die Rechtsgrundlage der *actio rei uxoriae*'. See further *Tit. Ulp.* 6.6: 'Divortio facto, si quidem sui iuris sit mulier, ipsa habet [rei uxoriae] actione[m], id est dotis repetitionem. Quod si in potestate patris sit, pater adiunct[a] filiae persona habet actionem re[i uxoriae]: nec interest, adventicia sit dos an profecticia'; *CJ* 5.18.10 (Diocletian and Maximian to Epigonus, AD 294): 'Si socero filiae tuae dotem dedisti, licet in eius positus potestate gener tuus rebus humanis exemptus sit, tamen non de peculio, sed in solidum a te consentiente filia conventum eum satis oportet facere.'   [8] Gell. 10.23.4, quoting speech *de dote*; cf. 3 and Corbett 187.
[9] Cic. *Top.* 23: 'Cum mulier viro in manum convenit, omnia, quae mulieris fuerunt, viri fiunt dotis nomine.' Cf. Corbett 109. See G 1.137a, on cancellation of *coemptio* by a married woman: 'haec autem [virum] repudio misso proinde compellere potest atque si ei numquam nupta fuisset.'   [10] G 2.63; *D* 23.3.7.3, cf. ht 9.3, Ulp., 69.8, Pap.

jurists tended to stress that dowry was only temporarily in the husband's possession, for the duration of the marriage, and always potentially reclaimable.[11] It has been argued that such views are as late as Justinian and have been interpolated in the classical texts.[12] But modern Romanists who take account of the literary evidence suggest that both the husband's ownership and the wife's potential claim coexist in classical legal texts.[13]

Literary sources as early as the second century BC show that the dowry could be thought of by non-jurists as belonging to the wife.[14] The whole concept of the *dotata uxor* would be empty if the woman were not seen as, in a sense, having control over her dowry. This point can be illustrated from Cicero's administration of Terentia's dowry. In April 59 he (and apparently Terentia) had inspected a forest belonging to her. But this was probably dotal, for he tells Atticus that only the oak of Dodona was missing to 'make us feel we own Epirus itself'.[15] In the crisis of 58, when Cicero was at least thinking of manumitting slaves in case his property was confiscated, he assures Terentia that he had only told her slaves that she would act in accordance with the deserts of each of them. Since he could not manumit slaves who were her private property, it sounds very much as if he must mean dotal slaves. Although the formal manumission would need to come from him, he implies the decision would be hers.[16] When Livy describes how the matrons in 207 BC joined together in dedicating an offering, he describes how all the women who lived within ten miles of Rome chose twenty-five of their number and brought to them contributions out of their dowries: he ignores the fact that this ought to have entailed authorization from all the husbands involved.[17]

The rights of both partners are expressed in the custom of *praelegatio dotis*, which allowed the husband to bequeath the dowry to the wife, before the estate as a whole was settled, bypassing slower legal processes: this clearly recognizes the husband's power of disposal and the wife's moral claim.[18]

---

[11] *D* 23.3.75, Tryph.: 'Quamvis in bonis mariti dos sit, mulieris tamen est.' Cf. Boeth. ad Cic. *Top*. 66 (Bruns ii. 74): 'Dos—licet matrimonio constante in bonis viri sit, est tamen in uxoris iure et post divortium velut res uxoria peti potest.'

[12] Albertario, 'La connessione dello dote con gli oneri del matrimonio'.

[13] e.g. Koschaker, 'Unterhalt der Ehefrau und Früchte der dos', esp. p. 26; Wolff, 'Zur Stellung der Frau im klassischen römischen Dotalrecht', esp. p. 357.

[14] Dixon, 'Polybius on Roman women and property', 161–2.   [15] *A* 2.4.5.

[16] *F* 14.4.4. See Dixon, 'Family finances: Terentia and Tullia' 80–2.

[17] Livy 27.37.8 ff.

[18] *D* 23.5.8, 33.2.27, 33.4 (see esp. ht 13, Paul on Labeo, saying that such legacies are customary), 35.1.40.4, 36.1.53, 37.5.10.1. On republican texts, Watson, *Persons* 25, *Succession* 96. Full treatment by Palazzolo, *Dos praelegata*.

2. *Liability*

The idea that dowry passes to the husband is clearly the original view. This is implied by republican modifications of practice which also attest the later view of the woman's potential right to restitution. Not only do praetors adjudicate claims for the return of all or part of the dowry after divorce, but by the time of Servius Sulpicius the husband was liable for negligence, as well as fraud. P. Mucius decided that C. Gracchus' widow Licinia should be able to get back her dowry, although dotal property had been destroyed in the disturbances for which her husband was responsible.[19] Allegedly Caesar secured their dowry to the wives of dead Pompeians.[20]

During the marriage, dowry is in the husband's hands and he can do almost anything he likes with it. He can for instance manumit dotal slaves and enjoy the resulting patronal rights as part of *dos*.[21] A considerable body of legal rulings, some of which go back to republican sources, confirmed that income produced by the dowry belonged to the husband. Dotal 'fruits' included interest on capital sums invested in loans, agricultural produce such as grain, grapes, and olives, young animals apart from those needed to keep the herds up to their original strength. The husband could use these profits as he pleased. If we imagine what would naturally happen in a peasant society, where the wife brings, say, ten ewes and a sow as dowry, some lambs, most if not all of the females produced in a year, will be kept as replacements; some of the male lambs and most of the piglets will be eaten by the family, and any surplus may be sold or exchanged.[22] Capital gains augment the *dos* so the husband might have to restore them.[23] He must use due care, *diligentia*, as much as he used for his own property,[24] although if he was brutal to his own slaves, that did not licence him to use equal brutality to dotal slaves.[25] He was responsible for both *culpa* and *dolus* (negligence and

---

[19] *D* 24.3.66 pr., Iav. 6 *ex post. Lab.* Cf. Watson *RPL* 26; Daube, 'Licinnia's dowry', *Aspects of Roman law* 154–5; Waldstein, 'Zum Fall der "dos Licinniae"'; Dixon, 'Family finances: Terentia and Tullia' 81. Cf. *CJ* 5.12.9. Imp. Decius Augustus et Decius Caesar Urbicanae (AD 250): 'Dotis tuae potiorem causam magis esse convenit quam rei p. cui postea (idem maritus obnoxius factus est.'

[20] Dio 43.50.2.

[21] *D* 24.3.24.4, 61, 62–3, 64, 38.16.3.2, 40.1.21, 48.10.14.2; *CJ* 5.12.3, 7.8.7; Buckland, *RLS* 263–4.

[22] *D* 23.3.7 pr., ht 10.2–3, cf. ht 7.1; Just. *Inst.* 2.1.37; Corbett 172 n. 1.

[23] *D* 24.3.67. *Ancillarum partus* go to *dos* unless the slave-women were *aestimatae*; if they were valued, then they are at the husband's risk and the babies go to him: Buckland, *RLS* 263, citing 23.3.10.2 and ht 69.9. See too 23.3.18, citing Labeo, and ht 58.1.

[24] *D* 23.3.17 pr., Paul: 'In rebus dotalibus virum praestare oportet tam dolum quam culpam, quia causa sua dotem accipit: sed etiam diligentiam praestabit, quam in suis rebus exhibet.' Cf. Corbett 171 and Buckland, '*Diligens paterfamilias*'.

[25] *D* 24.3.24.5, Paul.

malice).[26] Since he owned the dowry, he could invest cash or turn land
and moveables into cash. It might also simplify accounting, in the
event of restoration, if the dowry were valued, so that he was
responsible for a cash amount. But it was in the husband's interest
that items which were part of the dowry not be valued, since if they
were, he bore the risk of their depreciation. As Ulpian puts it with his
customary lucidity:

Plerumque interest viri res non esse aestimatas idcirco, ne periculum rerum
ad eum pertineat, maxime si animalia in dotem acceperit vel vestem, qua
mulier utitur: Eveniet enim, si aestimata sit et eam mulier adtrivit, ut
nihilominus maritus aestimationem eorum praestet. Quotiens igitur non
aestimatae res in dotem dantur, et meliores et deteriores mulieri fiunt.
(*Digest* 23.3.10 pr., Ulpian *xxxiv ad Sabinum*)

It is generally in the husband's interest that items not be valued, to avoid
their being at his risk, particularly if he receives animals as a part of the
dowry or clothing which the wife uses, for it will happen, if it is valued and
the wife wears it out, that the husband is nevertheless responsible for paying
their price at valuation. So when items are given in dowry and not valued,
their appreciation or depreciation affects the wife.[27]

Fungibles, such as cash, were at the husband's risk.[28]

These detailed rules were formulated gradually. From 230 BC
onwards, during the period when Roman prosperity grew out of
recognition, the upper class acknowledged, by custom rather than
law, the rights of widows and divorced women to their dowry. The
ideal still remained the *univira* who on widowhood would remain with
her husband's family and her children and who would not go, taking
her dowry with her, into a new marriage. But a woman perhaps in a
sine manu marriage, if widowed young and particularly if she was
childless, would normally want to remarry—or her own family would
want to redeploy her. If a husband divorced a blameless wife, he had
no moral claim on her dowry. Literary sources attest two instances
from this period when dowries were repaid at the cost of some
inconvenience. Aemilius Paullus, after divorcing his first wife Papiria

---

[26] *D* 23.3.17 pr.; 23.4.12.4; 24.3.18, ht 44.1, 67. Cf. 23.3.72.1 on similar responsibility for the husband's *paterfamilias*.

[27] Cf. *D* 23.3.11, ht 12, 17.1, 18; 23.4.29 pr. See Calonge, 'Aestimatio dotis'.

[28] *D* 23.3.42: 'Res in dotem datae, quae pondere numero mensura constant, mariti periculo sunt, quia in hoc dantur, ut eas maritus ad arbitrium suum distrahat et quandoque soluto matrimonio eiusdem generis et qualitatis alias restituat vel ipse vel heres eius.' See Corbett 172. Jurists distinguish various circumstances in which dowry was at the risk of one spouse rather than the other (*D* 23.3.10, ht 33, 35, 41.3, 46 pr., 56 pr., 58.1, 71, 23.4.6, ht 21, 29 pr., 24.3.66,7). These need not concern us here. But one excerpt is perhaps of interest: 'If the husband, not acting on orders from his wife, during the marriage, gave his father-in-law a receipt for the dowry, even though this was done because the father-in-law was needy, Labeo says that it is the husband's risk' (24.3.66.6).

and remarrying, died and left his heirs responsible for returning the dowry to his widow. Polybius tells us, as an edifying proof that Aemilius Paullus was no profiteer 'He left so small a private fortune that his sons could not pay his wife's jointure wholly from the sale of his personalty, and were obliged to sell some of his real estate also to do so.'[29] Note the distinction between liquid and non-liquid assets and how the dowry has merged with Paullus' own property. Another instance of frugality is less reliably attested. Paullus is said to have given a silver bowl from his booty as dowry to his son-in-law Q. Aelius Tubero. When Tubero died, his only farm had to be sold in order to provide cash to repay his widow.[30] Both sources recognize the social necessity of repayment.

Later, Augustus reduced the husband's power of absolute disposal of dotal property during a marriage by limiting his right to sell dotal land in Italy.[31]

While legal matters such as distinctions in the woman's status as *filiafamilias* or wife *in manu mariti* are left obscure, the social impact of dowry is often emphasized in Plautus and his contemporaries. A way of looking at the matter, usually from the husband's point of view, which had a long history in satirical writing and perhaps in the minds of most Romans, is reflected and reinforced. This is the idea that dowry is a powerful lever. Whatever her legal position, the wife with a big dowry was never really in her husband's control. Megadorus expresses this view in a long soliloquy in *Aulularia*. He is thinking of marrying the miser's daughter, starting from the premiss that if rich men married poor men's daughters without dowry, then there would be much more harmony in the city and much less expense for husbands. Even rich women could marry without dowry and bring better morals as their contribution instead. As it is, women who bring a big dowry expect to be extravagantly maintained: 'I brought you a dowry much bigger than your own property. So you ought in fairness to give me purple and gold, slave-girls, mules, muleteers, footmen, boys to carry messages, vehicles for me to ride in.' Then he paints an alarming picture of a house crammed with tradesmen of all sorts come

[29] Polyb. 32.8, cf. 18.35: 'I know that on his death, which occurred shortly after the war, when his own sons Publius Scipio and Quintus Maximus wished to pay his wife her dowry, amounting to twenty-five talents, they were reduced to such straits that they would have been quite unable to do so if they had not sold the household furniture and slaves, and some of the landed property besides' (trans. E. S. Shuckburgh). Cf. Livy *Epit.* 46: 'L. Aemilius Paullus, qui Persen vicerat, mortuus. Cuius tanta abstinentia fuit, ut, cum ex Hispania et ex Macedonia immensas opes rettulisset, vix ex auctione eius redactum sit, unde uxori eius dos solveretur'; Plut. *Aem. Paul.* 5. His first wife, Papiria, whom he divorced, was the mother of Scipio and Fabius; his second wife bore him two sons. There were also two daughters. See Dixon, 'Polybius on Roman women and property' 164–5.
[30] VM 4.4.9. [31] See esp. *D* 23.5; Paul *S* 2.21b.2.

to dun the unfortunate husband. 'These are only some of the draw-backs and unendurable expenses which go with big dowries. A wife without a dowry is in her husband's power. Women with dowries torment and ruin their husbands.'[32]

The same speaker earlier in the play makes the point that a *dotata uxor* demands heavy expenditure. The husband is enslaved by expense.[33] The point about the life-style required by a richly dowered wife is less frequently made[34] than the point that the wife treats her husband like a slave. This is often expressed with great economy, which shows how familiar it was.[35] Old women can earn husbands by their dowry; men sell their power for a dowry.[36] It is assumed that old women could not marry or stay married without a dowry.[37] *Dotatae* rely on their dowry and demand that their husbands serve them.[38] Husbands won over by dowries have to behave like maidservants to their wives.[39] It is worth choosing a dowerless girl in order to stay free.[40] *Dotatae* cannot be criticized for their faults;[41] they are naggers and give their husbands no rest.[42] Or, says Juvenal, their dowry buys them compliant husbands: the rich woman married to a greedy man has all the licence enjoyed by a widow.[43] They will queen it over their husbands but they can leave them when they wish.[44] 'If I start being a little too independent, if another's house has a brighter gleam, if I behave too roughly, she will go . . . she will want her money back.'[45] To support a poor wife was difficult, to bear a rich one was torture.[46]

The rich and disagreeable wife is not confined to the comic stage, the schoolroom, and satire. Cicero took advantage of the stereotype in his speech on behalf of Scaurus. Aris had a rich old ugly wife who (he says) conveniently died by hanging, either at her own hands or those of a freedman of her husband. The situation had been piquant:

Is enim cum hanc suam uxorem anum et locupletem et molestam timeret, neque eam habere in matrimonio propter foeditatem neque dimittere propter dotem volebat. (*pro Scauro* 7)

---

[32] *Aul.* 475ff., esp. 498ff., 532ff. On the *dotatae* see Schaps 76–7; Schuhmann, 'Der Typ der *uxor dotata* in den Komödien des Plautus'; Winterbottom on *Decl. min.* 301.20.

[33] 158ff., 169.   [34] e.g. *Men.* 120–1, 801–2.

[35] e.g. *Men.* 766–7. A Greek topos, e.g. Stob. 4.22.71, 4.22.118ff.

[36] *Most.* 281, cf. 703, *Asin.* 87: 'dote imperium vendidi.'

[37] Pompon. *Atellan.* 89: 'nupsit posterius dotatae vetulae varicosae vafrae.'

[38] Caec. *Ploc.* 142ff. ap. Gell. 2.23.10 with Williams, *Tradition and originality in Roman poetry* 363ff.; Plaut. *Men.* 767; cf. *Epig. Bob.* 22.1ff.: 'Uxorem duces si, Zoile, pauper egenam, pauperie iunges, Zoile, pauperiem; at si ⟨tu⟩ validam gaza dotisque superbam, | non illa uxor erit, sed violens domina.'

[39] Titin. *com.* 73.   [40] Sen. *Contr.* 1.6.5, 7; Juv. 7.224; Auson. *Epp.* 342.

[41] *Persa* 387, cf. *Asin.* 898.   [42] *Mil.* 681: *oblatratrices*, literally 'yappers'; *Most.* 703–4.

[43] 6.136–41.   [44] Hor. *O* 3.24.19–20; Juv. 6.224–5.

[45] Sen. *Contr.* 1.6.5.   [46] Jer. *adv. Iovin.* 1.47 = 313E.

Being afraid of this wife of his, who was an old woman and rich and disagreeable,[47] he did not want to stay married to her because she was so unattractive, nor could he divorce her because of her dowry.[48]

The *Digest* offers at least one reference to the immunity of the *dotata uxor*: a father-in-law withdraws an accusation of adultery because he does not want the dowry to pass out of the family.[49]

It was the husband's duty to keep his wife in the style to which her *dos* entitled her. Menaechmus tells his well-dowered wife that he has been too soft with her. He has been a good provider.[50] We have already seen how comic husbands interpret their duty as compulsion to give in to every extravagant whim which a wife might have. The list of luxuries became fairly standard:

> Quando ego tibi ancillas, penum,
> lanam, aurum, vestem, purpuram bene praebeo nec quicquam eges,
> malo carebis si sapis, virum opservare desines . . .
>
> (Plautus *Menaechmi* 120–2)

Since I provide you properly with slave-girls, food, wool, gold, clothes, purple stuff, and there is nothing you lack, you'll escape trouble if you have any sense, you'll stop keeping an eye on your husband . . .[51]

In the eyes of husbands and fathers, the requirements for luxurious living were gold, purple, and carriages, all mentioned in Livy's version of Cato's speech against the repeal of the Oppian Law as well as by Plautus, and an elaborate suite of slaves, not only *ancillae* but specialized male slaves.[52] The list may go back to a Greek original, for Jerome in his tirade derived from Theophrastus, on why the philosopher should not marry, says that he will be distracted by the needs of his wife:

Multa enim esse quae matronarum usibus necessariae sunt, pretiosae vestes, aurum, gemmae, sumptus, ancillae, supellex varia, lecticae et esseda deaurata. (Jerome *adversus Iovinianum* 1.47 = 313 C)

(He says) that there are many things which married ladies must use, expensive clothes, gold, gems, outlays, slave-girls, all sorts of household goods, litters, and a gilded chariot.

The saint has inflated earlier lists and embroidered his original.

---

[47] The classic word: cf. Metellus ap. Gell. 1.6.2.
[48] The fragmentary line Plaut. *Cist.* 305 probably refers to the same idea.
[49] 48.5.12.3.   [50] 61, 110ff.
[51] His father-in-law repeats the lesson: 'quando te auratam et vestitam bene habet, ancillas, penum | recte praebet' (801–2), also noticed by Dumont, 'Les revenues de la dot en droit romain' 32.
[52] Livy 34.3.9, cf. 7.6; *Aul.* 498ff., *Men.* 120ff., 801–2.

3. *Maintenance*

In legal thinking, maintenance and dowry were firmly linked. This must have been true from the beginning of marriage in which the wife did not enter *manus*. For, if the wife retained her rights in her family of birth, it was surely fair that her father or kin should reimburse her husband for the expense of supporting her. Enough thinking on the subject had been done for the jurist Servius Sulpicius Rufus to produce a book on dowry in the mid-first century BC. Cato the Censor, an obstinate opponent of the growth of women's financial independence and spending-power, had made a speech on dowry, but the context and exact date are unknown.[53] We know that the praetors in their edicts had concerned themselves with equity to both parties when the wife sued for return of dowry after divorce.[54] Jurists by the time of Cicero had defined the purpose of dowry and had considered many of the problems which it raised. Juristic evidence for the connection between dowry and maintenance is, however, comparatively late, unless we accept one restored fragment. The matter became unnecessarily controversial because scholars focused their attention on the technical phrase for the duty of supporting a wife, the *onera matrimonii*, which, it was argued, was not classical. A substantial set of clear statements on the matter was therefore ruled out as interpolated by the Justinianic compilers, who were operating with a different conception of the function of dowry.[55] But *onus* is frequently used in classical prose to describe duties such as those of guardians or heirs. The nearest parallel seems to be a reference by Quintilian to 'the burdens of marrying a wife and bringing up children'.[56] Besides, even if the phrase was invented by post-classical or even Justinianic lawyers, the concept could antedate it. The historical development of the law of dowry deserves reappraisal. Much of that history has been lost by the disappearance of sources. But if we postulate that the concept of the link between dowry and necessary expenses existed from the beginning, but was refined and developed over the centuries, and that certain problems were still matter for debate and disagreement even among classical lawyers, we shall see that many texts which do not mention *onera matrimonii* are consistent with the

---

[53] *ORF* 221–2 = Gell. 10.23.4–5. For his record cf. his opposition to the repeal of the Oppian Law and his approval of the Voconian Law (*ORF* 156–60, esp. 158 = Gell. 17.6.1, 8).

[54] Cic. *Top.* 66, *Off.* 3.61.

[55] For Justinian's very interesting new ideas, see *CJ* 5.12.29–31, 13.1.

[56] *Decl. min.* 298.4: 'ne haec quidem ducendae uxoris et educandorum liberorum onera recusavi, ut relictum [sc. rus paternum] a parentibus meis relinquerem filio meo' ('Nor did I shirk the charges of marrying a wife and bringing up children, so that I might leave to my son the paternal farm which my parents had left to me').

concept. The credit for dispersing clouds of controversy and for discussing the maintenance of wives and income from dowry together and in their full context goes to an admirable article by François Dumont.[57]

If a papyrus fragment is both correctly restored and uninterpolated itself, we can push back the concept of *onera matrimonii* at least as far as Labeo and probably Servius Sulpicius Rufus. The relevant part of the text is as follows:

> [Quia apud eum esse debet] q(ui) on[e]
> [ra sustinet; quod si iam di]ssoluto
> matrimonio [(societas) distrahatu]r, isdem dieb(us) prae
> [cipi debet qui]b(us) et solvi debet.
> [Ita Se]r(vius) et Lab(eo) scribunt.

(*P. Grenf.* 2.107 recto[58])

Because [sc. the dowry] ought to be with the person who carries the charges of a marriage; but if the partnership is broken up after the marriage has been dissolved, it ought to be taken out first [sc. taken by the married man from the assets of the partnership] on the same days on which it must be paid over [sc. to the divorced wife].

This fragment corresponds with a *Digest* text from Paul:

Si unus ex sociis maritus sit et distrahatur societas manente matrimonio, dotem maritus praecipere debet, quia apud eum esse debet qui onera sustinet: quod si iam dissoluto matrimonio societas distrahatur, eadem die recipienda est dos, qua et solvi debet. (*Digest* 17.2.65.16, Paul *xxxii ad edictum*)

If one of the partners is a married man and the partnership is broken up while the marriage continues in existence, the husband ought to take the dowry out first, because it ought to be with the man who carries the charges of the marriage; but if the marriage has already been dissolved when the partnership is broken up, the dowry must be recovered on the same day that it ought to be paid over.

The papyrus fragment corresponds in all essentials with the *Digest* text, except that it ascribes the opinion, though not necessarily the wording, to Servius (where the restoration is convincing) and Labeo (where the reading is not in doubt). So the ruling that, when partners divide their assets, a man's wife's dowry must first be taken out of the pool before the division is made must go back at least to the late

---

[57] 'Les revenues de la dot en droit romain'.

[58] Also called *Fragmenta Bodleiana* 1; text of Sierl, *Supplementum ad Othonis Lenel Palingenesiam iuris civilis ad fidem papyrorum* xxii no. 24a (p. 12). Cf. *FIRA* ii.423, Watson, *Persons* 16.

Republic or the time of Augustus. The reason given for it is very likely also to be ascribed to Servius Sulpicius or Labeo or both.

If all the scattered texts which refer to *onera matrimonii* had been systematically interpolated, it would say much for the energy and consistency of Tribonian's committee. The principal texts may be mentioned briefly. Pomponius (who flourished under Hadrian) cites his contemporary Julian for the ruling that if a woman promised as dowry money which she had lent to a third party to an intended husband who was also the surety for the debt and whom she has successfully sued for payment, then after the marriage he could sue the principal debtor 'because it is understood that the money is missing for the reason that he carried the charges of the marriage'.[59]

Ulpian refers quite often to *onera*. He related a decision by which Septimius Severus avoided splitting the income from a dowry from the charges of a marrige.[60] He makes a clear statement of the function of the income from dowry:

Dotis fructum ad maritum pertinere debere aequitas suggerit: cum enim ipse onera matrimonii subeat, aequum est eum etiam fructus percipere. (*Digest* 23.3 [*de iure dotium*] 7 pr., Ulpian *xxxi ad Sabinum*)

Equity suggests that the income from dowry ought to belong to the husband: for since he undergoes the charges of the marriage, it is fair that he should also draw the income.

Paul, Ulpian's contemporary, makes the same general point:

Ibi dos esse debet, ubi onera matrimonii sunt. Post mortem patris statim onera matrimonii filium sequuntur, sicut liberi, sicut uxor. (*Digest* 23.3.56.1–2, Paul *vi ad Plautium*)

The dowry ought to be where the charges of marriage are. After the death of his father [sc. his *paterfamilias*], the charges of his marriage at once follow the son, just as his wife and children do.

That is, when he becomes *sui iuris* and a *paterfamilias* on the death of his father, who had previously controlled him, his wife and children, as well as his wife's dowry, a man's acquisition of control is simultaneous for both his dependants and the dowry. Until the father died, the wife and the children which she bore to the *filiusfamilias* were in his household and the dowry was there too, as Paul and Ulpian's older contemporary Papinian made clear in discussing the private property of a soldier who was *filiusfamilias*: the dowry was not part of it.[61]

---

[59] D 17.1.47 pr.: 'Iulianus ait, si fideiussori uxor doti promiserit, quod ei ex causa fideiussoria debeat, nuptiis secutis confestim mandati adversus debitorem agere eum posse, quia intellegitur abesse ea pecunia eo, quod onera matrimonii sustineret.' For explanation of the circumstances see Dumont, 'Les revenues de la dot en droit romain' 30–1.

[60] D 23.4.11.   [61] D 49.17.16 pr.

When a *filiusfamilias* was his father's heir and executor, he, like the partner mentioned above, took his wife's dowry out of the estate before paying legacies.[62] Paul points out that he can do this immediately without waiting for formal institution as heir:

Quia mortuo patre quaedam filios sequuntur etiam antequam fiunt heredes, ut matrimonium, ut liberi, ut tutela. Igitur et dotem praecipere debet qui onus matrimonii post mortem patris sustinuit: et ita Scaevolae quoque nostro visum est. (*Digest* 10.2.46, Paul *vii ad Sabinum*)

Because on the death of the father certain things follow the children [sc. sons] even before they become heirs, for example marriage, children, guardianship. So he ought to take out the dowry first because he has carried the burden of marriage since his father's death: this was also the opinion of our colleague Scaevola.

This, like all the other texts which mention *onera matrimonii*, has been attacked. The use of *matrimonia* for 'wives' is challenged, but it is perfectly classical, since it occurs in non-juristic prose writers, including Tacitus and Suetonius. The argument is perfectly consistent with that of the other suspected texts and the phraseology is closely parallel to *Digest* 23.3.56.1–2.[63] Note the appeal to Cervidius Scaevola, which shows that the particular point at issue (but not the argument about *onera*) was controversial. Yet another text points up the connection between income from dowry and the charges of marriage. Paul again, commenting on an agreement made with the wife that the income from a dotal farm shall be used to pay a debt of hers, rules that if the agreement is made before the wedding, then the amount of her dowry is reduced by the amount paid from the income to settle the debt. But if the agreement is made after the marriage, then the husband is making his wife a gift of the money, since the income was supposed to offset the *onera*.[64] If the text is accepted as sound in all the above passages, then the concept of *onera matrimonii* was familiar to the great jurists of the late second and early third century and they frequently made appeal to it. I would conjecture that the idea and the expression were both present in Servius

[62] *D* 10.2.20.2: 'filius familias heres institutus dotem uxoris suae praecipiet, nec immerito, quia ipse onera matrimonii sustinet' ('a *filiusfamilias* who is instituted heir will first take out his wife's dowry, and this is proper, because he is the one who carries the charges of the marriage').

[63] *D* 10.2.46. *Contra*, Albertario, 'La connessione della dote con gli oneri del matrimonio' 302. Cf. *OLD* s.v. *matrimonium* 2b.

[64] *D* 23.4.28: 'Quaeris, si pacta sit mulier vel ante nuptias vel post nuptias ut ex fundi fructibus quem dedit in dotem creditor mulieris dimittatur, an valeat pactum. Disco, si ante nuptias id convenerit, valere pactum eoque modo minorem dotem constitutam: post nuptias vero cum onera matrimonii fructus relevaturi sunt, iam de suo maritus paciscitur ut dimittat creditorem et erit mera donatio.' There are two further texts on *onera*: *D* 23.3.75 (an interpolated text) and ht 76.

Sulpicius and in Labeo and that very probably they occurred in praetorian edicts on this topic. Some support for this conjecture may be drawn from the fact that the passage from Paul on partnership and two of the excerpts from Ulpian come from their commentaries on the edict.[65]

If the idea of the husband's obligation to support the marriage with the help of the income from dowry is old, though elaborated over the centuries, a converse practice grew up during the Principate, by which the wife or her family made a bargain with the husband that the income from the dowry should go directly to her, so that she could organize her own living expenses (or at least some of them). There was no doubt a good deal to be said for such an arrangement if, for instance, the husband was sent abroad on active service. The following passage makes the connection of this practice and the normal acceptance of *onera* quite explicit:

Si uxor viro dotem promiserit et dotis usuras, sine dubio dicendum est peti usuras posse, quia non est ista donatio, cum pro oneribus matrimonii petantur. Quid tamen, si maritus uxori petitionem earum remiserit? Eadem erit quaestio, an donatio sit illicita: et Iulianus hoc diceret: quod verum est. Plane si convenerat, uti se mulier pasceret suosque homines, idcirco passus est eam dote sua frui, ut se suosque aleret, expeditum erit: puto enim non posse ab ea peti quasi donatum, quod compensatum est. (*Digest* 24.1.21.1, Ulpian *xxxii ad Sabinum*)

If the wife has promised dowry and the interest on the dowry to her husband, without doubt we must say that the interest may be claimed, because it is not a gift, since the interest is claimed to balance the charges of marriage. But what if the husband remits his claim against his wife? It will be the same question, whether this is an illegal gift, and Julian would say so and it is right. Clearly if an agreement was made, that the wife should feed herself and her people and the husband allowed her to enjoy the revenue from her dowry, so that she could support herself and her people, then it will be solved: I think that it cannot be claimed from her as a gift, when it has been offset.[66]

Several other texts allude to the same custom, but without mentioning *onera* in relation to it. Scaevola writes of a father who promised a dowry and agreed to support (*aleret*) his daughter and all

---

[65] *D* 17.2.65.16, 10.2.20.2, 23.4.11.

[66] The style is clumsy in places and the final clause with its reference to *compensare* is suspect. However, as Dumont says ('Les revenues de la dot en droit romain' 24 n. 2), 'dans son ensemble il exprime une idée classique'. *D* 17.1.60.3, Scaev., has an agreement that the father will allow the husband the interest on the dowry and that the husband will support the wife. Dumont points out that the agreement meant that the husband could use only that part of the income which was needed to support the wife: the rest would revert to her father, whereas in the absence of an agreement the husband took all the income and used any residue as he liked (art. cit. 21 n. 1).

her people, but out of ignorance he also wrote promising the interest on the dowry to his son-in-law, who tried to tie him to his written word. Scaevola says that as the father had supported his daughter (*exhibuerit*) and the husband had had no expenses, the father can defend himself by charging the son-in-law with bad faith.[67]

Scaevola has two examples of fathers who make such arrangements and fail to pay up. One wife has to borrow from her husband in order to pay for herself and her father's slaves who attend her. After her death, the husband sues her father for his expenses.[68] The second case is exactly similar, with the added details that the allowance from her father is called a *salarium*, and that the wife had not only to borrow, but also to use some of her husband's own money, which she was able to do because his household affairs were entrusted to her care. There is no suggestion that she was abusing her trust. On her death her father refuses to pay and the husband holds on to property belonging to her.[69]

A more extreme expedient was for a wife to promise a dowry and then make an agreement that she should support herself (*se alat*) or hand over to her husband a sum sufficient for her support and that the dowry should not be claimed.[70] If a man took a wife in his absence, he could not, in Papinian's opinion, claim interest on dowry which she had used to support herself in his house until he came back.[71] On the other hand, it was possible for a husband not to claim the interest but to support his wife out of his own pocket.[72] It was also possible for a husband to pay his wife an allowance out of which she could meet her expenses. Ulpian links this again with dotal revenue:

Ex annuo vel menstruo, quod uxori maritus praestat, tunc quod superest revocabitur, si satis immodicum est, id est supra vires dotis. (*Digest* 24.1.15 pr., Ulpian *xxii ad Sabinum*)

Out of the annual or monthly allowance, which a husband makes to his wife, any surplus will be reclaimed if it is sufficiently excessive, that is, beyond the capacity of the dowry.

That is, if the husband allowed his wife much too much for her support and more than the income from her dowry, the extra would count as a gift and he could reclaim it.[73] Julian discusses a complicated case which begins with a husband and wife agreeing that the income

---

[67] *D* 44.4.17 pr. Cf. Dumont, 'Les revenues de la dot en droit romain' 21 n. 1.

[68] *D* 15.3.20 pr.

[69] *D* 15.3.21. The interpolated *D* 24.3.42.2 also confirms how common were specific agreements on maintenance and the interest from dowry.

[70] *D* 23.4.12.1.   [71] *D* 23.3.69.3.

[72] *D* 24.3.42.2, 24.1.21.1, ht 54.

[73] On this passage see Corbett 127.

from a farm which she had brought as her dowry or part of her dowry should go to her as an annual allowance.[74]

Diocletian and Maximian summed up the position in the late third century:

Pro oneribus matrimonii mariti lucro fructus dotis totius esse, quos ipse cepit, vel, si uxori capere donationis causa permisit, eum in quantum locupletior facta est posse agere manifestissimi iuris est. (*Codex Justiniani* 5.12.20, AD 294)

It is an absolutely clear point of law that the income from the whole dowry is to the profit of the husband, as compensation for the charges of marriage, and that, if he allows his wife to take it as a gift, he can sue her for the amount by which she has been enriched.

Again the husband, if he allows the whole income of the dowry to his wife, can reclaim anything not expended for her support.

Enough has been said to show that the basic responsibility of supporting the wife was the husband's and that he was expected to use the income of the dowry. As a corollary, the dowry was expected to be adequate to supply all the funds required for her support, perhaps with a surplus. There is a parallel in praetorian rulings on funeral expenses. The basic idea was that the person who took the dead woman's dowry should be responsible for her funeral. If the dowry did not cover the expenses, then her father might be held responsible for the balance.[75] But what exactly is covered by terms such as *onera matrimonii* or *exhibere uxorem*?[76]

A Victorian gentleman contemplating matrimony would take into account the probability that he would soon be called upon to set up a nursery and employ a nurse and a nursery maid and eventually governesses. Only one Roman legal text specifically links children with the *onera matrimonii*.[77] But Quintilian regards marrying and child-rearing as charges.[78] The strongest connection of children with dowry is provided by the institution of *retentio propter liberos*, which existed by the time of Cicero, and by which, if a divorce took place on the initiative of the wife or her *paterfamilias*, the husband could keep one-sixth of the dowry for each child up to a maximum of three. (This is the proportion established by the classical period.) *Retentio* did not

---

[74] *D* 23.4.22 pr. Cf. Dumont, 'Les revenues de la dot en droit romain' 21 n. 3.

[75] *D* 11.7.16ff., esp. ht 20.1 on *dos permodica*, 23.3.78 pr. Later, costs might be shared pro rata between heirs and whoever got the dowry.

[76] *D* 17.1.60.3, 24.1.54. The word replaces *alere* (15.3.20 pr., 44.4.17 pr.), which is common with words such as *filiam*, but not cited by *TLL* with *uxorem*.

[77] *D* 49.17.16 pr.

[78] *Decl.* 298.4. Ov. *M* 5.523 uses *pignus onusque* ('a pledge and a responsibility') of a daughter in relation to her parents.

apply if the motive for the divorce was the husband's misconduct or if the marriage was invalid.[79] But these texts do not amount to a proof that the living expenses of a couple's children were seen as a direct charge on the income from a dowry. The texts on *retentio* are rather an indication that children might have a claim on *capital* from the mother, if she deliberately cut her ties with them and their father. (There was no *retentio* if the marriage was broken by death. If that happened, it was expected that a mother would have provided for her children.) The basic rule was that children were a charge (*onus*) on their father, but this was not among the *onera matrimonii* as such.[80]

The most obvious charge covered by *onera matrimonii* is for food. But although the primary sense of the verb used in several texts, *alere*, is 'to feed', legacy of *alimenta* included also other means of subsistence, clothing and housing, without which a human being cannot survive, and it seems likely that the verb in legal texts also has this extended sense.[81] The wife's dependents, *sui*, had to be supported as well as herself.[82] This will mean her servants, her own slaves and freedmen, and on occasion slaves of other people who waited on her. For instance, a father who took over responsibility for his daughter's maintenance might supply her with slaves and then neglect to provide the money for their food.[83] The husband might give his wife money to supply provisions, food, and unguents to her staff and this would not count as a gift since she obtained no capital gains.[84] But there seem to have been precise limits to the servants for which the husband had to pay living expenses. This is made clear by two passages on food rations, *cibaria*, in the context of what counted as a gift between husband and wife. The husband had no claim for a refund of what he spent to supply the household staff or baggage-animals which belonged to his wife, as long as he used them too. On the other hand, he did have a claim if he fed a group of slaves which she kept for sale or her domestic staff, *familia domestica*, by which I understand those attached to a separate household of her own.[85] This produced the interesting irony that if a man and woman lived in concubinage, he could not reclaim what he spent on rations to her slaves; but if they subsequently became husband and wife, he could, unless the slaves were in common use by both (*in communi usu*).[86]

---

[79] Cic. *Top.* 19; *Tit. Ulp.* 6.9–10.

[80] *D* 25.3.8. Note, however, that Justinian apparently regarded the *retentio* as helping the father to bring up his young children by a divorced wife: *CJ* 5.13.1.5c.

[81] *D* 34.1.6, Iav.

[82] *D* 44.4.17 pr., 23.4.4, cf. 24.1.21.1: *pascere*. Terence uses *alere* for supporting a mistress and her staff (*Heaut.* 751).

[83] *D* 15.3.20 pr.   [84] *D* 24.1.31.9; cf. 24.1.7.1.

[85] *D* 24.1.31.10.   [86] *D* 24.1.58.1.

So it is not clear which of the wife's staff the husband was normally expected to supply out of the income from her dowry, except for those who worked for both of them. We might expect mention of the slaves which the husband supplied, who appear so often in the literary sources, and it is possible to suppose that husbands in comedy mean that they provided slaves and their keep. It is obviously no good giving your wife a slave if she does not have the funds to keep him. As Jorrocks says of a parallel chattel, ten couple of hounds, 'Con-found all presents wot eat!'[87]

It seems reasonable, however, to conjecture that one group of slaves whom the husband would normally be expected to maintain were those who were themselves part of the dowry. *Cibaria* (rations) for dotal slaves were a necessary expense, but not of that special sort which qualified as *impensae necessariae* for which a husband could claim a refund if he had to return the dowry. The husband had to pay for food as he did for moderate medical expenses. But major expenditure on the health of slaves would be a necessary expense which entitled him to compensation, like propping up a building in danger of collapse. Neratius says it is the job of the husband to look after (*tueri*) dotal property at his own expense, *suo sumptu*: so not necessarily out of income from the dowry.[88]

In the broader context, the husband's provision for his wife is frequently mentioned under the rubric of *uxoris causa parata*. These are things which he assigned to her use which he often legated to her in his will. So they do not appear to be linked with income from her dowry.[89]

4. *The Size and Nature of Dowry*

However attractive it might seem for a woman to marry a man from a richer family than her own or for a man to marry a woman with a large dowry or wealth of her own which he might hope would pass to their children or himself on her death, there was a strong school of thought which aimed at balance. We have seen already how a long tradition pointed out the risks to the husband in having a rich dowry. Ausonius is still hammering the point in the fourth century. 'Harm is done in marriage if the dowry is excessive.'[90]

It was also improper for the wife's family to overbid by offering a dowry disproportionate to their wealth and standing in order to achieve hypergamy. The clearest evidence for this is unfortunately

---

[87] Surtees, *Handley Cross* ch. 43. In the *Digest*, *manicipia* and *iumenta* are often paired.
[88] *D* 25.1.15.
[89] But they might be objects which had originally been part of the dowry: *D* 32.78.6.
[90] 12.7.1: 'Saepe in coniugiis fit noxia, si nimia est dos'; 342.1.

late, although it may be implied by Plautus' idea that old women bought husbands. Apuleius taunts his opponent with having had to borrow all the money for his daughter's dowry. Besides, it was a bigger one than his bankruptcy and quiverful of other children could possibly justify.[91] Sidonius puts it more clearly: Paconius, a man of modest background, in order to ally himself with a superior family, married off his daughter (admittedly an honourable woman) by offering a splendid dowry, in contravention of the norms of civil behaviour.[92] Sober and earlier evidence suggests that the amount of dowry necessary and proper to secure and celebrate a particular marriage for a particular girl was a matter for careful consideration of the status of each partner and the economic position of the bride. When a woman's father died before her marriage, Celsus says her *tutores* were to decide on the amount of the dowry, as a good man would determine it, in the light of the status (*dignitas*), resources (*facultates*), and number of children the testator had. This must have been the standard view.[93] Elsewhere Celsus says the amount is set with reference to the *facultates* and *dignitas* of both husband and wife; Papinian mentions the *facultates* of the wife's family and the *dignitas* of the husband and the *facultates* and *dignitas* of the woman's original family. Terentius Clemens talks of the woman's *facultates*, and the Vatican fragment of a woman who marries a man of greater *dignitas* and so gives him all her property as dowry.[94] This fits well with what Pliny had said earlier on this topic in a letter to an advocate called Quintilianus:[95]

Quamvis et ipse sis continentissimus et filiam tuam ita institueris ut decebat tuam filiam, Tutili neptem, cum tamen sit nuptura honestissimo viro Nonio Celeri, cui ratio civilium officiorum necessitatem quandam nitoris imponit, debet secundum condicionem mariti [uti] veste comitatu, quibus non quidem augetur dignitas, ornatur tamen et instruitur. Te porro animo beatissimum, modicum facultatibus scio. Itaque partem oneris tui mihi vindico, et tamquam parens alter puellae nostrae confero quinquaginta milia nummum plus collaturus, nisi a verecundia tua sola mediocritate munusculi impetrari posse confiderem, ne recusares. Vale. (*Epistulae* 6.32.1–2)

[91] *Apol.* 76 fin.: 'Dos erat a creditore omnis ad terruncium pridie sumpta et quidem grandior quam domus exhausta et plena liberis postulabat.'

[92] *Epp.* 1.11.5: 'Namque ut familiae superiori per filiam saltim quamquam honestissimam iungeretur, contra rigorem civici moris splendidam, ut ferunt, dotem Chremes noster Pamphilo suo dixerat.'

[93] *D* 32.43: 'boni viri arbitratu . . . ex dignitate, ex facultatibus, ex numero liberorum testamenti facientis aestimare'; cf. VM 4.4.10.

[94] *D* 23.3.60, ht 69.4; cf. 17.1.60.1, Scaev., 23.3.61, ht 69.5; *FV* 115.

[95] Cf. Dumont, 'Les revenues de la dot en droit romain' 29. The letter from bride's friend to bridegroom in *D* 17.1.60.1 provides a neat counterpart to Pliny's letter to the bride's father.

You yourself are not a self-indulgent man and have brought your daughter up as befitted your daughter and the granddaughter of Tutilius. Still, as she is about to marry that honourable man, Nonius Celer, whose career in the lawcourts imposes on him a certain obligation of éclat, she must adapt her clothes and attendants to the position of her husband, for although they do not increase a person's dignity, they equip and adorn it. I know you to be rich in spirit, but of moderate wealth. So I claim for myself part of your charge, and, as if I were a second father to her, I give our dear girl fifty thousand sesterces. I would give more, were I not sure that it is only because of the modesty of this little present that I can persuade you to suppress your instinct to refuse. Farewell.

Duncan-Jones[96] reckons this gift as *dos*, that is, a contribution to augment the dowry given by Quintilianus. Clothes and attendants could clearly be part of a dowry, the former in particular could equally be part of a bride's trousseau. But, since Pliny is giving the 50,000 sesterces to the girl herself, it would be impolite of him to suggest precisely how she is to allocate the money. Whichever she does, she will be doing the correct thing by her husband's position (*condicio*) and (whatever Pliny says) be maintaining the *dignitas* of her own family for which her father's *facultates* were inadequate.

A rich man could expect an *uxor dotata*; a poor man whose whole capital was less than her trousseau could not.[97] To marry a girl without a dowry into a rich family seemed improper.[98] It put the girl in a weak position. She might seem to be a concubine.[99] Often, it would simply be impracticable. The dowerless girl would be *inlocabilis* or have to marry a social inferior.[100] Ap. Claudius (consul 54) owed it to his birth and the generosity of Lucullus that he was able to marry his sister to him without a dowry.[101]

For the upper class at least, it was essential to give a respectable dowry. Cicero, arguing as a Stoic, provides a *locus classicus*. Riches are a state of mind, not of a man's exchequer:

Animus hominis dives, non arca [quae] appellari solet. Quamvis illa sit plena, dum te inanem videbo, divitem non putabo. Etenim ex eo, quantum cuique satis est, metiuntur homines divitiarum modum. Filiam quis habet, pecunia est opus; duas, maiore; pluris, maiore etiam; si, ut aiunt †Danaum quinquaginta sint filiae, tot dotes magnam quaerunt pecuniam. Quantum

---

[96] *ERE* 28, followed by Saller, 'Roman dowry and the devolution of property in the Principate' 200.

[97] Plaut. *Mil*. 679–80; Hor. *Epp*. 1.6.36–7; Juv. 3.160–1.

[98] Plaut. *Trin*. 605–6: 'sine dote ille illam in tantas divitias dabit? non credibile dices'; cf. *Aul*. 534.

[99] Plaut. *Trin*. 689 ff.; cf. Watson, *Persons* 2–6.

[100] Plaut. *Aul*. 191; cf. Ter. *Ad*. 345–6.   [101] Varro *RR* 3.16.2.

enim cuique opus est, ad id accommodatur, ut ante dixi, divitiarum modus. Qui igitur non filias plures, sed innumerabiles cupiditates habet, quae brevi tempore maximas copias exhaurire possint, hunc quo modo ego appellabo divitem, cum ipse egere se sentiat? (*Paradoxes* 44, from 'Only the wise man is rich')

It is the soul of man which is rich, not his money-chest, which is usually so called. Although it is full, as long as I see you are empty, I shall not think you rich. Men measure the extent of their riches by considering what is enough for each individual. If a man has a daughter, he needs money; if he has two, he needs more; if he has several, he needs more again; if he has fifty, like Danaus in the legend, that many dowries require a great deal of money. So the extent of riches is fitted to the individual's needs, as I said before. If a man has, not several daughters, but innumerable desires, which can rapidly exhaust great wealth, how can I call him rich, since he himself perceives that he is in want?

It is assumed here that desires can be limited, but not daughters' dowries. How burdensome was this obligation in general? We have seen that the amount of dowry given was expected to be proportionate to the resources of the bride's family and the *dignitas* of both sides. We have also seen that charitable people like Pliny might help swell the amount. One other example occurs in his letters, where he reminds Calvina that he had taken over all the debts of her father, becoming his only creditor. Part of her dowry had been paid by her father out of money which, in effect, he owed to Pliny, and 100,000 sesterces more had been a direct contribution from Pliny.[102] Dowry, as the legal terminology makes very clear, did not have to come from a male ascendant of the woman: it could be *adventicia* as well as *profecticia*.[103] Besides, it did not have to be paid over all at once. *Pacta dotalia* could stipulate long delays: for instance, that dowry was to be paid on the father's death. In the absence of *pacta*, cash could be paid over in three annual instalments, starting a year after the wedding.[104] In the light of these general observations, let us examine more closely the evidence on how burdensome the bride's family found the institution.

First of all, it was urgent to get a girl married off at the right age. So it was almost a topos as an example of misfortune if a daughter's marriageability coincided with a father's financial difficulties. Not to be able to produce a dowry was a terrible fate.[105] It was entirely proper for a man's friends to come to the rescue:

[102] Pliny *Epp.* 2.4.2. [103] Kinsmen were allowed to give dowry by the Cincian Law (FV 305). [104] *D* 23.4.19, Alf.; Polyb. 32.137.
[105] Cic. *Quinct.* 98; Hor. *Epp.* 1.17.46–7; Mart. 7.10.14; Apul. *M* 10.23, where a mother cannot dower her daughter in accordance with her birth. See Daube, 'The undowered bride'. I am not convinced that all *indotatae* in the *Digest* are interpolated.

Liberales autem, qui suis facultatibus aut captos a praedonibus redimunt aut aes alienum suscipiunt amicorum aut in filiarum collocatione adiuvant aut opitulantur in re vel quaerenda vel augenda. (Cicero *de officiis* 2.56)

But liberal men [sc. in contrast to *prodigi*, spendthrifts] are those who by their resources ransom those captured by pirates or take on their friends' debts or help them in establishing their daughters or aid them in acquiring or increasing wealth.

The charitable work of giving dowries to poor or orphaned girls is particularly appropriate for wealthy women: it is credited to women of the Ptolemies and then to Livia and other upper-class ladies.[106] It could be performed with delicacy by men and we are told that the senate had sometimes rescued upper-class girls from dowerless marriages.[107]

No law forbade a woman to give all her property as dowry.[108] But if she was under 25 and committed her whole patrimony to her dowry, or more than the estate could stand, she could claim redress.[109] Furthermore, a woman's kin, especially her children, might argue that a dowry was unfair to their interests. Constantine in AD 358 argued that a dowry which absorbed all of a woman's property and left nothing for her children to inherit was excessive and they could sue in defence of their right against an 'undutiful dowry' (*dos inofficiosa*), as they might against an 'undutiful will' which neglected their claims.[110]

Dowries are usually expressed, whether in comedy or in real life, in terms of a sum of money. Unfortunately, few real-life figures have been transmitted. We are told that Scipio's daughters each had 50 talents, approximately HS1,250,000 in the early second century BC. The second wife of Aemilius Paullus had HS600,000.[111] Terentia is said to have brought Cicero a dowry of HS400,000.[112] When the emperor Tiberius designed munificent consolation for a girl who was runner-up in a contest for the post of Vestal, he gave her a dowry of HS1,000,000. This must have been a substantial amount for a girl of

---

[106] Greece: Lys. 19.59; Dem. 18.268; Ptolemies: Pomeroy, *Women in hellenistic Egypt from Alexander to Cleopatra* 15–16; Livia: Dio 58.3; the anonymous addressee of the *Laudatio* '*Turiae*' and her sister, an obligation in fact taken over by their husbands: *Laud. Tur.* 1.45 ff.

[107] Delicacy: cf. Plaut. *Trin.* 734 ff.; Apul. *M* 10.23; men: Pliny *Epp.* 2.4.2, 6.32. According to DH *Ant.* 2.10.2, it was in early times a duty of clients to subscribe to dowries for daughters of their patrons if the latter were short of money. Senate: Dixon 'Polybius on Roman women and property' 152–3, on the legend invented about the daughters of Africanus; cf. Pliny *NH* 34.36; Frontinus *Str.* 4.3.15: daughter of L. Mummius. Cf. Schaps 79 ff.

[108] *FV* 115; cf. *D* 33.3.72 pr.   [109] *D* 4.4.9.1, ht 48.2.   [110] *CJ* 3.30.

[111] Polyb. 31.27, 18.35.6. See Dixon, 'Polybius on Roman women and property' 152, 164.

[112] Plut. *Cic.* 8.2.

her status.[113] The women helped by Pliny had over HS50,000 (if that was dowry) and over HS100,000. Apuleius' elderly wife brought him HS300,000 and his enemy's daughter allegedly had HS400,000 scraped together. A decurion of Oxyrhynchus gave each of his two daughters 4 silver talents.[114]

Labeo talks of a husband who leaves his wife a legacy of 50, saying that she had brought it as dowry, although she had only given him 40. The same applied if she had in fact brought him nothing. Labeo may be thinking of *aurei* as the unit of measurement (at the Augustan rate HS5,000 and HS4,000).[115] Other examples cited in the *Digest* are probably for verisimilitude rather than accuracy: HS100,000; 400, that is, probably, 400 *aurei*, which included two farms worth 200 together; and 50 or 100 *aurei*.[116] In literary sources, one million sesterces recurs several times as a conventional figure for a large dowry for the wealthiest class. This corresponds with the minimum capital required for a senator, just as HS400,000 may be meant to remind us of the equestrian minimum census.[117] But that one million might not be high for the really rich of the Principate is already suggested by the figures for Scipio. Petronius makes Trimalchio talk of 10 million as a dowry which he allowed to get away from him. This must be extremely large, especially in Trimalchio's social stratum, although Duncan-Jones is right to accuse Petronius of being uninventive in choosing figures. But well over one million seems likely for the more prosperous senator.[118] It is hardly credible that Pliny, with a fortune which he considered modest but which allowed him to be a generous benefactor to communities and individuals, could have offered as little as one million if he had had a daughter. The largest fortunes alleged for the early empire are of 400 million, a thousand times the equestrian minimum.[119] It is impossible to guess what proportion of that the freedman Narcissus would have had to offer to get a well-born senator for his daughter, or whether the equally wealthy Cn. Cornelius Lentulus would have offered less. What was the dowry of

---

[113] Tac. *A* 2.86. It is likely that both candidates were *senatoriae*. (For Domitius Pollio, see *PIR*² D159.) Fonteius Agrippa (*PIR*² F465), as accuser of Drusus Libo in AD 16, was, if already a senator, promoted to praetorian rank (Tac. *A* 2.30.1, 32.1); the consul of 58 (*PIR*² F466) was probably his son.   [114] *FIRA* iii.51.

[115] *D* 33.4.6, Lab. 'Ten' and 'one hundred' are commonly mentioned in this as in other contexts as a substitute for real figures (*decem*: 23.3.48 pr., ht 50 pr., 59 pr., 59.2; *centum* or *ducenta*: 24.3.31.1, ht 66.4, 66.5; 45.1.21).

[116] *D* 23.4.30, 33.4.2.1, ht 11, 17.1.

[117] Sen. *Cons. ad Helv.* 12.6, for a *pantomima*; Juv. 6.137: 'Bis quingena dedit. Tanti vocat ille pudicam', 10.335, for Messallina marrying Silius; Mart. 2.65.5, 11.23, the dowry necessary to persuade him to marry Sila, 12.75.8. Juv. 2.117 mentions HS400,000. See Saller, 'Roman dowry and the devolution of property in the Principate' 201.

[118] Duncan-Jones, *ERE* 27ff.   [119] Wells, *Roman Empire* 203.

Lollia Paullina, who wore pearls and emeralds worth 40 million to an ordinary party? It was not well bred for a bride to have more in her trousseau than she brought to her husband in dowry.[120]

Saller has recently argued that the passages from the moralists and satirists which mention dowries of one million 'would lack point if one million were not conventionally thought to be an exceedingly large dowry suitable for the wealthiest class'. He believes that dowries of 5–10 million were uncommon among senators.[121] The figures are isolated from the total capital of any actual father or family at the time of negotiation and apply to a class which showed a considerable range of fortunes. The only dowry figure which we can relate to a woman's fortune is Pudentilla's—a moderate dowry given to a second husband, intended to revert to her sons of her first marriage if she and Apuleius had no children. The figure was HS300,000 and her total fortune was 4 million (supposing we can trust the speech).[122] Saller suggests that the 'conventional very large dotal settlement of one million was of the same order (one year's income for moderately wealthy senators, such as Pliny)'.[123] Thus they were comparatively small compared with 3–5 times the annual income, which was common in early modern Europe.

Saller's hypothesis is attractive but perhaps too tidy. One difficulty may be that while our literary evidence suggests that fathers and outsiders could put an immediate price-tag on a dowry, we can see from the jurists that dowries often consisted in whole or in part of property which might not be valued for some time after it was transferred, or at all. Dowry might therefore be visualized as a particular farm or apartment block or group of slaves rather than as a year's income in cash. For the wealthy at least, many families would probably make up a package of cash, moveables, and real estate.

Saller's argument that families in the Roman world were less worried about the need to provide dowry than those in early modern Europe needs some qualification. It must be borne in mind that Roman families faced a strong possibility that more than one effort to provide dowry might be required. If a first marriage ended in divorce and the husband succeeded in retaining a fraction of the dowry—up to half for children plus an eighth or a sixth for misconduct—then the dowry would presumably need to be replenished if the woman was to marry again. Quite apart from *retentiones*, older women needed

---

[120] Pliny, *NH* 9.117–18; Sen. *Rem fort.* 16.6: 'Duc bene institutam . . . non cuius minus sit in dote quam in veste.'

[121] 'Roman dowry and the devolution of property in the Principate' 201, citing Sen. *Cons. ad Helv.* 12.6; Mart. 2.65, 11.23, 12.75; Juv. 2.117, 6.136, 10.335.

[122] Apul. *Apol.* 71, 77, 91, 92.

[123] 'Roman dowry and the devolution of property in the Principate' 201–2.

bigger dowries to make them attractive and at least one case is cited where a dowry was increased for a third marriage.[124]

Secondly, I doubt if he is right to play down the evidence for worries and difficulties about the provision of dowry. Some of the relevant passages have been cited above. It was a joke, but surely with a social stereotype behind it, when Caligula, as soon as his daughter was born, started an appeal for funds for her dowry.[125]

Notoriously, even rich Romans frequently had difficulty laying hands on ready money when they needed it. Cicero worried about paying the second instalment of Tullia's dowry to Dolabella, due on 1 July 48, and the following year the problem of finding the cash was one of the considerations when he thought about the advisability of a divorce.[126] This is exactly comparable with the difficulty husbands might have in repaying the dowry at the end of a marriage. Cicero, although repayments by his own debtors were due, was short of cash to pay an instalment of the dowry refundable to his divorced wife Terentia in 44. One of his debtors was Dolabella, who was also paying back a dowry, Tullia's. There had probably been the same problem for Terentia in 45 and with Dolabella in 46 and 45. Q. Cicero also agonized about repaying Pomponia.[127] The system of instalments for any cash component in a dowry, paid annually and starting a year after the marriage, presumably attests the inconvenience to capitalists of handing over a lump sum. Somewhere close to the origins of dowry there must lie the idea that a father over three years could earmark a fraction of the annual surplus profits of his land and give it as his daughter's portion. The Romans are more likely to have thought of dowry like this than as the total income from farming and other investments dated to any one year.

According to Pliny, clumps of cypress-trees had in the olden days commonly been called daughters' dowries: this presumably refers to the custom (still practised in Greece) of planting cypresses which would grow in time to be cut and sold when a daughter married, an expedient proper for a small farmer who could not afford to give away his land.[128] Not many farmers were as efficient as Paridius, a neighbour whom Graecinus (probably Agricola's father) in a book on vineyards made into an exemplar of consistent effort. He had two daughters and a farm planted with vines. When the elder married, he gave her one-third of the vineyard. Then, by intensive cultivation, he

[124] Apul. *Apol.* 92; *D* 32.41.7.   [125] Suet. *Cal.* 42.1.
[126] Cic. *A* 11.2.2, 11.23.3, 11.25.3.
[127] *A* 16.15.5, cf. *F* 6.18.5, 16.24.1, *A* 12.8, 12.1; 14.13.5. See Dixon, 'Family Finances: Terentia and Tullia' 88–97; Rauh, 'Cicero's business friendships: economics and politics in the late Roman Republic'.
[128] *NH* 16.141; cf. Walbank, *Comm. on Polyb.* iii. 507.

made the remaining two-thirds yield as much as the whole farm had done before. Then he gave half of his remaining land to the second daughter on her marriage—and still achieved the same yields with what he had kept.[129]

If the bridegroom demanded cash—and for certain purposes, for instance if he were standing for office, he might well be hungry for cash—then the bride or her family might have to borrow[130] or sell property.[131] Both solutions indicate that the pressure might be uncomfortable. (A bridegroom in less of a hurry might accept a piece of property as dowry, then have it valued and turn it into cash, the amount remaining on paper in the dowry but available for his use.) Occasionally, families got into worse difficulties. An unscrupulous father might trick his son-in-law into a marriage by offering a dowry which he could not and did not pay.[132] Or he might admit his complete lack of means and his son-in-law might make an entry in his accounts attesting that he had received a dowry which was in fact fictitious, but for which he then became liable.[133] Girls whose fathers failed to make provision for them would often be in a difficult situation. Paul calls attention to a special case: if a fatherless boy was a ward, his guardian was not authorized to make payment from his property for a dowry for his half-sister by a different father, even if she could not marry without it. She would have to wait until he came of age and decided whether he wanted to contribute.[134]

Saller is right to argue that the giving of dowry did not appear as crippling to Romans as it did to later aristocracies. But the expense involved was not inconsiderable and could present inconveniences to families in the short term.

5. *The Composition of Dowry*

What, apart from cash, was given as dowry? The immoveable property most frequently mentioned is, as one would expect, farming land. Cicero thinks of land as transferred by inheritance, sale, and dowry.[135] Conversely, it is farms, whether denominated as *fundi dotales*, described by the broader title of *praedia*, or more closely particularized as vineyards, olive orchards, and so on, which are the type of dotal property most often specified in the legal sources. This in part parallels the jurists' normal concentration on land as the most important investment for the property-owners with whom they dealt

---

[129] Col. 4.3.   [130] G 3.125; D 23.3.5.8.   [131] D 23.3.61.1.
[132] D 23.3.84. Cf., for repayment after divorce, Plaut. *Stich.* 204.
[133] D 24.3.66.6, Iav. citing Labeo; cf. 35.1.40.4.
[134] D 26.7.12.3, Paul. The guardian was also forbidden to disburse for wedding presents for the ward's mother or sister (ht 13.2, 27.3.1.5).   [135] *Off.* 2.81.

and in part reflects the peculiar complications which dotal land, like land in general, might present.[136] Although land need not have been—indeed is unlikely to have been—the most frequently given dotal property, it remains striking that land was routinely regarded as a component of dowry. In other societies land is the last thing that we would expect to be transferred.

Dotal farms, like any other farms, might contain a villa and farm buildings, marble quarries, clay- or sand-pits, gold- or silver-mines.[137] On the other hand, an estate might be 'urban', by which the lawyers meant built-up, and contain, for example, apartment blocks.[138] Shops and bakeries figure as dotal property, so do *horrea*, which might be urban store-rooms and warehouses or country barns.[139] Pleasure-gardens are mentioned.[140] Under Augustus' law, dotal estates in Italy might not be sold by the husband without his wife's consent.[141] The dowry might include houses: a dotal town house might even be the couple's principal residence.[142]

Moveable dotal property provoked less interest, except for slaves, who in this as in other areas created special problems. They seem to have been from early times a normal part of the dowry. It was natural that a young woman's closest personal attendants should accompany her on marriage, people such as her nurse, her maids, or her steward. The problems they presented might be social as well as legal, since their first loyalty would often be to the wife.[143] Dotal farms do not seem to be specifically mentioned as coming with their staff, livestock, and equipment (*cum instrumento*), but dotal livestock is

[136] *Fundi dotales*: e.g. App. *BC* 1.10; *D* 2.8.8.1, ht 15.3, 10.2.51 pr., 23.3.6.1, ht 46.1, 50 pr., 52, 56.3, 62, 75, 85, 23.4.4 pr., 23.5, 29.1.16, 33.4.1.14–15, ht 9, 35.1.40.4, 50.16.79.1; *CJ* 4.47.1, 5.12.18, 5.13.1.15, 5.12.12, 5.23.1, 5.23.2. *Praedia* (farming): *D* 25.1.14.1. Vineyards etc.: *D* ht 1.3, 3, 6, 12, 14.

[137] *D* 23.3.32, 23.5.18 pr., 24.3.7.13, ht 8, 50.16.77.1.

[138] *D* 24.3.7.11. For the definition of *praedia* as the general word for estates cf. 50.16.115. For the distinction between rustic and urban *praedia*, ht 198, cf. 8.1.1 ff. On urban investment property see Garnsey, 'Urban property investment', and Frier, *Landlords and tenants in imperial Rome*. Terentia's dowry seems to have included apartments on the Aventine and in the Argiletum, which passed to Cicero after their divorce and which were used to provide their son Marcus with an annual allowance of HS80,000 while he lived in Athens. See Cic. *A* 12.32.3, 14.7.2, 14.17.5, 15.17.1, 15.20.4, 16.1.5. Dixon in Rawson, *FAR* 108–10 (= *Antichthon* 18 [1984] 94–6).

[139] *Taberna* or *pistrinum*: *D* 25.1.6; *horreum* or *pistrinum*: ht 1.3. Both are mentioned as examples of additions to dotal property by the husband. *A fortiori* dotal property might already incorporate such improvements.   [140] *D* 30.43.1.

[141] G 2.63, cf. Just. *Inst.* 2.8 pr.; *D* 23.5.1 pr., ht 16, 31.77.5; *CJ* 5.13.1.15.

[142] Plaut. *Mil.* 1278; *Decl. min.* 347 *thema*.

[143] Cato ap. Gell. 17.6.10. Cf. Cicero's difficulties with Philotimus (Treggiari, *RFLR* 264). Dotal slaves are very often mentioned in the jurists, e.g. *D* 23.3.10.2, 5, ht 12.1, 18, 47, 58.1, 69.9, 23.4.21, ht 29.2, 23.5.3 pr., 24.3.7.10, ht 25.3, 26, 31.4, 58, 61–4, 66.3, 25.1.2, ht 6, 33.4.1.6.

occasionally mentioned.[144] Clothing, jewellery, and household goods could also be part of dowry.[145]

Cash, naturally, often figures.[146] The husband might choose to invest it in land[147] or slaves.[148] A debt could also be assigned as dowry.[149] Gold is mentioned.[150] Dotal property of any type is lumped together under the general title of *res dotales, res in dotem datae*, and so on.[151] It is not surprising that a miserly father, called upon to produce a dowry, felt that he was asked to part with 'insulam Chrysam, agrum Caecubum, Seplasia Capuae, macellum Romuli', roughly the equivalent of the Rand, Château Lafite, the Rue de la Paix, and Smithfield Market.[152]

6. Rules for Reclaiming Dowry

The general rules about what happened to dowry at the end of the marriage depended on the provenance of the dowry and how the marriage ended. Dowry which was given by a woman's father or male ascendant was called *profecticia* and returned to him (if he was still alive) if she died. If there were children of the marriage, the husband kept one-fifth of the dowry for each one, with no limit.[153] Pomponius chose to regard the restoration of the dowry to the father as consolation for the loss of his daughter, so that he would not lose his money as well as his child.[154] Nothing is said to suggest that the dowry was

[144] D 23.3.10 pr., 3.
[145] VM 4.4.9; *FIRA* iii.17; *PSI* 6.730; D 23.3.10 pr.
[146] e.g. Plaut. *Cist.* 561, *Trin.* 1158; Ter. *Andr.* 951; Varro *LL* 5.175; VM 4.4.10; D 23.3.48 pr., ht 49.1, 54, 56.3 (together with a farm), 60, 61.1, 67, 82, 23.4.21, ht 32.1, 25.1.5 pr., 33.4.1.9.   [147] D 23.3.58.1.
[148] Cic. *Caec.* 11; D 23.3.26–7; *CJ* 5.12.12.
[149] D 23.4.21.   [150] D 23.3.34.
[151] D 23.3.10.4 ff., ht 12, 14–17, 27, 42, 51, 54, 61.1, 69.7–8; 23.4.29.2.   [152] *Men.* 38.
[153] *Tit. Ulp.* 6.3–4: 'Dos aut profecticia dicitur, id est quam pater mulieris dedit, aut adventicia, id est quae a quovis alio data est. Mortua in matrimonio muliere dos a patre profecta ad patrem revertitur, quintis in singulos liberos in infinitum relictis penes virum. Quod si pater non sit, apud maritum remanet.' For the definition of *parens* as a male ascendant in the male line see *Tit. Ulp.* 6.2: 'parens mulieris virilis sexus per virilem sexum cognatione iunctus, velut pater avus paternus.' Cf. D 23.3.5 pr.: 'Profecticia dos est, quae a patre vel a parente profecta est de bonis vel facto eius' ('A *profecticia dos* is one which comes from a father or a *parens*, either from his possessions or by his act'). Ulpian goes on to discuss instances which might pose problems of definition: for instance, dowry could still count as *profecticia* if the father was mad and his guardian acted for him, or a prisoner of war and the civil authority acted for him (ibid. 1–8). On the other hand, it was not *profecticia* but *adventicia* if a mother gave her husband a sum for him to give as dowry (ibid. 9). It made no difference whether the daughter was or was not in her father's power, or adopted (ibid. 11–13). The expressions *dos profecticia* or *dos a patre profecta* (D 24.3.10 pr.) are not common in the *Digest*, but the father is the donor most frequently mentioned (e.g. *passim* in 23.3). See Gardner, 'The recovery of dowry in Roman law'; Söller, *Zur Vorgeschichte und Funktion der Actio rei uxoriae*.
[154] D 23.3.6 pr.: 'Iure succursum est patri, ut filia amissa solacii loco cederet, si redderetur ei dos ab ipso profecta, ne et filiae amissae et pecuniae damnum sentiret.'

expected to improve the fortunes of any other descendants of the donor. Often the father or grandfather might be expected to have predeceased the woman, so that her husband would retain the dowry. But if the dowry came from anyone other than a male ascendant, it was called *adventicia*. On the death of the wife, the husband kept this, unless the donor had stipulated for its return. If there was such a stipulation, the dowry came under the additional definition of *recepticia*.[155]

If a marriage ended in divorce, the wife by herself, if she were independent, or together with her *paterfamilias* could sue for the return of the dowry. If her husband was responsible for delay in refunding it and she subsequently died, her heirs also had the right to sue.[156] The classical lawyers insisted that the *paterfamilias* did not have the right to sue without the consent of his daughter, although that consent might be assumed unless she made it clear that she withheld it.[157] The action could lie either against the husband or his *paterfamilias* (or even against his owner, if the woman had by mistake 'married' a slave and given him what she thought was dowry).[158] The *actio rei uxoriae*, action for restoration of wife's property (which had until the divorce been dowry and belonged to the husband) is later than the divorce of Carvilius Ruga but probably in operation by the time of Plautus.[159] The formula appears to have been 'If it appears that Numerius Negidius ought to give back dowry or part of dowry to Aula Ageria, let the judge condemn Numerius Negidius (to pay) to Aula Ageria as much of it as will be better and more equitable; if it does not so appear, let him absolve him.'[160] Cicero in an enthusiastic passage in the *Topica* describes how legal experts brief advocates in the subtle definitions required in cases which rested on good faith and equity and the proper relationship between, for instance, partners and between wife and husband.[161] Since the relationship was one of trust,

[155] *Tit. Ulp.* 6.3 (quoted in n. 153) and 5: 'Adventicia autem dos semper penes maritum remanet, praeterquam si is qui dedit, ut sibi redderetur, stipulatus fuerit: quae dos specialiter recepticia dicitur.'   [156] *Tit. Ulp.* 6.6–7; *D* 24.3 *passim*; heirs: ht 27.

[157] *D* 24.3.2.1–2. Cf. ht 3, 4, 22.3ff., 9ff., 34, 37, 40, 42 pr. Cf. Corbett 184ff., Watson, *Persons* 73–4. Full discussion by Wolff, 'Zur Stellung der Frau im klassischen Dotalrecht' 301–21.

[158] *D* 24.3.22.12–13, cf. ht 25 pr., 53.   [159] Watson, *Persons* 67–8.

[160] Lenel, *Edictum Perpetuum* 305, quoted by Corbett 187 and Watson, *Law making* 175–6, *Persons* 67. Corbett points out that the edict implies that the previous norm was for the husband to keep the dowry. I think the important point is rather that the husband has not returned the dowry by himself and is being compelled to do so: since the dowry is with the husband, action is taken against him.

[161] Cic. *Top.* 66: 'In omnibus igitur eis iudiciis, in quibus EX FIDE BONA est additum, ubi [vero] etiam UT INTER BONOS BENE AGIER OPORTET in primisque in arbitrio rei uxoriae, in quo est QUOD EIUS AEQUIUS MELIUS, parati [sc. iurisconsulti] eis [sc. patronis] esse debent. Illi dolum malum, illi fidem bonam, illi aequum bonum, illi quid . . . alterum alteri praestare oporteret, quid

high standards of consideration for the partner's interests were required.

The exact rules for what happens on divorce can be found most clearly in the late *Tituli Ulpiani*: the fractions of dowry mentioned there may not be those applied in the Republic, but the *principle* of retention of part of the dowry by the husband is attested by Cicero. A husband could make deductions because of children or the wife's immorality or expenses, or gifts or property which she took away. All these were eventually abolished by Justinian.[162] An innocent divorcing husband who could prove his wife's adultery could keep one-sixth of the dowry, or one-eighth for lesser faults (immorality less serious than adultery).[163] If the wife or her *paterfamilias* were responsible for divorcing a husband who had committed no fault, then he could keep one-sixth of the dowry for each of up to three children, but if he were responsible he kept nothing.[164] The husband guilty of a major fault had to repay the dowry immediately; if the fault was minor, he had six months.[165] Otherwise he could pay cash in three annual instalments, although non-fungibles, such as farms, had to be restored at once.[166] To sum up, if the divorce was initiated by the wife without moral fault of the husband, or initiated by the husband because of moral faults on the wife's part, he might defend himself against the *actio rei uxoriae* by claiming up to half her dowry for children and up to one-sixth for immorality. If on the other hand he had laid *himself* open to charges of immorality—but the immorality threshold was higher for husbands—or if he divorced her without cause, she might be awarded the whole of her dowry. The basic feature is that the whole dowry is in principle recoverable, although the presiding magistrate might modify that principle by penalizing the woman for misbehaviour, to the advantage of the husband, or by recognizing the improvement in his claim made by the existence of children.

If this more or less indicates how a republican praetor might

virum uxori, quid uxorem viro tradiderunt.' Cf. Cic. *Off.* 3.61: 'Reliquorum autem iudiciorum haec verba maxime excellunt: in arbitrio rei uxoriae MELIUS AEQUIUS'; *D* 4.5.8, 24.3.66.7; Boeth. ad Cic. *Top.* 66 (Bruns ii.74–5): 'Quae quidem dos interdum his condicionibus dari solebat, ut, si inter virum uxoremque divortium contigisset, "quod melius aequius esset", apud virum remaneret, reliquum dotis restitueretur uxori, id est ut, quod ex dote iudicatum fuisset melius aequius esse, ut apud virum maneret, id vir sibi retineret, quod vero non esset melius aequius apud virum manere, id uxor post divortium reciperet. In quo iudicio non tantum boni natura spectari solet, verum etiam comparatio bonorum fit, ut non tam quod bonum, sed quod melius aequiusque est, id sequendum sit.'

[162] *Tit. Ulp.* 6.9; *CJ* 5.13.1.5, AD 530; Just. *Inst.* 4.6.29, 37.

[163] *Tit. Ulp.* 6.9, 6.12; Pliny *NH* 14 (13) 90. If, after 18 BC, the *Lex Iulia de adulteriis* came into operation, half the dowry was confiscated by the state.

[164] Cic. *Top.* 19; *Tit. Ulp.* 6.10. This applies only if it is the wife or her *paterfamilias* who causes the divorce. For *Digest* texts on *culpa* cf. 24.3.39, ht 44.1, 45, 47.

[165] *Tit. Ulp.* 6.13.   [166] *Tit. Ulp.* 6.8; *D* 23.4.19.

decide, it is an intriguing thought that our—partial—sources on the results of Terentia's divorce from Cicero and Tullia's from Dolabella show no trace of legal action *or retentiones*. Both divorces may have been bilateral, though Tullia at least had just cause to initiate a divorce.[167] At any rate, Dolabella did not have to speed up his repayment of the dowry: he did it in instalments. Nor do we hear of *retentio* because of the child, although Cicero planned to mention him in his will. Similarly, there is no indication of formal *retentio* from Terentia on account of her two children, though again Cicero expected them to benefit under her will.[168]

If the husband died, the widow needed to recover her dowry just as she did after divorce. The *actio rei uxoriae* could be used. The husband's heirs could not claim *retentio propter mores*, nor *propter liberos*.[169] It is logical that a divorcing husband who claimed to have been injured by his wife's misconduct might be allowed penal damages, but that if he died without rejecting his wife his heirs had no such claim. Any other system might have opened the door to false accusations. But the refusal to allow heirs to claim on account of children of the marriage is striking. It means that the most obvious category of heirs, children of the marriage, had no claim against their mother for any of the capital which she had brought into the family as dowry. The privilege of *retentio propter liberos* is reserved for the husband himself. This suggests that it is meant as a contribution to child support rather than to the endowment of joint offspring with capital. It is worth noting that the rights of the woman's heirs are almost symmetrical. If she died after a divorce and the bringing of an *actio rei uxoriae*, her heirs had a claim on the dowry only if her husband had been dilatory in restoring it to her.[170]

---

[167] Cic. *A* 11.23.3; 11.24.1; cf. *F* 14.10, 13. I do not agree with Watson, *Persons* 71–2, that *A* 11.23.3 refers to danger of *retentio* by Dolabella.

[168] For Terentia's will, made before the divorce and when Cicero was worried about Tullia's financial position and the dangers of confiscation: Cic. *A* 11.16.5 (3 June 47), 11.24.2, 11.22.2. For Terentia's interest in Cicero's will after the divorce (probably to be dated in early 46) see Cic. *A* 12.18a.2 (13 Mar. 45). On all this see Dixon, 'Family finances: Terentia and Tullia' 78 ff.

[169] *D* 24.3.15.1: 'Heredi mariti, licet in solidum condemnetur, compensationes tamen, quae ad pecuniariam causam respiciunt, proderunt, ut hoc minus sit obligatus, veluti ob res donatas et amotas et impensas: morum vero coercitionem non habet.' *Compensationes* is agreed to be an interpolation for *retentiones*. The text suggests that only deductions for expenses, gifts, and things the wife removed from the matrimonial home are allowed. Confirmation that *retentio propter liberos* was not allowed is found in the invalidity of agreements that they should be due if the husband died: *D* 23.4.2; 33.4.1.1; *CJ* 5.14.3 (AD 239). This is the view of Corbett 192. It is not invalidated by *FV* 97.

[170] *Tit. Ulp.* 6.7.

7. *Deduction of Expenses*

The husband could deduct certain expenses when he returned the dowry. These are again most clearly defined by the *Tituli Ulpiani*:

Impensarum species sunt tres: aut enim necessariae dicuntur aut utiles aut voluptuosae. Necessariae sunt impensae, quibus non factis dos deterior futura est, velut si quis ruinosas aedes refecerit. Utiles sunt, quibus non factis quidem deterior dos non fuerit, factis autem fructuosior effecta est, veluti si vineta et oliveta fecerit. Voluptuosae sunt, quibus neque omissis deterior dos fieret neque factis fructuosior effecta est, quod evenit in viridiariis et picturis similibusque rebus. (*Tituli Ulpiani* 6.14–17)

There are three kinds of expenses: they are called necessary or useful or for pleasure. Necessary expenses are those without which the dowry will deteriorate, for example, if someone repairs a house which is falling into ruin. Useful expenses are those without which the dowry will not have deteriorated, but which, if carried out, will make the dowry more profitable, for example, if he makes vineyards or olive orchards. Expenses for pleasure are those in the absence of which the dowry would not deteriorate and which do not make it more profitable if they are carried out: this is illustrated by evergreen gardens or paintings and such things.

The definitions of Ulpian and Paul in the *Digest* correspond.[171] Examples of the various types of expenditure were formulated quite early. Labeo counted the building of moles on the sea or a river among necessary expenditures. So was building a mill or a granary or shoring up a building which was about to collapse, restocking an olive orchard, curing a sick slave, propagating vines, looking after trees or making plantings, or building embankments.[172] Agricultural expenditure of short-term effect did not count, since the husband would reap the profits himself within the year.[173] Sowing wheat or other quick-yielding crops did not improve the dotal property and all profit belonged to the husband. He had to pay any tax incurred, since the income offset it.[174] Any expense was *necessaria* if without it the value of the dotal property would be reduced, and the husband would be liable to make good the loss.[175] The husband would keep the improved property until the wife had given him money to compensate him for the necessary expenses.[176] Moderate expenditure on maintenance

---

[171] *D* 25.1, ht 5.3, 7, expanded by ht 4, 6, etc.; 50.16.79, Paul. Bibliography in Thomas 430. Guizzi, 'La restituzione della dote e le spese utili', rightly rejects Latorre, 'Voluntas mulieris y reembolso de las impensas utiles dotales'.

[172] *D* 25.1.1.2, ht 3, 14 pr.

[173] *D* 25.1.1.3, ht 16, 24.3.7.16.

[174] *D* 25.1.13.

[175] *D* 25.1.4; cf. *Tit. Ulp.* 6.15.

[176] *D* 25.1.5 pr.–2, 23.3.56.3, 33.4.1.4; cf. Corbett 194.

such as everyday repair to buildings or food or medical attention for slaves was to be absorbed by the husband.[177]

Useful expenses made the dowry more profitable. For instance, the husband might start a vineyard, olive orchard, tree plantation, or nursery garden from scratch or put stock on land for the sake of their manure, or add a mill or shop on to a house, or teach skills to dotal slaves.[178] Some lawyers held that the wife could only be asked to reimburse the husband if she agreed to the improvements since she risked losing the improved property if she could not pay for the improvements.[179] A problem was posed to Augustan lawyers when the husband opened up a quarry on a dotal estate. Divorce followed. To whom did the marble belong which had been cut but not removed from the quarry? Who was liable for the money spent on opening the quarry? Labeo held that the marble belonged to the husband but the wife owed him nothing because the expenditure was not necessary and the farm had become less valuable (clearly because marble had been removed). Iavolenus held that the expenditure was useful and that the wife should pay (so he presumably assumed that she had consented to the work); moreover, the farm was not to be considered damaged if the quarries happened to be the sort where the marble grew back.[180] Ulpian later ruled that marble was not *fructus* (unless it was the sort which grew back, as in certain places in Gaul and Asia). But he seems to have agreed that discovering and opening up quarries made the estate more profitable, so was a useful expense. He solved the problem by allowing the husband to keep the cut marble but denying him compensation for his expenses. Paul held that if the quarry already existed when the wife gave the land as dowry, she intended the husband to profit from the stone as *fructus*.[181]

But to understand this we need to look at the *fructus* and the husband's right to keep them. Farms must from the beginning have been an important type of dotal property, and they presented particular problems and early gave rise to a good deal of juristic discussion.

The *fructus* were the profits left after the expenses were deducted.[182] Since crops such as grapes were harvested once a year, it would be unfair for the husband to take the full profit from the vintage if he divorced his wife a month later, or for her to take all the following vintage if they divorced in April. The amount of *fructus* taken by the husband was to be pro-rated by the number of months the vineyard had been dotal.[183] A comparable arrangement with a

[177] *D* 25.1.12, ht 15, 16, 24.3.7.16. [178] *D* 24.3.7.16, 25.1.6, ht 14, 50.16.79.1.
[179] *D* 25.1.8, 50.16.79.1; cf. *CJ* 5.13.5e. [180] *D* 23.5.18 pr.
[181] *D* 24.3.7.13, ht 8 pr. [182] *D* 24.3.7 pr.; cf. ht 42.1 n. 180.
[183] *D* 24.3.7 pr.–4; Paul 2.22.1.

different time-frame had to be made for land which was improved and produced two crops a year because it was irrigated, or land which produced less than one crop a year, for instance timber. If a husband received sheep as dowry just before lambing and shearing, and divorced when they had produced lambs and wool, it would obviously be unjust if he returned none of the profits. The principle also applied to the profits earned by a slave who was hired out by the year, or to urban rents. If the husband felled trees or took poles from a coppice, they either counted as *fructus* and the wife received a portion, or he was liable for depreciation. Marble was not *fructus* according to Ulpian. But the products of chalk-pits, silver- or gold- or other mines, and sand-pits were.[184]

Impensae voluptariae or *voluptuosae* were added luxury improvements for pleasure, not profit. Embellishments of property which was to be sold counted as useful. These included the addition of baths to a property or the making of gardens and fountains, coatings (such as marble panelling), incrustations (mouldings etc.), or paintings on walls.[185] The wife could not be compelled to compensate her husband for these expenses even if she had consented to the improvement.[186] But she had to allow him to remove the improvement if that could be done without damage to the property and to compensate him if she refused to let him remove it.[187]

A judge or an arbiter would decide how much the husband was entitled to keep for expenses.[188] The dowry was *ipso iure* (by operation of law) diminished by necessary expenses.[189] The husband's heir could claim.[190]

8. *Other Deductions*

Deductions on account of gifts made by the husband could be made from dowry by the defendant in an *actio rei uxoriae*.[191] For instance, if the husband lent his wife money in partial payment for a slave or gave her a cash gift, he could deduct from dowry.[192] The husband's heir could claim for invalid gifts.[193] This procedure was particularly convenient if the husband had given a cash amount, which could be kept back from a cash dowry (or portion of dowry). The alternative was to claim back the gift by *condictio* or *vindicatio*, a procedure also open to the wife and one which Justinian thought simple and adequate.

---

[184] *D* 24.3.7.   [185] *D* 25.1.10, ht 14.2, 50.16.79.2.
[186] *D* 25.1.7, ht 11 pr.; cf. *CJ* 5.13.5–6.   [187] *D* 25.1.9.
[188] *D* 25.1.4, ht 12.
[189] *D* 23.2.61, 25.1.5 pr., 33.4.1.4, ht 2 pr.   [190] *D* 24.3.15.1.
[191] *Tit. Ulp.* 6.9; *CJ* 5.13.1.5a; cf. Corbett 195.   [192] *D* 24.1.50 pr., ht 66.1.
[193] *D* 24.3.15.1.

Because of Justinian's abolition of the *retentiones*, evidence on deductions because of gifts is thin.

Similarly, he found *retentio* on account of things taken away otiose, since judicial procedures were available.[194] But more information on this retention survives indirectly from the classical period, since the *Digest* title on the action for restoration of things removed (25.2) can be exploited. Although the extracts in it have been revised in order to make them applicable only to the action, it is possible to deduce what were the classical rules on retention by the husband.[195] If the wife or her agent, intending a divorce, or because she knew she would be divorced, removed objects belonging to her husband or to his *paterfamilias*, he or his heir or *paterfamilias* could keep possession of equivalent dotal property.[196] If the wife died before the matter was settled, the husband could keep back dowry from her father or heir, at least if they had benefited from the theft. The objects removed might themselves be dotal.[197]

The *actio rerum amotarum*, unlike the expedient of retention of dowry, was available to the wife against the husband.[198] The action was used because the reverence due to husband or wife ruled out the use of an accusation of theft.[199] Juristic study of the *actio* and presumably of retention goes back a long way, to Labeo at least. The classical jurists treat it in commentary on the praetor's edict and on Sabinus.[200]

9. Contracts

Dowry could, however, be made returnable by contract. Surviving examples on papyri list dotal items.[201] The *pacta dotalia* mentioned as examples in the *Digest*, as we would expect, tend to take into account children of the marriage.[202] It might be arranged that if the marriage ended in divorce or the death of the wife, the dowry or part of it should remain with the husband if there were children[203] or that if the wife died the husband should keep one-third of the dowry for one or more surviving children and restore the rest to her father or, if he were dead, his *filiifamilias*,[204] or that on the wife's death the husband should keep the dowry (which Ulpian held should stand even if there were no children),[205] or that the husband should keep all the dowry if his wife left a child who survived to the age of 1 and part of it if there had been a child who predeceased her.[206]

---

[194] *CJ* 5.13.5b. See further Wacke, *Actio rerum amotarum*.   [195] Corbett 195–6.
[196] *D* 25.2 *passim*.   [197] *D* 25.2.3.4, ht 4, 5, 6.3, 24.   [198] *D* 25.2.6.2, ht 7, 11 pr.
[199] *D* 25.2.1, 2, ht 3.2.   [200] *D* 25.2.13 and ht *passim*.   [201] See ch. 5 nn. 41 ff.
[202] 23.4.2, ht 23, 24, 26 pr., 2, 4. I have not taken into account here the similar agreements and intentions mentioned in the title on bequests and trusts, e.g. the interesting 32.41.7.
[203] 23.4.2, ht 24.   [204] 23.4.23.   [205] 23.4.12 pr.   [206] 23.4.26 pr.

Alternatively, we hear of agreements that if the wife died the dowry should be repaid to her father or if he were dead, his son or heir,[207] or to her mother.[208] Some of these, particularly the favourite legal puzzle about what to do if child and mother perished in a shipwreck and there were no evidence about which died first,[209] may be hypothetical, but they still show what sort of wishes families might have. One case seems satisfactorily tied to the early third century.[210] An agreement was made that Baebius Marcellus should promise Baebius Marullus HS100,000 as his daughter's dowry but that this sum should not be claimed during the marriage and the father-in-law's lifetime. If the daughter survived her father and died still married but without children, half the dowry should go to the husband, Marullus, and half to the woman's brother. The father died, while both his son and his daughter were still alive, and he left the dowry to his daughter in his will. Subsequently she bore a daughter and Marullus divorced her. She then died, leaving her daughter and her brother as equal heirs. Marullus claimed the whole dowry from his brother-in-law, on the plea that the agreement was that if there were no surviving child he should have part of the dowry on his wife's death, but that if he had a child he should have the whole dowry. The case came before the praetor Petronius Magnus, a patron attested on the album of Canusium in AD 223, or possibly his father,[211] and was decided in favour of the brother, particularly in view of the fact that Marullus had divorced his wife before her death. The salient fact seems to be that if there were children, *intervenientibus liberis*, it was usual for the husband to keep at least part of the dowry. Tacitus approves of what he claims to be the custom of the Germans that a dowry was given to the bride but passed on to her children.[212] It was also, of course, usual for the wife to mention children in her will, as we shall see in the next chapter. Justinian regarded it as instinctive for both parents to provide for the rearing of their children.[213]

Estate-planning was often fairly complex, as in the following instance:

Testamento, quo filium et uxorem heredes instituerat, filiae per fideicommissum centum, cum in familia nuberet, legavit et adiecit ita: 'fidei tuae, filia, committo, ut, cum in familia nubas, et quotienscumque nubes, patiaris ex dote tua, quam dabis, partem dimidiam stipulari fratrem tuum et Seiam matrem tuam pro partibus dimidiis dari sibi, si in matrimonio eius cui nubes sive divortio facto, priusquam dos tua reddatur eove nomine satisfactum erit, morieris nullo filio filiave ex eo relicto.' Pater virginem filiam nuptum

[207] 23.4.9.   [208] 23.4.26.4.   [209] 23.4.26 pr.   [210] 23.4.30.
[211] *PIR*[2] P211.   [212] *Germ.* 18.2–5.   [213] *CJ* 5.13.1.5c.

collocavit eiusque nomine dotem dedit et post divortium eandem recepit et alii in matrimonium cum dote dedit et stipulatus est eam dotem sibi aut filiae suae reddi: manente filia in matrimonio secundo mortuus est eodem testamento relicto eique heredes exstiterunt filius et uxor: postea marito defuncto puella dote recepta nupsit alii praesentibus et consentientibus fratre et matre, quae etiam dotem eius auxit, et neuter eorum stipulati sunt dotem, mox matri filius et filia heredes exstiterunt: deinde in matrimonio filia decessit marito herede relicto. Quaesitum est, cum puella non ex causa legati pecuniam in dotem ab heredibus patris acceperat, sed mortuo secundo marito mater familias facta dotem reciperaverat, an heres eius ex causa fideicommissi fratri defunctae teneatur in eam pecuniam, quam percipere posset, si dotem stipulatus esset. Respondit secundum ea quae proponerentur non teneri. (*Digest* 32.41.7, Scaevola *xviii digestorum*)

In a will in which he had instituted his son and wife as heirs, a man bequeathed to his daughter one hundred, if she married in the family, and added, 'I charge you, daughter, as a *fideicommissum*, that when you marry in the family [*precise sense obscure*] and however often you marry, you allow your brother and your mother Seia to stipulate for half of the dowry you give to be given to them, half each, if you die while married to the man you are marrying or if you die after a divorce but before your dowry is returned to you or repayment made on account of dowry, leaving no son or daughter from that man.' The father gave his daughter in marriage as a virgin and gave a dowry on that account, and after a divorce received it back and gave her to another man in marriage with the dowry and stipulated that the dowry should be returned to himself or his daughter. While the daughter was still in that marriage, he died, leaving the same will, and his son and wife were his heirs. Afterwards, the girl's husband died and she received her dowry back and married another man, in the presence and with the consent of her brother and mother, who also increased her dowry, and neither of them stipulated for the dowry. Then the son and daughter became heirs of the mother. Then the daughter died, still married, and left her husband as heir. Since the girl had not received the money for her dowry from her father's heirs in accordance with the legacy, but on the death of her second husband having become a *materfamilias* had recuperated her dowry, the question was put, whether her heir in accordance with the *fideicommissum* was liable to the dead woman's brother for that money which he would have been able to obtain if he had stipulated for the dowry. He replied that, according to the facts which were put to him, he was not liable.

St John Chrysostom, Bishop of Constantinople AD 398–403, addresses some of the preoccupations of an upper-class congregation. In his homily on the kind of wife a man should marry, in which, in typical Greek philosophical style, he attacks the preference for riches, he describes the care devoted to the dotal contract:

When you are on the point of taking a wife you run after alien lawyers with great eagerness, sit beside them, and meticulously explore the question of

what will happen if your wife dies without issue, and what will happen if she
has a child, or two, or three, and how will she enjoy her property if her father
is alive, or if he is not, and what part of her share will go to her brothers and
what to her husband, and in what circumstances will the husband take
control of all her property, so that he does not have to give up any of it to
anyone, and when he will lose possession of it entirely. And you busy
yourself about many such things and you keep asking them questions,
searching round and about and up and down to make sure that in no way can
any of the wife's property go back to any of her relations.[214]

The law imposed various restrictions on *pacta*, in the interests of both
sides. For instance, the husband could not contract not to claim
retentio propter mores, *propter res donatas*, *propter res amotas*, or
propter impensas. The wife could not bind herself to exempt the
husband from liability for negligence in his administration.[215] But the
parties were free not to exercise their legal rights. The elaborate legal
rules for retentions and actions for restoration of dowry and the
individual arrangements of dotal contracts might have been expected
to provoke long and involved court battles. But there is practically no
evidence for this. Cicero considered antagonistic action possible
between Dolabella and Tullia, but in the event negotiations seem to
have been conducted amicably, without resort to retentions or a
suit.[216] In the early second century BC a judge in an *actio de moribus*
awarded the whole dowry to the husband because his wife drank
more wine than her health demanded or he permitted.[217] In 100 BC
Marius adjudicated between Fannia and her husband C. Titinius of
Minturnae, who had (we are told) married her deliberately because
she was rich and immoral, planning to divorce her and then strip her
of her patrimony. Marius judged her guilty and awarded Titinius a
derisory sum.[218] Although the framework of rules remained in force
down to the sixth century AD, it seems likely that the upper classes
from the late Republic on found that the more flexible *pacta* met their
needs better. The jurists themselves envisage the return of dowry by
the husband without any lawsuit.[219]

We have one surviving example of a legal document drawn up to
record the restoration by C. Valerius Gemellus, serving in the fleet of
Alexandria, to his divorced 'wife' Demetria daughter of Lucius of a
dowry consisting of clothes (on which a cash value had been set) and
802 drachmae. The couple had been 'married' some time, since they

---

[214] PG 51.226–7.   [215] Corbett 198ff.

[216] p. 463. There may be an instance in a condensed and therefore obscure reference in Cic. *A*
15.21.2.   [217] Pliny *NH* 14.90; cf. Watson, *Persons* 70.

[218] VM 8.2.3; Plut. *Mar.* 38; Watson, *Persons* 68–9.

[219] *D* 24.3.3, ht 31.4, where a subsequent action may be necessary to allow the wife to claim
fruits for part of the year, or children of her dotal slave-women or inheritances by slaves.

had sons aged 14 and 10. But the union, since it is dated to the second century, cannot have been valid, because he was a sailor.[220]

To sum up, the procedure following a divorce therefore seems to have been that (1) the husband might return the whole dowry or (2) might return the dowry minus retentions or (3) might keep the whole dowry. If (1), then he might subsequently bring an *actio de moribus*, claiming that a fraction of the dowry be restored to him. If (2) or (3), then the wife or her *paterfamilias* might bring an *actio rei uxoriae*, challenging the retentions if any. Since the schedule varied according to the content of the dowry (cash or real property) and who was responsible for the divorce, the course of events might vary. The probability that the husband was attempting (3) might become apparent when he defaulted on the first of an expected series of three instalments or missed a six-month deadline.[221]

10. Conclusions

What was the function of Roman dowry? The question is misconceived. The strength of the Roman dotal system was its adaptability: customs and rules changed and various purposes were served. In the archaic system of *manus*, where the wife and her portion were merged in the husband's family, she presumably received what her father considered an equitable share of the family property when she left his household. Children remaining under his *potestas* when he died would succeed to the rest: intestate succession would give them equal shares, and there was a tradition that brothers might for a time maintain a farm undivided. The 'dowry' given to daughters is likely to have consisted of surplus produce and to have been relatively modest in this peasant society. The development of marriage without *manus* and of divorce transformed this picture. Dowry now had to be kept distinguishable from the husband's other property, since he or his heirs might have to restore it. Growing wealth was matched by dowry inflation, at least among the great imperialist families, and accompanied by malaise as fathers found they had to offer more in order to marry their daughters off suitably, and husbands, though attracted by generous dowries, felt insecure because of their liability to repay.

---

[220] *FIRA* iii.20. Although the people mentioned are all citizens, they are no doubt influenced by the local legal systems. The dowry was strictly invalid; the children, called, significantly, Iustus and Gemellus, were illegitimate. Wooden tablets from Herculaneum (*Tab. Herc.* 86–9; Arangio-Ruiz and Pugliese-Carratelli, 'Tabulae (ceratae) Herculanenses') document a divorce in AD 70. For a judicious and full account see Dixon, *WRW* (forthcoming).

[221] The *actio de moribus* is poorly attested and is said to have been rare (*CJ* 5.17.11.2b). It may also have served when the dowry had not been received by the husband. See Corbett 130ff., 150.

Because of the old *manus*, Romans must have started with a tendency to see dowry as a final settlement of the daughter's claims on her family's estate.[222] The relatively high amount of dowry from the second century BC onward would also make such a view understandable, especially for families with other heirs. But the giving of dowry had now ceased to be a single event in a woman's life. It could now be given in instalments, added to by various donors at various stages, postponed until the father's death, retrieved if the husband died or the marriage ended in divorce, and so on. Instead of being given irrevocably to the husband at one moment, it now becomes an endowment of the woman, to be held by the husband for the time being, which needs to be preserved for her in case she needs to marry again.

Rei publicae interest mulieres dotes salvas habere, propter quas nubere possunt. (*Digest* 23.3.2, Paul *lx ad edictum*)

It is important for the commonwealth that women should have their dowries safe, since they enable them to marry.[223]

To some extent, the texts reflect the view that dowry represents a daughter's share of her natal family's property. A woman's funeral ought to be paid for from her dowry, as if it were her patrimony. A daughter must be defended against her father who cheats her out of her dowry, since her dowry is her own estate (what she leaves, rather than what is left to her). Valerius Maximus sees Titinius' contemptible plot as an attempt to cheat his wife out of her family property.[224] The praetor, by the institution of *collatio dotis*, allowed an emancipated daughter who wished to share in the intestate succession to her father to do so, providing she brought her dowry and other property back into the pool.[225] '*Collatio dotis*', as Saller points out, 'implies that dowries were substantial enough to be worth taking into account when dividing the estate on the father's death, but not to represent the woman's whole share.'[226] We also hear of daughters who refrained from accepting a family inheritance and contented themselves with their dowry.[227] Or a father might take account of the dowry and

[222] As in Greece and elsewhere. See Saller, 'Roman dowry and the devolution of property in the Principate' 195–6.

[223] Also *D* 24.3.1, Pomp.: 'Dotium causa praecipua est: nam et publice interest dotes mulieribus conservari, cum dotatas esse feminas maxime sit necessarium'; cf. 23.4.14; *Decl. min.* 360.3. *Favor dotium*: *D* 23.3.9.1, Ulp.

[224] *D* 11.7.16 (Schulz, *CRL* 125, claims that the wording is late), 4.4.3.5, Paul: 'quoniam dos ipsius filiae proprium patrimonium est'; cf. *CJ* 5.12.30 pr., 5.13.1.14; Corbett 179; VM 8.2.3.

[225] *D* 10.2.20 pr., ht 39.1, 37.7. See Crook 105, 119; Rawson, *FAR* 61; Saller, 'Roman dowry and the devolution of property in the Principate' 199; Gardner, 'The recovery of dowry in Roman law'.　　[226] 'Rowan dowry and the devolution of property in the Principate'.

[227] *D* 19.1.52.1, 37.7.9; cf. ht 8.

peculium which he had given his daughter and so disinherit her in his will.[228]

The custom with sons by the late Republic seems to have been to allow them a certain independence, even though they were *filiifamilias*. This might be achieved by paying them an allowance or giving them a *peculium*. Dowry, usually a lump sum, is comparable. Further property will accrue later, for both sexes, as inheritance from either parent or other kin. Launching a son, via foreign travel and higher education, on a political career will have been expensive compared with settling a daughter. But the dowry system might be exploited in favour of the father of a son. Cicero in two letters makes it clear that if a young man married, his father might be able to stop paying him an allowance.[229] The need for an injection of cash helps account for the fact that young Roman politicians tended to marry at the beginning of their careers, therefore at an earlier age in the Principate than in the Republic.

On balance, then, it seems that dowry can be treated as only partial settlement of a daughter's claim on her family. It also functions as a contribution to the expenses of her new household. It was assumed that a husband was morally obliged to support his wife, because he enjoyed the revenue from her dowry. *Pacta dotalia* which arranged that the wife's family or herself would be responsible for maintenance merely confirm this general assumption.[230] It is only late in the classical period that a lawyer asserts a wife's *legal* right to compel her husband to support her—as much as her dowry permitted.[231] By the late Republic, however, the idea that there must be a strict distinction between the private property of the husband and that of the wife meant that there was a defined area of expenses which the wife would have to pay for herself.[232]

The income goes to the husband; the capital may come back to the wife or her family. Eventually, the capital may stay with the husband, or his family, or the children of the marriage. There is some evidence that the giver of a dowry often had an eye to the bride's children.[233]

In the classical period life expectancy was relatively low and divorce easy. In negotiating dowry, the families on both sides had to think of the short term: what was a reasonable contribution from the wife's side to joint expenses, how much income would be necessary to defray the additional expenses which the husband incurred by being

[228] D 6.1.65.1.   [229] Cic. A 15.29.2; cf. 16.1 (SB 409) 5, with SB ad loc.
[230] D 15.3.21, 23.4.12.1, 24.1.21.1, 24.3.42.2, 44.4.17 pr.
[231] D 24.3.22.8 (on *furiosa*); cf. Corbett 127.
[232] Dixon, 'Family finances: Terentia and Tullia' 88–91.
[233] Cf. Dixon, 'The marriage alliance in the Roman elite' 363–4.

married, and to pay for the items of property, such as slaves and houses, which supported their standard of living? They also considered the long term: how much capital could the wife's family risk losing by allowing it to go to the husband, his heirs or children? Since in marriage without *manus* the wife retained her own property, a balance also had to be struck between the amount her family or friends gave her as dowry, at the outset of the marriage or later, and the amount which then or eventually she received as her own property.

11
Res: Property—Separation and Mixing

> Wedlock for them was an earthy business, the Solemnization of Matrimony differing but a little from the conveyance of land . . . Had they been bidden to witness a Livery of Seisin they would have gone in the same spirit.
>
> (Dornford Yates, *As other men are* [1925] 51–2)

Apart from dowry, legally his and potentially hers, a husband and, if not *in manu*, a wife would usually have separate property.[1] The husband was not expected to endow his wife by making a pre-marital settlement. A *donatio* from husband to wife before or, later, during, marriage, balancing *dos* (*donatio ante* or *propter nuptias*), comes in only in during the fifth and sixth centuries.[2] The Romans were aware that in some societies husbands gave a bride-price.[3] But in the classical period, at the beginning of a marriage, capital was usually transmitted from the bride and her family to the husband and perhaps his family.

Manus meant that the wife's dowry was absorbed into the pool of the property of her husband or his *paterfamilias* but that she might inherit a share if her husband predeceased her. This custom and philosophical ideals of sharing lie behind approval of non-division of marital property. Even where the property of the wife was clearly distinguished as hers, the husband might feel himself a quasi-owner.[4] The Cincian Law of 204 BC, which restricted gift-giving, allowed it between relations up to the fifth degree, *sobrini* (in the sixth degree), persons in the *potestas* or *patresfamilias* of these, relations by marriage (stepchildren, step-parents, parents- or children-in-law), wife, husband, *sponsus*, and *sponsa*.[5] The Voconian Law of 169 BC, which prohibited the institution of women as *heredes* by people in the first

---

[1] Cf. Gell. 17.6.4 ff.; Corbett 202 ff.   [2] Corbett 207 ff.
[3] e.g. Caes. *BG* 6.19; Strabo 3.4.18.
[4] Cic. *A* 2.4.5; cf. Plut. *Praec. conj.* 20 = 140F.   [5] *FV* 298 ff.; Corbett 115.

census class and ruled that no one receive as legacy or gift in view of death more than the heir took, checked the institution of daughters or wives as heiresses by men of the wealthiest strata in society. The law meant that even an only daughter or childless wife could not inherit more than half. But this intent was circumvented if a testator left a *fideicommissum* to the heir or heirs to hand over the residue to a woman, as well as her legacy. It may be surmised that some fathers would name a son-in-law as heir, either asking him to hand his share over to his wife, or trusting him to let his wife benefit from the inheritance, or a daughter's son might become the heir.[6] We know that Pompey was Caesar's heir from 59 until they were at open enmity. During the period of Pompey's marriage to Julia, Caesar's intention may have been that Pompey would hand over the inheritance to her, at once or in his own will.[7] By the time of Augustus, the Voconian Law seems to have had little effect.[8] The evasions of which we hear in the late Republic were, however, in the interest of daughters rather than wives and the great imperial concentrations of wealth in the hands of women chiefly exemplify the channelling of fortunes to female descendants. The primary Roman duty in transmitting property, for both sexes in the classical period, seems to have been to pass it on to children if they existed. The law encouraged the idea that property should stay, as far as possible, in the lineage where it originated.

1. Donatio

Ulpian and Paul express with great lucidity the orthodox view on transfer of property from husband to wife or wife to husband during marriage, as it existed during the Principate.[9]

Moribus apud nos receptum est, ne inter virum et uxorem donationes valerent. Hoc autem receptum est, ne mutuo amore invicem spoliarentur donationibus non temperantes, sed profusa erga se facilitate. (*Digest* 24.1.1, Ulpian *xxxii ad Sabinum*)

It is accepted by custom among us that gifts between husband and wife are invalid. The reason for this practice is to prevent them being plundered

---

[6] Cf. Cat. 68.119ff. See Crook, 'Women in Roman succession' 65ff.; Dixon, 'Breaking the law to do the right thing: the gradual erosion of the Voconian law in ancient Rome'.

[7] Suet. *DJ* 83.1; cf. *D* 34.9.25, with Johnston, *Roman law of trusts* 67–8.

[8] Crook, 'Women in Roman succession' 66–7; Dixon, 'Breaking the law to do the right thing' 530–1.

[9] See Buckland, *Textbook* 111–12; Corbett 114ff.; Watson, *Property* 229ff.; Thayer, *On gifts between husband and wife* (Digest *24.1* De donationibus inter virum et uxorem): *Text and commentary*; Misera, *Der Bereicherungsgedanke bei der Schenkung unter Ehegatten*.

reciprocally because of their mutual love, by not being moderate in gift-giving but by extravagant generosity towards each other.

. . . ne cesset eis studium liberos potius educendi. Sextus Caecilius et illam causam adiciebat, quia saepe futurum esset, ut discuterentur matrimonia, si non donaret is qui posset, atque ea ratione eventurum, ut venalicia essent matrimonia. (*Digest* 24.1.2, Paul *vii ad Sabinum*)

. . . lest they should lose interest in bringing up children instead. Sextus Caecilius adds another reason, that it would often happen that marriages would be broken up, if the person who was able to do so did not give gifts, and by this means it would come about that marriages were for sale.

Haec ratio et oratione imperatoris nostri Antonini Augusti electa est: nam ita ait 'Maiores nostri inter virum et uxorem donationes prohibuerunt, amorem honestum solis animis aestimantes, famae etiam coniunctorum consulentes, ne concordia pretio conciliari videretur neve melior in pauper-tatem incideret, deterior ditior fieret.' Videamus, inter quos sunt prohibitae donationes, et quidem si matrimonium moribus legibusque nostris constat, donatio non valebit, sed si aliquod impedimentum interveniat, ne sit omnino matrimonium, donatio valebit: ergo si senatoris filia libertino contra senatus consultum nupserit, vel provincialis mulier ei, qui provinciam regit vel qui ibi meret, contra mandata, valebit donatio, quia nuptiae non sunt. (*Digest* 24.1.3. pr.–1, Ulpian *xxxii ad Sabinum*)

This reason is also picked out in the speech of our emperor Antoninus, for he says 'Our ancestors forbade gifts between husband and wife, calculating honourable love by the heart alone, and also safeguarding the reputation of the couple, so that it should not seem that harmony was won by money and so that the richer partner should not fall into comparative poverty and the poorer partner become wealthier.' Let us see between whom gifts are prohibited. If a marriage is valid by our customs and laws, a gift will not be valid. But if some impediment intervenes to make the marriage non-existent, then the gift will be valid. So if a senator's daughter marries a freedman in contravention of the senatorial decree or if a provincial woman marries a man who is ruling the province or serving there, in contravention of imperial rulings, then the gift will be valid because the marriage does not exist.

The rule applied also to people in the *potestas* of the recipient, so that, for example, a woman might not make a gift to her son if he was in his father's power, or to his slave.[10] *Affines* were also included, so, for instance, a father-in-law could not make a gift to his daughter-in-law, although gifts were allowed between mother- and daughter-in-law.[11] But step-relations were exempt.[12] A husband could not transfer property to an intermediary who would pass it on to his wife, or vice

---

[10] *D* 24.1.3.2 ff., ht 38 pr.   [11] Plut. *QR* 8; *D* 24.1.32.16 ff., ht 53.
[12] *D* 24.1.60 pr.

versa.[13] Some of the examples of indirect giving may represent attempts to evade the law. Thus, if a husband asked a third party, to pay over to his wife a sum owed to himself, this amounted to a direct gift from husband to wife.[14] Similarly, if a wife promised to pay off her husband's creditor or if, after marriage, the husband agreed that a creditor of his wife's should be paid out of the income of a dotal farm (that is, his income), this was clearly a gift.[15] Imaginary sale was another dodge, and invalid. This meant that the husband pretended to sell something to the wife. If money actually changed hands, the price might be fixed at lower than the market value of the property. Neratius held that this was not a fake sale if the husband had previously had the intention of selling to someone, but that if the wife got the property cheap she was to pay the difference to the husband. The wife had been unjustifiably enriched. But if she bought something worth 15 for 5 and then the value dropped to 10, she only had to pay 5 more.[16]

Some arrangements were legal. Thus, a *coniunx* could give the other a burial place, for such a gift did not enrich.[17] For the same reason, presumably, a husband might give his wife a sum of money to rebuild a house which had burnt down: any surplus would, however, count as a gift.[18] It was also permissible, according to juristic interpretation, to divert an inheritance or legacy to the *coniunx*. For one was not made poorer by avoiding a windfall. As Proculus put it, their ancestors had banned *donatio* so that *coniuges* should not despoil themselves to benefit the other, but they had not wanted them to be malevolent and begrudge the other's enrichment.[19] It was also permissible to give a slave in order that he be manumitted. There were two reasons for this. One was that the recipient was not enriched (because he or she ceased to own the slave), the other was the view that the slave's hope of liberty should be safeguarded.[20] It was also possible to transfer property when one had reason to think one's death was imminent, *donatio mortis causa*. Such a gift took full effect on the death of the donor. (The donor could either intend the donee to take the gift at once, in which case it became reclaimable if the donor did not die, or he could grant that the thing be given when he died. If the donee died first, the gift lapsed.) Husbands and wives had the same rights to this kind of gift as anyone else. The gift failed if the

---

[13] *D* 24.1.3.9, ht 5.2; Paul *S* 2.23.3.   [14] *D* 24.1.3.13, 5.3, 46.3.38.1.
[15] *D* 24.1.5.4, 23.4.28.
[16] *D* 24.1.5.5, 32.25–6, 16.1.17 pr., 18.1.38; Paul *S* 2.23.4.
[17] *D* 24.1.5.8ff.   [18] *D* 24.1.14.   [19] *D* 24.1.5.13ff., ht 31.7.
[20] *D* 24.1.7.8–9, ht 8, 9; Paul *S* 2.23.2.

couple divorced before the donor died.[21] *Coniuges* also had the specific privilege of giving in contemplation of divorce (*divortii causa*).[22] Such gifts were revocable if divorce did not follow. We also hear of gift in contemplation of exile.[23]

The meticulousness with which jurists look for evidence of unjustified enrichment and the attempts to evade the law suggest that Roman husbands and wives frequently found these restrictions irksome. Strict accounting might theoretically be required. The rich, whose affairs were complex, could have employed several accountants on the task of documenting expenditures, profits, and manufactures. The slave staff of one might be mixed up with the other's.[24] Happily, if the wife used slaves or clothing belonging to the husband (or vice versa), Pomponius held that the gift was valid. Paul agreed, giving the reason used by Proculus in another context:

Si quas servi operas viri uxori praestiterint vel contra, magis placuit, nullam habendam earum rationem: et sane non amare nec tamquam inter infestos ius prohibitae donationis tractandum est, sed ut inter coniunctos maximo affectu et solam inopiam timentes. (*Digest* 24.1.28.2, Paul *vii ad Sabinum*)

If the slaves of the husband have carried out any tasks for the wife or vice versa, it is considered preferable that no account should be taken of these: for clearly the law of forbidden gift must not be applied harshly and as if between people who are hostile to each other, but as between people joined with the greatest affection, who are afraid only of poverty.

Similarly, no claim could be made for the slave's rations if both used the slaves' services.[25] But if the slaves' work involved manufacturing something, more complicated considerations arose. If the husband had a garment made for the wife with his own wool, then it was legally the husband's, even though the wife had overseen the making of it. If, on the other hand, the wife used her own wool, but employed her husband's maids, and made women's clothes, these were her own, and she owed nothing for the maids' work. But if she made men's clothes in the same way, they were her husband's, as long as he paid her for the wool. The work put in by the slave-women is excluded from consideration in all these examples, but the ownership of the unworked material is relevant.[26] Similarly, if the husband gave his wife a building-site and she built a block of flats on it, the building

---

[21] *D* 39.6.43, cf. ht 26, 27, 40, 24.1.9.2, ht 10, 11, 13 pr.–1, 20, 52.1; in general 39.6; Paul *S* 2.23.1, 5–6; Buckland, *Textbook* 257ff.; Thomas 193–4. Severus subjected such gifts to the Falcidian rule: *D* 24.1.32; *CJ* 6.50.5, 8.56.2. An SC of unknown date ruled that those incapable of taking legacies under the law (probably the marriage laws) could not benefit (*D* 39.6.35 pr.). The subject has been treated in detail by Santi di Paola, *Donatio mortis causa*.
[22] *D* 24.1.11.11, 12, 60.   [23] *D* 24.1.43, Paul.   [24] *D* 29.5.1.15.
[25] *D* 24.1.18, 58.1.   [26] *D* 24.1.31 pr.–1.

belonged to the husband, but he had to refund her expenses.[27] The key concept is enrichment: if the wife is given clothes made with wool which belongs to the husband, she is enriched by the value of the raw material. If, on the other hand, the husband gave his wife money for travel expenses, whether to enable her to join him or for her own business, then the money was used and the wife was no richer: such a gift was legitimate. But the fact that Ulpian and Papinian had to argue this point suggests that it had caused some trouble.[28] If a husband paid for something that was consumed, such as food or unguents for the wife's servants or the maintenance of a proper standard of living, some lawyers held that this did not enrich her.[29] According to Paul, this was because the thing had been consumed: it was at his risk and he had lost his own property.[30] If he incurred expenses on her behalf, for instance by repairing a building which belonged to her, he could naturally reclaim these under the rule about gifts.[31]

The customary rule (which ran counter to the Cincian Law of 204 BC) seems to have taken effect before the time of Augustus.[32] It cannot be ascribed to the Augustan legislation, since authorities agree that it was not laid down by statute. It may be that it grew up after Quintus Mucius Scaevola in the early first century BC laid down that if a woman acquired any property the provenance of which was unknown, it should be assumed that it came from her husband or someone in his power. This was to protect the lady's reputation.[33] Cicero speaks of the possibility of Terentia selling some property in order to help him when he was exiled, but he does not make it clear whether she intends to transfer it legally to him, so it is not certain that this would qualify as a gift according to later criteria. Sallust makes Catiline claim that he could rely on the generosity of his wife in settling debts by means of her own and her daughter's resources.[34] In any case, a few years later the jurists were giving their attention to the complications of the ban. It is discussed by Alfenus Varus (suffect consul 39 BC) and by Labeo.[35]

How was the law applied? Juristic interest suggests that it was applied. But the accounting and restitution or compensation would only become necessary if someone questioned the validity of a gift. The donor might do so if circumstances or feelings changed. So might his heir after his death. Otherwise the attention of lawyers might not be attracted and the gift might be treated as valid. For instance, there

---

[27] *D* 24.1.31.2.   [28] *D* 24.1.21 pr.

[29] *D* 24.1.31.9, Pomp., cf. ht 7.1, Ulp., and perhaps 5.17, Marcellus; *contra*, ht 58 pr., Scaev. The difference may have been made by the *Oratio*: ht 32.9, Ulp.

[30] *D* 24.1.28 pr.   [31] *D* 24.1.47, Celsus.   [32] Watson, *Property* 229.

[33] *D* 24.1.51. Cf. Gardner 73–4; *contra*, Watson, *Property* 230 n.1.   [34] *F* 14.1.5.

[35] *D* 24.1.38, ht 29.1, 32.27, 64, 65, 67.

was disagreement about whether a wife might acquire by usucapion after divorce if the husband had given her something during the marriage.[36] A wife might be left in possession of gifts during the marriage and the husband might confirm the gift by will. Labeo quotes a will in which the husband bequeathed to his wife what he had given or donated during his lifetime or procured for her use. He pedantically interprets this as meaning what had been given up to the time when the testator made his will.[37] It seems that it was common practice for husbands and wives to give each other pieces of property. In practice, the recipient treated them as his; in law they remained the donor's. As the younger Celsus (consul for the second time AD 129) wrote in his treatment of the matter, 'What a husband gives to his wife after marriage remains his and he can claim it.' He adds that it makes no difference if the wife left generous legacies to this husband. Clearly he is thinking of the legal situation following the wife's death: the husband could reclaim any gifts from her estate, as well as taking legacies.[38]

Plainly, if divorce followed the gift, it was likely that the donor might reclaim his or her property.[39] If the husband was the donor, he had the possibility of retaining part of the dowry to make up for what he had given.

It was difficult to apply the law with scrupulous fairness. If one partner manumitted a slave given by the other, for instance, he might benefit from services which the freedman vowed to give him. And if one paid for the reconstruction of the other's house which was accidentally destroyed, although the recipient was not enriched, it is hard to deny that the donor suffered expense.

The law was never intended to be applied to modest gifts made on the occasion of birthdays or the Matronalia.[40] Antoninus Pius loosened the law by permitting a wife to give her husband property which would bring him up to the census qualification for the Senate or equestrian order or allow him to give games. This was called *donatio honoris causa*.[41] But it seems to have been regarded as common, though not necessarily a good thing, for husbands to give wives substantial items of property, such as farms and slaves.[42]

It seems likely that in reforming the law in 206 Severus and Caracalla were bringing it into line with the sentiments of the ruling class. The imperial address, ratified by a senatorial decree, allowed a gift between husband and wife to be valid as long as the donor persevered in the wish to make the gift and he or she predeceased the

---

[36] *D* 41.6.1.2. [37] *D* 32.33.1. [38] *D* 24.1.48.
[39] Cf. *D* 20.1.1.4, 24.1.50, Iav., 57. [40] *D* 24.1.31.8.
[41] *D* 24.1.40ff.; *Tit. Ulp.* 7.1. [42] Juv. 6.149ff.; cf. 2.59.

recipient. Such a gift was independent of anything left by will, so that if the survivor was qualified to take only one-tenth by will, he or she suffered no such limitation in regard to a gift made during life.[43] If a divorce occurred or if the recipient died first, then the old law applied, that the gift was valid if the donor wished it to stand.[44] All gifts previously prohibited could now be confirmed.[45] Gifts between in-laws were now on the same footing as those between husband and wife.[46] The most delicate legal problem created by the reform was how to determine whether the donor had changed his mind. We find Gordian protecting a woman when her father-in-law attempts to take away her dead husband's gift and Diocletian and Maximian informing a son that he cannot interfere with his father's gift to his mother. Both take it for granted that the donor persevered in his intention.[47] But both the oration and Ulpian go into the difficulty:

Ait oratio 'fas esse eum quidem qui donavit paenitere: heredem vero eripere forsitan adversus voluntatem supremam eius qui donaverit durum et avarum esse.' Paenitentiam accipere debemus supremam. Proinde si uxori donavit, deinde eum paenituit, mox desiit paenitere, dicendum est donationem valere, ut supremum eius spectemus iudicium, quemadmodum circa fideicommissa solemus, vel in legatis cum de doli exceptione opposita tractamus, ut sit ambulatoria voluntas eius usque ad vitae supremum exitum. Sed ubi semel donatorem paenituit, etiam heredi revocandi potestatem tribuimus, si appareat defunctum evidenter revocasse voluntatem: quod si in obscuro sit, proclivior esse debet iudex ad comprobandam donationem. (*Digest* 24.1.32.2–5, Ulpian *xxxiii ad Sabinum*)

The speech says 'The giver has indeed the right to change his mind, but it is cruel and greedy for the heir to snatch away the gift perhaps against the final will of the giver.' By changing his mind we ought to understand a final change. For if he made a gift to his wife and then changed his mind and subsequently changed it back again, we must say that the gift is valid, when we look at his last decision, as we are in the habit of doing with *fideicommissa* or with the defence of fraud in relation to legacies, so that his wishes may be changed up to the very end of his life. But when the donor changed his mind only once, we allow the heir the opportunity to reclaim the gift, if it is clear that the dead man changed his mind. But if there is room for doubt, the judge should be more inclined to confirm the gift.

There could be evidence that the giver had changed his mind, for instance if he subsequently pledged the property.[48] The law and the jurists favoured upholding the validity of gifts whenever possible. As

---

[43] *D* 24.1.3 pr., ht 32 (Ulpian's detailed treatment of the difference between previous law and the new system); cf. 33.4.1.3; *FV* 276, 294.2; *CJ* 5.16.10.

[44] *D* 24.1.32.10ff.   [45] *D* 24.1.32.23.   [46] *D* 24.1.32.16ff.

[47] *CJ* 5.16.10; *FV* 276.   [48] *D* 24.1.32.5.

a further instance, if both giver and recipient died in circumstances, such as a shipwreck, which made it difficult to decide which died first, they preferred to hold that the donor had died first (particularly as he was no longer alive to reclaim his property). The gift would then stand and go to the recipient's estate.[49]

The essential difference between the situation before and after the reform is that before the gift needed to be confirmed by the donor's will and afterwards it took full effect automatically unless there was evidence that he had changed his mind. Confirmation after divorce was required both before and after 206.

Paul quotes a letter from a woman to her husband which gives the flavour of how the system worked, though it is not clear whether it applies to the situation before or after 206.

'Cum petenti mihi a te, domine carissime, adnuit indulgentia tua viginti ad expediendas quasdam res meas, quae summa mihi numerata est sub ea condicione, ut, si per me meosque mores quid steterit, quo minus in diem vitae nostrae matrimonium permaneat, sive invito te discessero de domo tua vel repudium tibi sine ulla querella misero divortiumque factum per me probabitur, tunc viginti, quae mihi hac die donationis causa dare voluisti, daturam restituturam me sine ulla dilatione spondeo.' Quaero an, si eadem Titio marito suo repudium miserit, pecuniam restituere debeat. Paulus respondit pecuniam, quam vir uxori donavit, ex stipulatione proposita, si condicio eius exstitit, peti posse, quoniam ex donatione in pecuniam creditam conversa est: quod si stipulatio commissa non probetur, tunc tantum peti posse, quanto locupletior ex ea donatione facta probetur. (*Digest* 24.1.57, Paul *vii responsorum*)

'When in response to a request from me, my dearest lord, you granted me of your indulgence 20 to arrange certain affairs of mine, a sum which was paid over to me on the condition that if it came about through me and my behaviour that our marriage did not last until the end of our lives, whether I left your house against your will or sent you a notice of divorce without any just cause of complaint and it is proved that I was responsible for the divorce, then I promise to give and restore to you without any delay the 20 which you have agreed to give me as a gift today.' I ask whether the woman ought to restore the money, if she sends Titius notice of divorce. Paul replied that if that condition is fulfilled the money can be reclaimed in accordance with the stipulation quoted, since it has been converted from a gift to a loan. But if it is not proved that the stipulation was made, then only the amount by which she is proved to have been enriched by the gift may be claimed.

Whether before or after the reform, such a gift was clearly reclaimable. What is interesting is to see that *coniuges* found it convenient to document such a transaction in order to simplify a refund, if it became

---

[49] *D* 24.1.32.14, 34.5.8.

necessary. There is also an interesting irony in the contrast between the dutiful (though legalistic) tone of the letter and the wife's subsequent actions. Whether the letter is genuine (as is suggested by the fact that someone was consulting Paul) or fabricated by the client or the lawyer as a convincing example of what this sort of document ought to be makes little difference. We have here a vivid example of financial arrangements between husband and wife. It should also be noted that the jurists usually considered gifts as going from man to woman. This will no doubt be due partly to male bias, partly to their feeling that this was in general a more proper direction for liberality, but partly also to the probability that an older husband would predecease his wife, circumstances in which dispute might arise.[50]

At all periods, the expedient of *donatio inter virum et uxorem* could give the donor the possibility of making a revocable transfer of property. A husband could thus give as a gift to his wife more property than she might be qualified to take under his will. Donation offered a way round the Augustan penalties against the childless. On the other hand, should the wife predecease the husband, he had the opportunity to reclaim the gift and not let it go with the estate. Similarly, if the marriage broke down he might take the gift back. The rules on donation thus offered much more flexibility than is suggested by the blunt statements of jurists on the invalidity of gift-giving between *coniuges* during their marriage and their life.

2. *Joint Enterprises*

(a) *Household administration*

As we have seen, it was generally held that a husband and wife living in the same house would share the services of each other's slaves and, no doubt, freedmen. Ulpian expresses this forcefully when saying that if either husband or wife is murdered, the slaves of either may be tortured for evidence, 'although the husband's slaves are not strictly speaking called the wife's or the wife's called the husband's. But because the staff is mixed and it is one household, the senate voted that the rule should apply to the slaves of the murdered person's spouse as well as to his own.'[51] There would be a general tendency for the more personal or confidential servants to be one's own slaves, whether acquired before marriage, like the nurse who is the normal confidante of the wife in drama, or bred, bought, or acquired by gift or bequest later. The mistress of a rich household tended to own her dressers, wet-nurses, and midwives.[52] Her husband owned his valet

---

[50] *D* 24.1.33.1, Ulp. (on annuities).   [51] *D* 29.5.1.15; cf. ht 3.2.

[52] Treggiari, 'Domestic staff in the Julio-Claudian period' 248.

and secretaries. But those who performed more general functions
could belong to one and work for both. The steward Philotimus,
Terentia's freedman, who ran Cicero's households, is a familiar
example.[53] We have already reviewed juristic references to slaves
whose services were shared.[54] Outdoor servants, gardeners, grooms,
litter-bearers, and couriers tend to belong to men. A husband might
lend his wife a team of litter-bearers or perhaps some young girls for
her exclusive use.[55] Since women slaves were of little use to him in
normal work-roles, he might lend her his own women and their
female offspring. Conversely, we can assume, some of the wife's
slaves might be chiefly employed by the husband. Further merging, in
practice if not law, must have occurred when either *coniunx* assigned
or gave slaves to their children or stepchildren, despite the legal
obstacles to the wife transferring ownership to a child in her
husband's power.

Because of the husband's duty to maintain the wife, discussed in
Chapter 10.3, he might buy or otherwise procure slaves especially
for her use. These were often bequeathed to her, presumably in part
because it was difficult to give them to her. We shall discuss property
procured for the wife's use in connection with legacies.

Whoever owned them, the women who performed tasks such as
spinning were likely to be taking their orders from the wife. The
product of their labours went to clothe not only master, mistress, and
their children, but the other members of the staff, and it must often
have been difficult to trace a fleece from the sheep's back to a
particular human's.[56] The wife in such matters might, to a lawyer, be
acting as the husband's agent, *viri negotium procurat*, but supervision
of wool-working was subsumed in her general duty to supervise the
running of the house. Her participation in domestic production might
be less menial than in the good old days, but Cicero expected Terentia
at least to give orders about such mundane details as provision of
wash-basins, and the ideal of the spinning housewife was still potent
throughout the Principate.[57] It surprised no one if the day-to-day
running of a large slave household, with control over funds belonging
to the husband, was entrusted to the wife.[58] It was her duty to
conserve and guard domestic resources.[59] Within the household,
there seems no reason to doubt that a husband would normally be
able to give orders to his wife's slaves and vice versa. Apart from
shared service, slaves owned by wife and husband might be drawn

[53] Treggiari, *RFLR* 263–4 (possibly dotal).   [54] *D* 32.49.2, cf. ht 45.
[55] *D* 32.49 pr.–2.   [56] Treggiari, 'Jobs for women' 81 ff.
[57] Col. 12 pr.; Cic. *F* 14.20.   [58] *D* 3.5.2, 15.3.21.
[59] Pearce, 'The role of the wife as *custos* in ancient Rome'.

into close relationships through quasi-marriage, *contubernium*. Since a higher proportion of women in any city household were likely to be in the ownership of the wife, it follows that many of them would find mates among the husband's slaves. The property rights which followed from *contubernium* interested the owner of the woman, for any children belonged to him or her. But the interest of the slaves in continuing their own union gave them an interest in the continued cohabitation of their respective owners.

Husband and wife might also own slaves in common, *servi communes* (in varying fractions).[60] The law takes no particular notice of common ownership between husband and wife. Such slaves might have been acquired by purchase (each putting up a fraction of the price) or by inheritance (where husband and wife might be coheirs, as Tiberius was heir to two-thirds of Augustus' estate and his mother to one-third, or co-legatees). Epigraphic evidence attests slaves jointly freed by husband and wife, especially in the middle range of society.[61]

It was considered usual for the upper-class husband to own the matrimonial home in Rome or the town where the couple normally resided. But the house might be part of the dowry or the wife's personal property. Each *coniunx* might also have other residences, villas in the country or at the seaside, lodges (*deversoria*) for short stays, farmhouses which they might occasionally visit, apartment blocks and warehouses for rent.[62] Productive property might include agricultural land, grazing, forests, lakes, quarries, clay-pits, shipping, and so on. Such items of property could more easily be regarded as belonging solely to one *coniunx* than the *domus* in which both spent much of the year and which was run by the wife. So it is easy for the lawyers to say that if a wife owns slaves for trading, the husband need not supply them with food.[63] A country villa and its staff might be sharply distinguished if necessary.[64] Even with such easily distinguished items, however, the marital relationship meant that either might take some responsibility, out of a sense of duty, for the affairs of the other. More specifically, either might in an emergency (for instance to shore up a building or treat a sick slave) act on the other's behalf without explicit authorization, *negotium gerere*.[65] Again there is nothing specific in the law on this which relates to husband and wife.

---

[60] Buckland, *Textbook* 311–12, *RLS* 372 ff.

[61] e.g. *CIL* 1.1570 = *ILLRP* 977; *D* 34.1.16.3.

[62] Cf. *D* 31.34.3.   [63] *D* 24.1.31.10.

[64] The line between *familia urbana* and *rustica* was drawn according to where a slave was expected to be employed (*D* 32.78 pr.) but especially by function, not location (31.65 pr., 32.60.1, ht 99, 50.16.166 pr.). However, the core staff of a specific farm or villa would be identifiable (e.g. 30.84.10, 31.1.32.2).

[65] *D* 3.5, esp. ht 3.1; Buckland, *Textbook* 537–8; Crook 236 ff.

We hear in the jurists of wives controlling their husband's property during marriage and after the husband's death and of husbands managing their wives' affairs even after a divorce.[66] The anonymous *laudata* wanted her husband, if they divorced, to continue to treat all their property as communal, and wished to let him continue to control it. She also hoped that he would want her to go on assisting.[67] A husband who administered all his wife's property during her lifetime was left as heir to the whole estate, with a *fideicommissum* (trust) that he should on his own death pass on five-sixths of it to their son and one-sixth to a grandson. An inscription praises a wife who took care of her husband's house and affairs.[68] Authorization to carry out specific business might be given by mandate. A woman could carry out this gratuitous service as well as a man.[69] A mandate might also authorize someone to act on someone's behalf as a general manager, called a *procurator*. Because of the limits on women's legal rights, a woman was not generally allowed to take on this role officially, but parents who had no other suitable agent might appoint their daughter to sue on their behalf. Husbands are not included on the list of close family members for whom women might take legal action.[70] A husband might appear in court on his wife's behalf and did not require an official mandate.[71] The husband might be his wife's official guardian, who interposed his verbal authorization for important transactions, such as alienation of land or slaves, bail, making a will, or making contracts which put her under an obligation. The anonymous *laudata* seems to have come into her husband's guardianship.[72] The emperors checked guardians who wanted to marry their wards, except when the woman's father had made previous arrangements. Although there was some risk of conflict of interest if the husband were also the guardian, the powers of a *tutor* had been so attenuated that the convenience of this arrangement probably outweighed the disadvantages. Only women required lifelong guardians (a protection eroded for favoured individuals), and naturally the task of acting as guardian was peculiarly masculine, so no woman could perform this service for her husband.[73]

All sorts of ordinary business transactions might take place between husband and wife. They could lend each other money.[74] They could buy things from each other.[75] If one damaged the other's property, he or she could be prosecuted for damages. A wife whose

[66] *D* 3.5.32, ht 34 pr.   [67] *Laud. Tur.* 1.37 ff., 2.36 ff.
[68] *D* 35.2.95 pr.; *CIL* 13.1597 = *CLE* 35.   [69] e.g. *D* 17.1.10.6.
[70] *D* 3.3.41, 54 pr., 50.17.2 pr.; cf. 3.1.1.5.   [71] *D* 46.7.3.3.
[72] *Laud. Tur.* 1.37 ff.; cf. 21 ff.   [73] *D* 26.1.18; cf. ht 16 pr.
[74] e.g. *D* 15.3.20 pr., ht 21, 23.3.82, 34.3.28.13.   [75] *D* 19.5.12.

husband gave her some loose pearls to use and who (very naturally) had them pierced and strung, without his knowledge or consent, could be sued whether she was still married or divorced.[76] The husband could be sued for fraudulently spending his wife's cash or a wife for corrupting her husband's slave.[77] A wife could not be sued for theft if she stole from her husband (although her accomplice could be) but only for removing property. A husband was similarly protected, because of the respect due to the relationship.[78]

Under the Republic, husbands and wives could freely stand surety for each other's debts. But Augustus and Claudius both prohibited women from making this risky commitment on behalf of their husband, and a senatorial decree under Claudius or Nero made a general ruling against women standing surety. These measures have convincingly been attributed to the need to protect women's property from a risk the extent of which they might be unable to predict when they accepted the obligation, and have been related to the erosion of guardianship under these emperors.[79] Paul cites the risk to their private fortune, *res familiaris*.[80] The decree did not prevent women from giving guarantees on behalf of others, but it allowed the praetor to protect them if, for instance, they had been deceived.[81] Women were still allowed to borrow money in their own names to lend to their husbands.[82] It seems likely that the decree did not greatly handicap women in engaging in business of all sorts, for plenty of activity in all kinds of affairs is discussed in the *Digest* title. Husbands were still allowed to stand surety for their wives.[83]

(b) Negotia

It was also possible for husband and wife to enter into a *societas* in order to administer their property communally or to engage jointly in business.[84] In humbler classes of society we can sometimes document and must often assume husbands and wives running businesses together. In the upper classes profit-making ventures were viewed as an extension of domestic economy, and it is hard to draw a firm line between exploitation of land for crops and the leasing of clay-pits to potters or between rearing of slave children and the sale of the surplus. So in lower social strata, where craftsmen and shopkeepers

---

[76] *D* 9.2.27.30, on which see Birks, 'Other men's meat' 164–5.   [77] *D* 10.4.14, 11.3.17.
[78] *D* 25.2.1, ht 2, 3, 47.2.52 pr.; Corbett 196.
[79] Talbert 442; Crook, 'Feminine inadequacy and the *senatusconsultum Velleianum*'; Gardner 75–6.
[80] *D* 16.1.1.1.
[81] *D* 16.1.2.2–3, ht 16 pr., 21. See Crook, 'Feminine inadequacy and the *senatusconsultum Velleianum*' 87.   [82] *D* 16.1.17 pr.   [83] e.g. *D* 16.1.28 pr.
[84] *D* 34.1.16.3 (for over 40 years). See in general Crook 229ff.

lived above the shop, the division between work and home life was fuzzy. A group of clothes-makers from the *Vicus Tuscus* is commemorated by one of its members, a freedwoman. The others are her patron, his patron, and her freedman and husband.[85] Husband and wife shared such trades as the making of nails, gold leaf, baking, and (probably) hairdressing (for men and women respectively) and the manufacture of purple cloth and of incense.[86] Other lower-class married women worked at trades independently of their husbands.[87] Some of these are cottage industries; others involved the woman in dealing with the public in the front of the workshop or shop, or in peddling goods around the town or from a market stall. It would be hard to imagine a Roman inn, tavern, or cook-shop without its hostess or the markets without women hawking the produce which their husbands grew or at least bought and transported. In large-scale production and trade, objects marked with the manufacturer's stamp such as bricks, Arretine ware, or lead pipes are more likely to reflect separation of property between husband and wife.[88] But Annia Faustina, the sister of M. Aurelius, and her husband C. Ummidius Quadratus were co-owners of an estate which produced bricks. So were Annia Fundania Faustina and T. Vitrasius Pollio (consul for the second time 176) and earlier Claudia Capitolina (daughter of Claudius Balbillus) and M. Junius Rufus (prefect of Egypt in the 90s). These couples are to be regarded as *societates*.[89]

3. Inheritance

The essential object of marriage was to produce children to inherit the father's estate. There was a clear link between *matrimonium* and *patrimonium* (the estate, strictly that of a *paterfamilias*).[90] A man had to be able to have confidence in the chastity of his wife in order to be sure that he was leaving his property to descendants of his own blood. 'Chastity is essential to the state. For you know that the state is held together by marriages, and by them are bonded peoples, children, the

---

[85] *CIL* 6.37826.

[86] *CIL* 5.7023, 6.9211, 6939, 8.24678, 37811, 37820 = *ILLRP* 809, 9934 = *ILLRP* 818. See further Treggiari, 'Lower-class women in the Roman economy'; Kampen.

[87] e.g. sewing: *CIL* 6.9884; spinning: Apul. *M* 9.5; perfumery: *CIL* 6.10006; dealing in grains and pulses: ibid. 9683; keeping a cook-shop (the wife of a sculptor): ibid. 9824; hairdressing (probably the wife of a goldsmith): ibid. 37469.

[88] See e.g. Setälä, *Private domini in Roman brick stamps in the empire* 24 ff. A third of the landowners, 49, are women (p. 211).

[89] Setälä, *Private domini* 59, 94–5, 121–2, 142, 203–4, 206 ff. 232–4.

[90] *OLD* s.v. Also inherited from *parentes* (Cic. *Red. Sen.* 2; cf. *Caec.* 75).

succession to estates and the degree of inheritances, and the safety of the home.'[91]

Roman rules on succession have been much studied both by Roman jurists and by modern scholars.[92] But the variety of practices within the framework of the law and the evolution of legal rules are only now being studied with the requisite tools.[93] Here we need only attempt a brief survey of succession between husband and wife, which should, in accordance with Roman ideals, have been of little importance compared with the continuity of the family line. We shall review the general rules where they are important for the context in which succession of husband or wife to the other's property might occur. Unless they were related to each other by blood or the wife was *in manu* and so gained the rights of a daughter, the right of husband and wife to inherit from each other as heirs on intestacy was slight. The civil law omitted them from consideration in listing those who would succeed; the praetors inserted them after *liberi*, *legitimi*, and *cognati*.[94] The first degree was represented originally by *sui heredes*, natural children and adoptive children *in patria potestate*, including the second and later generations in the male line. Wives *in manu mariti* come in this class. The praetors brought in here other *liberi*, those who would have been *sui* if they or their fathers had not been emancipated, given in adoption, or married with *manus*.[95] They are those who would also have a claim against a will. Failing *sui*, the Twelve Tables awarded the estate to the nearest agnates, brothers and sisters, or, failing these, the father's brothers and sisters or the brother's children.[96] The praetors widened this class to include more distant agnates, but no further than sisters in the female line. The jurists call them *legitimi*, those authorized by law or senatorial decree. If these were lacking, blood-relations, *cognati* (including women), had a claim.[97] While *sui* succeeded automatically, relatives in other grades had to make an application. Emancipated children

---

[91] *Decl. min.* 249.19.

[92] See in general Crook, 'Women in Roman succession'; Gardner 163 ff.; Corbett 117 ff.; on particular aspects, Boyer, 'Le droit successoral romain dans les œuvres de Polybe'; Dixon, 'Polybius on Roman women and property'; Csillag, 'I rapporti patrimoniali fra coniugi all'epoca di Augusto'; Corbier, 'Idéologie et pratique de l'héritage (1ᵉʳ s. av. J.-C.–IIᵉ s. ap. J.-C.)'.

[93] See e.g. Johnston, *Roman law of trusts*.

[94] *D* 38.6 ff.; Buckland, *Textbook* 365 ff. If the intestate person was a freed slave, patrons also took precedence over wives. For the strength of the feeling that *coniuges* were outsiders on intestacy see *CJ* 8.2.3 (AD 395).

[95] Crook 119; id., 'Women in Roman succession' 61.

[96] G 3.1 ff.; Watson, *XII Tables* 66–7.

[97] See Gardner 190 ff. *Cognati* take the place occupied under the Twelve Tables by *gentiles* (Watson, *XII Tables* 67 ff.).

and married daughters who had received a share of the family property already might have to put it back in the pool before taking their share on intestacy. After all these, the wife or husband might apply. In order to claim *bonorum possessio unde vir et uxor*, the marriage had to be valid and still in existence when one *coniunx* died. Furthermore, the claimant had to qualify under the *Lex Julia Papia*.[98]

The Romans of the upper class in the historic period seem to have disliked being intestate.[99] So if someone who was qualified to do so (being adult, sane, and so on) died without making a will it was probably because death came unexpectedly. But the rules on intestacy are important because they would come into play for succession to minors or if a will was broken (for instance by the heir refusing the inheritance or by the birth of a posthumous child of whom the testator had not taken account) or if children, for instance, applied to the praetor for possession against the terms of the will. The praetorian developments also show how strong was the feeling that all children should have a share in their father's estate. The general rules of the classical period avoid discriminating among children on the grounds of sex or primogeniture. If a child *in patria potestate* died, his or her *peculium* of course reverted automatically to the father. So did *dos profecticia*. The son of a *filiusfamilias* who died would eventually come in for his share of the grandfather's property. If an emancipated child died childless, his father (or hers if she had not passed into another family through *manus*) would benefit. The praetorian rules which allowed *sui* to appeal against a will did not apply to women's wills, since they had no *sui*.[100] We have seen that gradually under the Principate the reciprocal rights of mother and child were brought into line with those between father and child. The rules of intestacy put the rights of husband and wife at the opposite end of the spectrum from those of father and child.

If a will was made, the testator had a liberty of choice limited only by circumstance (such as the prior death of the person he wished to be his heir), social expectations, the legal incapacity of certain classes of person to take under wills, and by various statutes which have already been described. A woman needed (usually and down to Hadrian) to undergo *coemptio* and if under guardianship needed her guardian's consent to make a will, but he did not need to know the terms of the will or agree to them. In any case, a guardian could be compelled to give consent unless he was *legitimus*.[101] In practice, many women

[98] *D* 38.11 (significantly a title consisting of one extract); *Tit. Ulp.* 28.7; Just. *Inst.* 3.9.3ff.
[99] See Crook, 'Intestacy in Roman society', against Daube, 'The preponderance of intestacy at Rome'.   [100] *D* 37.4.4.2.   [101] Details in Gardner 167–8.

could probably act as if effectively independent (as far as legal constraints went) before the Augustan offer of freedom from guardianship to mothers, but the constraints must have been burdensome enough for relief to be welcome.

The Voconian Law of 169 BC, which disadvantaged women in the top property class, limited the amount that a man could leave to his wife or daughter or a woman to her daughter. But it is the injustice to daughters which came under attack. The law did nothing to stop a rich woman leaving all her property to her husband.[102] The Augustan rules on testamentary disposition between husband and wife (discussed in Chapter 2.II.1) illustrate again the privileged position of children, in contrast with wives as such. Husband and wife could leave each other one-tenth by reason of being married to each other, but the whole estate if they had a child. The effect of this might be that the surviving spouse would pass on the property to the child or children. But the law also allowed dead children to qualify the survivor to inherit. In such instances, the legislator would presumably be content if the once fecund survivor went on to remarry and produce other children, and the property might assist in this laudable aim. But the law is doing little to keep property in the testator's agnate group, except that it allows inheritance by kin (including *cognati*) within the sixth degree even if they did not qualify by reason of marriage or children. By this time, it would probably not have occurred to a legislator to dictate the directions in which property should pass. Augustus was concerned merely to encourage transmission to people who had children. He did not stop people leaving bequests or even whole estates to non-relatives, as long as they qualified.

Within the framework set up by law, how did testators try to leave property? Our literary, juristic, and papyrological evidence does not allow us to arrive at statistical probabilities for what a husband of 40 would decide to do if he had a wife of 30 and three children, of 14, 10, and 1. When, for instance, a jurist tells us that Titius left his son as heir, we often do not know if his wife was still alive or if she received legacies. If a jurist is concerned with a particular farm, we may not know if it represents the whole estate. The examples themselves instruct us chiefly about the range of possible dispositions.[103] The surviving brick-stamps document a sizeable group of landowners near Rome in the heyday of the Empire, roughly comparable with the social classes on whom the jurists and literary sources focus. Among

[102] Crook, 'Women in Roman succession' 69 ff.; Gardner 170 ff.

[103] Cf. Montevecchi, 'Ricerche di sociologia nei documenti dell' Egitto greco-romano I: i testamenti' 73; Humbert, *Remariage à Rome* 181 ff.; Amelotti, *Il testamento romano attraverso la prassi documentale*; Hobson, 'Women and property owners in Roman Egypt'.

that group of property-owners, continuity between parents and descendants is often attested. Transfer between husband and wife is convincingly deduced for three couples.[104] But of course it is easier to detect descendants (identifiable through nomenclature) than *coniuges*. This evidence shows the importance of transmission to children, but not whether, in the absence of children, transmission to wives would be thought more or less acceptable in general than transmission to such kindred as a brother or a nephew.

(a) Heredes

The *Digest* provides many references to those selected as *heredes*. It is important to remember that the *heres* or *heredes* were responsible for paying legacies and debts, carrying out manumissions, and so on. Although the Falcidian Law of 40 BC ruled that the heir was entitled to at least a quarter of the estate after payment of necessary expenses and legacies, entering an inheritance remained troublesome as well as potentially profitable.[105] Considerate men might sometimes hesitate to impose the burden on wives and daughters.[106] But there are plenty of instances where the wife is named. She might be heir to the whole estate.[107] As long as proper formalities were observed, the wife might be named *heres* and the children as substitutes in case she died first, or vice versa.[108] Similarly, a man who named posthumous children as heirs might name his wife in the second degree in case no child was born.[109] He might disinherit his children and name his wife as heir, but express a wish that she pay a legacy to the (adult) daughter and pass on the rest to the (under-age) son when he reached 20, or to the daughter if the son died before that age.[110] This particular settlement seems a sensible way of taking account of the risk that a child might die young and allowing a degree of flexibility within which the mother was trusted to work. It recognizes a unity of the group of mother and children, whereas the alternative, of leaving the under-age son as heir, under guardianship, with legacies to wife and daughter, would have introduced another responsible adult into the picture. This will makes the wife responsible for a trust, *fideicommissum*, which was, from the time of Augustus, enforceable at law.

A wife might be one of several coheirs. In particular, she might be coheir with her children.[111] Julian discusses a will in which the

---

[104] Setälä, *Private* domini 232 ff.

[105] Buckland, *Textbook* 342–3; Crook 124 ff.

[106] *D* 31.34.6 is a nice instance. Cf. Pliny *Epp.* 2.4.1.   [107] *D* 31.89.7.

[108] *D* 28.6.43.2, ht 47. It was most usual to substitute one child to another in case one died before reaching adulthood or parenthood. See *D* 28.6 *passim*.

[109] *D* 29.5.4.   [110] *D* 36.1.76.1.

[111] *D* 31.89 pr., 32.41 pr. Coheir with a son, with *fideicommissum* to the daughter: 32.41.7.

husband ordered that if his wife bore a son, he was to be heir to two-thirds and the wife to one-third. But if the child was a girl, she was to be heir to one-third and his wife to two-thirds. The man died and his wife had twins, one of each sex. The jurists decided that the testator's wishes would be most accurately reflected if the estate were divided into seven and the son took four-sevenths, the wife two-sevenths, and the daughter one-seventh.[112] A husband might leave his wife as heir and ask her (the wording indicates a trust) to pass on the property to their children or to his kin on her death. For example, 'I ask you, my dearest wife, that when you die you restore my inheritance to my children or one of them or my grandchildren or to whichever you wish or to my kinsfolk or to whichever you wish of all my kin.'[113] But equally (perhaps when he had no child or kin) he might think of her family as the eventual recipients. A man left his mother and wife as heirs and wrote, 'I ask you, my dearest wife, that you leave nothing to your brothers on your death: you have the children of your sisters to whom you can leave it. You know that one of your brothers killed our son, while robbing him. Another of them too has done worse to me.' One would like to know more of this deplorable family. The wife dying intestate, one of her brothers succeeded, but it was argued that the estate should go to the nephews.[114] Alternatively, a father might leave his children as heirs and ask a daughter to keep for herself from her inheritance a hundred gold pieces and an estate at Tusculum, but to pass on the rest to her mother.[115] Predictably, the *Digest* shows that it was normal for fathers to institute children as heirs. The possibility of posthumous children caused complications. Siblings might be heir to varying fractions, or one might be an heir and the other given a legacy.[116] Account may have been taken by the testator of what one child had received previously, for instance as dowry, or what he or she might expect from other sources.[117] Usually we know nothing of such context. But we do know that the principle of fair (if not precisely equal) shares for all children was widely endorsed. One prosperous citizen from North Africa boasts on his tombstone that he divided up his property among his children before his death and was careful to treat his daughter and his daughter-in-law equally with gifts of gold, silver, and clothing. Murdia made all her children equal heirs, though with a prior legacy to the son of her first marriage which reflected what she had received from her late husband.[118] A testator from Oxyrhynchus in the late third century left

---

[112] *D* 28.2.13 pr.   [113] *D* 36.1.59.2, 31.77.12; cf. Johnston, *Roman law of trusts* 156 ff.
[114] *D* 31.88.16; cf. Johnston, *Roman law of trusts* 175–6.
[115] *D* 31.77 pr.   [116] *D* 5.2.13.   [117] e.g. *D* 10.2.39.1.
[118] *CLE* 51; *CIL* 6.10230 = *FIRA* iii.70.

his five children as heirs. To the two daughters (one already married) he also legated their dowries. His wife, along with a guardian, was to take care of the property of the three children who were still under age. There was also a legacy to the wife (at least of farms already earmarked for her as equivalent of the dowry she had brought him).[119]

A wife might make her husband heir.[120] Like husbands, wives tied up property beyond the appointment of a first heir. One woman, in a case which caused a good deal of trouble, instituted her husband heir with a *fideicommissum* to leave the whole inheritance to their son on his own death. She then divorced the husband, recuperated her dowry, and died without changing her will, which meant that the son would eventually receive the dowry with the rest.[121] 'A woman put down her husband Seius as heir and substituted to him her foster-child Appia, with a *fideicommissum* to her heir to restore her inheritance to that same foster-child after his death, or, if the child died first, that he should restore the same inheritance to Valerianus, her brother's son.'[122] Here the husband owns the property for his lifetime, but it reverts either to the foster-child (replacing the child whom presumably she did not have) or to the wife's own kin. A child might be a woman's preferred heir, but she might fall back on her husband and brother if he died.[123] Sometimes husband and children inherited jointly.[124]

Appointment of husband or wife might be invalidated if the marriage was *iniustum*. Lawyers held that if a condemned adulterer married his alleged (even if uncondemned) partner, he could not validly make her his heir, nor she him.[125] Sometimes there was an asymmetry between the sexes. An administrator who married a provincial woman was presumed to have exploited her. Therefore, it was argued, she could be his heir but he could not be hers.[126] An emperor might intervene to deprive the husband of his inheritance if he had negligently and culpably contributed to his wife's death.[127]

The jurists seem to take more interest in children as heirs to their mothers than in husbands. But this may be partly because plans for young lives might more often go wrong and because more legal complications (such as guardianship of minors) might be involved. We hear, as we expect, of mothers naming children *in patria potestate* on condition that the father emancipated them. If the father agreed, it showed his respect for his wife's last wishes. This custom is not

---

[119] *FIRA* iii.51 (AD 276).   [120] *D* 28.7.20 pr., 35.2.6.
[121] *D* 36.1.80.9.   [122] *D* 32.41.12.   [123] *D* 34.4.30.4.
[124] *D* 20.4.19, including her children by a previous husband; 35.2.25.
[125] 34.9.13.   [126] *D* 34.9.2.1–2f.   [127] *D* 34.9.3.

necessarily a sign that the wife disapproved of her husband.[128] An instance occurred under Marcus Aurelius when the divorced wife of a Spartan and *praetorius* named Brasidas left a *fideicommissum* for property to be transferred to their children once they had become independent by their father's death. She had not expected Brasidas to emancipate them, but he did so and the emperor then allowed the children to claim the property at once. Here it is apparent that relations between the former wife and husband were strained. There is another variant on this situation when a wife left a *fideicommissum* to her husband to hand over the inheritance to her children by her previous, divorced husband when the latter died. The first husband emancipated them instead. Ulpian holds that this case is to be resolved in the same way as that of Brasidas' children.[129]

Women might seek to take care of various family members in different ways: we hear of one woman dividing the inheritance equally between two sons by one husband and one daughter by another and asking them to give a usufruct to her mother. Another leaves one son heir to five-twelfths, a daughter to three-twelfths, and another son to four-twelfths, and asks this last, if he should die without issue before the age of 20, to restore his inheritance to his brother and sister.[130] According to circumstances, heirs might be found among grandchildren, great grandchildren, parents, brothers, sisters, and even parents-in-law.[131] Foster-children are occasionally mentioned and freed slaves often. An owner could free his own slave and institute him heir, or could institute another person's slave (which enriched his owner, unless arrangements were made also for the slave to be freed). One's own freedmen, who took the same gentile name, were seen as substitute descendants.[132]

(*b*) *Legatarii*

Individual legacies may be as substantial as the residue left to the heir. They go to the same sort of people as do *hereditates*. (Apart from close family, this includes friends, dependants, communities, the emperor, and other eminent people.) Testators often wished to leave particular items to particular people. A specific legacy would be needed. One of the criteria was that something the testator had received from one relation should revert to that side of the family: we

---

[128] *D* 35.1.70; cf. 77 pr., 93 (grandchildren). Humbert (*Remariage à Rome* 225) finds 11 examples ('dans 11 cas exactement') or, more accurately, references to an instance or the possibility of a mother imposing this condition: *D* 5.3.58, 26.5.21.1, 29.7.6 pr., 32.50 pr, 35.1.70; *CJ* 3.28.25, 6.25.3, 8.54.5; Pliny *Epp.* 4.2.2; Suet. *Vit.* 6. He counts also *D* 36.1.23 pr. He takes it as a sign of hostility.

[129] *D* 36.1.22 pr.   [130] *D* 33.2.32.1, 36.1.80.5.   [131] *D* 30.104.7, 34.9.25.

[132] e.g. *CIL* 3.8143 = *CLE* 401: '"non fui maritus et reliqui liberos." servi domino.'

have seen this at work in an obvious form when Murdia leaves one son what had been his own father's property. A father might bequeath to his daughter her mother's property.[133] As we have seen, such instincts were often regulated by *fideicommissa* from the first testator.[134]

If children were heirs, a legacy might be left to the *coniunx*.[135] Legacies to husbands rarely provoke juristic discussion; legacies to wives are frequently mentioned. One reason may be that legacies to wives seem often to fall into specific categories or to be conditional. We find legacies on condition that the wife bore children. This condition clearly relates to the Augustan Law, for motherhood would qualify her to take the legacy. The children might be either those she bore to the testator after the will was made or those born in a subsequent marriage after his death.[136] She might be left a usufruct, to become ownership when she bore children and became able to take.[137] We also hear of the condition that she lived with the testator's child.[138] A general condition that she did not remarry was usually held unenforceable under the Augustan Law. But Julian held that if a husband left his wife an annuity on condition that she did not marry while the children were under age, the condition would be valid, since the husband was enjoining his wife to look after the children rather than to remain a widow. A condition 'as long as she does not marry Titius, Seius, or Maevius' (which might be imposed by a husband or another testator) was held to be valid, since she could marry anyone else and celibacy was not imposed on her. If the condition was 'if she marries Titius', it was valid as long as Titius was a suitable match. If not, the condition was unenforceable and she could marry anyone, thanks to the law.[139]

The traditional categories into which many legacies to wives fit include restoration of her dowry (which would give her probably enough to support herself and, if necessary, to remarry) and various types of allowance.

(*i*) *Legacy of dowry* According to Labeo, it was customary for a husband to bequeath the dowry to his wife as a prior charge on his estate.[140] This gave the wife the advantage that the dowry would be paid over to her immediately.[141] Expenses might be deducted.[142] If a

---

[133] *D* 31.77.19.
[134] But *legata* and *fideicommissa* were distinguishable. See Johnston, *Roman law of trusts* 256ff.
[135] e.g. *FIRA* iii.47.28ff. (AD 142). See on all types of beneficiaries Boyer, 'La fonction sociale des legs d'après la jurisprudence classique'.
[136] *D* 35.1.25, ht 61, 62 pr.   [137] *D* 22.1.48.   [138] *D* 35.1.8.
[139] *D* 32.1.14 pr., 35.1.62.2, ht 63, 64. But Gaius upholds the condition: 32.14 pr.
[140] *D* 33.4.13.   [141] *D* 33.4.1.2.   [142] *D* 33.4.1.4.

husband instructed the heir to give his wife the Cornelian farm 'which she brought me as dowry', the legacy stood even if the farm had not been part of the dowry, for the name identified it sufficiently.[143] The dowry or money or property in lieu of the dowry could also be paid as an ordinary legacy.[144] All these types of legacy allowed the wife to obtain her dowry with less trouble and waste of time than would have been involved in an *actio rei uxoriae*. They also made possible a dodge by which the husband attempted to transfer his own property to his wife more quickly than usual, or when she was not qualified to receive so much under the law.

(*ii*) *Legacy of* uxoris causa parata In contrast to food rations, which the husband might provide for his wife to consume, these are relatively durable items, clothes, woollen, linen, or purple cloth, jewellery and accessories, gold, silver, vessels, slaves, horses, mules, litters, sedan-chairs, sleeping-carriages.[145] They were assigned to her rather than transferred as a gift.[146] They were procured for her (this includes purchase) or for a previous wife or a daughter, grand-daughter, or daughter-in-law and then handed over to her to use.[147] Naturally, if the husband then took the objects back or if there was a divorce, legacy of things procured for his wife was no longer valid.[148] They had to be things which were obtained for the wife to use rather than for joint use (by wife and husband: *communis usus*) or for general use (by other people as well: *promiscui usus*),[149] but this could be quite liberally interpreted: if it could be said that the husband was in the habit of, as it were, borrowing things from his wife so that they came under the heading of things in general use rather than things reserved for her, they could still be regarded as procured for her benefit.[150] Both *uxoris causa parata* and dowry could be taken out of the estate before the other legacies, and this was specifically allowed by the Falcidian Law.[151] A typical legacy to a wife might run 'mundum muliebrem omnem, ornamenta et quidquid vivus dedi donavi eius causa comparavi confeci, id omne dari volo' '(I will that all her *mundus muliebris*, ornaments, and everything of whatever description that I gave during my lifetime or donated or procured or made for her be given [to my wife]').[152] Here the husband confirms the gifts which he had made to his wife, legates everything he had procured for

---

[143] *D* 35.1.40.4; cf. Just. *Inst.* 2.20.15.   [144] Details in Corbett 188ff.
[145] *D* 32.45, ht 49 pr., 58, 60.2, 78.6, 100.2, 34.2.2, ht 10, 13, 23.2, 34.1–2.
[146] For the contrast see *D* 32.33.1, 34.2.13.
[147] *D* 32.47, ht 49.3, 6.
[148] *D* 32.48, ht 49.6, 34.2.2.   [149] *D* 32.45.   [150] *D* 32.49.2.
[151] *D* 33.4.17 pr., 35.2.81.2.   [152] *D* 34.2.13, cf. 32.2.100.2.

her use, and adds the specific items (which might fall into the other categories too) of her *ornamenta* and *mundus*.

(*iii*) *Legacy of toilet articles and valuables* Various articles which might be bequeathed as part of the *uxoris causa parata* might equally form a separate bequest. Legacies of jewellery and other feminine luxuries were often appropriate. The *mundus muliebris* and *ornamenta* are often linked, but are distinguished as follows:

Feminine ornaments are those with which a woman is adorned, for example ear-rings, bracelets, armbands, rings (apart from signet-rings), and everything which is procured for no other purpose than to adorn the body. This category also includes gold, gems, and stones, which have in themselves no other use. Women's toilet equipment is what is used to make a woman better groomed. It includes mirrors, pots, unguents, unguent-containers, and anything similar, such as washing-vessels and storage-chests. The following are categorized as *ornamenta*: fillets, turbans, half-turbans, a head-dress, a pin with a pearl of the sort which women are accustomed to have, nets, woven accessories for the hair. A woman can be groomed, but not adorned, as commonly happens when women have groomed themselves by washing at the baths, but have not adorned themselves. Or the opposite can happen, as when someone rises from sleep and adorns herself but does not wash. (*Digest* 34.2.25.10, Ulpian *xliv ad Sabinum*)

Ulpian performs very creditably with these feminine arcana. Some of the items in *mundus muliebris* might have considerable value, for the material might be silver. A will might leave the *mundus* to one legatee and the silver to another: in such instances silver basins and ewers and such would count as part of the former.[153] A husband might bequeath to his wife all her *mundus muliebris* and *ornamenta*, everything he had provided for her, and everything he had given her, or her toilet equipment and ornaments, with clothes and the gold and silver he had procured for her.[154] Legacy of precious metals had seemed natural as early as Cicero. He argues that a legacy of silver included any coin left in the house.[155] Such legacies left house and lands untouched.

(*iv*) *Legacy of stores* As Dumont has pointed out, it is also typical of Roman recognition of the husband's duty to provide for his wife's needs that legacy of *penus*, stores including food, 'everything which human beings eat', was usual.[156] It was defined by Mucius Scaevola and later writers as things to eat and drink used by the *paterfamilias*,

---

[153] *D* 34.2.1, 19.8. [154] *D* 32.100.2, 34.2.13.
[155] *Top*. 13, cf. 16.
[156] 'Les revenues de la dot en droit romain' 29–31; Cic. *ND* 2.66.

his wife, children, their attendants and animals.[157] Early lawyers had a field-day adding to this list. For instance, Aelius Catus (*pace* Q. Mucius Scaevola) included incense and candles, and Servius Sulpicius added writing-paper and unguents; some thought that fuel to cook the food was included.[158] There was some argument about the status as eatables of honey and spices but none about vinegar—unless of course it was kept for putting out fires. Labeo did not deny that mackerel in their brine were victuals.[159] Containers which were absolutely essential to hold the food and drink were included.[160] Supplies intended for slaves and animals who worked on farms rather than in personal attendance on the family were excluded at least by Mucius.[161] If the testator traded in such provisions, then the legacy was limited to a year's supply.[162] Rather than leave his wife all the stores which he had at the time of his death, the testator might tell the heir to give her a certain quantity of *penus* as an annual allowance.[163] Such legacies were not, of course, confined to wives.[164]

(*v*) *Other legacies* The furniture of a house, with or without the house or the right to live in it, might also be bequeathed to a wife.[165] A husband wishing his wife's way of life to continue as unchanged as possible might bequeath 'that part of the house in which we were accustomed to dwell'. Did that mean just the bedrooms? No, for it was shown that husband and wife had used the whole house, without letting any rooms. The wife received the whole house in which the couple and staff had lived.[166]

Another way of securing continuity for the wife as long as she lived was to bequeath her a usufruct of a house, which would then automatically revert to the husband's heir on her death. Such arrangements could include all sorts of property, such as farms or slaves.[167] Cicero seems to regard it as normal for a wife to inherit a life interest in her husband's entire estate. M. Fulcinius the banker left his son heir, but gave his wife a usufruct together with the son. This was a great honour and pleasure to the wife, who intended to make the son her own heir. But unfortunately he died young, leaving a male heir, but silver to his wife and a major legacy to his mother.[168] As we have seen, the Augustan legislation allowed a *coniunx* to take a usufruct of one-third of the estate and to acquire full ownership if she (or he)

---

[157] Gell. 4.1, esp. 17; D 33.9.3 pr.   [158] Gell. 4.1.20, 22; D 33.9.3.9, 10.
[159] D 33.9.3.1 ff., ht 5.1.   [160] D 33.3.11, ht 4 pr.   [161] D 33.9.3.6–7.
[162] D 32.60.2, Alf., 33.9.4.2.   [163] D 33.9.1.   [164] D 33.9.7.
[165] D 33.10.8, ht 10, 13.   [166] D 32.33 pr.
[167] Cic. *Top*. 21; D 33.2.32.2; cf. Humbert, *Remariage à Rome* 233 ff.
[168] Cic. *Caec*. 11–12; cf. *Top*. 17. See Frier, *The Rise of the Roman jurists. Studies in Cicero's pro Caecina* 13 ff.; Crook 'Women in Roman succession' 77.

subsequently had children. We also hear of wives leaving usufructs to their husbands, for instance of property which had been part of the dowry.[169]

Annual allowances (*annua*) were also legated to wives. Ten *aurei* is the sum given in one text, and in another the same amount as when the husband was alive, with an immediate cash gift of one hundred.[170] An allowance paid to the wife might also be intended for the education of a minor child.[171]

It was often considered that, even if the bulk of the estate went elsewhere, the honour of being named in the will was due to the *coniunx* as a guarantee of the testator's continued good opinion (*iudicium*). Fulcinius paid a great compliment to his widow. Murdia left a certain sum to her husband (who automatically retained her dowry), so that he enjoyed *honos iudicii*. Pontianus left his wife some linen—an insult according to Apuleius.[172] In the wills quoted in the *Digest* a courteous and affectionate tone and references to the beneficiary's deserts demonstrate propriety.[173]

Our information often suggests that legacies were used to 'top up' the wife's wealth so that she would be well taken care of. Another man, who left his under-age son as heir, gave his wife a prior legacy of her dowry and added legacies of jewellery and slaves and a sum of ten gold pieces.[174] It may well be assumed that she would live with the son.

(c) Appeals against undutiful wills

According to Ulpian complaints against undutiful wills were frequent between parent and child. But it was not worth while for relations beyond the degree of brother or sister to attempt to prove in the courts that they had been unjustly excluded.[175] The plaintiff needed to show that the will had been made without due regard for family ties, 'non ex officio pietatis', and successful appeals were often made by children on the grounds that they had been disinherited or passed over by mistake. In the second century complaints could be brought against a mother's will as well as a father's.[176] A parent could also complain about a child's will, 'for even though the inheritance of children is not owed to parents because parents want children and have a natural love for them, yet when the natural order of death is upset property ought to be left to parents as much as to children out of a sense of duty'.[177] Gaius assigns one particular cause for fathers to pass over children unjustly: 'they usually do this, passing a malignant

[169] D 31.34.7.   [170] D 33.1.5, ht 10.2.   [171] D 33.1.21.5.
[172] CIL 6.10230 = FIRA iii.70; Apul. Apol. 97.
[173] e.g. D 34.2.32.4, ht 35 pr., 36.   [174] D 31.88.7.   [175] D 5.2.1.
[176] D 5.2.2–6; cf. Humbert, Remariage à Rome 191 ff.   [177] D 5.2.15 pr.

judgment on their own blood, because they have been corrupted by the blandishments or promptings of stepmothers.'[178] The rest of the title does not focus on stepmothers or stepfathers. We hear of inheritances going to unspecified outsiders and to other children or grandchildren, and of complaints brought by children no doubt accidentally excluded, such as *postumi* or children thought to be dead.[179] Gaius' generalization (which was probably diluted by further remarks in its original context) is too sweeping and has a strong flavour of the 'stepmother topos'. What is clear is that the Romans were on their guard against the danger that fathers would be unfair to children of an earlier marriage because of the influence of a second wife, especially if she bore children of her own. It is not so clear that injustice because of the remarriage of parents was widespread.[180] Instances are occasionally attested: we hear of these because the injustice was reversed.[181]

If it was not worth while for relatives beyond siblings in the second degree to complain of wills, clearly it was useless for a husband to complain against his wife's will or vice versa, since husband and wife came after blood-relations in the sixth degree.

Putting the evidence of *hereditates* and *legata* together, Humbert has analysed the *Digest* evidence provided by Scaevola, Papinian, and Modestinus as if it were statistical.[182] He finds 72 instances where the wife benefits by her husband's estate as heir or legatee. In 39 of these cases steps are taken to protect the interests of children: in 10 the method is by *fideicommissum* that the wife shall pass on the property. In 33 nothing is heard of the children and Humbert postulates that there were none. The husband benefits in 21 instances, in 12 of which the interests of children are secured. In 9 instances the husband has full power over what he takes; children are known in 5 of these. Humbert finds little difference of treatment between husband and wife. By reason of the nature of the *Digest*, such a statistical approach is invalid, particularly when only three jurists are used. Moreover, the information given by Humbert is not fully reliable.[183] Erudite and interesting though his discussion is, he does not succeed in proving his thesis that there was a widespread danger of injustice to the children of a first marriage. Rather, the evidence which he cites tends to show that the Romans were sensitive

---

[178] *D* 5.2.4. The style of the extract has aroused suspicion. See Humbert, *Remariage à Rome* 196.   [179] *D* 5.2.6 pr., ht 13 pr., 14, 16 pr., 19, 23 pr., 27.4.

[180] On the topos see Jer. *Epp.* 54.15.4: 'omnes comoediae et mimographi et commune rhetorum loci in novercam saevissimam declamabunt'; Humbert, *Remariage à Rome* 198–9; Noy, 'Wicked stepmothers and unjust wills'.

[181] VM 7.7.4; Pliny *Epp.* 6.33.   [182] *Remariage à Rome* 208 ff.

[183] For instance, of the four *annua* (p. 210 n. 12) two are left to the child, not the wife.

to such a possibility and that the legal and moral safeguards of children's interests were effective.

4. Conclusions

A sense of the identity of interest of husbands and wives emerges from such statements as that of the man who left his daughter as heir, with her son as substitute, and wrote, 'I leave 200 gold pieces to Lucius Titius my brother's son, my son-in-law. I know he will be content with this legacy, since by making my daughter and grandson heirs to my entire estate, I have arranged that he will share all of it with them. I commend them to one another.'[184] Unfortunately, the wife divorced the husband, so the father's expectations came to nothing. But the sharing by mother and son presumably worked. We have many instances of conscientious attempts to strike a proper balance between duty to *coniunx* and to children. As nowadays, particular care might be taken when second marriage was involved, with the possible clash of interest between children of the first marriage and a second *coniunx* and perhaps more children. For instance, a woman who was remarrying arranged that her two sons should be able to recover the dowry she was giving to her second husband. When one of the sons died she changed the arrangement and asked the survivor to leave half to the husband.[185] Apuleius claims that when Pudentilla married him, after rearing the sons of her first marriage, she arranged that all her dowry should revert to them, unless she had another child. If she did have one surviving child by Apuleius, then he or she was to inherit half, leaving the rest to the elder sons.[186]

It would often be assumed that a husband could trust his wife to look after her children's interests. This might lead a testator to be too trusting.

Item Marcus imperator rescripsit verba, quibus testator ita caverat, 'non dubitare se, quodcumque uxor eius cepisset, liberis suis redditturam', pro fideicomisso accipienda. Quod rescriptum summam habet utilitatem, ne scilicet honor bene transacti matrimonii, fides etiam communium liberorum decipiat patrem, qui melius de matre praesumpserat: et ideo princeps prudentissimus et iuris religiosissimus cum fideicommissi verba cessare animadverteret, eum sermonem pro fideicommisso rescripsit accipiendum. (*Digest* 31.67.10, Papinian *xix quaestionum*)

So the emperor Marcus laid down in a rescript that when the testator stated that 'he did not doubt that his wife would return to his children whatever she had taken' his words should be taken as a *fideicommissum*. This rescript is

---

[184] *D* 36.1.80.8–9.   [185] *D* 32.37.4.
[186] Apul. *Apol.* 91 fin.–92 init. On the textual question of her age, ibid. 89.

extremely useful in ensuring that the honour due to a well-conducted marriage and the trust established by their having children in common should not lead the husband mistakenly to assume that the mother will do what he expects. So the emperor, who was far-sighted and scrupulous about the law, when he observed that the proper wording of a *fideicommissum* had not been observed, laid down that the expression should be treated as a *fideicommissum*.

The passage is eloquent for the normal assumptions about the good faith of widowed mothers, based on their conduct as wives.

Despite the tradition that a second wife or husband could turn a parent against children of the first marriage or cause favouritism towards the new family, there is evidence for an atmosphere of trust. The rhetorical scenarios about stepmothers poisoning young children or seducing stepsons give a lurid and no doubt improbable picture of the home life of a man who married again after the death or divorce of his first wife. There might, if the divorce was not *bona gratia*, be hard feelings towards a surviving ex-wife, but no reason why these should affect his attitude towards the children, who, if they were young, probably continued to reside chiefly with him. The risk of the alienation of the divorced wife from her first family might tend to be greater, especially if she had a numerous family by a second husband. But affection and close contact are not the only factors involved. Duty and equity were expected to control the testamentary dispositions of a parent, unless the child was demonstrably undutiful.[187] Even when a first marriage was broken by divorce, the ex-wife might be trusted with her own children, as Livia was by Nero. In their wills fathers trusted mothers and stepmothers indifferently with looking after children under 25.[188]

Praelegatio allowed pieces of property to be taken out of the estate and legated to people who were among the heirs. This has been shown to have been used when a parent wished to ensure that children received the property of his or her dead *coniunx*. So a woman who had been heir to her husband asked her two sons to take everything which had come to her by her husband's will.[189] Julius Phoebus appointed as heirs two children, Phoebus and Heraclia, by one wife and one, Polycrates, by another. He gave them equal shares, but asked Polycrates to take a certain estate for himself and in exchange give his share of the whole to his brother and sister. He also gave a *fideicommissum* to the first two that if either of them died

---

[187] See the full and convincing discussion of Dixon, *RM* 51 ff.
[188] For trust in mothers see *D* 31.67.10 (with Johnston, *Roman law of trusts* 161–2); *D* 33.1.21.2, 36.1.59.2, ht 76.1, 36.2.26.2; stepmother: 33.1.21.2.
[189] *D* 31.88.2; cf. 32.34.2; Humbert, *Remariage à Rome* 254 ff.

childless, he or she should restore his share to the survivors or survivor, except what had come from the mother or grandparents. This obviously means that the maternal property of the elder children (which had passed through the hands of their father) was not to go to the stepbrother. A document was also left with Polycrates' mother, to be opened only if her son died under age: this no doubt dealt with his share. Or a father told his daughter to take her mother's property, or picked out two out of several children who were his heirs and gave them their grandmother's property. These instances too can perhaps be explained by supposing that the father had children by more than one wife.[190] But other reasons of sentiment no doubt came into play. A mother might leave a *fideicommissum* that all her jewellery, gold, silver, and personal clothing should not be sold but kept for her daughter. When a woman leaves her 'darling daughter' all her feminine ornaments, gold and other feminine accessories, we may perhaps assume that she was the only daughter. Such mothers are presumably concerned that their personal treasures shall be kept in the family and continue to be used and appreciated.[191]

The testator's perceptions of what was proper would be measured by others in accordance with their perceptions. Pliny's letter on the death of Domitius Tullus is a *locus classicus*. Tullus had encouraged outsiders to hope for inheritances, but in his will he unexpectedly appointed his brother's daughter, his own adoptive daughter, as heir and left legacies to grandchildren and a great granddaughter. Pliny attacks the legacy-hunters for complaining that their hopes had been disappointed, as if Tullus were not a father, grandfather, and great grandfather. Besides, he was merely restoring his wealth to the daughter, since it had come from her maternal grandfather, who had wanted it to go straight to her and not to her natural father, but whose plans had been neatly frustrated by the two Domitii. But despite his previous dishonourable behaviour, Tullus redeemed himself by writing a will dictated by *pietas*, *fides*, and *pudor* (duty, faith, and conscience). He showed appreciation to all his relations by marriage, including his excellent wife, who had married him late, nursed him in his old age, and was left beautiful villas and a large sum of money. The will generated much talk. Pliny is no doubt expressing opinions which would be generally accepted: a testator's first duty was to blood-relations if they existed. Provision should be made for the maintenance of the wife in suitable style, but ancestral property should as far as possible be kept for the lineage. Bequests to *affines* were a mark

---

[190] *D* 36.1.83, 31.77.19, 33.7.2 pr.; Humbert, *Remariage à Rome* 258 ff.
[191] *D* 34.2.16, ht 32.4, cf. 15, where the motive is unfathomable.

of proper respect and it was always proper to mention friends, either for bequests or as reversionary heirs (a mark of honour even though they had little chance of succeeding).[192]

If there were no children or close kin, the wife's moral claims against *externi heredes* were felt to be strong in the classical period. Even practices of dubious legal validity which secured her the inheritance might be connived at.[193] Papinian held that when a wife, during her last illness, changed her mind and wanted to write codicils cutting her husband out of her will, it was normal and permissible for him to persuade her to change her mind, placating her with affectionate talk, *maritali sermone*.[194] If there were children of a marriage, it was expected that their fortunes should incorporate property from both sides of the family.[195] If the couple had been equally matched in the first place, the *bona paterna* and the *bona materna* might be in equilibrium. But the chances of family composition (how many qualified heirs survived?), the good fortune of some individuals in increasing their fortunes from external sources, by inheritance from outsiders, by investments, or by war and administration, and delicate considerations of need, merit, and sentiment ensure that the pattern of the flow of wealth was hardly ever neatly symmetrical.

[192] Pliny *Epp.* 8.18; Dixon, *WRW*, forthcoming.
[193] Quint. *Inst.* 9.2.73–4.   [194] *D* 29.6.3.
[195] Cf. Wallace-Hadrill, 'Family and inheritance in the Augustan marriage laws' esp. 64–5.

12
Domus

As for feast of reason and for flow of soul, is it not a question whether any such flows and feasts are necessary between a man and his wife? How many men can truly assert that they ever enjoy connubial flows of soul, or that connubial feasts of reason are in their nature enjoyable? But a handsome woman at the head of your table, who knows how to dress, and how to sit, and how to get in and out of her carriage—who will not distress her lord by her ignorance, or fret him by her coquetry, or disparage him by her talent—how beautiful a thing it is! For my own part, I think Griselda Grantly was born to be the wife of a great English peer.

(Trollope, *Framley Parsonage*, chapter 48)

Women have their uses for historians. They offer relief from warfare, legislation, and the history of ideas; and they enrich the central theme of social history, if and when enough evidence is available.

(Syme, *The Augustan Aristocracy* 168)

We have discussed people's plans for an ideal or acceptable match, the ideology of the good wife or husband, and the evidence for how people thought about each other's behaviour in real life and dispositions of property aimed at security and continuity. We shall go on to discuss the breakdown and the end of marriage. All this is peripheral to the central relationship and daily conduct of the two *coniuges* during their married life. That is precisely the area which is most difficult to investigate. Since we may observe the same phenomenon in our understanding of the marriages of those nearest to us, as well as in literary, historical, or sociological accounts of contemporary or comparatively recent marriages in our own society, and since the lack of suitable sources on this area of life in the Roman period is notorious, no apology is needed for the tentative nature of this chapter. I shall attempt merely to indicate the results of modern scholarship which give us the vital demographic and physical background to Roman family life, to suggest lines of further inquiry, and to assemble some fragments of evidence about the banalities of everyday life and rarer crises and the circumstances and conduct of some upper-class *coniuges*.

1. Demography

(a) Mortality and age at marriage

The relationship of husband and wife was vitally affected by demographic patterns unfamiliar to twentieth-century Westerners. The current view is that we may put Roman life expectancy at birth at between 20 and 30. Model life-tables are constructed for a stable population. It is agreed that the population of Roman citizens in the late Republic and early Empire was not stable. But the tables will give a rough idea. If we adopt the hypothesis of a life expectancy at birth of 25, then there is high infant mortality. One-third of children die before the age of 1, and half before the age of 10. Of those who reach 10, about one in three live to 60 and about one in seven to 70.[1] As we know from our unsystematic literary evidence, the death of a child *sponsus* or *sponsa* was not a remote possibility, nor was that of a couple's own children. Cicero quotes a passage from Euripides on the human condition: many people have to bury their children and then produce more. Fronto tells us that this was precisely what happened to him: he lost five children and each time a child died there was no survivor. So he and his wife always produced the next child while still mourning for its predecessor. Yet, says Seneca, so many die young, but we still think about how our infants will grow up to take the *toga virilis*, to serve in the army, to inherit our property.[2]

A high percentage of the population would not reach an age to marry, and of those who did many women would not survive to the end of what might have been their child-bearing years and many men would not reach 50.[3] In a modern stable population where females' life expectancy at birth is 25, of an original cohort of 100,000 females born, about 46,000 would reach 15, about 43,000 live to 20. So well under half of all girl babies would reach the age which Romans considered normal for first marriage. But a girl who survived to 10 had an average expectation of life of forty more years and at 20 of

---

[1] Saller, '*Patria potestas* and the stereotype of the Roman family' 12, based on Coale, Demeny, and Vaughan, *Regional model life tables and stable populations*, South Level 3.

[2] Cic. *Tusc.* 3.59; Fronto *de nepote amisso* 2 (Loeb ii.222 ff.); Sen. *ad Marciam* 9.2; *Rem.* 13: 'ducuntur ex plebeia domo inmatura funera, ducuntur ex regia. Non est idem fati ordo, qui et aetatis.'

[3] Coale, Demeny, and Vaughan, *Regional model life tables and stable populations*, South Level 3. Cf. Hopkins, *DR* 72, for male survival rates.

thirty-seven, so that it would be reasonable for a Roman girl who survived the perils of childhood to look forward with some confidence to marriage and child-bearing. Approximately 27,000 of the hypothetical cohort, just over a quarter of all females born, would reach 50, by which time they can be regarded as having completed and survived their child-bearing years. About 20,000 would survive to 60.

Among males in the same model population, about 44,000 would reach 20, about 40,000 25, about 37,000 30, 26,000 50 and 18,000 60. A boy who reached 10 could expect another forty years of life and at 20 his expectation is another thirty-three, at 30 twenty-eight.

None of the ancient data, whether epitaphs (which provide a profile of commemorative practice rather than a demographic portrait of an actual population) or jurists' theories of mortality rates, or specific samples of skeletal evidence, can generate statistics.[4] We lack average figures for the whole Roman Empire, or for the citizen population isolated from the rest, or for socio-economic classes or professions, or for specific cities, areas, or provinces. For Rome itself, as for other cities, it is reasonable to hold that general mortality rates were relatively high.[5]

High mortality can be compensated by high fertility, which is achieved when women's reproductive powers are utilized as fully as possible. The age of marriage of women is strongly correlated with fertility (where pre-marital chastity is general or where pre-marital pregnancy is a prelude to a wedding). The age of marriage of men has some effect on fertility. For our present purposes, the age of marriage of each sex is relevant because of its effect on the individual's experience of life and on the relationship between *coniuges*, and its probable effect on the shape of the family.

A recent study has taken account of all epitaphs set up in the Latin West by a commemorator whose relationship was identified to males whose age was attested and over 10. This demonstrates that the normal age of marriage for men in those classes in society which could afford epitaphs falls in the late twenties or early thirties. Of the 128 men in the sample who died between 15 and 19, most were commemorated by parents and none by wife or child. In the age-group from 20 to 24 (total 108) the proportion of parents commemorating goes down (no doubt because of the increase in parental mortality) but still only 2 were commemorated by wives. Wives start appearing as commemorators for husbands of 25 and over and preponderate

[4] Cf. Frier, 'Roman life expectancy: Ulpian's evidence'; id., 'Roman life expectancy: the Pannonian evidence'; Hopkins, 'Graveyards for historians'.
[5] Brunt, *IM* 133 ff.

overall for husbands of 30 and over. Since in most areas commemoration by wives was apparently preferred where possible, it is
reasonably deduced that most of those men under 25 who are
commemorated by parents had no wives.[6]

Using the same method and comparable data, it has been demonstrated that women begin to be commemorated by husbands from the
age of about 15, but increasingly from the late teens onwards. An age
in the late teens seems typical for first marriage of girls as attested by
inscriptions in the Western Empire. (The epigraphic evidence ignores
those too poor to put up inscriptions and those who had not acquired
the Roman 'epigraphic habit', so it does not reflect the total population.) In Rome itself, 'Parents seem well in evidence until the early
twenties; husbands first appear at about age 15, but do not take over
until the mid-twenties.'[7] Women tended to marry after 15, men after
25. Women would then be expected to be physically mature and
about to enter on their years of peak fertility. Men would perhaps be
economically well established. (The labourers who would reach a
peak of their earning-power at a rather younger age are unlikely to
afford an inscription.) The age for women fits well with that at which
Augustus encouraged members of the wealthier classes to achieve
parenthood: 20.

This pattern of relatively early marriage for women and relatively
late marriage for men corresponds with the 'Mediterranean marriage
pattern' distinguished by students of more recent epochs.[8] It is
contrasted with the north-western European pattern, in which both
sexes tended to marry in the mid- to late twenties, and with the
pattern of teenage marriage for both sexes frequently found in
eastern Europe and the Balkans.[9] The consequence of the Roman
pattern is that the age-gap between husband and wife in a first
marriage would tend to be about a decade. The effect of this would
often be to emphasize the husband's authority and the difference in
tastes and maturity.[10] However, it is a gap which in societies such as
modern Britain (where a slighter age-difference is normal) wives who
are ten or fifteen years younger than their husbands are often able to
obliterate or exploit. A much more important difference is created

[6] Saller, 'Men's age at marriage and its consequences in the Roman family'. He omits the city
of Rome. On commemorative practice see MacMullen, 'The epigraphic habit in the Roman
Empire'.
[7] Shaw, 'The age of Roman girls at marriage: some reconsiderations'. I agree that the
inscriptions of Rome disproportionately reflect freed slaves of aristocratic households.
[8] Laslett, 'Family and household as work group and kin group: areas of traditional Europe
compared'. The Roman pattern does not correspond to the later Mediterranean type in all the
features conveniently listed by Laslett (pp. 526–7).
[9] Hajnal, 'European marriage patterns in perspective', and 'Two kinds of pre-industrial
household formation system'.   [10] e.g. Pliny *Epp.* 1.16.6; Quint. *Inst.* 6 pr. 6.

when a man, previously married or long a bachelor, marries a young girl at her first marriage. Here the gap might be as much as between father and daughter or even grandfather and granddaughter. Pompey and Julia, Cicero and Publilia, Pliny and Calpurnia are instances. The disparity may also occur even when the woman is not at her first matrimonial experience. Julia, widowed at 16, next married Agrippa, who was a contemporary of her father. There seems to have been a clear preference among middle-aged men who lost a previous wife by death or divorce to seek a match with a woman near the beginning of her child-bearing years and consequently at the height of her physical attractiveness.

The second effect of this pattern is to create a considerable generation-gap between most fathers and their children.[11] The gap between mothers and their eldest children would normally be shorter, though the ancients observed that sometimes a woman's fertility was not demonstrated until several years after the beginning of a marriage.[12] A stepmother could be as young as her stepchildren or even younger, as Publilia was younger than Tullia. Hence the phobia, or at least rhetorical theses, about adultery between stepmother and stepson.

Some couples were closely matched in age. This seems more likely to happen if the woman was at her second or subsequent marriage and the man at his first. Presumably the ages would have been close if young Quintus Cicero (born late 67 or early 66) had married a divorcee in 44.[13] The woman might even in such marriages be slightly older. Pomponia was almost the same age as her brother (born 110), which suggests she was older than Q. Cicero (born c.104/102) and that she had been married before she married him in c.68.[14] Approximate equality also occurs when both had been previously married, as when Livia, almost 20, married Octavian, aged 24. But a considerable age-gap still seems to be the usual pattern. Mark Antony (born c.83) becomes the second husband of Octavia (born 69) in 40 (after previous marriages perhaps to Fadia and certainly to Antonia and Fulvia).

The most eligible women of the imperial family and senatorial class sometimes married younger than the normal age.[15] Augustus' daughter Julia was born in 39 BC and married in 25, at about 14. Agrippina

---

[11] Saller, 'Patria potestas and the stereotype of the Roman family' 14ff., 'Men's age at marriage and its consequences in the Roman family' 30.

[12] Sen. Contr. 2.5.8, 14; Decl. min. 251.6.   [13] Cic. A 15.29.2.

[14] Nep. A 17.1; Cic. A 1.6.2.

[15] See Hopkins, 'The age of Roman girls at marriage', for these and for a group of 145 epitaphs which attest early ages, with a mode of 12 to 15.

the Younger, born in AD 15 or 16, married in 28. Claudius' daughter Octavia, who was born by AD 40, married in 53. But Antonia the Younger, born in 36 BC, did not marry until 16. Some women at least probably married before the legal minimum age of 12. Dynastic considerations also sometimes hastened the marriage of men in the imperial family. Julia's first husband Marcellus, married in 25, had been born in 42 BC. Nero, born in AD 37, was about 16 when he married Octavia. Antonia's Drusus, however, was near the newly set senatorial norm at around 22. Such an age was encouraged by the privileges extended by Augustus to office-seekers and heirs and legatees who were parents. To take fully under wills of testators who were not close kin, a man of 25 needed to be a father. Before Augustus' law the senatorial norm seems to have been in the late twenties, at about the time a young man sought office in Rome.[16] Both in the Julio-Claudian family and in the senatorial aristocracy of the Principate in general, the age-gap between husband and wife in a first marriage might be narrower than in the broader population above the poorer classes. Among the labouring classes, men (if they married at all) might marry younger than was usual among the more affluent, but women later (when they had attractions of strength and perhaps savings).[17]

The Augustan marriage legislation will have tended to reduce the gap in age between husband and wife if both were marrying for the first time, among the prosperous classes affected by its incentives. It is tempting to conjecture that a relationship will start out on more equal terms where the bride is about 18 and the bridegroom a mere three or four years older. Supposing, as women mature physically earlier than men, that, despite their lack of formal higher education and their more restricted social experience, their emotional maturity came earlier than to their more privileged brothers, we might think that a difference of three or four years at this stage of life meant that husband and wife met on almost equal terms.

Because the law probably lowered the age of marriage for upper-class men but not women, men who before might have died without marrying were now more likely to marry. There would be more men available for marriage. Nuptiality would increase for men. On the model life-tables, there would be just over 43,000 women and about

---

[16] Syme, 'Marriage ages for Roman senators', collects examples of precocious marriage for some patricians and plebeian *nobiles* and of deferral to quaestorian age for others.

[17] Cf. Brunt, *IM* 136 ff.; den Boer, 'Demography in Roman history: facts and impressions'. Shaw, 'The age of Roman girls at marriage' 42, suggests that the Christian inscriptions, which show a later age of marriage for women, document a class which previously had not had the epigraphic habit.

43,500 men aged 20, about 40,000 of each sex at 25, and about 37,000 at 30. So the sexes are nearly in balance. The table may suggest a rough idea of the greater proportion of men who might marry if their normal age at marriage dropped from the late twenties to the early twenties. Because virtually all women who reached marriageable age seem to have married, both before and after Augustus' law, a drop in men's age must have meant that more men were available for the same number of women. This should have increased the chances of swift remarriage for widows and divorcees. It should also have meant that men had to broaden their search to women they might previously have considered ineligible, for instance those in a lower social class than their own. It is tempting to connect this with Dio's statement that there was a shortage of well-born women and so Augustus allowed free-born (but non-senatorial) men to marry freedwomen: the shortage could have been created by his encouragement to men to marry younger. But for this to be right, one needs to rate Dio's accuracy and the percipience of Augustus' informants and drafters quite high.[18]

(b) Reproductivity

The child-bearing years of a woman are obviously far more tightly restricted than those during which a man may reproduce himself.[19] Unfortunately we lack the data which would allow us to judge the average fertility of a Roman woman who was married at 18 and continued married until after menopause. Because of high infant mortality, if a stable population was to be maintained each woman who survived to adulthood needed to bear five or six children.[20] But this approaches the average attested in highly fertile populations such as that of eighteenth-century Geneva.[21] The idealized peasant woman in Juvenal, recovering from childbirth, had three infants (and a slave child) playing around her as she watched over the saucepans in which supper was simmering for the bigger sons who worked in the fields. The peasant soldier Ligustinus' wife is portrayed as having six sons and two daughters surviving. We are told by our sources of women of conspicuous fertility: Cornelia Gracchi who bore twelve and reared three; Agrippina the Elder, of whose nine babies six grew up.[22] Claudia Fortunata, who lived to the age of 50, is commemorated as

[18] 54.16.2. For the effect of a fall in the age of marriage of men see Habbakuk, 'The economic history of modern Britain' 152 ff.
[19] Pliny NH 7.61–2. Cf. Amundsen and Diers, 'The age of menopause in classical Greece and Rome'. [20] Garnsey and Saller, REESC 138.
[21] Cf. Hopkins, DR 100 ff. At Crulai between 1674 and 1742, the mean number of children for a woman married at 20 was eight. See Henry, 'The population of France in the eighteenth century' 450. [22] Livy 42.34.3–4; VM 7.1.1; Pliny NH 7.57.

the mother of twelve.[23] Pliny assures us that Eutychis of Tralles (honoured in an inscription in the Theatre of Pompey) had thirty children, of whom twenty carried her to her pyre.[24] But surely even Cornelia and Fortunata appeared to contemporaries quite exceptional. Augustus set targets of three (or four or five) children to men and women in some contexts. These seem to have been thought of as relatively high. We have seen that children who died young allowed parents to count equivalences in terms of fractions. It is noteworthy that although a husband had more chances of achieving a higher number of children by serial marriages over his longer physical prime, a smaller number of children sufficed to gain him certain privileges (for example, two to enable a freedman to avoid *operae*, but four for a freedwoman to escape *tutela*). For many of the more generally useful privileges, one child sufficed. All this makes it hard to believe that Roman women achieved the *average* of six live births. Our literary evidence is undoubtedly poor on children who died soon after birth, on boys who died before they entered a public career, on girls at any age. We do not know the obstetrical history of any woman, even Cornelia or Agrippina. We do not know if Tullia had any pregnancies other than the two which produced the premature child (who presumably died almost immediately) and the boy Lentulus (who is unrecorded after the first few months of his life). We do not know if Terentia had any pregnancies or live-born children between Tullia, in the first half of the 70s, and young Marcus in 65. For very prominent men, emperors for instance, posterity is more likely to record children who died untimely, stillborn babies, and even the miscarriages of their wives. For men like Pliny or Tacitus, we may know that they married (Pliny three times) and had no surviving child. Most of the men and women of completed fertility of whom we know something from the literary record between the time of Cicero and that of Pliny had one, two, or three children who lived to adulthood. The evidence is that this was seen as typical. Germanicus (father of six surviving children) was remarkable. Pliny picks out Q. Metellus Macedonicus (consul 143), who had six children and eleven grandchildren (so the pattern did not continue in the next generation), and the free-born plebeian of Augustus' time, C. Crispinius Hilarus, father of eight (with twenty-seven grandchildren), as striking for their reproductive success.[25] It seems that better or more recent records were unknown to him. Numerous children scarcely ever appear in family groups in tomb inscriptions. This is only partly explicable by high mortality of infants and young children who might be commemorated separately.

---

[23] *AE* 1934.67, Algeria.   [24] Pliny *NH* 7.34.   [25] *NH* 7.59–60; cf. VM 7.1.1.

Nor (for what it is worth) do jurists see fit to discuss the succession of more than two or three children to their parents' estates or the need for testators to provide for the guardianship or support of more than one or two children. Shortly stated, the argument is that, even when we take into account the various inadequacies of our ancient evidence, it is still significant that our sources regard a total of twelve children born to a woman as exceptional and none as not unusual. Yet these two extremes should roughly balance each other out if six births are to be average. It seems unlikely that the prosperous classes of citizens represent a stable population which succeeded in reproducing itself. The difficulty of achieving replacement was particularly severe for the upper classes and the inhabitants of the city of Rome. Higher fertility might have been achieved by peasants. The citizen population was recruited from outside, from foreigners and enfranchised slaves, as well as from births.[26]

The children of Cornelia and Agrippina were all by one husband. Other women, such as Pompey's Mucia, Cato's Marcia, or Servilia the mother of Brutus, bore children to two successive husbands.[27] The most famous instance of a numerous progeny by multiple husbands is Vistilia's. She produced seven children in six marriages.[28] Like Marcia, Cato had children by two *coniuges*.[29] Antony was as productive as Vistilia: more than one by his alleged first wife Fadia, a daughter by Antonia, Antyllus and Iulus by Fulvia, two daughters by Octavia, not to mention three acknowledged children by Cleopatra.[30] In contrast, Caesar was married three times and had only one child (by his first wife); Agrippina the Younger bore a child to only the first of her three husbands (and that after many years of marriage).[31] Serial marriage did not ensure fecundity, any more than stable monogamy did.

The deliberate limitation of families has been effectively studied. Various contraceptive methods were recommended, but it was impossible to distinguish whether a woman failed to become pregnant because she was wearing a charm on her ankle or whether a pessary which did not on a particular occasion prevent impregnation would always be useless. It is unlikely that contraceptive devices were

[26] Cf. Brunt's conclusion that the free population of republican Italy failed to reproduce itself (*IM* 133) and the corresponding view of the élite of Hopkins and Burton (*DR* 74, 78 ff.).

[27] Mucia: Cn. and Sex. Pompeius and Pompeia by Pompey; a son by Scaurus, Marcia: a son and two daughters by Cato, others (who died young: Schol. ad Lucan 2.339) by Hortensius; Servilia: M. Brutus by Brutus (d. 78), three Juniae by D. Silanus.

[28] Syme, *RP* ii.805 ff.   [29] Young Cato and Porcia Bruti were borne by Atilia.

[30] Fadia: Cic. *Phil.* 2.3, 3.17, 13.23, *A* 16.11.1. See Bradley, 'Dislocation in the Roman family' 42 ff. Fulvia had three other children by her previous husbands Clodius and Curio.

[31] Agrippina: born AD 15, married Cn. Domitius Ahenobarbus 28, bore Nero 37; later married Crispinus and (49) Claudius (d. 54).

effective in preventing all conception for fertile couples, but the frequent use of pessaries might reduce the number of pregnancies, just as modern prophylactics do, though less reliably.[32] It seems impossible to prove whether or not the Romans practised *coitus interruptus*. Silence in the sources is consistent with the idea either being too familiar to mention or not generally known.[33] If the method was known, questions might still be raised about whether Romans would have thought it acceptable, if they felt that pleasure was sacrificed. Abstinence during the period at which conception was most likely would have been fairly effective. Unfortunately, since ancient scientists misdated this period to immediately after the end of the menses, the Romans could not have limited their families efficiently by periodic abstinence.[34] Neglect of wives because the husbands' attentions were diverted to women who could not bear them legitimate children is always a possibility, particularly in a slave-household. But such neglect was considered improper by society as well as by wives. Sleeping apart seems to have been unusual enough to provoke comment. What was later regarded as unilateral 'denial of conjugal rights' does not seem to have occurred to Romans as a likely factor in their failure to reproduce. Such denial would have logically led to divorce in pre-Christian Rome.[35]

Induced abortion was not sharply distinguished from contraception. Abortion might be effected by instruments or drugs.[36] The ancients were well aware of the risk of killing the mother as well as the foetus.[37] It was particularly feared that women would abort in order to deprive their husbands of offspring. Indeed, there seems to have been a phobia that women could control their own fertility secretly, either by contraception or by procuring abortions.[38] The most frivolous conceivable reason was most commonly ascribed: that women wanted to avoid damage to their figures.[39] The law took cognizance of

[32] Hopkins, 'Contraception in the Roman Empire'; cf. Eyben, 'Family planning in Graeco-Roman antiquity'.

[33] The Romans were well aware of all the ways in which a male achieves orgasm without vaginal penetration. The question whether they practised such methods with their wives in order to avoid procreation seems unanswerable.

[34] See Jones, 'Morbidity and vitality: the interpretation of menstrual blood in Greek science' 184 ff. In general, Blayney, 'Theories of conception in the ancient Roman world'.

[35] Jewish law and Solon of Athens established minimum standards of love-making by husbands (Plut. *Solon* 20, *Mor.* 769 A ff.). The greater freedom of Roman women to initiate divorce made such rules otiose in Rome.

[36] e.g. Ov. *Am.* 2.14.27–8. In general see Nardi, *Procurato aborto nel mondo greco romano*; Dickison, 'Abortion in antiquity'.   [37] e.g. Ov. *Am.* 2.13.1–2, 14.38.

[38] e.g. Cic. *Clu.* 32 ff. (cf. Quint. *Inst.* 8.4.11; *D* 48.19.39), 125; Ov. *Am.* 2.13.3, *F* 1.621 ff.; Tac. *A* 14.63.1; Juv. 6.594 ff.

[39] Ov. *Nux* 23–4, *Am.* 2.14.7. Taken seriously by, e.g. Hopkins (*DR* 94).

abortion when it defrauded people of their rights, for instance a
divorced or dead husband of his expected progeny, and when a third
party supplied a dangerous drug.[40]

It is impossible to establish whether or to what extent couples
attempted to limit the number of their children, or to space births, by
these means. It seems unlikely that any couple, or *coniunx*, aimed at
complete sterility.[41] Authors occasionally imply that Romans wanted
to limit their children, *numerum liberorum finire*.[42] But it is less clear
that they could achieve this by contraception or abortion.

Once born, unwanted children might be abandoned, normally in
the hope that they would be rescued and reared by someone else. This
practice avoided the risks to the mother associated with abortion, but
left her with the fatigues and dangers of pregnancy and childbirth. It is
attested for married couples of some degree of prosperity.[43] The
incidence of abandonment is said by our sources to have increased in
times of crisis. It has been held that in normal times daughters may
have been more likely than sons to be abandoned at birth and the
possibility has been demonstrated that citizen parents could have got
rid of a significant percentage of girls.[44] Abandoned children might be
brought up as free persons by the benevolent, but were more likely to
be reared as slaves and so removed (at least for a time) from the free
population. In either case they were normally lost to their family of
birth.[45] The impact on the parents of a decision to abandon a child,
especially if the decision was imposed by the father, can only be
imagined.

Natural checks on fertility also operated. Women cease to ovulate
for an indeterminate period after the birth of a child. This period is
normally lengthened by lactation. Women of the wealthier classes
(and sometimes slave-women in large households) often seem to have
handed their babies over to a wet-nurse, so for them this natural
period of infertility will have been curtailed.[46] The occasional separa-
tions of husband and wife, and particularly the long absences of

[40] *D* 40.7.3.16, 47.11.4, 48.8.8, 48.19.38.5, 39.
[41] An imaginary scenario: *Decl. min.* 327.4.
[42] Tac. *G* 19.5. It is a frequent charge by Christians against pagans.
[43] Boswell, '*Expositio* and *oblatio*: the abandonment of children in the ancient and medieval
family'; id., *The kindness of strangers. The abandonment of children in Western Europe from
late antiquity to the Renaissance* chs. 1, 2. The probable effect on the wife's emotions was
appreciated, e.g. Afran. *com.* 346–7: 'Non dolorum partionis veniet in mentem tibi | quos ‹tu›
misera pertulisti, ut partum proiceret pater?' ('Will the pains of childbirth not come to your
mind, which you, poor wretch, endured so that the father should cast out the child?').
[44] Harris, 'The theoretical possibility of extensive female infanticide in the Graeco-Roman
world'; cf. Golden, 'Demography and the exposure of girls at Athens', against Engels, 'The
problem of female infanticide in the Greco-Roman world'.
[45] See e.g. *D* 22.6.1.2, 25.3.4, 40.4.29.   [46] Bradley, 'Wet-nursing at Rome' 212.

republican husbands on provincial duties or military campaigns (which applied also to *milites gregarii*), must have spaced children.[47] I would not endorse the view that the availability of slave-women or any other type of sexual partner has much effect on the number of children a man gives his wife. We hear of amenorrhea as a problem even among the patients of the medical writers, who must have been the more prosperous classes and their servants. We have no means of guessing how many women in the poorer classes whose diet was inadequate or whose work was too heavy stopped ovulating. It has also been suggested that lead poisoning (from cooking-vessels and women's cosmetics) and hot baths (which would lower the sperm-count) severely reduced the fertility of both sexes. Gonorrhea is a more convincing factor, but not conclusively proven.[48]

In their perceptions of how people produced and reared children, ancient writers were affected by stereotypes. The rich were selfish and preferred not to incur the expense of establishing their children properly. Beautiful women preferred frivolity to motherhood. The poor could not afford to bring up their offspring.[49] Everyone feared to rear children under a tyrant. Then it was a happiness not to be a mother and women would abort children they had conceived or avoid conceiving altogether. Men would avoid marriage or at least paternity.[50] Under a despotism those who had never acknowledged children were fortunate and the grief of those who lost children was lessened.[51] Conversely, if a good prince ruled people would seek to have children, convinced that their future would be happy. Mothers would delight in their fertility and bear sons to serve in the army of a good emperor. Parents would expect freedom and security for their children.[52] Such generalizations spring in part from the commonplace that families were threatened by despots: no wife or virgin would be safe, so no man could trust in the continuity of his family.[53] It was a necessary deduction that *spes liberorum* would revive with good government. How far any of these generalizations were confirmed by observation of the deliberate increase or decrease in the number of children reared is highly doubtful.

Complaints that people deliberately chose not to produce or rear

---

[47] For *peregrinatio* cf. Sen. *Contr.* 2.5.14.

[48] Lead: critiques by Phillips, 'Old wine in old lead bottles: Nriagu on the fall of Rome'; Needleman and Needleman, 'Lead poisoning and the decline of the Roman aristocracy'. Baths: Krenkel, 'Hyperthermia in ancient Rome'; Gonorrhea: Needleman and Needleman, art. cit.; Grmek, *Diseases in the ancient Greek world* 144 ff.   [49] e.g. *CTh* 11.27.1.

[50] Sen. *Contr.* 2.5.2, 13 ff.; Pliny *Epp* 10.2.2–3. Sinful times in general might deter people from raising children: *Decl. min.* 327.4.   [51] Cic. *F* 4.5.3, 5.16.3; cf. *A* 10.4.5.

[52] Vell. 2.103.5; Sen. *Clem.* 1.13.5; Pliny *Pan.* 22.3, 26.5 ff., 27.1.

[53] Sen. *Contr.* 2.5.2. Contrast *Pan. lat.* 2.37.4, 3.13.3, 4.38.4.

children come from moralists, satirists, and rhetoricians. The emphasis in less tendentious sources is rather on the inability of people to become parents when they wished to do so or on the grief of those who lost children. Adoption, normally of adults and normally of males, remedied a man's lack of descendants. But, although a man might adopt a person with whom he already had a tie of kinship and affection, for instance a sister's son, the adoption itself did not fill the need for a child to love. The affection of both husband and wife was likely to find an object in their own household in *alumni*, children (sometimes foundlings) whom they chose to rear, and in the children of their slave-women, *vernae*.[54] The rich often had favourite slave-children, some of whom are called *delicia*.

As we mentioned above, there is a possibility that over the population as a whole there was a tendency to choose to abandon a fraction of the girl babies born. Many such girls would then, if rescued, not be brought up as free citizens. It is also sometimes suggested that girls, if reared, might be given a smaller share of available resources than boys. If food was short in a labouring family, the working man and boys might get a better diet. Although, no doubt, in the Roman population, as in all others known to us, more boys were born and the mortality of boys would in natural circumstances have been higher in childhood, the expected rough balance of the sexes in early adulthood would not have been achieved, since an abnormally high proportion of girls would have disappeared from the population. The sex ratio would show a preponderance of men.[55] We would therefore expect that the available women would be highly valued because of their scarcity. We would see a situation which has been termed 'women at a premium', in contrast to 'women at a discount'. 'Women at a premium' can mean that men pay bride-price instead of receiving dowries. This is not true for the classical period. On the other hand, the practice of giving substantial dowries does not, in the Roman context, prove that women were at a discount, if we are right in holding that dowries were not very high in relation to the donor's capital, that they were meant for the subsistence of the wife and often returned to her family or children, and therefore did not operate merely as an incentive to the bridegroom. It does not seem to me that any deductions can be made about the sex ratio from

[54] B. Rawson, 'Children in the Roman *Familia*'.

[55] On normal sex ratio at birth (102/106 males : 100 females) and the Roman male's greater chance of epigraphic commemoration (in his sample 135 : 100) see Hopkins, 'On the probable age structure of the Roman population' 260 ff. On the sex ratio in *alumni* and *vernae* inscriptions see Rawson, 'Children in the Roman *Familia*' 179–80, 191–2. The preponderance of males probably reflects the higher value set on them, which meant that boys were more likely to be regarded as *alumni* and to be commemorated in either group.

Roman economic practices, useful as such evidence can be in less complex societies.[56]

2. *Family and Household*

It has been demonstrated in recent work that the Romans regarded the 'nuclear family' as central to their experience.[57] That is, the mature male was expected to live with his wife and eventual children (up to the age at which the children moved away), independently of other close relatives. Sons moved out of the parental home for long periods of military service or study and perhaps, in the lower classes, to find work. Young men of the upper classes set up bachelor establishments in Rome. Marriage meant the founding of a new household, if this had not happened before. It was unusual for sons on marriage to bring their wives into the parental home, a system which may have obtained for landowners in earlier times. Daughters left the parental home on marriage, though not before. For both sexes, marriage was neo-local, unless the husband had already inherited the family house. Such, at least, was the way of life of the prosperous classes. Labourers, without property and able to afford little for accommodation, may have been similarly mobile, moving in search of work and rooming with non-kin. But people of small property, peasants and shopkeepers, may have behaved differently. The son may have remained working on the land or in the family trade and brought his bride into his parents' household. But such arrangements, because of the demographic facts, would be of short duration. We would expect such co-residence to result, for instance, in joint dedications by a dead man's parents and wife.[58] Two other groups are very different from those considered by modern historians. Soldiers living in barracks cannot have spent much time with their unofficial wives in the settlements outside the camps. But that they shared meals and other home comforts with them is suggested by the women's title of *focariae*, from *focus*, a fireplace. Slave *contubernales* probably often continued to live in quarters in the household to which they both belonged, although some, like some single slaves, may have

[56] Goody and Tambiah, *Bridewealth and dowry*.

[57] Saller and Shaw, 'Tombstones and family relations in the Principate: civilians, soldiers and slaves'; Saller, '*Familia, domus* and the Roman conception of the family'. Cf. Shaw, 'The concept of family in the later Roman Empire: *familia* and *domus*'.

[58] e.g. the dedication of a husband and his parents to his wife, their freedwoman, suggests a joint household (*ILLRP* 977), but this may be exceptional, since the young wife is said to have run the household from her girlhood. Joint dedications cannot be traced through Saller and Shaw, 'Tombstones and family relations in the Principate' 124 ff. (cf. 131–2). The subject might repay further study.

'lived out'. *Contubernales* who belonged to different households may not have 'lived together', but merely visited each other.[59]

But this reality of the nuclear family cut across concepts, such as those described by the words 'familia' and 'domus'. Both words have multiple connotations, none of which coincide with 'husband, wife, and children'.[60] Everyday life for the upper classes was centred on a house in Rome or their city of residence, a *domus*, which was also home to a household of servants (one of the senses of *familia*) and perhaps other dependants. The complex household was an important part of their experience. Within it, some people, such as nurses and their children (*collactanei*), might be particularly closely connected with the children of the family. Some slave children might be the natural children of the *dominus*. But the Romans had no difficulty in sharply distinguishing the legitimate nuclear family from the other members of the household. Instead of using one word, they describe them as individual members of the group, usually in relation to the father: a man and his *uxor* (or *coniunx*) *liberique*.[61] Commemorative practice shows the overwhelming importance of the ties between parents and children and husbands and wives.[62] But this does not mean that other blood-kin might not sometimes reside with the core group of *coniuges* and their children. For instance, the widowed mother of one of the couple might do so, as Caesar's mother apparently lived with him and Pompeia.[63] Married children and their *coniuges* might frequent the houses of their parents. Tullia, although married, is often to be found with Cicero or her mother. The early death of one *coniunx* or divorce, either followed by remarriage, meant that the nuclear group was frequently dissolved and reconstituted. The modern nuclear family is not static, but moves through various phases from the founding couple to the couple with young children at various ages and finally to the couple whose children are no longer 'at home'. There are multiple variations on this basic theme. Serial marriage makes successive nuclei more various. A Roman husband's marital career could show distinct phases marked by successive wives, each of whom might have children by him and might also have children by other husbands (who, if their father was alive, would normally reside in another household). Such a man could successively form several 'nuclear' families. How far these

---

[59] Cf., for later patterns, Laslett, 'Mean household size in England since the sixteenth century'; id., *Family forms in historic Europe* 513 ff.; Herlihy, *Medieval households*.

[60] Saller, '*Familia, domus* and the Roman conception of the family' 344.

[61] e.g. Ter. *And.* 891; Cic. *Quinct.* 97, *Sex. Rosc.* 96; Livy 8.37.11.

[62] Saller and Shaw, 'Tombstones and Roman family relations in the Principate: civilians, soldiers and slaves'.   [63] Plut. *Caes.* 10. Cf. Dixon, *RM* 200.

overlapped in one household would depend on the spacing of children and the intervals between marriages. By the time Pompey married Cornelia (his last wife), for instance, his children by Mucia were adult. A similar discontinuity might mark a woman's experience, heightened for her by the tendency to leave children of a divorced husband to his control and domicile. Children might experience home life with both parents and then one parent and a step-parent. If their second home was with their father, they might live with a succession of stepmothers. If, after a divorce, they lived with their father and he subsequently died, they might then return to their mother and her new husband, as did the sons of Livia and Ti. Nero.

In such circumstances, the stability which might be represented by non-kin within the household and with blood-kin outside the household must have become especially important.[64] The Romans conceptualized the structure of the family (both agnatic and cognatic and *affines*) stretching up, down, and sideways from each individual.[65] In normal practice, it was siblings, perhaps coeval cousins, aunts, uncles, grandparents, and grandchildren who would, at various stages of an individual's life, constitute an inner group. Such people had a claim on affection, social duty, inheritance, and commemoration. The original concept of who counts as a close relative may be illustrated by the old *ius osculi*, which prescribed that a wife must kiss all her husband's relations on each meeting, down to the children of his cousins.[66] Such 'kissing kin' did not in the classical period usually live with each other, but they were recognized as 'family' (under various titles according to their relationship) and easily distinguished from non-kin (such as servants) who did live in the same household.

(a) Couples

In the context of this book and the current state of our data, it has not seemed that much new light would be cast on marriage as an institution or marital relationships between *coniuges* by a systematic collection of all known married couples, even if the search was restricted to defined areas such as the republican senatorial class or epigraphic evidence in specific cities or provinces. Scholars have already established that there was comparatively frequent intermarriage between senatorial and equestrian families, between ex-slaves and persons of servile descent, between old and new citizens.[67]

---

[64] Bradley, 'Dislocation in the Roman family'.   [65] Ibid. 51 ff.

[66] Polyb. 6.2.6 = Ath. 10.440–1. Other authorities are less specific on degrees of kinship.

[67] See e.g. Wiseman, *NMRS* 53 ff.; Weaver, *FC* 112 ff., 179 ff. But Raepsaet-Charlier, 'Égalité romaine sous le Haut-Empire', regards 'mixed' marriage with equestrians as quite rare in the 1st cent. AD.

Intermarriage between citizen and non-citizen has also been investigated.[68] Monographs on particular areas may be expected to cast light on such topics as social and geographical mobility and acculturation. We know, for instance, that in Roman Britain it was possible for a man from Palmyra to take to wife his freedwoman who came from Colchester. What could better exemplify the meeting of two ends of the Empire? The form of commemoration is Roman. The tomb which he erected combines oriental motifs with the proper accessories of a Roman matron.[69] Yet such informative inscriptions are rare and scattered. Very often we have only the bare names. Literary sources may be almost as spare. As Asconius pointed out, the identity of wives of even prominent men was often hard to discover.[70] If we take one of the best-documented decades of the late Republic, 60–50 BC, and the best-documented group of men, those who held magistracies above the quaestorship during those eleven years, we can identify 108 men.[71] Thirty-five have wives whom we can name. Seventy-three have not. Of the thirty-five, we have complete lists attested for the best-known men, for instance Pompey, Caesar, Mark Antony. There are fifty named wives but twenty-one of these belong to eight husbands (and Pompey, Caesar, and Antony account for a dozen). Often the wives of men's youth are shadowy or dubious figures, for instance the daughter of a freedman who is said to have been Antony's legal wife or Clodius' Pinaria. It is not surprising that we can identify the wives of Lepidus, Cassius, or Brutus or the husbands of Clodia and Fulvia, but it is striking that we know so little of the wife of Crassus (only a nickname). For many marriages our information rests on chance and uncorroborated mention, such as Asconius' passing reference to Cornelia Lepidi.[72] For obscure individuals like Coelius Vinicianus, it is sheer chance if the wife's name survives. Often we have only a bare and unilluminating name. Our information on the date and duration of a particular marriage is usually thin and often deducible only by conjecture about the date of birth of sons. It seems likely that many of these men had other unattested wives, just as we know that of the seventy-three remaining magistrates most were married at least once. Our information for other periods is similarly limited.[73]

[68] Cherry, 'The marriage of Roman citizens and non-citizens: law and practice'.
[69] *RIB* 1065; Birley, *The people of Roman Britain* 147.   [70] *Pis.* 10c.
[71] The data, detailed in Appendix 4, were compiled for me by Alice Pellegrino.
[72] See Marshall on *Mil.* 43c.
[73] Raepsaet-Charlier, *Prosopographie des femmes de l'ordre sénatorial (Ier–IIe siècles)*, provides a basis for further research. So will S. Dixon's forthcoming data on property-owning women. Collections like these should give the impetus to the study of women in society which *RE* and *PIR* gave to historical work from the 1920s onwards.

3. *Married Life*

(a) *The social role and activities of wives*

When a man married, he ceased to be *caelebs* and became *maritus*, but if he was a *paterfamilias* before marriage he was no more of a *paterfamilias* after. For a woman, the change was much more striking. She was now a man's wife and *materfamilias*, and to the outside world a *matrona*. If it was her first marriage, she had now made the important transition from *virgo* to *mulier*, a change which Romans conventionally regarded as significant, natural, and auspicious, rather than, as ascetics later held, a loss and spoiling.[74] Her way of life was now dominated by her position of authority in the household and her potential motherhood. His occupations would continue much as before, except that he now had the support of a wife, who might be more or less involved in his business, the running of his estates, and his political career. Now if he had a dinner-party, respectable women might be invited and his wife would issue the invitations to them. If he went out to dinner, she might accompany him.

A woman might be identified as so-and-so's wife, most conveniently by adding the husband's name in the genitive to her own, for instance 'Terentia Ciceronis'. But there was no legal change of name, and she might still be identified by reference to her father. In public speeches, an orator would avoid offence by identifying a woman as the wife of so-and-so, without giving her personal name. A woman's social status (*dignitas*) was theoretically determined by her husband's although her own family's continued to count.[75] During the Principate, rules of precedence became more rigid and honorific titles were gradually attached to certain offices. A woman married to a consul was *consularis femina*, a woman married to a *vir clarissimus* was *clarissima*.[76] In the Principate, we find husbands and wives addressing each other by their titles as master or mistress of the household, as *domine* and *domina*. This usage appears in the formal context of epitaphs and wills. A husband might also refer to his wife as 'domina mea'.[77] The manners of a simpler age had allowed Cicero to write to Terentia as 'mea Terentia' or Augustus to Livia as 'mea Livia'.[78]

---

[74] Cf. Hor. *O* 3.14.10–11.

[75] Livy 1.13.7; *D* 37.9.1.19; *FV* 104.

[76] *D* 1.9.1, ht 8, 12 pr.; *CJ* 5.4.10, 12.1.13. Such titles were lost if the woman married a second husband of lower rank. See Raepsaet-Charlier, *Prosopograhie* 8 ff.

[77] *CIL* 6,11252, 11458; *D* 32.41 pr.; Ov. *Tr.* 4.3.9, 5.5.1; Petr. 66.5.

[78] Cic. *F* 14.1.5, 2.2, 3.1, etc.; Suet. *Cl.* 4.1, 4, 6.

Legal domicile depended on that of the husband.[79] In the Principate faithful wives even accompanied the husband into exile.[80]

Roman houses, whether they were small or large, had no areas designated as for women only (like the Homeric inner room) or areas which excluded women (like the Victorian smoking-room). In small houses, there was no scope for privacy and the one or two rooms had multiple uses. In apartment blocks a household might occupy a set of rooms and share a large communal room with other tenants. In the ordinary houses of Pompeii, as in those of classical Greece, we cannot usually determine who used particular rooms, children, servants, or tenants who did not strictly belong to the household.[81] In grand houses, the *atrium* is both the most communal and the most public area: it is one particularly associated with the mistress of the household, because she directed the servants at work there and because it was sanctified by the presence of the symbolic marriage-bed.[82] In the upper-class town houses and villas described by Cicero and Pliny, there are clearly rooms regarded as peculiarly belonging to wife or husband, such as Calpurnia's room or apartments (*diaeta*) or Cicero's libraries and galleries.[83] Rich women had somewhere relatively private where their maids helped with their toilette (though since the equipment was portable the place might vary). The *cubiculum*, particularly designated for sleeping, might in grand houses be large and light enough to be used for other purposes as well. But it was felt to be private. Admission to it was a privilege, controlled by chamberlains. It was this privacy which made it so undesirable for public business to be conducted there.[84] It is impossible to tell from archaeological remains whether a bed (the base of which survives) was occupied by one person or two. But the matrimonial bed was a familiar concept, represented by the *lectus genialis* in the atrium. It emerges from literary and juristic sources that it was the accepted practice for husband and wife to occupy the same room and bed.[85] If they slept apart, it would often be because of a quarrel or

[79] *D* 50.1.22.1, ht 37.1–2, 38.3.
[80] Tac. *A* 15.71.7, *H* 1.3.1; Pliny *Epp.* 9.10; cf. Apul. *M* 7.7. See Raepsaet-Charlier, *Prosopographie* nos. 41, 259, 338 (Agedia Quintina, Artoria Flaccilla, Fannia, Egnatia Maxmilla); cf. 72 (Antistia Pollitta).
[81] See Hermansen, *Osita. Aspects of Roman city life* 17 ff.; Thébert, 'Private life and domestic architecture in Roman Africa', 319 ff.; Wallace-Hadrill, 'The social structure of the Roman house'. Cf. Walker, 'Women and housing in classical Greece: the archaeological evidence'; Cohen, 'Seclusion, separation and the status of women in classical Athens'; Jameson, 'Private space in the Greek city'.   [82] Asc. *Mil.* 43c.
[83] Pliny *Epp.* 7.5; Cic. *A* 1.4.3, 8.2.
[84] e.g. Cic. *A* 6.2.5, *Phil.* 8.29.
[85] Lucan 5.806 ff.; Tac. *A* 4.60.4; Plut. *Praec. conj.* 34 = 142 F; *D* 29.1.3.2.

estrangement.[86] But pregnancy was a proper reason.[87] The bed was also a place where quarrels might take place and annoyance be shown by turning one's back.[88] But it figures more prominently as the place for love-making.[89] Husband and wife were not always the only people in their bedroom. Slaves might be there or in an adjacent room. But it does not appear that slaves slept in the same room when master and mistress went to bed together, though in other circumstances a man might, for instance, have a slave-boy sleeping at the foot of his bed.[90]

The daily routine of men has been frequently described. But that of women is less familiar.[91] How the routines of a husband and wife relate to each other has not, as far as I know, been examined in detail. I shall begin with two specific marriages, those of Cicero and Terentia and of Atticus and Pilia, and examine the information which Cicero gives us in the letters about the wife's role in relation to the husband's social life, a very one-sided view.

Tu autem qui saepissime curam et angorem animi mei sermone et consilio levasti tuo, qui mihi in publica re socius et in privatis omnibus conscius et omnium meorum sermonum et consiliorum particeps esse soles, ubinam es? Ita sum ab omnibus destitutus ut tantum requietis habeam quantum cum uxore et filiola et mellito Cicerone consumitur. Nam illae ambitiosae nostrae fucosaeque amicitiae sunt in quodam splendore forensi, fructum domesticum non habent. Itaque cum bene completa domus est tempore matutino, cum ad forum stipati gregibus amicorum descendimus, reperire ex magna turba neminem possumus quocum aut iocari libere aut suspirare familiariter possimus. (Cicero *ad Atticum* 1.18.1)

Where are you now? You have so often lightened the pain and anxiety of my heart by talking to me and counselling me. You have been my ally in public matters and my confidant in all my private affairs and have shared in all my talk and plans. But now where are you? I am so abandoned by everyone that the only relaxation I have is the time I spend with my wife and darling daughter and sweet little Cicero. For those ambitious and artificial friendships give prestige in public life but bring no profit at home. So when my house is well filled in this morning, when I go down to the forum packed in the midst of a flock of friends, I can't find anyone in that great throng with whom I can joke casually or risk a sigh.

This is a *locus classicus* on Cicero's friendship with Atticus rather than on the joys of family life. In January 60 Cicero was feeling excluded

---

[86] Lucil. 685; Cat. 61.100–1, 64.379–80; Cic. *A* 5.1.4; Suet. *Tib.* 7.3.
[87] *Decl. min.* 277.9; cf. 306.29.
[88] Juv. 6.268–9, 475–6; Plut. *Praec. conj.* 39 = 143 E.   [89] Plut. *Praec. conj.* 39.
[90] *D* 29.5.1.27, ht 3.2, 14. Mart. 11.104.13–14 imagines slaves outside the door while *domini* make love. Cf. Veyne, 'The Roman Empire' 73.
[91] Balsdon, *LLAR* 17 ff.; *RW* 252 ff. (excellent on toilette, visits to baths, dinner-conversation).

from high politics, and some irritations to do with the family (perhaps the strained relations of his brother Quintus and his wife Pomponia and her brother Atticus) were nagging at his mind. He wrote to Atticus, who was in Epirus, from Rome, regretting that he had no confidant at hand. Quintus had gone to govern Asia, another possible candidate was no good. His grand political supporters were not people with whom he could act naturally to express light-heartedness or sadness, and even if there was a moment for a joke or a sigh during the *salutatio* or *deductio*, Cicero would scarcely attempt a confidential conversation then. So the only time when he could be himself was with his family. Cicero needs Atticus because he can talk to him about both public and private matters. In a letter to him, he naturally emphasizes his need in warm terms. But his brother is also mentioned as someone to whom Cicero would normally have turned, as Cicero claims elsewhere when writing to Quintus himself.[92] In inserting the sentence about Terentia and the children, Cicero leaves the precise point about conversation and counsel and begins to move towards the lack of people with whom he can relax. He can only relax with his family. This remark seems to stress what is most important to him at this moment, the ease and naturalness of being in the family group. It does not exclude the possibility of serious conversation with Terentia. Since young Marcus was now four, Cicero could enjoy delightful chats and games with him, but not confidences about his own worries. Tullia was probably already a married woman but only in her late teens. A couple of years later, Cicero praises her intelligence and conversation and it is likely that he already found comfort in talking to her.[93] There are indications that Terentia took a great interest in Cicero's political career and it seems unlikely that he wants Atticus to understand that she could not be a confidante. Indeed, it is quite interesting that he does not say, 'Terentia is a mere woman and so I cannot talk about politics with her.'[94] But instead he is concerned to conjure up a picture of the intimate family group (without the son-in-law) focused on the small son. This focus continues as Marcus grows up and through succeeding marriages of Tullia, who sometimes remains 'Tulliola'. Cicero writes letters to or about all three from his exile and to Terentia, closely conjoined with Tullia when he and Marcus were abroad later.[95]

In writing to a friend, it would be a solecism for Cicero (except in moments of high emotion) to praise Terentia, for it must be assumed normal for a Roman to approve of his wife. In writing to Atticus, who

---

[92] *QF* 1.3.3.   [93] Ibid.   [94] Plut. *Cic.* 20.2.
[95] *F* 14.1–3 seem really addressed to Terentia, with messages to the children, 4 to all; 5, 7, 9, 19 to Terentia with inquiries about Tullia; 14, 18 from both men to both women.

was long a bachelor and who was the brother of Pomponia, of whose
performance as a wife Cicero was known to disapprove, it would be
tactless. In the small coin of social intercourse, Cicero relays an
invitation from Terentia to Pomponia for the day before the Com-
pitalia of 59, presumably for dinner and a short stay, since Atticus was
going to be with Cicero for a bath on the first day and a walk on the
feast-day itself.[96] He keeps Atticus informed of her health, sends her
greetings to him and sometimes his sister and mother, and lets Atticus
know that she had enjoyed one of his letters. In later letters such
commonplaces are taken for granted and not expressed.[97] During the
crisis of 58 Cicero constantly sends Terentia's thanks for the services
Atticus performed.[98] After Atticus eventually married Pilia in February 56, Cicero and she often exchange greetings through Atticus. The
new baby, Caecilia Attica (born 51), a precocious sender of messages, and sometimes Cicero's children, are included in these affectionate but conventional exchanges.[99] Later Cicero asked Pilia not to
grieve for Tullia's death.[100] He expresses his concern for Atticus' wife
and child not only by constant solicitude whenever either of them was
ill and by keeping informed about them from other sources, but by
acts of kindness such as lending his villa at Puteoli to Pilia.[101] This
arrangement is described by him as if it was a routine matter.[102] He
was enjoying a round of visits to his properties and friends in
Campania in that abnormal spring after Caesar's murder in 44, and
had been at his villa on the Lucrine lake for some time before he
writes to Atticus (who was in Rome or Lanuvium with Attica) that he
is handing over the house and its contents, which included bailiffs,
agents, and stores, to Pilia on 2 May. Cicero himself had left the
house on 1 May and gone to dine with Cluvius, *en route* for Pompeii.
There he spent the period 3–10 May, before sailing round to dine and
stay with Lucullus on the 10th. He called on Pilia on the 11th and then
went off to dine with Vestorius, again by boat. Soon after that, he
returned to the villa at Puteoli and stayed until the 17th. Pilia appears
to have moved to Cicero's Cumanum, keeping in touch with Cicero
about couriers to Atticus. Cicero called on her there on the 17th and
subsequently saw her also at a funeral in the town, before he set off
towards Arpinum, breaking the journey at his own place near

[96] *A* 2.3.4.   [97] *A* 1.5.8, 2.7.5, 9.4, 12.4.   [98] *A* 3.5, 8.4, 9.3.
[99] *A* 6.1.22, 2.10, 3.9, 4.3, 5.4, 8.5 (50 BC), 12.3.2 (46 BC), 17, 24.3, 26.2, 27.3, 28.3; 13.22.5
(45 BC), 14.3.2, 16.1.6, 3.6, 6.4 (44 BC). Terentia is left out, perhaps because Pilia was more
intimate with Tullia (*A* 4.4a.2, 12.3.2, 14.4) and perhaps more her age. Cf. Bowman and
Thomas, 'Vindolanda 1985: the new writing-tablets' 123.   [100] *A* 12.14.3.
[101] *A* 7.5.1, 8.6.4, 10.15.4, 12.6a.2, 11, 13.1, 17, 23.3, 24.3, 33.2, 37.1, 40.5, 45.1, 48.1,
13.12.1, 13.3, 13/14.3, 14/15.2, 17, 18.1, 19.1, 21a.3, 27.2, 44.2, 49.1, 51.2, 14.16.4.
[102] *A* 14.15.3, 16.1, 17.1, 19.6, 20.1 and 5, 22.1, 15.1, 1a.1.

Sinuessa and at a friend's house near Vescia and arriving on the 19th. By the 27th or 28th he had left Arpinum and reached his villa at Tusculum. He went off again in early June to see Brutus at Antium, then perhaps for a few days to Astura and then back to Tusculum.[103] It is clear that Cicero was systematically visiting his properties, not only because this was a normal spring duty and pleasure, because he loved them and needed to inspect them, but because he might need at any moment to go abroad. Since the Puteolanum and Cumanum had been put in order for his own visit and for the reception of callers, it no doubt made sense to let Pilia use them too. It is interesting that, without making a great fuss about it to Atticus, Cicero arranged his programme so that he did not sleep in either house while Pilia was there. This must be at least partly because of etiquette: Cicero had no hostess to receive her and ensure propriety. But it was also partly because Pilia was to treat the house and facilities as if they were her own, not as if she were a guest.

His own rapid tour, punctuated by entertainment at the houses of male friends, may be compared with his spring tour of 59, undertaken in company with Terentia. They were at the seaside house at Antium at the beginning of April, after a visit to an estate belonging to Terentia.[104] Then they planned to go to the villa at Formiae, back to Antium from 1 May until about the 6th for some games (which Tullia wanted to see), then to Tusculum, then to Arpinum and back to Rome by 1 June. This plan was frequently changed. Eventually Cicero, with Terentia and Marcus and presumably Tullia, left Antium on 19 April, decided not to return there after all, and established himself at Formiae, where the local gentry came to call. Cicero politely called on Atticus' uncle Caecilius. But social equals from Rome were in short supply and Cicero was presumably having a quiet family dinner when he nearly fell asleep at the table. Atticus was invited to Formiae, Antium, or Tusculum, but decided to join them at the less sophisticated old house at Arpinum on about 10 May.[105] In all this we see that Terentia's business interests and Tullia's desire to watch the games are taken into account, and Cicero writes as if the plan to stay at Formiae is theirs as well as his, but we do not hear if there were dinner-parties in which they took part at Formiae or if they went calling on the local ladies. The invitation to Atticus to come to Arpinum and enjoy rustic hospitality, since he scorned the seaside, is put in the first-person plural. The pace and nature of this holiday are markedly calmer than those of the tour of 44.

[103] A 15.5, 11.
[104] A 2.4.5–6. Presumably they went on to Tusculum and then back to Rome.
[105] A 2.8.2, 12.2, 14.2, 15, 16.1 and 4, 17.1, 19.5.

In Rome during the working-year the *salutatio* and *deductio*, important formal duties in a man's day, are all-male events in Cicero's time. The levee began around dawn and attracted particularly large crowds when a man was a candidate or a consul. The requirements fluctuated over a year or a lifetime. At times even senior friends would need to attend at another's house. Politics aside, the *salutatio* provided an occasion for clients to pay their respects or to request favours. They might also receive gifts as a reward for attendance. We are not told if the *materfamilias* slept later than her husband or if she avoided the atrium during the time the *salutatores* were received. Under the Principate, the emperor's morning reception was enormous and carefully regulated. On occasion the Senate attended *en masse*. Sometimes the women and children were involved.[106] It appears that wives went with their husbands to claim *sportulae* from their patrons.[107]

Some, at least, of the great ladies of the imperial family held their own official receptions. Dio claims that Livia in her widowhood received the Senate and others at her house, and the fact was entered in the public records. Nero in AD 55 removed his mother from his own residence, so that she could not be visited by the crowds who came to salute himself. It seems that she had held such *salutationes* before, early in her son's reign and presumably when she was married to Claudius. Julia Domna, who also took a major share in public appearances and was overtly responsible for administration in the absence of her son Caracalla, also, as a widow, received the Senate.[108] But noble and wealthy ladies, including those of the imperial family, must always have had receptions at which normal private business was transacted. Juvenal mocks at the praetor who rushes off in the dark to pay his respects to a couple of early-rising childless women.[109] Were it not for this couple and Agrippina, one would have thought that women might have held their receptions later than men, especially since authorities agree that it took a considerable time for a lady to be made presentable. Some visitors might be admitted to the private rooms during her toilette, but surely this was not the norm for the ordinary client or friend.[110] Men, on the other hand, could receive favoured friends even before they got out of bed.[111] There were other occasions later in the day at which clients or friends could make requests. Men were often accosted as they went about their business

---

[106] Suet. *Cl.* 35.2, *Galba* 4.1. In general see for recent accounts Millar, *ERW* 15 ff.; Saller, *PPEE* 128 ff.   [107] Juv. 1.120 ff.

[108] Dio 57.12.2, 78.18.2–3; Tac. *A* 13.18.5; cf. Jer. *Epp.* 22.16.1.   [109] 3.128 ff.

[110] Ov. *AA* 3.209 ff.   [111] Dio 65.10.4–5: Vespasian (cf. Pliny *Epp.* 3.5.9).

or amusements.[112] But they would also receive callers at home. The great jurists of an earlier day had advised all their fellow citizens about any problem, while they were crossing the forum or when they were sitting at home.[113]

Women, who spent more of their time at home, must have expected to see both their social inferiors and their friends there. A Caecilia Metella would have local notables among her clients. As patroness, the daughter of Metellus Balearicus and the wife of Ap. Claudius Pulcher could offer Sextus Roscius the shelter and hospitality of her house.[114] The *matrona* could conveniently receive callers of all kinds during the working-day while she supervised the household from a chair or couch in the atrium. These would include tradesmen to whom she had given commissions, pedlars who laid their wares at her feet, men and women asking for favours, her own servants, agents, bailiffs, procurators, or legal guardian.[115] Social equals and friends would be hospitably entertained, no doubt often away from the bustle of the atrium, in the private apartments, peristyle, or gardens. We have seen that Cicero paid a courtesy-call on Pilia. The younger Hortensius called on Terentia at Cumae. The young future consul, L. Vinicius, who called on Augustus' daughter Julia at Baiae, was rebuked, but this was an unusually severe father.[116] A married woman or a widow was entitled to receive gentlemen. A wife was bound by the same rules of hospitality as her husband, a point of etiquette which made it difficult for Lucretia to refuse to be at home either to a group of drunken male cousins or to two. On the first occasion, Livy implies that the visitors were admitted to the atrium, where they found Lucretia sitting among her maids, who were working despite the lateness of the hour. But it is her husband, arriving with them, who issues the invitation to eat or drink. When Sextus returns (with one companion) Lucretia invites him to dine and stay the night.[117] Although we hear little of women entertaining, there could normally be no objection to visits from women friends and relations. Young married women visited and received their mothers, their husband's kinswomen and their own, older matrons and widows, their own contemporaries, and unmarried girls. It was, of course, a courtesy for younger or socially inferior women to call on their elders and superiors and for friends to call on the sick or pregnant and women in childbed.[118] Cicero is careful to let Atticus

---

[112] See Millar, *ERW* 22 ff.   [113] Cic. *de or.* 3.133.   [114] Cic. *Sex. Rosc.* 27.
[115] Ov. *AA* 1.421–2.   [116] Cic. *A* 10.16.5; Suet. *DA* 64.2.
[117] Livy 1.57.9 ff., with colour from the heroic age.
[118] Lucil. 992 ff., 1056 ff.; Ov. *AA* 3.641–2; Sen. *Cons. ad Marciam* 16.6 ff.; Juv. 6.235 ff. For contacts between daughters and mothers see Dixon, *RM* 217 ff.

422 Paterfamilias *and* Materfamilias

know, at a time when bonds between them were being tightened by the recent marriage of Quintus and Pomponia, that Terentia had grown fond of Atticus' mother and sister: it is clear that there was social intercourse between the women of the households.[119] Women as well as men attended birthday-parties, betrothals, weddings, and funerals. They went away to stay with each other.[120]

One invitation issued by a married woman actually survives. By a happy coincidence this is the earliest Latin autograph by a woman. It is a letter on wooden tablets sent by Claudia Severa to ask Sulpicia Lepidina (wife of Flavius Cerialis, stationed at Vindolanda) to spend her birthday with her.[121] We have seen that it was correct for married women to extend invitations to ladies while their husbands invited the male guests. The rule even applied when husband and wife were to entertain their slaves on a feast-day.[122] This does not mean that Cicero could not invite Atticus and Pilia without a mention of female support.[123] Livia, as a widow, expected (if Dio may be trusted) to invite senators, *equites*, and their ladies to a banquet to celebrate the dedication of a statue of Augustus, a semi-public occasion. But Tiberius prevented her and invited the men himself.[124] Apparently in the absence of Terentia, Cicero makes it clear that his daughter Tullia joins him in inviting Atticus' bride Pilia.[125] It was clearly correct for ladies to know that there would be a hostess to receive them at a mixed party. There could of course be no objection to a married woman holding parties for women only. But for an elderly widow to invite men, even with their wives, was more delicate. But it seems that young wives invited guests of both sexes in the absence of their husbands, though they were probably thought 'fast'. The ladies of the young Tarquins were giving a feast to people of their own age when their husbands dropped in from the wars. Clodia, as a widow, is alleged to have attracted susceptible young men up from the river to her elegant house: dinner-parties for bachelors are presumably to be deduced. Luxurious houses surrounded by gardens were the proper setting for raffish parties of this sort.[126] But there also seems to have been a difficulty when an unmarried, divorced, or widowed man wished to receive guests of both sexes. In decent society he would need to bring in his mother or sister to receive the ladies; in indecent society, such as that which the sources attribute to the emperor Gaius, the proprieties were outraged by worse things than the

[119] A 1.5.8 (Nov. 68).   [120] Fronto *ad M. Caes.* 2.8, 9, *Ep. gr.* 2 (Loeb i.144ff.).
[121] Bowman and Thomas, 'Vindolanda 1985' 122–3.
[122] Cic. A 2.3.4, 5.1.3: Pomponia makes it clear that this is the function of the lady of the house.   [123] A 4.4, 13.47a.1.   [124] Dio 57.12.5.
[125] A 4.4a.2. It is not so clear that Tullia was to be present when Junia Tertia, Cassius' wife, came to dinner (F 16.17.1).   [126] Cic. *Cael.* 36. Cf. Messallina: Tac. A 11.31.

absence of a hostess.[127] It was, of course, a gaffe for a hostess to fail to
be at home at the right time to receive her guests.[128] It was normal
Roman practice (though it shocked the Greeks) for husbands to take
their wives to parties.[129] Women by the late Republic reclined at
dinner and seem normally to have shared a couch with their husbands. T. Flavius Clemens, better known as Clement of Alexandria,
who instructed Christian converts around AD 200, warned men that it
was prudent not to recline next to a married woman.[130] Married
women remained for the *convivium* (wine, conversation, and other
amusements) which might follow the dinner.[131] The old-fashioned
held that unmarried girls should withdraw, and young people of both
sexes might be kept to stricter standards at dinner than their elders,
sitting, not reclining, and given a smaller allocation of wine and
plainer food.[132] Women in the classical period were allowed to drink
wine, but excess was bad manners as well as incontinence. Juvenal
chooses to assume that a husband would have no control over his
wife's drunkenness.[133] Even respectable women might display their
skills in dancing, singing, or music, although professional standards
and provocative movements were disparaged.[134] Clement told Christian upper-class women that if they were obliged (by social pressures)
to attend banquets, they should make sure that their clothes covered
them completely. To both sexes he gave exhortations on the avoidance of gourmet tastes, excessive drinking, luxury, the provision at
dinner of sensual music, erotic songs, and comedians. He combines
this with worldly advice on refined manners, reminiscent of Ovid's
tips to lovers. His ideal matron would accept invitations to banquets,
as her social position made it necessary for her to do, but would
attend discreetly clad in neutral colours (not purple) but in softer
cloth than a man would wear (though not silk), without a garland,
perfume, make-up, or jewels. She would drink politely and avoid
blowing her nose, spitting, or belching.[135]

The social activities of the earlier part of an upper-class matron's
day include all those which Ovid describes for the instruction of the
predatory man and prescribes for the man-hunting woman of dubious
social and moral status but of elegant and attractive behaviour.
Women frequented galleries and colonnades, temples, synagogues,
theatres, the circus, the games, triumphs, resorts outside Rome.[136] An

---

[127] Suet. *G* 36.2; cf. Cic. *2 Verr.* 5.137.   [128] Juv. 6.418ff.   [129] Nep. *Praef.* 6.
[130] VM 2.1.2; Ov. *Am.* 1.4.15–16, 35ff.; Tac. *A* 11.2.5; Tert. *ad uxorem* 2.6; Clem. *Paed.*
2.54.1.   [131] Cf. Ov. *Am. 1.4, AA* 1.229ff., 3.749ff.; Clem. *Paed.* 2.40ff., esp. 54.2.
[132] Varro ap. Non. 372L; Suet. *Cl.* 33; Tac. *A* 13.16.1; cf. Plut. *QR* 33.   [133] 6.425ff.
[134] Balsdon, *RW* 274–5.   [135] *Paed.* 2.3ff., 33, 54ff., 104ff., 107ff.
[136] *AA* 1.67ff., 255ff., 3.387ff., 633ff.; cf. Juv. 9.22ff.

accomplished woman should play dice and board-games and be adept at cultivated but delightful conversation.[137] Married women would go out to visit their women friends' houses, or to meet them at the baths, stroll with them in the places of public resort, sit with them in the theatre and amphitheatre (where women were segregated from the time of Augustus), or attend religious gatherings, of which the nocturnal rites of the Bona Dea, exclusively for women, were the most worrying for men.[138] It was proper for eminent women to be attended by their women friends on important occasions. Just as men were escorted on their way out of Rome or welcomed back when they returned by their male friends and supporters, so Plancina, when she and her husband returned in disgrace from their province, was welcomed and attended by a group of women, *feminarum comitatu.*[139] Ladies of the imperial family had courtiers of both sexes, friends of their own age.[140]

In short, Roman wives had the first position in their own homes and took a full part in social occasions there.[141] This is consistent with a very marked division of social activities for husband and wife at all or some stages of their married lives and for much or most of their time. Cicero does not portray women as participants in his fictitious dialogues, but Scipio and his sons-in-law. He constantly mentions male friends whom he visited, without mentioning whether or not their wives were present. He and Terentia seem frequently to have been separated when he paid brief visits to his villas and for long periods, for instance when he stayed at Brundisium in 47 and Tullia (herself a married woman, but having problems with her husband) joined him.[142] Even the most respectable married men might go to mixed dinner-parties to which wives were not invited.[143]

For most married women only a small proportion of their day or year will have been devoted to social occasions with their equals. Although only lower-class women cleaned and cooked for their families, the supervision of domestic work must have involved time and thought for the *domina*, even though she had slave or freed supervisors to carry out her orders.[144] Petronius portrays the wealthy

[137] Ov. *AA* 3.353ff.; Juv. 6.434ff.
[138] Balsdon, *RW* 277ff.; Wiseman, *Cinna the poet and other Roman essays* 130ff. On seating see E. Rawson, '*Discrimina ordinum*: the *Lex Julia Theatralis*' 89ff.
[139] Tac. *A* 3.9.2.   [140] Macr. *S* 2.5.3, 6.   [141] Nep. *Praef.* 6–7.
[142] *A* 11.17.1, 17a.1, 21.2.   [143] Cic. *F* 9.26.
[144] Tert. *Exhort. cast.* 12.1, *ad uxorem* 2.4. Sources allude to working housewives only rarely, to evoke a simpler past or idealized present: e.g. Verg. *G* 1.293ff.; Ov. *M* 8.629ff.; Col. 12 pr.; Stat. *S* 5.1.122ff.; Plut. *Comp. Aristides & Cato mai.* 4.5. Cato on the duties and permitted recreation of the slave *vilica* suggests something of the routine of a farmer's wife (*Ag.* 143). Work in the domestic sphere included wool-work as well as cooking and cleaning and might involve tasks in farmyard and garden. Cf. Maurin, 'Labor matronalis: aspects du travail féminin à Rome'.

ex-slave Fortunata as vulgarly fussy during her dinner-party. She runs around everywhere and Trimalchio claims that she never joins the guests until the silver has been put away and the slaves have been fed with the left-overs. She takes her place with the guests at dessert, boasting of her housewifely zeal: she is *diligens materfamilias*.[145] A married woman must have spent some time with small children or in the education of daughters, and on her own bath (perhaps at one of the great public baths) and toilette. If husband or child was ill, though the menial duties of nursing were performed by slaves, the wife was expected to tend him.[146] And some time must have been devoted to the husband. Jerome has a highly coloured passage on the distractions of a married woman's life, which made asceticism preferable:

Quae vero nupta est, cogitat quae sunt mundi, quomodo placeat viro (1 Cor. 7.34). Idem tu putas esse diebus et noctibus vacare orationi, vacare ieiuniis; et ad adventum mariti expolire faciem, gressum frangere, simulare blanditias? Illa hoc agit, ut turpior appareat, et naturae bonum infuscet iniuria. Haec ad speculum pingitur, et in contumeliam artificis conatur pulchrior esse quam nata est. Inde infantes garriunt, familia perstrepit, liberi ab osculis et ab ore dependent, computantur sumptus, impendia praeparantur. Hinc cocorum accincta manus carnes terit, hinc textricum turba commurmurat: nuntiatur interim vir venisse cum sociis. Illa ad hirundinis modum lustrat universa penetralia, si torus rigeat, si pavimenta verrerint, si ordinata sint pocula, si prandium praeparatum. Responde, quaeso, inter ista ubi sit Dei cogitatio? et hae felices domus? Caeterum ubi tympana sonant, tibia clamitat, lyra garrit, cymballum concrepat, quis ibi Dei timor? Parasitus in contumeliis gloriatur: ingrediuntur expositae libidinum victimae, et tenuitate vestium nudae impudicis oculis ingeruntur. His infelix uxor aut laetatur, et perit: aut offenditur, et maritus in iurgia concitatur. Hinc discordia, seminarium repudii. Aut si aliqua invenitur domus, in qua ista non fiant—quae rara avis est—tamen ipsa dispensatio domus, liberorum educatio, necessitates mariti, correctio servulorum, quam a Dei cogitatione non avocent? (*adversus Helvidium*, PL 23.214)

But she that is married careth for the things of the world, how she may please her husband (1 Cor. 7.34). Do you think it is the same thing to be at leisure for prayer and fasting day and night and to make up your face ready for your

---

[145] Petr. 37, 67. *Diligens paterfamilias* is a familiar phrase. Cf. *Decl. min.* 301.20 on wives in modest households serving dinner to husband and guest; Suet. *de poetis* 6.7 for upper-class responsibility. Trollope neatly (if ironically) characterizes the women of the English leisured classes as having more occupations than the men: 'A woman is so different! Darning will get through an unlimited number of hours. A new set of underclothing will occupy me for a fortnight. Turning the big girls' dresses over there into frocks for the little girls is sufficient to keep my mind in employment for a month. Then I have the maidservants to look after and to guard against their lovers. I have the dinners to provide, and to see that the cook does not give the fragments to the policeman' (*Mr Scarborough's family* ch. 62).

[146] Pliny *Epp.* 3.16.3 ff., 8.18.9–10.

husband's arrival and mince about and fake endearments? The ascetic is concerned to appear uglier and to darken her natural beauty by suffering. The wife paints herself at the mirror and in despite of the Creator attempts to make herself more beautiful than she was born. There the babies are chattering, the staff are making a din, her children are hanging about her for kisses, the accounts are being totted up, expenses are being prepared. Over here an aproned band of cooks is pounding meat, over there a crowd of weaving-women is murmuring together. Now there is an announcement that her husband has arrived with his companions. She flits around all the corners of the house like a swallow, to see if the couch is smooth, if the floors have been swept, if the cups are arrayed, if the dinner is ready. Tell me please, where is thought of God in all this? Are these happy homes? But when the drums beat, the pipe shrills, the lyre chatters, the cymbal clashes, what fear of God is there? The parasite shows off in insults, the victims come in, exposed to lust, the target of unchaste looks, naked in their transparent clothes. If the wretched wife takes pleasure in this, she is lost. If she is offended, then her husband will quarrel with her, and this leads to discord, the seed-bed of divorce. But if you can ever find a house in which that sort of thing does not happen—and such houses are rare—yet how can a woman not be distracted from thoughts of God by the governance of her house, the upbringing of children, the needs of her husband, and the regulation of slaves?[147]

Wives accompanied their husbands on their journeys to estates and coastal resorts. They might also go alone to the country for recreation or the sake of their health or for safety and comfort in time of civil war.[148] That extensive travel by women without their husbands was perfectly normal is demonstrated by Cicero's light remark to Atticus in late November 54, after a trip to Asia, that no doubt he expected to find his womenfolk (his wife and perhaps sister, for Q. Cicero, her husband, was in Britain) in Apulia on his return, but that they are not there.[149] The sources take it for granted that women took journeys, without explaining if they usually went by litter or carriage and whether the presence of a lady implied a slower pace. During the Republic, wives did not normally accompany their husbands to provincial governorships. But there was nothing except the risks and hardships of travel to prevent their making journeys on private occasions. During the civil war of 49–48 BC Cornelia accompanied Pompey to the east, though she was kept away from the fighting. In

[147] Cf. Frassinetti 170 ff., who believes Tertullian to be the source. Household cares were a topos: Jer. *Epp.* 22.2 (CSEL 54.145 ff.): 'me . . . nec enumeraturum molestias nuptiarum, quomodo uterus intumescat, infans vagiat, cruciet paelex, domus cura sollicitet, et omnia quae putantur bona, mors extrema praecidat.'

[148] Cic. *F* 14.14.1, 18, *A* 7.12.6, 13.3, 14.3; Pliny *Epp.* 6.4.1–2.

[149] Cic. *A* 4.19.1. Atticus, who had left Rome in May (*A* 4.14.1), had been to Buthrotum (4.16.1) and then went on to Asia, leaving (apparently) his wife and child, presumably at Buthrotum, whence they returned to Italy independently (4.16.9, 15.2, 17.1; cf. 18.5).

the early Principate it became established custom for wives to go out to the provinces, a practice which was upheld by the Senate in Tiberius' time in the face of the anxiety (which continued to be expressed) that women would abuse their power, be rapacious, and meddle in military matters.[150] A rigidly virtuous woman might aspire to being unknown to her husband's subjects: Seneca claims that his aunt during the sixteen years when her husband governed Egypt was never seen in public, never admitted a provincial to her house, never petitioned her husband, and never allowed herself to be petitioned.[151] But most wives, like those of Pilate and Felix, undoubtedly appeared on public occasions. It is assumed that a husband going abroad for any purpose would wish his wife to accompany him.[152] There seems to have been nothing abnormal about a woman travelling without her husband, either to join him or for her own purposes.[153] An upper-class woman would have a considerable retinue. Obviously governors' ladies and imperial women had military escorts and proper attendance.[154] Pliny's wife, returning from Bithynia alone to be with her aunt on the death of her grandfather, was even permitted to use the imperial post.[155]

(b) Behaviour of coniuges

The major shared activity common to husbands and wives was the procreation of children. Conceiving and carrying a child was a natural function of women. If a couple failed to have children, it was usual to assume sterility in the wife.[156] Expectant fathers displayed anxious care for mother and child.[157] Sound medical advice on a healthy regimen for a pregnant woman was available, although medical practice if complications occurred was less reassuring.[158] The dangers of miscarriage and childbirth and complications after childbirth were vivid and real.[159] A woman in childbirth was attended by women, even male doctors apparently remaining at a distance.[160] But husbands might be near at hand: C. Octavius is said to have arrived late at the

---

[150] e.g. Tac. A 3.33–4; Juv. 8.128 ff. A similar topos applied to lovers and confidential freedmen. See Marshall, 'Tacitus and the governor's lady: a note on Annals iii.33–4'; id., 'Roman women and the provinces'. Senatorial women in the provinces have been listed in Raepsaet-Charlier, Prosopographie 692–5.

[151] Cons. ad Helv. 19.6.   [152] Juv. 6.94 ff.

[153] Cic. A 11.17, 17a.1; D 24.1.21 pr.; CJ 9.9.14. Seneca mentions travel for pleasure as a distraction to his widowed mother: Cons. ad Helv. 17.2.

[154] Tac. A 1.41.2.   [155] Pliny Epp. 10.120.2, 121.

[156] D 21.1.14 pr.–3; Soranus 1.42; Decl. min. 251; Jer. Epp. 54.15.3.

[157] Cf. Pliny Epp. 8.10–11.   [158] Soranus 1.64 ff., esp. 78 ff.; 2.66 ff.

[159] Pliny Epp. 8.10.1, 11.1–2; Juv. 6.592; Balsdon, RW 195–6.

[160] Galen Fac. nat. 3.149, 151; cf. Emperor Leo VI, Novellae 48 ed. P. Noailles and A. Dain, Les Novelles de Léon le Sage (Paris, 1944).

Senate on the day his son was born.[161] In any case, a Roman father needed to be present soon after the birth to perform the ceremonial act of raising the baby from the floor. This meant that he accepted the responsibility of rearing it.[162] Presumably the mother normally watched this event. Religious ceremonies followed, of which the name-giving, on the eighth day for girls and the ninth for boys, was a social event which no doubt the mother attended if she was well enough.[163] If the mother died during pregnancy, an attempt was made to save the child by Caesarean section.[164] The father must have been the person most keenly interested.

A divorced wife had to inform her husband if she found she was pregnant, within thirty days from the divorce.[165] The husband might deny that the child was his: then he need not recognize it when it was born. Or he might send observers: if his wife did not co-operate, then again the husband could refuse to acknowledge the child. If he sent observers, then he retained the right to refuse to acknowledge the child after it was born. These rules were established by the *Senatus-consultum Plancianum*, probably Hadrianic.[166] A little later, under Marcus Aurelius, there was an interesting twist to this theme, when a husband claimed that his divorced wife was pregnant and she claimed she was not. The emperor's rescript made new law to protect the interests of all concerned, modelled on the earlier regulations about examination.[167] The jurists take into account the probability that the husband is anxious to have children. Care was taken to safeguard the child's rights to belong to his father as well as the father's interests in the child. Praetorian edicts had already laid down procedures to ensure that when a husband died the widow who claimed to be pregnant was carefully supervised. She was to report the pregnancy within thirty days to interested parties (those who would benefit if there was no posthumous child), undergo an examination by up to five free-born women (who could, however, touch her only if she agreed) to determine whether she was in fact pregnant, and, if so, give thirty days' notice before the expected date of delivery and allow three free-born men and three free-born women to keep guard outside her door, and during delivery up to five free-born women inside her room. Including her own friends and attendants and those

---

[161] Suet. *DA* 94.5.   [162] Dixon, *RM* 106–7, 237 ff.

[163] Brind'Amour and Brind'Amour, 'Le *dies lustricus*, les oiseaux de l'aurore et l'amphi-dromie'.

[164] *D* 5.2.6 pr., 6.2.11.5, 11.8.2 (law of regal period), 28.2.12, 38.8.1.9, 38.17.1.5, 50.16.132.1, ht 141; cf. Verg. *A* 10.315.

[165] *D* 25.3.1.   [166] Talbert no. 85. p. 445.

[167] *D* 25.4. pr.–9. Cf. W. Williams, 'Individuality in the imperial constitutions: Hadrian and the Antonines' 79.

sent by the husband's family, there were not to be more than ten free-born women, six slave-women, and two midwives in the birth-chamber. All these women could be searched in case they were pregnant. The room had to have at least three lights. The baby was to be shown to the interested parties or their agents. These precautions must have been sufficient to prevent any introduction of supposititious children into the lineage. The rules were in the interest of the child as well as to prevent fraud.[168] Similarly, the widow might obtain from the praetor possession of the dead husband's estate on behalf of her unborn child or children.[169] The jurists refer to children in the womb as 'the belly', *venter*. The usage may seem to dehumanize the mother or even the unborn child, but it is a useful technicality, since the lawyers could not be sure how many children the mother was carrying. They sensibly decided that, when an estimate was necessary, it should be assumed that the number would not be more than three, although instances were quoted of quadruplets and quintuplets (and allegedly septuplets).[170]

Through sons and their careers women could achieve ambitions which could otherwise find no outlet.[171] Shared children strengthened a marriage: it was *liberis subnixum*.[172] Children were pledges of love and fidelity.[173] If a child died, the husband was the person best qualified to comfort the wife: the words of philosophers and poets could not be as efficacious as those which came from a dear mouth and a united heart.[174] As we have seen, the Romans thought of a happy home life as represented by *coniunx* and children, not by either alone. The strong and affectionate interest in small children which is a constant theme in the correspondence of Marcus Aurelius and Fronto is paralleled in earlier art and literature and is not a sign of any new sensitivity in the second century.[175]

(c) Relations between coniuges

It was expected that normal courtesies would be observed between husband and wife. A hand-clasp and a kiss were exchanged when they

[168] *D* 25.4; cf. *Decl. min.* 377.8. See Gardner, 'A family and an inheritance: the problem of the widow Petronilla'. [169] *D* 25.5–6, 37.9.
[170] *D* 5.4.3, cf. ht 1.5, 34.5.7 pr., 46.3.36. In the interests of the child, a pregnant woman was granted stay of the death sentence (like early modern English women who pleaded their bellies) and of torture (*D* 48.19.3). Y. Thomas, 'Le "ventre": corps maternel, droit paternel', collects the evidence.
[171] Sen. *Cons. ad Helv.* 14.2. [172] *D* 43.30.1.5.
[173] e.g. Prop. 4.11.73; Ov. *F* 3.218; *Cons. ad Liviam* 324; Suet. *Tib.* 7.3.
[174] Fronto *de nepote amisso* 2.7 (Loeb ii.228). Cf. Golden, 'Did the ancients care when their children died?'
[175] e.g. Fronto *ad M. Caes.* 1.6.7, *ad Antoninum imp.* 1.3, 4, *ad amicos* 1.12 (Loeb i.162, ii.118ff., 170–1).

met. Enquiries or exhortations about the other's health were proper then or in letters, and not often neglected.[176] Pleasantness in conversation was prized. We have representations in literature of objurgation between husband and wife, but in real life public criticism of a *coniunx* was clearly a breach of morality as well as of manners.[177] However, it was clearly recognized that quarrels occurred, whether in private or in public. The function of the shrine of Viriplaca was to provide a place where a husband could be placated after a quarrel. The couple were supposed to make offerings to the goddess so that harmony might be restored and also 'to say what they wanted to say'.[178] This may sound like a modern psychiatric treatment, but the emphasis on the need to sweeten the husband is probably more essential to the republican attitude. Juvenal and others perpetuate the notion that it is wives who are responsible for quarrels.[179] Juster authorities divide the blame.[180] If a couple split up after a quarrel, but then resumed their cohabitation, the jurists regarded the separation not as a divorce but as a *iurgium* or *frivusculum* which had calmed down.[181] The ideal remained a marriage without quarrels or serious disagreement. Completed marriages are praised as having been free from quarrel or offence or complaint.[182]

There is evidence from Christian Africa of wives who were familiar with physical abuse.[183] It is hard to document such behaviour in the pagan period. This does not prove an absence of wife-beating. In rhetorical exercises wives might sue for mistreatment, *mala tractatio*. The causes mentioned do not include physical abuse of the wife herself. The husband has deprived his wife of her children in a variety of improbable ways.[184] Or he has aspersed his wife's honour.[185] Or he has failed to consummate the marriage.[186] These cases were much more interesting than those motivated by banal failings such as failure to supply the wife with clothes or jewels, grieving her by keeping a mistress, or neglecting to make love to her. In such a list of boring complaints degrading treatment of the wife's body, *corporum contumeliae*, makes a rare appearance. So the vulgar possibility of insulting and even violent treatment of Roman ladies by their husbands existed on the fringes of the consciousness of teachers of

---

[176] Plaut. *Amph.* 711 ff.; cf. *Decl. min.* 279.11; Cic. *F* 14.1.6, 2.3, 3.2, 4.6, 6, 10, 21, 22, 23, 24.
[177] Petr. 74.8 ff.; Cic. *A* 5.1.3–4.   [178] VM 2.1.6.
[179] Juv. 6.35, 268 ff. (with sources cited by Courtney).
[180] Ov. *AA* 2.151 ff.   [181] *D* 24.1.32.12, 50.17.48.
[182] Pliny *Epp.* 8.5.1: a 39-year marriage *sine iurgio sine offensa*; Cf. *sine offensa: CIL* 6.8438. *Sine ulla querela:* 6.8737, 11778, 15606, 17856. Cf. Lattimore, *Themes in Greek and Latin epitaphs* 279; von Hesberg-Tonn 215.
[183] Aug. *Conf.* 9.8–9 with Shaw, 'The family in late antiquity: the experience of Augustine' 31–2.   [184] Sen. *Contr.* 3.7, 4.6, 5.3; Quint. *Inst.* 9.2.79; *Decl. mai.* 8, 10, 18, 19.
[185] *Decl. min.* 363.   [186] Sen. *Contr.* 1.2, 22; cf. Calp. Fl. 51 (a yet wilder scenario).

rhetoric and the boys they taught.[187] But cases of *mala tractatio* were merely school exercises. The law which provided their background was Greek rather than Roman. In real life they were parallel to actions for restoration of dowry, which followed divorce.[188] This suggests that the remedy for bad treatment in the Roman upper class was divorce or the threat of divorce or pressure brought by the wife's family.[189] When the possibility of divorce is remote, as it may in practice have been for the lower classes in the classical period and as unilateral divorce became in the Christian empire, violence and hostility will tend to rise.

Perhaps for the same reason, accusations of the murder of a wife are rare.[190] The poisoning of a husband is more frequently alleged. Poison was naturally blamed for sudden unexplained death, and members of the household, especially wives, were the obvious suspects. It would tend particularly to be ascribed to women whose position made divorce impossible, such as Livia or Agrippina the Younger.[191] During the proscriptions of 43 BC some wives are alleged to have betrayed their husbands. The wife of Septimius, who was having an affair with a friend of Antony, had her husband put on the proscription list and then kept him until he could be arrested. She remarried on the day of his death. The wife of Salassus brought the executioners upon him.[192] Such violent ways of disposing of a husband suggest that effective ill treatment of a husband could only be imagined in its extremest form. Since it would be held that a woman was unlikely to succeed if she expressed her dissatisfaction by physically abusing her husband, only plots to compass his death through third parties or hidden means would seem feasible.

These accounts of betrayal during the proscriptions are balanced by the equally moralistic tradition that wives were conspicuous (along with children, brothers, and slaves) by their devotion to proscribed husbands. Valerius Maximus cites Turia, who hid Q. Lucretius above the ceiling of their bedroom and so saved him, and Sulpicia, who, despite her mother, disguised herself as a slave-girl in order to follow Lentulus Cruscellio to Sicily. Appian adduces the wife of Ligarius, who concealed him and killed herself when he was killed, and Dio tells the story of Tanusia, the wife of T. Vinius, who hid him in a chest at the house of a faithful freedman and later successfully

[187] *Decl. mai.* 8.6, 10.9, 18.5
[188] Quint. *Inst.* 7.4.11. Cf. Bonner, *Declamation* 94–5.
[189] Quint. *Inst.* 7.8.2 has an incidental reference to frequent beatings as the reason why a wife first gave her husband a love-potion, then divorced him.
[190] Tac. *A* 4.22; Quint. *Inst.* 7.2.24.
[191] Livia: Tac. *A* 1.5.1; Dio 56.30.1–2; Agrippina: Tac. *A* 12.66–7; Suet. *Cl.* 44; Dio 61.3.2ff.
[192] App. *BC* 4.23, 24.

obtained a pardon for him from Octavian.[193] In a survey of the proscriptions, Velleius held that wives were the most loyal of all, freedmen showed moderate loyalty, slaves some, and sons none.[194] The rhetorical narratives may be suspect, but credence is usually given to the heroism of the anonymous lady whose tombstone attests that (along with her sister and brother-in-law) she found a hiding-place for her husband and so ensured his survival.[195]

Such daring and ingenuity were not often required of Roman wives. The ordinary course of work, child-bearing, and care for their families demanded the moral and intellectual qualities they demand in any age and might evoke emotions recognizable to us. The major difference in the experience of marriage compared with our own was produced by demography: the relatively high probability that young people's marriage would be broken within a few years by death and punctuated by the deaths of children. Like twentieth-century husbands and wives and unlike Europeans of the medieval and early modern periods, Romans also lived in a society in which any marriage might conceivably end in divorce.

[193] VM 6.7.2–3; App. *BC* 4.23; Dio 47.7.4.
[194] Vell. 2.67.2.   [195] *Laud. Tur.* 2.5 ff.

PART V
Separation

13
Divorce

If . . . other remedies may not be had, they must in the last place
sue for a divorce: but that is somewhat difficult to effect, and not
all out so fit. For as Felisacus urgeth, if that law of Constantine
the great, or that of Theodosius and Valentinian, concerning
divorce, were in use in our times, we should have almost no
married couples left.

> (Robert Burton, *Anatomy of melancholy*, part 3, sect. 3,
> memb. 4, subs. 2)

1. Introduction: terminology

A *matrimonium* was dissolved in various ways.[1] Jurists and people
making arrangements about dowry took account of the possibility of
the death of either partner and of divorce, as well as the more remote
hazard that a change in the status of either—capture in war, enslave-
ment, or judicial deportation—would remove the capacity to be
married.

Dirimitur matrimonium divortio, morte, captivitate, vel alia contingente
servitute utrius eorum. (*Digest* 24.2.1, Paul *xxxv ad edictum*)

A marriage is sundered by divorce, death, captivity, or other slavery which
happens to either of them.

Si quis sic stipuletur a marito: 'si quo casu Titia tibi nupta esse desierit,
dotem dabis?' hac generali commemoratione et ab hostibus capta ea com-
mittetur stipulatio vel etiam si deportata fuerit vel ancilla effecta, hac enim
conceptione omnes hi casus continentur. (*Digest* 24.3.56, Paul *vi ad
Plautium*)

---

[1] The neutral words used by jurists are *matrimonium solvitur, dissolvitur, dirimitur* (*D*
23.5.12, 24.2.11.1, 24.3.29.1; *dirempto matrimonio*: 23.3.84, 23.5.12), occasionally *nuptiae
dirimuntur* (24.3.22.7: 'nuptias esse diremptas'), rarely *distrahitur* (e.g. 23.3.9.3: 'cum distrac-
tum fuerit matrimonium cf. *CJ* 5.4.14, where *distrahendi* balances *contrahendi*). Ablative
absolute constructions are especially frequent. *Solvere matrimonium* is the most usual phrase
(e.g. 24.2.7, 24.3.44.1), also *solvere nuptias* (24.1.53 pr). *Soluto matrimonio* is the opposite of
constante matrimonio (24.2.5, 24.3.22.7, ht 24 pr.) or *manente matrimonio* (23.3.85, 23. 4.18;
24.3.66.6). Titles in the *Digest and Code* on the recovery of dowry when a marriage ends are
identical: *soluto matrimonio dos quemadmodum petatur* (*D* 24.3.; *CJ* 5.18).

If anyone makes the following stipulation to the husband: 'If by any occurrence Titia ceases to be married to you, will you give (back) the dowry?', in this general phrase the stipulation includes her being captured by the enemy or being deported or made a slave: all these occurrences are included in this wording.

Paul decides that it is humane to equate this obliteration of the wife's legal personality with her physical death rather than with divorce.

Dotal contract naturally took into account the various ways in which marriage could be brought to an end.[2] *Capitis deminutio* (loss of citizenship and *conubium*) of either partner must have been relatively rare under the *Pax Romana*; death was (normally) nobody's fault and unavoidable. Divorce was the eventuality for which the more detailed and specific arrangements had to be made.

When jurists, especially in discussion of property settlements, mention that divorce occurred without entering into detail, they made use of such terms as *divortium factum est* ('a divorce was made'), *divortium intercedit* ('a divorce intervenes'), *divortio facto* ('when a divorce had been made').[3] Or responsibility for divorce may be allocated: a marriage may be dissolved by the wife's fault or a divorce brought about without the husband's fault, and so on.[4]

Where our sources express the action of either husband or wife in a divorce, their vocabulary is, with a few exceptions from the second century AD, determined by sex.[5] To start with the husband, since it is agreed that the husband had powers of unilateral divorce from the beginning, we may look at the verb *repudiare* and its associated noun *repudium*. In republican Latin these words were used to describe rejection of a *sponsa*, most often in comedy.[6] They are not used in relation to divorce by Plautus, Terence, Cicero, Livy, or Ovid.[7] But *repudiare* then becomes the normal prose word to describe the husband's action in divorce. Velleius and Suetonius remark that Caesar refused to repudiate Cinna's daughter.[8] The verb is used of husbands by prose writers in general and by jurists.[9] The use of the

---

[2] e.g. *D* 23.4.29.1, 24.3.29.1.

[3] e.g. *D* 10.2.46, 24.3.5, ht 66.1, 24.1.32.10, ht 32.12, 41.6.1.2; also *divortium intervenit* (24.3.57) or *sequitur* (24.3.7.2, 25.2.25); also *divortio secuto* (23.4.26.5, 23.4.29.1, 24.1.32.9; *FV* 114) or *facto* (3.5.34 pr., 6.2.12 pr., 15.1.38.1; *FV* 106) or simply *post divortium* (*D* 11.7.29, 23.4.18, contrasted with *manente matrimonio*). [4] *D* 24.3.38, cf. 24.3.22.7, 35.1.101.3.

[5] I shall for the moment ignore the role of the *paterfamilias* in producing divorce. The following discussion of terminology took as its starting-point Robleda, 'Il divorzio in Roma prima di Costantino' 347–55, but his account is frequently misleading. The Greek terminology which he cites is only marginally relevant to Roman concepts of divorce.

[6] Above, ch. 4.4.   [7] I rely here on the standard concordances.

[8] Vell. 2.41.2; Suet. *DJ* 1.1.

[9] Suet, *DJ* 74, *Gaius* 25, *Cl.* 26.1; Quint. *Inst.* 4.2.98; *Decl. min.* 251, 262, 330, all *passim*, 257.6, 338 *thema*, 368 *thema*; *Rhet. lat. min.* p. 351.6; probably Tac. *A* 6.49.2; *D* 22.3.29.1, 23.2.12 pr., 24.2.4, 24.3.22.7, 40.4.29, 48.5.12.13, 48.5.14.9.

abstract noun, *repudium*, is parallel, where the husband divorces[10] or when notice of divorce is sent in his name.[11] However, it later became possible to speak of a wife or her *paterfamilias* or even her new husband sending a *repudium* to her husband.[12] *Repudiare* with a wife as subject is rarer.[13] The absence of *repudiare* of divorce in our earlier Latin sources seems surprising, especially as the comic writers use it of broken engagements, and both Cicero (often) and Caesar (occasionally) use it in a more general sense.

Let us turn for the moment to the wife's part. Here we need to concentrate on the verb *divertere/divortere*. This is used either absolutely or with *ab* and the ablative to describe the wife's action in separating from her husband and adopting a different path in life, literally 'diverging'. The usage appears as early as Plautus[14] but is absent from the prose writers of the late Republic. It occurs in Apuleius and Tertullian and is used with great consistency by the jurists.[15] But in time *divortere* came to be used also of the husband. There is an example in Apuleius and two secure instances in the jurists.[16] The noun *divortium* does not precisely parallel this usage. In one of our earliest sources, the Elder Cato, it is the husband who 'makes the divorce'.[17] Novius (early first century BC) in a farce apparently referred to both *coniuges* making a divorce.[18] The wife may also make a divorce.[19] The ceremonious divorce with which Cicero alleged Antony dismissed his mistress is summarized as 'he made a divorce with the mime-actress'.[20] The reason for this difference between verb and noun is presumably that either husband or wife or both may produce the condition of separation, though that separation tends to be seen as the departure of the wife (who normally would be leaving the matrimonial home rather than sending

[10] Sen. *Contr.* 2.2.6, 2.5.17; Pliny *NH* 7.122; Tac. *A* 3.22.3; Quint. *Inst.* 7.4.38; *Decl. min.* 251, 262 *passim*, 257.7, 347.1; *Rhet. lat, min.* p. 351.6; *D* 24.3.59; 40.9.14.2, 48.5.17; *FV* 107.

[11] Suet. *Tib.* 11.4, *Gaius* 36.2.

[12] *D* 24.1.57 pr., 24.2.4, 24.3.38; (?) G 1.137a; *FV* 116; *D* 24.2.8.

[13] *D* 24.2.4.   [14] *Men.* 635.

[15] Apul. *M* 5.26; Tert. *Monog.* 10; perhaps Gell. 4.3.1 (if 'nullis etiamtunc matrimoniis divertentibus' is to be taken as equivalent to '. . . uxoribus divertentibus'; *D* 5.1.42, 7.8.8.1; 23.2.45.5, 24.1.62.1, 24.3.7 pr., ht 19, 41, 45, 24.2.3, ht 5, 11.2, 25.2.21 pr., 25.4.1 pr., 33.4.7.3, 34.2.2, 36.1.80.8, 40.9.14.2, 46.3.65, 50.17.48.

[16] Apul. *Apol.* 99; *D* 23.4.30, Tryph., 34.2.3, Celsus. In 24.3.44.1, Paul, there may be a change of subject.

[17] Gell. 10.23.4: 'Vir . . . cum divortium fecit.' Cicero says *divortium* is the right word in connection with a wife, as *pes* (sheet) is good nautical language: 'si res suum nomen et vocabulum proprium non habet, ut pes in navi . . . ut in uxore divortium' (*de or.* 3.40). This does not help us much.

[18] *Com.* 89–90: 'Postquam se vidit [esse] heredem, desubito divortium | fecerunt.'

[19] *D* 24.1.64, Iav. 24.2.11 pr., Ulp.

[20] *Phil.* 2.69: 'cum mima fecit divortium.' This construction with *cum* is normal: cf. Cic. *A* 13.7; Suet. *Cl.* 26.2.

her husband away from it). The husband may produce his wife's departure by dismissing her. *Dimittere* is the proper and neutral word, which is used by Cicero and good prose authors of the early Principate.[21] It seems to have been the word used by the Julian Law on Adultery of the husband who divorced a wife taken in adultery.[22] The husband who failed to do this was said to keep his wife, *retinet*.[23]

The comic writers naturally use more picturesque words to describe the husband throwing the wife out of doors. Prose writers also use them for melodramatic effect. *Exigere* ('to drive out') is the commonest.[24] Plautus uses it comically of a wife sending away her husband from her dotal house, Cicero mock-seriously of Antony's divorce of his mistress, Suetonius to heighten the drama of Pompey's divorce of a woman who had borne him three children.[25] *Expellere* is at least as dramatic,[26] but *exturbare* ('to turn out') and *extrudere* ('to push out') or *eicere* ('to throw out') are more vivid.[27] Conversely, the wife can go away from her husband or marriage or leave him or, more dramatically, desert him.[28] Not all these pathetic desertions need comprise divorce. The husband may also abandon his wife, and, very commonly, the lover the lover, and the separation of *coniuges* may be involuntary.[29] *Separari* in the context of divorce is very rare.[30] Nor do Roman women often seem to have been obliged to run away.[31] Finally, it should be noted that *nuntium* (*re*)*mittere* ('to send a messenger') is a fairly common expression, emphasizing one event in divorce.[32]

The Latin sources on divorce are notably patchy: allusions in comedy, sporadic references in Cicero, and a passage in the Elder Cato typify the evidence for the Republic. At that period the language used tends to be informal: the husband dismisses his wife, she

---

[21] Cic. *Scaur.* 8: 'neque dimittere uxorem propter dotem volebat'; Ov. *AA* 3.33; Vell. 2.41.2; VM 2.1.4, 6.3.10, 9.1. ext. 5; Sen. *Contr.* 1.6 thema, 1.6.5, 2.1.34, etc.; Asc. *Scaur.* 19, 20c; Lucan 5.765; Suet. *DJ* 1.1, *DA* 62.1, *Tib.* 49.1; *Decl. min.* 251 thema, 257 thema, 262.7; Tert. *Pudic.* 16.17, adv. *Marc.* 4.34.6; *HA Hadr.* 11.3.
[22] Paul *S* 2.26.6, 8 = *Coll.* 4.12.5ff.
[23] *D* 48.5.2.2, 6, ht 30 pr.
[24] Plaut. *Merc.* 822: 'uxor . . . exigitur matrimonio; Ter. *Hec.* 242; Afr. *com.* 167.
[25] Plaut. *Mil.* 1277; Cic. *Phil.* 2.69; Suet, *DJ* 50.1, cf. *Cl.* 26.3.
[26] Cic. *Clu.* 14, 188; *D* 25.2.11 pr: 'sive vir uxorem sive uxor virum domo expulit'; *Decl. min.* 257.7 (of father-in-law).
[27] Cic. *Clu.* 14; Tac. *A* 14.60.1, cf. 11.12.2 (of the adulteress); Plaut. *Poen.* 1220, *Cist.* 530, cf. *Rud.* 1046, where a wife might throw out a husband; Cic. *Phil.* 2.99. ἐκβάλλειν is a common Greek expression.
[28] *Abire*: Plaut. *Men.* 722–3, *Mil.* 1164–5, cf. 1167 for the husband leaving a dotal home. *Discedere*: Cic. *Clu.* 189; Cael. ap. Cic. *F* 8.6.2; Sen. *Contr.* 2.2 (10) 5; *D* 24.1.57 pr., 24.2.10. *Digredi*: Suet. *DJ* 43.1. *Relinquere*: Sen. *Contr.* 2.2.5. *Deserere*: Plaut. *Amph.* 888; Ter. *Ad.* 477; Pomp. *Atell.* 132; Verg. *A* 2.572; Mart. 4.9.2, 7.58.5, 10.41.2.
[29] Ter. *Ad.* 477; Plaut. *Most.* 196, 202, etc.; Ov. *M* 7.710, *Tr.* 1.3.95.
[30] *D* 36.1.23 pr.   [31] *Fugere*: cf. Cic. *Clu.* 189.   [32] Below, n. 70.

leaves him, a divorce is made. *Repudiare* is used rather for the breaking of an engagement. In the Principate *repudiare* becomes comparatively common (though this is partly because Suetonius uses it regularly) and is the normal technical word in the jurists. *Divortere*, similarly, is the normal technical word for what the wife does. Less precise usages of course continue. This terminology reflects the legal informality of divorce at all periods. I conjecture that in the society of the late Republic and early Empire, where, as I shall argue, the husband rarely alleged moral grounds for divorce, the precise connotation of repudiation for shameful behaviour which Roman etymologists (rightly) gave to *repudium*[33] made authors avoid the word. We would expect it to have been more current in an earlier period before the divorce of Carvilius Ruga, when husbands divorced women for adultery and other moral transgressions, but there is no evidence.

An important point which has not been emphasized by scholars is that verbs normally associated with the husband's action are transitive, but those describing the wife are usually intransitive. He repudiates or dismisses her, she goes her separate way or departs. (Authors achieve pathos when they say she abandons him.) This parallels the notorious syntactical asymmetry of the two verbs which describe the initiation of marriage: *ducere uxorem* (literally 'to lead a wife') of the husband, *nubere viro* of the wife. *Divortium* is the obverse of *deductio in domum*.[34]

The distinction drawn here between *repudiare* and *divortere* is not new, though it has been made too hard and fast. The further observation that *repudium* was used of divorce and breaking an engagement and *divortium* only of marital rupture was made by the Roman jurists:

'Divortium' inter virum et uxorem fieri dicitur, 'repudium' vero sponsae remitti videtur. Quod et in uxoris personam non absurde cadit. (*Digest* 50.16.101.1, Modestinus *ix differentiarum*)

'Divorce' is said to take place betweeen man and wife, but 'repudiation' seems to be sent to a fiancée. However, this word can without absurdity be applied to a wife.

Inter 'divortium' et 'repudium' hoc interest, quod repudiari etiam futurum matrimonium potest, non recte autem sponsa divortisse dicitur, quod divortium ex eo dictum est, quod in diversas partes eunt qui discedunt. (*Digest* 50.16.191, Paul *xxxv ad edictum*)

There is this difference between 'divorce' and 'repudiation', that a future marriage (as well as a present one) can be repudiated, for it is incorrect to say

---

[33] Fest. s.v. 350–1L: derivation from *pudet*.
[34] Robleda, 'Il divorzio a Roma prima di Costantino' 352.

that an engaged woman has 'divorced', because the word 'divorce' derives from the fact that those who separate go different ways.

Some scholars have emphasized another distinction, that *repudium* is an action and divorce the resulting state.[35] Isidore takes this further, to the point where the divergence of a couple is made firm by the formation of a new marriage by at least one of the divorced people.

Repudium est quod sub testimonio testium vel praesenti vel absenti mittitur. Divortium est quotienscumque dissoluto matrimonio alter eorum alteras nuptias sequitur. Divortium autem dicitur a flexu viarum, hoc est, viae in diversa tendentes. (Isidore *Etymologiae* 9.7.24–5)

A *repudium* is what is sent to a person absent or present, with the attestation of witnesses. *Divortium* takes place whenever after a marriage has been dissolved one or other of the two proceeds to a new marriage. *Divortium* is so called from the turning of the ways, that is, roads going in different directions.

The modern distinction between action and resulting state, though worth making philosophically, does not fit the Latin vocabulary and was not prominent in the minds of jurists. What does worry them is that sometimes the formula of divorce (which would be equivalent to *repudium*) might be spoken in the heat of the moment and soon repented. In such cases, they denied that *divortium* had happened.

Yet another distinction may be suggested by a definition given by Gaius:

Divortium autem vel a diversitate mentium[36] dictum est vel quia in diversas partes eunt, qui distrahunt matrimonium. In repudiis autem, id est renuntiatione, comprobata sunt haec verba: 'tuas res tibi habeto', item haec: 'tuas res tibi agito.' (*D* 24.2.2 pr.–1, Gaius *xi ad edictum provinciale*)

Divorce is so called from the difference of intent or because those who break up the marriage go in different directions. In repudiations, however, that is, renunciation, the following words are approved: 'Take your things for yourself' or 'Look after your own affairs.'

He goes on to discuss how to break an engagement. There is an odd shift here between the etymology of the first sentence and the instructions on proper formulae of the second. What seems to underlie these remarks is a distinction between bilateral and unilateral divorce. It would be logical enough to keep a distinction between *repudium*, where one partner, but usually, even in classical law, the husband, rejects the other, and *divortium*, which is used of rivers and

---

[35] For the *status quaestionis* see ibid. 349–50.
[36] An interesting contrast with the mutual consent, *mens coeuntium*, which produces marriage.

roads splitting into two[37] and might therefore suggest mutual assent. When wives *in manu* began to divorce, they must have needed the consent, however unwilling, of husbands, so even *mulier divortit* could imply a sort of bilateral agreement. But this must not be pressed.[38]

Whether or not this text makes clear a distinction between unilateral and consensual divorce, we shall see that the difference was of practical importance to Romans of the classical period.

The abstract noun *discidium*, literally 'cleaving asunder', is also frequent in prose of all periods as a paraphrase for *divortium*. It is, however, broader. It can be used of the separation of friends, allies, or kin and of the temporary separation of husband and wife by circumstance or misunderstanding, or of permanent separation by death. But it is a convenient synonym for divorce, perhaps sometimes slightly euphemistic, sometimes more vivid, elsewhere used merely for variety.[39]

2. *Historical Development: Capacity to Divorce*

It is generally accepted that from the earliest times husbands had the right to divorce their wives at least for matrimonial offences. According to Plutarch a law of Romulus allowed husbands to divorce wives for adultery, poisoning children (including abortion?), and substituting keys (failure in their duty to be good *custodes*). If a husband divorced for any other reason, his property was forfeit, half to his wife and half to Ceres.[40] Stories about early lawgivers should be treated with scepticism, but it is inconceivable that a husband with *manus* could not divorce his wife for such causes. A suspect passage of Dionysius of Halicarnassus should not make us believe that all Roman marriages or even all patrician marriages were initially indissoluble.[41] That divorce existed in the fifth century can safely be argued from an allusion by Cicero to a regulation in the Twelve Tables. Cicero inflates Antony's dismissal of his mistress into an archaic divorce:

illam suam suas res sibi habere iussit, ex duodecim tabulis clavis ademit, exegit. (*Philippics* 2.69)[42]

[37] Cic. *Or.* 3.69, *F* 2.10.2; Tac. *Ag.* 19.4.
[38] Any such distinction is blotted out in *CJ* 5.17.8.
[39] Friends etc.: Cic. *A* 1.17.7, 4.1.1, *Am.* 78, *Har. resp.* 45; Tac. *A* 14.60. Temporary: Cic. *Dom.* 96. Also of the forcible separation of lovers: Cic. *Phil.* 2.45. Death: Ov. *M* 14.79. Divorce: Ter. *And.* 697, *Hec.* 476; Cic. *A* 11.23.3, 15.29.2, *Clu.* 190, *Cael.* 61; Tac. *A* 2.86.2, 3.34.10, 11.30.5, 12.40.3; Suet. *Dom.* 3.1; *D* 48.5.12.13, 49.15.8; *FV* 106. The verb *discindo* is usually used literally and does not connote divorce.
[40] *Rom.* 22.3, Cf. Watson, 'The divorce of Carvilius Ruga' 44–5.
[41] *Ant.* 2.25. Cf. Corbett 219–23; Watson, 'The divorce of Carvilius Ruga' 38, 49–50.
[42] I follow Corbett 218, Watson, 'The divorce of Carvilius Ruga' 42–3, and recent editors

He ordered that lady of his to take her things for herself, in accordance with the Twelve Tables he took the keys from her, he drove her out.

One divorce is attested as dated to the interval between the Twelve Tables and the notorious divorce of Carvilius Ruga, which is convincingly put about 230 BC.[43] L. Annius was said to have been removed from the Senate by the censors of 307/6 for divorcing his wife (who had come to him a virgin) without consulting friends. Ruga was not the first man to divorce his wife. But his divorce was a landmark. The innovation introduced when he divorced a beloved wife for sterility (because he could not otherwise tell the censors that he was married for the sake of procreating children) was that he suffered no financial penalty. From now on it therefore became necessary to allow the wife action for restoration of dowry.[44] Gellius specifically states that Cicero's contemporary, the jurist Servius Sulpicius Rufus, in his book on dowry said that this divorce showed that *cautiones rei uxoriae* were needed. Sulpicius should be authoritative on such a point.

Let us summarize what seems now to be an accepted reconstruction, although the sources on which it relies are scarcely satisfactory. Tradition postulated that originally all marriage involved *manus*. Only the husband (or his *paterfamilias*) could bring about a divorce. If the wife was divorced for an offence, she lost her dowry; if the husband divorced her for no good reason or arbitrarily he was penalized. But this inflexible system must have seemed increasingly unsatisfactory. Husbands must sometimes have wanted to divorce blameless but childless wives or wives whom they wished to replace. The precedent of Ruga established the rule that the husband would not be punished for divorcing an innocent wife, but that she could claim her dowry. A wife's rights to restoration of dowry must have seemed more obvious as marriage without *manus* grew more common between (at latest) the fifth and the third century. As it became customary for some married women to remain *in patria potestate*, divorce initiated by the wife's father would come into use. This development must have led to a situation in which a wife who had emerged from power and was *sui iuris* could divorce unilaterally. The course of these developments is obscure, for our evidence on the

---

(including Shackleton Bailey), in punctuating after *iussit* and *ademit*, rather than taking *ex duodecim tabulis* with *iussit*.

[43] DH *Ant.* 2.25.7; Gell. 17.21.44; VM 2.9.2; cf. Livy 9.43.25 for the date. Cf. Watson, 'The divorce of Carvilius Ruga' 40.

[44] Watson, 'The divorce of Carvilius Ruga' 38–50, who is widely accepted, e.g. by Gardner 48–9, 83–4. The texts are DH *Ant.* 2.25.7; Plut. *QR* 14, *Theseus–Romulus* 35 (6) 3, 4, *Lycurgus–Numa* 25 (3) 12, 13; VM 2.1.4; Gell. 4.3.1, 17.21.44.

period in which the major changes must have taken place in this area of private law as in all others is practically non-existent. We must argue from the better-attested late Republic back towards the late third or early second century.

By the time of Cicero, it seems to have been unusual for women to enter *manus*. Wives whose fathers survived might therefore be *in patria potestate*. Conversely, in the time of Plautus marriage in which the wife entered *manus* was still a vigorous institution.[45] When it was dramatically important for him to portray daughters appealing to fathers for support against their husbands or fathers deciding to break up a marriage against their daughters' will[46] (themes which may have been present in his Greek original), Plautus probably relies on his audience to equate the situation with that of a woman married but not *in manu*, whose father retains control of her. *Patria potestas* over married children of either sex continued to be a live legal issue until the end of the classical period. But we must not concentrate on the state of law as it may be reflected in comedy and forget that affection and duty may equally control the dramatic interaction between fathers and daughters.

But many fathers will have died before or soon after their children married.[47] Since daughters usually married younger than sons, for the first few years of marriage they had a higher chance of being *in patria potestate*. The extent to which either sons or daughters were emancipated from *patria potestas* cannot be ascertained. *Emancipatio* is frequently mentioned by the jurists, but literary sources never (I think) tell us whether a particular daughter is *emancipata* or *in patria potestate*. Modern scholars have deduced from indications in the evidence that Tullia was in Cicero's power during her marriage to Dolabella or Julia in Augustus' during her marriage to Tiberius. Their arguments are convincing.[48] But many married women in the late Republic must have been *sui iuris*. It is unthinkable that a woman who was married without *manus* was able to persuade her father to initiate a divorce or authorize her divorcing, but that when he died and she became *sui iuris* there was no way she could bring about a divorce except by nagging her husband. It is generally held that by the late Republic women who were independent and not under the husband's control could legally divorce as simply as their husbands could.

[45] Watson, *Persons* 21, 29–31. He takes *Merc.* 700ff., 817ff., as describing marriage *cum manu* where the wife cannot divorce.

[46] *Stich.* 11ff., *Men.* 719ff.; Enn. ap. *Rhet. ad Her.* 2.38. Cf. Watson, *Persons* 48–53.

[47] Saller, 'Men's age at marriage and its consequences in the Roman family'.

[48] Dixon, 'Family finances: Terentia and Tullia' 90ff., for Tullia; S. Jameson, 'Augustus and Agrippa Postumus' 306–7, and Linderski, 'Julia in Regium' 185, for Julia.

Already Plautus could portray some wives as able to divorce. They are imagined as turning their husbands out of the matrimonial (but dotal) home or pronouncing a formula of divorce against them.[49] Divorce by women never actually happens in a Plautine comedy, but then neither does divorce by a husband or a *paterfamilias*. The point is that the possibility that a *sui iuris* wife could divorce her husband had been raised—if only for dramatic effect. Alcmena in *Amphitruo* plays a responsible and dignified part, as an ideal matron. It does not seem right to see her use of the divorce formula simply as the topsy-turvydom of comedy. In the *Miles*, where the divorce is merely part of the tale spun to the braggart warrior, the wife's right to initiate it is taken for granted once it is explained that the house (in which she has to stay if the plot is to work) is part of her dowry.

For the Ciceronian period, we have little evidence on divorces by *sui iuris* wives. Cluentia and Aemilia divorced their husbands: they had no fathers alive. Valeria Paulla was also presumably *sui iuris*: Caelius certainly regards her as acting of her own initiative, and her presumed father C. Valerius Triarius, praetor 78, is unlikely to have been still alive in 50. Dolabella's wife also probably divorced him and we know nothing about her father. (See Appendix 5.) Divorce by women acting alone is relatively rare. Our information could be affected by two factors. The first is that, even though women's legal right to divorce may already have been well established, social reasons may still have made them reluctant to exercise it. The unfortunate Aemilia was a pawn controlled by her mother and stepfather. Cluentia, according to Cicero, was driven to divorce by her husband's flagrant misconduct. If this factor was influential, the comparatively small proportion of attested divorces initiated by women may reflect the actual situation. The second point to bear in mind is that our sources are all men, who tend to assume that whenever a divorce takes place the husband has initiated it. Most of them would only be inclined to mention that a wife had divorced a husband if the circumstances were scandalous. This might mean that divorces by women are under-represented. So it is difficult to see how far women may have been responsible for unilateral divorces. But the theory of consensual marriage, with the corollary that either *coniunx* could break the union, seems well established for marriage without *manus* by the time of Cicero.

A *filiafamilias* who entered *manus* passed out of her father's power. By the time of Gaius, even a wife *in manu mariti* could divorce.

---

[49] *Mil.* 1164ff., *Amph.* 928; Watson, *Persons* 49–52; McDonnell, 'Divorce initiated by women in Rome: the evidence of Plautus', adds some useful refinements to the technique of using Plautus, but I am not convinced by his main arguments.

What were the rights in classical law of the *filiafamilias* who married but did not enter her husband's control and of the *filiusfamilias* when his wife was in his father's control and when she was not? Neither son nor daughter could possess property of their own. The daughter in power depended on her father for her dowry, for even if it were given to her by someone else, it would theoretically belong to her father except during the marriage, when it belonged to the husband.[50] Her children would be outside her father's power and in her husband's (or that of his *paterfamilias*). The dowry brought by the wife of a *filiusfamilias* would belong to his father for the duration of the marriage. If she were *in manu* (which is unlikely in the classical period) then all her property would be dowry. Any children would be in the grandfather's power. It is clear, then, that the divorce of a *filiusfamilias* would involve his father in the repayment of dowry, while that of a *filiafamilias* would mean that her father recovered dowry.

As a father's consent to the marriage of a *filiafamilias* could be assumed unless he evidently dissented, it seems that his consent to her divorce was assumed. A father could sue for return of dowry only if his daughter consented.[51] She could sue by herself. Classical lawyers writing of the divorce of a *filiafamilias* often ignore the father. Several passages are most easily explained as referring to unilateral divorce by a *filiafamilias*. We have no instance in the jurists of a *paterfamilias* opposing a divorce willed by his daughter. The father's consent in these passages may have been formally given, and the lawyers omit to mention it, or it may be so taken for granted that it was tacit. Corbett regards half a dozen texts as clear evidence of a *filiafamilias* divorcing without reference to her father. Some of his instances do not seem cogent.[52] But several are convincing:

cum . . . Seia . . . sine culpa sua divorterit vivo patre suo, in cuius potestate est . . . (*Digest* 24.3.45, Paul *vi quaestionum*)

after Seia divorces[53] without fault on her part, during the lifetime of her father, in whose power she is . . .

Si filia familias nuptura ex peculio, cuius administrationem habet, dotem viro dedit, deinde, cum in eadem causa peculium eius esset, divortium

---

[50] The donor could avoid this problem by stipulating for the return of dowry to himself or the woman: *D* 24.3.45.

[51] *D* 24.3.34; *Tit. Ulp.* 6.6.

[52] pp. 242–3. *D* 24.3.34, Afr.: a dispute arises after Titia divorces because Titius says she is in his power and asks for the dowry to be restored to him. She claims that she is *sui iuris*; 46.3.65, Pomp.: the father is mad. The daughter divorces without his consent; dowry may be paid either to her, with the curator's consent, or to the curator, if she wishes.

[53] The *Philadelphia Digest* translates this 'is divorced', but I disagree.

fecerit, dos ei recte solvitur, quasi a quolibet peculiari debitori. (*Digest* 23.3.24, Pomponius *xv ad Sabinum*)

If a *filiafamilias* who is about to marry gives the husband a dowry out of her *peculium*, which she is allowed to administer, and then, when the *peculium* is in the same condition, makes a divorce, then the dowry can properly be paid to her, as might any kind of debt to the *peculium*.

Filia familias divortio facto dotem patri reddi iusserat. (*Digest* 24.3.66.2, Iavolenus *vi ex posterioribus Labeonis*)

A *filiafamilias* after a divorce had been made had ordered the dowry to be returned to her father.[54]

The last example is less certain than the others, but the action described in the ablative absolute may be attributed to the subject of the sentence. It seems fair for Corbett to claim that these texts presuppose the freedom of the *filiafamilias* to divorce and that the contexts practically exclude any parental concurrence. At the very least, they show what is of more interest, that people could regard daughters in power as the main agents in their own divorces. Taken together with Cicero's letters on Tullia's divorce, these texts suggest that it was practically inconceivable for a father to oppose the wishes of a daughter in such a matter. Even if the consent of the father was legally necessary, his silence was all that was expected of him.

A *filiusfamilias* by divorcing could inflict loss on his father. We might expect his consent to be more important in law. But this is not a preoccupation of the classical jurists. It was left to Justinian to take measures against children who defrauded their fathers by divorcing.[55]

3. Procedure

A verbal formula is a familiar element in Roman divorce. If we punctuate Cicero's account of Antony's divorce as above, the words *tuas res tibi habeto* ('take your things for yourself') are not there said to have been prescribed by the Twelve Tables. But Cicero at least implies that they are consecrated by tradition. Plautus had known this formula, for he makes Alcmena say to her presumed husband 'valeas, tibi habeas res tuas, reddas meas' and a lover uses it to get rid of Love, 'apage te, Amor, tuas res tibi habeto'.[56] The Elder Seneca quotes the formula as *res tuas tibi habe*, Apuleius as *tibi . . . res tuas habeto*.[57] Gaius says the approved formula was either *tuas res tibi habeto*

---

[54] Mistranslated in *Philadelphia Digest*.
[55] *CJ* 5.17.12; *Nov.* 22.19.   [56] *Amph.* 928, *Trin.* 266.
[57] Sen. *Suas.* 1.6; Apul. *M* 5.26. Cf. Mart. 10.41.2: 'iubes res sibi habere suas'; *Decl. min.* 262.6: 'res suas sibi habere iussa est.'

(exactly Cicero's version, which also occurs in Plautus: other authors vary the order of words) or *tuas res tibi agito*.[58]

Gaius connects the formula with *repudia*, so probably with the husband's initiative. He implies that the formula was not essential, a point which had been a matter of controversy in the mid-second century BC. Did divorce have to be validated by some fixed form of words or did a new marriage demonstrate that a divorce had taken place? Nothing shows that any verbal formula was essential. If Cicero uses the formula to send up Antony's non-divorce, it suggests that the words are so loaded with tradition that authors will use them for solemnity or mock solemnity. When Plautus puts them into the mouth of the dignified Alcmena, he achieves solemnity, as does Apuleius when Cupid divorces Psyche.[59] But Martial uses the solemn words to mock Proculeia's facile divorce. The pasquinade in the form of a mock bill of divorce which was written on a statue of Antony at the time of his 'marriage' to Cleopatra ran: 'Octavia and Athene to Antony. Keep your things for yourself.'[60] None of these fictitious examples proves the actual use of the formula by real women.

The original application of *res tuas* was probably to personal belongings, such as clothes, since a husband, even when his wife was not *in manu*, will hardly have used such vague terms to allow her to remove her dowry. It was reasonable to allow her to take personal effects.[61]

The use of the formula by husbands had become traditional by the time of Plautus and continued to be regarded as solemn form well into the second century AD, probably followed by surrender of the keys (prescribed by the Twelve Tables) and the wife's departure from the house, which the husband might also explicitly order. But, as Gaius said, the formula, though approved, was not essential. It is hard to imagine Cicero—or even Caesar, when he certainly took the initiative in divorcing Pompeia—going through this rigmarole. Cicero provides our evidence for the view that divorce in the second century BC might be very informal. In the *de oratore*, the dramatic date of

[58] *D* 24.2.2.1, G. There may also have been a variant on the lines of 'Leave the house', which is mentioned in humorous poetry as *ei foras*, *mulier* or *baete foras* (Plaut. *Cas.* 210; Varro *Men.* [Bücheler] 553; Mart. 11.104.1). Cf. Titin. *com.* 51–2: 'nuntiet | Geminae ut res suas procuret et facessat aedibus'; *Decl. min.* 262.6.

[59] Plaut. *Amph.* 928; Apul. *M* 5.26. There is bitter irony when a husband who has raped a virgin and is compelled to marry her divorces his innocent wife with full ceremony. The rhetorician contrasts the moment when the husband orders his wife to take her things and go with the moment when he took an action inconsistent with his being her husband (*Decl. min.* 262.6: 'Tunc repudiatam tu credis uxorem cum res suas sibi habere iussa est, cum egredi domo?'). [60] Mart. 10.41; Sen. *Suas.* 1.6.

[61] Watson, 'The divorce of Carviluis Ruga' 48–9. *Contra*, Yaron, 'Minutiae on Roman divorce) 1 ff.

which is 91 BC, he makes the orator L. Crassus (born 140) discuss the importance of disputes on a person's civil status.

Quid, quod usu, memoria patrum, venit, ut paterfamilias, qui ex Hispania Romam venisset, cum uxorem praegnantem in provincia reliquisset, Romaeque alteram duxisset, neque nuntium priori remisisset, mortuusque esset intestato, et ex utraque filius natus esset; mediocrisne res in controversiam adducta est, cum quaereretur de duobus civium capitibus, et de puero, qui ex posteriore natus erat, et de eius matre? Quae, si iudicaretur, certis quibusdam verbis, non novis nuptiis, fieri cum superiore divortium, in concubinae locum duceretur. (Cicero *de oratore* I.183)

What about what occurred in the living memory of our fathers, when a *paterfamilias* who had come from Spain to Rome, leaving his wife in the province pregnant, married another woman at Rome and did not send a notice of divorce to his previous wife? He then died intestate and each wife bore a son. It was not a trivial matter which was disputed, for an investigation was made about the civil rights of two citizens, both about the child born of the second wife and about his mother. She would have been reduced to the position of a concubine if judgment were given that divorce from an earlier wife takes place because of some fixed form of words, not because of a new marriage.

Cicero's language here is not technical enough to satisfy modern lawyers. M. Antonius (praetor 103) replies that the law is often uncertain and the orator need not study technicalities.

Quibus quidem in causis omnibus . . . atque in eo puero, qui ex altera natus erat uxore, non remisso nuntio superiori, fuit inter peritissimos homines summa de iure dissensio. (Ibid. 238)

In all these cases [sc. which Crassus cited] and in the case of the boy who was born from the second wife, when a message of divorce had not been sent to the first wife, there was an intense disagreement on points of law among experts.[62]

The problem in this case (as often in instances cited in the *Digest*)[63] was that one protagonist had died without leaving evidence of his interpretation of the status of his relationship with the second woman. She could presumably attest that she regarded him as her husband, and probably bring witnesses that he treated her as a wife (for example, there may have been a wedding ceremony). But if he already had a wife, a second marriage would not be valid. Her advocate (or her son's) would therefore argue that the man had intended to be married to her and that this intention was inconsistent

[62] For bibliography see Corbett 224; Watson, *Persons* 53; Robleda, 'Il divorzio a Roma prima di Costantino' 377 n. 151.
[63] e.g. *D* 24.1.3.1.

with the will to continue as the husband of the first woman (*affectio maritalis* in later juristic terminology). The second marriage demonstrated that he *had* divorced his first wife, even though he had neglected to inform her of the fact. The form and dating of this divorce are foggy but it must antedate the time the lawyers would argue that he regarded the second women as his wife. But Cicero expresses this argument more simply as 'novis nuptiis fieri cum superiore divortium', as if the new marriage did not merely prove but actually produced the divorce.

The opposing lawyers argued that it was essential to inform the divorced spouse and that this had to be done in a prescribed form of words. Since no message had been sent to the first wife, the second woman was merely a concubine and her son illegitimate, with no right of intestate succession.[64]

The requirements for valid divorce were disputable even to legal experts (let alone the orators, who, as M. Antonius is made to argue in reply, were quite capable of doing a good job for their clients without technical legal knowledge). It is unclear whether the question was resolved in this famous case. It was in most people's interest to make their intention of divorcing perfectly clear to their *coniuges*. But some possibility of doubt remained. If the words signifying divorce were spoken in anger or action taken which constituted divorce and the separation proved to be temporary, that counted as a quarrel, *frivusculum* or *iurgium*.[65] Perseverance of intention was required to make it a divorce.

If a husband and wife were rapidly reconciled and subsequently divorced, the question might arise whether the first separation had in fact constituted a true divorce. If, for instance, there was a divorce, then the husband gave a gift to the wife to secure her return, and she returned and subsequently divorced him, a question might arise about the validity of the gift. The husband had to argue that the marriage had in fact survived the first divorce, that is, it was no true divorce, so that he could revoke the gift after the second, true divorce, because gifts between husband and wife were revocable if

---

[64] See Corbett 224–6; Robleda, 'Il divorzio a Roma prima di Costantino' 374 ff.; Watson, *Persons* 53–4.

[65] *D* 24.2.3, Paul *xxxv ad edictum*: 'Divortium non est nisi verum, quod animo perpetuam constituendi dissensionem fit. Itaque quidquid in calore iracundiae vel fit vel dicitur, non prius ratum est, quam si perseverantia apparuit iudicium animi fuisse: ideoque per calorem misso repudio si brevi reversa uxor est, nec divortisse videtur.' The text from *quidquid* on is repeated at 50.17.48. *Frivusculum*: *D* 24.1.32.12, Ulp.; Isid. *Etym.* 9.7.26: 'Frivolum est cum eo animo separantur, ut rursum ad se invicem revertantur. Nam frivolus est velut quassae mentis et fluxae, nec stabilis. Proprie autem frivola vocantur fictilia vasa inutilia.' *Iurgium*: *D* 23.3.31, Pap., 23.4.27, cf. 24.2.3, Paul. Cf. Ov. *Rem. am.* 663 ff.

the donor changed his mind (as he often did after a divorce). The wife would argue that the first was a true divorce, so the gift was final. This apparently happened in a notorious case between Maecenas and Terentia, when Labeo reports that Trebatius said that if the first was a genuine divorce, then the gift was valid, but if it was faked, then the opposite was true. Proculus and Caecilius held (followed by Iavolenus) that it would only be proved to be a true divorce and the gift would only be valid if another marriage (sc. to a new partner) followed, or if the woman remained single for so long that it was obvious that her resumption of marital life with her former husband constituted a new marriage.[66] Remarriage of a previously divorced couple is a phenomenon frequently discussed in the jurists.[67]

Valid marriage to someone else confirmed divorce from a former partner. This is not to say that it constituted such a divorce. (The divorced person would need to be capable of remarriage and also to intend marriage. The case in the *de oratore* turned partly on the man's intentions.) This was particularly significant when a freedwoman divorced her patron against his will. The Augustan legislation refused her the right to make another valid marriage, as long as her patron did not consent to the divorce. Ulpian quotes the clause 'let there be no power of making a divorce for the freedwoman who is married to her patron'. He argues that this does not make such a divorce null (*infectum*), for the marriage is partly broken. Because the marriage is not wholly dissolved, she cannot claim her dowry. Nor has she the right to remarry. Conversely, we can take it that the divorce had some validity. But if the patron married again or even became engaged, the divorce at once became fully valid and so did any second marriage into which she might have entered. Here the second marriage of the patron shows that he now accepts the divorce, which becomes valid, so the freedwoman's second marriage also starts to be valid. The logical chronology is that the patron's changed attitude to the unilateral divorce precedes his remarriage, for if he were not divorced he could not remarry, but since it is the remarriage which proves his

---

[66] *D* 24.1.64, Iav. *vi ex post. Lab.*: 'Vir mulieri divortio facto quaedam idcirco dederat, ut a se reverteretur: mulier reversa erat, deinde divortium fecerat. LABEO: Trebatius inter Terentiam et Maecenatem respondit si verum divortium fuisset, ratam esse donationem, si simulatum, contra. Sed verum est, quod Proculus et Caecilius putant, tunc verum esse divortium et valere donationem divortii causa factam, si aliae nuptiae insecutae sunt aut tam longo tempore vidua fuisset, ut dubium non foret alterum esse matrimonium: alias nec donationem ullius esse momenti futuram.' Cf. Watson, *Persons* 54 n. 6. On this problem of donation during interruption of marriage see *D* 24.1.32.11, Ulp. Yaron, 'De divortio varia' 533–42, argues convincingly that divorce normally took immediate effect and its genuineness was only questioned in exceptional cases, particularly when donation was involved.

[67] Below, n. 225.

changed attitude the chronology easily becomes tangled. (Similarly, the divorce was ratified if the patron sued the freedwoman for adultery or removal of his property, which showed that he had ceased to regard her as his wife.[68])

Since cohabitation usually accompanied marriage, long physical separation might seem to imply a divorce. But if the couple each still honoured the marriage, they were to be regarded as married.[69]

The usual method of initiating a divorce from the late Republic onwards seems to have been formal notification by a letter or a messenger or both: *nuntium remittere/mittere* or *repudium mittere/remittere* ('to send a message/messenger/repudiation').[70]

It seems sometimes to be taken for granted that a freedman of the *coniunx* who took the initiative would deliver the message.[71] The employment of a freedman (an agreeable luxury available to the more prosperous classes) put the divorce on a businesslike footing, since he could give evidence of it, and avoided the embarrassment of direct communication. It is hard to imagine husbands in the late Republic uttering the archaic formula. If a man, in the heat of a quarrel with his wife, announced in some form of words that he repudiated her and then maintained his intention (for instance by facilitating her departure from his house) then the divorce no doubt dated from his words. Similarly, if a wife took the decision in the heat of the moment she might tell her husband directly. But otherwise she would probably leave the matrimonial home and then send a message announcing that she was divorcing. An announcement known to third parties was necessary to protect her since otherwise any absence might be construed as divorce. Or announcement of divorce might follow a period of apparently normal absence from the marital home.[72] When Valeria Paulla made a divorce on the day her husband (whose name is unknown to us) was due to return from his province, she presumably left the house and arranged for him to be welcomed home by a message.[73]

---

[68] *D* 24.2.11, Ulp., cf. ht 10, Mod., 23.2.45, Ulp.; *CJ* 5.5.1, 6.3.9, both Alexander. For bibliography on the divorce of the freedwoman see Robleda, 'Il divorzio a Roma prima de Costantino' 387 n. 180.

[69] *D* 24.1.32, 13, Ulp.

[70] *Nuntium remittere*: Cic. *de or.* 1.183, 238, *Top.* 19, *A* 1.13.3, 11.23.3, *F* 14.13. *Nuntium mittere*: *D* 24.1.32.19, 20, 24.3.22.7, 9. *Repudium mittere*: G 1.137*a*; *D* 24.1.57 pr., 24.2.3, 24.3.38, ht 59, 48.5.17, ht 44; *FV* 107; cf. Suet. *Gaius* 36.2. *Repudium remittere*: Suet. *Tib.* 11.4 Also *denuntiare*: Cic. *A* 11.23.3. *Nuntium remittere* may be used even in low life, when the couple were in the same house, before the husband threw his wife out: Apul. *M* 9.28. The written notice might, if the text is original, be called a *libellus divortii* (*D* 24.2.7, Pap.).

[71] *D* 24.2.9; Juv. 6.146: '"collige sarcinulas", dicet libertus, "et exi"' Cf. Cat. 11, with Mayer, 'Catullus' divorce'.

[72] Cf. Cic. *A* 11.17.   [73] Cic. *F* 8.7.2.

The method of announcing the divorce does not seem to be different when a *paterfamilias* took the initiative to inform the *coniunx* of his daughter or son. A message was probably more usual than a personal declaration.[74]

Did the divorced *coniunx* have to receive and comprehend notice of divorce in order to make it valid? There might sometimes be difficulties, for instance if he or she had gone mad and was unable to understand the notice. It was clear that a sane partner could divorce a mad one.

Iulianus libro octavo decimo digestorum quaerit, an furiosa repudium mittere vel repudiari possit. Et scribit furiosam repudiari posse, quia ignorantis loco habetur: repudiare autem non posse neque ipsam propter dementiam neque curatorem eius, patrem tamen eius nuntium mittere posse. (*Digest* 24.2.4, Ulpian *xxvi ad Sabinum*)

Julian in the eighteenth book of his Digests asks whether a mad woman can send notice of repudiation or be repudiated. And he writes that a mad-woman can be repudiated, because she is in the same position as a person who does not know: but neither she herself nor her curator can repudiate her husband, although her father can send notice of divorce.

The equation of a mad person (who cannot understand the notice) with a person *who does not know* about the notice shows that a *coniunx* could be unaware that he had been divorced, presumably because he had not received a notice. Another passage of Ulpian confirms that the ignorance of the divorced spouse did not matter except when the freedwoman divorced her unwilling patron.[75] Diocletian and Maximian in AD 294 ruled that a marriage was dissolved even if the notice (*repudii libellus*) was not delivered or known to the husband.[76]

There would be practical difficulties if a husband or wife were far away. It might well take two months to contact a campaigner on the frontiers and as long again for the wife to be informed that her husband had received notice. It was sensible of Valeria Paulla to avoid these difficulties by waiting until her husband got home. (On the other hand, she divorced him in time to preclude any resumption of marital life: this presumably allowed her to remarry at once, since no one could wonder if any child she might conceive was by her former husband.) Or the whereabouts of the *coniunx* might be unknown.

This must often have been the situation of prisoners of war. Julian

[74] *D* 24.1.32.19; *FV* 116 etc.; cf. *D* 24.2.2.3.
[75] *D* 23.2.45.5. Cf. Corbett 238–9; Yaron, 'Divortium inter absentes'.
[76] *CJ* 5.17.6.

probably argues that wives of captives had to be careful about marrying again. The underlying fact (not stated in our extract) is that *captivi* lost citizenship and *conubium* with their wives (if the text is authentic).[77] Nevertheless, he holds that if the husband is known to be a prisoner the wife should terminate the marriage by a formal divorce (of which she would count as the initiator) before remarrying. It is extremely unlikely that the husband could be informed.[78]

Bilateral divorce, that is, divorce agreed *bona gratia* by husband and wife, which seems to have been quite common, though specific instances are rarely attested, was probably the least formal of all. The *coniuges* and their friends knew what was going on. They made whatever practical arrangements were necessary. But there would be no need for a message or messenger. It was only in AD 449 that Theodosius and Valentinian required a formal *repudium* beyond the consent of both partners.[79]

There are two major and linked controversies in this connection. Did Augustus introduce tighter formalities? Did Messallina later divorce Claudius and fail to notify him? It is unlikely that a generally accepted solution to these questions will be found. A number of disparate texts have been mustered to support the view that the Augustan legislation prescribed a formal procedure. Suetonius says that when Augustus found his marriage law was being evaded by engagements to under-age girls and by frequent changes of marriage partners, he reduced the time during which an engagement secured the same privilege as marriage and 'he set a limit on divorces'.[80] By itself, this would suggest that he permitted only a limited number of divorces. But there is no evidence or likelihood that Augustus could restrict freedom to divorce, attractive though that might have been in the context of the new laws. The only known restriction is on freedwomen who wished to divorce their patrons.[81] If Suetonius is

---

[77] ch. 2.3.

[78] *D* 24.2.6. The text adds the probably post-classical rule that, if it was dubious whether the husband was alive and a prisoner, or dead, the wife should wait five years before remarrying and the divorce should be regarded as *bona gratia* (the *Philadelphia Digest* is misleading). Cf. *CJ* 5.17.7, AD 337.

[79] *CJ* 5.17.8. For a recent account of the post-classical situation see Arjava, 'Divorce in later Roman law'.

[80] *DA* 34.2: 'Cumque etiam inmaturitate sponsarum et matrimoniorum crebra mutatione vim legis eludi sentiret, tempus sponsas habendi coartavit, divortiis modum imposuit.'

[81] Levy refers Suetonius either to this or to penalties on dowry (*Der Hergang der römischen Ehescheidung* 48–52). Shuckburgh *ad loc.* holds that Augustus, stepping up the penalties against the person who was responsible for the divorce, mentioned in Cic. *Top.* 19, made a person who divorced capriciously forfeit the dowry. (There is no evidence for such a penalty against wives.) He also refers to the new formal procedure. Csillag (129), Robleda ('Il divorzio a Roma prima di Costantino' 376), and Gardner (85) think that *modum imponere* can mean to 'impose a form', connecting it with Ulpian's *certo modo*. But the usage of *modum imponere* is

right to link this with the limit on the privileges given to *sponsi*, then we might think of a temporal limit and in particular of the interval allowed to divorced wives before they had to remarry in order to claim privileges under the marriage law. The chronology of the modifications to the marriage law is unclear, but it might be possible to relate the introduction of two years for the privileges of engaged people to the rule that divorcees had six months to remarry (later increased to eighteen months) while widows had one year (later increased to two).[82] But this did not set a limit on divorces, but only on the time a divorced woman should remain single. There was no grace-period for men. Nor did it tackle the problem of frequent change: it only encouraged substitution of a new *coniunx* after divorce. Frequent change must include rapid divorce, which the law in fact encouraged since some people married to qualify for office or bequests and divorced almost immediately. Then the obvious solution was to refuse to allow valid divorce until a couple had been married for a minimum term. But this would be impossible to impose in the Roman context of free divorce and would anyway not have prevented separation and consequent loss of reproductivity. It seems that Suetonius does not give us enough information for a secure interpretation to be found. In any case, Suetonius' statement on the limit set to divorces cannot be related to the legal texts on formalities of divorce which follow. These receive no mention in the literary sources.

(1) Nullum divortium ratum est nisi septem civibus Romanis puberibus adhibitis praeter libertum eius qui divortium faciet. (*Digest* 24.2.9, Paul *ii de adulteriis*)

No divorce is ratified unless seven adult Roman citizens are brought in as witnesses as well as a/the freedman of the person who is making the divorce.

(2) Ut autem haec bonorum possessio [sc. unde vir et uxor] locum habeat, uxorem esse oportet mortis tempore. Sed si divortium quidem secutum sit, verumtamen iure durat matrimonium, haec successio locum non habet. Hoc autem in huiusmodi speciebus procedit. Liberta ab invito patrono divortit: lex Iulia de maritandis ordinibus retinet istam in matrimonio, dum eam prohiberet alii nubere invito patrono. Item (lege) Iulia de adulteriis, nisi certo modo divortium factum sit, pro infecto habet. (*Digest* 38.11.1.1, Ulpian *xlvii ad edictum*)

clearly 'to impose a limit or check, set bounds' (*OLD*). Cf. Livy 21.44.5, 23.23.3; Suet. *DA* 27.2: 'ita modum se proscribendi statuisse.' Thomas tentatively asks whether Suetonius means that the adultery law did not prohibit divorce as such, but penalized 'its most common ground' (p. 426). I cannot accept this, since the law compelled divorce for adultery.

[82] Engagements: Dio 56.7.2, cf. 54.16.7; Suet. *DA* 34.2. Divorcees and widows: *Tit. Ulp.* 3.14. See Brunt, *IM* 560.

For this type of *bonorum possessio* between husband and wife to apply, she must be the man's wife at the time of his death. But if divorce has occurred, but in law the marriage still exists, this type of succession does not apply. This happens in instances of the following sorts. A freedwoman divorces her patron against his will: the Julian Law on the intermarriage of the orders keeps her in the marriage, since it forbids her to marry another man against the will of her patron. In the same way, the Julian Law on adultery holds a divorce to be null unless it is made in a certain way.

(3) Si non secundum legitimam observationem divortium factum sit, donationes post tale divortium factae nullius momenti sunt, cum non videatur solutum matrimonium. (*Digest* 24.1.35, Ulpian *xxxiv ad edictum*)

If a divorce has not been made according to the procedure established by law, gifts given after such a divorce will have no effect, since the marriage does not appear to have been dissolved.

(4) Si ex lege repudium missum non sit et idcirco mulier adhuc nupta esse videatur, tamen si quis eam uxorem duxerit, adulter non erit. Idque Salvius Iulianus respondit, quia adulterium, inquit, sine dolo malo non committitur, quamquam dicendum [? videndum] ne is qui sciret eam ex lege repudiatam non esse dolo malo committat. (*Digest* 48.5.44, Gaius *iii ad legem xii tabularum*)

If the repudiation has not been sent in accordance with the law and it therefore seems that the woman is still married, yet, if someone marries her, he will not be an adulterer. This was the opinion of Salvius Julian, on the grounds that adultery is not committed without malicious intent, though it must be said (? ensured) that a man who knows that she was not repudiated in accordance with the law must not act with malicious intent.

The plain sense of Paul's comment on the Julian Law on adultery (1) is that seven witnesses are needed and that these do not include the freedman of the divorcing *coniunx*, who is assumed to be the messenger. The phrase 'eius qui divortium faciet' might refer to wife as well as husband.[83] Corbett holds that the witnesses attest the dispatch of the messenger and would attach their seals to the written message if there was one.[84] If this was a requirement of the adultery law, then it is natural that we should think of the husband who must divorce his adulterous wife in order to avoid an accusation of *lenocinium*. He had to make an abrupt and public break.

The second and third passages, which have clearly been reworked, may still be taken to mean that unless certain formalities were followed—and it is tempting to identify these with those in (1)—a divorce was not fully valid. Ulpian in (2) is discussing *bonorum possessio unde vir et uxor*. To claim this privilege,[85] a husband or wife

[83] Cf. *D* 24.2.7.   [84] p. 238.   [85] ch. 11.3.

had to be validly married at the time of the other partner's death. If there had been a divorce but the marriage still continued in law, that was not enough to allow a claim of *bonorum possessio*. An example of such a situation was provided by the freedwoman who divorced her unwilling patron: according to the Julian Law on marriage, she was still married and could not validly marry anyone else. In the parallel of the freedwoman who is half-married and half-divorced the flaw is not procedural. The flaw under the adultery law was procedural.

(3) raises a new question, *donationes*. Nothing shows that this was part of the adultery law. It might better fit the *Lex Julia et Papia*.[86] We seem again to be in the area of Maecenas' divorce, where it is not clear if a genuine divorce has produced validity of a gift. Evidence of formal divorce would clarify such a situation.

(4) is a comment on the Law of the Twelve Tables and it is that law, and not an Augustan law, which Gaius' usage suggests is referred to in *ex lege*.[87] But the extract was placed by the compilers under the Julian adultery law, and this has naturally led scholars to refer *ex lege* to the Julian Law and relate this passage to (1). But its relevance to the adultery law lies in its discussion of the remarriage of a woman not divorced in proper form. Gaius is probably referring to the clause on procedure mentioned by Cicero,[88] although he may have in mind rules for *sending* notice rather than the personal confrontation which Cicero envisages. Gaius is saying that without proper formalities the divorce is not perfect; the woman is still technically married but the logical effect of this, that a new husband would be an adulterer, is held not to follow. The wife here is in an ambiguous position, like the freedwoman whose second marriage is *iniustum* until her patron consents to her divorce.

So far we can conjecture that some formality was necessary for ratification of a divorce if the husband was disembarrassing himself of an adulteress[89] or if either *coniunx* wished to make a valid gift to the other or to marry again. Both the Augustan Law and the Twelve Tables on these matters were *minus quam perfectae*. Some legal effects such as removal from rights to *bonorum possessio* follow on this invalid divorce. Such formalities were a normal part of divorce, expressed by other phrases describing part for whole (such as *dimittere uxorem* or *discedere*): they served to date and ratify it. But they did not constitute divorce and they were not compulsory in all instances.

[86] ch. 11.1.
[87] Cf. *D* 47.22.4. For this view see Levy, *Hergang der römischen Ehescheidung* 46; *contra*, Robleda, 'Il divorzio a Roma prima di Costantino' 381, and Yaron, 'De divortio varia' 554–7.
[88] Above, pp. 441–2.
[89] Corbett 229–33 disposed of Levy's argument that (1) refers to breaking of *manus*.

The attestation by seven witnesses was of the statement of the divorcing party, not that the notice had been served on the other partner.[90]

The language in which the rule is expressed is general: *Nullum divortium* . . . Assuming the text is not reworked, I am inclined to think that this procedure did not apply only to the husband who divorced his wife for adultery. It was equally important for a woman to make a clean break: not only would she thus be sure of avoiding an adultery charge because of a remarriage, but it would simplify recovery of dowry. Provisions about dowry were an important part of the Julian Law on adultery.[91] Nevertheless, this short sentence is torn from a context in which the circumstances must have been more fully explained. Ulpian may have said why a divorce needed to be ratified. If a divorce was consensual and the couple came to a private agreement about the dowry, would they need to follow this formal procedure? I think not. A divorce which is not ratified is not the same as an invalid divorce.

On balance, then, I would agree with those who think that Augustus tightened up procedures which proved that one partner had divorced the other. There is nothing to show that seven witnesses were used for bilateral divorce and there is some indication (4) that the formalities prescribed by the Twelve Tables coexisted with the procedure which called for seven witnesses. But for *fully* valid unilateral divorce by husband or wife some formal procedure seems to have been required. The scarcity of sources may suggest that, like marriage ceremonies, a procedure was taken for granted, and that, like marriage ceremonies, it was evidential, not essential.[92] One might also remark that, as so often, the Augustan legislation seems to have made a fuzzy situation still fuzzier. One expects the jurists to comment on *inelegantia iuris*.

As the anonymous Roman from Spain shows that the Twelve Tables were imperfect law on this point, so the interesting case of Messallina suggests that the Augustan Law did not enforce universal observance of formal divorce.

---

[90] This may be confirmed by Isid. *Etym.* 9.7.24: 'Repudium est quod sub testimonio testium vel praesenti vel absenti mittitur.'

[91] e.g. the *Lex Julia de fundo dotali* was a section of the adultery law (Paul *S* 2.21b.2; cf. Corbett 180).

[92] Bonfante, *Corso* i.338, argues that seven witnesses were needed for unilateral divorce; *contra*, Robleda, 'Il divorzio a Roma prima di Costantino' 383. Corbett 239, Volterra, 'Intorno a D. 48.5.44 (43)', Thomas 425 and '*Lex Julia de adulteriis coercendis*' 643–4 hold that seven witnesses were required for divorce of an adulteress. Yaron, 'Divortium inter absentes' 59, conjectures that the *Lex Julia de adulteriis* contained the clause 'nullum inter absentes divortium ratum est nisi VII civibus Romanis puberibus adhibitis'.

According to Tacitus, Messallina, incredible as it might seem, celebrated a public marriage with Silius.

. . . consulem designatum cum uxore principis, praedicta die, adhibitis qui obsignarent, velut suscipiendorum liberorum causa convenisse, atque illam audisse auspicum verba, ⟨subisse,⟩ sacrificasse apud deos; discubitum inter convivas, oscula complexus, noctem denique actam licentia coniugali. (Tacitus *Annals* 11.27.1)

The consul designate, with the wife of the emperor, announced the day in advance, invited witnesses to affix their seals, came together as for the rearing of children, and she listened to the words of the *auspices*, [*text corrupt*] sacrificed to the gods. Then they reclined among the guests, there were kisses and embraces, and the night was then passed in the licence allowed to husband and wife.

Later, when the news is given to Claudius, Tacitus makes Narcissus ask him if he knows he is divorced.[93] The story, as Tacitus admits, is improbable. But since it obtained credence, it is worth asking if such a divorce and remarriage were theoretically possible.[94] Tacitus himself believed that a real marriage was intended: Messallina was not play-acting as Nero was later said to have done.[95] I discard the view that the marriage to Silius is supposed to constitute divorce from Claudius. According to Guarino no one holds that, only that Tacitus presents divorce as 'the implicit consequence of the marriage to Silius'.[96] But divorce must precede marriage. Nor does the cessation of *affectio maritalis* towards Claudius inside Messallina's head suffice, even if that logically preceded her new marriage.[97] Some outward sign of her divorcing should have been given. Had she left the palace and removed her personal belongings? Had she even left written notice on Claudius' desk while he was at Ostia? If she had taken some positive step to demonstrate that she *divortit*, then she would have had some justification for regarding her marriage to Claudius as dissolved and her union with Silius as *matrimonium*. Julian (4 above) might have thought Silius innocent of adultery. But a new marriage was, even on Messallina's terms, scandalous because of its rapidity.[98]

---

[93] *A* 11.30.5: '"An discidium" inquit "tuum nosti?"'

[94] Tac. *A* 11.27, backed by Juv. 10.329ff.; Suet. *Cl.* 26.2, cf. 29.3, whose details on the formalities of the wedding (dowry, *auspices*, and dotal contract in Suetonius, veil, wedding-bed in the gardens, dowry, witnesses, *auspex* in Juvenal) are suspiciously similar to those in Tacitus. Cf. Dio 61.31.3.

[95] Suet. *Nero* 28 (mentioning veil, dowry, and *deductio*), 29; Tac. *A* 15.37. 8–9 (veil, auspices, dowry, 'genialis torus', torches).

[96] Guarino, 'In difesa di Messallina' 18.: 'la conseguenza implicita del matrimonio con Silio.'

[97] Robleda, 'Il divorzio a Roma prima di Costantino' 385–8, though he is neither lucid nor cogent.

[98] Cf. Suet. *DJ* 62.2; *Decl. min.* 347; *D* 24.2.8.

4. Patresfamilias

The most important feature of Roman divorce throughout the classical period is that it was free. Pacts not to divorce and penalties on the divorcing partner were ruled void in a rescript of Alexander Severus, on the grounds that ancient usage made marriages free.[99] Divorce depended on the will of at least one of the *coniuges* and public authorization was not required. But various qualifications should be made. In archaic times, when the power of the husband and *paterfamilias* was strongest and he alone could repudiate his wife, it was nevertheless expected that he would summon a domestic council, which would show that his action was not hasty or ill-judged.[100] At least informal consultation of trusted friends and kinsmen no doubt continued as a normal preliminary to divorce as to any important action.

It is not clear when wives *in manu mariti* won the legal right to compel divorce. They could legally do so by the time of Gaius.[101] In the classical period, to judge from the silence of our sources, there seems to have been no problem. This may be because wives rarely entered *manus* or because wives were able to persuade husbands to divorce them or because the legal right was obtained long before Gaius or because wives *in manu* were so conditioned that they rarely wanted divorce.

The main legal limitation on the freedom of *coniuges* to divorce or not was *patria potestas*. The *paterfamilias* of either wife or husband could send notice of divorce.[102] Notice of divorce might also be given by one *coniunx* to the *paterfamilias* of the other.[103] Or the action of the wife's *paterfamilias* may be expressed by saying that he takes away his daughter, *abducere*.[104] In Plautus the *pater* of the wife has two roles. He may want to break up a daughter's marriage against her will or she may appeal to him to put pressure on her husband after a quarrel. Although in both cases the father in the Roman context could unilaterally declare a divorce, this is not how things work in practice. The father in *Stichus* has two daughters, who want to remain married although the husbands have been abroad for a long time. They are afraid he wants to take them back home. He has more power;[105] but it is not just his power but propriety which makes it wicked and

---

[99] *CJ* 8.38.2, AD 223: 'Libera matrimonia esse antiquitus placuit, Ideoque pacta, ne liceret divertere, non valere et stipulationes, quibus poenae inrogarentur ei qui divortium fecisset, ratas non haberi constat.' Cf. *D* 45.1.134 pr., Paul.

[100] Corbett 226–7.   [101] 1.137a.

[102] *D* 24.1.32.19 (to wife); *FV* 116 (to husband). Cf. Giannetto Longo, 'Sullo scioglimento del matrimonio per volontà del paterfamilias'.   [103] *D* 24.2.2.3.

[104] Plaut. *Stich.* 17; Ter. *Hec.* 545, 748; Afran. *com.* 301; Sen. *Contr.* 2.2.10; *D* 43.30.1.5.

[105] 69, apparently *patria potestas*.

dishonourable for his daughters to oppose him. They must attempt to win him round by persuasion—which they do.[106] Conversely, in *Menaechmi* and *Mercator* it is the woman who summons her father in order to complain to him or even to ask him to take her away.[107] It is unexampled in the literary sources that a *paterfamilias* forces divorce on an unwilling son or daughter. Even Cato refrained from disturbing his daughter's marriage in order to give her to Hortensius.[108] A father who had authority greater than that of an ordinary *paterfamilias* might well meet with co-operation from even reluctant daughters when he manipulated their marriages. Augustus brought about the divorce of his daughter Julia in the name of her husband, not as her father. He could also arrange the divorce of Agrippa and Marcella or of Tiberius and Vipsania although he did not stand in the relation of a *paterfamilias* to them.[109]

But the legal sources naturally discuss the imposition of divorce by *patresfamilias* on unwilling children. Down to the time of Antoninus Pius the *pater* had legal power to break up his child's marriage. Pius is said to have forbidden the father to 'separate' a harmonious marriage.[110] This was confirmed by Marcus Aurelius, who ruled that if the *paterfamilias* had once consented to the marriage he could not, if he changed his mind, impose his will on a daughter who got on with her husband, unless for very serious reason.[111] It was unreasonable of a *pater* to dissolve a *bene concordans matrimonium*, particularly if it was supported by children. But the *filius/filiafamilias* should avoid a head-on collision and persuade the father not to exercise his power harshly.[112] If the father sent notice of divorce to his son-in-law against his daughter's will, he could not sue for the return of dowry without her consent and probably could not make her leave her husband either. As far as the couple was concerned, the marriage remained, although the relationship between the *pater* and his son-in-law was broken.[113] The right of *paterfamilias* to dissolve a marriage for serious reason continued until the time of Justinian.[114]

It appears that a *filiafamilias* could in classical law divorce her husband without explicit permission from her father,[115] but it seems likely that his consent to divorce was assumed if he did not express dissent. If he was mad, he could not consent.[116] It is argued that a

---

[106] 68 ff. A similar dialogue seems to have occurred in Ennius Cresphontes (*Rhet. ad Her.* 2.38).   [107] *Men.* 734 ff., esp. 782, *Merc.* 787–8.   [108] Plut. *Cato min.* 25.4 ff.
[109] pp. 169, 259.   [110] Paul *S* 5.6.15; cf. Buckland, *Textbook* 117.
[111] *CJ* 5.17.5; cf. Paul *S* 2.19.2.   [112] *D* 43.30.1.5, Ulp.
[113] *D* 24.1.32.19–20, Ulp. According to Severus and Caracalla gifts from daughter-in-law to father-in-law therefore became invalid, as if he had died.   [114] *CJ* 5.17.10, AD 528.
[115] *D* 23.3.24, 24.3.34, ht 45, 66.2; *Tit. Ulp.* 6.6. Cf. Corbett 242.
[116] *D* 46.3.65. This parallels the rules on consent to marriage.

filiusfamilias had long had this right, at least when the wife was not *in manu* and so was not in the power of his father. We would expect that the consent of the *paterfamilias* was necessary if his daughter-in-law had to be released from his control. But when most marriages were without *manus* and divorce was informal, from the late Republic onwards, it is likely that even husbands who were *filiifamilias* enjoyed considerable freedom to divorce. They certainly had the legal right before Justinian changed the law in AD 534. He found it scandalous that young people could dissolve their marriages unadvisedly and thus penalize their parents by taking the dowry away from them. He therefore limited their right, as Pius and Marcus Aurelius had limited the right of *patresfamilias*.[117] It appears that Justinian believes that *filiifamilias* had had this right at least since the second century AD. The only other evidence adduced is the alleged inability of the father in Terence's *Hecyra* to stop his son divorcing.[118] This is shaky. At most, it will show that it would already seem natural for a Roman audience to accept that a father would attempt persuasion and, if that failed, acquiesce in his son's decision. A *paterfamilias* might have legal rights but hold them in abeyance. When we observe the behaviour of Marcus and Quintus Cicero, who probably had *patria potestas*, we never find them invoking it. As social customs changed, the right of a *paterfamilias* to prevent his son divorcing might wither away. But it is hard to think of a time when it would have seemed appropriate for a legislator to attack his privilege, since it was closely connected with his ownership of the dowry.

Interference by the state is most sharply present in the laws of Augustus, which intervened to compel a husband to divorce an adulterous wife and to limit the power of the freedwoman to divorce her patron unilaterally.

5. *Causes of Divorce*

It was accepted that divorce should not take place without due cause.[119] The earliest law allowed divorce when the wife had committed a fault, such as adultery. Drinking wine is also alleged to have been a serious offence during the archaic period.[120] Antiquarians catalogue wives divorced for going out with their heads covered or

[117] *CJ* 5.17.12; *Nov.* 22.19. [118] Corbett 241–2; Watson, *Persons* 53, *RPL* 23.
[119] Cf. Dixon, 'Family finances: Terentia and Tullia' 98–100 (or in Rawson, *FAR* 112–13).
[120] Cato ap. Pliny *NH* 14.90; Varro *de vita populi romani* 1.38 (with Riposati ad loc.), cited by Gell. 10.23.1–2; VM 2.1.5b, 3.9; Pliny *NH* 14.89; Serv. ad *A* 1.737; Plut. *QR* 6; Tert. *Apol.* 6.4–5; Non. 96L. Moderns usually connect this prohibition with the risk of sexual misconduct (e.g. Minieri, 'Vini usus feminis ignotus'). See also MacCormack, 'Wine drinking and the Romulan law of divorce'. Durry, 'Les femmes et le vin', and 'Sur le mariage romain' 187–8, argues unconvincingly that the reason was that wine was regarded as an abortifacient. Oswyn

bare, for talking to a vulgar freedwoman, or for going to the games without the husband's knowledge.[121] Plautus makes a woman complain that a wife could be divorced simply for leaving the house without permission.[122] Such ideas relate to Greek standards of wifely behaviour and interest later authors chiefly because they are held to reflect the rigorous morality of a lost age. Wives might still be divorced if they were thought to be compromised. Caesar divorced Pompeia, not for any proved misconduct of her own, but because of the suspicion that Clodius had planned to meet her in compromising circumstances. (See Appendix 5.)

Suspected adultery was always good reason for divorce.[123] Pompey's divorce of Mucia was warmly approved.[124] Where the husband had proof of adultery, the Augustan Law tried to coerce him into divorcing. Claudius divorced Urgulania for sexual scandal and suspicion of murder, and later alleged that her child was not his, but seems not to have prosecuted her.[125] Divorcing a wife convicted of adultery in a previous marriage was entirely proper.[126]

After Carvilius Ruga, a husband might unilaterally divorce his wife for sterility. Sulla allegedly repudiated Cloelia for this reason. It was the cause alleged by Caligula for divorcing Lollia Paullina—a motive which was lent some colour by his remarriage to Milonia Caesonia either immediately after or a month before she presented him with a child.[127] The rhetorical schools took as a favourite theme an imaginary law that a wife could be divorced after five years if she had not borne a child.[128] Sterility could also be good reason for consensual divorce, as the anonymous *laudata* suggested.[129]

It was also expected that a wife would have reasonable cause before she divorced a husband. Sexual misconduct is the reason most commonly mentioned. A slave-woman in Plautus complains that a man can bring a mistress home and get away with it, while a woman can be divorced for a trivial fault:

Murray has recently made the attractive suggestion that accounts of the prohibition are a reaction to Greek disapproval of the Roman custom of having wives at the dinner-table ('Symposium and genre in the poetry of Horace' 48–9).

[121] The wives of Sulpicius Gallus (Plut. *QR* 14; VM 6.3.10), of Antistius Vetus (Plut. loc. cit.; VM 6.3.11), of P. Sempronius Sophus (presumably the censor of 252, Plut. loc. cit.; VM 6.3.12). Attending shows without the husband's knowledge against orders is still an offence in *Nov.* 117.8.6.   [122] *Merc.* 821–2.

[123] e.g. Plut. *Cato min.* 24.3 *Luc.* 38.1, *Ant.* 9.1–2 Cf. Cat. 11.17.   [124] Cic. *A* 1.12.3.

[125] Suet. *Cl.* 26.2, 27.1. For (suspected) adultery as a valid reason cf. Suet. *Dom.* 3.1; *SHA Marcus* 19.7–8.   [126] *D* 48.5.12.13, Pap.

[127] Plut. *Sulla* 6.11; Suet. *Cal.* 25.2–3; Dio 59.23.17; cf. Tac. *A* 12.2.2.

[128] Sen. *Contr.* 2.5; *Decl. min.* 251, cf. 327. Cf. Bonner, *Declamation* 122–4.

[129] *Laud. Tur.* 2.31 ff.; *D* 24.1.60.1.

I say women, poor wretches, live under a hard law, and one much more unfair to them, than men do. For if a man brings in a tart unbeknownst to his wife, even if his wife finds out about it, the man gets off scot free. But if a wife, unbeknownst to her husband, goes out of the house, it gives the husband a reason to drive her out of the marriage. If only there was the same law for wife and husband; for if a wife who is good is content with one man, why should not a man be content with one wife? I say I'd see to it that, if the men copped it in the same way, if one of them unbeknownst to his wife brought his tart home, just as women are driven out for committing a fault, there would be more divorced men than there are divorced women nowadays. (*Mercator* 817–29)

Despite this claim that men enjoy impunity, as soon as the *matrona* hears that her husband has brought a girl in, she sends for her father. Another comic husband is convinced that as soon as he takes a girl to his house his wife will jump to the wrong conclusion and divorce him.[130] Bringing mistresses into the matrimonial home was an aggravated form of sexual misconduct, commonly mentioned in literature.[131] It seems to have had some relevance to Roman practice, for in AD 449 Theodosius and Valentinian mention it as particularly exasperating for chaste wives and allow it as just cause for divorce, in a list which includes a husband's adultery with a married woman, murder, conspiracy, the attempted murder of his wife, or wifebeating.[132] Similarly, it was proper for Cluentia to divorce Melinus for his affair with her own mother. When Cicero was considering the advisability of a divorce between Tullia and Dolabella (where he, presumably as her *paterfamilias*, would have taken the initiative), he thought they had grounds either in Dolabella's political activity or in his notorious sexual misconduct, which included an affair with Metella and, allegedly, forced entry into houses (*nocturnae expugnationes*).[133] Sexual licence was probably included when a divorcing wife raised the question of her husband's *mores*.[134]

The cause of a divorce might be formally alleged when the wife sued for return of her dowry. Responsibility for the divorce had to be established. The *coniunx* responsible was not necessarily the one who initiated divorce, but the one who gave cause. The question was *utrius culpa divortium factum sit*, 'by whose fault was the divorce made?' or about the person *qui discidii necessitatem inducit*, 'who brings about the necessity for divorce'.[135] The husband could retain one-sixth of the

[130] Plaut. *Merc.* 785 ff., 923 ff., *Rud.* 1046–7.
[131] e.g. [Andoc.] *Contra Alcib.* 14; Ovid *H* 9.121; Sen. *Ag.* 258.
[132] *CJ* 5.17.8.2; Cf. *Nov.* 117.9.5.
[133] Cic. *Clu.* 14, *A* 11.23.3. For Metella cf. Wiseman, *Cinna the poet and other Roman essays* 112, 176, 188 ff.   [134] *D* 24.3.39; cf. 32.50 pr.
[135] Quint. 7.4.11; *FV* 121; cf. Cic. *Top.* 19; *Decl. min.* 262.8.

dowry if the divorce was brought about by fault of the wife or her *paterfamilias*; one-sixth for serious moral offences, *graviores mores*, which meant adultery; one-eighth for lesser offences, *leviores mores*, which meant all the rest.[136] If serious moral offences were proved against the husband, he had to repay in six months.[137] It is not quite clear how these faults in the husband were defined. But since Constantine disallowed drunkenness, gambling, or flirtation as reasons for a wife to divorce a husband, it seems likely that these were previously included among recognized reasons.[138]

An idea of 'matrimonial offences' was thus enshrined in praetorian law. But there seems in historic times to have been a tension between two duties. The divorcing *coniunx* owed a duty to equity, to conjugal faith, and to his own reputation for *gravitas* to divorce his wife only for serious reasons. Terence makes a young man say that it is arrogant to send a young wife back to her father when you cannot accuse her of fault.[139] It was shocking to divorce a virtuous, obliging, and faithful wife.[140]

On the other hand, it might also seem good or expedient to spare the reputation of the divorced *coniunx*. According to Plutarch, though Pompey was sure of Mucia's adultery and both advertised his indignation against her seducer at the time and later resented her new husband, he did not formally allege adultery as a reason for the divorce.[141] This no doubt saved trouble with her family. He could well afford to do without *retentiones*. Ungentlemanly behaviour is attributed to M. Antonius. A political quarrel between Antony and Dolabella, who had been friends, was rumoured to have its roots in suspicion of adultery between Dolabella and Antony's wife Antonia, daughter of his uncle Hybrida. Cicero later accused Antony of having trumped up the charge against his irreproachable wife and even, to compound the dishonour, of having alluded to it in the Senate in front of her father, in order to cloak his real reason for an unjust divorce, that he wanted to marry Fulvia.[142]

Unilateral divorce for incompatibility was less acceptable. Disobliging temper or incompatibility of character were occasionally alleged against a wife. But such claims might be seen as unconvincing or irresponsible. Trimalchio claims to be behaving like a good guy because he tolerates his infuriating wife instead of looking light-

---

[136] *Tit. Ulp.* 6.9ff. Claudius divorced Aelia Paetina *ex levibus offensis*, contrasted with Urgulania's grave transgressions, and could consider remarrying her (Suet. *Cl.* 26.2; Tac. *A* 12.2.1–2).
[137] *Tit. Ulp.* 6.13.   [138] *CTh* 3.16.1.   [139] *Hec.* 154–5.   [140] *Decl. min.* 262.8.
[141] Plut. *Pomp.* 42.7; Asc. 19–20c. Cf. Dixon, 'Family finances: Terentia and Tullia' 99–100 (or in Rawson, *FAR* 114–15).   [142] *Phil.* 2.99. Plut. *Ant.* 9.1–2 accepts Antony's reason.

minded by divorcing her. When Octavian divorced Scribonia and alleged that she had a bad temper, this invited her riposte that this meant she was unwilling to tolerate his mistress. But Plutarch could understand how it was small faults rather than grave offences or deficiencies which might make a marriage unendurable.[143]

As it was later thought undesirable that a *paterfamilias* could break up a successful marriage, so outside interference was deplored. Caesar is praised for refusing to divorce Cinna's daughter at Sulla's request, while M. Piso is criticized for having got rid of Cinna's former wife to please Sulla.[144]

Bilateral divorce, with *bona gratia*, might be for sound practical reasons and leave no bitterness.[145] There is one classic passage in the jurists:

Divortii causa donationes inter virum et uxorem concessae sunt: saepe enim evenit uti propter sacerdotium vel etiam sterilitatem, (*Digest* 24.1.60.1, Hermogenianus *ii iuris epitomarum*)

Gifts between husband and wife are allowed because of divorce: for it often happens that because of a priesthood or even sterility,

vel senectutem aut valetudinem aut militiam satis commode retineri matrimonium non possit: (ht 61, Gaius *xi ad edictum provinciale*)

or old age or ill health or military service it is inconvenient to maintain a marriage

et ideo bona gratia matrimonium dissolvitur. (ht 62 pr., Hermogenianus *ii iuris epitomarum*)

and therefore the marriage is dissolved with good will.

Certain examples of consensual divorce are hard to find, apart from the especially generous one projected by the *laudata*.[146]

The legislation of Christian emperors as they attempted to limit unilateral divorce reminds us of ugly possibilities which only occasionally find mention in the literature of the pagan upper class. Wife-beating was listed as a valid reason for the wife to divorce.[147] Cruelty, habitual violence, or individual acts of physical violence such as attempted murder would undoubtedly have constituted solid reason for divorce in pagan thinking, whether the violence was directed against the *coniunx* or against others.[148]

---

[143] Petr. 74.16: 'At ego dum bonatus ago et nolo videri levis, ipse mihi asciam in crus impegi.' Suet. *DA* 62.2, 69.1; cf. Dio 59.23.7; *SHA Hadr.* 11.3; Plut. *Paullus* 5.3–4, for contemporaries attitude to Paullus' divorce, a related anecdote, and his own view.   [144] Vell. 2.41.2.
[145] *D* 24.1.32.10, 40.9.14.4   [146] *Laud. Tur.* 2.31ff.   [147] *CJ* 5.17.8.2.
[148] Cf. Suet. *Cl.* 26.2.

6. *Effects*

The legal effect of divorce was normally considered to be the physical separation of the *coniuges* and the restoration of dowry, apart from whatever the husband retained on account of children, fault, expenses, gifts, or things taken away. There was no community of property resulting from the marriage, unless the wife had fused her property with her husband's because she had entered *manus*: this would now have to be regarded as *dos* and restored to her in some form. But husband and wife might have become joint owners of various possessions, such as real estate or slaves, and it might now be convenient for one to buy the other out of his share.

Although the dowry system was partly designed to insure the woman against the severe economic consequences of divorce, and although she might have other property and might even be able to increase her dowry in order to attract a new husband,[149] her capital was likely to be decreased by a divorce. She might be lucky if the ideal of *aequitas* or aristocratic liberality made her husband more generous than the law demanded, so that he did not take full advantage of the *retentiones*. It is also clear from the jurists that gifts might be given to either *coniunx* in view of divorce.[150] Gifts given during the marriage were expected to be reclaimed, but if they were not reclaimed then they might be turned into valid transfers.[151] The Romans, like us, seem to have regarded an amicable property settlement as part of a 'civilized' divorce. When Nero divorced Octavia on the grounds of sterility, he was at first anxious to give their separation the appearance of a *civile discidium*, and he made substantial gifts to her, the house of Burrus and the estates of Rubellius Plautus. Ovid, who recommended an unemotional separation at the end of any love relationship, advised young men not to go from the bedroom to the courts in order to reclaim the presents they had given to wives or mistresses. It was better—and showed more indifference—to let her keep everything. Sulla dismissed Cloelia with gifts.[152] As we have seen, the law allowed gifts in view of divorce. (Conversely, gifts given during marriage might be reclaimed on divorce.) A divorce would usually have a more concrete effect on the wife's life-style than the husband's. He might have to raise cash to pay back her dowry and might consequently face some inconvenience. But unless they had been living in a dotal house, she would usually have to leave a house to which she had become accustomed. Her position as mistress of a

---

[149] pp. 346–7.   [150] *D* 24.1.60.   [151] Above, pp. 370–4.
[152] Tac. *A* 14.60.5; Ov. *Rem. am.* 669f.; Plut. *Sulla* 6.11. Cf. Plaut. *Miles* 1125–6.

household which centred on the social life of a man would disappear. A pattern of existence would be disrupted.

Particularly if a couple had children, their economic interests might continue to be linked. Although the original agnatic system made the husband primarily responsible for looking after their interests, by the time of Cicero it was recognized that a mother might have a duty to contribute economically to the fortunes of her children by a divorced husband.[153]

The introduction of *retentio propter liberos* suggests that the husband was always expected to be responsible for the support of children. Since they belonged to his family, not his ex-wife's, the norm was for them to be brought up in his household. This meant that many children of divorced parents must have lived with a stepmother. But there were departures from the norm. It might be convenient for babies to remain with their mother for some time. A particular variant is presented by the child who was unborn at the time of the divorce. The *Senatusconsultum Plancianum* ordained that a divorced wife should, if she found herself pregnant, send notice to the ex-husband within thirty calendar days of the divorce. He might then (1) deny the child was his, in which case he was not obliged to recognize it, though he might if it turned out to be his, (2) send guards, which left his options open, (3) do nothing, in which case he was compelled to recognize the child and provide for its support.[154] A child whom the father refused to recognize became the mother's responsibility.[155] Unless she exposed it when new-born, she had a duty to provide for its support.[156] There was a novel occurrence under Marcus Aurelius when a husband claimed that his divorced wife was pregnant and she denied it. The emperor decided on an equally novel procedure of inspection and verification to protect everyone's interest.[157] Ulpian says that up to the time of birth the child is part of the mother; only when it is born can the husband present a claim to see the child or take it away.[158] When a widow bore a child, her dead husband's *paterfamilias* (if any) had in principle the right to decide where and by whom the child was to be brought up.[159] Presumably the husband had

---

[153] Dixon, 'Family finances: Terentia and Tullia' 93 ff., cf. 87 (or in Rawson, *FAR* 108 ff., cf. 101).

[154] *D* 25.3.1, Ulp. The guards would presumably act along the lines set out in the praetor's edict on the watching of pregnant widows (*D* 25.4.1.10). The SC is shown to be pre-Hadrianic by 25.3.3.1, Ulp. Salvius Julianus (*c.*100–69) was an authority on the matter. Y. Thomas, 'Le "ventre": corps maternel, droit paternel', explores the concept but adds little to the texts on the law.

[155] Suet. *Cl.* 27.1.   [156] *D* 25.3.5.4, Ulp.

[157] *D* 25.4.1, Ulp. Cf. W. Williams, 'Individuality in the imperial constitutions: Hadrian and the Antonines' 79–82.

[158] *D* 25.4.1.1   [159] *D* 25.4.1.10.

the same right if he acknowledged the child of a divorced wife. The son whom Livia bore after her divorce from Nero went to his father for his early years.

When a child was supported by his father (in the father's house or elsewhere) it was still expected, at least by Marcus Aurelius, that his mother would spend some of her own money on him too, out of maternal affection. The same rescript shows that she might pay for support of the child, perhaps though not certainly in her own house, in which case she could claim reimbursement of expenses by the husband.[160] Probably such arrangements go back to the late Republic. When Dolabella and Tullia divorced, she turned out to be pregnant and the child appears to have been duly acknowledged, or so Cicero, an interested party, implicitly claims when he calls him Lentulus. But Dolabella was away and Tullia dead, so Cicero, the maternal grand-father, took some steps to support the baby in a suitable establish-ment. He would presumably be able to claim expenses from Dolabella, but there is no sign that he meant to do so. This was family affection and duty, not legal obligation.[161]

Evidence concerning the mother's financial and other involvement in the rearing of young children after a divorce is hard to come by. But the social set-up of the late Republic did not encourage monopoly of children by a father and stepmother. He might take a particular interest in the education of sons over the age of about 7, and the stepmother might take responsibility for the domestic training of girls. But children spent most of their time under the care of servants and moved around a good deal between their father's house and the establishments of various relations, between Rome and the country and the seaside. Fathers might be away in the provinces as much after a divorce as before. There might be a gap between their divorce and their remarriage. The possibility that young children would live sometimes with their mother cannot be discarded.[162]

The best-attested instance—and an extreme one—is that of the upbringing of the children of M. Antonius. Octavia, who had earlier refused to leave Antony's house when her brother asked her to, took his children with her to her own house when he finally sent her notice of divorce in 32 BC. The children of whom she then took charge were

[160] *D* 25.3.5.14.

[161] Cic. *A* 12.28.3. Dixon, 'The marriage alliance in the Roman elite' 368, suggests the baby was born at the home of 'her ex-husband's father-in-law'. The maternal grandfather was legally obliged to support a child only when other *alimenta* were missing, at least later (*D* 25.3.5.5, Ulp. citing Pius).

[162] One of Oppianicus' children is said to have lived with his mother at Teanum: he was old enough to visit his father on festivals (Cic. *Clu.* 27). The effect of divorce and death on the upbringing of children is explored by Bradley in 'Dislocation in the Roman family'.

her two daughters by Antony (born 39 and 36) and his younger son by his previous wife Fulvia, who was dead. Antony was in no position to look after young children. After his death, she brought up his three children by Cleopatra too. She already had the three children she had borne to the dead Marcellus.

Livia, after an amicable divorce from Ti. Claudius Nero, took their two sons, aged 9 and 5, into Augustus' house when their father died in 33. Augustus is said to have had an important influence on their upbringing (just as Livia had on her stepdaughter, Julia). Nero was given due honour: the 9-year-old Tiberius pronounced his funeral oration and later, when he had grown up, gave magnificent games in honour both of Nero and of his maternal grandfather, funded by his mother and stepfather.[163] It is interesting that there seems to have been particularly close affection between Augustus and his younger stepson, born after his own marriage to Livia. A contemporary witticism, which became proverbial, suggesting that Drusus was his natural son, can be discounted. But despite Augustus' even-handedness in distributing public honours between his two stepsons, it was Drusus whom he had named joint heir with his adoptive sons.[164] A similar paternal feeling may have been engendered in Asinius Gallus, when he took over the pregnant Vipsania from Tiberius and presumably saw the younger Drusus as the eldest child of his own household. According to Dio, he claimed Drusus as his own son, a statement which cannot be taken literally.[165]

The emperors in the second century took an interest in child custody. The general preference remained that the father should have the child in his control—and, it is understood, living with him. But if there were just cause, particularly the wickedness of the father, a judge was allowed to let the mother keep the child in her care, although the father retained *patria potestas*.[166] A rescript of Diocletian and Maximian in AD 294 found that no emperor had ever divided children up by sex, so that the girls lived with their mother and the boys with their father.[167] But they ruled that a judge could decide with which parent children should live and be brought up.[168] Christian emperors were particularly anxious to safeguard the economic and other interests of the children in case of divorce: 'favour to children

---

[163] Suet. *Tib.* 6.4, 7.1.
[164] Suet. *Cl.* 1.1, 5; cf. *DA* 62.2, *Tib.* 4.3; Vell. 2.95.1; Tac. *A* 1.10.4, 5.1.3; Dio 48.44.
[165] 57.2.7. For the numerous sons of Gallus and Vipsania see *PIR*² A1229.
[166] *D* 43.30.1.1, 5, Ulp. citing Pius, M. Aurelius, and Severus.
[167] Such a division was applied by the anonymous statute altered by Vespasian, that if a free man cohabited with a slave-woman whom he thought to be free, her male children were free, but the daughters were slaves (G 1.85).   [168] *CJ* 5.24.

commands that the dissolution of marriage should be rather difficult.'[169]

Emotional ties between mother and child seem often to have survived divorce. We do not know the nature of the relationship between Scribonia and Julia from the day of Julia's birth, when Octavian divorced Scribonia, but we are told that the mother voluntarily accompanied her daughter into exile 37 years later. We must assume that they kept in touch during the interval. Ties to mothers were not forgotten, even though the relationship between *coniuges* had been dissolved. No one ignored the fact that Drusus, who might have succeeded Tiberius as emperor, was the son of Vipsania and the grandson of Agrippa.[170] The rhetoricians make much of the indestructible bond between mother and children.[171]

If the divorce was consensual, there was no reason why all concerned should not remain on good terms. Even if some cause for bitterness existed, it could still be expected that the kinsmen of the injured *coniunx* would maintain friendly relations with their former *affines*. Cicero preserved the *convenances* with Dolabella and, after an interval, was again friendly with Tullia's previous ex-husband, Crassipes.[172] Social expectations of civilized tolerance could be extreme. Although Pompey had divorced Mucia without formally complaining of adultery, but openly aspersing her, Aemilius Scaurus apparently thought that in marrying her he strengthened his link with Pompey.[173] Breeding children who were half-siblings of Pompey's was especially important. Pompey, however, is said not to have thought that this relationship put him under any new obligation to Scaurus.[174] Such a bond was supposed to hold between Hortensius and Cato, since Cato divorced Marcia specifically so that she could marry Hortensius, strengthening the friendship between the two men and producing stepsons for Cato.[175]

Pompey resented Mucia and her new husband. We have some information on the emotional impact of divorce on two other husbands. M. Aemilius Lepidus (consul 78 BC) was expelled from Italy after his rebellion. In Plutarch's highly coloured account, he went to Sardinia and there died of despondency caused by accidentally coming across a document which indicated that his wife was an adulteress.

[169] *CJ* 5.17.8 pr., and cf. 7, ht 11.1c.

[170] Tac *A* 2.43.7, 3.19.4. Further instances in Dixon, *RM* 169, 218.

[171] e.g. *Decl. min.* 338; Calp. *Decl.* 35: '"Repudiata es" inquit; mariti haec culpa non filii est, nec matris officium repudio deponitur, sed uxorium nomen amittitur.'

[172] See Dixon, 'The marriage alliance in the Roman elite' 368; SB *F* on 139.

[173] He already had a bond as a legate to Pompey and a former brother-in-law. See Gruen, *LGRR* 62–3, 148–9.

[174] Asc. *Scaur.* 19–20c.   [175] Plut. *Cato min.* 25.2ff.

According to Pliny, Lepidus was an example of strong affection. Whereas his other exemplar, Ti. Gracchus, when it was fated that either his wife or he must die, chose to die himself, sacrificing himself for Cornelia, Lepidus actually died of love. He repudiated his wife Appuleia and died of the anxiety caused by the divorce.[176] To add to the pathos, things went badly wrong at his cremation. It is interesting that elaborate stories about private disaster attached to men who incurred political calamity.

A more convincing account is given of the effect on Tiberius of the breaking up of his *bene concordans matrimonium* with Vipsania by order of Augustus. He still loved her and conceived a lifelong resentment of her new husband Asinius Gallus. Domitian is said not to have been able to endure his divorce from Domitia, although he had divorced her because she was in love with an actor, and to have found a pretext for taking her back.[177] Whatever the historicity of these stories, they show that heart-broken husbands had a certain appeal to rhetorical historians and their largely male audiences.

The emotional impact on the wife is harder to assess. We are told nothing of Tullia's reactions or Vipsania's or Marcella's when Agrippa divorced her. Since forgiveness of a husband's faults was sanctioned up to a point,[178] while condonation of a wife's adultery was condemned, the wife might be expected to feel or feign reluctance to divorce even a delinquent husband. Cicero captures this ladylike attitude neatly when he describes the divorce of Cluentia: 'So there was a rapid divorce, which looked as if it would console her for all her sufferings. Cluentia left Melinus, not unwillingly because of her injuries, but not gladly since she was leaving her husband.'[179] The rhetoricians make the most of the pathos of the repudiation of a blameless wife, driven from the house to which she had gone as a virgin bride.[180]

7. *Attitudes*

Divorce of a virtuous wife or frivolous divorce of a husband was conventionally condemned. Light divorce by women was condemned by philosophers and satirists.[181] To divorce irresponsibly was to injure

---

[176] Plut. *Pomp.* 16.6; Pliny *NH* 7.122, 186. Appuleia is presumably a kinswoman of the tribune Saturninus. But Hirschfeld, *KS* 685, thinks this is Appuleia Varilla, condemned for adultery in AD 17. Syme, *Augustan Aristocracy* 126, suggests that the couple are this Appuleia or, better, a close relative and M. Lepidus.

[177] Above, p. 259; Tac. *A* 1.12.6; Suet. *Dom.* 3.1.

[178] Plaut. *Men.* 768–9.   [179] *Clu.* 14.

[180] *Decl. min.* 338.9, 28; cf. Tac. *A* 14.63.4.

[181] Sen. *Ben.* 3.16.2; Mart. 6.7, 10.41; Juv. 6.224 ff.; Tert. *Apol.* 6.6.

the sanctities of marriage.[182] A wife who had borne children of undoubted legitimacy had a particular claim on her husband's loyalty, even if her subsequent behaviour justified suspicion of adultery.[183] But for a husband to divorce the mother of his children when no suspicion of infidelity attached to her or because he had a mistress was thoroughly deplorable.[184] The divorce of a wife who was about to bear her husband a child was also shocking.[185] The reason for this attitude is not the welfare of the children but the husband's duty to a wife who had done her duty.

It was easy to attack the impropriety of a husband who remarried rapidly and brought his wife into a bed warm with the traces of the woman he had divorced.[186] Irresponsible divorce by men is less of a target than the levity of wives who divorce. But the man who brought about divorce by seducing a married woman is condemned as adulterer and abductor.[187] When Sulla in 89 BC gave Cloelia an honourable divorce, with gifts and testimonies to her character, but claiming that he was dismissing her because she was childless, he was thought to have trumped up a reason, since he married Metella a few days later.[188]

Roman society never looked on divorce as anything other than a sad necessity. It provided a way out of difficulties but it was not a solution to be lightly adopted.[189] When Vestal Virgins were chosen in AD 19, the daughter of Domitius Pollio was preferred to the rival candidate, the daughter of Fonteius Agrippa, 'because her mother had remained in the same marriage: for Agrippa had reduced his house by divorce'.[190]

Although the misconduct of a husband or wife might make it impossible to remain happily or honourably married, the line between divorce which social peers would accept as unfortunate but justified and divorce which would be seen as irresponsible and self-seeking was hard to draw. The divorced woman might be regarded as unfortunate, like a widow, and the noun which describes her is the same, *vidua*.[191] Apuleius has a highly rhetorical passage, which suited his case but cannot have pleased his wife, that to marry a widow proves altruism, not avarice. People prefer virgins as brides. Both types of *viduae* present problems:

[182] VM 2.9.2: 'coniugalia sacra . . . iniuriose tractata.'

[183] Suet. *DJ* 50.1 (Mucia and Pompey); Plut. *Cato min.* 24.3 (Servilia and Lucullus, Atilia and Cato).

[184] Dio 46.18.3 (Calenus on Cicero); Ov. *AA* 3.33; Plut. *Paullus* 5.1 ff.; Tac. *A* 4.3.5.

[185] Afran. *com.* 165–7; Dio 54.31.2 (Vipsania Tiberii); cf. Plut. *Cato min.* 25.5. But it is attested surprisingly often: Aemilia, Tullia, Livia, Vipsania.   [186] *Decl. min.* 338.28.

[187] *D* 24.2.8; cf. Dio 54.16.6.   [188] Plut. *Sulla* 6.11; cf. Cic. *Phil.* 2.99.

[189] Cf. e.g. Ter. *And.* 567–8; Cic. *A* 11.23.3, *Clu.* 14.   [190] Tac. *A* 2.86.2.

[191] Plaut. *Men.* 726; Tac. *A* 14.64.2; *D* 24.1.64, Labeo. For *viduus* see Plaut. *Merc.* 829.

But a *vidua* goes away after a divorce in the same condition in which she came to the wedding: she brings nothing which cannot be asked for again, but she comes already deflowered by some other man. Certainly she is not at all teachable for what you want; she suspects her new house as much as she ought to be suspected because of her previous divorce, whether she lost her husband by death, which makes her a woman of evil omen and ill-fated marriage and so not at all to be courted, or whether she went away because of a *repudium*, which means that blame attaches to her, either because she was so unbearable that she was repudiated, or so arrogant that she divorced (*repudiaret*). (*Apology* 92)

8. Frequency

According to moralizing sources, divorce was frequent and frivolous in the late Republic and early Empire. Modern scholars have often accepted this view of things.

Robleda, for instance, claims that there is abundant information for the early period, citing Plautus, apparently without the slightest glimmer of doubt which might have been caused by the limited range of love scenarios available to comic writers.[192] I take a different view, that married men, whether young like Menaechmus of Epidamnus or old like Lysidamus in the *Casina*, who pursue hetaerae or slaves are rare in Plautus and their love-affair is either ignored or punished in the denouement. Divorce never occurs in extant comedy, whether for this or any other reason. There is no justification for supposing, as Costa did long ago, that Plautus proves that divorce, not the death of a *coniunx*, was already at this date the commonest cause for the end of a marriage.[193]

Two allusions in Terence and the divorce of Aemilius Paullus do not add up to much for the second century BC. For the first century, Robleda cites Cicero and Valeria Paulla, for the first century AD two generalizations in the sources, to show that divorces 'dilagavano quasi spudoratamente'.[194]

But for the late Republic Robleda is relying on F. Piccinelli, who in 1885 drew up a cursory list of eminent politicians who were known to have divorced—Sulla, Pompey, Caesar, Cicero, Antony, Brutus —and Aemilia, in order to marry Pompey, and Valeria Paulla.[195] By the standards of Italian Catholics in the late nineteenth century, this no doubt represents an epidemic of divorce, as it might to an

[192] 'Il divorzio a Roma prima di Costantino' 365 ff.
[193] *Il diritto privato nelle commedie di Plauto* 177, cited with approval by Robleda, 'Il divorzio a Roma prima di Costantino' 365. Costa's collection of Plautine texts under various headings still has some usefulness. See now Schuhmann, 'Ehescheidungen in den Komödien des Plautus'.   [194] p. 366.
[195] 'L'evoluzione storico-giuridica del divorzio in Roma da Romolo ad Augusto' 468.

Englishman earlier in that century. He might find parallels between sparsely documented divorce by husbands in archaic Rome—striking examples of severe moral standards or of husband's irresponsibility punished by the censors—and the period from the late seventeenth century to 1857 when divorces were granted with extreme difficulty by the House of Lords.[196] The liberalization of English law in 1857 allowed husbands and even wives greater freedom to apply for a divorce.[197] In 1923 the grounds became the same for both. Both Acts led to an increase in the number of divorces. In 1860 127 were granted; in 1887, 390. Such figures must have seemed alarming compared with what England had seen before. But they were not high compared with the rate in revolutionary France, where in 1797 there had been more divorces than marriages, or in the contemporary United States. There private Acts of state legislatures originally granted individual divorces. This system gave way to varying patterns in different states. Only in South Carolina was divorce not recognized. Grounds for divorce differed and were looser than in England, including 'marital cruelty'. In 1867 there were 9,937 divorces; in 1886, 25,535 in the whole of the United States, an increase of 157 per cent. Sir James Bryce, who in 1901 conveniently quoted these figures, and who discussed, with scholarly objectivity, the question of whether the English law should be liberalized, was shocked by the American figures. 'The total number granted in these twenty years (and the record is probably not quite complete) is 328,716, a ghastly total, exceeding all the divorces granted in the same years in all other Christian countries. The population of the Republic increased about 60 per cent within the same twenty years.'[198] Moreover, two-thirds of these divorces were granted to wives. European countries not controlled by the Roman Catholic Church such as Germany and France (after 1884) also showed a significant and increasing divorce-rate. It is not surprising that scholars thought to compare secular ancient

---

[196] During this period 'a little over 200 . . . divorces' were granted. 'Of these only about half a dozen were granted at the suit of a woman' (K. Thomas, 'The double standard' 201). The first divorce by a wife took place in 1801.

[197] In 1857 husbands could divorce for one act of infidelity, wives only for bigamy, incest, adultery made worse by cruelty or two years' desertion. Misconduct by the husband, however, debarred him from divorcing his wife.

[198] 'Marriage and divorce under Roman and English law'. Between 1870 and 1880 the US population increased 30.1% and the divorce-rate 79.4%. For a succinct and scholarly account of divorce law in England and Wales in the 20th cent. see Parkinson, *Conciliation in separation and divorce* 11 ff. The Matrimonial Causes Act 1937 added cruelty, desertion, and incurable insanity to the grounds for divorce. The Divorce Law Reform Act of 1969 introduced 'irretrievable breakdown of marriage' as the only grounds, but this was to be proved by arguments which might impute blame to one partner in the pattern established by the old grounds of adultery etc. For the separate development of American divorce practice and law see Friedman, *A History of American Law* 204 ff., 498 ff.

Rome. Bryce himself, who thought that Roman marriage in the Principate was characterized by equality, not the subordination of the wife, held that women should have the same rights as men in English divorce law, but that the permanence of marriage must be defended. He found it difficult to point to any decline in morality as a cause for contemporary divorce and found that a desire for independence was a more likely cause than infidelity. He finds the causes of divorce in the decline in religious belief, industrialization, individualism, higher standards for marriage, the pursuit of happiness, urbanism, and newspaper-reading, a list which is refreshing after the sweeping attacks on sexual licence offered by many writers.

Acceptance of divorce by society, preceding and following legislation, came most slowly in Catholic countries. In Italy the introduction of civil divorce in 1970 unleashed a surge of cases, many of them a backlog from couples who had long been separated. Despite the opposition of the Catholic Church to such changes in the civil law, it too has adjusted to the changing situation in Italy and elsewhere by making it far easier than before for Catholics to obtain decrees of nullity. But the scandal which this provokes now or a few generations back among scholars brought up in a society which made marriage virtually indissoluble—and never yet dissoluble at the mere will of one partner—should not lead us to project our own preoccupations back into pagan Rome.[199] In Western countries at the present time the divorce-rate has reached unprecedented levels. In England and Wales it is predicted, on current trends, that one recent marriage in three will end in divorce. In the United States, in 1985 there were 10.2 marriages and 5 divorces per 1,000 people.[200] Would we argue that Roman rates were comparable in the first century BC?

As we have seen, the history of Roman divorce shows a gradual development from the early period when unilateral divorce by the husband was practised for grave fault, to the classical period when either party could divorce the other with relative freedom. *Mores*, not *leges*, determined the social rules. The development of rules about

---

[199] Piccinelli, 'L'evoluzione storico-giuridica del divorzio', was particularly shocked by consensual divorce, which showed how far corruption had gone and gave an incentive to abuse. Because women could divorce capriciously, men avoided marriage (p. 468). See too Salvatore, 'L'immoralité des femmes et la décadence de l'Empire selon Tacite'.

[200] Parkinson, *Conciliation and separation in divorce* 1: 'It is well known that divorce increased sharply during the 1970s. The number of couples who divorced in England and Wales (1.2 million between 1971 and 1980) was three times the number who divorced in the 1960s (0.4 million between 1961 and 1970). The divorce rate increased sixfold in England and Wales between 1960 and 1980 and although it has levelled out since 1979, the level remains very high, since on current trends it is predicted that one in three marriages will end in divorce within 35 years of marriage.' US rate: *New York Times* 15 Apr., 1986. In California the divorce-rate is now estimated at 80% or higher (*Palo Alto Weekly*, 11 Feb. 1987).

restoration of dowry belongs principally to the period when our evidence is scantiest and attested divorces therefore rarest. But the process of change was fairly gradual and no one piece of legislation will have opened the floodgates to a sudden spate of divorces, as in modern times. In assessing the frequency of divorce, we would have to have statistics which are unobtainable. We have only two sorts of evidence: generalizations by ancient authors and references to individual divorces. Let us assess the generalizations first.[201]

Cicero in the speech on behalf of Cluentius remarked that new enmities among families often led to divorces and the breaking of ties by marriage. But he is not talking about the high rate of divorce in general, only about the frequency of divorce for this reason. And his reason for the generalization is to make a hit at Sassia, that, with her, enmities lead to marriages.[202] But this text may have some value in explaining some upper-class divorces, as we shall see later.

Moderns rehearse a number of passages from authors whose adherence to genre is more striking than their exact observation of contemporaries.[203] Seneca's diatribe on how adultery leads to divorce has already been quoted. In another famous passage, he argues that if vices, such as ingratitude, are published, they become common. The trend can be seen in women's attitude to divorce.

Is any woman now ashamed because she is divorced, when various illustrious and nobly born women count their age not by adding up consuls but by husbands, and go away [i.e. divorce] in order to marry and marry in order to divorce? As long as divorce was rare, it was feared. But now there is a divorce in every issue of the *Daily News*, women have learnt to do what they keep hearing about. (*De beneficiis* 3.16.2)

This leads to adultery.[204] An unpredictable switch from love to hate also led even elderly ladies to abandon their husbands:

Veterum matrimoniorum repudia cognovimus et foediores divortio male cohaerentium rixae. Quam multae quos in adolescentia amaverunt, in senectute communi reliquerunt! Quotiens anile divortium risimus! Quam multarum notus amor odio notiore mutatus est. (*De remediis fortuitorum* 16.5 ed. Loth, *Revue de philologie* NS 12 (1888) 118–27)

We have seen long-standing marriages end in repudiation and the quarrels of inharmonious couples which are more shameful than divorce. How many

---

[201] Raepsaet-Charlier, 'Ordre sénatorial et divorce sous le haut-empire: un chapitre de l'histoire des mentalités' (which came to hand after I had formulated views which support hers), has a similar review of the ancient texts at 162 ff.

[202] *Clu.* 190.

[203] Raepsaet-Charlier, 'Ordre sénatorial et divorce' 161 n. 1, collects representative examples.

[204] *Ben.* 3.16.3.

women have, when both were old, deserted the husbands they loved in youth! How often have we laughed at an old woman's divorce! How many women noted for love have exchanged it for even more noteworthy hatred!

The epigrams make an excellent sermon, but Seneca's purpose is to preach, not to inform. Martial exaggerated the same motifs into grotesque jokes: Telesilla has had ten husbands in the month since the Julian Law was revived. Serial marriage is adultery.[205] Juvenal says that dominant wives leave, remarry, and return to the previous husband with enormous rapidity. Eight husbands in five years—worth putting on her epitaph.[206] Finally, a hostile source from the late second century. Tertullian attacks the decline of women's morality from archaic simplicity. Once women did not drink, wore no gold except an engagement ring, and there was no divorce. Now they are laden with gold, they cannot be kissed because they smell of wine, and they look forward to divorce as the fruit of marriage (apparently expecting to profit from it).[207]

There is a different slant in two *incidental* remarks, which might have rather more weight, though again we must attend to the context. The anonymous *laudator* claims that he and his wife were exceptional —both fortunate and good?—in having enjoyed a marriage of forty-one years uninterrupted by divorce. He was tempted to generalize: 'Such long unions, uninterrupted by divorce, are uncommon.'[208] The essential point is that long happy marriages are rare, which is why people boast of them on epitaphs. By definition a happy marriage must not end in divorce. If he implies anything about the point at which divorce might normally be expected, if neither *coniunx* had been carried off by death, it is very imprecise. The statistical probability of death before the fortieth wedding anniversary was undoubtedly high.

Another virtuous *coniunx* makes a similar remark in a different context. When Lucan describes how Pompey felt compelled to send his wife Cornelia away to safety in Lesbos, he gives her a splendid speech. She laments that it is not death which breaks their love. She will be without her husband, dismissed (like a divorced wife), a fate which is common and vulgar.[209] She is expressing aristocratic revulsion from a banal experience, in order to stress her love and fidelity, and playing on the idea of lifelong marriage. We are back in the

---

[205] 6.7. Proculeia divorces her husband because he is about to become expensive as a praetor (10.41). This text, though often used, does not tell us anything about how often she divorced.

[206] 6.224 ff.   [207] *Apol.* 6.3 ff.

[208] 'Rara sunt tam diuturna matrimonia, finita morte non divortio in[terrupta]' (*Laud. Tur.* 1.27–8). 'Forty-one years' is perhaps lower than the figure originally inscribed: there is a lacuna after xli.

[209] 5.764–8: 'sed sorte frequenti | plebeiaque nimis careo dimissa marito.'

context of the ideology of marriage, not of an objective assessment of divorce. Such literary allusions attest nothing more than conventional disapproval of divorce. They tell us nothing about its incidence in the late Republic and early Empire, only that moralists thought it was too high. We turn to the attested divorces. Let us confine our attention to relatively well-documented times and begin with the age of Cicero.[210]

In the period covered by Cicero's letters (68–43 BC), L. Lucullus divorced Clodia perhaps soon after his return from the east in 66. Despite the later scandalous allegations of incest, the main reason may have been his annoyance with the behaviour of her brother when he served under him: the incest charge was meant to damage Clodius.[211] Lucullus then married Servilia, presumably the niece of Cato, and divorced her for adultery at an unknown data but after she had given him a son.[212] Cato's divorce of his first wife is also attributed to sexual misbehaviour. Pompey divorced his third wife Mucia in 62. It was common knowledge that he accused her of adultery with Caesar, but this was not the official motivation. Modern scholars connect the event with Pompey's need for new alliances to consolidate his position on his return from the east. He attempted to connect himself with Cato's family, but this failed, so he remained *caelebs* until the marriage with Julia in 59.[213] Soon after this, Caesar divorced Pompeia, to whom he had been married since 67. Her childlessness and the need for new political support may have been the reasons which underlay his overt scrupulosity about her impaired reputation. In 60 M. Lucullus divorced his wife (identity unknown) for adultery with Memmius. Memmius' own long-standing marriage to Sulla's daughter Fausta may have lasted until 55, when she married Milo. We

---

[210] See Appendix 5.

[211] Wiseman, *Cinna the poet and other Roman essays* 113; Dixon, 'The marriage alliance in the Roman elite' 370. The allegations of incest were made by Lucullus at the trial of Clodius in spring 61, when he claimed that he had taken evidence from slave-women under torture (Cic. *Mil.* 73: 'eum, quem cum sorore germana nefarium stuprum fecisse L. Lucullus iuratus se quaestionibus habitis dixit comperisse'; cf. Plut. *Cic.* 29.3, *Caes.* 10.5; *Luc.* 34.1 does not date the accusation; ibid. 38.1 has the generic 'accusation about brothers'). Cicero does not use incest in his exchange of repartee with Clodius in the Senate on 15 May reported in *A* 1.16.8ff. When he introduces that theme, which was to become such a favourite with him, in mid-60, the sister to whom he refers is the wife of Metellus Celer (*A* 2.1.5).

[212] Plut. *Luc.* 38.1, who is probably wrong to think Servilia is Cato's sister. See Wiseman, *Cinna the poet and other Roman essays* 113–14, citing Cic. *Fin.* 3.8–9 for the relationship and also Plut. *Cato min.* 24.3, 29.3, 54.1, Cic. *A* 1.18.3 (of 20 Jan. 50, implying that Memmius seduced her as well as her sister-in-law). Note that Memmius' wife Fausta, Sulla's daughter, had been the ward of L. Lucullus. Memmius prosecuted M. Lucullus in 66 and opposed L. Lucullus' triumph (SB *A* on 18.3). Servilia's son L. Lucullus became Cato's ward; mother and son accompanied Cato to the east in 49. (Andréev, 'La Lex Iulia de adulteriis coercendis' 180, inexplicably dates both the divorces of L. Lucullus to 74.)

[213] Syme, *RR* 113; Gruen, 'Pompey, the Roman aristocracy and the Conference of Luca' 82–3; Leach, *Pompey the Great* 112–13; Seager, *Pompey. A Political biography* 73, 96.

do not know the reason for this rupture, nor for the break-up of Tullia's relatively brief marriage with Furius Crassipes (betrothed 56, divorced by spring 51 and after December 54), although that is thought to have produced a break in the friendship between Cicero and his son-in-law.[214] In 50 Dolabella's wife (presumably the wife attested in an anecdote as Fabia) left him and Valeria Paulla sent her husband (who is unidentified) formal notice of divorce in order to marry D. Brutus. The outbreak of civil war in 49 was not attended by formal marital break-ups: these cluster in the aftermath of war, when couples were reunited. In 47 or 46 Antony discarded his cousin Antonia, chiefly perhaps in order to marry Curio's widow Fulvia. Dolabella and Tullia and Cicero and Terentia split up, perhaps consensually, in 46. In 45 Spinther divorced Metella; Cicero and Publilia abandoned their marriage after a few months; and Brutus divorced Claudia, to whom he had been married probably since about the time of her father's consulship in 54, a step which was not approved by his friends, probably because it seemed to mark a break with the *boni*.[215] The marriage of Q. Cicero and Pomponia was almost conterminous with the extant letters of M. Cicero. The attitude of Quintus to his wife was being nervously monitored by his brother in the first surviving letters to Atticus in late 68 and early 67. The divorce, heralded by an embarrassing quarrel in front of Marcus in 51, did not occur until early 44.[216] Soon after, the younger Quintus was hoping to make a match with a lady, perhaps called Tutia, whose divorce was said to be decided upon. In the period after Cicero's death three divorces can be laid at the door of the rapidly rising young Octavian.

These examples do not add up to very much. Some divorces may have been caused by a rapidly discovered incompatibility—Tullia's from Crassipes or Cicero's from Publilia. Others were long postponed. Cicero approved of Terentia almost up to the end. L. Lucullus is said to have borne Servilia's infidelities for years out of respect for Cato. Other divorces seem to have been primarily motivated by political advantage: Sulla's from Cloelia, Pompey's from Antistia and Mucia, Caesar's from Pompeia, Brutus' from Claudia, Octavian's from Clodia and Scribonia. All formed new alliances which in different ways reflected their new standing or alignments. Sexual motivation occurs, and is naturally hinted at for divorcing women like Valeria. It may be one of the reasons why their husbands discarded the ageing Terentia or Mucia. But if we look at even the most married

[214] Cf. SB *F* on 139.
[215] Cn. Pompeius the Younger was married to Claudia's sister. Their father had died in 48.
[216] See esp. Cic. *A* 1.5.2, 1.6.2, 1.10.5, 5.1.3–4, 14.10.4, 14.13.5.

politicians of the late Republic, they did not resort to divorce repeatedly. Pompey married five times and was noted for his affection towards Julia and Cornelia. He divorced the unfortunate Antistia under pressure from Sulla and Metella, in order to marry Metella's daughter Aemilia. He divorced Mucia after long separation caused by his campaigns. He lost Aemilia and Julia by death. Sulla had also married five times according to Plutarch. But 'Ilia', his alleged first wife, is probably a doublet for 'Aelia', his second.[217] The fate of this lady or ladies is unknown, not necessarily divorce; the third, Cloelia, he divorced in order to marry a Caecilia Metella. He remained loyal to her until she was dying during the festival or Hercules in 82. Then he was advised to avoid ritual pollution by not visiting her or conducting the funeral from his house. He not only arranged for her to be taken to another house to die, but sent her notice of divorce, later making up for this by giving her a magnificent funeral.[218] Caesar married three times and divorced once. M. Lucullus divorced both his wives and so did Cato (but the arrangement with Marcia, whom he later remarried, was peculiar). Crassus stuck to his brother's widow Tertulla, disregarding attacks on her reputation, which were probably fabricated in order to drive a wedge between him and Caesar.[219] Caesar kept the apparently virtuous but certainly childless Calpurnia for about fifteen years (hardly any of them spent together). Even Octavian, after a ruthless youth, was resolutely wedded to Livia in spite of her failure to give him children. Among prominent ladies, Servilia (Cato's half-sister), Clodia Metelli (despite alleged disputes), and Fulvia lost husbands by death, not divorce. D. Brutus and the notorious Sempronia seem to have remained married.

A discreditable divorce was often good ammunition against a political opponent. Cicero's divorce of Terentia and Antony's of Antonia were publicly attacked. We would expect to hear of more, for gentlemanly reticence is unlikely to have restrained Cicero from adding marital delinquencies to the more interesting vices such as seduction, pathic homosexuality, or incest in his attacks on Catiline, Clodius, Piso, or Vatinius. We might also expect more instances in the gossipy letters of Cicero and Caelius. Caelius refers once to a rash of scandals since Cicero's departure, but this should not be taken as solemn evidence for a higher rate of adultery and divorce.[220] Much of

---

[217] See Münzer in *RE* ix/1.1000 s.v. *Ilia* (2). Ilius appears not to be a *gentilicium*. The names are also suspiciously similar to 'Cloelia'. But Plutarch claims that Ilia was the mother of Cornelia, who married Q. Pompeius Rufus and died in the year of his consulship, leaving two children. If Sulla divorced Cloelia for barrennes, we cannot identify Ilia and Cloelia. We could identify Aelia and Cloelia.

[218] Plut. *Sulla* 35.2.   [219] Plut. *Cr.* 1.1; Suet. *DJ* 50.1.   [220] Cic. *F* 8.7.2.

our evidence on divorce, as on marriage, is owed to the conscientious gleanings of Plutarch. On most of the lesser figures we are simply uninformed. What we see is divorce working as a safety-valve: socially defensible where there was serious cause, often deplored when the responsible *coniunx* acted lightly or for improper reasons. Certain great men were prepared to manipulate marriage and divorce cynically for their social and political advancement: Cato is as striking an instance as Sulla or Pompey. Others, consistently or sometimes, kept conjugal faith separate from political life.

A similar pattern continues in the early Principate. Augustus manipulated divorce as coldly as Sulla. Attested divorces in the upper class are scattered and involve chiefly those closest to the dynasty. After the Julio-Claudian period the evidence is thinner still. The apparent high-water mark of divorce in the first century BC and first century AD almost certainly reflects the availability of sources, though a reaction to old-fashioned values discerned by Tacitus and reflected in the home life of Antoninus Pius and Marcus Aurelius, as well as the fact that the right to rule of Hadrian and M. Aurelius depended (at least in part) on their wives, may have meant that the post-Julio-Claudian aristocracy was more disposed to longer marriages. M.-T. Raepsaet-Charlier has shown that many of the divorces known from the early Principate occur in the ruling house: an indication not only of the focus of the sources but of the emperors' manipulation of marriage. Her thorough study of the senatorial class from 10 BC to *c.* AD 200 produces 27 attested divorces for 562 known women. (There are also 12 attested remarriages, which might indicate up to 24 further divorces, but I leave these out of account since I believe death is frequently the cause of the dissolution of the first marriage.) Of the 27 certain divorces, 15 occurred in the imperial family or in families closely related to it, and 24 occurred under the Julio-Claudians. I would modify her calculations slightly, but her main arguments are cogent. (Appendix 6.)

Divorce initiated by women is no more commonly attested in the early Principate than in the late Republic. Divorce by men is not normally attested in the literary sources as a result of the operation of the Julian Law on adultery. Dynastic planning or the errant appetites of an emperor account for a high proportion. It is not possible to generalize these data in order to argue for a high frequency of divorce among the senatorial or equestrian class in general during the period *c.* 100 BC to AD 200.[221] Nor is it possible to argue with confidence that the propertied classes outside the imperial house and its immediate

---

[221] *Pace* Humbert, *Remariage à Rome* 80–92, in a discussion of attested remarriages which obscures the distinction between divorce and the death of a *coniunx*.

circle were less inclined to divorce. Our literary sources (except Pliny) almost ignore them and tombstones (on which so many of our sample of women are attested) do not document divorce.

In the absence of evidence, either a higher or lower incidence of divorce has been postulated for the lower classes.[222] Since the evidence is from tombstones, divorce is unlikely to be attested unless it was unusually amicable. A handful of epitaphs to wives dedicated by two living husbands are probably to be explained as attesting first marriages, probably *contubernia*, broken by third parties (such as slave-owners).[223]

We have, then, no statistics for nuptiality or divorce. On balance, the divorce-rate seems much less rapid and the habit of divorce less widespread than has commonly been thought. But the legal sources show clearly that divorce was always a possibility and an option. Both marriage and divorce were free. No automatic social stigma attached to the *coniunx* who divorced or the *coniunx* who was divorced. The upper class, at least, may show a tendency towards not attributing blame in unilateral divorce and towards preferring bilateral divorce *bona gratia*.

Our evidence on what happens to divorced people is thin. Men probably had no difficulty in marrying again, though Q. Cicero preferred not to. It is hard to discern in the upper class the feeling that for a woman to remarry while her former husband was still alive was dishonourable which Plutarch saw as a reason for comparatively quiet weddings.[224] The Augustan legislation discouraged women between the ages of 20 and 50 from delaying remarriage for more than eighteen months. Valeria Paulla had her next marriage arranged before she divorced. Young divorced women like Tiberius' Vipsania or Agrippa's Marcella were compensated by new husbands (one, Marcella's, arranged by Augustus and his family, the other probably not). Women still of child-bearing age and with good connections like Pompey's Mucia remarried creditably enough. But an older woman like Terentia or Apicata might have had more difficulty in finding a new husband.[225] It must be admitted that, whatever suffering the Roman system of divorce entailed, it fell more heavily on the woman.

[222] Grimal, *L'amour à Rome* 323–6; Kajanto, 'On divorce among the common people of Rome', approved by Raepsaet-Charlier, 'Ordre sénatorial et divorce' 161.

[223] Treggiari and Dorken, 'Women with two living husbands in *CIL* 6'. T. R. Bryce, 'Lycian tomb families and the social implications' 301, allows for the burial in the same tomb of two successive husbands, possibly both alive when the inscription was carved. I owe this reference to L. A. Curchin.   [224] Plut. *QR* 105, Cf. Humbert, *Remariage à Rome* 6.

[225] Remarriage to the same *coniunx* is a fairly popular topic in the jurists, but probably not common in real life. See e.g. *D* 23.2.33, 23.4.26.5, ht 29.1, 24.1.32.11, 24.3.19, ht 29.1, 25.2.23; *FV* 107. Domitian is said to have put Domitia away only temporarily, bringing her back (he claimed) by popular demand (Suet. *Dom.* 3.1).

14
Death

Two graves must hide thy and my corse,
If one might, death were no divorce.

(Donne, 'The Anniversarie')

When widows exclaim loudly against second marriages, I would always lay a wager that the man, if not the wedding-day, is absolutely fixed on.

(Fielding, *Amelia* VI.8)

1. Mors

Losing a wife by death was a major misfortune. A philosophical topos compared it with the subjugation of one's country or the loss of children. Only the wise man could rise above it to account himself happy.[1] Since a woman had fewer pleasures in life than a man, and less philosophy, the Romans must have felt that loss of a *coniunx* was even more disastrous for women. But the nature of the sources tends to obscure this. We even lack formal letters of condolence or consolatory essays addressed to women on the deaths of husbands, although our authors must have been in the habit of writing them.

The Romans chosen by ancient biographers often died by violence. Great interest attached to whether they made a good end, but circumstances precluded the presence of wives and children. Outsiders knew less about those whose end was more peaceful. A natural death, from illness or old age, was surrounded by ritual and etiquette and we know a good deal about externals. The Romans approved of friends and family attending death-beds. A dying man might summon kinsmen and friends. So Atticus, when suffering from a painful illness, called his son-in-law, Agrippa, and two male friends to hear his resolve to starve himself to death: 'I am determined to stop feeding my disease.' Cicero claims that he visited Metellus Celer and

---

[1] Sen. *Epp.* 9.18, *Rem.* 16, *Prov.* 3.2; cf. Stob. 4.22.3.79.

held discussion on high politics as he lay dying.[2] Final messages and, especially, last words were important.[3] We are sometimes told that it was the wife to whom the last words were addressed. Augustus was said to have made an excellent end. Death came as he and Livia were kissing, and he asked her to live remembering their marriage and bade her farewell. 'Repente in osculis Liviae et in hac voce defecit: "Livia, nostri coniugii memor vive, et vale!" '[4] The strength of the feeling that a *coniunx* was an appropriate person to receive the last words is illustrated in Statius' highly artificial consolation to Abascantus, in which a long speech is put into the mouth of the dying Priscilla.[5] But both the intimacy of the marital relationship and the ignorance of biographers tend to keep the reality private.

The ideal was that a close relative or *coniunx* be present to exchange a last kiss and to catch the dying person's last breath.[6] Cicero, in classifying oratorical complaints (*conquestiones*), identifies the eighth type as saying that something which should not have happened had happened, or something which should have happened had not happened. For instance, 'I was not present, I did not see him, I did not hear his last words, I did not catch his last breath.'[7] Romans dreamt of dying in the arms of their wives—although a friend would do. A married woman would look for her husband at her death-bed.[8] There was a horror of breathing one's last without those one loved or under the eyes of enemies or alone.[9] At the peaceful and well-conducted death-bed of Agricola, his loving wife sat beside him and others were there to pay due respect, but something was missing which he would have wished to see and there were fewer to weep for him, because his daughter and her husband were far away. They, for their part, were sad not to have been there to comfort him in his illness, to store up memories of his face and of his final embrace, and to hear his bidding and last words.[10]

When a person died, someone closed his eyes. It was right that this should be a close relative. Mothers are often mentioned, to pathetic

---

[2] Sen. *Contr.* 2.4.3–4; Nep. *Att.* 21.4ff.; Cic. *Cael.* 59.

[3] Sen. *Cons. ad Marc.* 3.2; Tac. *Ag.*45.3.

[4] Suet. *DA* 99.1; cf. Tac. *A* 2.72.1 (the last *mandata* of Germanicus). It is a pity, since Suetonius liked reporting last words, that so few dutiful wives were available for the death-beds of Caesars.   [5] *S* 5.1.177ff.

[6] e.g. Cic. *2Verr.* 5.118; Quint. *Inst.* 6 pr. 12; *Cons. ad Liv.* 95ff.; Sen. *Cons. ad Marc.* 3.2, *Cons. ad Polyb.* 15.5, *Cons. ad Helv.* 2.5; Stat. *S* 5.1.195–6; 195–6; Vives 5792.

[7] Cic. *Inv* 1.108.

[8] Wife's arms: Cic. *F* 14.4.1; cf. *Cons. ad Liv.* 307–8. Friend's: Cic. *Phil.* 12.22. Husband's: Stat. *S* 5.1.171ff.; *CIL* 11.6606 = *CE* 386; Vives 5792.

[9] Cic. *Inv.* 1.108; *Cons. ad Liv.* 307; Tac. *A* 2.70.2. It goes back to Homer: cf. Plut. *Mor.* 117B, quoting *Il.* 11.452–3.

[10] Tac. *Ag.* 45.4ff.

effect, for the young, but it depended on who was present, and a husband or wife might take that role. A kiss was a normal expression of love and of leave-taking.[11] Everyone called the dead by name, a ritual which might be repeated at the funeral.[12] The body would be laid out in the house and mourned by relations, friends, and servants.[13] Women might lay locks of hair on the body.[14] Displays of grief were expected of close members of the family: at least tears and breast-beating.[15] It was thought proper (according to literary descriptions of scenes of mourning) to address the dead aloud, using a number of standard complaints according to circumstances, such as that the mourner should have died first. Some of these recur on epitaphs. Human beings no doubt instinctively try to continue their relationship by at least imagining conversation with the dead. But for lack of eyewitness reports or diaries or letters written immediately after the writer suffered the loss of someone he loved, we cannot get beyond the conventional laments to what people really thought or uttered on these occasions.[16] Such realistic accounts of death and its sequel as we have emphasize rather a matter-of-fact attention to decent care of the corpse and consideration of the feelings of the living.[17] Visits or letters and condolences from friends and relations followed a death.[18] Restraint and comforting ritual were the outward accompaniments of bereavement, at least for the upper classes.

When death was violent, we are more likely to obtain a description, which need not mean that it is realistic. Historians delighted in describing dramatic death-scenes between husband and wife. Occasionally a husband is said to have been murdered in the arms of his wife.[19] Joint suicides proved conjugal devotion and provide a frequent theme. A friend from Como vouched to Pliny for the story that a husband and wife had voluntarily leaped to their death in the lake because the husband had incurable ulcers. Pliny thought the deed as fine as the more famous suicide of Arria.[20] Rhetoricians played with the idea of joint suicide.[21]

[11] *Premere oculos* etc.: Verg. *A* 9.487, Ov. *Am.* 3.9.49, *Tr.* 3.3.44; Val. Flacc. 1.334; *Cons. ad Liv.* 94, 160; Stat. *S* 5.1.196 (husband for wife). Kiss: Prop. 2.13b.29; Tib. 1.1.62; Petr. 74.17.
[12] *Conclamare* etc.: Verg. *A* 3.68; Livy 4.40.3; Ov. *Tr.* 3.3.43; *Cons. ad Liv.* 75–6, 219; Sen. *Contr.* 4.1; Lucan 2.23; Stat. *S* 2.6.5.
[13] Toynbee, *Death* 43–4; Prieur, *La Mort dans l'antiquité romaine* 18ff.
[14] *Cons. ad Liv.* 98; Petr. 111.
[15] e.g. Ov. *Tr.* 1.3.21–2; Stat. *S* 5.1.20ff., 5.5.11ff.
[16] Lucian *On grief* 12ff., quoted by Hopkins, *DR* 219; Lattimore, *Themes in Greek and Latin epitaphs* 217ff., on the device of making the dead address survivors.
[17] e.g. Cic. *F* 4.12 on the death and obsequies of M. Marcellus.
[18] e.g. Cic. *F* 4.5.1; Stat. *S* 5 pr.; Pliny *Epp.* 10.120.2.
[19] Pliny *Epp* 3.16.9, but the cause of death was obscure: possibly poison (Tac. *A* 12.52.3).
[20] *Epp* 6.24. [21] Sen. *Contr.* 6.4.

Sometimes husband and wife killed themselves together because the husband was ruined. Plutarch says Fulvius (he means Fabius Maximus) determined to kill himself because he had lost the friendship of Augustus by his and his wife's indiscretion over Augustus' visit to Agrippa Postumus. His wife rebuked him for not having learnt that she could not control her tongue, told him she must die first, and stabbed herself. Tacitus' more conservative version is that Maximus might or might not have died by suicide and that Marcia at the funeral accused herself of having caused his death. The discrepancy shows how such heroic stories could attach themselves even to women as eminent and as unlikely to be victims of the regime as a cousin of Augustus.[22] According to Tacitus, in the flood of executions and suicides at the end of Tiberius' reign Pomponius Labeo, former governor of Moesia, opened his veins and his wife Paxaea emulated him. The motive for this and other suicides was to avoid prosecution and consequent confiscation of property and denial of burial. (Tiberius claimed Paxaea had had no cause to fear.) Mamercus Scaurus also anticipated condemnation by killing himself, his wife encouraging him and sharing his death.[23] Calvisius Sabinus and his wife Cornelia were both accused after his government of Pannonia and killed themselves under Caligula.[24] In 42 Caecina Paetus, implicated in conspiracy, hesitated to commit suicide. His wife, the heroic Arria, took the sword and stabbed herself, with the famous words, 'It does not hurt, Paetus.'[25] According to the account given to Pliny by her granddaughter Fannia, on a previous occasion she had discussed suicide with her son-in-law Thrasea. He had asked her if she would wish her daughter to die with him, if he had to die. She replied that she would wish it, if they had had such a long and happy marriage as she and Paetus had enjoyed. Her immediate attempts to kill herself by hitting her head against the wall were frustrated by her family.[26] Noteworthy in the accounts of Marcia and Arria is the theme that the wife sets the example of masculine courage and dies to support her husband.

If a wife could not die with her husband, it was proper for her to kill herself afterwards. Again, this provides a theme for rhetorical exercises.[27] Most of the attested instances in Roman history are set in a context of political or judicial crisis. In 82 BC, when the Sullan partisan Antistius was assassinated by the praetor Damasippus, his

[22] Plut. *Mor.* 508A–B; Tac. *A* 1.5.3 ff.   [23] *A* 6.29.7; Dio 58.24.
[24] Dio 59.18.4.   [25] Pliny *Epp* 3.16.6; Mart. 1.13; Tac. *A* 16.34.3; Dio 60.16.6.
[26] Pliny *Epp* 3.16.10 ff.
[27] Sen. *Contr* 8.1, 10.3. On suicide from grief see Grisé, *Le suicide dans la Rome antique* 74 ff. She also lists all attested suicides (pp. 34 ff.) and has a useful but not exhaustive treatment of suicide in Latin literature (pp. 225 ff., including suicide of lovers).

wife Calpurnia stabbed herself.[28] In the proscriptions of 43 BC some
wives betrayed their husbands but others showed devotion. Arruntius was killed, but his son escaped. The mother returned to bury her
husband and then heard that her son too had been killed. She starved
herself to death. Ligarius went into hiding and his whereabouts were
known only to his wife and a slave-woman, who betrayed him. When
his severed head was taken away, his wife accused herself of having
sheltered him, and when nobody killed her she denounced herself to
the triumvirs, who pretended not to see her. Like Arruntius' wife, she
then starved herself.[29] The heroism of Porcia was thought to excel
even that of her father Cato, the noble suicide.[30] The hagiography is
retailed assiduously. Nicolaus of Damascus and Valerius Maximus
(followed by moralists, poets, and historians) said that she killed
herself after she heard of Brutus' death at Philippi in 42. According to
the most detailed versions, a strict watch was kept on her, but she
succeeded in swallowing live coals from a brazier (in one version, as a
servant was carrying it). Plutarch is inclined to disbelieve this account
because an extant letter from Brutus shows (if it is genuine) that she
died before Brutus. In the letter he lamented her death and put it
down to neglect by her friends and her wish to die because of an
illness.[31] Plutarch's sceptical view explodes the legend that she killed
herself in grief for her husband. His dating must be right, for Cicero
sent a letter of condolence to Brutus, probably in June of 43.
Although Porcia is not named, Brutus' grief is as bad as Cicero's for
his daughter and he has lost 'something unequalled on earth'. This
must mean the loss of his wife. Cicero makes no allusion to suicide
and the letter is consistent with death through illness. The letter
Plutarch knew may also have meant that Porcia succumbed to disease
because she had no will to live: given her husband's danger depres-
sion would be natural.[32] In any case it seems that the whole edifice of
suicide from wifely devotion is fiction.

When the younger Lepidus' plot was crushed in 30 BC, his wife
Servilia, daughter of Isauricus, killed herself, allegedly by swallowing
fire.[33] This method of suicide is rare and unlikely. Rationalists suggest
that Porcia and Servilia inhaled poisonous fumes.[34] The coincidence
of method and the further coincidence of relationship (for Servilia

[28] Vell. 2.26.3; Plut. *Pomp.* 9.3.   [29] App. *BC* 4.21, 23.

[30] The story of how she wounded herself in 44 to show her courage and self-control is an
example of *fortitudo*: she was not at all of a womanish disposition (VM 3.2.15).

[31] Plut. *Brut.* 54–5, cf. *Cato min.* 73.4; VM 4.6.5; Sen. ap. Jer. *adv. Iovin.* 1.46 = 312 D:
'vivere . . . Porcia sine Bruto non potuit'; Mart. 1.42; App. *BC* 4.136; Dio 47.49.

[32] Cic. *ad M. Brut.* 17. If Plutarch is right in saying that Antony sent Brutus' ashes to Servilia,
not Porcia, this is also consistent with her having died first.

[33] Vell. 2.88.3.   [34] Grisé, *Le suicide dans la Rome antique* 123.

was the daughter of Junia and her husband the son of another Junia, both daughters of Cato's half-sister Servilia, the mother of Brutus, so that Porcia and Servilia were half-cousins once removed) cast suspicion on the whole story. The legends about the wives of defeated republicans were in circulation by the time of Tiberius and encouraged emulation, whether by women or writers is unclear. So, the story goes, in the mopping-up of supporters of Sejanus in AD 30, C. Fufius Geminus anticipated arrest by stabbing himself at home. His wife Mutilia Prisca then smuggled a dagger into the senate-house and killed herself there.[35] After the execution of Sejanus and his children the following year, his wife Apicata committed suicide.[36]

Other wives wished to kill themselves but were prevented. In the highly wrought account of Seneca's death, the husband embraces his wife and begs her to be moderate and philosophical in mourning, but she declares that she too is determined on death, so he agrees that they shall both give an exhibition of fortitude, although her glory will be the greater. They open their veins, and since Seneca's blood runs slowly and he fears to see her sufferings or to break her courage by letting her see his, he eventually has himself taken into another room and later into the bath to die. The agents of Nero arrive in time to bind up Paullina's arms, and she recovers, but her lifelong pallor bears witness to the loss of blood.[37] The younger Arria also wished to commit suicide with her husband Thrasea, following her mother's example, but Thrasea persuaded her to live for their daughter's sake.[38]

Suicide by husbands out of grief for wives is rarely mentioned. The senator C. Plautius Numida killed himself on hearing of the death of his wife. The admiral M. Plautius, when his wife was taken ill and died at Tarentum, pretended to anoint and kiss her body on the pyre and fell on his sword. They were burnt together and on the tomb the Tarentines wrote 'The Two Lovers'.[39]

Such stories of matrimonial devotion belong in a context of romantic idealization of suicide for motives of love or honour which runs from Greek mythology and literature through parodies in Roman comedy to moral tales in epic and history. It is clear that the reading public, like Pliny, found them moving. Some suicides (like that of Atticus, whose justification to son-in-law and friends is reported but whose wife does not appear in Nepos' narrative) are well attested and there seems no doubt that the Roman upper class had a tendency to resort to self-slaughter when life or execution or disgrace presented less attractive alternatives. Death by the sword might provide good

[35] Dio 58.6.   [36] Dio 58.11.6; *CIL* 14.4533.15 ff. = EJ p. 42 n.
[37] Tac. *A* 15.63-4.   [38] Tac. *A* 16.34.3.   [39] VM 4.6.2, 3.

evidence of suicide. But can we trust the dramatic detail? Did Arria really pronounce those last words? If she did, there must have been eyewitnesses other than Paetus present. If so, this is a telling instance, like the deaths of Seneca or Petronius, of the use of suicide as a public statement. But the unexplained death of a woman in her own house, after that of her husband, may often have been due to natural causes, not poison or 'swallowing coals'. It was tempting for outsiders to claim a dramatic and moral cause.

2. Funus

The funerals of the rich were often grand, involving considerable expense. The cost was supposed to be in proportion to the dead person's fortune and position.[40] Among things which normally had to be paid for were unguents for the body, transport costs, a site for the burial, a tomb.[41] Attendance at funerals was a social duty for friends and dependants.[42] The basic pattern of a decent ceremony was that friends and relatives, wearing black, followed the bier to the place of cremation or burial. The procession might include musicians and professional mourners, but close family, particularly children and the *coniunx*, would follow immediately behind the bearers of the body. The widow and female relatives would wear their hair loose. Although the sources rarely stress the share that women took in the proceedings, it is clear that if there was a widow, she had a special place. As we say that a woman buries her husband, so Romans describe wives as carrying their husbands out for burial.[43] The use is figurative but shows the widow's role in ordering the funeral and taking a leading part in it. Since in some cultures women do not attend funerals of their nearest relatives, this acknowledgement of the widow's role has some importance.[44] Husbands too are described as protagonists in burial.[45] Because, for the richer classes, professional female mourners took the duty of dramatic and stylized displays of grief, dignity and self-control were the part of the matron.[46] It seems, however, to have been correct for participants of both sexes to beat their breasts and weep. Even Augustus might groan and shed tears

---

[40] *D* 11.7.12.5, ht 21.
[41] *D* 11.7.37.   [42] Toynbee, *Death* 43 ff.; Hopkins, *DR* 201 ff.
[43] Mela 2.20; Juv. 1.72; Mart. 8.43.1. For representations of funerals in art and discussion of funerary practices see Prieur, *La Mort dans l'antiquité romaine* 21 ff.
[44] Tacitus makes much of the absence of his grandmother and perhaps mother from the entry into Rome of the ashes of Germanicus (*A* 3.3). This has nothing to do with sex, but with the absence of Tiberius (the adoptive father).
[45] Plaut. *Epid.* 174; Sen. *Prov.* 3.2; Mart. 8.43.1; Stat. *S* 5.1.216–17; *CIL* 6.6976: 'hoc tumulo cineres atque ossa novissima coniux | Terpsichor(a)e grata condidit ipse manu, | hic fudit lachrumas, hic verba novissima dixit, | hic viduom questus per sua damna torum.'
[46] The *praeficae* tore their hair (Lucil. 955).

for a kinswoman.[47] The Twelve Tables forbade women to scratch their cheeks. Since this temporary disfigurement is mentioned in conventional descriptions of formal mourning, it cannot be confidently maintained that Roman matrons consistently obeyed the rule.[48] Writers also conceive that female mourners tore their loosened locks.[49] Criticism of ostentatious display rather suggests that, in some circles at least, it was a familiar sight.[50]

Since it involved a long walk and hours of standing (especially for cremations), the funeral must have been a considerable ordeal. Upper-class ceremonies involved a pause at the Rostra for a eulogy to be delivered; state and particularly imperial funerals were the most elaborate of all and might involve more than one speech. After the funeral of Augustus, we are told that his widow, then 71 years of age, spent five days at his pyre. This must mean, not that she never left the place for the whole of that time, but that, like the sons of George V guarding his catafalque, she kept ritual watch for long periods during those days. Similar feats were expected of exemplary imperial widows when the funerary rituals were prolonged because a prince died far from Rome. When Germanicus died in the east, the cremation ceremonies took place at Antioch soon after (without the trappings of ancestral images, says Tacitus—naturally, since although officials on tour might carry mourning-clothes in case they had to attend someone else's funeral, they could hardly have travelled equipped for their own). His ashes were brought back to rest in Augustus' mausoleum in Rome. His widow Agrippina took the leading part in the ceremonial and the towns of Italy along the route from Brundisium to Rome saw the funeral procession.[51] We are told that Agrippina herself carried the urn, clasped in her hands.[52] But military tribunes and centurions also took turns to carry it on a bier. Germanicus' older children (who had been in Rome) and his brothers came to join the procession.[53] Seneca's heroic aunt was admired, like Agrippina, for bringing her husband's body safely through storms at sea and performing his obsequies.[54] So dutiful and dignified behaviour was expected of the widow at the final ceremonies. Some lingering by the pyre was proper at any funeral.[55] Ovid, incorrigible as ever, points

[47] Tac. *A* 3.1.5; Stat. *S* 5.5.16–17; Prop. 4.11.57ff.; *Cons. ad Liv.* 65, 442.
[48] Cic. *Legg* 2.64 = *FIRA* i.2.10.4; Livy 1.13.1; Ov. *Tr.* 3.3.51; *Cons. ad Liv.* 318; Lucan 2.36ff.; Apul. *M* 5.11.
[49] Ov. *Am.* 3.9.52; *Cons. ad Liv.* 317; Apul. *M* 4.34; *CIL* 11.6507 = *CE* 424.3.
[50] Hopkins, *DR* 218–19.   [51] Tac. *A* 2.73, 75, 83.3, 3.1ff.
[52] Tac. *A* 2.75.1, 3.1.5.
[53] Tac. *A* 3.2.2, 4. Caligula is said to have made his sister carry the ashes of her lover all the way from Germany to Rome, in imitation of her mother (Dio 59.22.8). For Plotina and the ashes of Trajan see *SHA Hadr.* 5.9.   [54] *Cons. ad Helv.* 19.4–5.   [55] Ov. *Am.* 3.9.54.

out that the widow might find a new husband at her dead husband's funeral: tears and loose hair could be attractive.[56] The funeral did not put an end to mourning, but, as in more recent societies, it gave opportunity for the most intense public expression of grief.

Funeral expenses were charged against the estate. If someone other than the heir undertook to arrange the funeral, he could normally recover his expenses. In this context, we hear of people being asked by the testator to handle the funeral or of family members who might act out of a sense of duty.[57] A married woman's funeral expenses were seen originally as a charge on her dowry. So if the dowry stayed with the husband he was responsible and if it returned to her father (or any other donor) he would pay. That remained the main outline of what was supposed to happen, but we can see the jurists in their discussions carefully weighing questions of moral and financial responsibility and financial capability. Presumably as it became normal for a woman's property to be greater than her dowry, it was felt unfair that the whole burden should fall on the husband and we hear of the view that expenses should be split between dowry and estate in proportion to their size.[58] But the husband might still have a duty because of his relationship, not because of property. Pomponius, thinking of what should happen when someone else had already paid for the funeral, argues, 'But if there was no dowry, then Atilicinus says that the father should pay all the expenses, or the woman's heirs (supposing she is emancipated). But if she has no heirs and her father is insolvent, the husband ought to be sued for as much as he can afford, so that it cannot seem as if his wife was left unburied because of his bad behaviour to her.' If a woman divorced and remarried and then died, even though the first husband profited from the dowry he had no responsibility to pay for the funeral. It may be assumed that the second husband had a moral duty to pay.[59] Nero gave Poppaea a public funeral and delivered a formal eulogy from the Rostra, praising, in the absence of virtues, her beauty and production of a daughter.[60] The particular duty of one *coniunx* to provide for the proper burial of the other is illustrated by the provision that gifts for the purpose of burial were allowed.[61] *Pietas* ought to have ensured that a wife would bury her husband, though legally she would have a claim on his estate.

After the funeral, the family would continue to visit the tomb. Such visits would naturally be most frequent in the period immediately after a death. The Widow of Ephesus provides an extreme fictional

[56] *AA* 3.431–2.   [57] *D* 11.7.12.2ff., 14.6ff.
[58] *D* 11.7.16ff., 22ff., 46.1, 24.3.60; Paul *S* 1.21.11; *FIRA* iii.49.18ff.
[59] *D* 11.7.28, ht 29 pr; cf. 35.2.6.   [60] Tac. *A* 16.6.   [61] *D* 24.1.5.8.

example of a woman watching at her husband's tomb.[62] Later, visits were made on particular anniversaries and ritual offerings were made and ritual meals shared.[63] In the natural course of events, close family would often be able to commemorate several dead kin together, in one tomb-chamber, or by making visits to separate, but not distant, burial-places, as Italian families today visit *i morti*.

The primary group of the dead reflects the family and household groups of the living. Free-standing tombs were usually dedicated to husband, wife, and descendants. Failing children, freed slaves, who bore the same name, might be granted the privilege of sharing the tomb and carrying on the cult of the dead while they lived.[64] Very grand tombs might be intended for several generations. Augustus himself planned to include everyone associated with the dynasty: not only his daughter (in the event excluded) and descendants, but his son-in-law Agrippa and his stepson Drusus.[65] At the other extreme, burials in the *columbaria* show wives, husbands, and young children sharing the same plaque, niche, or urn. Husband or wife often took the primary role in dedicating epitaph or tomb to the other *coniunx*. The statistics which illustrate who commemorates whom have been carefully assembled and analysed.[66] They show that commemoration of wife by husband and vice versa are common in all strata of society in the West. But conjugal commemoration is not in all strata the most frequent form. Many of those commemorated by parents must have been as yet unmarried; many of those commemorated by children had no surviving *coniunx*. The duty of the heir to commemorate may also explain the higher frequency of commemoration of parent by child in the senatorial and equestrian classes.[67] But the importance of the conjugal duty to commemorate is clearly demonstrated. When there was a surviving *coniunx* he or she would normally, in most areas and social groups, take precedence over parents or children or patron.[68] The rules about who was responsible for paying for the epitaph are included in the arrangements about the funeral. Occasionally, a dedicator specifically states on the inscription that he used his own money to pay for it.[69] Husband or wife may have done this

---

[62] Petr. 111.   [63] e.g. *D* 34.1.18.5. See Toynbee, *Death* 61 ff.

[64] e.g. *CIL* 6.22915; *FIRA* iii.49.

[65] *Cons. ad Liv.* 67 ff. Prieur, *La Mort dans l'antiquité romaine* 49 ff., is especially useful on monuments.

[66] Saller and Shaw, 'Tombstones and family relations in the Principate' 124 ff.

[67] Ibid. 138. For an example of commemoration by heirs see the epitaph to Q. Volusius Antigonus from his wife and stepfather (*CIL* 6.7377).

[68] Cf. Saller, 'Men's age at marriage and its consequences in the Roman family' 27–8; e.g. *CIL* 6.7370: 'L. Volusio Paridi . . . Claudia Helpis cum Volusia Hamilla et Volusio Paride filiis suis coniugi suo.'   [69] *CIL* 6.1883b.

often without documenting the fact. The normal assumption is that (unless the survivor remarried) husband and wife will be together in the tomb.[70]

3. Luctus

For nine days after a death the household observed a period of purification, the *feriae denicales*, during which men were exempt from public duties. At the end of this time a funeral feast was celebrated.[71] There was a view that men should suppress grief.[72] Cicero did not wish it thought that he was avoiding parties after his daughter Tullia's death.[73] But he did keep away from people as far as possible for some time, especially the first month, although he had some companions in his solitude.[74] Pliny, while grieving over the loss of his second wife, followed a different etiquette. We cannot tell if fashions had changed or whether he alludes to a time so soon after his loss that seclusion was still proper, as it might have been for Cicero for a limited time after Tullia died. He may even have been referring to the nine days after the funeral. Pliny in fact says that his fresh mourning kept him inside his house, so that when he needed to talk to the widowed Anteia about his resolve to avenge her husband, he was obliged to invite her to visit him, instead of calling on her as courtesy would normally have required.[75]

Formal mourning involved abstention from religious and social festivities and the wearing of dark clothes. Men might grow their beards and women their hair.[76] The praetorian edict expected completion of a period of mourning by widows.[77] Ancient custom seems to have prescribed a maximum period of ten months.[78] This became the *normal* period, *legitimum tempus*, for which widows should mourn their husbands. This period, the archaic year, probably seemed sufficient to avoid offence to the spirit of the dead husband.[79] But it later represented also the interval amply sufficient to ensure that the dead man's child was not attributed to a second husband.[80] If the widow produced a child, the mourning was at an end.[81] A joyful event naturally interrupted the display of grief. On various occasions public

[70] ch. 8 nn. 133–4.   [71] Balsdon, *LLAR* 127; Toynbee, *Death* 50–1.

[72] Cic. *Tusc.* 3.70ff.; Sen. *Rem.* 16.8.

[73] *A* 12.13.2; cf. 12.20.1, 21.5, 23.1, 28.2, 38a.1, 40.2–3.

[74] *A* 12.18.1, 34.1, 40.2–3, 13.26.2.   [75] *Epp.* 9.13.4–5.

[76] Paul *S* 1.21.14. Cf. Kübler in *RE* xiii/2 (1927) 1697ff. s.v. *Luctus*.

[77] *FIRA* i.65.16; *D* 3.2.8ff.; Lenel, *Edictum Perpetuum* 78.

[78] *FV* 321; Plut. *Numa* 12.2; Sen. *Epp.* 7.1.13, *Cons. ad Helv.* 16; Ov. *F* 1.33–4. See Rasi, 'Tempus lugendi' 394ff.   [79] Apul. *M* 8.9.

[80] Ov. *F* 1.33ff.; *D* 3.2.11.1. See Humbert, *Remariage à Rome* 113ff.; Rasi, 'Tempus lugendi'.   [81] *D* 3.2.11.2: Pomponius and Ulpian held that she could also remarry.

authorities ruled that the bereaved should reduce their mourning in order to participate in celebrations.[82] In the later rationalistic view, a woman who bore a child to her dead husband was free to remarry, since confusion of blood-lines was no longer possible.[83]

Otherwise a widow was not to remarry within ten months. If she did, Numa's law demanded the sacrifice of a cow which was in calf. The praetor's edict penalized those responsible for the remarriage of a widow within the statutory mourning-period. In historic times the remarriage of Octavia to Antony within ten months of the death of her previous husband made a senatorial decree necessary to allow her to cut short her mourning.[84] Later, permission might be obtained from the emperor. A woman might become engaged during the period of mourning.[85] In any case, neither the edict nor the opinion of jurists made mourning compulsory.[86] But neglect of due mourning was, or might be, penalized, although not forbidden. *Infamia* might be the inconvenient result if the widow publicly demonstrated that she had cut short her mourning by making a new marriage.

Observance of *luctus* was both more proper and more practicable for women than for men (who might be involved in public life).[87] Periods of mourning were longest for those most closely related. Paul says that the periods of mourning could be one year for parents and children over 6 (or 10 according to Pomponius), ten months for a husband, eight for close kin, and one month for a child below 6. Pomponius, probably rightly, held that the 'one year' here meant the archaic year of ten months, so husbands were given the same rights as parents or children.[88] Mourning ran continuously from the date of death: if notification that a person had died arrived late it was theoretically possible for the mourner to put on and put off mourning on the same day.[89] All this applies to women: there were no established periods for men. The Julian Law on marriage, in allowing widows a one-year exemption from the requirement to marry, was presumably inspired by the period of mourning attributed to King Numa. The Roman limits come close to English nineteenth-century

---

[82] Livy 22.56.5; *FIRA* i.57; cf. Dio 59.7.5. Traitors were not to be mourned at all (e.g. *D* 11.7.35).

[83] Yaron, 'Ad secundas nuptias convolare' 272 ff., dates this reason late, pointing out that *turbatio sanguinis* (*D* 3.2.11.1) is *hapax legomenon*. For post-classical law see *CTh* 3.8.1 = *CJ* 5.9.2; *CJ* 5.17.8–9.

[84] Plut. Numa 12.2, *Ant.* 31.3; cf. Dio 48.31.3; *FV* 320. Cf. ch. 5 n. 89. Octavia bore a posthumous daughter to Marcellus: the birth took place after she married Antony (*PIR*[2] C1103).

[85] *D* 3.2.10.   [86] *D* 3.2.9.   [87] Rasi, 'Tempus lugendi' 401–2.

[88] Paul *S* 1.21.13; *FV* 321, Ulp. Plut. *Cor.* 39.5 says Numa made ten months the maximum, for father, son, or brother.   [89] *D* 3.2.8.

practices rather than to the recent extended wearing of black by Italian and Greek widows, which has often been lifelong.[90]

4. Maeror

Giving way to grief was, said the philosophers, characteristic of the less rational types of human being, slaves, barbarians, and women.[91] Nevertheless, some admiration was given to inconsolable widows. Paullina was admired for keeping the memory of Seneca fresh and Seneca praises the widow who claimed that her dead husband was still alive for her.[92] The bitterness of others was more violent. Antistia Pollitta, the widow of Rubellius Plautus, the Stoic who had calmly awaited execution by Nero's agents in AD 62, was a striking instance of the widow who prolonged and advertised her mourning. Tacitus describes her as having seen the assassins and having cradled her husband's lifeless trunk in her arms. She caught and saved his blood and kept their bespattered clothes. She wore black and kept her hair unkempt and only ate enough to keep herself barely alive. When her father too was threatened, she waylaid Nero every time he went out and upbraided him in the best traditions of Roman *flagitatio*. In the sequel, she, her father, and grandmother committed suicide, opening their veins and dying decently in the bath, in order of seniority.[93]

In the epitaphs, both sexes say they would have wished to die for the other or before the other and that their survival is sadder for them than death would have been.[94] This feeling, that life is no longer worth living, that accustomed occupations have lost their savour, and that no other human being can replace the dead, seems a natural human reaction. But just because the survivor carves it in stone we need not assume that it is a permanent feeling.

Cicero's letters to Atticus after Tullia died give a classic picture of a man's real reactions to bereavement, quite unlike the statutory responses of philosophers, whose advice Cicero was careful to read. A striking feature is that Cicero feels he has a duty to Tullia to commemorate her in a special way, by building a 'shrine' to her and claiming a sort of apotheosis.[95] And he avoids the show of grief, but cannot, and does not wish to, reduce his actual pain.[96] Fronto's letters

---

[90] Queen Victoria herself set new standards.

[91] For moderation and excess in mourning children cf. Rutilia mother of Cotta: Cic. *A* 12.20.2, 22.2; Sen. *Cons. ad Helv.* 16.7. Livia, contrasted with Octavia: Sen. *Cons. ad Marc.* 2.3 ff.; cf. *Cons. ad Liv.* 474. For a Greek list see Plut. *Mor.* 118 D. Philosophers praised women for controlling their grief: Sen. *Cons. ad Helv.* 16.2.

[92] Tac. *A* 15.64.2; Jer. *adv. Iovin.* 1.46 = 313 A–B.   [93] Tac. *A* 14.57 ff., 16.10.

[94] Lattimore, *Themes in Greek and Latin epitaphs* 203 ff.

[95] *A* 12.18.1, 38a.2, 41.4, etc. See SB *A* vol. v, app. 3.

[96] *A* 12.28.2.

on his grandson give some sense of the individual he missed.[97] Cicero's instinct to remember a beloved daughter as she was, or at least for what she meant to him, to imagine some kind of continuing existence for her and some kind of continuing relationship to himself, and to experience his own grief seems deeply rooted in human nature. The preachings of philosophers about the general fate of mankind conflict with the natural instinct of an individual to mourn another whom he loved and to see what was especially precious and irreplaceable in that person. The Roman epitaphs, like the Book of Common Prayer, in setting the value of the individual in the context of common mortality, provide more comfort than the moralists.

Latin literature is not rich in the reflections of widowers or even in consolations addressed to people bereaved of a *coniunx*. Little comfort could be got from the reflection that a man who lost his wife might replace her: a wife was *adventicium*. A good sister who died might be irreplaceable: a wife was not.[98] By the accident of survival and the identity of the addressee, we have a private but formal letter from Sulpicius Rufus to Cicero on his daughter's death, with Cicero's equally accomplished reply, and such philosophical essays and rhetorical effusions as Seneca's consolations to his mother on his own exile (a quasi-death), to Marcia on the loss of a son, and to Polybius on that of a brother, or the anonymous poem to Livia about the death of her son.[99] It is normal for formal consolations to refer to the comfort to be found in surviving relatives or to the grief which they also feel.[100] But naturally in a poem dedicated to Livia even Tiberius, who had been present at his brother's death, must take a secondary place, and so must Drusus' wife, Antonia, who is left unmentioned for three hundred lines. Statius' *epicedion* to Domitian's freedman Abascantus is a sickly example of consolation to a widower: 'You love her shade and honour her remains. This is a chaste passion, a love which deserves the approval of your master the imperial censor.' It happens that, while the literature of consolation for the death of a child or sibling created lists of stoical parents and brothers, similar lists for brave widows and widowers are lacking.[101]

Traces survive of deep grief at the death of wives. Fronto lost his

[97] Fronto *de nepote amisso* 2 (Loeb ii.222 ff.).

[98] Sen. *Rem.* 16.9. Cf. Soph. *Ant.* 909 ff.

[99] Cic. *F* 4.5, 6. None of Pliny's letters is a direct consolation. See also Plut. *Mor.* 101 F ff. (to Apollonius), 608 A ff. (to his wife) on children. For background see Kassel, *Untersuchungen zur griechischen und römischen Konsolationsliteratur*, Johann, *Trauer und Trost*, for philosophy; Esteve-Forriol, *Die Trauer- und Trostgedichte in der römischen Literatur*.

[100] e.g. Sen. *Cons. ad Polyb.* 12.1–2 (surviving brothers, wife, son).

[101] Cic. *A* 12.20.2, 22.1; Sen. *Cons ad Marc.* 12.6 ff., *Cons. ad Polyb.* 14.4 ff.; Stat. *S* 5.1, esp. 40 ff.

wife Gratia (to whom he refers tenderly during her life): the surviving correspondence does not preserve his immediate reactions to his loss. He mentions it a short time afterwards when he was suffering deeply from the new blow of the death of his daughter's son. 'I am crushed by almost unbroken griefs, for within a very few months I have lost my dearest wife and my three-year-old grandson.'[102] Quintilian too describes the loss of his wife, but in a published work and years after the event. Deep feeling can be sensed under the conventional language:

. . . erepta prius mihi matre eorundem, quae nondum expleto undevicesimo anno duos enixa filios, quamvis acerbissimis rapta fatis, ‹non› infelix decessit. Ego vel hoc uno malo sic eram adflictus ut me iam nulla fortuna posset efficere felicem. Nam cum, omni virtute quae in feminas cadit functa, insanabilem attulit marito dolorem, tum aetate tam puellari, praesertim meae comparata, potest et ipsa numerari inter vulnera orbitatis. Liberis tamen superstitibus et—quod nefas erat sed optabat ipsa—me salvo, maximos cruciatus praecipiti via effugit. (*Institutio oratoria* 6 *prohoemium* 4–5)

. . . their mother had earlier been snatched away from me. She had not yet reached her nineteenth birthday and she had borne two sons. She was carried off by bitter fate, but died not unhappy. I was so crushed by this one disaster that no good fortune could make me happy. She had every virtue a woman could have and she brought her husband incurable grief. Besides, it was like the loss of a child, because she died in her girlhood and she was so young compared with me. But she left her children surviving and me alive (which was wrong but what she wished) and by going so hastily she escaped the most dreadful sufferings.

Just as what Quintilian says about his wife's good qualities, her good fortune in being a mother, and the unnaturalness of her dying before him parallels points so often made by epitaphs, so his inconsolability is like that of commemorators who claimed they could never be happy again or who promised not to remarry.[103]

Both the epitaphs and Quintilian show that it was proper for the widower to say he was afflicted. The same assumption is made when third parties refer to the death of someone else's wife. So Pliny writes of the serious wound suffered by Macrinus when his exemplary wife died after thirty-nine years of marriage without quarrel or disagreement. Although it might be a solace to have enjoyed such a long marriage, this also meant that he would miss her worse. Only time would bring healing.[104] Like the rest of us, the Romans tended to think of the metaphor of wound and scar-tissue and to believe that no

---

[102] *ad Verum imp.* 2.9 (Loeb ii.232); cf. *de nepote amisso* 1, 2 (Loeb ii.220 ff.).

[103] e.g. *CE* 440, 498, 512, 545, 634.

[104] *Epp* 8.5. Pliny also grieved for the husbands of the two Helvidiae, both dead in childbirth (4.21), and the wife of Junius Avitus (8.23.7–8).

cure was so efficacious as time. Reading Cicero's letters after Tullia's death, one must believe that violent grief is gradually assuaged.

5. Viduus *and* Vidua

The bereft state of widow or widower was indicated by the words by which they were described, though these also applied to divorced people. *Viduus* is used only adjectivally, *vidua* as adjective or noun.[105] The word implies the *coniunx* of which one is deprived. But Latin does not refer to a woman as the *vidua* of so-and-so. A man's widow will continue to be described as, for instance, 'C. Cassii uxor' or 'quae Cinnae uxor fuerat' or 'nupta olim Cn. Pisoni'.[106] The concept of *vidua* is thus not sharply defined. It is contrasted with *virgo* and sometimes with *nupta*, but not with a divorced woman, and the man from whom the widow is separated is not specified.

The widow was a more noticeable phenomenon than the widower. Given the usual discrepancy in age of *coniuges*, there must have been a strong likelihood that the wife would survive the husband. Solitary women, *viduae*, formed a permanent enough class to be worth listing separately with orphans on the census.[107]

The widow in Judaeo-Christian culture has been regarded as pitiable, capable of laudable spirituality, and deserving of special consideration and charity. There is little trace of similar feelings in Roman culture. But the word *vidua* is occasionally used to connote 'a defenceless woman'.[108] A teenage widow might, according to Jerome, complain that she needed a man to look after her: 'My little property is shrinking day by day, my inheritance from my ancestors is being scattered, a slave was rude to me, my maid took no notice of my orders. Who will appear for me in court? Who will answer for my land-tax? Who will educate my little children? Who will train my slaves?'[109] The widow might be the prey of fortune-hunters.[110] Admiration was given to some great ladies, whose motherhood, family connections, wealth, and survival guaranteed their position. The mothers of Coriolanus, the Gracchi, and Julius Caesar and the widows of Scipio Africanus, Cassius, and Augustus are obvious examples. Age and authority, rather than their widowed state, were important. In the Republic they retained the prestige of their dead husbands. So at the funeral of his aunt Julia Caesar displayed the image of her husband Marius, dead nearly twenty years, which had

[105] *Caelebs* can do duty for 'widower': Livy 1.46.7; Tac. *A* 12.1.1.
[106] Vell. 2.41.2; Tac. *A* 3.76.1, 6.26.4. But *nupta* and *vidua* are contrasted to denote currently and previously married women (e.g. Plaut. *Curc.* 37).
[107] Brunt, *IM* 22.   [108] Cic. *Caec.* 14; Petr. 95.3.
[109] *Epp.* 54.15.   [110] Hor. *Epp* 1.1.78; Mart. 2.32.6, 4.56.1.

not been on show since Sulla's dictatorship, and revived Marian memories. Even more strikingly (though the portrait was absent) did the funeral of Junia, the widow of Cassius, remind the onlookers of the tyrannicide sixty-three years after his suicide at Philippi.[111]

Some men who lost their wives when they themselves were comparatively old are known to have decided to live unmarried. This tends to be stated in conjunction with the remark that, rather than create a new family, they preferred to live with concubines. Remarriage at an advanced age was remarkable.[112] If a widower had no official concubine, that does not mean he lived celibate. But usually we are simply uninformed about the emotional or sexual life of elderly widowers. For many, their own death will have followed rapidly. It is more remarkable that some younger men, like Quintilian, seem not to have thought of remarrying. The Augustan legislation suggests that a considerable proportion of men who could beget children failed to remarry after divorce (as did Tiberius himself) or the death of a wife. Men in their twenties or thirties, faced with the death of a wife in childbed or from sickness and needing more children or a mother for existing children, were probably most likely to remarry.

It is rare for women in epitaphs to be praised for having lived as widows. This may suggest not that the occurrence was rare, but that it was not often of great interest to the commemorator (who by definition was not the widow's *coniunx*) or praiseworthy unless she was young and attractive when her husband died. Although the women themselves could have ordered their tombs in advance and mentioned perpetual widowhood, they tend not to tempt fate or incur the expense. Widows are also likely to escape commemoration altogether. Children are most likely to mention deliberate continuance of the widowed state.[113] Hadrian in his eulogy of his mother-in-law Matidia underlines her long years of widowhood.[114] Aemilia Valeria, who died at 54, had lived happily without a husband for eighteen years because of her devotion to her five grandchildren.[115] Aemilia Pudentilila similarly chose to remain a widow for fourteen years until her sons were grown up. But it could be argued that this was against her will, and in fact she then remarried.[116] Older women might remain in the widowed state. Helvia's children were at least in

---

[111] Plut. *Caes.* 5; Suet. *DJ* 6; Tac. *A* 3.76.
[112] Plut. *Cato mai.* 24; Treggiari, 'Concubinae' 75.
[113] Humbert, *Remariage à Rome* 68, finds five examples. The aspiration to remain faithful to the memory of a dead *coniunx* is more frequently expressed on tombs, but we cannot tell if it was realized (ibid. 68 ff.).   [114] *CIL* 14.3579.23.   [115] *CIL* 13.2056.
[116] Apul. *Apol* 67 ff. For a mother remaining a widow, perhaps for a period, cf. *CIL* 6.12372.

their thirties by the time her husband died. Her sister also presumably did not remarry.[117]

It does not seem to have been the norm in the upper classes for young women to have been encouraged to live in widowhood. Tullia's first husband died in 57: she was re-engaged in April 56. The exemplary Porcia was widowed in 48 and remarried in mid-45. (The civil war, in which her father played a major part, will have made greater speed difficult.) Cornelia lost the younger Crassus at the battle of Carrhae in 53 and married Pompey in 52; Fulvia twice remarried promptly.[118]

It has been claimed that the stereotypical merry widow, free to love where she would and happy in the control of her life and fortune, existed in Rome.[119] Certainly Clodia, as portrayed by Cicero, fills that role a few years after the death of her husband. Her shocking behaviour combined with her unmarried state (*non nupta mulier*) laid her open to imputations of behaving like a courtesan.[120] Other young widows sought chaperonage, as did Antonia (born in 36, widowed in 9 BC) when she went to live with her mother-in-law. The risk of allegations of misconduct was high for the highly placed, like Livia Julia (born between 14 and 11 BC, widowed in AD 23) and Agrippina the Elder (widowed at about 33), the prolongation of whose widowhood is explained by the danger their remarriage would have posed to Tiberius.[121] Gossip did not of course spare the reputation of even slightly senior widows like Agrippina the Younger, who was almost 39 when her last husband, Claudius, died. But such allegations are not launched especially against widows.

Because of the working of the Julian Law on adultery, a woman who conducted an illicit affair while clinging to her widowed state (*in viduitate perseverare*) was as much at risk as a married woman and could be prosecuted more directly.[122] This circumstance means that widows during the Principate were not, as far as the law went, in a position of greater sexual freedom than married women. Nor was there such a striking contrast in the economic position of married and

---

[117] Sen. *Cons. ad Helv.* 2, 19. The Elder Seneca died between 37 and 41; the Younger, the second son, was born between 4 BC and AD 1.

[118] Cic. *Sest.* 68, *QF* 2.4.2, 5.1; *RE* xxii/1.216–18 (Miltner); Wiseman, *Catullan questions* 58.

[119] Veyne, 'The Roman Empire' 75 ff., on the unrestricted eroticism of widows and widowers. As usual, he does not cite sources.

[120] *Cael* 49.

[121] Antonia: VM 4.3.3. All these women had done their duty by producing children. But Antonia is unique among young widows in Augustus' family in not being redeployed as a dynastic match. Her personal wishes may have been the main cause. Tiberius' daughters-in-law are said to have wished to remarry (Tac. *A* 4.39–40, 53). Tiberius will have been more alert to the dangers of importing stepfathers to his rival heirs presumptive.

[122] *D* 48.5.16.8, cf. ht 6.1.

widowed women as there was, for instance, in nineteenth-century England. A Roman woman did not attain greater control of her property by the mere fact of her husband's death. She might increase her property by inheriting from him; she might, on the other hand, see her standard of living diminished. It is evident that the rich widow who was chased by *captatores* might wield influence over them.[123] But nothing suggests that widows with strings of amenable lovers were the norm, even in the late Republic. Young widows, like Violentilla, would remarry, just as enterprising young divorced women like Valeria Sullae remarried. The freedom of widowhood was not an attractive escape from the trammels of marriage.

6. *Remarriage*

The norm was remarriage for women who could bear children, or men who had not reached the age when more children were not needed and the desire for affection could be solaced by a concubine. The topic of remarriage has been thoroughly treated.[124] Here is it sufficient to underline the propriety of the remarriage of widows and widowers. Love for a second *coniunx* need not suggest lack of love for a first. Epitaphs which commemorate two *coniuges*, although naturally rare compared with those which attest only one, attest the continuing emotional tie with the first, a tie which his or her successor was expected to accept and even share.[125] P. Vibius Verissimus commemorated his wife Statilia Tigris, who died at 36. Her first husband would have commemorated her if he had conquered fate and outlived her. But the task fell to Verissimus after sixteen years of happiness.[126] Usually, if any comment is made it is that both marriages were successful. For instance, the dead wife is made to claim that she was loved by both husbands or worthy of both.[127] One well-adjusted widower says on his tombstone that he had had three wives who died before him. He grieved for them, but they were no more. He was also lucky in his fourth wife, who survived (and no doubt approved the wording of the inscription).[128]

For widowers, who were not bound to any particular period of

---

[123] Mart. 1.49.34.

[124] Humbert, *Remariage à Rome*. Cf. for examples to demonstrate remarriage as the norm Wiseman, *Catullan questions* 58 ff.

[125] Susan Dorken (cf. ch. 1 n. 25) collects 12 examples from 527 epitaphs mentioning *uxores* in *CIL* 6. Among 10 in the category of free/freed people, there are 5 examples of a wife and two husbands (1899, 8429, 8601 and 8602, 21098, 38833) and 5 of a husband and two wives (7547, 15113, 15488, 32292, 37146).   [126] *CIL* 5.7453 = *CE* 1578.

[127] Paci, 'Nuovi documenti epigrafici dalla necropoli romana di Corfinio' 48 ff.; *CIL* 6.7873 = *CE* 1024. Cf. Humbert, *Remariage à Rome* 106–7.

[128] *CIL* 6.18659. Cf. Lattimore, *Themes in Greek and Latin epitaphs* 271–2.

mourning, remarriage could be timed to suit their convenience. Pompey lost Julia in 54 and married Cornelia in 52. Among the consuls of the period 80–30 BC, Humbert notes that M. Crassus (consul 70) married his brother's widow; D. Iunius Silanus (consul 62) married the widowed Servilia; L. Marcius Philippus (consul 56) married the widowed Atia. P. Sulla (consul designate 65) and L. Murena (consul 62) married women who had been married before and who may have been widows. The widows of Bibulus (consul 59) and C. Marcellus (consul 50) remarried. Scribonia, widowed or divorced wife of Cn. Lentulus Marcellinus (consul 56), married again. Pompey lost two wives by death and Caesar one; both remarried. Philippus and Mark Antony remarried when their wives died. The following remarried, after the death or divorce of their wives: Valerius Messalla Niger (consul 61), P. Vatinius (consul 47), perhaps M. Lepidus (consul 46), L. Munatius Plancus, M. Agrippa, M. Valerius Messalla Corvinus (consul 31).[129] We have already mentioned other examples of widows who married again.

Remarriage created a new *matrimonium*, new *affines*, new patterns of property, and the possibility of new progeny. The *viduus* or *vidua*, whether the previous marriage had been ended by death or by divorce, would take to the new relationship the experience of a previous *coniunx* and family connections, perhaps property acquired through the previous marriage, perhaps children. A second or subsequent marriage might therefore be more complex than a first. But the basic range of possibilities which it offered was the same. The cycle began again.

---

[129] Humbert, *Remariage à Rome* 85 ff.

15
Conclusions

BIRTH and death are inescapable biological facts. Sexual intercourse and procreation are biological experiences which may or may not fall to the lot of each human being who is born. Marriage is a human institution which has historically been linked with sexuality and the production and rearing of children.

The Roman state defined narrowly the marriages which were valid for its citizens and which produced a new generation of citizens. It was possible for a legislator to think of interfering in the sexual conduct of citizens by penalizing adulterers and to attempt to deter those who chose not to marry or avoided procreation. The law would also intervene between married people and their kin to protect equity in property matters (and here ideas about what was equitable evolved). But the state played no role in ratifying a marriage (though it set the criteria for validity). Nor did any other official. Important as the approval and knowledge of family and friends were in practice, in theory a marriage depended on the will of the husband and wife alone (unless either was *in patria potestate*). The same holds true of divorce, but here the will of either *coniunx* sufficed to end the marriage. Although the vital importance of consent survived in canon law, the Church encouraged a public sacrament and modern states have superimposed requirements of public ratification and registration on marriage. The Christian Church limited and then abolished divorce and in the twentieth century it remains something granted by outside authority.

The legal centrality of the couple was matched by moral and affective ties. Although the original Roman agnatic system and philosophical theory stressed the vertical relationships running from father to child and back, the insoluble blood-tie, still the soluble link formed by the conjugal relationship acquired, both in ideology and through the affection generated in the constantly changing group of parents and children, a strength of its own. By the time of Cicero this family group, rather than the agnatic line, is the focus of strong feelings. Affection and duty are reflected in such practical matters as living-arrangements and disposal of property. Children, even daughters, assert and are allowed individual choices. A closely knit family and a devoted married couple remain the ideal from the first century BC to the third century AD and beyond: no evolution of ideas can be discerned within this period. This is not to deny that there is constant tension between belief and practice. Theorists differed from each other on the relative importance of moral qualities and still more on the right choice of action in specific circumstances. Individuals found their choices circumscribed by their own character, brute facts, and other human beings. No doubt the home life of Cicero was different from that of Antoninus Pius. But it was not different because ideals had changed.

Changes may be discerned in law. The trend is never purely in one direction. It cannot be labelled as 'the gradual emancipation of women' or 'the assertion of the priority of the nuclear family'. Statutes are passed from time to time because legislators diagnose a social problem (such as too much property passing to women or rampant adultery). At other times a legislator, judge, or jurist may attempt to give weight to a new consensus in society about what is equitable (as, for instance, the praetors developed theories of equity in relation to dowry or the emperors recognized the reciprocal rights of mother and child). But it is not the task of law to promote the interests of any one group against another.

It may be admitted that, before the period for which we have reasonably full evidence, there was a development in individualism. In the period under discussion the individual was as free to make his or her own choices as at any period before the twentieth century. Biological facts, social expectations, accepted ideology, and family pressures, not (usually) *patria potestas*, controlled his or her actions. So instead of one simple pattern into which lives or marriages might theoretically fit, there were many. In the study of marriage, as in that of, for instance, politics, the fascination lies in seeing the interplay of individuals in a given context. How does a common experience work out in the life of a particular couple? Only a fragmentary answer to this question can be attempted for a few marriages in the Roman period. If a full answer were possible, it would be as complex as those given by modern sociologists for the small samples to whom they administer questionnaires.

Before the so-called 'sexual revolution' of the 1960s, it had been fashionable to recommend 'companionate marriage', of which the distinctive components were sexual intercourse and companionship. But the development and acceptability of reliable methods of birth-control enabled couples to achieve these purposes without marriage.

The custom of cohabitation without connubial links seems to be widespread in the 1980s and in the Western world. The primary motive for choosing to marry rather than merely cohabit would therefore seem to be the wish to procreate legitimate children. We seem to be approaching once more the original Roman concept. As the reasons for the institution of marriage are called in question and as our ideals for relationships between individuals change, it may be salutary, or at least interesting, to see how the complexities of the marital relationship worked in Rome.

Appendix 1
Some Alleged *Adulteri*

This selection represents gossip and allegations of various types, to indicate the range of slander and the vulnerability of public figures to charges of sexual immorality.

C. Julius Caesar and Postumia Ser. Sulpici. [Suet. *DJ* 50.1]
                 Lollia A. Gabini. [ibid.]
                 Tertulla M. Crassi. [ibid.]
                 Mucia Cn. Pompei. [ibid.]
                 Servilia. [ibid. 50.2]
                 Tertia Cassi [ibid.]
                 various foreign ladies. [ibid. 51–2]
Clodia and various men. [Cic. *Cael.* 48 ff.]
P. Clodius Pulcher and Pompeia Caesaris. [Sen. *Epp.* 97.2–11 etc.]
Fulvius, son of a fuller, and Pompeius Macula and Fausta Milonis. [Macrob. *S* 2.2.9]
Cn. Sallustius and Fausta Milonis. [Gell. 17.18; *Inv. in Sall.* 15–16]
Plancus and Maevia Galla. [Macrob. *S* 2.2.26]
C. Memmius and wife of M. Lucullus. [Cic. *A* 1.18.3, 60 BC]
Vedius and Iunia Lepidi and four other ladies: suspected [Cic. *A* 6.1.25]
Augustus and Tertulla, Terentilla, Rufilla, Salvia Titisenia (according to Antony), and others. [Suet. *DA* 69]
Julia Aug. f. and many lovers.[Pliny *NH* 7.46; Sen. *Ben.* 6.32.1; Macr. 2.5.9; etc.]
Decius Mundus *eques* and Paulina Saturnini [Jos. *Ant.* 18.65–80] by trick. Mundus exiled.
Wife of an *eques* with son-in-law. [Suet. *Tib.* 35.1]
Julius Postumius and Mutilia Prisca. [Tac. *A* 4.12.6]
Agrippina the Elder and Asinius Gallus [Tac. *A* 6.25.2], according to Tiberius.
Livia Julia and various men. [Dio 58.24.5]
Urgulanilla Claudi. [Suet. *Cl.* 26.2, 27.1]
Gaius and Ennia Macronis. [Suet. *G* 12.2]
Silius and Messallina Claudi. [Tac. *A* 11.12, 26]
Vettius and Messallina. [Tac. *A* 11.30.3]
Mnester and Messalina. [Tac. *A* 11.36.1 ff.]
Montanus and Messalina. [Tac. *A* 11.36.4]

Plautius Lateranus and Messallina. [Tac. *A* 11.30.3, 11.36.5, 13.11.2]

Seneca and someone in Germanicus' house. [Tac. *A* 13.42]

Seneca and Agrippina. [Dio 61.10.1]

Lepidus and Agrippina. [Tac. *A* 14.2.4]

Faenius Rufus and Agrippina. [Tac. *A* 15.50]

Antonius Pallas and Agrippina. [Tac. *A* 12.65, 14.2.4]

Julia Germanici f. [Dio 60.8.5]

Atimetus and Domitia Lepida. [Tac. *A* 13.21.5]

Iunia Silana and Iturius and Calvisius [Tac. *A* 13.21.3–4, cf. 14.12.6–7], alleged by Agrippina.

Octavius Sagitta and Pontia. [Tac. *A* 13.44]

Salvius Otho and Poppaea Sabina. [Tac. *A* 13.45]

Nero and Poppaea Sabina. [Tac. *A* 14.1]

Eucaerus, a slave, and Octavia Neronis. [Tac. *A* 14.60.3–4]

Anicetus and Octavia Neronis. [Tac. *A* 14.62]

Nero (among others) and Statilia Messallina Vestini. [Tac. *A* 15.68.5]

Appendix 2
Some Adultery Prosecutions or Sentences under the Julio-Claudians

Julia Aug. f. 2 BC. Relegated first to Pandateria, then to Rhegium. [Tac. *A* 1.53.1; Suet. *DA* 65.3, *Tib.* 11.4, 50.1; Dio 55.10.14–15]

Julia Aug. n. AD 8. Died on Trimera. [Suet. *DA* 65.1; Tac. *A* 3.24 5ff., 4.71.6–7]

Laetorius. After AD 14. Tried by Senate. [Suet. *DA* 5]

Appuleia Varilla (granddaughter of Octavia) and Manlius. Also charged with *maiestas*. Appuleia relegated 200 miles by kin; Manlius banished from Italy and Africa. [Tac. *A* 2.50]

Vistilia. Relegated to Seriphos. [Tac. *A* 2.85.1 ff.]

Decius Mundus. AD 19. ? Tried by Senate. [Jos. *Ant.* 18.65 ff.; cf. Garnsey, *Social status* 22]

Aemilia Lepida. AD 20. Also charged with poisoning. Tried in Senate and banished. [Tac. *A* 3.22 ff.; Suet. *Tib.* 49.1]

Antistius Vetus. AD 21. *Quaestio*, under Tiberius. Acquitted. [Tac. *A* 3.38.2]

Aquilia and Varius Ligus. AD 25. Aquilia exiled by Tiberius, though condemned under *Lex Julia* by consul designate. [Tac. *A* 4.42]

Claudia Pulchra and Furnius. AD 26. Accuser Domitius Afer. Both condemned. [Tac. *A* 4.52.1 ff.]

Sex. Marius. AD 33. For incest. Executed. [Tac. *A* 6.19.1; Dio 58.22]

Mam. Aemilius Scaurus for adultery with Livia Julia. AD 34. Also charged with magic. Suicide. [Tac. *A* 6.29.6–7; Dio 58.24.5]

Aemilia Lepida (widow of Drusus Caesar) and a slave. AD 36. Suicide. [Tac. *A* 6.40.4]

Albucilla Satri Secundi and Cn. Domitius Ahenobarbus, C. Vibius Marsus, L. Arruntius, Carsidius Sacerdos, Pontius Fregellanus. AD 37. Before the Senate. Also charged with impiety towards Tiberius. Arruntius committed suicide; Albucilla attempted suicide unsuccessfully and was imprisoned; Carsidius was relegated to an island, Pontius demoted from Senate. [Tac. *A* 6.47.2 ff.; cf. Dio 58.27.2]

Agrippina and Julia. AD 39. Accused of adultery with Lepidus. Banished to Pontia. [Dio 59.22.6 ff.]

Ofonius Tigellinus. AD 39. Charged with corrupting Agrippina. Banished. [Dio 59.23.9]

Julia and L. Annaeus Seneca. AD 41. Banished, Seneca to Corsica. [Dio 60.8.4–5, 61.10.1 ff.]

D. Valerius Asiaticus. AD 47. Accused in Claudius' *cubiculum* of corrupting soldiers and of homosexual *stuprum* and adultery with Poppaea Sabina P. Corneli Lentuli Scipionis. Messallina drove Poppaea to suicide. Claudius allowed Asiaticus to choose the manner of his death. [Tac. *A* 11.1 ff.]

Two *equites*, surnamed Petra, for lending house to Poppaea and Mnester for adultery. AD 47. Before Senate. (One also accused of predicting a disaster.) [Tac. *A* 11.4.1 ff.]

Anicetus Neronis l. AD 62. Persuaded to confess to adultery with Octavia, before a council of Nero's friends. Banished to Sardinia, where he died. [Tac. *A* 14.62.3 ff.]

Octavia Neronis. AD 62. Declared by Nero in an edict to have aborted illegitimate child and attempted to tamper with the loyalty of the fleet. Confined on Pandateria, then killed. [Tac. *A* 14.63–4]

Appendix 3
Philosophers on Sexuality

This selection of sources, with quotation of the more interesting passages, is intended to illustrate philosophers' teaching on the sexuality of married people. I cite a few key texts in approximate chronological order.

Charondas *Proem. legum* according to Stobaeus 4.2.24.

Pythagoras according to Iamblichus *Vita Pyth*. 45–50 (with paradigm of Odysseus, 57).

Plato *Legg*. 838 E–841 D: prohibiting homosexuality and extra-marital intercourse and especially the begetting of bastards.

[Aristotle] *Oec*. 1 (? late 4th/early 3rd century BC) 1344ᵃ: husbands not to wrong wives by 'outside relationships'.

[Aristotle] *Oec*. 3 (? 3rd century BC), Rose pp. 143–4: 'Maximus autem honor sobriae mulieris, si videt virum suum observantem sibi castitatem et de nulla alia muliere curam magis habentem, sed prae ceteris omnibus propriam et amicam et fidelem sibi existimantem. Tanto enim magis studebit se talem esse mulier.' Also avoidance of degenerate bastards who would dishonour legitimate children and wife (p. 146: Odysseus as paradigm).

Bryson (? 3rd century BC) *Oeconomicus*, in Thesleff, *Texts* 58.

Zeno (early 3rd century BC): cf. *SVF* 729.

Chrysippus (late 3rd century BC) cf. *SVF* 728.

Ocellus of Lucania (*c*.150 BC) 4: sexual intercourse only for procreation.

Philo (early 1st century AD) *On special laws* (commentary on Ten Commandments) 3.11, 3.64ff.: adultery destroys hope of children and falsifies families. Death penalty.

Seneca *Epp*. 94.26: 'Scis inprobum esse, qui ab uxore pudicitiam exigit, ipse alienarum corruptor uxorum; scis ut illi nil cum adultero, sic tibi nil esse debere cum paelice, et non facis.' Ibid. 95.37: 'sciet in uxorem gravissimum esse genus iniuriae paelicem, sed illum libido in contraria inpinget.' Cf. ibid. 88.7 on Odysseus.

Musonius Rufus 12 'On sexual indulgence' = Lutz 84–9 at 87–9: 'Men who are not wanton or immoral are bound to consider sexual intercourse justified only when it occurs in marriage and is indulged in for the purpose of begetting children (ἐπὶ γενέcει παίδων), since that is lawful, but unjust and unlawful when it is mere pleasure-seeking, even in marriage. But of all sexual relations those involving adultery are most unlawful, and no more tolerable are those of men with men, because it is a monstrous thing and contrary to nature. But, furthermore, leaving out of consideration adultery, all intercourse with women which is without lawful character is shameful and is practiced from lack of self-restraint. So no one with any self-control would think of having relations with a courtesan or a free woman apart from marriage, no, nor even with his own maidservant . . . "That's all very well," you say, "but unlike the adulterer who wrongs the husband of the woman whom he corrupts, the man who has relations with a courtesan or a woman who has no husband wrongs no one for he does not destroy anyone's hope of children." I continue to maintain that everyone who sins and does wrong, even if it affects none of the people about him, yet immediately reveals himself as a worse and a less honorable person . . . In this category belongs the man who has relations with his own slave-maid, a thing which some people consider quite without blame, since every master is held to have it in his power to use his slave as he wishes. In reply to this I have just one thing to say: if it seems neither shameful nor out of place for a master to have relations with his own slave, particularly if she happens to be unmarried, let him consider how he would like it if his wife had relations with a male slave. Would it not seem completely intolerable not only if the woman who had a lawful husband had relations with a slave, but even if a woman without a husband should have? And yet surely one will not expect men to be less moral than women, nor less capable of disciplining their desires, thereby revealing the stronger in judgment inferior to the weaker, the rulers to the ruled. In fact, it behooves men to be much better if they expect to be superior to women, for surely if they appear to be less self-controlled they will also be baser characters. What need is there to say that it is an act of licentiousness and nothing less for a master to have relations with a slave? Everyone knows that.' Ibid. 4 (pp. 44–5): 'Again, it is recognized as right for a woman in wedlock to be chaste, and so it is likewise for a man; the law, at all events, decrees the same punishment for committing adultery as for being taken in adultery.'

Epictetus *Discourses* 2.4: the adulterer denies his nature.

Quintilian *Inst.* 8.5.31: '"Occidisti uxorem ipse adulter; non ferrem te, etiamsi repudiasses" divisio est.'

? Quintilian *Decl. min.* (ed. Winterbottom) 262.8: 'Pessimus maritus videreris si amorem in aliquam meretricem deflexisses, si ancillarum cupiditas a geniali te toro avocaret. Iam, tum non eras maritus cum animus tuus spectabat vacantes.'

Plutarch *Praec. conj.* 42 = *Mor.* 144B: neither husband nor wife to have intercourse with others, nor with anyone from whom they do not want children or would be ashamed of having children (cf. *de educ. liberis* 1.2). *Praec. conj.* 43–4 = 144 C–D: husbands to avoid affairs, which upset wives. Ibid. 47 = 144F–145A: 'The man who enjoys the very pleasures from which he tries to dissuade his wife is in no wise different from him who bids her fight to the death against the enemies to whom he has himself surrendered.'

Nicostratus *On marriage* (Stob. 4.23.65): adultery prohibited because it produces loss of reputation for both sexes and bastards born of *akolasia* and *hubris*.

Ulpian, *D* 48.5.14.5: 'Iudex adulterii ante oculos habere debet et inquirere, an maritus pudice vivens mulieri quoque bonos mores colendi auctor fuerit: periniquum enim videtur esse, ut pudicitiam vir ab uxore exigat, quam ipse non exhibeat: quae res potest et virum damnare, non rem ob compensationem mutui criminis inter utrosque communicare.'

Appendix 4
Magistrates 60–50 BC with Identified Wives

M. Aemilius M. f. Lepidus aed. 53 m. (1) Cornelia (2) Junia Silani f.

M. Aemilius Scaurus aed. 58, pr. 56 m. Mucia Q. Scaevolae f. (divorced wife of Pompey).

T. Ampius Balbus pr. 59 m. Eppuleia.

T. Annius Milo pr. 55 m. Fausta Sullae f. (divorced wife of C. Memmius).

M. Antonius M. f. qu. 52 m. (? 1) Fadia (2) Antonia C. Antoni f. (3) Fulvia M. Bambalionis f. (4) Octavia C. Octavi f.

M. Atius Balbus pr. c.60 m. Julia C. Caesaris f.

Q. Caecilius Q. f. Metellus Celer pr. 63 cos. 60 m. Clodia Ap. Pulchri f.

Q. Caecilius Metellus Pius Scipio pr. 55 cos. 52 m. Aemilia Lepida.

M. Calpurnius C. f. Bibulus cos. 59 m. Porcia Catonis f.

L. Calpurnius L. f. Piso Caesoninus cos. 58 m. Atilia/Rutilia Nudi f.

C. Calpurnius Piso Frugi qu. 58 m. Tullia Ciceronis f.

C. Cassius Longinus qu. 53 m. Junia Tertia D. Silani f.

C. Claudius Marcellus cos. 50 m. Octavia C. Octavi f.

Ap. Claudius Pulcher pr. 57 cos. 54 m.? a Servilia Caepionis f.

P. Clodius Pulcher qu. 60 tr. pl. 58 aed. 56 m. (1) Pinaria (2) Fulvia Bambalionis f.

M. Coelius Vinicianus qu. c.56 m. Opsilia.

L. Domitius Ahenobarbus pr. 58 cos. 54 m. Porcia Catonis f.

Faustus Cornelius Sulla qu. 54 m. Pompeia Cn. Magni f.

Furius Crassipes qu. 51 m. Tullia Ciceronis f. (widow of C. Piso Frugi).

A. Gabinius A. f. cos. 58 m. Lollia M. Palicani f.

C. Julius C. f. Caesar cos. 59 m. (1) Cornelia Cinnae f. (2) Pompeia Q. Rufi f. (3) Calpurnia L. Pisonis f.

M. Junius Brutus qu. 53 m. (1) Claudia Ap. Pulchri f. (2) Porcia Catonis f.

M. Licinius M. f. Crassus qu. 54 m. Caecilia Cretici f. Metella.

P. Licinius M. f. Crassus qu. ? 55 m. Cornelia Q. Metelli Scipionis f.

M. Licinius P. f. Crassus cos. 55 m. 'Tertulla' (widow of his brother).

L. Marcius L. f. Philippus cos. 56 m. (2) Atia Balbi f.

C. Memmius pr. 58 m. Fausta Sullae f.

Cn. Pompeius Magnus cos. 55, 52 m. (1) Antistia P. f. (2) Aemilia Scauri f. (3) Mucia Scaevolae f. (4) Julia Caesaris f. (5) Cornelia Scipionis f.

M. Porcius Cato pr. 54 m. (1) Atilia Serrani f. (2) Marcia L. Philippi f.

C. Sallustius Crispus ? qu 55 m. ? Terentia (divorced wife of Cicero).
C. Scribonius Curio qu. 54–3 m. Fulvia (widow of Clodius).
P. Servilius Isauricus pr. 54 m. Junia D. Silani f.
P. Sestius pr. 54 m. (1) Albinia C. f. (2) Cornelia Scipionis Asiatici f.
Ser. Sulpicius Q. f. Rufus cos. 51 m. Postumia.
P. Vatinius pr. 55 m. (1) Antonia Cretici f. (2) Pompeia.

Appendix 5
Attested Divorces during the Republic

> husband initiates; < wife initiates; / initiator unknown or unclear; +
bilateral

Early and middle Republic

307/6   L. Annius > ? [VM 2.9.2; cf. Livy 9.43.25]
C. Sulpicius Gallus > ? [VM 6.3.10]
Q. Antistius Vetus > ? [VM 6.3.11]

early 3rd cent.   P. Sempronius Sophus > ? [VM 6.3.12]
*c.*230   Sp. Carvilius Ruga > ? [p. 325]
2nd cent.   Aemilius Paullus > Papiria ? C. Papirii Masonis
(cos. 231) f. [Plut. *Paull.* 5.1] No cause attested, but
Plut. suspects that she irritated him.

Late Republic

1st cent.   C. Titinius of Minturnae > Fannia. [VM 8.2.3] Q.
Servilius Caepio (pr. 91) / Livia M. Drusi (cos. 112)
f. She subsequently married M. Porcius Cato *c.*98.
[*RE* Livia 35; Syme, *Augustan Aristocracy* 25]

89   L. Cornelius Sulla > Cloelia. [Plut. *Sulla* 6.11]
Sterility/to marry Metella.

82   Cn. Pompeius > Antistia. [Plut. *Pomp.* 9.2–3, *Sulla*
33.3] To marry Aemilia.

82   M'. Acilius Glabrio (cos. 67) < Aemilia Scauri f.
[Plut. locc. citt.] To marry Pompeius.

81   L. Cornelius Sulla > Caecilia Metella Delmatici f.
[Plut. *Sulla* 35.2] To avoid pollution because she was
dying.

?   M. (Calpurnius) Piso (consular) > Annia (widow of
Cinna). [Vell. 2.41.2] To conciliate Sulla.
? / Valeria. [Plut. *Sulla* 35.3–4]

?   A. Aurius Melinus ? < Cluentia. [Cic. *Clu.* 14]
?   Oppianicus / Papia. [Cic. *Clu.* 27]
? 77   M. Aemilius Lepidus > Appuleia. [Plut. *Luc.* 38.1,
but see Syme, *Augustan Aristocracy* 126, 'Marriage
ages of Roman senators' 331]

? 66   L. Licinius Lucullus > Clodia [Plut. *Luc.* 38.1] ?

	Adultery with Clodius not publicly alleged until 61 (see ch. 13 n. 211).
?	M. Porcius Cato > Atilia [Plut. *Cato min.* 24.3] 'Unseemliness' after two children.
late 62	Cn. Pompeius > Mucia [Cic. *A* 1.12.3]
bef. 25 Jan. 61	C. Julius Caesar > Pompeia [Cic. *A* 1.13.3; Suet. *DJ* 6.2; Plut. *Caes.* 10.6]
? bef. Jan. 60	L. Licinius Lucullus > Servilia Caepionis f. [Plut. *Luc.* 38.1; *Cato min.* 24.3]
? Jan. 60	M. Licinius Lucullus > ? [Cic. *A* 1.18.3] Adultery with Memmius.
? 55	C. Memmius > Fausta Sullae f. [Asc. 28C] She then married T. Annius Milo.
? 51	Furius Crassipes / Tullia Ciceronis f. [Cf. SB *F* on 139]
50	P. Cornelius Dolabella? < ? Fabia. [Cic. *F* 8.6.1]
50	? < Paulla Valeria. [Cic. *F* 8.7.2] To marry D. Brutus (cf. Cic. *F* 11.8.1).
47/6	M. Antonius > Antonia C. Antoni Hybridae f. [Cic. *Phil.* 2.99] Alleged adultery with Dolabella.
46	P. Cornelius Dolabella / Tullia Ciceronis f. [p. 347]
46	M. Tullius Ciceronis / Terentia. [Plut. *Cic.* 14.4]
May 45	P. Cornelius Lentulus Spinther > Caecilia Metella. [Cic. *A* 12.52.2, 13.7]
45	M. Tullius Cicero / Publilia. [Plut. *Cic.* 14.5]
? June 45	M. Junius Brutus? > Claudia Ap. f. [Cic. *A* 13.9.2; cf. 13.10.3] To marry Porcia Catonis f.
44, bef. 22 Apr.	Q. Tullius Cicero / Pomponia. [Cic. *A* 14.13.5]
44, after 6 July	? / (*or* >) (Tutia). [Cic. *A* 15.29.2; cf. 16.2.5]
41	C. Julius Caesar Octavianus > Clodia P. Clodi Pulchri f. [Suet. *DA* 62.1]
39	C. Julius Caesar Octavianus > Scribonia. [Suet. *DJ* 62.2, 69.1] Complained of her character; married Livia at once.
Late 39/bef. 17 Jan. 38	Ti. Claudius Nero ? + Livia Drusilla. [Suet. *Tib.* 4.3]

Appendix 6
Attested Divorces in the Early Principate

I list, with references, revisions, and comments where necessary, the 27 women who divorced or were divorced in the period from Augustus to Domitian, in alphabetical order, according to the catalogue of Raepsaet-Charlier, 'Ordre sénatorial et divorce sous le haut-empire: un chapitre de l'histoire des mentalités' 171–3.

1. Aelia Paetina, divorced by Claudius.
2. Aemilia Lepida, divorced by P. Sulpicius Quirinus.
3. Atria/Satria Galla, taken away from Domitius Silius by his friend C. Calpurnius Piso (Tac. *A* 15.59.8). I would list her as Satria. Raepsaet-Charlier implies that she divorced, but the arrangement may have been consensual.
4. Claudia Marcella Maior, divorce imposed by Augustus.
5. Claudia Octavia, divorced by Nero.
6. Claudia Livia Orestina/Orestilla, taken from her husband by Caligula. (Again we cannot tell whether she took the initiative in divorce.)
7. Domitia, divorced by C. Sallustius Passienus in 41/2.
8. Domitia Longina, taken from her husband by Domitian. (Cf. 6.)
9. Fabia Numantina: divorce from M. Plautius Silvanus. Doubts, suggested by misreading Syme, *History in Ovid* 152, are unfounded: since Silvanus was married to the defenestrated Apronia during the lifetime of Fabia, his *prior uxor*, there must have been a divorce (Tac. *A* 4.22).
10. Julia Drusilla, separated from C. Cassius Longinus by Caligula.
11. Julia Calvina (*PIR* I856) divorced L. Vitellius (cos. 48).
12. Junia Silana (*PIR* I864) divorced by C. Silius.
13. Marcia Furnilla, divorced by future emperor Titus.
14. ? Milonia Caesonia, divorced probably to marry Caligula. All we know is that she already had three daughters by another (Suet. *Cal.* 25.3.4). She may equally have been a widow. Our only other information is ibid. 33; Dio 59.23.7.
15. Petronia, divorced by Vitellius.
16. Plautia Urgulania, divorced by Claudius.
17 and 18. Poppaea Sabina: two divorces, from Rufrius Crispinus and Salvius Otho.
19. Publilia, divorced by Cicero. Before the relevant period.
20. ? Silia, left her husband for Nero (? or divorced for adultery in 66). Tac.

A 16.20 mentions her as a short-term mistress of Nero, at some unidentified time the wife of a senator. There is no evidence of divorce.

21. Valeria Messallina divorced Claudius. Dubious.
22. Vipsania Agrippina, divorced by Tiberius on orders of Augustus.
23. Vistilia. Number of divorces hard to determine, none demonstrable; even Syme, *RP* ii.804 ff., does not deal with this part of the problem.
24. Anonyma, mother of Sex. Papinius, divorced by anonymus (Tac. *A* 6.49). (I have emended this item.)
25. Anonyma: divorce from Brasidas, praetorius under M. Aurelius (*D* 36.1.23 pr.). Later period.
26. Anonyma: divorce from Fonteius Agrippa (Tac. *A* 2.86).
27. Anonyma, divorced by *eques* for adultery (Suet. *Tib.* 35).

From this list I would drop 14, 19, 20, 23, 25 and regard 9 as secure. I would also add (though at least one woman is probably excluded from Raepsaet-Charlier's prosopography as not *senatoria*):

(i) Apicata, divorced by Sejanus.
(ii) Domitia, daughter of L. Domitius Ahenobarbus (cos. 16 BC) and the elder Antonia. She divorced or was divorced by C. Sallustius Crispus Passienus (cos. suff. AD 27) *c.* AD 40.
(iii) Domitia, divorced by Domitian (Suet. *Dom.* 3.1).
(iv) Julia, divorced from Tiberius in his name by Augustus (Suet. *Tib.* 11.4).
(v) Lollia Paulina, divorced by Caligula (Suet. *Cal.* 25.2; Dio 59.23.4).

These additions do nothing to upset Raepsaet-Charlier's hypothesis of the strong connection between dynastic manipulation and the majority of our attested divorces. My provisional total of divorces will be 27.

Chronological Chart

Dates are AD unless specified. Emperors are given in capitals. Authors and jurists are inserted approximately in the position appropriate to their literary floruit, with their dates of birth and death, when known.

trad. 753–510 BC PERIOD OF THE KINGS

509 BC REPUBLIC FOUNDED

451–450 BC Twelve Tables
445 BC *Lex Canuleia*
204 BC *Lex Cincia de donis et muneribus*
234–149 BC M. Porcius Cato the censor
195 BC Repeal of *Lex Oppia*
before 90 BC *Lex Minicia*
90–89 BC Enfranchisement of Italians
82–79 BC L. Cornelius Sulla dictator
106–43 BC M. Tullius Cicero (cos. 63)
Ser. Sulpicius Rufus (cos. 51), d. 43 BC; jurist
100–44 BC C. Julius Caesar (cos. 59)
86–? 34 BC Sallust, historian
? 84–? 54 BC Catullus, poet
P. Alfenus Varus (cos. 39 BC), jurist
C. Trebatius Testa, jurist
49–44 BC Civil wars and dictatorship of Caesar
44 BC Murder of Caesar

27 BC–AD 235 PRINCIPATE

27 BC–AD 14 AUGUSTUS
70–19 BC Vergil, poet
65–8 BC Horace, poet
59 BC–AD 17 Livy, historian
Q. Aelius Tubero, jurist
c.55 BC–AD 37/41 Seneca the Elder, rhetorician
43 BC–AD 17 Ovid, poet
M. Antistius Labeo, jurist
C. Ateius Capito (cos. 5), d. 22, jurist
18 BC *Lex Julia de maritandis ordinibus*
c.18 BC *Lex Julia de adulteriis*
4 *Lex Aelia Sentia*
9 *Lex Papia Poppaea*

14–37 Tiberius
Masurius Sabinus, jurist
Valerius Maximus, writing 20s and 30s.
*c.*20 BC–after AD 30 Velleius, historian
*c.*30 BC–AD 45 Philo of Alexandria, Jewish theologian
37–41 Gaius (Caligula)
41–54 Claudius
C. Cassius Longinus (cos. 30), died under Vespasian, jurist
*c.*4 BC–AD 65 Seneca the Younger (cos. 56), philosopher
54–68 Nero
before 18–after 65 Columella, writer on agriculture
? 20–66 Petronius, satirist
before 20–before 101/2 Musonius Rufus, Stoic teacher
39–65 Lucan, epic poet
68–9 Galba
69 Otho, Vitellius
69–72 Vespasian
23/24–79 Pliny the Elder, encyclopaedist
79–81 Titus
81–96 Domitian
*c.*40–after 112 Dio Cocceianus Chrysostom, orator and philosopher
*c.*35–100 Quintilian, rhetorician
*c.*40–*c.*104 Martial, epigrammatist
*c.*82–3 *Lex Malacitana, Lex Salpensana*
Iavolenus Priscus·(cos. 90), jurist
96–8 Nerva
98–117 Trajan
before 50–after 120 Plutarch, biographer and essayist
*c.*55–*c.*135 Epictetus, Stoic philosopher
*c.*56–after 112/13 Tacitus (cos. 97), historian
*c.*61–*c.*112 Pliny the Younger (cos. 100), orator and writer of letters
? 60–after 127 Juvenal, satirist
Neratius Priscus, *fl.* under Trajan and Hadrian, jurist
*c.*69–after 121 Suetonius, biographer
117–38 Hadrian
Salvius Iulianus (cos. 149), jurist
Sextus Pomponius, jurist
138–61 Antoninus Pius
*c.*123–after 158 Apuleius, novelist, orator
*c.*100–*c.*166 Fronto, rhetorician and letter-writer
Terentius Clemens, jurist
161–80 Marcus Aurelius
161–9 L. Verus (co-emperor)
*c.*130–*c.*180 Aulus Gellius, antiquarian and essayist
Gaius, d. after 178, jurist
Q. Cervidius Scaevola, *fl.* under M. Aurelius to Septimius, jurist.
176–93 Commodus (co-emperor 176–80)

193 PERTINAX, DIDIUS IULIANUS
193–211 SEPTIMIUS SEVERUS
c.160–c.240 Tertullian, Christian apologist
Tryphoninus, *fl.* under Septimius and Caracalla, jurist
Cassius Dio (cos. c.205, 229), *fl.* under Septimius to Alexander, historian
198–217 CARACALLA (co-emperor 198–211)
209–12 GETA (co-emperor)
212 Edict of Caracalla
217–18 MACRINUS
218–22 ELAGABALUS
222–35 SEVERUS ALEXANDER
Iulius Paulus, *fl.* under Commodus to Alexander, jurist
Domitius Ulpianus, killed 223, jurist
Marcianus, jurist
Macer, jurist
Modestinus, d. 244, jurist

235–8 MAXIMINUS
238–84 About twenty emperors
284–305 DIOCLETIAN and colleagues
306–37 CONSTANTINE
Hermogenianus, early 4th cent., jurist
Historia Augusta, late 4th cent.
354–430 Augustine
527–65 JUSTINIAN
533 *Digest*

Stemma of the Julio-Claudian Family

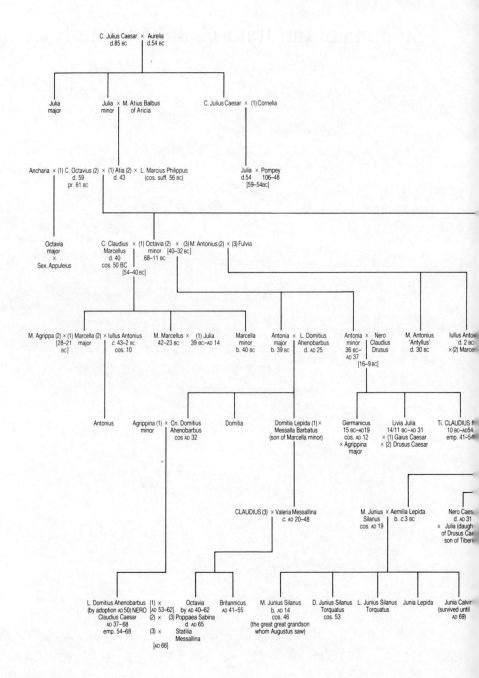

C. Julius Caesar × Aurelia
d.85 BC   d.54 BC

Julia
major

Julia × M. Atius Balbus
minor   of Aricia

C. Julius Caesar × (1) Cornelia

Ancharia × (1) C. Octavius (2) × (1) Atia (2) × L. Marcius Philippus
                d. 59   d. 43   (cos. suff. 56 BC)
                pr. 61 BC

Julia × Pompey
d.54   106–48
[59–54BC]

Octavia
major
×
Sex. Appuleius

C. Claudius × (1) Octavia (2) × (3) M. Antonius (2) × (3) Fulvia
Marcellus   minor   [40–32 BC]
d. 40   68–11 BC
cos. 50 BC
[54–40 BC]

M. Agrippa (2) × (1) Marcella (2) × Iullus Antonius
[28–21   major   c. 43–2 BC
BC]   cos. 10

M. Marcellus × (1) Julia
42–23 BC   39 BC–AD 14

Marcella
minor
b. 40 BC

Antonia × L. Domitius
major   Ahenobarbus
b. 39 BC   d. AD 25

Antonia × Nero
minor   Claudius
36 BC–   Drusus
AD 37
[16–9 BC]

M. Antonius
'Antyllus'
d. 30 BC

Iullus Anto
d. 2 BC
×(2) Marce

Antonius

Agrippina (1) × Cn. Domitius
minor   Ahenobarbus
               COS AD 32

Domitia

Domitia Lepida (1) ×
Messalla Barbatus
(son of Marcella minor)

Germanicus
15 BC–AD19
cos. AD 12
× Agrippina
major

Livia Julia
14/11 BC–AD 31
× (1) Gaius Caesar
× (2) Drusus Caesar

Ti. CLAUDIUS
10 BC–AD54
emp. 41–54

CLAUDIUS (3) × Valeria Messallina
                c. AD 20–48

M. Junius × Aemilia Lepida
Silanus   b. c.3 BC
COS. AD 19

Nero Caes
d. 31
× Julia (daugh
of Drusus Cae
son of Tiberi

L. Domitius Ahenobarbus (1) ×
(by adoption AD 50) NERO [AD 53–62]
Claudius Caesar   (2) ×
AD 37–68
emp. 54–68   (3) ×

                        [AD 66]

Octavia
by AD 40–62

(3) Poppaea Sabina
d. AD 65

Statilia
Messallina

Britannicus
AD 41–55

M. Junius Silanus
b. AD 14
cos. 46
(the great great grandson
whom Augustus saw)

D. Junius Silanus
Torquatus
cos. 53

L. Junius Silanus
Torquatus

Junia Lepida

Junia Calvir
(survived until
AD 69)

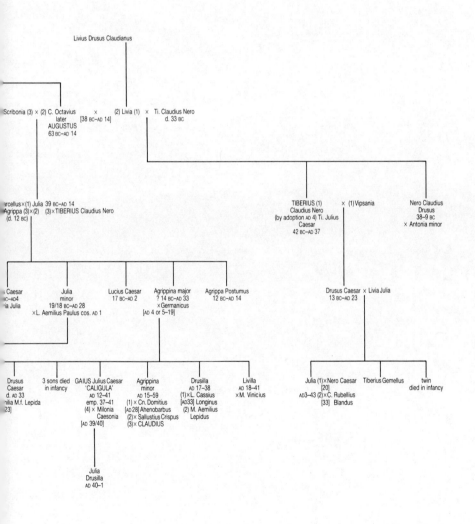

Livius Drusus Claudianus

Scribonia (3) × (2) C. Octavius   ×   (2) Livia (1) × Ti. Claudius Nero
                  later   [38 BC–AD 14]   d. 33 BC
                  AUGUSTUS
                  63 BC–AD 14

arcellus × (1) Julia 39 BC–AD 14   TIBERIUS (1)   × (1) Vipsania   Nero Claudius
Agrippa (3) × (2)   (3) × TIBERIUS Claudius Nero   Claudius Nero   Drusus
(d. 12 BC)   (by adoption AD 4) Ti. Julius   38–9 BC
                                                          Caesar   × Antonia minor
                                                          42 BC–AD 37

 Caesar   Julia   Lucius Caesar   Agrippina major   Agrippa Postumus   Drusus Caesar × Livia Julia
  –AD4   minor   17 BC–AD 2   ? 14 BC–AD 33   12 BC–AD 14   13 BC–AD 23
 ia Julia   19/18 BC–AD 28   × Germanicus
            × L. Aemilius Paulus COS. AD 1 [AD 4 or 5–19]

 Drusus   3 sons died   GAIUS Julius Caesar Agrippina   Drusilla   Livilla   Julia (1) × Nero Caesar Tiberius Gemellus   twin
 Caesar   in infancy   'CALIGULA'   minor   AD 17–38   AD 18–41   [20]   died in infancy
 d. AD 33   AD 12–41   AD 15–59   (1) × L. Cassius × M. Vinicius AD3–43 (2) × C. Rubellius
 ilia M.f. Lepida   emp. 37–41   (1) × Cn. Domitius [AD33] Longinus   [33] Blandus
 23]   (4) × Milonia   [AD 28] Ahenobarbus (2) M. Aemilius
                           Caesonia   (2) × Sallustius Crispus Lepidus
                           [AD 39/40]   (3) × CLAUDIUS

                              Julia
                              Drusilla
                              AD 40–1

Bibliography

Albertario, Emilio, 'La definizione del matrimonio secondo Modestino', in *Studi di diritto romano* i. *Persone e famiglia* (Milan, 1933) 179–93.
—— 'La connessione della dote con gli oneri del matrimonio', in *Studi* i.295–316.
Allestree, Richard, *The ladies calling* by the Author of *The whole duty of man* (12th impression, Oxford, 1727).
Amelotti, M., *Il testamento romano attraverso la prassi documentale* (Florence, 1966).
Amundsen, D. W., and Diers, C. J., 'The age of menarche in classical Greece and Rome', *Human Biology* 41 (1969) 125–32.
—— —— 'The age of menopause in classical Greece and Rome', *Human Biology* 42 (1970) 79–86.
Andréev, M., 'La lex Iulia de adulteriis coercendis', *Studi clasice* 5 (1963) 165–80.
Anné, L., *Les rites de fiançailles et la donation pour cause de mariage sous le bas-empire* (Louvain, 1941).
Arangio-Ruiz, V., *Istituzioni di diritto romano*, 14th edn. (Naples, 1960).
—— and Pugliese-Carratelli, G., 'Tabulae (ceratae) Herculanenses', *Parola del passato* 5 (1955) 448–77.
Arjava, Antti, 'Divorce in later Roman law', *Arctos* 22 (1988) 5–21.
Astolfi, Riccardo, 'Femina probrosa, concubina, mater solitaria', *SDHI* 31 (1965) 15–60.
—— *IP* = *La lex Iulia et Papia* (Padua, 1970).
—— 'Il fidanzamento nella "Lex Iulia et Papia" ', in *Studi Volterra* iii (Milan, 1971) 671–94.
—— 'Note per una valutazione storica della "Lex Iulia et Papia" ', *SDHI* 39 (1973) 187–238.
Badian, E., 'A phantom marriage law', *Philologus* 129 (1985) 82–98.
Bailey, D. R. Shackleton, 'The Roman nobility in the second civil war', *CQ* 10 (1960) 253–67.
—— *Cicero* (London, 1971).
—— 'Who is Junia?', *AJAH* 7 (1982) 40–1.
Balch = Balch, David L., *Let wives be submissive. The domestic code in I Peter* (The Society of Biblical History Monograph Series 26; Chico, Calif., 1981).
Baldwin, Barry, 'Horace on sex', *AJP* 91 (1970) 460–5.
Balsdon, J. P. V. D., *RW* = *Roman women. Their history and habits* (London, 1962).

Balsdon, J. P. V. D., *LLAR* = *Life and leisure in ancient Rome* (London, 1969).

——'Dionysius on Romulus: a political pamphlet?', *JRS* 61 (1971) 18–27.

——*RA* = *Romans and aliens* (London, 1979).

Barnes, T. D., *Tertullian. A historical and literary study* (Oxford, 1971).

——'Cassius Dio's *Roman History*', *Phoenix* 38 (1984) 240–55.

Bauman, R. A., 'Some remarks on the structure and survival of the *quaestio de adulteriis*', *Antichthon* 2 (1968) 68–93.

——'Criminal prosecution by the aediles', *Latomus* 33 (1974) 245–64.

Beard, Mary, in Joyce Reynolds, Mary Beard, and Charlotte Roueché, 'Roman inscriptions 1981–5', *JRS* 76 (1986) 124–46.

Bell, H. I., 'A Latin registration of birth', *JRS* 27 (1937) 30–6.

Besnier, R., 'L'application des lois caducaires d'Auguste d'après le gnomon de l'idiologue', *RIDA* 2 (1949) 93–118.

Biondi, Biondo, 'La *poena adulterii* da Augusto a Giustiniano', in *Scritti di diritto e di economia in onore di F. Mancaleoni* (Studi Sassaresi *16*; Sassari, 1938) 63–96 = B. Biondi, *Scritti giuridici* ii (Milan, 1965) 47–74.

Birks, Peter, 'Other men's meat: Aquilian liability for proper user', *Irish Jurist* 16 (1981) 141–85.

Birley, A., *The people of Roman Britain* (London, 1980).

Blayney, Jan, 'Theories of conception in the ancient Roman world', in Rawson, *FAR* 230–6.

Boer, W. den, 'Demography in Roman history: facts and impressions', *Mnem.* 26 (1973) 29–46.

Bonfante, *Corso* = Bonfante, Pietro, rev. by Giuliano Bonfante and Giuliano Crifó, *Corso di diritto romano* i. *Diritto di famiglia*, rev. edn. (Milan, 1963).

Bonner, S. F., *Declamation* = *Roman declamation in the late Republic and early Empire* (Liverpool, 1949; repr. 1969).

Boswell, J. E., '*Expositio* and *oblatio*: the abandonment of children in the ancient and medieval family', *AHR* 89 (1984) 10–33.

——*The kindness of strangers. The abandonment of children in Western Europe from late antiquity to the Renaissance* (New York, 1988).

Bourdieu, P., 'Marriage strategies and strategies of social reproduction', in R. Forster and O. Ranum (eds.), *Family and society* (Baltimore, 1976) = *Annales ESC* 27 (1972) 1105–25.

Bouvrie, S. des, 'Augustus' legislation on morals—which morals and what aims?', *SO* 59 (1984) 93–113.

Bowersock, G. W., *AGW* = *Augustus and the Greek world* (Oxford, 1965).

Bowman, A. K., and Thomas, J. D., 'Vindolanda 1985: the new writing-tablets', *JRS* 76 (1986) 120–3.

Boyer, G., 'Le droit successoral romain dans les œuvres de Polybe', *RIDA* 4 (1950) 169–87.

——'La fonction sociate des legs d'après la jurisprudence classique', *RHDFÉ* 43 (1965) 333–408.

Bradley, K. R., 'Ideals of marriage in Suetonius' *Caesares*', *Riv. stor. ant.* 15 (1985) 77–95.

—— 'Wet-nursing at Rome', in Rawson, *FAR* 201–29.
—— 'Dislocation in the Roman family', *Historical Reflections/reflexions historiques* 14 (1987) 33–62.
Bradshaw, A. T. v. S., 'Horace, *Odes* 4.1', *CQ* 20 (1970) 142–50.
Brind'Amour, P. and L., 'Le *dies lustricus*, les oiseaux de l'aurore et l'amphidromie', *Latomus* 34 (1975) 17–58.
Brini = Brini, Giuseppe, *Matrimonio e divorzio nel diritto romano*, 3 vols. (Bologna, 1887–9; repr. Rome, 1975).
Broudéhoux, Jean-Paul, *Mariage et famille chez Clément d'Alexandrie* (Paris, 1970).
Brown, Christopher G., 'Ares, Aphrodite and the laughter of the gods', *Phoenix* 43 (1989) 283–93.
Brown, Peter, *The Body and Society. Men, women and sexual renunciation in early Christianity* (American Council of Learned Societies Lectures on the History of Religions 13; New York, 1988).
Brunt, P. A., *IM* = *Italian manpower 225 BC–AD 14* (Oxford, 1971).
—— 'Evidence given under torture', *ZSS rom.* 97 (1980) 256–65.
—— '*Nobilitas* and *novitas*', *JRS* 72 (1982) 1–17.
—— *The Fall of the Roman Republic and related essays* (Oxford, 1988).
Bryce, Sir James, 'Marriage and divorce in Roman and in English law', in *Studies in history and jurisprudence* ii (Oxford, 1901) 381–474.
Bryce, T. R., 'Lycian tomb families and their social implications, *Journal of the economic and social history of the Orient* 22 (1979) 296–313.
Buchan, John, *Augustus* (London, 1937).
Buckland, W. W., *RLS* = *The Roman law of slavery. The condition of the slave in private law from Augustus to Justinian* (Cambridge, 1908; repr. 1970).
—— '*Diligens Paterfamilias*', in *Studi in onore di P. Bonfante* (Milan, 1930) ii.85–108.
—— *Textbook* = *A Textbook of Roman law*, 3rd edn., rev. P. Stein (Cambridge, 1963).
Burkert, W., Review of Thesleff, *Texts*, in *Gnomon* 39 (1967) 548–56.
—— 'Zur geistesgeschichtlichen Einordnung einiger Pseudopythagorica', in *Pseudepigrapha* i (Geneva, 1971) 25–55.
Cairns, F., 'Propertius on Augustus' marriage law', *Grazer Beiträger* 8 (1979) 185–205.
Calonge, A., 'Aestimatio dotis', *Anuario de historia del derecho español* 35 (1965) 5–57.
Campbell, J. B., *The Emperor and the Roman army 31 BC–AD 235* (Oxford, 1984).
Campbell = Campbell, John Kennedy, *Honour, family and patronage. A study of institutions and moral values in a Greek mountain community* (Oxford, 1964).
Cantarella, Eva, 'Sui rapporti fra matrimonio e conventio in manum', *Rivista italiana per le scienze giuridiche* 10 (1959–62) 184–228.
—— 'Adulterio, omicidio legittimo e causa d'onore in diritto romano', in *Studi in onore di Gaetano Scherillo* (Milan, 1972) 243–74.

Carcopino = Carcopino, Jérôme, *Daily life in ancient Rome*, trans. E. O. Lorimer (London, 1941; repr. 1956).

Castelli, G., 'Il concubinato e la legislazione augustea', in *Scritti giuridici* (Milan, 1923) 143–63.

Castello, C., *In tema de matrimonio e concubinato nel mondo romano* (Milan, 1940).

Chafe, William H., *Women and equality. Changing patterns in American culture* (New York, 1977).

Chastagnol, A., 'Les femmes dans l'ordre sénatoriale', *Rev. hist.* 531 (1979) 3–28.

Cherry, D. A., 'Studies in the marriage legislation of Augustus' (diss. University of Saskatchewan, Saskatoon, 1981).

——'The marriage of Roman citizens and non-citizens: law and practice' (diss. Ottawa, 1985).

Coale, Ansley J., and Demeny, Paul, with Barbara Vaughan *Regional model life tables and stable population*, 2nd edn. (New York and London, 1983).

Cohen, David, 'Seclusion, separation and the status of women in classical Athens', *G&R* 36 (1989) 3–15.

Collins, J. H., 'Tullia's engagement and marriage to Dolabella', *CJ* 47 (1952) 164–68, 186.

Corbett = Corbett, P. E., *The Roman law of marriage* (Oxford, 1930).

Corbier, Mireille, 'Idéologie et pratique de l'héritage (Ier s. av. J.-C.–IIe s. ap. J.-C.)', *Index* 13 (*Gérard Boulvert tra noi*; 1985) 501–28.

Corte, F. della, 'Le *leges Iuliae* e l'elegia romana', *ANRW* ii/30.1 (1982) 539–58.

Costa, E., *Il diritto privato nelle commedie di Plauto* (Turin, 1890; repr. Rome, 1968).

Cotton, Hannah, 'The concept of *indulgentia* under Trajan', *Chiron* 14 (1984) 245–66.

Courtney, E., *A commentary on the Satires of Juvenal* (London, 1988).

Crook = Crook, J. A., *Law and life of Rome* (London, 1967).

——'Intestacy in Roman society', *PCPS* NS 19 (1973) 38–44.

——'Women in Roman succession', in Rawson, *FAR* 58–82.

——'Feminine inadequacy and the *senatusconsultum Velleianum*', in Rawson, *FAR* 83–92.

Csillag, P., 'I rapporti patrimoniali fra coniugi all'epoca di Augusto', in *Studi Volterra* iv (Milan, 1971) 303–23.

Csillag = ——*The Augustan laws on family relations* (Budapest, 1976).

Curchin, L. A., 'Familial epithets in the epigraphy of Roman Spain', in *Mélanges Étienne Gareau* (Ottawa, 1982) 179–82.

Daube, David, 'The accuser under the *Lex Julia de adulteriis*', *Hellenika* 9 (1955) 8–21.

——'Licinnia's dowry', in *Studi in onore di Biondo Biondi* i (Milan, 1963) 199–212.

——'The preponderance of intestacy at Rome', *Tulane law review* 39 (1965) 253–62.

——*Aspects of Roman law* = *Roman law. Linguistic, social and philosophical aspects* (Edinburgh, 1969).

—— 'The undowered bride', in *Aspects of Roman law* 102–16.

—— 'The *Lex Julia* concerning adultery', *Irish jurist* NS 7 (1972) 373–80.

—— *The duty of procreation* (Edinburgh, 1977).

—— 'Historical aspects of informal marriage', *RIDA* 25 (1978) 95–107.

—— 'Fraud no. 3', in N. MacCormick and P. Birks (eds.), *The legal mind. Essays for Tony Honoré* (Oxford, 1986) 1–17.

Davidoff, L., *The best circles. Society, etiquette and the Season* (Totowa, NJ, 1973).

Davies, Kathleen M., 'Continuity and change in literary advice on marriage', in R.-B. Outhwaite (ed.), *Marriage and Society. Studies in the social history of marriage* (New York, 1982) 58–80.

Dickison, S., 'Abortion in antiquity', *Arethusa* 6 (1973) 158–66.

Dixon, Suzanne, 'Family finances: Terentia and Tullia', *Antichthon* 18 (1984) 78–101 (abridged in Rawson, *FAR* 93–120).

—— '*Infirmitas sexus*: womanly weakness in Roman law', *TvR* 52 (1984) 343–71.

—— 'Breaking the law to do the right thing: the gradual erosion of the Voconian law in ancient Rome', *Adelaide law review* 9 (1985) 519–34.

—— 'Polybius on Roman women and property', *AJP* 106 (1985) 147–70.

—— 'The marriage alliance in the Roman elite', *J Fam Hist* 10 (1985) 353–78.

—— *RM* = *The Roman mother* (London and Sydney, 1988).

—— *WRW* = *Wealth and the Roman woman* (forthcoming).

Dorey, T. A., 'Adultery and propaganda in the early Roman empire', *University of Birmingham historical journal* 8 (1961) 1–6.

Dorken, Susan, and Treggiari, S., 'Women with two living husbands in *CIL* 6', *LCM* 6/10 (1981) 269–72.

Dumont, F., 'Les revenues de la dot en droit romain', *RHDFE* 21 (1943) 1–43.

Duncan-Jones, R., *ERE* = *The economy of the Roman Empire. Quantitative studies*, 2nd edn. (Cambridge, 1982).

Durry, M., 'Les femmes et le vin', *RÉL* 33 (1955) 108–13.

—— 'Sur le mariage romain', *Gymn.* 63 (1956) 187–90.

Duyvendak, N., 'Restraining regulations for Roman officials in the Roman provinces', in M. David, B. A. Van Groningen, and E. M. Meijers (eds.), *Symbolae ad ius et historiam antiquitatis pertinentes Julio Christiano Van Oven dedicatae* (Leiden, 1946) 333–48.

Earl, D. C., *The moral and political tradition of Rome* (London, 1967).

Engels, Donald, 'The problem of female infanticide in the Greco-Roman world', *CP* 75 (1980) 112–20.

Esmein, A., 'Le délit d'adultère à Rome et la loi *Julia de adulteriis*', in *Mélanges d'histoire du droit et de critique. Droit romain* (Paris, 1886) 71–169.

Esteve-Forriol, José, *Die Trauer- und Trostgedichte in der römischen Literatur* (Munich, 1962).

Evans-Grubbs, Judith, 'Abduction marriage in antiquity: a law of Constantine (*CTh* IX. 24. 1) and its social context', *JRS* 79 (1989) 59–83.

Eyben, Emil, 'Antiquity's view of puberty', *Latomus* 31 (1972) 677–97.

——'Family planning in Graeco-Roman antiquity', *Anc. Soc.* (Louvain) 11–12 (1980–1) 5–82.

Falcão, M., *Las prohibiciones matrimoniales de carácter social en el imperio romano* (Pamplona, 1973).

Fantham, Elaine, 'Sex, status and survival in Hellenistic Athens: a study of women in New Comedy', *Phoenix* 29 (1975) 44–74.

——'The mating of Lalage: Horace *Odes* 2.5', *LCM* 4 (Mar. 1979) 47–52.

——'Women in antiquity: a selective (and subjective) survey 1979–84', *EMC/CV* 30 NS 5 (1986) 1–24.

Flory, M. B., 'Sic exempla parantur: Livia's shrine to Concordia and the Porticus Liviae', *Historia* 33 (1984) 309–30.

Foucault, M., *L'histoire de la sexualité* ii. *L'usage des plaisirs*; iii. *Le souci de soi* (Paris, 1984).

Fraenkel, E., 'Zur Geschichte des Wortes *Fides*', *RhM* 71 (1916) 187–99.

——*Elementi plautini in Plauto* (Florence, 1960).

Franciosi, G., *Clan gentilizio e strutture monogamiche. Contributo alla storia della famiglia romana* i (Naples, 1975).

Frank, R. I., 'Augustus' legislation on marriage and children', *CSCA* 8 (1975) 41–52.

Fraser, Antonia, *The weaker vessel. Woman's lot in seventeenth-century England* (London, 1984).

Friedländer, Ludwig, *Darstellung aus der Sittengeschichte Roms*, 4 vols., 9th/10th edn. rev. G. Wissowa (Leipzig 1919–21).

Friedman, Lawrence, M., *A History of American law* (New York, 1973; 2nd edn. 1985).

Frier, B. W., *Landlords and tenants in imperial Rome* (Princeton, 1980).

——'Roman life expectancy: Ulpian's evidence', *HSCP* 86 (1982) 213–51.

——'Roman life expectancy: the Pannonian evidence', *Phoenix* 37 (1983) 328–44.

——*The Rise of the Roman jurists. Studies in Cicero's* pro Caecina (Princeton, 1985).

Furneaux, H., 'Excursus on the Lex Papia Poppaea', in *The Annals of Tacitus*, 2nd edn. (Oxford, 1896) i.483–8.

Gabba, E., 'Studi su Dionigi di Alicarnasso I: la costituzione di Romolo', *Ath.* 38 (1960) 175–225.

Galinsky, Karl, 'Augustus' legislation on morals and marriage', *Philologus* 125 (1981) 126–44.

Gardner, Jane F., 'A family and an inheritance: the problems of the widow Petronilla', *LCM* 9/9 (Nov. 1984) 132–3.

——'The recovery of dowry in Roman law', *CQ* 35 (1985) 449–53.

Gardner = ——*Women in Roman law and society* (London and Sydney, 1986).

——'Proofs of status in the Roman world', *BICS* 33 (1986) 1–14.

Garnsey, Peter, 'Adultery trials and the survival of the *quaestiones* in the Severan age', *JRS* 57 (1967) 56–60.

—— *Social status* = *Social status and legal privilege in the Roman Empire* (Oxford, 1970).

—— 'Urban property investment', in M. Finley (ed.), *Studies in Roman property* (Cambridge, 1976) 123–36.

—— and Saller, Richard P., *REESC* = *The Roman Empire. Economy, society and culture* (Berkeley, 1987).

Gaudemet, J., 'La conclusion des fiançailles à Rome à l'époque préclassique', *RIDA* 1 (1948) 79–94.

—— 'Justum matrimonium', *RIDA* NS 2 (*Mélanges de Visscher*; 1949) i.309–66.

—— 'Observations sur la manus', *RIDA* NS 2 (1953) 323–53.

—— 'Origine et destin du mariage romain', in *L'Europa e il diritto romano: Studi in mem. Paolo Koschaker* ii (Milan, 1954) 511–57.

—— 'Les transformations de la vie familiale au Bas-Empire et l'influence du christianisme', *Romanitas* 4 (1962) 58–85.

—— 'Tendances nouvelles de la legislation familiale au IVme siècle', *Antiquitas* 1 (1978) 187–207.

Geiger, J., 'Tiberius and the Lex Papia Poppaea', *Scripta classica israelica* 2 (1975) 150–6.

Gelzer, M., *RNob* = *The Roman nobility*, trans. R. Seager (Oxford, 1969).

Gide = Gide, Paul, *Étude sur la condition privée de la femme dans le droit ancien et moderne et en particulier sur le sénatus-consulte Velléien* (Paris, 1867).

Gilliam, J. F., 'Some Roman elements in Roman Egypt', *Illinois classical studies* 3 (1978) 115–31.

Glass, D. V., and Eversley, D. E. C., *Population in history. Essays in historical demography* (London, 1965).

Golden, Mark, 'Demography and the exposure of girls at Athens', *Phoenix* 35 (1981) 316–31.

—— 'Did the ancients care when their children died?', *G&R* 35 (1988) 152–63.

González, J., 'The Lex Irnitana', *JRS* 76 (1986) 147–243.

Goody, J. R., *The development of the family and marriage in Europe* (Cambridge, 1983).

—— and Tambiah, S. J., *Bridewealth and dowry* (Cambridge Papers in Social Anthropology 7; Cambridge, 1973).

Gordon, A. E., 'On reversed C (Ɔ = Gaiae)', *Epigraphica* 40 (1978) 230.

Gouge, William, *Of domesticall duties*, 2nd edn. (London, 1626; first pub. 1622).

Gratwick, A. S., 'Free or not so free? Wives and daughters in the late Roman Republic', in E. M. Craik (ed.), *Marriage and property* (Aberdeen, 1984) 30–53.

Green, Peter, *Ovid. The erotic poems* (London, 1982).

Greenidge, A. H. J., *The legal procedure of Cicero's time* (Oxford, 1901).

Griffin, Jasper, 'Augustan poetry and the life of luxury', *JRS* 66 (1976) 87–105 = *Latin poets and Roman life* 1–31.
——'Propertius and Antony', *JRS* 67 (1977) 17–26 = *Latin poets and Roman life* 32–47.
——*Latin poets and Roman life* (London, 1985).
Grimal, Pierre, *L'amour à Rome*, trans. as *Love in ancient Rome* by Arthur Train (New York, 1967).
Grisé, Y., *Le suicide dans la Rome antique* (Paris, 1982).
Grmek, Mirko, *Diseases in the ancient Greek World* (Baltimore and London, 1989).
Gruen, E. S., 'Pompey, the Roman aristocracy and the Conference of Luca', *Hist.* 18 (1969) 71–108.
——*LGRR = The last generation of the Roman Republic* (Berkeley, 1974).
Guarino, A., 'Tagliacarte', *Labeo* 13 (1967) 124.
——'In difesa di Messalina', *Labeo* 20 (1974) 12–26.
Guizzi, F., 'La restituzione della dote e le spese utili', *Labeo* 3 (1957) 245–50.
Günther, Rosmarie, *Frauenarbeit-Frauenbindung. Untersuchungen zu unfreien und freigelassenen Frauen in den stadtrömischen Inschriften* (Munich, 1987).
Habbakuk, H. J., 'The economic history of modern Britain', in Glass and Eversley, *Population in history* 147–58.
Habinek, T. N., 'The marriageability of Maximus: Horace, *Ode* 4.1.13–20', *AJP* 107 (1986) 407–16.
Hajnal, J., 'European marriage patterns in perspective', in Glass and Eversley, *Population in history* 101–43.
——'Two kinds of pre-industrial household formation system', in Wall, Robin, and Laslett, *Family forms in historic Europe* 65–104.
Hallett, Judith P., 'The role of women in Roman elegy: counter-cultural feminism', *Arethusa* 6 (1973) 103–24.
——*Fathers and daughters in Roman society. Women and the elite family* (Princeton, 1984).
Harris, W. V., 'The theoretical possibility of extensive female infanticide in the Graeco-Roman world', *CQ* 32 (1982) 114–16.
Harrod, Samuel G., *Latin terms of endearment and of family relationship. A lexicographical study based on Volume VI of the* Corpus inscriptionum latinarum (Princeton, 1909).
Harvey, F. D., 'The wicked wife of Ischomachus', *EMC* NS 3 (1984) 68–70.
Henry, Louis, 'The population of France in the eighteenth century', in Glass and Eversley, *Population in history* 434–56.
Herlihy, D., *Medieval households* (Cambridge, Mass., 1985).
Hermansen, G., *Ostia. Aspects of Roman city life* (Edmonton, 1982).
Hesberg-Tonn, von = Hesberg-Tonn, B. von, *Coniunx carissima. Untersuchungen zum Normcharakter im Erscheinungsbild der römischen Frau* (diss. Stuttgart, 1983).
Highet, Gilbert, *Juvenal the satirist* (Oxford, 1954).
Hirschfeld, Otto, *KS = Kleine Schriften* (Berlin, 1913).

Hobson, D., 'Women and property owners in Roman Egypt', *TAPA* 113 (1983) 311–21.
Honoré, Tony, *Ulpian* (Oxford, 1982).
Hopkins, M. Keith, 'Contraception in the Roman Empire', *Comparative studies in society and history* 8 (1965) 124–51.
——'The age of Roman girls at marriage', *Population studies* 18 (1965) 309–27.
——'On the probable age structure of the Roman population', *Population studies* 20 (1966) 245–64.
——'Brother–sister marriage in Roman Egypt', *Comp. studies in society and history* 22 (1980) 303–54.
——*DR = Death and renewal* (Sociological studies in Roman history 2; Cambridge, 1983).
——'Graveyards for historians', in *La mort, les morts et l'au-delà dans le monde romain* (Actes du Colloque de Caen 1985; Caen, 1987).
Horsfall, Nicholas, 'Some problems in the "Laudatio Turiae"', *BICS* 30 (1983) 85–98.
Huber, Josef, *Der Ehekonsens im römischen Recht* (Rome, 1977).
Humbert, M., *Le remariage à Rome. Etude d'histoire juridique et sociale* (Milan, 1972).
——'Hispala Fecenia et l'endogamie des affranchis sous la République', *Index* 15 (1987) 131–48.
Humphrey, J., 'The three daughters of Agrippina maior', *AJAH* 4 (1979) 125–43.
Jameson, M. H., 'Private space in the Greek city', in O. Murray and S. Price (eds.), *The Greek city from Homer to Alexander* (Oxford, 1990) 169–93.
Jameson, Shelagh, 'Augustus and Agrippa Postumus', *Hist.* 24 (1975) 287–315.
Johann, Horst-Theodor, *Trauer und Trost* (Munich, 1968).
Johnston, David, *The Roman law of trusts* (Oxford, 1988).
Jones, A. H. M., *The criminal courts of the Roman Republic and Principate* (Oxford, 1972).
Jones, Lesley A.,'Morbidity and vitality. The interpretation of menstrual blood in Greek science' (diss. Stanford, 1987).
Jörs, P., *Die Ehegesetze des Augustus* (Marburg, 1894).
Kajanto, Iiro, 'On divorce among the common people of Rome', *RÉL* 47 bis (1969) 99–113.
——*Classical and Christian. Studies in the Latin epitaphs of medieval and Renaissance Rome* (Annales Academiae Scientiarum Fennicae B203; Helsinki, 1980).
Kampen = Kampen, N., *Image and status. Roman working women in Ostia* (Berlin, 1981).
——'Biographical narration and Roman funerary art', *AJA* 85 (1981) 47–58.
Kaser, M., 'Die Rechtsgrundlage der *actio rei uxoriae*', *RIDA* 2 (1949) 511–50.

Kassel, Rudolf, *Untersuchungen zur griechischen und römischen Konsolationsliteratur* (Zetemata 18; Munich, 1958).

Kleiner, D. E., *Roman group portraiture. The funerary reliefs of the late Republic and early Empire* (New York and London, 1977).

Koschaker, P., 'Unterhalt der Ehefrau und Früchte der dos', in *Studi P. Bonfante* (Milan, 1930) iv.3–27.

——'"Univira" in Inschriften', in W. den Boer *et al.* (eds.), *Romanitas et Christianitas. Studia Iano Henrico Waszink oblata* (Amsterdam, 1973) 195–206.

Krenkel, Werner A., 'Hyperthermia in ancient Rome', *Arethusa* 7 (1974) 381–6.

——'Prostitution', in M. Grant and R. Kitzinger (eds.), *Civilization of the ancient Mediterranean* ii (New York, 1988) 1291–7.

Krueger, P., 'Anekdoton Livianum', *Hermes* 4 (1870) 371–2.

Krummrey, H., 'Zu dem Grabgedicht für Aelia in Nikopoli a.d. Donau (*CLE* 492)', *Klio* 63 (1981) 527–49.

Kunkel, W., *Untersuchungen zur Entwicklung des römischen Kriminalverfahrens in vorsullanischer Zeit* (Abhand. Bay. Akad. Wiss., Phil.-hist. Klasse 56; Munich, 1962).

——'Das Konsilium im Hausgericht', *ZSS rom.* 83 (1966) 219–51.

Kupiszewski, Henryk, 'Das Verlöbnis im altrömischen Recht', *ZSS rom.* 77 (1960) 125–59.

Lacey, W. K., *The family in classical Greece* (London and Ithaca, 1968).

Lafont, Hubert, 'Changing sexual behavior in French youth gangs', in Philippe Ariès and André Béjin, *Western sexuality Practice and precept in past and present times* (Oxford, 1985) 168–80.

Lanfranchi, F., *Il diritto nei retori romani. Contributo alla storia dello sviluppo del diritto romano* (Milan, 1938).

Laslett, P., 'Mean household size in England since the sixteenth century', in P. Laslett (ed.), *Household and family in past time* (Cambridge, 1972) 125–58.

——'Family and household as work group and kin group: areas of traditional Europe compared', in Wall, Robin, and Laslett, *Family forms in historic Europe* 513–63.

Last, Hugh, 'The social policy of Augustus', *CAH* x (Cambridge, 1934) 425–64.

Latorre, A., 'Voluntas mulieris y reembolso de las impensas utiles dotales', *Iura* 5 (1954) 209–12.

Lattimore, Richmond, *Themes in Greek and Latin epitaphs* (Urbana, 1942).

Laurenti, R., *Studi sull'Economico attribuito ad Aristotele* (Milan, 1968).

——*Filodemo e il pensiero economico degli epicurei* (Milan, 1973).

Leach, John, *Pompey the Great* (London, 1978).

Levick, Barbara, 'The *senatus consultum* from Larinum', *JRS* 73 (1983) 97–115.

Levy, E., *Der Hergang der römischen Ehescheidung* (Weimar, 1925).

Lévy, Jean-Philippe, 'Les actes d'état civil romains', *RHDFE* 30 (1952) 449–86.

——'Nouvelles observations sur les *professiones liberorum*', in *Études J. Macqueron* (Aix-en-Provence, 1970) 439–49.

Lilja, S., *Homosexuality in republican and Augustan Rome* (Comm. hum. litt. 74; Helsinki, 1983).

Linderski, J., 'Julia in Regium', *ZPE* 72 (1988) 181–200.

Longo, Giannetto, 'Sullo scioglimento del matrimonio per volontà del paterfamilias', *BIDR* 40 (1932) = *Ricerche* 281–99.

——*Ricerche* = *Ricerche romanistiche* (Milan, 1966).

Longo, Giovanni E., '"Common-law marriage" statunitense e matrimonio romano: prospettive di una comparazione', in *Studi Volterra* iii (Milan, 1971) 247–62.

Lowe, N. J., 'Sulpicia's syntax', *CQ* 38 (1988) 193–205.

Lutz, Cora, 'Musonius Rufus: the Roman Socrates', *YCS* 10 (1947) 3–147.

Lyne, R. O. A. M., *The Latin love poets from Catullus to Horace* (Oxford, 1980).

MacCormack, G., 'Wine drinking and the Romulan law of divorce', *Irish jurist* 10 (1975) 170–4.

——'Coemptio and marriage by purchase', *BIDR* 20 (pub. 1978) 179–99.

McDonnell, Myles, 'Divorce initiated by women in Rome: the evidence of Plautus', *AJAH* 8 (1983) 54–80.

——'The speech of Numidicus at Gellius, *N.A.* 1.6', *AJP* 108 (1987) 81–94.

MacFarlane = MacFarlane, Alan, *Marriage and love in England. Modes of reproduction 1300–1840* (Oxford, 1986).

McGinn, Thomas A. J., 'The taxation of Roman prostitutes', *Helios* 16 (1989) 79–110.

MacKenzie, D. C., 'The wicked wife of Ischomachus—again', *EMC* NS 4 (1985) 95–96.

MacMullen, Ramsay, 'The epigraphic habit in the Roman Empire', *AJP* 103 (1982) 233–46.

Manning, C. E., 'Seneca and the Stoics on the equality of the sexes', *Mnem.* 26 (1973) 172–6.

Marchi, Attilio de, 'Le virtù della donna nelle iscrizioni sepolcrali latine', *RIC* 42 (1909) 771–86.

Marquardt, J., *PL = Das Privatleben der Römer* (Handbuch der römischen Alterthümer 7; Leipzig, 1886); trans. = *VP: La vie privée des romains* (Paris, 1892–3).

Marshall, Anthony J., 'Tacitus and the governor's lady: a note on Annals iii.33–4', *G&R* 22 (1975) 11–18.

——'Roman women and the provinces', *Ancient society* (Louvain) 6 (1975) 109–27.

——'Roman ladies on trial: the case of Maesia of Sentinum', *Phoenix* 44 (1990) 46–59.

Marshall, B. A., 'The engagement of Faustus Sulla and Pompeia', *Ancient society* (Louvain) 18 (1987) 91–101.

Martino, F. de, 'L'"ignorantia iuris" nel diritto penale romano', *SDHI* 3 (1937) 387–418.

Matringe, G., 'La puissance paternelle et le mariage des fils et filles de famille en droit romain (sous l'empire et en occident)', in *Studi in onore di E. Volterra* v (Milan, 1971) 191–237.

Maurin, Jean, 'Labor matronalis: aspects du travail féminin à Rome', in *La femme dans les sociétés antiques* (Univ. des Sciences humaines de Strasbourg, Contributions et travaux de l'Institut d'histoire romaine 2; Strasburg, 1983) 139–55.

Mayer, Robert, 'Catullus' divorce', *CQ* 33 (1983) 297–8.

Mayer-Maly, Th., 'Studien zur Frühgeschichte der usucapio', *ZSS rom.* 78 (1961) 221–76.

Meise, Eckhard, *Untersuchungen zur Geschichte der Julisch-Claudischen Dynastie* (Vestigia. Beiträge zur alten Geschichte 10; Munich, 1969).

Meunier, M., *Femmes Pythagoriciennes: Fragments et lettres de Théano, Perictioné, Phintys, Mélissa et Myia* (Paris, 1932).

Millar, Fergus, *A Study of Cassius Dio* (Oxford, 1964).

——*ERW = The Emperor in the Roman World (31 BC–AD 337)* (London, 1977).

Minieri, L., 'Vini usus feminis ignotus', *Labeo* 28 (1982) 150–63.

Misera, Karlheinz, *Der Bereicherungsgedanke bei der Schenkung unter Ehegatten* (Forschungen zum römischen Recht 33; Cologne and Vienna, 1974).

Mitchell, T. N., *Cicero. The ascending years* (London, 1979).

Mommsen, T., *Römisches Strafrecht* (Leipzig, 1899).

Montevecchi, O., 'Richerche di sociologia nei documenti dell'Egitto greco-romano I: i testamenti', *Aegyptus* 13 (1935) 67–121.

Moreau, Philippe, 'Structures de parenté et d'alliance à Larinum d'après le *Pro Cluentio*', in *Les bourgeoisies municipales italiennes aux IIe et Ier siècles av. J.-C.* (Paris and Naples, 1983) 99–123.

Morris, Desmond, *The illustrated Naked Ape* (London, 1986).

Münzer, F., *Römische Adelsparteien und Adelsfamilien* (Stuttgart, 1920).

Murray, Oswyn, 'Symposium and genre in the poetry of Horace', *JRS* 75 (1985) 39–50.

Nagle, Betty Rose, *The poetics of exile. Program and polemic in the* Tristia and Epistulae ex Ponto *of Ovid* (Coll. Latomus 170; Brussels, 1980).

Nardi, Enzo, *La reciproca posizione successoria dei coniugi privi di conubium* (Milan, 1938).

——'Sui divieti matrimoniali delle leggi augustee', *SDHI* 7 (1941) 112–46.

——*Procurato aborto nel mondo greco romano* (Milan, 1971).

Needleman, L. and D., 'Lead poisoning and the decline of the Roman aristocracy', *EMC/CV* NS 4 (1985) 63–94.

Nicholas, Barry, *An introduction to Roman law* (Oxford, 1962).

Nicolet, C., 'Le cens sénatorial sous la République et sous Auguste', *JRS* 66 (1976) 20–38.

Nörr, D., 'The matrimonial legislation of Augustus: an early instance of social engineering', *Irish jurist* 16 (1981) 350–64.

North, Helen, *Sophrosyne. Self-knowledge and self-restraint in Greek literature* (Cornell Studies in Classical Philology 35; Ithaca, 1966).

North, J. A., 'These he cannot take', *JRS* 73 (1983) 169–79.

Noy, David, 'Matchmakers and marriage-markets in antiquity', *EMC* ns 9 (1990), forthcoming.
——'Wicked stepmothers and unjust wills', forthcoming.
Orestano, R., 'Sul matrimonio presunto in diritto romano', in *Atti del congresso internazionale di diritto romano e di storia di diritto* iii (Milan, 1948) 49–65.
Oro, A. dell', 'Il divieto del matrimonio fra funzionario romano e donna della provincia', in *Studi in onore di Biondo Biondi* ii (Milan, 1965) 525–40.
Paci, Gianfranco, 'Nuovi documenti epigrafici dalla necropoli romana di Corfinio', *Epigraphica* 42 (1980) 31–64.
Palazzolo, Nicola, *Dos praelegata* (Milan, 1968).
Paola, Santi di, *Donatio mortis causa* (Naples, 1969).
Parkinson, Lisa, *Conciliation in separation and divorce* (London, 1986).
Pearce, T. E. V., 'The role of the wife as *custos* in ancient Rome', *Eranos* 72 (1974) 16–33.
Peristiany, J. G. (ed.), *Honour and shame. The values of Mediterannean society* (Chicago, 1966).
——*Mediterranean family structures* (Cambridge, 1976).
Phillips, C. R., 'Old wine in old lead bottles: Nriagu on the fall of Rome', *CW* 78 (1984) 29–33.
Piccinelli, F., 'L'evoluzione storico-giuridica del divorzio in Roma da Romolo ad Augusto', *Archivio giuridico* 34 (1885) 424–72.
Pieri, G., *L'histoire du cens jusqu'à la fin de la République romaine* (Paris, 1968).
Pitkäranta, R., 'Formule sepolcrali', in V. Väänänen (ed.), *Le iscrizioni della necropoli dell'autoparco vaticano* (Acta Instituti Romani Finlandiae 6; Helsinki, 1973) 113–23.
Pitt-Rivers, Julian, *The fate of Shechem or the politics of sex. Essays in the anthropology of the Mediterranean* (Cambridge, 1977).
Plessner, M., *Der Οἰκονομικὸς des Neupythagoräers 'Bryson' und sein Einfluss auf die islamische Wissenschaft* (Orient und Antike 5; Heidelberg, 1928).
Pomeroy, Sarah B., *GWWS = Goddesses, wives, whores and slaves. Women in classical antiquity* (New York, 1975).
——'The relationship of the married woman to her blood relatives in Rome', *Ancient society* (Louvain) 7 (1976) 215–27.
——'Technikai kai mousikai', *AJAH* 2 (1977) 51–68.
——*Women in hellenistic Egypt from Alexander to Cleopatra* (New York, 1984).
Price, S. R. F., *Rituals and power. The Roman imperial cult in Asia Minor* (Cambridge, 1984).
Prieur, Jean, *La Mort dans l'antiquité romaine* ([Rennes], 1986).
Purcell, N., 'Livia and the womanhood of Rome', *PCPS* 212 ns 32 (1986) 78–105.
Quartuccio, Donatella, 'Sull'origine dell'"adfectio maritalis"', *Labeo* 24 (1978) 51–6.

Rabinowitz, J. J., 'On the definition of marriage as a consortium omnis vitae', *Harvard theol. rev.* 57 (1964) 55–6.
Raditsa, L. F., 'Augustus' legislation concerning marriage, procreation, love affairs and adultery', *ANRW* ii/13 (1980) 278–339.
Raepsaet-Charlier, M. T., 'Ordre sénatoriale et divorce sous le haut-empire: un chapitre de l'histoire des mentalités', *Acta classica Debrecen.* 17–18 (1981–2) 161–73.
——'Égalité et inégalités dans les couches supérieures de la société romaine sous le Haut-Empire', *L'Égalité* 8 (1982) 452–77.
——*Prosopographie des femmes de l'ordre sénatorial (Ier–IIe siècles)* (Louvain, 1987).
Rage-Brocard, M., '*Deductio in domum mariti*' (diss., Paris, 1933).
Raschke, Wendy, 'The early books of Lucilius', *JRS* 69 (1979), 78–89.
Rasi, Piero, *Consensus facit nuptias* (Milan, 1946).
——'Tempus lugendi', in *Scritti Ferrini* i (Milan, 1947) 393–409.
Rauh, Nicholas K., 'Cicero's business friendships: economics and politics in the late Roman Republic', *Aevum* 60 (1986) 3–30.
Rawson, Beryl, 'Roman concubinage and other *de facto* marriages', *TAPA* 104 (1974) 279–305.
——*FAR = The family in ancient Rome: new perspectives* (London and Ithaca, 1986).
——'Children in the Roman *familia*', in Rawson, *FAR* 170–200.
Rawson, Elizabeth, *Cicero. A portrait* (London, 1975).
——*ILRR = Intellectual life in the late Roman Republic* (Oxford, 1985).
——'*Discrimina ordinum*: the *Lex Julia Theatralis*', *PBSR* 55 (1987) 83–113.
Reekmans, L., 'La "dextrarum iunctio" dans l'iconographie romaine et paléochrétienne', *Bulletin de l'Institut historique belge de Rome* 31 (1959) 23–95.
Reynolds, Joyce, Beard, Mary, and Roueché, Charlotte, 'Roman inscriptions 1981–5', *JRS* 76 (1986) 124–46.
Reynolds, R. W., 'The adultery mime', *CQ* 40 (1946) 77–84.
A. Richlin, 'Approaches to the sources on adultery at Rome', in H. P. Foley (ed.), *Reflections of women in antiquity* (New York, 1982) 379–404.
——*The Garden of Priapus: sexuality and aggression in Roman humor* (New Haven and London, 1983).
Robleda, Olis, *El matrimonio en derecho romano. Esencia, requisitos de validez, efectos, dissolubilidad* (Rome, 1970).
——'Il divorzio a Roma prima de Costantino', *ANRW* ii/14 (1982) 347–90.
Rossiaud, Jacques, 'Prostitution, sex and society in French towns in the fifteenth century', in Philippe Ariès and André Béjin (eds.), *Western sexuality. Practice and precept in past and present times* (Oxford, 1985) 76–94.
Rudd, Niall, 'Romantic love in classical times?', *Ramus* 10 (1981) 140–58.
Ste Croix, G. E. M. de, *The class struggle in the ancient Greek world* (London, 1981).

Saller, Richard P., 'Anecdotes as historical evidence for the Principate' *G&R* 27 (1980) 69–83.
——*PPEE = Personal patronage under the early Empire* (Cambridge, 1982).
——'Roman dowry and the devolution of property in the Principate', *CQ* 34 (1984) 195–205.
——'*Familia, domus* and the Roman conception of the family', *Phoenix* 38 (1984) 336–55.
——'*Patria potestas* and the stereotype of the Roman family', *Continuity and change* 1 (1986) 7–22.
——'Slavery and the Roman family', *Slavery and abolition* 8 (1987) 65–87.
——'Men's age at marriage and its consequences in the Roman family', *CP* 82 (1987) 21–34.
——'*Pietas*, obligation and authority in the Roman family', *Alte Geschichte und Wissenschaftsgeschichte. Festschrift für Karl Christ zum 65. Geburtstag* (Darmstadt, 1988) 393–410.
——and Garnsey, Peter, *REESC = The Roman Empire. Economy, society and culture* (Berkeley, 1987).
——and Shaw, B. D., 'Close-kin marriage in Roman society?', *Man* NS 19 (1984) 432–44.
—— ——'Tombstones and Roman family relations in the Principate: civilians, soldiers and slaves', *JRS* 74 (1984) 124–56.
Salvatore, A., SJ, 'L'immoralité des femmes et la décadence de l'empire selon Tacite', *RÉC* 22 (1954) 254–69.
Sanders, H. A., 'A Latin marriage contract', *TAPA* 69 (1938) 104–16.
Schaps, David M., 'The women least mentioned: etiquette and women's names', *CQ* 27 (1977) 323–30.
Schaps = *Economic rights of women in ancient Greece* (Edinburgh, 1979).
Schuhmann, Elisabeth, 'Ehescheidungen in den Komödien des Plautus', *ZSS rom.* 93 (1976) 19–32.
——'Der Typ der *uxor dotata* in den Komödien des Plautus', *Philologus* 121 (1977) 45–65.
Schulz, F., *Principles of Roman law* (Oxford, 1936).
——'Roman registers of births and birth certificates', *JRS* 32 (1942) 78–91; 22 (1943) 55–64.
——*CRL = Classical Roman law* (Oxford, 1951).
Seager, Robin, *Pompey. A political biography* (Oxford, 1979).
Setälä, P., *Private domini in Roman brick stamps in the empire* (Helsinki, 1977).
Shaw, Brent D., 'The age of Roman girls at marriage: some reconsiderations', *JRS* 77 (1987) 30–46.
——'The family in late antiquity: the experience of Augustine', *P&P* 115 (1987) 3–51.
——'The concept of family in the later Roman Empire: *familia* and *domus*', forthcoming.
——and Saller, R. P., 'Close kin marriage in Roman society?', *Man* NS 19 (1984) 432–44.

Shaw, Brent D., and Saller, R. P., 'Tombstones and family relations in the Principate: civilians, soldiers and slaves', *JRS* 74 (1984) 124–56.

Sherwin-White, A. N., *Pliny = The Letters of Pliny. A historical and social commentary* (Oxford, 1966).

——*RC = The Roman citizenship*, 2nd ed. (Oxford, 1973).

——'The *Tabula* of Banasa and the *Constitutio Antoniniana*', *JRS* 63 (1973) 86–98.

Sider, David, 'The love poetry of Philodemus', *AJP* 108 (1987) 310–23.

Skinner, M., 'Pertundo tunicamque palliumque', *CW* 73 (1980) 306–7.

——'Pretty Lesbius', *TAPA* 112 (1982) 197–208.

Slater, M., 'The weightiest business: marriage in an upper-gentry family in seventeenth century England', *P&P* 72 (1976) 25–54.

Smith, Nicholas D., 'Plato and Aristotle on the nature of women', *Journal of the history of philosophy* 21 (1983) 467–78.

Solazzi, S., 'Studi sul divorzio I: il divorzio della "filiafamilias"', *BIDR* 34 (1925) 1–28 = *Scritti di diritto romano* iii (Naples, 1960) 1–21; 2: 'Il divorzio della liberta', *BIDR* 34 (1925) 295–319 = *Scritti di diritto romano* iii.21–33.

——'Divortium bona gratia', *RIL* 71 (1938) 511–24 = *Scritti di diritto romano* iv (Naples, 1963) 23–33.

Söller, Alfred, *Zur Vorgeschichte und Funktion der Actio rei uxoriae* (Cologne, 1969).

Spurr, M. S., *Arable cultivation in Roman Italy c. 200 B.C.–c. A.D. 100* (*Journal of Roman Studies* Monographs 3; London, 1986).

Städele, Alfons, *Die Briefe des Pythagoras und der Pythagoreer* (Meisenheim am Glan, 1980).

Stone, Lawrence, *The family, sex and marriage in England 1500–1800*, abr. and rev. edn. (London, 1979).

Strachan-Davidson, J. L., *Problems of the Roman criminal law*, 2 vols. (Oxford, 1912; repr. Amsterdam, 1969).

Sumner, G. V., 'The *Lex annalis* under Caesar', *Phoenix* 25 (1971) 246–71, 357–71.

——*Orators = The orators in Cicero's 'Brutus': prosopography and chronology* (*Phoenix* supp. 11; Toronto 1973).

Syme, Ronald, *RR = The Roman revolution* (Oxford, 1939).

——*Tac. = Tacitus*, 2 vols. (Oxford, 1958).

——'Bastards in the Roman aristocracy', *Proc. Amer. Philosoph. Soc.* 104 (June 1960) 323–7 = *RP* ii.510–17.

——'Domitius Corbulo', *JRS* 60 (1970) 27–39 = *RP* ii.805–24.

——*History in Ovid* (Oxford, 1978).

——'No son for Caesar?', *Hist.* 29 (1980) 422–37 = *RP* iii.1236–50.

——*RP = Roman Papers* i, ii (Oxford, 1979), iii (Oxford, 1984).

——'Dynastic marriages in the Roman aristocracy', *Diogenes* 135 (1986), 1–10.

——*The Augustan Aristocracy* (Oxford, 1986).

——'Marriage ages for Roman senators', *Hist.* 36 (1987) 318–32.

Talbert = Richard J. A. Talbert, *The Senate of imperial Rome* (Princeton, 1984).

Taubenschlag, R., *The law of Greco-Roman Egypt in the light of the papyri 332 B.C.–640 A.D.* (New York, 1944).

Thayer, James B., *On gifts between husband and wife* (Digest 24.1 De donationibus inter virum et uxorem): *Text and commentary* (Cambridge, 1929).

Thébert, Y., 'Private life and domestic architecture in Roman Africa', in P. Veyne (ed.), *A History of private life* i. *From pagan Rome to Byzantium* (Cambridge, Mass., and London, 1987) 313–409.

Thesleff, Holger, *Introduction* = *An introduction to the Pythagorean writings of the Hellenistic period* (Abo, 1961).

——'On the problem of the Doric pseudo-Pythagorica: an alternative theory of date and purpose', in *Pseudepigrapha* i (Geneva, 1971) 59–87.

Thomas, J. A. C., '*Lex Julia de adulteriis coercendis*', in *Études J. Macqueron* (Aix-en-Provence, 1970) 637–44.

Thomas = —— *Textbook of Roman law* (Amsterdam, 1976).

Thomas, Keith, 'The double standard', *Journal of the history of ideas* 20 (1959) 195–216.

Thomas, Yan, 'Mariages endogamiques à Rome: patrimoine, pouvoir et parenté depuis l'époque archaïque', *RHDFÉ* 58 (1980) 345–82.

——'Le "ventre": corps maternel, droit paternel', *Le genre humain* 14 (1986) 211–36.

Torelli, M., *LR* = *Lavinio e Roma. Riti iniziatici e matrimonio tra archeologia e storia* (Rome, 1984).

Townend, G., 'The Augustan poets and the permissive society' (W. J. Knight Memorial Lecture 5; Abingdon on Thames, 1972).

Toynbee, J. M. C., *Death* = *Death and burial in the Roman world* (London and Ithaca, 1971).

Tracy, V. A., 'The *leno-maritus*', *CJ* 72 (1976) 62–4.

Treggiari, Susan, *RFLR* = *Roman freedmen during the late Republic* (Oxford, 1969).

——'Domestic staff in the Julio-Claudian period', *Histoire sociale* 6 (1973) 241–55.

——'Jobs for women', *AJAH* 1 (1976) 76–104.

——'Lower-class women in the Roman economy', *Florilegium* 1 (1979) 65–86.

——'Questions on women domestics in the Roman West', in *Schiavitù, manomissione e classi dipendenti nel mondo antico* (Università degli studi di Padova, Pubblicazioni del Istituto di Storia antica 13; Rome, 1979) 185–201.

——'*Contubernales* in *CIL* 6', *Phoenix* 35 (1981) 42–69.

——'*Concubinae*', *PBSR* 49 (1981) 59–81.

——'Consent to Roman marriage: some aspects of law and reality', *EMC/CV* NS 1 (1982) 34–44.

——'*Digna condicio*: betrothals in the Roman upper class', *EMC/CV* 27 NS 3 (1984) 419–51.

Treggiari, Susan, 'Iam proterva fronte: matrimonial advances by Roman women' in J. W. Eadie and J. Ober (eds.), *The craft of the ancient historian. Essays in honor of Chester G. Starr* (Lanham, 1985) 331–52.

——'Ideals and practicalities in match-making', in D. Kertzer and R. P. Saller (eds.), *The family in Italy from antiquity to the present* (New Haven, 1991).

——and Dorken, S., 'Women with two living husbands in *CIL* 6', *Liverpool classical monthly* 6/10 (1981) 269–72.

Vatin = Vatin, Claude, *Recherches sur le mariage et la condition de la femme mariée à l'époque hellénistique* (Paris, 1970).

Veyne, Paul, 'Le folklore à Rome et les droits de la conscience publique sur la conduite individuelle', *Latomus* 42/1 (1983) 3–30.

——'The Roman Empire', in Veyne (ed.), *A History of private life* i. *From pagan Rome to Byzantium*, trans. A. Goldhammer (Cambridge, Mass., 1987) 5–233.

Villers, Robert, 'A propos de la disparition de l'usus', *RHDFÉ* 28 (1950) 538–47.

——'Manus et mariage', *Irish jurist* 4 (1969) 168–79.

Visscher, F. de, 'Conubium et civitas', *RIDA* NS 1 (1952) 401–22.

Volterra, E., 'In tema di accusatio adulterii', in *Studi Bonfante* ii (Milan, 1930) 109–26.

——'Quelques observations sur le mariage des filii familias', *RIDA* 1 (1948) 213–42.

——'Il preteso tribunale domestico', *RISG* NS 2 (1948) 105–13.

——'L'acquisto della cittadinanza romana e il matrimonio del peregrino', in *Studi Enrico Redenti* ii (Milan, 1951) 403–22.

——'Sulla condizione dei figli dei peregrini cui veniva concessa la cittadinanza romana', in *Studi Cicu* ii (Milan, 1951) 645–72.

——'La nozione giuridica del conubium', *Studi Albertario* ii (Milan, 1953) 347–84.

——'Sulla D. 1.5.24', in *Symbolae Taubenschlag* = *Eos* 48 (1956) 541–52.

——'Intorno a D 48.5.44 (43)', in *Studi in onore di Biondo Biondi* ii (Milan, 1965) 123–40.

——'Nuove ricerche sulla *conventio in manum*', *Atti Accad. Lincei*, Memorie, ser. 8, 12/4 (1966), 251–355.

——Review of Watson, *Persons*, in *Iura* 19 (1968) 161–70.

——'La "conventio in manum" e il matrimonio romano', *RISG* NS 12 (1968) 205–26.

——'Iniustum matrimonium', in *Studi in onore di G. Scherillo* ii (Milan, 1972) 441–70.

——'Sull'unione coniugale del funzionario della provincia', in *Festschrift Erwin Seidl* (Cologne, 1975) 169–78.

——'Precisazioni in tema di matrimonio classico', *BIDR* 78 3rd ser. 17 (1975) 245–70.

——*Enciclopedia* = 'Matrimonio: diritto romano', in *Enciclopedia del diritto* (Milan, 1975) 727–807.

Wächter, H., *Über Ehescheidung bei den Römern* (Stuttgart, 1882).

Wacke, Andreas, *Actio rerum amotarum* (Cologne, 1963).

Waldstein, W., 'Zum Fall der "dos Licinniae"', *Index. Quaderni camerti di studi romanistici* 3 (1972) 343–61.

Walker, Susan, 'Women and housing in classical Greece: the archaeological evidence', in Averil Cameron and A. Kuhrt (eds.), *Images of women in antiquity* (London, 1983) 81–9.

Wall, R., Robin, J., and Laslett, P., *Family forms in historic Europe* (Cambridge, 1983).

Wallace-Hadrill, Andrew, 'Family and inheritance in the Augustan marriage laws', *PCPS* 27 (1981) 58–80.

——'The social structure of the Roman house', *PBSR* 56 (1988) 43–97.

Waltzing, J. P., *Étude historique sur les corporations professionnelles chez les Romains jusqu' à la chute de l'empire d'occident*, 4 vols. (Louvain, 1895–6).

Watson, Alan, '*Captivitas* and *matrimonium*, *TvR* 29 (1961) 243–59.

——'Usu farre(o) coemptione', *SDHI* 29 (1963) 337–8.

——'The divorce of Carvilius Ruga', *TvR* 33 (1965) 38–50.

——*Persons = The law of persons in the later Roman Republic* (Oxford, 1967).

——*Property = The law of property in the later Roman Republic* (Oxford, 1968).

——*LAR = The law of the ancient Romans* (Dallas, 1970).

——'The development of the praetor's edict', *JRS* 60 (1970) 105–19.

——*Succession = The law of succession in the later Roman Republic* (Oxford, 1971).

——*RPL = Roman private law around 200 B.C.* (Edinburgh, 1971).

——*Law making in the later Roman Republic* (Oxford, 1974).

——*XII Tables = Rome of the XII Tables. Persons and property* (Princeton, 1975).

——'Two notes on *manus*', in J. E. Spruit (ed.), *Maior xxv annis* (Assen, 1979) 195–201.

Weaver, P., *FC = Familia Caesaris. A social study of the emperor's freedmen and slaves* (Cambridge, 1972).

Weiss, Egon, 'Endogamie und Exogamie im römischen Kaiserreich', *ZSS rom.* 29 (1908) 340–69.

Wells, C. M., *The Roman Empire* (London, 1984).

Westrup, C. W., *Introduction to early Roman law. Comparative sociological studies: the patriarchal joint family*, 4 vols. (Copenhagen, 1934–54).

Whitehorne, J. E. G., 'Ovid *AA* 1.101–132 and soldiers' marriages', *LCM* 4/8 (Oct. 1979) 157–8.

Wicker, K. O'Brien, 'First century marriage ethics: a comparative study of the household codes and Plutarch's conjugal precepts', in J. W. Flanagan and A. W. Robinson (eds.), *No famine in the land. Studies . . . J. L. MacKenzie* (Missoula, 1975) 141–53.

Wiedemann, T. E. J., Review of B. Manuwald, *Cassius Dio und Augustus: Philologische Untersuchungen zu den Büchern 45–56 des Dionischen Geschichtswerkes*, in *JRS* 71 (1981) 201–3.

Wilhelm, Friedrich, 'Die Oeconomica der Neupythagoreer Bryson, Kallik-ratidas, Periktione, Phintys', *RhM* 70 (1915) 161–223.

Williams, Gordon, 'Evidence for Plautus' workmanship in the *Miles Gloriosus*', *Hermes* 86 (1958) 79–105.

——'Some aspects of Roman marriage ceremonies and ideals', *JRS* 48 (1958) 16–29.

——'Poetry in the moral climate of Augustan Rome', *JRS* 52 (1962) 28–46.

——*Tradition and originality in Roman poetry* (Oxford 1968; repr. 1985).

——*Change and decline. Roman literature in the early Empire* (Berkeley, 1978).

——*Figures of thought in Roman poetry* (New Haven and London, 1980).

Williams, Wynne, 'Individuality in the imperial constitutions: Hadrian and the Antonines', *JRS* 66 (1976) 67–83.

Wilson, Harriette, *Harriette Wilson's memoirs*, selected and edited by Lesley Blanch (London, 1985).

Wiseman, T. P., *Catullan questions* (Leicester, 1969).

——*NMRS = New men in the Roman Senate 139 B.C.–A.D. 14* (Oxford, 1971).

——*Cinna the poet and other Roman essays* (Leicester, 1974).

——'Factions and family trees', *LCM* 1/1 (Jan. 1976) 1–3.

——'The wife and children of Romulus', *CQ* 33 (1983) 445–52.

——*Catullus and his world. A reappraisal* (Cambridge, 1985).

——*RPL = Roman political life 90 B.C.–A.D. 69* (Exeter, 1985).

Wistrand, Erik, *The so-called* Laudatio Turiae (Studia Graeca et Latina Gothoburgensia 34; Göteborg, 1976).

Wolff, H. J., 'Zur Stellung der Frau im klassischen römischen Dotalrecht', *ZSS rom.* 53 (1933) 297–371.

——'Trinoctium', *TvR* 16 (1939) 145–83.

Yaron, R., 'Minutiae on Roman divorce', *TvR* 28 (1960) 1–12.

——'Divortium inter absentes', *TvR* 31 (1963) 54–68.

——'De divortio varia', *TvR* 32 (1964) 533–57.

——'Ad secundas nuptias convolare', in J. A. Ankum, R. Feenstra, and W. F. Leemans (eds.), *Symbolae iuridicae et historicae Martino David dedicatae* i (Leiden, 1968) 263–79.

Index of Principal Texts
Quoted, Cited, or Discussed

Index of Persons
(including characters in literature and mythology)

Caesar (cont.)
marital history 413, 478–80, 502
only one child 405
marries Cornelia 156
refuses to divorce Cornelia 436, 465
divorce from Pompeia 311, 447, 462, 473,
478, 479, 480
breaks Julia's engagement with
Caepio 156
marriage to Calpurnia 480
relations with Pompey 366
offers to marry Pompeia 109
secures dowries 327
condemns adulterer 277
encouraged to improve birth-rate 59, 277
Caesar, C., grandson of Augustus, husband
of Livia Julia 117
Caesar, L., grandson of Augustus 117
betrothed to Aemilia Lepida 157
Caesonia, wife of Gaius 57
Calidius of Bononia 276 n. 74
Caligula, *see* Gaius
Callicles in Plautus *Trinummus* 108
Callicratidas of Sparta 89, 195–6, 202, 204
Calpurnia, wife of P. Antistius:
suicide 486–7
Calpurnia, daughter of L. Calpurnius Piso
Caesoninus (*cos* 58 BC)
married to Caesar 480
Calpurnia wife of Pliny the Younger 102–3,
401, 427
character as a wife 257
his letters 256–7, 258
Calpurnius Bibulus, M., *cos.* 59 BC 110, 500,
502
Calpurnius Piso, C., bridegroom of Livia
Orestilla 57
Calpurnius Piso, C., conspired against
Nero 89
Calpurnius Piso L. *cos.* 58: 207, 480
Calpurnius Piso, L., adopted son of
Galba 91
Calpurnius Piso Frugi, C., qu. 58 BC
engagement to Tullia 128
marries Tullia 92
dies 500
Calvina, debtor of Pliny the Younger 343
Calvisius Sabinus, C. 486
Caracalla (M. Aurelius Antoninus), the
emperor 420
on adultery 294
on *donatio* 367
increases penalty for adultery 296
enactments 43 n. 32, 147, 280; *see also*
Septimius Severus for joint
enactments
Carbo Attienus, an adulterer 271 n. 46

Carvilius Ruga, Sp.:
his divorce 58, 212, 237, 325, 351, 442
Cassius Longinus, C. 413, 498–9
Cato, *see* Porcius
Catullus, the poet 229, 260, 303–5, 307, 308
Celius or Cloelius, P., a patrician 112 n. 170
Celsus, P. Iuventius, jurist 341, 371 (book
on *donatio*)
Ceres 164, 441
Cerennius, P., an adulterer 271 n. 46
Cerinthus, addressee of Sulpicia 121–2,
302–3
Charite in Apuleius *Metamorphoses* 118–19
Charmides, in Plautus *Trinummus* 140–1
Charondas 192–4
Chloe in Horace 40
Chremes in Terence *Andria* 126
Chrysippus 218
Cicero, *see* M. Tullius
Claudia, in epitaph 243, 247
Claudia, role model in Seneca 216, 218, in
Plutarch 226
Claudia, daughter of Ap. Claudius Pulcher,
wife of M. Brutus 413
divorce 110, 178, 479
Claudia, wife of Statius 235, 257–8
Claudia Acte 315 n. 294
Claudia Capitolina 379
Claudia Fortunata 403–4
Claudia Helpis 492 n. 68
Claudia Marcella, elder daughter of
Marcellus and Octavia 469
epigram on remarriage 216, 218
marries twice 235
married to Agrippa 102
divorced from Agrippa 138, 169, 460, 471
married to Iullus Antonius 109, 116, 138,
482
Claudia Marcella, younger daughter of
Marcellus and Octavia, wife of Messalla
Appianus, 117, 469
Claudia Pulchra, daughter of Messalla
Appianus and Marcella the
Younger 157
Claudia Severa 422
Claudius, the emperor 490
discussed in letters 255–6
betrothed to Aemilia Lepida 156
betrothed to Livia Medullina 157
divorces Urgulania 462
betrothes Octavia to Silanus 154
breaks engagement to Silanus 156, 158
marriage to Messallina 453
marries Agrippina 101, 102, 112, 157
attends weddings 162–3
gives no public holiday for Octavia's
betrothal 148

Proiectus 88
Propertius, Sex., the poet 303–5
Psyche in Apuleius *Metamorphoses* 24
  divorced 447
Ptolemies 344
Publicia, wife of Postumius Albinus,
  executed 266
Publilia, wife of Cicero:
  age 410
  marriage to Cicero 96, 102, 119
  divorce 479
Publilius Syrus 207
Pudentilla, wife of Apuleius, *see* Aemilia
Pudicitia 233
Pyrgopolynices in Plautus *Miles* 137
Pythagoras, the philosopher 192, 200
Pythagoras, mock-bride of Nero 169

Quinctilius Varus, son of Varus *cos.* 13 BC
  and Claudia Pulchra:
  abortively engaged to a daughter of
    Germanicus 157
Quintilian:
  mourns his wife 258, 497, 499
  as source 272–3
Quintilianus, correspondent of Pliny 341

Romulus 3–4, 34, 59, 211, 212, 264, 265, 268
  alleged law of 441
Roscius, Sex. 421
Rubellius Plautus, son of Julia Drusi f. 91,
  466
  execution 495
Rufrius Crispinus, Praetorian Prefect 102
Ruga, *see* Carvilius
Rutilia, mother of Cotta 495 n. 91

Sagittarius 88
Salassus, proscribed by triumvirs 431
Sallust (C. Sallustius Crispus) expelled from
  Senate 277
  on moral decline 211, 307
(Salvia), daughter of L. Salvius Otho, *cos.*
  suff. AD 33, sister of future emperor
  Otho, 157
Sassia 101, 135, 145, 270, 476
Satriena P. l. Salvia 239
Scaevola, *see* Mucius
Scaevola, Q. Cervidius, late 2nd-cent.
  jurist 335–7
Scaurus, *see* Aemilius
Scribonia, wife of Cn. Cornelius Lentulus
  Marcellinus 502
Scribonia, wife of Octavian:
  divorced 120, 465, 470, 479
  relationship with Julia 470
Scribonius Curio, C. 413

Scribonius Laetus 303
Sejanus, *see* Aelius
Seleucus of Rhosus 48
Semonides 185
Sempronia, wife of D. Brutus 480
Sempronius Gracchus, Ti., *cos.* 177, 163 BC
  146, 219, 471
Sempronius Gracchus, Ti., *tr.* 133 BC, 92
Sempronius Musca, a wronged
  husband 271 n. 46
Sempronius Sophus, P. 462 n. 121
Seneca, *see* Annaeus
Septimius, proscribed by triumvirs 431
Septimius Severus, L., the emperor 66 n. 105
  allows *sponsae* to be accused of
    adultery 158, 280
  constitution on adultery 296
  decisions on *donatio* 371–4; on
    dowry 334; on Paulinus 56
  reforms law on gifts 371–3
  ?responsible for mandata on intermarriage
    between provincial official and
    provincial woman 47
  rules governors should compel fathers to
    marry off their *filiifamilias* 65, 147
Sergius Catilina, L. 119, 177, 370
Servilia, mother of Brutus 480, 502
  children 405
  as widow 304
  involved in search for husband for
    Tullia 127–8
  disapproves of marriage of Brutus and
    Porcia 178
Servilia, wife of M. Lucullus 478, 479
Servilia, daughter of Isauricus and Junia:
  repudiated by Octavian 156
Servilia, daughter of Isauricus and Junia,
  perhaps the same as the preceding:
  married to Lepidus 487
  alleged suicide 487–8
Servilius Ahala, C. a tyrannicide in 439 BC
  91 n. 35
Servilius Caepio, Q.:
  abortively engaged to Julia 156, 158
  then to Pompeia 158
Sestius, P., *tr.* 57 BC 127
Sextius Africanus 106
Silius, C., lover of Messallina 165, 169, 458
Simo in Terence *Andria* 126
Solon 189 n. 28, 226
Stasimus, in Plautus *Trinummus* 139
Statia Crescentina 245
Statilia Messallina, wife of Nero:
  marriage to Vestinus 106
Statilia Tigris 501
Statius, father of the poet:
  marries once 235

Index of Subjects